Museums in a Digital Age

The influence of digital media on the cultural heritage sector has been pervasive and profound. Today museums are reliant on new technology to manage their collections. They collect digital as well as material objects. New media is embedded within their exhibition spaces. And their activity online is as important as their physical presence on site.

However, 'digital heritage' (as an area of practice and as a subject of study) does not exist in one single place. Its evidence base is complex, diverse and distributed, and its content is available through multiple channels, on varied media, in myriad locations and in different genres of writing.

It is this diaspora of material and practice that this Reader is intended to address. With over forty chapters (by some fifty authors and co-authors), from around the world, spanning over twenty years of museum practice and research, this volume acts as an aggregator drawing selectively from a notoriously distributed network of content. Divided into seven parts (on information, spaces, access, interpretation, objects, delivery and futures), this book presents a series of cross-sections through the body of digital heritage literature, each revealing how a different aspect of curatorship and museum provision has been informed, shaped or challenged by computing.

Museums in a Digital Age is a provocative and inspiring guide for any student or practitioner of digital heritage.

Ross Parry is Senior Lecturer in Museum Studies at the University of Leicester, a scholar of digital heritage and a historian of museum media and technology. He is the author of *Recoding the Museum: digital heritage and the technologies of change*, the first major history of museum computing.

Leicester Readers in Museum Studies
Series editor: Professor Simon J. Knell

Museum Management and Marketing
Richard Sandell and Robert R. Janes

Museums in a Material World
Simon J. Knell

Museums and their Communities
Sheila Watson

Museums in a Digital Age
Ross Parry

Museums

in a

Digital

Age

Edited by

Ross Parry

 Routledge
Taylor & Francis Group

LONDON AND NEW YORK

First published 2010
by Routledge
2 Park Square, Milton Park, Abingdon, Oxon OX14 4RN

Simultaneously published in the USA and Canada
by Routledge
270 Madison Ave, New York, NY 10016

Routledge is an imprint of the Taylor & Francis Group, an informa business

Typeset in 11.5/12.5pt Perpetua by Saxon Graphics Ltd, Derby
Printed and bound in Great Britain by MPG Books Group, UK

British Library Cataloguing in Publication Data
A catalogue record for this book is available from the British Library

Library of Congress Cataloguing in Publication Data
A catalog record for this book has been requested

ISBN 10: 0-415-40261-1 (hbk)
ISBN 10: 0-415-40262-X (pbk)

ISBN 13: 978-0-415-40261-3 (hbk)
ISBN 13: 978-0-415-40262-0 (pbk)

In memory of Charles 'Bill' Pettitt

(1937–2009)

first chair of the Museums Computer Group

Contents

Series Preface

Leicester Readers in Museum Studies provide students of museums – whether employed in the museum, engaged in a museum studies programme or studying in a cognate area – with a selection of focused readings in core areas of museum thought and practice. Each book has been compiled by a specialist in that field, but all share the Leicester School's belief that the development and effectiveness of museums relies upon informed and creative practice. The series as a whole reflects the core Leicester curriculum which is now visible in programmes around the world and which grew, forty years ago, from a desire to train working professionals, and students prior to entry into the museum, in the technical aspects of museum practice. In some respects the curriculum taught then looks similar to that we teach today. The following, for example, was included in the curriculum in 1968: history and development of the museum movement; the purpose of museum; types of museum and their functions; the law as it relates to museums; staff appointments and duties, sources of funding; preparation of estimates; byelaws and regulations; local, regional, etc. bodies; buildings; heating, ventilation and cleaning; lighting; security systems; control of stores and so on. Some of the language and focus here, however, indicates a very different world. A single component of the course, for example, focused on collections and dealt with collection management, conservation and exhibitions. Another component covered 'museum activities' from enquiry services to lectures, films, and so on. There was also training in specialist areas, such as local history, and many practical classes which included making plaster casts and models. Many museum workers around the world will recognise these kinds of curriculum topics; they certainly resonate with my early experiences of working in museums.

While the skeleton of that curriculum in some respects remains, there has been a fundamental shift in the flesh we hang upon it. One cannot help but think that the museum world has grown remarkably sophisticated: practices are now regulated by equal opportunities, child protection, cultural property and wildlife conservation laws; collections are now exposed to material culture analysis, contemporary documentation projects, digital capture and so on; communication is now multimedia, inclusive, evaluated and theorised. The museum has over that time become intellectually fashionable, technologically advanced and developed a new social relevance. *Leicester Readers in Museum Studies* address this change. They deal with practice as it is relevant to the museum today, but they are also about expanding horizons beyond one's own experiences. They reflect a more professionalised world and one that has thought very deeply about this wonderfully interesting and significant institution. Museum studies remains a vocational subject but it is now very different. It is, however, sobering to think that the Leicester course was founded in the year Michel Foucault published *The Order of Things* – a book that greatly influenced the way we think about the museum today. The writing was on the wall even then.

Simon Knell
Series Editor

Acknowledgements

In its scope, its opening essay, its choice of texts and its interleaved introductory commentaries, a publication of this kind will always be the result of clear and distinct research activity, and a product of a particular research focus. However, in spite of the single editor's name that appears on the front cover, a volume of this complexity is never entirely the work of one individual. Instead, it represents the contribution of a range of people, groups and institutions over a long period of time.

For their role as research assistants, and aiding in the sourcing of some of the original texts for this volume, I am grateful to Konstantinos Arvanitis, Areti Galani, Lena Maculan and Alex Whitfield. My thanks also go to Paul Marty for his incisive and encouraging review at the inception of this project, as well as Andy Sawyer for working closely with me (over the last two years) on how a volume of this kind could not only be wired into a new Masters degree programme in digital heritage but also for reminding me how it must also stand alone as a 'critical edition'. Simon Knell and Richard Sandell have not only steered me through the challenging process of selection and ordering but also, as heads of school, have provided vital financial support for the research and compiling of this volume.

I am also grateful to the successive groups of students (campus-based and, increasingly, via distance learning) who have taken my classes in the School of Museum Studies at the University of Leicester, and particularly the first cohort of Digital Heritage Masters students. These course members have been the first to read some of these chapters in these particular combinations and the first to respond to the pathways and linkages that I have suggested exist within them. In the assignments they have written and the arguments they have built (drawing upon the evidence base presented in this book and, indeed, in earlier drafts of other selections), these postgraduates have helped to test and shape this compilation into what I hope is now a coherent and useful Reader for any student or researcher of the subject.

Leading up to publication, I have also been fortunate to share the typologies and narratives expressed in this volume at several international events and symposia at which the subject and curricula of digital heritage has been the focus. In particular my thanks go to the organisers of: *Locating the Past: Ownership of and Access to Cultural Heritage*, a joint symposium between the Arts and Humanities Research Council (AHRC) and BT Innovate, Adastral Park, Ipswich (22 November 2007); *Technologies for Cultural Heritage,* held at the University of Oxford, with Microsoft Research Cambridge and the Italian Embassy (1 October 2008); *Fiamp 2008*, hosted at Université du Québec en Outaouais, Gatineau, Canada (16 October 2008). I am grateful to all these organisations for their kind invitations and for allowing me to use those events as a means to work through publicly my reasoning for this project.

Owing to the logistical complexity of choreographing the sourcing, rights and printing of over forty articles, involving some fifty authors, published over twenty years, the skill and role of the publisher has been invaluable throughout this project – but perhaps most so in the last stages of production. In particular, my deep gratitude goes to Matthew Gibbons, Lalle Pursglove and Geraldine Martin at Routledge (for their encouragement, but particularly for their patience), as well as to Fiona Cairns for her excellent work on negotiating the permissions for the works included here.

However, most of all, I am indebted to all the authors themselves included in this volume. Thanks are due not only for granting permission to reproduce their work here but also for the insight, knowledge and creativity exhibited by each of them in the chapters that follow.

Ross Parry

1. Information: data, structure and meaning

Williams, D. (1987) 'A brief history of museum computerization' in Williams, D., *A Guide to Museum Computing*, American Association for State and Local History, 1–5. Reproduced by kind permission of the American Association for State and Local History (www.aaslh.org), Nashville, TN.

Roberts, A. (2001) 'The changing role of information professionals in museums' *MDA Information*, vol. 5, no. 3, 15–17. Cambridge © Collections Trust, 2001. All rights reserved. Reproduced with kind permission.

Orna, E. and Pettitt, C. (1998) 'What is information management in museums?' in Orna, E. and Pettitt, C. *Information Management in Museums*, Aldershot & Broomfield, Gower, 19–32. Reproduced by kind permission of Ashgate Publishing Limited.

Chenhall, R. and Vance, D. (1998) 'The world of (almost) unique objects' in Chenhall, R. and Vance, D. *Museum Collections and Today's Computers*. ©1998 Robert G. Chenhall and David Vance, 3–13. Reproduced by permission of Greenwood Publishing Group, Inc., Westport, CT.

Bearman, D. (1995) 'Standards for networked cultural heritage' *Archives and Museums Informatics: Cultural Heritage Informatics Quarterly*, vol. 9, no. 3, 279–307. Reproduced with kind permission.

Manovich, L. (1999) 'Database as symbolic form' *Convergence*, vol. 5, no. 2, 80–99. Reproduced by kind permission of Sage Publications.

MacDonald, G. and Alsford, S. (1991) 'The museum as information utility' *Museum Management and Curatorship*, vol. 10, 305–11. Reproduced by permission of Taylor & Francis Ltd, http://www.tandf.co.uk/journals

Cameron, F. (2005) 'Digital futures II: museum collections, documentation and shifting knowledge paradigms' *Collections – A Journal for Museum and Archive Professionals*, vol. 1, no. 3, February, 243–59. Reproduced by permission of Altamira Press.

Parry, R. Poole, N. and Pratty, J. (2008) 'Semantic dissonance: do we need (and do we understand) the semantic web?' in J. Trant and D. Bearman (eds) *Museums and the Web 2008: Proceedings*, Toronto: Archives & Museum Informatics. Reproduced with kind permission.

Lévy P. (2005) 'Building a universal digital memory', report prepared for the Virtual Museum of Canada in Steve Dietz, Howard Besser, Ann Borda and Kati Geber (eds) *Virtual Museum (of Canada): the next generation*, Canadian Heritage Information Network, 55–62. Reproduced by kind permission of CHIN (Canadian Heritage Information Network) and Professor Lévy.

2. Space: visits, virtuality and distance

Huhtamo, E. 'On the origins of the virtual museum'. Reproduced by kind permission of Erkki Huhtamo.

Battro, A. (1999) 'From Malraux's imaginary museum to the virtual museum', Xth World Federation of Friends Congress, Sydney, September 13–18.

Bandelli, A. (1999) 'Virtual spaces and museums' *Journal of Museum Education* vol. 24, no. 1/2, 20–22. © Museum Education Roundtable, available from www.LCoastPress.com.

Jackson, R. (1996) 'The virtual visit: towards a new concept for the electronic science centre', paper presented at the conference *Here and Now: improving the presentation of contemporary science and technology in museums and science centres*, Science Museum, London, 21–23 November. Reproduced with kind permission.

Galani, A. and Chalmers, M. (2005) 'Empowering the remote visitor: supporting social museum visits among local and remote visitors' in Alexandra Bounia, Niki Nikonanou and Maria Economou (eds) *I Technologia stin Ipiresia tis Politismikis Klironomias (Technology for Cultural Heritage)*, Athens, Kaleidoskopio, 2008 (ISBN 978-960-471-001-0) (articles in Greek and English). Reproduced by permission of Kaleidoscope Publications.

Arvanitis, K. (2005) 'Museums outside walls: mobile phones and the museum in the everyday' in IADIS International Conference: Mobile Learning 2005, Qawra, Malta. Reproduced with kind permission.

3. Access: ability, usability and connectivity

Abungu, L. (2002) 'Access to digital heritage in Africa: bridging the digital divide' *Museum International* vol. 54, no. 3, 29–34. Reproduced by permission of Wiley-Blackwell.

Carey, K. (2004) 'My dream of an accessible web culture for disabled people', UK Museums and the Web Conference, University of Leicester. Reproduced with kind permission.

Carey, K., 'My dream of an accessible web culture for disabled people: a re-evaluation'. Reproduced with kind permission.

Kelly, B., Phipp, L. and Howell C. (2005) 'Implementing a holistic approach to e-learning accessibility' in Cook, J. and Whitelock, D. *Exploring the Frontiers of E-Learning: Borders, Outposts and Migration*, ALT-C 2005 12th International Conference Research Proceedings, ALT Oxford. © Association for Learning Technology. Reproduced by kind permission of the Association for Learning Technology.

Cunliffe, D., Kritou, E. and Tudhope, D., (2001) 'Usability evaluation for museum web sites' *Museum Management and Curatorship* vol. 19, no. 3, 229–52. Reproduced by permission of Taylor & Francis Ltd, http://www.tandf.co.uk/journals.

Makkuni, R. (2003) 'Culture as a driver of innovation', ICHIM (Paris, France, Archives & Museum Informatics Europe, 2003). Reproduced with kind permission.

4. Interpretation: communication, interactivity and learning

Walsh, P. (1997) 'The web and the unassailable voice' *Archives and Museum Informatics* vol. 11, no. 2, 77–85. Reproduced with permission.

Frost, O.C. (2002) 'When the object is digital: properties of digital surrogate objects and implications for learning' in Paris, Scott G. (ed.) *Perspectives on Object-centered Learning in Museums*, Mahwah, NJ: Lawrence Erlbaum Associates, Inc., 79–94. Reproduced by permission of Taylor & Francis Ltd, http://www.tandf.co.uk/journals.

Roussou, M. (2004) 'Learning by doing and learning through play' *Computers in Entertainment*, vol. 2, no. 1, 1–23. Reproduced by kind permission of ACM Publications.

Heath C. and vom Lehn, D., *Interactivity and Collaboration: new forms of participation in museums, galleries and science centres*. Reproduced with kind permission.

Gammon, B. (1999) 'Visitors' use of computer exhibits. Findings from five grueling years of watching visitors getting it wrong' *The Informal Learning Review* 1112-a. Reproduced by kind permission of the Informal Learning Experiences Inc.

5. Object: authenticity, authority and trust

Müller, K. (2002) 'Museums and virtuality' *Curator*, vol. 45, no. 1, 21–33. Reproduced by kind permission of Altamira Press.

Trant, J. (1998) 'When all you've got is 'The Real Thing': museums and authenticity in the networked world' *Archives and Museum Informatics*, vol. 12, 107–25. Reproduced with kind permission.

Clifford, L. (2000) 'Authenticity and integrity in the digital environment: an exploratory analysis of the central role of trust' in *Authenticity in a Digital Environment* ed. by Council on Library and Information Resources. Reproduced with the kind permission of the Council on Library and Information Resources, Washington, DC.

Pachter, M. (2002) 'Why museums matter', keynote address to *Common Threads*, MDA Conference. Reproduced with permission.

Lyman P. and Besser, H. (1998) 'Defining the problem of our vanishing memory: background, current status, models for resolution' in Margaret MacLean and Ben H. Davis (eds) *Time and Bits: managing digital continuity*, Los Angeles: Getty Conservation Institution, Getty Information Institute and The Long Now Foundation, 11–20. Reproduced with kind permission.

Gansallo, M. (2002) *Curating New Media*, Third Baltic International Seminar 10–12 May 2001, Sarah Cook, Beryl Graham and Sarah Martin eds, Gateshead: Baltic, 61–72. Reproduced with permission.

6. Delivery: production, evaluation and sustainability

Stiff, M. (2002) *Managing New Technology Projects in Museums and Galleries*, 13–25. Cambridge © Collections Trust, 2002. All Rights Reserved. Reproduced with kind permission.

Conway, P., (2000) 'Rationale for digitization and preservation' in Maxine K. Sitts (ed.) *Handbook for Digital Projects: A Management Tool for Preservation and Access*. © 2000 Northeast Document Conservation Center. Reproduced with permission.

Colson F. and Colson, J., 'Speaking for themselves: new media' and 'Making the modern world'. Reproduced with permission.

Economou, M.(1998) 'The evaluation of museum multimedia applications: lessons from research' *Museum Management and Curatorship* vol. 17, no. 2, 173–87. Reproduced with permission.

Zorich, D.M. (2003) *A Survey on Digital Cultural Heritage Initiatives and Their Sustainability Concerns*, Washington DC: Council on Library and Information Resources, June, pp. 22–32.

7. Futures: priorities, approaches and aspirations

Šola, T. (1997) 'Making the total museum possible' in Tomislav Šola (ed.) *Essays on Museums and Their Theory*, Finland: Finnish Museums Association, 268–275. Reproduced by kind permission of the Finnish Museums Association.

Castells, M. (2001) 'Museums in the information era: cultural connectors of time and space' *ICOM News*, special issue vol. 54, no. 3, 4–7. Keynote Address at the nineteenth General Conference of the International Council of Museums (ICOM), Barcelona. Reproduced with kind permission.

Knell, S. (2003) 'The shape of things to come: museums in the technological landscape' *Museum and Society* vol. 1, no. 3, 132–46. Reproduced with kind permission.

Parry, R. (2005) 'Digital heritage and the rise of theory in museum computing' *Museum Management and Curatorship*, vol. 20, no. 4, 333–48. Reproduced by permission of Taylor & Francis Ltd, http://www.tandf.co.uk/journals.

Chapter 1

The Practice of Digital Heritage and the Heritage of Digital Practice

Ross Parry

The evidence of change

Museums have much to show for their four decades of computing. And like any professional sector that has learned the hard way to assimilate 'new technology', there is equal measure of factors to rue as there are to celebrate. As *institutions* they can reflect upon several decades of caution provoked by a set of technologies that for a long time, for most museums, were seen as expensive, high-risk, over-hyped and requiring an unfamiliar up-skilling of the workforce. Just as easily, however, many of these same museums can today equally point to new directorates, new workflows and new strategic aims within their organisations, as well as new funding streams and government priorities externally, that are now shaped and driven by the presence and push of digital provision. In a similar way – as *venues* – museums might recall some of their initial defensiveness to Internet technologies that appeared to encourage an arms-length proxy contact with collections and that seemed to threaten even the primacy of the physical visit event itself. And yet, two decades after the birth of the Web, museums increasingly see their distributed online audiences as important as those physically on site. Ever more these same museums see their remit as supporting collection-based experiences wherever those experiences may take place (be it gallery space or domestic space, city centre or school), and through whatever medium is most appropriate (be it exhibition or publication, blog or documentary). As *exhibitors*, museums will remember the reticence and suspicion once showed to digital resources and to digital interactives, and how problematic it first seemed to accommodate the 'new media' within environments whose credence was understood to come principally from the presence of genuine, material objects. Yet, today, the contemporary museum sector is one in which digital culture is now actively collected, where computer-based interpretive media allows exhibitions to support experiences in more flexible, creative and empowering ways, and where institutions are tuning their modes of delivery and audience engagement to the emerging channels of our evolving digital society. As *keepers* and *researchers* of collections, museums can look back on what (at least with the privilege of hindsight) might appear as the awkwardness and contrivance of some of the first attempts to make the free-playing and expressive world of individual curatorship fit into the new standardised systems and data models that first accompanied museum computing. However, since then, more vivid and much more important has been the way these new computer-based systems have buttressed a more efficient approach by museums to fulfilling their ethical responsibility of managing their collections data. With the case now soundly made for digital collections management systems (databases in the museum), what strikes us today is both the growing willingness and the increased ability of museums to interrogate, inter-connect, share and (even) let go of their collections data within and without the sector. Today, it is irrefutable that computing has had a profound effect on how museums manage and make visible their collections. In each of these cases – as *organisation* and *attraction*, as *communicator* and *collector* – there is for the museum an abundance of evidence (as indeed will become clear in the chapters that follow in this volume) to illustrate almost a half-century of development enabled by digital technology.

Unfortunately, sourcing this evidence has tended to be far from straightforward. The resources and the literature, the examples and evidence, the dialogues and debates that together constitute 'digital heritage' have tended to be dispersed – located in some quite different forums and media. For instance, a curator attempting to locate and identify precedent and best practice in digital heritage, might initially reach for published guides and manuals – much like those represented in Chapter 35 (on project management) or Chapter 36 (on digitisation). However, this practitioner is also likely to turn to the several professional curators groups, such as the Museum Computer Network (MCN) and the Museums Computer Group (MCG) and special interest web communities and professional network sites whose activity and membership is focused on museum technology. Typically, the regular meetings and conferences of these sorts of communities (along with their newsletters and publications, their email discussion lists and website resources) offer colleagues in the sector practical and candid advice and support; Carey's presentation to the MCG (Chapter 19) is an illustration of one such interaction. It is within the meeting halls and blogrolls of such groups that an important part of the principles and practice of digital heritage are shared and (constructively) opened to scrutiny. Alternatively, a student or scholar attempting to undertake and investigate digital heritage research may also gravitate towards journals with a commitment to publishing in this area (as in the case of Cameron's paper, Chapter 9), or, increasingly, to the growing bookshelf of volumes now positioned by authors and publishers alike as being distinctively 'digital heritage' titles (MacDonald 2006; Cameron and Kenderdine 2007; Din and Hecht 2007; Kalay et al. 2007; Marty and Burton Jones 2007; Parry 2007; Tallon and Walker 2008). As an expanding corpus of literature, these texts are testimony to digital heritage's maturing identity and intellectual confidence as a subject; as described, for example, in Chapter 43's discussion on the 'cultural turn' in museum computing. However, a commercial developer trying to determine the needs and drivers of a client's sector is (alongside these computing groups and academic publications) just as likely to mine the proceedings of international congresses that have routinely acted as a nexus of project reporting, professional networking and product promotion. Annual conferences (such as *ICHIM, EVA, UKMW, DISH* and, perhaps most notably of all, *Museums and the Web*) have over many years established their meetings as seminal events for digital heritage), their proceedings highly referenced sources for the subject. However, a policy maker aiming to plan and anticipate future provision based upon existing evidence, might also refer to commissioned consultation and strategic reports; consider, for instance, the vision paper by a national cultural organisation such as of the Canadian Heritage Information Network (Chapter 11). Likewise, they might also look towards the work of global bodies such as the International Committee for Documentation (CIDOC) and the International Committee for Audiovisual and New Image and Sound Technologies (AVICOM) – both constituted under a formal mandate from the International Council of Museums (ICOM), and UNESCO. The 'working groups' of committees such as CIDOC (in areas such as digital preservation, documentation standards, and multimedia) bring together international expertise around specific topics and, consequently, can be influential reference points in national digital heritage practice across the world; as illustration, see Roberts' cross-reference to the influence of CIDOC in Chapter 3. Therefore, the reality for anyone working in digital heritage is of an evidence and literature base that is complex, diversified and distributed, with relevant content available through multiple channels, on varied media, within myriad locations, and different genres of writing.

Digital heritage as diaspora

The cause of this diasporic body of literature is manifold. It has much to do with the diverse professional roles and identities of the people who engage with the subject, and not least what each of them choose to call it. Digital heritage practice and research may just as easily attract an educationalist as it may a subject curator. It could equally draw to it the attention of a museum director as it could attract the curiosity of a PhD student. Likewise, it might seize the interest of a technologist and computer scientist as it might a designer or exhibition developer. Put simply, there is no typical digital heritage practitioner or scholar. Then, to multiply and accentuate this scattering of activity, each of these individuals typically has their own subject community or community of practice with which they routinely confer. This community may then be located in very different discursive spaces – curatorial/non-curatorial, academic/non-academic, technological/non-technological. Furthermore, each of these communities may have its own conventions for publishing and debate – be it high profile, international, peer-reviewed journals with high readerships, or more localised, face-to-face meetings and symposia. (Consider, for instance, how MacDonald and Alsford, Chapter 8, publish in *Museum, Management and Curatorship* – an international periodical that has had editors specifically assigned to the area of digital heritage, signalling the journal's commitment to publishing in that area. And yet, the Gansallo piece, Chapter 34, is a transcript of a small, closed colloquium on digital curation.) Exacerbating matters still further is the fact that there is no single consensual term to describe activity in this area. Here, for consistency, we choose the term 'digital heritage' – a recognised label with credibility and currency for research councils, universities, governments and professional bodies in many parts of the world; see, for instance, Abungu's foregrounding of the term in Chapter 18. However, at times, practice and writing indistinguishable from such work presents itself instead as 'digital cultural heritage' – as, for instance, the Council on Library and Information Resources does in Chapter 39. And yet, to complicate matters still further, for some professional communities 'digital heritage' and 'digital cultural heritage' are the specialist terms used specifically (and only) to describe those aspects of our heritage that are 'born' in (and in some cases may only ever exist within) digital form – that is, our digital 'heritage' of such objects as emails, websites, wordprocessed documents, digital images, as well as digital video and sound files; see, for instance, the terminology of the Getty Conservation Institute used in Chapter 33. Cognate to (but self-consciously distinctive from) the term 'digital heritage' is the closely related area of 'museum informatics' (the parlance, for instance, of an influential writer such as Trant in Chapter 30), a label more recognisable perhaps to American readers, and implying a genealogy more grounded in information studies than, say, the more humanities-based subjects of museology and museum studies. Alternatively, many parts of the French-speaking world are more familiar with framing and searching this area of practice and scholarship as 'cybermuséologie'. Work that might be considered 'digital heritage' might even still tag itself as 'humanities computing' or 'museum computing' – the latter undoubtedly the term preferred by Pettitt (the co-author of Chapter 4) as the first chair of the Museums Computer Group. As the products and projects, practices and protocols of using digital media in museums migrate across different cultural and linguistic spaces, their disciplinary allegiances are thus open to realignment, and their emphases and significances can migrate with subtlety. More practically (for our curator, student, commercial developer and policy maker trying to find this material), there still remains the basic problem therefore of what, simply, to call the subject for which they suspect they may be looking.

In other words 'digital heritage' (as practice and as a subject) does not exist in one single place; a consequence perhaps of its modernity, of its emergence after and outside the traditional scholarly silos of disciplinarity. Instead, digital heritage's activity and presence both inside and outside these subject demarcations (we might even say, as a *post-discipline*) is what makes it a challenging and complex subject with which to engage, but it is also what makes it so attractive and liberating for those who practise and study within it. The digital heritage practitioner or researcher may or may not see themselves as part of a 'subject of digital heritage' in the same way an archaeologist, an art historian, a palaeontologist or an engineer might relate to their own disciplines. Similarly, the digital heritage practitioner and researcher may need to learn different modes of delivery in order to communicate with the different professional and academic communities to which they might (simultaneously) belong: learning to speak comfortably to the academy as well as to the cultural heritage sector in the language of technology as well as, perhaps, the languages of the social sciences or humanities. It is this dispersion (of literature, of activity, of personnel) that this Reader is intended to confront. For a subject that is decentred and defused in this way, it is hoped that there is a useful role for tools and interventions (such as this) that can offer a judicious collection and meaningful collation of the far-flung sources available.

This book as collage

The selection criteria for these texts have been varied – but specific and consistent. First, and perhaps out of step with some digital media literature, every attempt has been made here not to dismiss articles simply on the grounds that they do not represent the *state of the art*. On the contrary, the aim here has been to set out what is seen as a series of longer and significant developments that help explain museums' (and their visitors') current usage and expectation of digital media. Frequently discourse of technology (especially digital technology) can be permeated with the values of *progress* and *development, improvement* and *advancement*. It is, as such, an area of activity that can all too readily fetishise the future, and neglect the past – even the immediate past. By impatiently awaiting a new upgrade, automatically migrating to the next version, reflexively signing up to the latest Web phenomenon, and quixotically chasing the leading edge, digitality can all too often be fixated by the cultures of 'now' and 'what's next?' – and delete (if not deride) past practice. Yet, in digital heritage (as indeed in any subject related to technology), we discount our technical and professional history at our own risk. After all, it is in the patterns and trajectories of previous endeavour, and in the decisions and designs of earlier iterations, that we can trace and understand the assumptions and motives, as well as the politics and personalities, whose imprint remain deeply encoded within the later instantiations of technology that we might use today. In this way, in its conspicuous inclusion of articles and extracts across several decades of computing in the museum, this Reader is making a conscious statement about the value of historicised approaches to digital heritage. (Consider, for instance, Williams on the early days of museum computing in Chapter 2, Jackson on museums' first impressions of the Web in Chapter 15, or indeed Walsh's initial questioning of trust and authenticity in the new digital landscape, in Chapter 24.) In valuing history in this way, this volume makes a plea for digital heritage to look to its past as much to its present and future.

The second point regarding the selection criteria used is that some articles and excerpts have been included here as much because of who has written them as the subject on which they are writing. There has been an attempt here (as will be indicated in the commentaries that introduce each 'Part' of the volume) to highlight the work and influence of a number of key writers on the subject over the first four or five decades of museum computing – for example, Chenhall and Vance (Chapter 5), Bearman (Chapter 6), Lynch (Chapter 31) and Besser (Chapter 33). As well as attempting to acknowledge the role that some authors have occupied (and to give to a wider and later readership the recognition these authors perhaps deserve), it is hoped that their inclusion here might serve as an impetus for a reader to explore more of these individuals' oeuvre. Equally, several articles are included by authors not immediately synonymous for their research on digital heritage – but whose work here shows that each, excitingly, has something important to contribute to this subject.

We think here in particular of Knell (Chapter 42), Šola (Chapter 40), Lévy (Chapter 11), Cunliffe (Chapter 22) and Lyman (Chapter 33). Furthermore, in the profile of authors assembled, an attempt has been made here to present something approaching a representative sample of the types of writers on digital heritage. It is for this reason that the volume intentionally contains contributions from scholars based in universities (Cameron, Economou, Heath, Huhtamo, Kelly, Frost), some of whom might position themselves first and foremost as digital heritage scholars (Galani, Arvanitis, Parry), as well as consultants and researchers based in industry (Colson and Colson, Battro, Bandelli, Makkuni, Miller, Zorich). But, crucially, we also hear the voice of the curator and practitioner (Williams in Chapter 2, Gammon in Chapter 28, Jackson in Chapter 15), including the perspectives of various forms of directorate (such as Pachter in Chapter 32, Poole in Chapter 10, and Abungu in Chapter 18). Finally – and in some ways most excitingly – the volume also includes instances of when highly influential writers on digital media have turned their attention to the relationships between it and cultural heritage. We see here, for example, the sociologist Manuel Castells (in Chapter 41) addressing the International Council of Museums on the opportunities afforded to the sector by the 'information era'. Likewise, in Chapter 7, we encounter another new media giant, Lev Manovich, reflecting on the socio-cultural implications of the database. It is commentaries such as these that offer us a glimpse of digital heritage writing in some of its most intellectually confident and creative modes.

Third, it is not the intention here simply to reproduce texts that are readily accessible elsewhere, either in high-circulation printed publications or as readily discoverable and persistent online sources. Consequently, some well-know authors and communicators in the field might, to some readers, be conspicuous by their absence. Individuals such as Peter Samis, Bruce Wyman, Richard Light, Seb Chan, Susan Chun, Suzanne Keene, Paul Marty, Angelina Russo, Nina Simon, to name but a few, have contributed (and continue to contribute) much to the teaching, practice and research of this subject area, and yet are not included here. This is less an oversight and more a comment (if not a compliment) on how sourceable their work already is to practitioners and students of digital heritage. Equally, the scarcity of articles from the *Museums and the Web* and *ICHIM* conferences (in fact, just Chapter 10 and Chapter 24) should in no way be interpreted as a sleight on the importance of these online and printed proceedings – quite the opposite in fact. It is, instead, testimony to the success and status of these two meetings that their impressive archive of past papers (unparalleled in fact in this subject area) still remains openly accessible online and usable by any practitioner or scholar of the subject. Instead, this volume has tried to pull together in one place articles that may be more difficult to source, but are of no less value – including several unpublished papers (Chapters 12, 17, 19, 20 and 37), papers no longer available (such as Chapter 15), as well as papers that originally appeared in specialist publications or more limited print runs.

The strata and clouds of the blogosphere are another place (if more nebulous) that has much to offer any study and curricula of this subject – yet do not appear here. It is through the tagging, blogging, microblogging and syndication of these social media sites, that those within the community of digital heritage (who feel comfortable working or lurking in this environment) keep connected, promote, spread news and share their work in progress. Symmetrically, the museum community's growing interest in the social Web for its public-facing services has been reflected in these modes of interaction within its internal professional communication. Some of these blogs have a high readership (some not so), some adhere to high editorial standards (some less so), some persist (some do not). However, for this volume, the length of a typical post, their frequently intense topicality, and the high frequency of cross-referencing, linking and media interactivity within them, does, unfortunately, preclude their useful inclusion here. The absence of blog posts in this volume should not be seen as an undervaluing or an underestimation of the vitality that they bring to digital heritage discourse. It is simply, instead, that their natural place remains within the fluidity, multimediality and live exchanges of the Web, rather than here as record on the fixed printed page.

Finally, it would be advisable not to approach these forty chapters (and fifty authors and co-authors) as the 'premiere' articles on digital heritage, or as a definitive collection, or indeed as a complete survey of all the debates, technologies and applications within the subject and sector. More rewardingly, it might be best to see this volume as a discerning *aggregator* of digital heritage research and literature drawn selectively from a notoriously distributed network of content. And yet, it may also be helpful to see this book as a *map* – showing the boundaries and landmarks (historical and modern), as well as the communication systems and communities (established and ephemeral) that make up the shifting post-disciplinary landscape of digital heritage.

However, *Museums in a Digital Age* might best be viewed as a *collage* – an assemblage of some quite unexpected writings, normally not found together, but here framed, overlaid and (in some instances) juxtaposed to illustrate, to provoke and also – it is hoped – to inspire.

References

Cameron, F. and Kenderdine, S. (eds) (2007) *Theorizing Digital Cultural Heritage: A Critical Discourse*, Cambridge MA and London: MIT.

Din, H. and Hecht, P. (eds) (2007) *The Digital Museum: A Think Guide*, Washington DC: American Association of Museums.

Kalay, Y., Kvan, T. and Affleck, J. (eds) (2007) *New Media and Cultural Heritage*, New York: Routledge.

MacDonald, L. (ed.) (2006) *Digital Heritage: Applying Digital Imaging to Cultural Heritage*, Amsterdam and London: Butterworth Heinemann.

Marty, P.F. and Burton Jones, K. (2007) *Museum Informatics: People, Information and Technology in Museums*, New York and London: Routledge.

Parry, R. (2007) *Recoding the Museum: Digital Heritage and the Technologies of Change*, New York and London: Routledge.

Tallon, L. and Walker, K. (2008) *Digital Technologies and the Museum Experience: Handheld Guides and Other Media*, Lanham, MD and Plymouth: Alta Mira.

PART ONE

Information: data, structure and meaning

Introduction to Part One

THIS VOLUME IS DIVIDED INTO SEVEN 'Parts', each of which attempts a different cross-section through the body of digital heritage literature. Each Part holds up a different polarising lens to the same subject, in each case filtering out (and leaving in view) different issues and themes. There are, of course, many ways this corpus of material could have been divided in a book such as this. We could have presented ostensibly a history and a linear 'walk through' of the last few decades of research and development: the first adopters of 'automation' (as it was called) in the 1960s; the emergence of standards and of professional bodies related to museum information management in the 1970s; the rise of local networks, multimedia and microcomputing in the 1980s; the advent of the Web, interoperability and mass digitisation in the 1990s; and the evolution of the mobile and social media at the start of the new century. Alternatively, we could have rationalised the internal organisation of these articles according to different types of digital media, with different sections on: digitisation equipment; collections and content management systems; websites and Internet technologies; mobile devices; and in-gallery interactives and audio-visual media. There may even have been a case for marshalling the voices and perspectives of this volume according to different professional and cultural contexts, be that sections on various subject museums ('the art museum and digital media', 'the science centre and digital media'), or types of museums (national museums, independent museums, local and regional museums). However, rather than organising this subject along formal chronological, technological or cultural lines, the approach taken here, instead, is one embedded in the assumptions and rhythms of professional work. Each part of the Reader takes, therefore, a different aspect of curatorship and museum provision

and draws out the ways that area of the sector has been informed, shaped or challenged by computing. Consequently, our typology here is not that of *hardware*
and *software, old* and *new, national and international* but rather of *space, access,
interpretation, learning, objects, production and sustainability* – in other words,
the vocabulary of museum practice itself.

Part One focuses on the role of information within the museum. The opening
two chapters consider the history and context of the move to computerisation.
In Chapter 2, we have a first-person account by a registrar amidst the computer
revolution of the 1980s, taking stock of the progress and change that the sector
has seen in the previous decade or so. In this small extract from his book on
museum computing, David Williams not only reminds us of just how far back
museums' relationship with computing goes but also captures some of the excitement as well as the uncertainty and risk that were (and perhaps can still be) associated with undertaking digital media projects within the sector. Williams' brief
history also helps us to evidence how the advent of computing within the museum
came initially through databases and information management systems. It was
largely computers' potential to automate collections and records management
that first saw curators experiment with their use. In Chapter 3, we see another
information management professional taking a moment (if over a decade later)
to reflect upon the progress that museums had made with digital technology.
Andrew Roberts' list, which first appeared in *MDA Information* in 2001, sees
the former director of the Museum Documentation Association (MDA) and a
professional with a career in museum computing dating back to the early 1970s,
charting a series of key developments in the sector's growth. Significantly, the
trajectory Roberts plots (admittedly from a UK vantage point) is one of increased
collaboration between national and international organisations around the use of
collections-based technology, and a rise in the strategic importance of information management and the information professional within the sector.

With this historical wireframe sketched out, the next three chapters allow us
an opportunity to focus on some of the definitions and principles that underpin
computer-enabled information management systems within the museum. Reading
Chapter 4 (an extract from Elizabeth Orna and Charles Pettitt's 1998 book on
museum informatics) alongside Chapter 5 (Robert Chenhall and David Vance's
book from a decade earlier on the same subject), we are given a demonstration
of the clear and logical thinking that can (and must) take place at the heart
of museum informatics. Returning, as they do, to first principles, both of these
extracts rehearse thought processes that will withstand the progress of time, as
other technologies and strategies come and go. In the case of Vance and Pettitt,
their legacy is not just intellectual but also practical – with each being part of
the founding group of, respectively, the Museum Computer Network (in the US
in 1967) and the Museums Computer Group (in the UK in 1982). These, we
remember, were museum informational professionals not only exploring the
possibilities of these new technologies but, as they did so, forging new professional networks within the sector. It is then a later chair of the MCN that is the

author of Chapter 6; David Bearman's discussion on the role (and need) for standards for networked cultural heritage offers perhaps an even stronger example of 'first principle' thinking that deserves to be returned to and reflected upon. As well as being a key reference point for any subsequent discussion of the role of digital standards within the sector, this extract from a longer 1995 article for the *Archives and Museum Informatics* quarterly, also reminds us of the personal role that Bearman has taken for some two decades in helping the digital heritage community to think deeply about its approach to information architecture and data modelling.

Chapters 7 and 8 help us to turn our gaze outwards, and lead us into considering some of the broader social and cultural significances of using digital technology to manage information within the museum. In Lev Manovich we witness a renowned new media writer offering a critique of the database, alerting us to technology's (including software's) cultural contingency. Reading Manovich we become equipped to 'read' information management systems (including those in museums) as cultural constructs – a product of their time and context. We become mindful of how laden each can become with the ideologies and assumptions of individuals and communities that designed and shaped them, and also (Manovich's main point) how some of these iconic technologies can shape the way we see the world. Likewise in the article by George MacDonald and Stephen Alsford (Chapter 8), we see a national museum director recognising the political and sociological significance of the information revolution for museums. If information becomes a 'utility' (like gas, electricity and water), they ask, what role does that create (demand even) for museums. We read MacDonald and Alsford wondering whether the information society presents a threat (rendering the museum an anachronism, to a by-gone age when knowledge and power were wrapped up in materiality) or an unparalleled opportunity (identifying the museum as a unique and trusted editor and broker within this era of information massification and digitality).

It is this look to current and future trends and developments that provide the focus for the last three chapters of Part One. All three chapters look forward and highlight some of the key developments that are (and will) affect the next generation of collections management and information management systems in the museum. Fiona Cameron (in Chapter 9) skilfully reappraises the philosophical thinking upon which previous and future collections management systems could be built; what, in other words, would a post-structuralist database look like, and do our intrinsically hierarchical datasets in museums allow us to reflect the polysemy (the multiple and shifting meanings) that our intellectual and museological frameworks now expect. Chapters 10 and 11 step cautiously into the realms of some very different technologies and rationales for conceiving and facilitating information management, particularly online. Both make reference to the Semantic Web – an 'intelligent', machine-processable Web, more efficient at identifying and inferring relevant content, and more equipped to relationally connect and cross-reference online resources, and potentially more able to accommodate different ways of making meaning. One is a conference paper based on the work of a national 'think tank' involving Culture 24 (publishers of the '24 Hour Museum', the UK's national virtual museum) and Collections Trust, the other is more of an editorial piece within a national strategic report for the Canadian Heritage Information Network. But both temper their intellectual ambition with caution, both aware of the technical, intellectual and political factors that can still moderate development in this area – as much as they did, indeed, for Williams, Vance, Chenhall almost three decades earlier.

Chapter 2

A Brief History of Museum Computerization

David Williams

A DISTINCT PATTERN IN THE DEVELOPMENT of museums is discernible. When a museum is young, it concentrates on acquiring objects and building a collection; the more mundane tasks of documentation and record keeping often take a back seat. The institution establishes it *own* information management system, based primarily on the whims of the person – a registrar or curator – responsible for dealing with the records on a daily basis and influenced by the type of objects the museum is collecting at the time. Traditionally, little communication has existed either within the museum or between museums regarding proper record-keeping procedures. Consequently, a museum may suddenly realize that its records system is inadequate and its collection poorly documented because the registrar or curator was not informed in such matters and the administrator was concerned with other issues.

As the collection grows and routine museum functions become increasingly difficult because of the inaccessible records, the need for thorough documentation and efficient record keeping becomes painfully apparent. Because the collection continues to grow while the museum searches for a cure to its ailments, a backlog of poorly documented objects and unorganized records accumulates.

The museum using traditional paper-based practices for information management frequently becomes overwhelmed by collection growth. So inadequate are most initial information systems that the museum cannot keep up with the production of new records. Usually the next sign of failure is when the museum can no longer maintain up-to-date records on the locations of objects. As the situation worsens, cross-referencing becomes difficult, and lists of objects for research or exhibits seldom include every applicable object. Finally, the staff

Source: *A Guide to Museum Computing*, Nashville, TN: American Association for State and Local History, 1987, pp. 1–5.

begin to spend all its time *producing* paper records rather than *using* them to support the museum's other activities.

For the typical museum the shortcomings in a records system are at first mitigated by collection information stored in that invaluable repository – the curator's memory. Despite this supplemental source of collection data, museum staff members can seldom be absolutely certain they are making the most of the objects and information under their control.

Such problems have affected a great many museums in the past and continue to plague countless museums today. However, today's museums can benefit from changes in attitudes, awareness, and communication – changes that are occurring as a result of several factors.

Museums in operation during the 1960s found that they were not immune to the social and cultural changes affecting the rest of the country. As a more transient life style developed in America, museum professionals began to change jobs and relocate much more frequently than in the past. With these relocating professionals went valuable collection information previously recorded in their memories and relied on to fill the gaps in faulty record-keeping systems.

The 1960s also saw an awakening of Americans to their cultural and ecological past. Museums began to be recognized and appreciated as repositories of our heritage. With this recognition, however, museums were pressured to increase their activities and to use the resources at their disposal fully. To complicate matters further, museums were faced with a new kind of audience. The television generation demanded information presented in a sharp, snappy, modern manner. Museums were pressured to "jazz up" their acts.

Accompanying the new attention paid by the public to museums came a new public scrutiny of museum practices. Once the quiet, undisturbed sanctuary of scholars and researchers, museums were seen now as public trusts with duties and responsibilities to their collections, to their communities, and to future generations. As the demand for museum accountability increased, so did the demand for efficient information management.

These demands were by no means unreasonable. Museums were expected to be able to locate objects in a moderate amount of time and to maintain adequate records on the methods by which items in their collections were acquired. And museums were expected to document properly the disposal of items within their collections. As more and more museums failed to carry out their duties as public trusts, the search for a way out of the information management morass intensified.[1]

Initial attempts at museum computerization in the United States were undertaken in the 1960s – a commendably rapid response to the new computer technology, considering the traditionally isolated nature of museums. Because these early efforts were limited to museums that could afford expensive equipment, a popular misconception arose that only museums with large collections could justify using computers, especially for collections management. This misconception was so prevalent during the 1960s that remnants of it exist today. The technology had not yet advanced to the point where computers were readily adaptable for other museum uses, such as their integration into educational exhibits. In fact, many of the first applications of computers in historical organizations have been for financial operations, such as accounting and payroll processing.

Referred to as "mainframes," the early computers used in museums were very large and costly and required the services of highly trained data-processing operators, programmers, and systems analysts. Information was entered in the computers via keypunch cards or paper tape and stored on large reels of magnetic tape. Museums had to create special rooms for the computers to keep them cool and clean. Information processing was cumbersome, and operation of the computers was far from uncomplicated.

As unwieldy as those early computers were, there was an aura surrounding them. They were perceived as magical; their operators, as wizards of the modern age endowed with extraordinary scientific prowess. Computers were status symbols – badges to be worn proudly, announcing to the world that the museum that owned one had finally entered the twentieth century. Museum staff members saw computers as electronic cornucopias, loaded with cures for the museum's every ill.

Several museums that entered the computerization arena became de facto leaders of the movement by making the computer programs they had created for their projects available to the rest of the museum community. The most prominent of these programs was SELGEM, created by the Smithsonian Institution. An acronym for "SELf GEnerating Master," SELGEM was a replacement for an even earlier Smithsonian information management system, SIIR. Developed during the 1960s and first placed in operation at the Smithsonian in 1970, SELGEM was soon made available to nonprofit organizations free of charge. Composed of thirty-three unique programs, the package was issued as "a generalized system for information storage, management, and retrieval especially suited for collection management in museums."[2]

The system required data to be entered in the computer in batch-mode (keypunch cards), and the programs were written in COBOL, a widely used programming language for business applications. The use of COBOL made the package operable on a wide variety of computers. Over a period of years, museums across the country adopted SELGEM for a multitude of projects. However, technical requirements restricted SELGEM's use to institutions with access to large mainframe computers. Although many museums still use SELGEM, the Smithsonian Institution has recently discontinued distribution of the program and is in the process of designing a new package for information processing.

Another big name program package of the early days was GRIPHOS, an acronym for "General Retrieval and Information Processor for Humanities Oriented Studies." (Acronyms and verbose titles were in vogue; they helped to perpetuate the computer mystique.) Originally developed and used for library bibliographic record keeping at the Indexing and Retrieval Division of the United Nations, GRIPHOS was first adapted for museum use in 1968. Like SELGEM, it had its benefits and drawbacks. GRIPHOS allowed direct access to records and provided for the creation of indexed files on items in the collection. (An example of an indexed file is a file of all a museum's paintings listed alphabetically by artist's name.) Like SELGEM, GRIPHOS required access to a large computer system. The documentation accompanying the package was difficult to understand, and there was limited support available to help new users get started. Users of the GRIPHOS package were required to pay an annual fee to the

Museum Computer Network, Inc., a nonprofit organization, which marketed and supported the system. In an attempt to maintain uniformity, users were prohibited from modifying the GRIPHOS programs to meet their particular information needs better.

In the late 1960s, a group of New York museums formed the Museum Computer Network to serve as a clearing-house of information on museum computerization.[3] Many of the original members of MCN adopted GRIPHOS and endorsed it for use in museum information management. The package is still in use today in some museums, but its popularity has decreased significantly in light of technological advancements and of the failure of attempts to establish a national network of GRIPHOS users.

The third heavyweight program for museums in the early days was REGIS. The full name was "Arizona State Museum's Interactive REGIStration System." As its name implies, the program was designed for use in the various tasks associated with the registration of museum objects. Placed in operation at the Arizona State Museum in Tucson in 1975, the system was interactive with the user in that it provided screen prompts to aid the user in its operation. While the museum is not actively marketing the system for use by others, it can be adaptable to a variety of collections. As with SELGEM and GRIPHOS, however, REGIS requires access to a large computer system.

The success rate of the first computerization projects was relatively high, considering the obstacles posed by the developing technology and the fact that there were few models for museums to follow. But what do we mean by "success"? In this instance, success is measured by the computerized system's ability to perform the operations demanded of it with no more time and with at least as much efficiency as was required by a manual system. Record keeping of museums differed significantly from that of businesses and even varied from museum to museum. The projects that ultimately failed did so primarily because of poor planning and unrealistic expectations on the part of their instigators. Having become bogged down with their attempts to do too much, many organizations abandoned their projects before completion. These early pitfalls serve as valuable lessons for us today.

In the 1970s, as technology evolved, another generation of computing came of age – the generation of minicomputers. Less expensive and easier to operate, minicomputers rivaled the power and capacity of many mainframes while occupying only a portion of the space required by the older leviathans. The early minicomputers were still quite complex, however, and required the services of skilled data processors.

The advent of minicomputers placed electronic information management within reach of a new segment of the museum community – the mid-sized museums. Disillusioned with earlier failures or problems, hundreds of museums purchased or leased minicomputers and initiated projects to fill their information needs. Because of the greater number of projects attempted, and the do-it-yourself approach taken by many, the number of successful computerization projects during this era was low.

Unfamiliar with the basic concepts of data processing and uninformed of the pitfalls of previous projects, scores of museums secured funds, bought computers, and entered their records only to discover that they had neglected to plan for success.

Many museums found that they could not retrieve the information in the way they had hoped to once it was in the computer. Some became bogged down in entering information, while others completed the process only to find that they had created inadequate electronic versions of their inadequate manual systems.

Not all projects were failures though. Record keeping and registration at some museums were greatly improved as a result of fewer technological barriers and the dissemination of information. Here and there, museums began incorporating computers into exhibits or typesetting copy for publications via computers. During this second phase of museum computerization, museum staff members entered information in minicomputers directly from typewriter-styled keyboards rather than using keypunch cards. Rotating disks replaced reels of tape as the most popular storage medium.

During this time, more publications on computerizing collections began to emerge, and occasional sessions at museum conferences were dedicated to the subject. These sessions were attended mostly by those already involved in computer projects, however. Though somewhat diminished, the computer mystique still had an influence on the majority of professionals and caused most to shudder at the thought of attempting to computerize their museums. In addition, there were too many horror stories and too few success stories for most organizations to be convinced of the merits of computerization. Finally, though lower than ever before, costs were still prohibitive to the greater part of museums and historical institutions across the country.

Museum computerization projects proliferated, but there was still a conspicuous absence of canned programs specifically related to museum operations for use on minicomputers. The leading museum program to emerge during this time was not aimed at minicomputers at all. The "Detroit Arts Registration Information System," DARIS, was first made available to the public in 1982 but was limited to use on Burroughs mainframe computers, thereby placing the system out of reach of the majority of museums and historical organizations. DARIS was billed as "an extensive, interactive computerized system designed for cataloguing, research and collections management."[4] The system is very extensive, incorporating more the eighty-five fields or categories, and can be used by art, history, and archaeology museums.

DARIS comes with another package of business programs called "DAMIS," or the "Detroit Arts Management Information System." DAMIS includes programs for accounting, membership, fund raising, monitoring a museum gift shop, and merging correspondence with mailing lists. The entire system is available to nonprofit organizations free of charge, but there is an annual maintenance fee. A user's group of staff members from museums that employ the system meets regularly to share information and help each other.

The current museum computerization scene, an era which many believe to be yet another generation in the evolution of computing, is almost as diverse as the computer market itself. The 1980s have seen the proliferation of microcomputers. These machines and their programs are easier to use than minicomputers or mainframes, and micros do not require the services of trained data processors. And because costs for micros are not insurmountable barriers, historical institutions of every size and scope are entering the computer age as never before.

Microcomputers have brought the power of gigantic mainframes to the desktop. The technology has advanced so much that computers with display screens and disk drives can now fit in briefcases for use practically anywhere.[5]

Unfortunately, the information problems that plagued the first two generations of computer projects continue to plague today's generation as well. Although the need to computerize is still present, no central source yet exists to coordinate museum projects or to disseminate information. Although significantly less imposing and easier to use than minis or mainframes, microcomputers are still a foreign technology to the museum profession. As a result, thousands of museums are undertaking computerization projects despite a lack of understanding of even the basic principles involved.

As was the case during the preceding era of minicomputers, today there is lack of commercially available programs intended expressly for museum management with microcomputers. It is almost as if the museum community is a generation behind. Two of the most promising packages for museum management to emerge recently are intended for use on minicomputers, not micros. The continuing development of programs for minis can be attributed to the limited capabilities of many early microcomputer systems. Micros have evolved rapidly since their inception and are becoming suitable for larger and larger museum projects. We can expect to see commercially available packages for museum management in the near future for use on microcomputer systems.

A point that we should make clear deals with obsolescence. We frequently hear the word "obsolete" bantered about in discussions of museum computerization. The word readily catches the attention of museum professionals who are searching for computer systems that will meet their institutions' needs not only today but also well into the future. An automated system is never obsolete so long as it satisfactorily performs the functions required of it. Many museums have delayed the decision to computerize out of fear that the system they select will be obsolete in a short time. Meanwhile, these museums continue to suffer under inadequate manual systems while they could be enjoying the benefits of computers that would serve them well for many years to come.

The proliferation of micros throughout modern society has generated a positive attitude and done much to destroy the intimidating aura surrounding computers. People are slowly coming to see computers as tools that increase daily productivity with a minimal amount of expense and effort.

Despite increasing exposure to computers, however, anxiety remains among nonusers. And nowhere is anxiety more prevalent than within the academically oriented museum community. For the majority of museum professionals, the most frequent and lengthy contacts with automated systems are their periodic transactions with their local bank card machines. A novice is often quite intimidated when placed in front of a computer. The resulting anxiety can be a severe handicap during the initial stages of a museum computerization project. As computers continue to expand into even more aspects of daily life, especially the home environment, anxiety will decrease and ultimately disappear. Until then, first-time computer users need help. "Computerphobia" is merely a lack of understanding.

Notes

1   For a more detailed history of the events contributing to museum computeriza-
    tion, see Lenore Sarasan, "Why Museum-Computer Projects Fail," *Museum News* 59:4
    (January–February 1981): 40–9.

2   Reginald A. Creighton and James J. Crockett, *SELGEM: A System for Collection Manage-
    ment*, Smithsonian Institution Information Systems Innovations, 2:3 (August 1971).
    It was later reported in *MESH 1* (the SELGEM newsletter) that as of January 1976
    sixty-seven institutions were using the package of programs. Not all SELGEM users,
    however, were museums.

3   The Museum Computer Network, though recently hindered by lack of financial
    support, actively disseminates valuable information on computerization to the
    museum community. In addition to annual conferences, MCN publishes an informa-
    tive newsletter, *Spectra*. Of particular interest to first-time computer users are the
    lists of museums using various systems. For more information about this worthwhile
    organization, write to the Museum Computer Network, P.O. Box 2018, Empire
    State Plaza Station, Albany, New York 12220. Both individual and institutional
    memberships are available.

4   A prospectus on DARIS may be obtained by writing to The Founders Society, Detroit
    Institute of Arts, 5200 Woodward Avenue, Detroit, Michigan 48202.

5   Many of today's portable computers are more powerful than the early mainframes.
    The Radio Shack Model 100 portable computer, for example, has thirty-two times the
    memory capacity of ENIAC, the world's first computer with electronic switching.

Chapter 3

The Changing Role of Information Professionals in Museums

Andrew Roberts

Introduction

This research presents evidence of changes in the role of information professionals in museums during the last three decades and expectations for changes in the next decade, based on experience in the UK. The evidence is presented as a series of bullet points.

The research focuses on three themes across four decades, 1971–2010:

- Influences on museums: the external influences that have directly or indirectly affected the way museums work (commercial, government and social pressures), plus internal organisational and professional influences within museums (museum community pressures).
- The development of national co-ordination and the involvement of UK participants in international organisations and initiatives.
- Museum responses and trends: the ways in which museums have changed their priorities, organisational structures, documentation staffing and procedures.

1970s

Influences

- Strong pressures for museums to demonstrate accountability for the collections in their care, from internal and external auditors, such as the National Audit Office.

Source: *MDA Information*, vol. 5, no. 3, 2001, pp. 15–17.

- Early availability of large-scale external IT systems, including those in universities and local authorities.
- Trend towards organisational change and role specialisation in the public sector.

National co-ordination and international involvement

IRGMA and the MDA, 1967–

- Information Retrieval Group of the Museums Association (IRGMA), active from 1967–77.
- IRGMA supported by a research project based at the Sedgwick Museum, Cambridge, 1974–7, funded by the British Library.
- Developments pursued by the Museum Documentation Association (MDA), established in 1977, with UK-wide support from the national museums and the Area Museum Councils, initially staffed by the research staff from the Sedgwick Museum project, based at the Imperial War Museum branch at Duxford Airfield.
- These three initiatives result in active national collaboration, including:
    - Development of the IRGMA/MDA museum cataloguing standard.
    - System development based on the standard (a range of manual catalogue cards and computer software (GOS)).
    - Central advice and training support from the IRGMA team then the MDA specialists.
- Publications about museum documentation principles, the standard and manual systems.

CIDOC, 1963–

- ICOM's International Committee for Documentation (ICOM-CIDOC) on a small scale until late 1970s (20–30 participants acting as national representatives, two or three from the UK).
- Initial UK involvement by IRGMA then the MDA.
- Focus on international standards work, based on national initiatives.

Museum responses and trends

- Museum priority on cataloguing and basic procedural control, but with growing pressures for accountability.
- Main emphasis on the use of manual cataloguing systems.
- Development and small-scale use of the first computer systems for information management, typically in university museums.
- Introduction and take up of IRGMA/MDA systems and standard: 400 museums are active users within a year of the release of the manual cards.
- The staff responsible for documentation are mainly curators, as part of their general role.
- Very few specialist documentation staff, apart from temporary posts funded by government employment schemes.

- A few information specialists moving from libraries or information science backgrounds.
- Local input by individual staff into IRGMA/MDA developments.

1980s

Influences

- Following the election of the Conservative government, a strong emphasis on managerialism (structural, organisational and managerial changes which focus on the application of private sector systems and techniques into the public sector).
- Need for public bodies to demonstrate effectiveness.
- Early availability of in-house IT systems, including the first microcomputers.
- Acceleration of role specialisation.

National co-ordination and international involvement

MDA

- MDA develops a range of services and resources, with a team of specialists, moving from Duxford Airfield into Cambridge.
- National advisory service, with staff providing support in specific geographic areas.
- Continued development of the MDA standard.
- Wider range of systems (catalogue cards, new procedural controls, computer software (MODES)).
- Publications, including Planning the Documentation of Museum Collections.
- Conferences and conference proceedings, starting with Collections Management in Museums, 1987.

CIDOC

- Active involvement by the MDA staff plus growing membership by other individuals.
- Input into standards work and publications.
- Input into annual meetings and conferences, including two held in the UK (1983 in London, as part of the ICOM Triennial Conference, and 1987 in Cambridge, adjacent to the first MDA conference).

Museum Computer Network (MCN)

- Active participation by MDA staff, including Board membership.

Museum responses and trends

- Emphasis on inventory control and accountability.
- More active collections management.

- Growing use of external computer services for cataloguing support.
- Tentative use of in-house microcomputers.
- Gradual appointment of more documentation and registration specialists, usually from a curatorial background.
- Some movement of specialists between museums and to and from the MDA.
- Wider and more active involvement with MDA standards work, such as the design of procedural controls.
- Increased opportunity to take part in conferences (MDA, CIDOC, MCN, CHIN, etc.).
- Growth of the UK Registrars Group.

1990s

Influences

- Government and public perception of the importance of an information society.
- Newly elected Labour government (1997) with an emphasis on education and access.
- Changes in visitor expectations: high quality services.
- Focus on a series of standards-setting and monitoring initiatives across museums: Registration, Designation, strategic planning, collections management standards (Museums & Galleries Commission, MGC) and training standards (Museum Training Institute, MTI (now the Cultural Heritage National Training Organisation, CHNTO).
- Widespread availability of IT systems within organisations and development of external networks.
- Emphasis on the interplay between museums, libraries and archives (Museums & Galleries Commission to be succeeded by the Museums, Libraries and Archives Commission, MLAC):
- Investment in lottery-supported heritage projects, including the development of content and access

National co-ordination and international involvement

MDA

- MDA moves within Cambridge, and undergoes staff changes, including losing its original staff and outsourcing some functions.
- National advisory and training service covering wider remit, including IT.
- Renewed emphasis on standards, particularly SPECTRUM (the UK Museum Documentation Standard) and terminology work.
- Systems (procedural controls, computer software (MODES), now supported by a separate company).
- Publications.
- Conferences and conference proceedings.

MGC

- New responsibility for IT strategy.

CIDOC

- Active involvement by the MDA and UK individuals.
- Standards work and publications, including CIDOC Guidelines.
- Input into annual meetings and conferences, including one held in the UK (1999 London).

MCN

- Continued active participation by MDA staff, including Board membership.

Computer Interchange of Museum Information (CIMI) project

- Active support and involvement.

European initiatives

- Development of Memorandum of Understanding.
- Launch of European Museums' Information Institute (EMII).

Museum responses and trends

- Continued stress on inventory control, matched in later years by a growing concern to support public and research access.
- Significant increase in the emphasis on effective collections management and the use of standards.
- Significant increase in the use of computer systems, with improved performance, functionality and usability, including the first stages of exploiting external networks.
- Increased availability of standards and information systems.
- Changes in expectations, procedures and systems leading to greater demands on staff expertise.
- Development of documentation departments in larger museums and a continued focus on the appointment of junior and senior documentation and registration specialists.
- Job mobility and career progression within the information profession.
- Increased movement of specialists between museums and the MDA.
- Limited movement between museums and libraries and archives.
- Wider and more active involvement with MDA standards work, leading up to the publication of *SPECTRUM* and its subsequent widespread adoption.
- Continued opportunities for taking part in conferences, training and professional development within and beyond the sector.

2000s

Influences

- Pervasive use of computer systems and networks.
- Government policy in support of access.
- Public expectations for access to information.
- Convergence of museum, library and archive interests.
- Collaboration between museum-based and academic-based initiatives.

National co-ordination and international involvement

MDA and MLA
- MLA likely to focus on convergence and IT strategic planning and to re-assess the role of the MDA alongside that of similar library and archive agencies.
- Integration of museum, library and archive standards as part of a national and international development process.
- Re-focusing of advisory services.
- Development of national resources (SCRAN, common knowledge authorities, etc.).

Re-focusing of ICOM
- Role of ICOM and the International Committees under review.

Museum responses and trends

- Greater and on-going investment in systems.
- Move from inventory focus to information focus.
- Development and delivery of access resources.
- Significant increase in the use of content and syntax standards.
- Collaborative work across museums, across the museum, library and archive sectors and the museum and academic sectors.
- Organisational change from inventory and documentation work to active information management and access.
- Emphasis on supporting the use of networks and information by staff and users.
- Additional information specialists needed to support greater level and complexity of work.
- Greater emphasis on in-house training.
- Greater job mobility within museums and across the sectors.

Chapter 4

What is Information in the Museum Context?

Elizabeth Orna and Charles Pettitt

Any organization – including any museum – that is serious about using information to help it to achieve its aims has first to make its own definition of what information means for it, in the light of what those aims are. The idea that 'information' can mean different things for different organizations is perhaps an unfamiliar one, but it grows out of the general definition of information as the 'essential food of knowledge' which is adopted in our research. That definition relates information to knowledge in the minds of human beings, because it is only when information is transformed into knowledge and consciously applied to purposes defined by humans that it has value and power to bring about desired changes. In organizations like museums, different groups and individuals need to apply different kinds of knowledge to do their work, and so they have particular 'stakes' in different kinds of information. If a museum is to make productive and profitable use of information, it needs not only to define what information means for it, but also to understand itself as a community of users of information, to recognize the 'stakeholders' in information, and to provide them with the means of negotiating over the use of information.

Knowledge and information – some theory

While the avowed orientation of our research is a practical one, because this is our sense of what the readers we are addressing mainly wish to have, that is not to say that there is no theory underlying the ideas about information and its management which we propose. For those readers who are interested in knowing something about it,

Source: *Information Management in Museums*, Aldershot and Broomfield: Gower, 1998, pp. 19–32.

we shall say something here about its derivations; those who want to get on with the business can safely move on to the definitions.

We claim no originality for the theoretical basis. Its roots lie mainly in information science and the thinking of some of its founding fathers who went on contributing into the 1980s (in particular Brookes 1980a and b; Farradane 1980) as well as such contemporary theorists as Ingwersen 1992; Belkin 1990; Ginman 1988; and Saracevic 1992. Their ideas underlie the emphasis we place on the transformations which human minds make of external information into internal knowledge, and of internal knowledge into information which can in turn be put into the outside world for others to transform to knowledge for their own purposes. The other contributing strand – which again is quite mainstream – comes from modern theories of organizations as what Eason (1988) calls 'socio-technical systems'. It draws on such concepts as the soft systems approach (see, for example, Checkland 1969, 1985) and organizational learning (see, for example, Argyris and Schon 1978; Fiol and Lyles 1985; Senge 1990; Garratt 1994).

This strand underlies the attempt in this chapter to define what information means for a given organization. Organizations are seen essentially as consisting of human beings who are grouped together in socio-technical systems for explicit or implicit purposes. They interact both internally and with their 'outside world'; the interactions are of human beings with one another, and of human beings with technology. They create 'offerings' of products or services for their outside world; they have to seek 'sustenance' to keep in being; and they have a structure and a boundary. If these are the features singly necessary and jointly sufficient to make an organization, we can define the knowledge and the know-how they need in order to survive. They need to know what is happening inside their own boundaries, and in the 'outside world' on which they depend for sustenance; and they need to know how to recognize, interpret and act on significant changes within and without, how to create their 'offerings', and how to communicate. The actual content of the knowledge and know-how, and so the nature of the information they need to sustain it, will depend on their definition of their aims, of what they are in business for.

A general definition of knowledge and information

Knowledge is what we acquire from our interaction with the world; it is the results of experience organized and stored inside each individual's own mind in a way that is unique to each (though there are features common to how we all do it). It comes in two main kinds: knowledge *about* things, and *know-how*. We make it our own by *transforming* the experience that comes from outside into internal knowledge. Knowledge belongs to us more surely than most of our possessions, and is indeed the most precious and essential of all.

Information is what human beings transform their knowledge into when they want to communicate it to other people. It is knowledge made visible or audible, in written or printed words, or in speech, and put into external 'containers' like books, articles, conference papers, or databases. We can also usefully think of it as the *food of knowledge* because we need information and communication to nourish and maintain our knowledge and keep it in good shape for what we need to do in the world. Just as we have to transform food into energy before we can derive benefit from it, so we have to transform information into knowledge before we can put it to productive use.

As this general definition of information implies, the information required to feed knowledge has to be selected to meet the requirements of what we need to do with it – and they depend on our aims, purposes or objectives. The information that individuals and institutions need in order to maintain their knowledge will consist of different elements, according to their understanding of what they most need to do, that is, according to their value system.

Information is often spoken of today as a valuable resource, but in applying this description we need to be aware of some peculiarities and unique features which distinguish it from other material resources, and which are relevant to its value.[1]

Given those characteristics, organizations, including museums, need to be aware of the importance of interchange and negotiation among those with a stake in information. They also need to know what their information assets consist of, and to realize their potential for adding value and avoiding risk.

Why organizations need to define information for themselves

For most organizations, the idea that they need to define information in their own terms, or indeed that they need to define it at all, is an unfamiliar one. Most discussion of information systems, information resources, etc. assumes that everyone knows what information is, and that they all agree on what it is. But the definitions that emerge by implication from what organizations say about themselves, or explicitly from the answers of managers if they are asked what information means to them, are mostly rather thin and impoverished, usually with an emphasis on such things as IT, MIS (management information systems), or financial results. And there is no agreed organization-wide definition – individuals will define information in differing ways, from the point of view of their own immediate experience, and some people may not recognize that they actually use information at all, because their understanding of the concept is so restricted. Richer, more comprehensive and so more useful definitions start to develop only if organizations ask themselves: 'What do we need to *know* to survive and prosper?'

Aims and their knowledge implications – an example

A typical set of aims or objectives for a museum might be expressed in terms similar to those in the left-hand column of Table 4.1. The right-hand column sets out the 'knowledge-about' and the 'know-how' which it needs to have – in the minds of the people who work in the museum – in order to act effectively to achieve its aims.

Questions essential for survival

A complementary way of arriving at a museum's knowledge requirements is to list the questions to which it needs to know the answers in order to survive.

The collections

1 What is in the collections?
2 Why was it collected?
3 Where did it come from?
4 Where is it now?
5 What has happened to it since it came into the museum?

People on whom the museum depends

1 Who are the visitors to the museum?
2 What do they do there?
3 What questions do they ask?
4 Who are the potential visitors?
5 Who does the museum need to influence?
6 Who are its key contacts?
7 Who are its suppliers?
8 Who are its 'competitors' and its potential 'collaborators'?
9 Who are its 'customers' and 'markets'?
10 What knowledge and expertise do its staff possess? What else do they need to know about?

Finance to support the museum

1 What are the museum's present sources of funding?
2 What is its financial situation?
3 Where can it find additional funding?

Table 4.1

Aims	Knowledge required to meet them
Displaying collections	Of collections themselves Of technologies relevant to display of museum objects Know-how relevant to display
Adding to them via gift, transfer, purchase	Of potential and actual donors Of other potential sources Of market prices, vendors, etc. Of 'acquisition history' of items in collection Of value of items Of the terms of gifts
Documentating, researching, publishing collections; encouraging development of scholarship	Of collection, and of subject background; of developments in scholarship in relevant fields Of modern documentation practice, and of technologies to support it Of 'history' of all items since they became part of the collection Publishing know-how

contd.

Aims	Knowledge required to meet them
Providing suitable housing and storage, in keeping with modern conservation requirements	Of modern conservation techniques, environmental requirements of materials/object
Complementing the collections by loan exhibitions from other museums	Of collection of similar museums, in all countries
Interpreting the collections so as to engage the interest of visitors, provide education and inspiration and encourage them to continue to visit	Of the subject areas of collections, of collections themselves, of 'visitor profile', of interpretation methods Of the education system Know-how in presentation of information
Promoting the museum to a range of audiences, from first-time visitors to scholars	Of actual and potential visitor profile (including local population) Of strengths of collections, and ways in which they can engage interest of different audience Of PR know-how and skills
Securing resources from a range of sources to allow maintenance and development of the museum's activities	Of museum's actual financial and other resources, and of its financial position Of potential sources and methods of approaching them Of relevant legislation
Observing and contributing to the development of standards which affect the museum's field of interest	Of existing standards, requirements, regulations, legislation Of bodies concerned with developing and maintaining standards

Note: The aims in this table are based on those of the Tate Gallery, as set out in the gallery's *Forward Plan / Biennial Report*. Permission to use them in this context is gratefully acknowledged

Standards and obligations

1 What legal obligations does the museum have to meet?
2 What standards must it meet?
3 What conditions must its collections be kept in?

Scientific and technological support

1 What areas of scientific knowledge does it need to keep abreast of?
2 What is the state of the relevant technologies to support its work?

The knowledge base and the information to support it

We can describe the knowledge which a museum needs to master if it is to achieve its objectives as its 'requisite knowledge base'; it forms a useful standard against which to test its 'actual' knowledge base. We can also derive from it a statement of the kinds of information which it needs to take in so as to maintain its knowledge, and again, that forms a standard against which to set the *actual* information which the museum collects and uses in its work.

The heart of the knowledge base

At the centre of the museum's requirements for knowledge and information are the collections; all the other kinds of knowledge and information which any museum requires depend on them. If that core is not properly maintained, none of the aims can be achieved; instead of a rich store which justifies and rewards all the promotional, interpretive, commercial, financial and administrative uses of information, there will be a black hole in the middle. Current developments in the technology will certainly bring new ways of using collections and of creating 'offerings' based on them, and their form may also change, but they will still remain the core.

A threefold store of information and knowledge

We can think of the core of a museum as a threefold store of information and knowledge. The immediately visible store is what confronts us as soon as we enter a museum. Within that store – in art treasures, objects of daily life, machinery, mineral specimens, or dinosaur bones – is a store of 'embodied' information: what artefacts are made of, who made them, how, where and for what purpose they were made; where natural objects originate from, how and when they were formed, the material of which they are composed; how once-living organisms functioned, where and when they lived. Behind that again is an invisible store of knowledge in the minds of the people who are responsible for the care and presentation of the collections – supported by information sources that feed their knowledge, and made visible in the form of products that help visitors to relate to what they see before them, from captions and labels to catalogues, from interactive displays to guided lectures.

Similar ideas were expressed by Lytle (1981) in his 'recommendations for development of information resources at the Smithsonian Institution':

> The Smithsonian Is Information ... Museums select objects because they convey information. Artifacts, specimens, models, paintings, photographs and texts all are chosen because they convey information through their uniqueness or representativeness, their historical significance, or their aesthetic appeal. Museums conduct research to add information to their holdings, whether by identifying them more precisely or by discerning more accurately their relationship to human society. Museums disseminate

Table 4.2

Requisite knowledge for meeting aims	Information required to feed the knowledge	
	Information content	Container or vehicle for information
Of collections themselves	Comprehensive and complete details	Records, manual or in database
Of technologies relevant to display of museum objects; Know-how relevant to display	Current developments	Periodicals, conference papers, communication with professionals
Of potential and actual donors	Comprehensive and complete details	Records, manual or in database
Of other potential sources; Of market prices, vendors, etc.	'Current awareness'	Press, conversation, contacts database
Of 'acquisition history' of items in collection	Comprehensive and complete details	Records, manual or in database
Of value of items	Valuations plus 'current awareness'	Records, manual or in database; other documents
Of the collections, and of subject background; knowledge of scholarly developments in relevant fields	Past and current literature	Books, periodicals, conference proceedings – held in libraries and personal collections; communication with professionals
Of modern documentation practice and of technologies to support it	'Current awareness'	Periodicals, conference proceedings, products of specialist organizations
Of 'history' of all items since they became part of collections	Comprehensive and complete details	Records, manual or in database
Publishing know-how	'Current awareness' of developments in technology; past and current literature	Periodicals, books, trade literature, training courses, communication with professionals
Of modern conservation techniques, environmental requirements of materials/objects	'Current awareness' of scientific and technological developments	Periodicals, books, communication with professionals

contd

Requisite knowledge for meeting aims	Information required to feed the knowledge	
	Information content	Container or vehicle for information
Of collections of similar museums, in all countries	'Current awareness'	Periodicals, conference proceedings, communication with professionals
Of 'visitor profile'	Complete and comprehensive	Records; survey results details of visitors
Of interpretation methods	'Current awareness' of methods	Periodicals, conference proceedings, communication with professionals
Of the education system	'Current awareness' of developments in curriculum, teaching methods, etc.	Press, periodicals, communication with professionals
Know-how in presentation of information	'Current awareness'	Books, periodicals, training courses
Of actual and potential visitor profile (including local population)	'Current awareness' of local demography, employment, etc.	Local press, local organizations
PR know-how and skills	'Current awareness'	Communication with professionals, training courses
Of museum's actual financial and other resources, and of its financial position	Complete and comprehensive financial details	Records of transactions; accounts
Of potential sources and methods of approaching them	'Current awareness'	Press, contacts databases
Of existing standards, requirements, regulations, legislation	'Current awareness'	Government publications, published standards; database of organizations
Of bodies concerned with developing and maintaining standards		

Note: This table, like Table 4.1, is based on the aims of The Tate Gallery information through scholarly and popular publications, films, lectures and exhibits. One objective in their educational programs is to bring objects together in a way which increases their information content.

The full range of knowledge and information as described in Tables 4.1 and 4.2, and not merely that relating to the collections themselves, is essential if the three-fold store which forms the core of museums is to function properly. The relationship between information about the collections and information about the visitor profile, or sponsorship funding, or the latest interactive multimedia technology, is one of mutual support – not only are all the kinds of knowledge and information essential, they have to interact if the museum is to gain full value from them.

Who owns museum information?

There is a good deal of fairly loose talk at present about 'ownership' of information in organizations. If we define knowledge and information as they have been defined in this chapter, we can perhaps arrive at a clearer view of who owns what. Besides the concept of owners of information, we also need to consider two other groups – 'stakeholders' and 'guardians'.

Ownership

The museum is the owner of all *information* that it acquires and generates as an institution (though it must pay due regard to copyright in the case of what it acquires). Individual *knowledge* is the property of the person who holds it in his/her mind. The *information products* into which individuals who work for the museum transform their knowledge in the course of their work become the property of the museum.

'Guardians' and 'stakeholders'

The museum as an institution delegates responsibility for managing certain kinds of information to particular individuals or groups. In exercising responsibility for particular types of information (for example, information about donors, or about enquiries received), they have authority over acquiring, recording, and amending the information in question, and oversight of the ways in which it is used. They are, in effect, the 'guardians' of this information.

In addition to the guardians of any particular kind of information, there are usually many people who have a vital stake in it, because they need it in order to maintain their essential knowledge for doing their job. A documentation department, for example, may be the guardian of the master records of the objects in the collection. The stakeholders will include curators who provide cataloguing information, the registrar's department which is responsible for the inventory, acquisition and accessioning aspects of the records database and for keeping movement and location information up to date, conservators who provide conservation details, and the fund-raising department which needs information from the database for developing its strategy and products.

Organizations of all kinds should take into account the position of guardians and stakeholders in relation to information, but often their 'organizational culture' does not recognize it, and the way in which they are managed does not provide a forum where stakeholders and guardians can negotiate about their access to and use of essential information. That creates the potential for conflicts of interest and brings the danger of information not being well used to support the aims of the organization. It is essential for those who manage museums to be aware of the multiple and legitimate interests of information stakeholders and guardians, and to develop equitable organizational forms which ensure that they meet one another and negotiate over the information they need.[2]

Notes

1   This description of the peculiarities of information is based on Orna (1996).
   1.   In order to have value, information has to be transformed by human cognitive processes into human knowledge, without which no products of tangible value can be produced or exchanged.
   2.   If it is hoarded for the exclusive use of a limited number of people, it can actually fail to achieve its full potential value for those who hoard it, but if it is exchanged and traded, the value resulting from its use increases for all parties to the transactions.
   3.   Information has no inherent value of itself. 'Its value lies in its use' (Abell, 1993: 53) and the parable of the talents is applicable to it.
   4.   Information is a diffused resource, which enters into all the activities of organizations and forms a component of all products and services. As McPherson (1994: 203) puts it, 'Information permeates all organizations; it is the raw material of cognitive activity ... and ... the means whereby the organization obtains its window on the world.'
2   While the ideas set out here arose from discussions with colleagues in museums, they find an interesting echo from the world of business in a report from the Hawley Committee (1995) on the use and value of information assets by businesses, which also distinguishes the roles, rights and responsibilities of three groups of people: owners, custodians and users of information.

References

Abell, A. (1993) 'Business Link Hertfordshire', *Business Information Review*, 10(2): 48–55.

Argyris, C. and Schon, D. (1978) *Organizational Learning: A Theory of Action Perspective*, Reading, MA: Addison Wesley.

Belkin, N. (1990) 'The cognitive viewpoint in information science', *Journal of Information Science*, 16: 11–15.

Brookes, B. C. (1980a) 'Informatics as the fundamental social science', in P. Taylor (ed.) *New Trends in Documentation and Information*, Proceedings of the 39th FID Congress, University of Edinburgh, September 1978, London: Aslib.

Brookes, B. C. (1980b) 'The foundations of information science, Part 1. Philosophical aspects', *Journal of Information Science*, 2: 125–33.

Checkland, P. B. (1969, 1985) 'Systems and science, industry and innovation', reproduced in *Journal of Information Science*, 9: 171–84.

Eason, K. (1988) *Information Technology and Organisational Change*, London: Taylor & Francis.

Farradane, J. (1980) 'Knowledge, information and information science', *Journal of Information Science*, 2: 75–80.

Fiol, C. M. and Lyles, M. A. (1985) 'Organizational learning', *Academy of Management Review*, 10(4): 803–13.

Garratt, B. (1994) *The Learning Organisation*, London: HarperCollins.

Ginman, M. (1988) 'Information culture and business performance', *IATUL Quarterly*, 2(2): 93–106.

Hawley Committee (1995) *Information as an Asset. The Board Agenda. A Consultative Report*, London: KPMG Impact Programme.

Ingwersen, P. (1992) 'Information and information science in context', *Libri*, 41(2): 99–135.

Lytle, R. (1981) *Recommendations for Development of Information Resources at the Smithsonian Institution*, Washington DC: Smithsonian Institution.

McPherson, P. K. (1994) 'Accounting for the value of information', *Aslib Proceedings*, 46(9): 203–15.

Orna, E. (1996) 'Valuing information: problems and opportunities', in D. Best (ed.) *The Fourth Resource: Information and its Management*, Aldershot: Aslib/Gower.

Saracevic, T. (1992) 'Information science: origins, evolution and relations', in B. Cronin and P. Vakkari (eds) *Conceptions of Library and Information Science. Proceedings of the First CoLIS Conference*, Tampere, Finland, August 1991, London: Taylor Graham.

Senge, P. M. (1990) 'The leader's new work: building learning organizations', *Sloan Management Review*, 32(1): 7–24.

Chapter 5

The World of (Almost) Unique Objects

Robert Chenhall and David Vance

Electronic computers can be useful tools in the performance of many different functions within a nonprofit institution, just as they are now considered the basic implements of word processing, accounting, graphics design, and other activities in business, scientific, and other types of organizations. The application that is distinct to museums, however, is the use of computers to record and control activities having to do with physical objects that comprise museum collections: accessioning, registration, cataloging, inventorying, lending, exhibiting, research, etc. The use of now relatively inexpensive computers to store, process, and retrieve the verbal (and sometimes visual) symbols that represent artifacts in a museum's collection can greatly aid in the performance of these essential activities. In fact, even in modest-sized museums, it is now virtually impossible (a good case can be made for it having always been so) to maintain control of museum collections and activities without tools such as the computer.

Having made a case for the use of computers, we must quickly add the admonition that the computer alone will not automatically bring the collections of any museum under control. In twenty years of work in this field, we have both seen numerous cases of hopes dashed and money misspent pursuing the elusive dream of a "perfect" system that will take artifact records created by many different people over thirty years or more and distill them into exactly what is needed to run a museum. We must constantly remind ourselves that (1) it is only human intelligence that makes a computer function at all, (2) it is only museum people who can make a computer perform so as to accomplish the needs of museums, and (3) it is only the individuals in particular museums who make it possible to utilize a computer to accomplish the particular information needs of that institution.

Source: *Museum Collections and Today's Computers*, New York, Westpoint, Connecticut, London: Greenwood Press, 1988, pp. 3–13.

Most of the mistakes that have been made over the years have been the result of smart, sometimes brilliant, computer scientists designing systems to accomplish what *they* thought museums needed in the way of information to perform their functions. Often this occurred not as a result of arrogance on the part of the computer scientists – though this has at times interfered as well – but rather because the museum people with whom they were working were either unable to think in the precise, consistent terms demanded by computer technology or were unwilling to discipline themselves sufficiently to think through the kinds of information they really needed to do their jobs. "Give us everything you can, we might need it some day," is an all too typical response illustrating what we will sometimes do to avoid really hard thinking.

Somewhat related to the desire of the computer scientist to create the perfect museum system is the frequent suggestion that museums should adopt a computer system that has demonstrated its utility in another discipline, perhaps medicine, law, or, most often, the library field. To the uninitiated, it seems entirely logical that since libraries have highly developed schemes for the recording of physical objects – books – it should be simple to adapt one of these schemes for the recording of museum collections. The structure of a library catalog record is theoretically quite similar to the structure of a museum catalog record, so an understanding of the former provides a good starting point for understanding the latter.

Years ago, through the activities of committees composed of members of the ALA (American Library Association) and similar organizations, librarians agreed among themselves that most of the time people search for books in only one of three ways: by author name, title, or subject. The complete catalog record on any book, of course, requires additional information such as publisher and date and place of publication, but these committees reasoned correctly that if they recorded a precise but limited quantity of data on 3" × 5" cards and filed one copy of the card in alphabetical order by author, another copy in alphabetic order by title, and a third according to subject, they would then have resolved for all time the needs of library patrons in searching for library books. In later years, refinements of this basic system have been made and two subject classification schemes are now in use, the Dewey system and the Library of Congress (LC) system. However, the initial scheme has worked and continues almost unchanged to this day.

It has been recognized for a long time that the most difficult and expensive part of library cataloging was the cost of having a specialist prepare the initial record to begin with. Reasoning that this would not have to be repeated over and over in all the libraries in the country if a means could be found to do it once and reproduce catalog cards to send to libraries led to the Library of Congress becoming the central source of cataloging data. Today, all major publishers provide essential catalog data shown on the inside cover of every book as "Library of Congress Cataloging in Publication Data."

Whether the catalog in a particular library is made available in the form of 3" × 5" cards filed manually by author, title, and subject or through some form of electronic search device, the basic record on each book consists of a limited number of *fields* of data. For each such field, there is a precisely defined method for recording information: alphabetically, numerically (perhaps with a limited number of digits, and possibly in a tightly structured data code form), in a prescribed syntactic arrangement, or using only words or phrases that are listed in an authority file such as a word list or thesaurus. In other words, even though the cataloging of a book may require only a few fields of data, both the fields and the content of what is recorded are highly structured. A moment of reflection regarding how these files are used reveals why this tight structuring and control of the input was desirable even in the days when the records were prepared manually (including on typewriters); with computers, however, such structure and control is essential because there is no longer a human element intervening to pick up misspellings or errors in content. Catalog files contain records specifically intended to be placed in some kind of order, usually alphabetic according to the contents contained in one or more fields. A computer is essentially a "dumb" machine that with mechanical dependability looks at each letter, number, character, or blank space in sequence and performs functions such as searching, sorting, or filing on the basis of what is found. Therefore, if the ultimate retrieval of needed records is to be accurate and complete (and retrieval is what this kind of file is all about), it is essential that the contents of each record be structured the same way and have dependable terminology, word order, spelling, and meaning.

If libraries have been so successful in converting their catalog records from typed cards to electronic storage, why have museums been so slow to adopt more modern technology? There are several answers to this question, each of them correct in itself but accounting for only part of the problem.

The basic reason for maintaining library catalog files and museum artifact catalog files is the same: to assist in locating physical objects by providing written records that represent those objects. The physical objects in libraries, though, are sufficiently uniform that it was possible long ago to develop standardized systems for the storage of the objects and for their representation in written records. Library catalogs, basically, are quite simple: each record contains a limited number of precisely defined fields of information, and searching the file of records is usually done according to no more than three of these fields (author, title, and subject). To some extent, this simple structure is arbitrary, created by the common consent of librarians, but for the most part it serves the needs of library patrons adequately.

By contrast, those who use museum collections (not the visiting public, but museum registrars, conservators, curators, and scientists) differ among themselves in what they consider to be the important attributes of an artifact or specimen. The registrar, for example, is primarily interested in inventory control, which involves fields of information such as storage location, object number and name, source (donor, vendor, etc.), condition, and valuation. The scientist, on the other hand, will normally concentrate on an in-depth study of only a small part of the collection, which, in an archaeological collection for example, requires the recording of attributes such as the precise location where an artifact was originally found, by whom and with what associations, the material(s) out of which it is made, and implied techniques of fabrication. Because these different groups of users see different purposes for maintaining artifact files, the usual practice is to attempt to include *all* of the different fields of data that *may* be important to *any* of the probable users in the initial record.

If one adds to this complexity the wide diversity in types of museums and the differences between what is important, for example, in a university geological museum as contrasted with a large, public, fine arts museum, it is easy to see why progress in standardization has been so slow. The inevitable result has been an almost complete lack of uniformity among museums in what should be included in a catalog record, other than in situations such as within the National Park Service, where a governmental authority can dictate what information a number of museums must maintain for inventory control purposes, or where there are special files developed because of comparable interest within a particular part of the scientific community. In sum, the multiple purposes served by museum catalog files lead inevitably to the recording of many artifact attributes in place of the no more than six to ten attributes sufficient to catalog a book, and to a complexity of catalog records unknown to the library profession.

As a further extension of these differences, library science is a discipline ideally suited to the adoption of this advanced technique, whereas among museums there is still no common acceptance of the benefits that museums could derive from networks. In a library, when a catalog card is required for a new acquisition, it can be a duplicate of the same card required by every other library and, thus, can be printed, say, in Peoria from a computer file located anywhere in the country. With museum catalog records, it might occasionally be possible to produce a usable card (or another document) from a record in a file at a remote location, but in the majority of cases a museum object does not exactly duplicate any object that exists in any other museum, nor will cataloging in a central museum file adequately serve the information needs of other museums.

In this discussion, a good deal of emphasis will be placed upon the creation of information systems that are unique to the artifacts and information needs of each particular museum. Contrary to what was once believed, it is not feasible to develop one "ideal" cataloging system that will adequately serve a large number of museums and, in the process, allow the free and easy electronic interchange of all data about all objects in all the museums. The Canadian Heritage Information Network has demonstrated that a single system can serve an entire country, but even with this system it is still necessary for each institution to determine the information that it needs or wants to put into the system.

There are several reasons for this emphasis on creating individualized information systems for each institution (or organizational subdivision in the case of a large institution):

1   There are many different kinds of museums in terms of the kinds of objects that make up the collections. The information that is important, say, to an art museum, is very different from what is important to a history museum; and a natural history museum is just as different from both art and history museums as the latter are from each other. In addition to these general kinds of museums, however, are many other, more specialized, institutions. A photography museum such as the George Eastman House in Rochester, New York, for example, is in most ways similar to an art museum, but subject matter in the cataloging of photographs demands a precision that is unknown to most art historians. What is regarded as significant information in the recording of one category of museum object will always be different to some degree from what is significant for other categories.

2   Even when museums collect and exhibit identical or similar objects, the emphasis placed upon those objects – and, in turn, the information that is considered
important about those objects – may be quite different. The best example of this
is probably the archeological museum and the art museum. In the archeological
museum, collections and exhibitions emphasize primarily the historical chronology and functional utility of the objects against a background of what is known
about the society that made and used them. In the art museum it is the aesthetic
importance and craftsmanship that are most often highlighted.

3   Prior to the era of modern industrialization, every human artifact and every
specimen of nature was essentially unique. While preindustrial physical objects
are always in some ways similar to other objects – it is this similarity that makes
classification possible – they are never identical in the sense that machine-made
nuts and bolts are identical to one another.

It is essential that we constantly maintain a clear distinction between the techniques
of computerization, which can well be standardized across the bounds of most
museums (the size of the collections being the major limiting factor), and the data
fields and content of the information that any particular institution requires in order
to fulfill its objectives and goals in the best manner possible. The latter are, in truth,
almost unique in every museum because the objects themselves in each museum are
almost unique. The more widely accepted the classification systems for the objects in
a particular museum, the less need there is for creating new data structures. Geological specimens are probably described by classification categories and terminology
that are more precise than for any other discipline. In a geology museum, therefore,
the recording of specimens should be a very simple procedure, at least conceptually.
At the other extreme, however, are art and photography museums, where subject
access to visual resources creates all kinds of problems. The majority of the world's
museums lie somewhere between these two extremes. Computers can help manage
information, but the structure of the information that is important about collections
must be determined separately for each institution.

Museum activities – the need for artifact records

Museum activities may conveniently be grouped, on the basis on when they are
performed, into three major categories:

Initial Activities. When an artifact is first acquired, a number of things happen.
The object must be accessioned, identified, registered, and, possibly, restored. In
some museums, a photograph is routinely taken as part of these initial activities.

Ongoing Activities. Once the first surge of activity is over, most museum objects
rest in storage until such time as they are needed for a research project or exhibit,
either at home or on loan in some other museum, or until a noticeable deterioration
in the condition of the object indicates that some conservation effort is needed. It is
these ongoing activities that are the essential business of the museum. Even though
most of the artifacts or specimens will remain in storage, untouched for the life of
the institution, appropriate groups must be readily locatable in order for the ongoing

activities to be performed efficiently, and this is possible only if the initial activities were carried out properly to begin with.

Terminal Activity. Eventually, practically all museum objects are disposed of in one way or another. The terminal activity of decessioning (or deaccessioning) must be mentioned in order to make the cycle complete, but it is not a significant activity for this discussion.

The only reason for creating any sort of artifact record is to provide various individuals with information they will probably need to carry out certain defined activities – primarily information that is necessary or helpful to employees in the process of performing the ongoing activities of the museum. Ordinarily, research, exhibits, conservation, and loans cannot be based solely upon artifact records without physical examination of the objects themselves. Historically, however, card catalog files and the reliable(?) memories of good curators have been the only tools available to assist in locating the groups or artifacts that might be appropriate for any of these activities.

In order to lay the groundwork for what is to come, it is important to understand something about files in general, the kinds of files museums have maintained in the past, and the severe limitations the latter have imposed upon the ability of museum employees to efficiently perform their essential activities.

The word *file* comes from the Latin word for "thread" by way of the French word for "row." Thus it implies anything that is lined up in a series. Traditional examples include the pages of a ledger and cards in a file box, but the principle is the same whether we are looking at folders lined up in a filing cabinet, 3" × 5" typed cards to represent the artifacts in a museum collection, or an electronic file of the same information hidden from view within some kind of computer storage. The physical nature of these different kinds of files is distinctive, but their logical structure and content may be identical.

A file consists of from one to many *records*, with the information in each record representing all of the verbal (and sometimes visual) data available about one object or person. In museums, in addition to other records, there will almost always be a file of records containing available data on each artifact in the collection.

The structure of all records within a file should always be the same, i.e., each record should contain the same defined *fields*, or data categories, one for each type of discrete observation, kind of data, or category of information that will probably be required to record the objects that are the subject matter of that particular file.

Finally, the *content* of the data recorded in each field must be controlled in a consistent manner in all of the records contained in a particular file. There are several ways this can be accomplished, depending upon the nature of the data. For example, in recording dates, the structure of the field can be limited to a fixed number of numeric digits with punctuation to separate year, month, and day. In recording precise terminological fields such a object name or materials, the acceptable content can be controlled by word lists or thesauri, perhaps stored in computer memory. In like manner, the content of other fields can be controlled by various combinations of field length, alpha-numeric character limitations, syntax, and thesauri.

The important thing to remember at this stage is not the details, but the immutable structure of files: each file contains records with a fixed number of defined fields; and in each defined field the content is controlled in a precise manner.

The most common museum artifact file – probably the earliest in point of time – is what we now call an *accession file*. These files, of course, are not at all uniform. Some are maintained in massive ledgers, some are in less pretentious books, and some are simply file folders containing the paperwork (letters, signature sheets, etc.) associated with each acquisition that the museum has made. Generally, accession files contain *fields* of information such as the following:

- Accession Number – most often a two-part number corresponding to the year in which objects were acquired and the chronological number of their accession within that year
- Accession Date
- Source – name and address of the donor or vendor from whom objects were acquired
- Source of Funds – if the objects were purchased
- Method of Acquisition – donation/purchase/loan
- Number of Objects in the Lot.

Notice that this file ordinarily does not include any object descriptions at all. If it did, a large bequest would require many accession records, and descriptions of each individual object would mean repeating a large quantity of accession information – which would not accomplish anything in terms of the activities of the museum.

Early on, curators and registrars conceived the idea of not repeating any more data than was necessary by creating a separate artifact *catalog file* in which the accession is referenced by the two-part number and each object is given a distinctive, third number (thus, 1925.23.7 would be the seventh object within accession number 23 during 1925). This innovation provided not only the possibility of separately describing each object without the redundancy of including accession data in each object record, but it also produced a convenient and brief system of code numbers that could be applied to the objects themselves as a permanent and positive form of identification.

Museum catalog files, like accession files, come in many forms. Some are little more than a card with the artifact number and a lengthy textual description of the object. Most provide for the separation of the textual description into a number of discrete fields of information. As one might expect, if the entire description is reduced to discrete fields or categories of data, the result is a catalog file with many distinct fields. A minimal catalog file, which can be maintained without too much work on 3" × 5" cards, might contain the following fields:

- Artifact Number – the three-part number described above
- Object Name
- Provenience – where did the object originate?
- Price/Value
- Artist/Creator
- Location – within the museum.

Although most small museums are able to maintain both an accession file and a catalog file somewhat like those described, both files are usually organized in numerical sequence, which does nothing to aid employees in the performance of their work. The activities of the museum require the ability to find artifacts by such characteristics as object name, storage location, or artist name, not by a basically arbitrary number comparable to a social security number.

There are two basic organizations of itemized data. One can make a list of entities such as objects or persons, and attach a list of attributes to each entity, thus:

Artifact Number 1925.23.7
    Object Name
    Storage Location
    Etc.

Artifact Number 1925.23.8
    Object Name
    Storage Location
    Etc.
    Etc.

Alternatively, one may list the attributes and attach to each one a list of entities:

Object Name <1>
    Artifact Number
    Artifact Number
    Artifact Number

Object Name <2>
    Artifact Number
    Etc.
    ———

    ———

Storage Location <1>
    Artifact Number
    Etc.

Storage Location <2>
    Artifact Number
    Etc.

The former organization seems natural to us as humans. We perceive a world of things, each of which exhibits certain attributes ("this *tree* is green"), not a world of attributes that show up in certain things ("*green* is manifest in this tree"). Therefore the first form of organization is referred to as *normal*, whereas the second is described as *inverted*. The inverted form of data organization, however, is invaluable for research. Indexes are the most familiar example, and finding artifacts appropriate to museum activities is, in fact, the same thing as a form of indexing.

In some of our larger museums the utility of inverted indexing was recognized early, if not by name, at least in practice. In the Henry Francis DuPont Winterthur

Museum, for example, three copies of each artifact catalog card were prepared for many years. One was filed numerically, by artifact number; one was filed alphabetically, by object name; and the third was filed alphabetically, by provenience. This was clearly a great improvement over the maintenance of the artifact catalog solely in numeric sequence – at least the records on objects that had the same name could be located easily and it was possible to conveniently find records describing artifacts from the same locality. However, the system still had several drawbacks. It is possible to prepare three artifact cards without too much trouble, but when the number of discrete, indexable data categories is, say, ten or more, the clerical task of creating, filing, and controlling so many cards very quickly gets out of hand and the system breaks down completely.

Enter the computer and a totally new way of thinking about artifact records. No longer does one have to worry about the mechanics of what physically happens in the preparation and filing of cards. Once the information about each accession and each artifact is organized and entered into the computer files in the precise format demanded by the system, what happens physically, within the computer, is of no concern. The files can be reorganized on demand to fit almost any conceivable data need.

With the advent of database management systems that can be used on relatively small and inexpensive computers, it is possible for the first time to concentrate initially on what kinds of records one wants to maintain: to begin – from the top down – with the objectives and activities of the institution; to outline a framework of records that will probably provide the greatest aid in carrying out those activities; to list the discrete types of data (the fields) that need to be present in each of the records; and finally, to organize the whole into a complete system that will provide the needed data to each employee in the most efficient and dependable manner possible.

Top-down organization such as this means, of course, that there must be a clear, communicated statement of institutional objectives and activities, and that someone must have a sufficiently organized mind to delineate the records and record fields that will be required in order for the total system to work. Although these needs appear to be obvious, in fact, failure to consider them at the beginning of the project is probably the biggest cause of problems with computer-based cataloging systems; success requires that the director and governing board must first do the hard thinking about their mission statement and the kinds of records that will be necessary to fulfill their mission most efficiently.

Chapter 6

Standards for Networked
Cultural Heritage

David Bearman

The enthusiasm with which cultural institutions have embraced the latest developments in computer-based communications as reflected in their adoption of the World
Wide Web, stands in great contrast to their conservatism and hesitancy in the face
of computing over the past twenty years. While this enthusiasm is naive, seasoned
computing professionals should be alerted that it reflects the importance to museums
of public accessibility and of the visual image, neither of which was enabled by the
past generation of systems which made few inroads. Obviously heritage information professionals should welcome the change of attitude, and especially the implicit
recognition of the power of visual surrogates of primary materials. At the same time,
we must be aware that the WWW will not contribute to enabling useful access to
cultural heritage information without a clearer sense of which standards are critical to the provision of functional access in the near-term and to the preservation of
content over the long-term. In this paper I will discuss the nature of the standards
required for the international cultural heritage community to succeed in implementing computer-based communications and the role leading cultural heritage organizations could play in bringing their programs into line with these standards. I hope the
argument will contribute to getting commitment from museum directors and their
counterparts in other cultural institutions to standards-based information management strategies.

Over the next two decades we can expect to see a growing penetration of interactive, broadband services into homes, schools and businesses and the emergence of
a facility for information and entertainment of an importance equal to that of television today.[1] Information services with this degree of market impact will only occur

Source: *Archives and Museum Informatics*, vol. 9, no. 3, 1995, pp. 279–307.

if the user is "coddled" and "assisted" and the information can be provided with a minimum of reprocessing to support a variety of "points-of-view". The coddled user expects his software to diagnose its environment, locate the elements it needs to run, update itself and automatically back up his activity. The assisted user will not read manuals or lists of headings, will use her own language in making inquiries and will expect relevant, weighted, and usefully formatted results that can easily be utilized with a range of available tools. Users will be almost unaware that information has been provided to support other points-of-view than their own because what they will see, as results of their searches, will employ language appropriate to their level of expertise and display it using metaphors with which they are already comfortable, such as maps or timelines. Information suited to their point-of-view will have been compiled from sources, such as dictionaries of national biography, national bibliographies, historical atlases and the like which expand the contextual linking opportunities of the users own search.

Recent developments in computing could contribute towards enabling us to serve these users, but the objective of making our information systems work in these ways will have to be accompanied by reassessment of the kinds of standards we support and how we implement them. There is no question in my mind that if cultural heritage institutions are to succeed in the next century, they will need to provide easy, one-stop electronic access to their collections and programs. For this reason, I have confidence that they will only succeed if they act collectively and if appropriate standards are developed and employed. Unfortunately, I'm equally convinced that the standards we have been promoting until recently are not appropriate for the strategies we need to enable.

Why standards?

A standards-based information management strategy should help individual museums acquire information less expensively and with greater functionality but its real pay-off is for the cultural heritage community as a whole. There it promises to make our information collectively useful, enabling us to become players in the emerging consumer communications environment. The benefits of such a strategy, however, will only be realized if the strategy can capitalize on three sources of potential value:

- it must reduce the cost of capturing digital representations of the collections, in text, image and sound or multimedia; and it must make possible capturing existing source materials and making new source materials in equally cost effective ways,
- it must support the functionality required for public access to meaningful information about cultural heritage while at the same time enabling museum applications, and
- it must substantially increase the size of the audiences we can reach both by enabling us to reach a broader audience, satisfy special requirements of narrower audiences, and tailor content to previously unreachable audiences.

In each case, adopting the right standards can play a significant role in reducing risks, increasing benefits and reducing costs, but in each case also the speed at which the technology is changing makes any decision complicated. Not deciding, of course, is making a decision too. Therefore consciously addressing the implications of specific technical decisions is crucial. It will be much easier to know what actions to take in the context of an overall strategy.

To reassess our strategy we need first to understand the strategy we have been pursuing and to identify its strengths and weaknesses.

Simply put, our strategy has been to make special purpose representations of cultural objects (catalog entries for artifacts and bibliographic entities), and to use specialized interchange protocols to combine these into union lists. The implications are that the representations needed to be uniform in content and often in data values. The major functional purpose we were trying to serve locally was accountability, and therefore the premium was placed on comprehensiveness. Ideally each object would have a record. It was acceptable for those records to contain a small quantity of well structured information used essentially for control (bibliographic control or collections management), and because comprehensiveness was important, the result was that our community invested in thin representations.[2]

This strategy has produced a legacy of records and of standards that fail to serve either the needs of broader audiences or those of specialized niche markets. In addition, our approach has been financially and intellectually costly for the heritage community because it doesn't exploit the major investments we make in interpretive content or make our richest value-added resources available to the public. And because it relies of standards that are not generally used by other database creators, this strategy does not help us exploit the investments made by those others (cartographers, makers of national biographies and bibliographies, companies creating sales catalogs, and the like), who employ other standards in construction of databases that document other aspects of society with which we would like to link.

Museum professionals, perhaps because they have sensed this or perhaps because they are simply uncooperative types, have been discussing the question of what standards to employ in creating digital representations of their collections but have made little progress in the past decade. We've held a variety of conferences on data value standards and while these have helped us become aware of many different thesauri and classification systems, there is still little agreement about the value of ICONCLASS, no widespread use of the Art and Architecture Thesaurus (AAT), and most of the systems ever presented are still being used by those who originally promoted them.[3] There has been no agreement proposed or accepted regarding data value standards based on rules (AACR II for example) or formats common to other disciplines (ISSN, longitude/latitude, Greenwich time etc.). The community has organized numerous committees to define content standards. Some of these have attempted to create a standard for all kinds of objects and others have proposed standards for specific types of objects only. To date there is no widely accepted content standard, although the SPECTRUM standard may be on its way towards acceptance as a generic framework for data required to support museum processes and functions.[4]

The issue of encoding has not been addressed by the community so the standards generally followed by business have prevailed. The approach we've taken to encoding standards may have been, and still be, the only one we could have taken because operating systems and utility software are not specific to museums and the market has dictated ways in which systems will read. For text, today, this has meant capturing in ASCII. In the future, when systems generally can manage it, we may choose UNICODE. For image, the standard solution is still to get the best photographic images we can and delivering digital representations only as "use" copies for specific applications regardless of the standards they employ.[5] For sound, digital recordings in audio CD standards are quality intermediaries if the human voice or instruments designed for human ears are the subjects.

At the level above encoding characters, pixels and tones, we've been promoting standards without articulating the specific success criteria that should be employed in evaluating their effectiveness. Indeed, museums have generally only attended implicitly, rather than explicitly, to standards designed to ensure the functionality of the data we capture. Those engaged in the somewhat arcane task of developing data value standards for museums, especially the companies that delivered collections management software, have long had to re-present the data, re-encode it, in order for it to do the jobs that museums want it to perform. It's still essentially impossible to bring data from existing museum automation systems into a common view for use for non-collections management purposes as the experience of the Museum Educational Site Licensing (MESL) and RAMA (Remote Access to Museum Archives) projects have demonstrated. Soon most museums will face the equally important question of how they can afford to re-use their own multimedia data in new products, and they will find that the standards we have promoted in the past are inadequate to the task.

The fundamental incentive for museums to adopt standards-based information management strategies are, simply, that museum data is very long lived and information systems, generally, are not. Standards for cultural heritage information are the bridge between systems over time. Of all the levels of standardization to which museums could become committed, the most promising is content. But adopting standards should not mean standardizing in the narrow sense of making the content conform to specific values. Widespread adoption of content representation standards, rather than adoption of common content value standards, should be the objective. Some of the most promising standards we could adopt to ensure the longevity of museum content, such as SGML together with museum community defined DTDs, do not dictate data values. Other standards, such as terminology standards or thesauri, can be used in ways that exploit the variability of the data content rather than requiring its homogeneity. Nor should adopting standards, although designed to create quality data, be confused with making all content conform to someone else's "high quality" standard. Effectiveness stands above purity in the hierarchy of values we need to promote – in standards the best is too often the enemy of the good. There is no evidence that use of "good" terminology will improve access or usability of the data we create and much theoretical reason to believe that a "preferred" term or form is less likely to be found than any term in a system that recognizes the relations between all terms.

The premise of standardization is that it will enable us to provide information to others in an effective manner. This means it must support appropriate retrieval and enable effective reuse without massive reconfiguration or re-authoring. In order to choose strategies, therefore, we need to understand how data will be served to the public and in what ways they will use it. But the excitement engendered by the World Wide Web and its multimedia browsers should be an object lesson in how quickly the nature of the delivery environment changes. It reminds us that in thinking about how data will be served we should not be tied to *http* any more than we were to *gopher* or *ftp* clients. The failure of numerous experiments with interactive television over the past few years should be further cause for concern. The fact is that a decade from now the content we are making today will be used by people through technical mechanisms we cannot now envisage. Nevertheless we can know what conceptual purposes they will be using it for and what means of intellectual access they will require to locate the information of value to their inquires.

We must not forget that adopting standards is an investment which typically costs organizations a considerable amount up front. The gamble is that it will pay off for them or their clients down the road. Those who invest in making standards take an even greater risk – the pay off will only come if many, and usually, most, others adopt the standards over time.

Which standards?

In the search for strategic approaches to standards, it is useful to distinguish between four different "levels" of standards which do different types of work: data value standards, data content standards, data structure standards and systems standards.[6]

Data values: knowledge representation and authority control

Computers store and process data which is designed to represent knowledge. How we represent that knowledge should be determined by the processes we intend to support. Ultimately, certain processes will not be possible if they cannot use the data in the system. Because we are used to paper data storage and the human mind as our information processing system, we frequently identify the wrong data values to control. For example, humans can easily read and process the prose phrase from our wildlife encyclopedia – "In early autumn, the pelt of the arctic hare thickens ..." – but a computing system will need to translate the concepts of "early autumn" and "thickens" into a calculable period of time (for example, 22 September–21 October) and a calculable percentage of additional bulk (for example, +10%) and to link to an authority file in order to recognize that "arctic hare" is a term used to designate a species of mammal, a type of hare, and that hares are closely related to rabbits. These expressions, when "re-presented" for computation, may be accompanied by degrees of certainty (for example, circa or approximately equal +/– 5%), which are, of course, fundamental to the prose they stand for, but even with such (equally calculable) qualifications the substitute representation is usable for searching and for comparative assessment of pelt in a way that the prose expression is not. The relationship between hares and rabbits may be needed to locate this or any other data about this specimen for a lay person.

Providing computing systems with appropriate knowledge representations to serve business needs is a critical strategic concern. It is increasingly clear that two very distinct questions must be answered along the way: which data will serve our business needs, and how should we go about getting data to conform to knowledge representations that can be used for the processing purposes we envisage. Cultural institutions to date have probably answered both of these questions in a way that we will not want to continue in the future.

For example, in the above case, in order to ensure that the data was processable, we could:

- instruct data entry staff to create a record with the data formatted in fields for "time of capture" and "pelt thickness" according to structured data entry rules (Rule-Based Data Validation) and to check the term "arctic hare" in a thesaurus (Authorized Term Entry).
- create a lookup table which translates "early autumn" into a date range and puts the date range value in the field and another table which looks up "arctic hare" and places the scientific name of the arctic hare into another field of the database and the terms hare, rabbit, etc. into a related terms field (Vocabulary-Based Term Substitution).
- create a knowledge-base linked to at the time of searching and processing to translate "early autumn" into a date range but which leaves the prose in the computer record and which can translate searches for "rabbits" or "hares" into searches for the narrower term or scientific name for arctic hare (Knowledge-Assisted Search and/or Processing).
- build an application that accepts the terms "early autumn" and "arctic hare" as valid input and operates on them according to proprietary rules (Software-Dependent/Enhanced Data Validation).

Managers of business information systems, who rarely need to worry about the use of knowledge representations outside their applications or address issues which occur due to the instability of technology standards over time, will choose the first or fourth options because their efficiency can be optimized. To date, standards proponents in cultural heritage have opted for the third approach, but institutions holding cultural heritage information have resisted imposing uniformity on their data content. It is now evident that the cultural heritage information to which we want to support access will continue to reside in many systems created for many different local purposes. While we hope the aggregate will satisfy our collective needs, it is also clear that documentation is labor intensive and there are many objects in the collections of museums so we need to define tactics that allow us to exploit the information that exists rather than adopting tactics that would require making data uniform across the world. It is now obvious that we couldn't, and shouldn't, demand that everyone use the same application even if we were in a position to give it away for free.

The first rule of data value standardization strategies for networked cultural heritage, therefore, ought to be to invest in knowledge representations to translate between disparate data values assigned by individuals with different backgrounds, perspectives, and local cataloging conventions rather than in technologies dependent on data uniformity. This strategy was adopted by the Getty Art History Information Program in constructing the Union List of Artists Names, which eschewed the concept of "preferred" name in favor of a cluster of names all used by different authority sources to represent the same individual. Earlier and in a quite different technical environment, AHIP, like others, had invested in vocabulary and terminology development that promoted "authority control" as a means toward data uniformity. I believe that as a consequence the museum community standard efforts have been less successful than they might have been, and much less successful than they need to be if the method for achieving the benefits depends on uniformity. It is critical to understand what has changed; later we can explore how the current products can best be promoted with the new tactics.

In a more centralized data storage and data processing environment, and an environment in which specific application requirements for control were the objective of new data capture, terminology standards were typically implemented in systems that employed term substitution and rule-based validation. The new computing paradigms for which we are now planning suggest that these tactical choices will no longer deliver the efficiencies we imagined we could achieve in the previous implementation environment but the full implications of these shifts have not yet been taken into account in vocabulary standardization work.

Even if we adopt appropriate approaches to ensuring processability, we still need to examine what data values we have been trying to control. Here it seems that we have too often chosen to control the easiest things, proper nouns, rather than the data values most important to the applications we want to support. From the world of art databases, I have chosen two examples of data representation problems relating to physical description which are important and two examples relating to logical to identify some further questions we need to address.

Museums typically record the size of objects in their collections, but in human readable fields the display is processable by a human mind regardless of the consistency (or inconsistency) of the presentation. Thus a person has little trouble making sense of the measurements $10'' \times 4'' \times 300'$, or 10 inches (height), 4 inches (width), 300 feet (length), or 'about ten by four inches and over three hundred feet long when fully extended', while a computer will not be able to make much sense of these or necessarily even be able to recognize them as measures within a body of text. In most collections management systems, a method of representing size has been developed that allows the museum professional to calculate the size of a crate or frame or to inform a colleague from another gallery of the installation requirements of a traveling piece. These application processes are supported by the knowledge representation used. But what if we want to show various objects from different museum collections in relative proportion to each other? The representation of size in each museum's information system may help a person answer all such questions but they will fail a computer because they will be different from one system to the next and because their translation into processable form is typically software dependent. Yet size is one of the truly critical points of information used by human beings to understand the world and without it our data will be of limited use for the generalist or public user. We can immediate perceive the size of objects by bringing images of them into a single frame of reference, and this will presumably be one of the application requirements of our distributed image search and display systems, but how will knowledge representations support it?

Color is, of course, another characteristic that we use to understand and appreciate the physical world. Indeed the world of art is to a very large extent defined by color and other properties of reflected light. Digital representation of objects may contain textual descriptions of color or representations of pixels encoded to capture color values. In either case, the degree of accuracy in the representations would seem to be an important measure of the value of the digital surrogate. Yet museums have not widely adopted standards for describing or representing color and the computing systems in use today are notoriously poor at rendering color consistently. Simple standards could be adopted that would enhance the value, and quality, or museum data to the public and would make searching by color easy.

Beyond physical description, the objects of our cultural heritage have meaning to us by their associations. In the past we have focused on conformity in naming the objects of these associations, the things (people, places, buildings, ships, etc.), with which the objects were associated. Increasingly it seems that we should have concerned ourselves with the relationships (creating, selling, designing, using, critiquing) between the objects and the proper nouns on which we lavished so much attention because as we examine the queries being put to us by our publics, it is obvious that each user community needs to know about quite different relations (and, as argued earlier, the nouns could be "controlled" without imposing conformity anyway).[7] The difference between interests in where a group of objects were made, or found, or used, reflects the profound differences in intellectual perspective between the art historian, archaeologist and anthropologist. Our different publics are interested in exploring these kinds of associations in themselves, rather than in the compilation of lists of things with any association to a person or place. Types of objects, by their functions and their cultural meanings, and types of events, by their personal, societal or corporate significance, are currently hidden in the data structures we have built to hold nouns, preventing the association of items used with religious rituals, objects given as tribute from conquered peoples, or designs realized by different creators.

Finally, people associate objects with specific, as well as with generic, events because it is through their relationship to events that many objects obtain their significance to us. Specific public events do not necessarily have proper names, rather they take their names from a combination of event types and the individual or organization at the center of the event, such as the Rabin funeral, the Kennedy inauguration, or the christening of a private person whose name would be meaningful only to family members tracing their genealogy. Whether events have names (World War II) or only constructed titles (the first Sputnik mission) or no regular means of identification, they occurred at a time and in a location and can therefore be searched and organized according to date and place if their knowledge representations enable it. Very little effort has gone into the creation of authority databases to permit access by events to date, but it will need to be a major concern in the future if we are to reach new audiences.

In general, the community has placed a great emphasis on making vocabularies which it urges professionals to use in place of their existing terminology and on making secondary data records to represent primary materials which use pre-approved language in their structured fields. Two important points should be made about this programmatic focus:

1   the information elements which terminology standardizers have chosen to control are no less important than those in the examples above which have not been emphasized to date, and
2   the pre-occupation with terminology control has reflected the state of computing which, until very recently, required controlled terminology. But we must acknowledge that some of the resistance to the use of controlled vocabularies at the front end of database was simply a reflection of the fact that individuals employed in museums rely on their professional training and expertise and do not take well to formal rules. For these reasons they often resisted prescribed lists of terms and thesauri even when these reflected the very best thinking within their own professions. Nevertheless, there are legitimate reasons for resisting the use of prescribed terminologies. Often there is nuance in the choice of particular local or historically correct terms to describe an object, sometimes the "literary" requirements of a piece of text justify variety in the choice of terms, and sometimes the functional requirements of a particular application demand a different representation of the information than is suggested by the controlled terminology.

Until several years ago, the appropriate strategy for museums with standards-based commitments to reducing risks and increasing their opportunities to exploit the value of their data would have been to override the objections to imposing controlled vocabularies in the face of the greater advantages to be gained from its imposition. Recently the advent of alternative approaches and new computing technologies which do not depend on rigid structures of the more limiting databases of the past, have led to reconsideration of the way in which controlled vocabularies can best contribute to standards-based strategies. Instead of emphasizing their role in imposing values on data entered into databases, the new approach sees the value of such vocabularies in intermediating access to uncontrolled database language.

Instead of making such vocabularies in a quality controlled workshop staffed by a highly specialized central staff, the new approach envisions making vocabularies through distributed linking of practice as it is reflected in usage of all users.

It is worth noting that the value of both "term switching" or "vocabulary enhancing" search strategies and of distributed database construction are not well proven. Nevertheless, there are some good reasons to believe that in the future terminologies will be used primarily to enhance access rather than to control data entry and it is self-evident that the limits of centrally staffed database construction are finite and have been reached. Cautious managers will want to continue to exercise some control over data input as well as watching for implementable terminology solutions in search and retrieval systems.

Content standards

In order to enable the distributed construction of data resources, the museum community has expended substantial effort on defining data content standards such as the CHIN data dictionaries, the CIDOC Data Model, and the AITF Categories for Description of Works of Art. These data content standards addressed only one of two issues which such standards must resolve: how to locate information of a particular type, but not how to act on it. We could label these two problems as "content designation" and as "supporting processable data types". The approach to data content standardization reflected in the physical, logical and conceptual models referred to above presumed that the aim was to standardize, in the sense of homogenize, the defined elements of information managed by a Database Management System (DBMS) with field labels as markers served only as content designation. While the approach was adequate in a world of central computing systems and union databases where common functionality was dictated by common processing environments, the disadvantages of assuming such structures for distributed access are now apparent. Even if interchangeability of data between DBMSs could be achieved, it is not clear that museums would be willing or well advised to make the sacrifices necessary to achieve homogeneity based on physical equivalence of data structures across different institutions and platforms.

An alternative method of content designation which additionally addresses the support of processable data types, and enables the modularization of functional attributes of data types so that the same data can be used from a multiplicity of perspectives, is to "mark up" the data with SGML (Standard, Generalized, Markup Language) labels. Because SGML parsers (systems designed to read SGML-tagged data) are designed to accept "arbitrary" Document Type Definitions (DTDs), they are able to read SGML-tagged information without regard to the software dependencies of the systems that created it and the nature of the language is that it should be readable over time even as SGML and other standards change. Unlike interchange formats developed for special reasons, like the MARC format or EDI, SGML does not have limits on the modalities of data it can hold, on length of records, or on types of receiving systems. Furthermore, it can be easily transformed into MARC, EDI or the proprietary data structures of the locate DBMS.[8]

One of the benefits of using SGML as a standard, and adopting community agreements on how to label objects using SGML standards, is that it brings the museum community into congruence with other humanities which have adopted SGML as a way to mark up full texts of humanistic primary source materials, such as archives and manuscripts, as well as published texts. This permits a variety of users, over time, to mark the same information from numerous distinctive intellectual perspectives, or at different depths for specialized application needs, while benefiting from and building on the effort of previous analysts.

However, the mere choice of SGML as the means of locating data types in cultural heritage information systems (a choice endorsed by the Committee for Computer Interchange of Museum Information in 1993 and being pursued by the Consortium for Interchange of Museum Information today), does not help us to determine what content to mark or how to represent it. The choices involved in implementing SGML will determine the degree to which it is accepted by the community and the benefits (if any) from its use. So far the suggestions made by potential "standardizers" oriented toward SGML-based solutions have not demonstrated sufficient sensitivity to application requirements, and, at the same time, have been overly driven by physical rather than logical data content. An SGML-based strategy for interchange of cultural herit-age data will be successful *if and only if* the DTDs it advances serve the application purposes of the data contributors and support the cumulative construction of cultural knowledge-bases. Only tactics that enable the aggregate work of many people over time to populate the fullest possible content designation will succeed in producing documentation which reflects the sum of the perspectives of many disciplines and is affordable to the community.[9]

For example, in the title of the painting "The Constitution in Newport Harbor" there is a reference to a ship and to a place. In databased computing environments we would have identified this as the title of a painting (by placing the data in the field with that label), and the ship name and place reference would be lost. Thinking more care-fully about representation of the data, we could "mark" the internal contents of this field to allow for retrieval of references to ships and to cities independently of where the reference takes place. This would allow us to create indexes by place and proper names of ships thereby satisfying several potential uses that otherwise would be lost. If these uses can justify the added cost of mark-up, or better serve the mission of our particular organization, then the aspects of the DTD which permit deeper mark-up of content elements within content elements will be exploited. If not, the organization doing the mark-up would not use the deeper markings, although others might later add value by inserting such markup for their own purposes or re-use. If the title of the above painting was contained in a paragraph of text which noted that the artist was, at the time of creating the work, actually visiting with the Stephenson family in Charleston and used as his model "The Maiden", a civilian fishing vessel, the value of both the ability to mark deep content and to ignore it becomes clearer. A maritime museum which had the anchor of "The Maiden" among its holdings would almost certainly consider this important enough to warrant detailed content designation while an art museum holding the original painting would likely settle for marking the entire paragraph as "history of creation". Ideally, knowing that "The Maiden" was a boat out of Charleston should allow linking to registers of vessels and to footnotes in literary criticism which reference the same boat.

Not only should any DTD allow the markup of content from different intellec-tual perspectives and uses, thereby serving different audiences, but we need to alter our expectations about when and by whom "documentation" occurs. Specifically we need to accept that documentation takes place over time and that everything which is written (spoken, drawn) about a cultural artifact ought to be brought meaningfully into the sphere of documentation. We need to begin to see documentary and inter-pretive acts as a continuum rather than as different and accept that any "facts" about an object should be attributed to someone, some time and place, and some authori-ties if relevant. This purpose was central to the Architectural Documents Advisory Group (ADAG) data model. I was highly critical of it at the time of its production because it was advanced as an implementation which presumed, despite the obvious and insupportably immense overhead, that each documenting agency would capture all such information in a single pass even if it needed, for its own purposes, only a small amount of that information.[10]

If we are to have rich cultural documentation it must be the consequence of inde-pendent, and subsequently integrated, actions of many documentalists and interpreters over the lifetime of the cultural object. Early in my professional career, I encountered a natural history museum which held a painting of a beaver that it had documented by recording the species name in Latin and the date of the painting but had not felt it necessary to record the "artist", "title", or "provenance" of the work. Needless to say, a visiting art historian was scandalized and felt that this was evidence of poor curatorial and documentation practices. But I believe it reflected a sound documentary practice for that museum, while I simultaneously felt that it would be important that the art historian be able to add information of significance to his perspective without having to create a new record or new system. After all, the art museum documented similar paintings without reference to species or other elements of information essential to the natural history curator. As a rule, our methods and systems should enable each user or institution to research items from their perspective and record information to serve their needs. If we can design standards that enable this to take place and information to flow from one model to the other, then we have achieved a method for cultural heritage knowledge base construction that can be widely adopted to the benefit of all. Over time, documentation will be broader and deeper than it can be if only one source of cataloging and one authority prevails.

Another of the more exciting properties of SGML is that if we adopt DTDs with sufficient power to capture the content desired by the most demanding researcher, the hierarchical structure of the SGML language allows us to equally well (and more frequently) capture content at a very general level. This kind of facility is not available in fielded databases, where either we must have some fields whose content will be sometimes very general and sometimes very specific (making them virtually unusable) or require users of the structure to enter data at a level of detail they do not know and cannot afford to research. At the extremes, SGML or full text hierarchically sensitive markup, allows the equivalent of designating a document without any further markup (full-text) and designating a document with such complete markup that no fielded data structure could accommodate it without incredible redundancy and extraneous data input. Since we want standards that permit efficient and cost effective capture of primary content and which allow content to be rendered for users according to their point-of-view rather than simply the point-of-view of the documenting agency, these features of SGML are of great value.

Finally, as the acceptance of the WWW should tell us, cultural heritage institutions, and the audiences for their information resources, are almost unconsciously aware that multimedia is the more powerful and potentially more profitable content than text surrogates. SGML has the great advantage in this regard in that it allows for the objects being marked to be text, sound, graphics or image and, even more importantly, provides for meaningful links between them. We know that such multimedia data will be of greater importance in the future, and that the National Inventory, or Index to Canadian Heritage, would be greatly enriched by images of the primary documents and objects to which they refer.

Application interfaces

For the past decade, thinking about museum standards has been dominated by the hope that either a museum network standard for museums could be developed into which commercial applications would fit (the RLG-AMIS project and the Remote Access to Museum Archives-RAMA project both imagined this as a successful outcome) or the hope that museum collections management applications developers could be persuaded by the market to implement museum community specific common interfaces (the Z39.50 museum data set, EDI museum object loan data set, etc.). Not only have these solutions not worked to date, they are increasingly looking like the wrong answers.

Probably the most important development of the past few years in the potential for a standards-based museum information management strategy has been the adoption by museums of a range of commercial utilities or generic application services which support their broad missions. This has meant that the ultimate benefits of automation to museums will be realized through a variety of commercially vended applications that support specific business functions of the museum such as authoring tools and presentation managers for exhibition and interactive education, desktop publishing tools for museum publications, commercial store inventory support and fulfillment systems for museum shop sales, and general purpose fund-raising tools for membership and development. Software developed for these application areas is sold by commercial firms with disincentives to adopt common standards within their niches (and none to adopt museum community standards) but substantial incentives to adopt cross-application standards. Now, because museums are like other clients of the software applications, the potential standardization can occur through layered architectures which are becoming the industry standards.

The implications of these developments for a new standards-based strategy need to be spelled out further. Either layered architectures or client-server architectures allow the creation of another piece of software (technically a "client" or an API service) which takes the data from the vendor application and passes it to a different vendors' applications. In many respects this will be the biggest breakthrough for museum computing, if it can be implemented, because it would not only enable museums to save the value in their data but enable them to engage in cooperative applications with others. Client/server approaches can further insulate the end-user from the specific requirements of different application software while communication between software of different origins is enabled.

Standards that enable different software applications to exchange data in a format suitable for manipulation would enable suites of application software to be acquired from a variety of sources and still exchange data using SGML. This would allow museum consortia to develop "museum workstation" tools that acquired data from numerous sources and performed tasks such as displaying them in 3-D mockups of exhibition spaces, arranged for their custom brokerage, delivered them to classroom teachers, and provided them to value-added resellers in a variety of commercial sectors.[11] An example of such a standard would be a protocol that supported the requirements for end to end licensing of museum controlled intellectual property including data interchange and directory services. Without such a standard, museums will not be able to easily make their properties known to the potential user community. With it they could link a range of separate databases into a service.

Another example, which the AHIP Vocabulary Control Systems (VCS) project has already proposed to address, would be to develop interfaces that allow applications which create databases to take advantage of remote authority files controlling the content of different fields within the authority and to update remote authority files with new terms which represent found uses of concepts in the literature. This kind of two-way interaction has been envisioned in a model for the prototype of the VCS system.[12]

Systems environment

In the new distributed computing environment the purpose of creating database/imagebases is as much to support re-use of the data content as to provide the "published" product. The ability of the end user to link to, copy, transform, or otherwise exploit relevant pieces of information is a critical measure of the value of the product. Standards for known or knowable data structures only go part of the way toward ensuring that valuable data will be able to support multiple uses. Making information reusable also requires making the content of the data malleable, especially algorithmically, to support different points of view.

To date, most of our discussion has been of documented data structures rather than true "inter-operability" with the emphasis on the kinds of operations we can expect to support. Here we cover the issue which I have elsewhere discussed under the dual headings of the "fungibility" of museum data and the issue of "re-usable quality".

The fundamental question we must answer here is how much we should invest in making our data more standard than it needs to be for the specific application in which we are going to use it next? The answer, logically, is that we should make additional investments if:

- there is reason to expect we will want to re-use this data for another purpose in the future, and
- the cost of the additional investment is significantly less than the cost of re-manipulating the data for a different purpose later.

Economically, of course, we must also answer in the context of the cost and availability of capital for this investment. These measures become more complex, but the ultimate gamble is that we will save substantially in the future by making the data we use more functional now.

A single example will suffice, I believe, because it is so widely shared. Cultural heritage organizations are making substantial investments in digitizing their collections for publication, exhibition, and education. How much effort will be required the second time the same data (an image and accompanying text) is needed? Is there anything we do now that would reduce the likelihood that we'll need to recapture from the same source in a decade?

We can't answer this obvious, and critical, question without examining current practice from a new perspective. We need to ask how often we are able to take analog images and existing text prepared for one purpose – say a catalog raisonée – and use it for another, such as, for example, an exhibit catalog or school tour unit? If we currently edit the content of each node (the image, the caption, the introductory text) for each application, how could digital technology change our practices? An example of a kind of re-use not enabled by analog technologies is that paper-based systems do not give us the option of organizing our text by artist for one user, by period for another, or by geography for a third. This luxury could be supported in digital content source databases if we used appropriate standards for node naming and for linking. In principle, content could be refashioned without each re-use being expensively reauthored.

Typed data allow us to exploit the promise of formal design methodologies, such as Hypertext Design Methodology (HTDM), in authoring content in the future. The premise of HTDM is that if we focus on links, we can support re-use of data through algorithmic and dynamic authoring. It seems obvious to me that we should be testing this hypothesis, and if it proves plausible, we should be examining what qualities of the original data make it most or least suitable for re-use. We should be defining markup strategies that support editing on the fly and investigating the points-of-view of our audiences to understand the "frames of reference" which would need to be similar to AI frames in that their slots could be filled from existing knowledge schemas developed for other purposes. While this may present us with a series of research issues for the very long-term future, the medium-term issues will have to do with the kinds of standards that could support link structures created by different applications.

Notes

1 For reflections on how this will impact cultural institutions, see David Bearman, ed., *Hands On: Hypermedia and Interactivity in Museums* (Pittsburgh, Archives & Museum Informatics, 1995): 293pp. and *Multimedia Computing in Museums* (Pittsburgh, Archives & Museum Informatics, 1995): 388pp.

2 The clearest example of how we thus became victims of our success is the 25 million object National Inventory of the Canadian Heritage Information Network which contributes little that will be of interest to the publics whom we increasingly want to serve with our information.

3 The situation today has changed little from the chaos reported in Andrew Roberts, ed., *Terminology for Museums: Proceedings of an International Conference* (Cambridge, MDA, 1988).

4 Museum Documentation Association, SPECTRUM (Cambridge, MDA, 1994).

5 For further ideas on the state of imaging standards, see Jennifer Trant, "The Getty AHIP Imaging Initiative: A Status Report", *Archives and Museum Informatics*, 9(3): 262–278.

6 For further discussion, see David Bearman and John Perkins, "The Standards Framework for Computer Interchange of Museum Information," *Spectra* 1993, 20(2&3): 1–61.

7 My preliminary analysis of some of these issues is reported in "Data Relationships in the Documentation of Cultural Objects", in Jane Sledge, ed., *Categories for Description of Works of Art*. The paper is scheduled for *Visual Resources* vol.11. In page proofs it

carried the pagination of pp. 295–306. Additional work in exploring these relations is scheduled for a meeting in Crete in the spring of 1996.

8   For more on SGML in the museum context, see David Bearman, "Issues involved in Using SGML for Data Interchange", *Archives and Museum Informatics*, 8(1): 74–9.

9   The current proposal for "Encoded Archival Description" is an example of a proposed DTD that fails these tests.

10 David Bearman, "Buildings as Structures, as Art and as Dwellings: Data Exchange issues in an Architectural Information Network", in Lawrence McCrank, ed., *Databases in the Humanities and Social Sciences*, vol. 4 (Medford NJ, Learned Information, 1989) pp. 41–8.

11 The Canadian Heritage Information Network and some commercial and museum sector partners have recently been awarded a grant from CANARIE Inc., the "Information Superhighway" funding agency in Canada, to develop just such a set of tools.

12 For further information on the design and purposes of the VCS prototype, contact Joseph Busch, Program Manager, Getty Art History Information Program – jbusch@ getty.edu.

Chapter 7

Database as Symbolic Form

Lev Manovich

The database logic

After the novel, and subsequently cinema, privileged narrative as the key form of cultural expression in the modern age, the computer age introduced its correlate – database. Many new media objects do not tell stories; they don't have a beginning or an end; in fact, they don't have any development, thematically, formally or otherwise, which would organise their elements into a sequence. Instead, they are collections of individual items, where every item has the same significance as any other.

Why do new media favour database forms over others? Can we explain its popularity by analysing the specificity of the digital medium and of computer programming? What is the relationship between the database and another form that has traditionally dominated human culture – narrative? These are the questions I will address in this article.

Before proceeding I need to comment on my use of the word 'database'. In computer science database is defined as a structured collection of data. The data stored in a database is organised for fast search and retrieval by a computer and therefore it is anything but a simple collection of items. Different types of databases – hierarchical, network, relational and object-oriented – use different models to organise data. For instance, the records in hierarchical databases are organised in a tree-like structure. Object-oriented databases store complex data structures, called 'objects', which are organised into hierarchical classes that may inherit properties from classes higher in the chain.[1] New media objects may or may not employ these highly structured database models; however, from the point of view of the user's experience a large proportion of them are databases in a more basic sense.

Source: *Convergence*, vol. 5 no. 2, 1999, pp. 80–99.

They appear as collections of items on which the user can perform various operations: view, navigate, search. The user experience of such computerised collections is therefore quite distinct from reading a narrative or watching a film or navigating an architectural site. Similarly, literary or cinematic narrative, an architectural plan and database each present a different model of what a world is like. It is this sense of database as a cultural form of its own which I want to address here. Following art historian Ervin Panofsky's analysis of linear perspective as a 'symbolic form' of the modern age, we may even call the database a new symbolic form of the computer age (or, as philosopher Jean-Francois Lyotard called it in his famous 1979 book *The Postmodern Condition*, 'computerised society'),[2] a new way to structure our experience of ourselves and of the world. Indeed, if, after the death of God (Nietzsche), the end of grand Narratives of Enlightenment (Lyotard) and the arrival of the web (Tim Berners-Lee), the world appears to us as an endless and unstructured collection of images, texts, and other data records, it is only appropriate that we will be moved to model it as a database. But it is also appropriate that we would want to develop a poetics, aesthetics, and ethics of this database.

Let us begin by documenting the dominance of this database form in new media. The most obvious examples of this are to be found in popular multimedia encyclopedias (which are collections by their very definition), as well as other commercial CD-ROM titles which are also collections – of recipes, quotations, photographs, and so on.[3] The identity of a CD-ROM as a storage medium is projected onto another plane, becoming a cultural form of its own. Multimedia works which have 'cultural' content appear particularly to favour the database form. Consider, for instance, the 'virtual museums' genre – CD-ROMs which take the user on a 'tour' through a museum collection. A museum becomes a database of images representing its holdings, which can be accessed in different ways: chronologically, by country, or by artist. Although such CD-ROMs often simulate the traditional museum experience of moving from room to room in a continuous trajectory, this 'narrative' method of access does not have any special status in comparison to other access methods offered by a CD-ROM. Thus the narrative becomes just one method among others of accessing data. Another example of a database form is a multimedia genre that does not have an equivalent in traditional media – CD-ROMs devoted to a single cultural figure such as a famous architect, film director or writer. Instead of a narrative biography we are presented with a database of images, sound recordings, video clips and/or texts which can be navigated in a variety of ways.

CD-ROMs and other digital storage media (floppies, and DVD-ROMs) proved to be particularly receptive to traditional genres which already had a database-like structure, such as a photo-album; they also inspired new database genres, like a database biography. Where the database form really flourished, however, is on the internet. As defined by original HTML, a web page is a sequential list of separate elements: text blocks, images, digital video clips, and links to other pages. It is always possible to add a new element to the list – all you have to do is to open a file and add a new line. As a result, most web pages are collections of separate elements: texts, images, links to other pages or sites. A home page is a collection of personal photographs. A site of a major search engine is a collection of numerous links to other sites (along with a search function, of course). A site of a web-based TV or radio station offers a collection of video or audio programmes along with the option to listen to the current broadcast; but this current programme is just one choice among many other programmes stored on the site. Thus the traditional broadcasting experience, which consisted solely of a real-time transmission, becomes just one element in a collection of options. Similar to the CD-ROM medium, the web offered fertile ground to already existing database genres (for instance, the bibliography) and also inspired the creation of new ones such as those sites devoted to a person or a phenomenon (Madonna, the Civil War, new media theory, etc) which, even if they contain original material, inevitably revolve around a list of links to other web pages on the same person or phenomenon.

The open nature of the web as medium (web pages are computer files which can always be edited) means that websites never have to be complete; and they rarely are. The sites always grow. New links are being added to what is already there. It is as easy to add new elements to the end of a list as it is to insert them anywhere in it. All this further contributes to the anti-narrative logic of the web. If new elements are being added over time, the result is a collection, not a story. Indeed, how can one keep a coherent narrative or any other development trajectory through the material if it keeps changing?

Data and algorithm

Of course not all new media objects are explicitly databases. Computer games, for instance, are experienced by their players as narratives. In a game, the player is given a well-defined task – winning the match, being first in a race, reaching the last level, or reaching the highest score. It is this task which makes the player experience the game as a narrative. Everything which happens to him/her in a game, all the characters and objects she encounters either take her closer to achieving the goal or further away from it. Thus, in contrast to the CD-ROM and web databases – which always appear arbitrary since the user knows that additional material could have been added without in any way modifying the logic of the database – in a game, from a user's point of view, all the elements are motivated (i.e. their presence is justified).[4]

Often the narrative shell of a game ('you are the specially trained commando who has just landed on a Lunar base; your task is to make your way to the headquarters occupied by the mutant base personnel ...') masks a simple algorithm well-familiar to the player: kill all the enemies on the current level, while collecting all treasures it contains; go to the next level and so on until you reach the last level. Other games have different algorithms. Here is an algorithm of the legendary *Tetris* (Spectrum Holobyte, 1989): when a new block appears, rotate it in such a way so it will complete the top layer of blocks on the bottom of the screen making this layer disappear. The similarity between the actions expected from the player and the computer algorithm is too uncanny to be dismissed. While computer games do not follow a database logic, they appear to be ruled by another logic – that of the algorithm. They demand that a player executes an algorithm in order to win.

An algorithm is the key to the game experience in a different sense as well. As the player proceeds through the game, s/he gradually discovers the rules that operate in the universe constructed by this game. S/he learns its hidden logic, in short its algorithm. Therefore, in games where the play departs from following an algorithm, the player is still engaged with an algorithm, albeit in another way: s/he is discovering the algorithm of the game itself. I mean this both metaphorically and literally: for instance, in a first person shooter, such as *Quake*, the player may eventually notice that under such and such condition the enemies will appear from the left, i.e. s/he will literally reconstruct a part of the algorithm responsible for the game play. Or, in a different formulation by the legendary author of *Sim* games Will Wright, 'Playing the game is a continuous loop between the user (viewing the outcomes and inputting decisions) and the computer (calculating outcomes and displaying them back to the user). The user is trying to build a mental model of the computer model.'[5]

What we encounter here is an example of the general principle of new media: the projection of the ontology of a computer onto culture itself. If in physics the world is made of atoms and in genetics it is made of genes, computer programming encapsulates the world according to its own logic. The world is reduced to two kinds of software objects that are considered complementary to each other: data structures and algorithms. Any process or task is reduced to an algorithm, a final sequence of simple operations that a computer can execute to accomplish a given task. And any object in the world – be it the population of a city, or the weather over the course of a century, a chair, a human brain – is modelled as a data structure, i.e. data organised in a particular way for efficient search and retrieval (such as arrays, linked lists and graphs).[6]

Algorithms and data structures have a symbiotic relationship. The more complex the data structure of a computer program, the simpler the algorithm needs to be, and vice versa. Together, data structures and algorithms are two halves of the ontology of the world according to a computer.

The computerisation of culture involves the projection of these two fundamental parts of computer software – and of the computer's unique ontology – onto the cultural sphere. If CD-ROMs and web databases are cultural manifestations of one half of this ontology, data structures and computer games are manifestations of the second half – the algorithmic half. Games (sports, chess, cards, etc) are a good example of a cultural form that requires algorithm-like behaviour from the players. Consequently, many traditional games were quickly simulated on computers. In parallel, new genres of computer games came into existence such as first-person 'shootem-ups' like *Doom* or *Quake*. Thus, as it was with database genres, computer games both mimic already existing games and create new game genres.

It may appear at first sight that data is passive and algorithms are active – another example of the passive–active binary categories so loved by human cultures. A program 'reads in' data, executes an algorithm, and writes out new data. We may recall that before 'computer science' and 'software engineering' became established names for the computer field, it was called 'data processing'. This name remained in use for a few decades during which computers were mainly associated with performing calculations over data. However, the passive/active distinction is not quite accurate since data does not just exist – it has to be generated. Data creators have to collect data and to organise it, or create it from scratch. Texts need to be written, photographs need to be taken, video and audio need to be recorded – or they need to be digitised from already existing media.

In the 1990s, when the new role of the computer as a Universal Media Machine became apparent, already computerised societies went into a digitising craze. All existing books and video tapes, photographs and audio recordings started to be fed into computers at an ever increasing rate. Steven Spielberg created the Shoah Foundation which videotaped and then digitised numerous interviews with Holocaust survivors; it would take one person forty years to watch all the recorded material. The editors of *Mediamatic* journal, who devoted a whole issue to the topic of 'the storage mania' wrote: 'A growing number of organisations are embarking on ambitious projects. Everything is being collected: culture, asteroids, DNA patterns, credit records, telephone conversations; it doesn't matter.'[7] Once it is digitised, the data has to be cleaned up, organised, indexed. The computer age brought with it a new cultural algorithm: reality → media → data → database. The rise of the web, this gigantic and always changing data corpus, gave millions of people a new hobby or profession: data indexing. There is hardly a website that does not feature at least a dozen links to other sites. Therefore every site is a type of database. With the rise of internet commerce, most large-scale commercial sites have become real databases, or rather front-ends to company databases. For instance, in autumn 1998 Amazon.com, an online book store, had 3 million books in its database; and the maker of leading commercial database Oracle has offered Oracle 8i, fully integrated with the internet and featuring unlimited database size, natural-language queries and support for all multimedia data types.[8]

Jorge Luis Borges' story about a map which was equal in size to the territory it represented has been re-written as a story about indexes and the data they index. Now the map has become larger than the territory. Sometimes, much larger. Porn websites exposed the logic of the web to its extreme by constantly re-using the same photographs from other porn websites. Only rare sites feature the original content. On any given date, the same few dozen images would appear on thousands of sites. Thus, the same data would give rise to more indexes than the number of data elements themselves.

Database and narrative

As a cultural form, database represents the world as a list of items which it refuses to order. In contrast, a narrative creates a cause-and-effect trajectory of seemingly unordered items (events). Therefore, database and narrative are natural 'enemies'. Competing for the same territory of human culture, each claims an exclusive right to make meaning out of the world.

In contrast to most games, most narratives do not require algorithm-like behaviour from their readers. However, narratives and games are similar in that the user, while proceeding through them, must uncover the underlying logic – the algorithm. Just like a game player, a reader of a novel gradually reconstructs an algorithm (here I use it metaphorically) which the writer might have used to create the settings, the characters, and the events. From this perspective, I can re-write my earlier equations between the two parts of the computer's ontology and its corresponding cultural forms. Data structures and algorithms drive different forms of computer culture.

CD-ROMs, websites and other new media objects which are organised as databases correspond to the data structure; narratives, including computer games, correspond to algorithms.

In computer programming, data structures and algorithms need each other; they are equally important for a program to work. What happens in a cultural sphere? Do databases and narratives have the same status in computer culture?

Some media objects explicitly follow database logic in their structure while others do not; but behind the surface practically all of them are databases. In general, creating a work in new media can be understood as the construction of an interface to a database. In the simplest case, the interface simply provides the access to the underlying database. For instance, an image database can be represented as a page of miniature images; clicking on a miniature will retrieve the corresponding record. If a database is too large to display all of its records at once, a search engine can be provided to allow the user to search for particular records. But the interface can also translate the underlying database into a very different user experience. The user may be navigating a virtual three-dimensional 'city' composed of letters, as in Jeffrey Shaw's interactive installation *Legible City*.[9] Or s/he may be traversing a black and white image of a naked body, activating pieces of text, audio and video embedded in its skin, as in Graham Harwood's CD-ROM *Rehearsal of Memory*.[10] Or s/he may be playing with virtual animals which come closer or run away depending upon her/his movements, as in the VR installation *Menagerie* by Scott Fisher et al.[11] Although each of these works engages the user in a set of behaviours and cognitive activities that are quite distinct from going through the records of a database, all of them are databases. *Legible City* is a database of three-dimensional letters which make up the city. *Rehearsal of Memory* is a database of texts, audio and video clips which are accessed through the interface of a body. And *Menagerie* is a database of virtual animals, including their shapes, movements and behaviours.

The database becomes the centre of the creative process in the computer age. Historically, the artist made a unique work within a particular medium. In this sense, the interface and the work were the same, i.e. the level of an interface did not exist. With new media, the content of the work and the interface become separate. It is therefore possible to create different interfaces to the same material. These interfaces may present different versions of the same work, as in David Blair's WaxWeb.[12] Or they may be radically different from each other, as in Moscow WWWArt Centre.[13] This is one of the ways in which the already discussed principle of *variability* of new media manifests itself. But now we can give this principle a new formulation. *The new media object consists of one or more interfaces to a database of multimedia material*. If only one interface is constructed, the result will be similar to a traditional art object; but this is an exception rather than the norm. This formulation places the opposition between database and narrative in a new light, thus redefining our concept of narrative. The 'user' of a narrative is traversing a database, following links between its records as established by the database's creator. An interactive narrative (which can be also called 'hyper-narrative' in an analogy with hypertext) can then be understood as the sum of multiple trajectories through a database. A traditional linear narrative is one, among many other possible trajectories, i.e. a particular choice made within a hyper-narrative. Just as a traditional cultural object can now be seen as a particular case of a new media object (i.e. a new media object that only has one interface), traditional linear narrative can be seen as a particular case of a hyper-narrative.

This 'technical' or 'material' change in the definition of narrative does not mean that an arbitrary sequence of database records is a narrative. To qualify as a narrative, a cultural object has to satisfy a number of criteria, which literary scholar Mieke Bal defines as follows: it should contain both an actor and a narrator; it also should contain three distinct levels consisting of the text, the story, and the fabula; and its 'contents' should be 'a series of connected events caused or experienced by actors'.[14] Obviously, not all cultural objects are narratives. However, in the world of new media, the word 'narrative' is often used as an all-inclusive term, to cover up the fact that we have not yet developed a language to describe these strange new objects. It is usually paired with another over-used word – interactive. Thus, a number of database records linked together so that more than one trajectory is possible is assumed to constitute an 'interactive narrative'. But just to create these trajectories is, of course, not sufficient; the author also has to control the semantics of the elements and the logic of their connection so that the resulting object will meet the criteria of narrative as outlined above. Another erroneous assumption frequently made is that by creating her own path (i.e. choosing the records from a database in a particular order) the user constructs her own unique narrative. However, if the user simply accesses different elements, one after another, in a usually random order, there is no reason to assume that these elements will form a narrative at all. Indeed, why should an arbitrary sequence of database records, constructed by the user, result in 'a series of connected events caused or experienced by actors'?

In summary, database and narrative do not have the same status in computer culture. In the database/narrative pair, database is the unmarked term.[15] Regardless of whether new media objects present themselves as linear narratives, interactive narratives, databases, or something else, underneath, on the level of material organisation, they are all databases. In new media, the database supports a range of cultural forms which range from direct translation (i.e. a database stays a database) to a form whose logic is the opposite of the logic of the material form itself – a narrative. More precisely, a database can support narrative, but there is nothing in the logic of the medium itself which would foster its generation. It is not surprising, then, that databases occupy a significant, if not the largest, territory of the new media landscape. What is more surprising is why the other end of the spectrum – narratives – still exists in new media.

Notes

1   Database: 'Britannica Online', http://www.eb.com:180/cgi-bin/g?DocF–icro/160/23.html (27 November 1998).
2   Jean-Francois Lyotard, *The Postmodern Condition: A Report on Knowledge*, trans. Geoff Bennington and Brian Massumi (Minneapolis: University of Minnesota Press, 1984), p. 3.

3 As early as 1985 Grolier Inc. issued a text-only 'Academic American Encyclopedia' on CD-ROM. The first multimedia encyclopedia was 'Compton's MultiMedia Encyclopedia' published in 1989.

4 David Bordwell and Kristin Thompson define motivation in cinema in the following way: 'Because films are human constructs, we can expect that any one element in a film will have some justification for being there. This justification is the motivation for that element.' Here are some examples of motivation: 'When Tom jumps from the balloon to chase a cat, we motivate his action by appealing to notions of how dogs are likely to act when cats are around.' 'The movement of a character across a room may motivate the moving of the camera to follow the action and keep the character within a frame.' Bordwell and Thompson, *Film Art: an Introduction* (New York: The McGraw-Hill Companies Inc., 1997, fifth edition), p. 80.

5 Chris McGowan and Jim McCullaugh, *Entertainment in the Cyber Zone* (New York: Random House, 1995), p. 71.

6 This is true for a procedural programming paradigm. In an object-oriented programming paradigm, represented by such computer languages as Java and C++, algorithms and data structures are modelled together as objects.

7 *Mediamatic*, 8, no. 1 (Summer 1994), p. 60.

8 See http://www.amazon.com/exec/obidos/subst/misc/company-info.html/ and http://www.oracle.com/database/oracle8i/ (28 November 1998).

9 http://artnetweb.com/guggenheim/mediascape/shaw.html (28 November 1998).

10 Harwood, *Rehearsal of Memory*, CD-ROM (London: Artec and Bookworks, 1996.)

11 See http://www.telepresence.com/MENAGERIE (22 October 1998).

12 See http://jefferson.village.virginia.edu/wax/ (12 September 1998).

13 See http://www.cs.msu.su/wwwart/ (22 October 1998).

14 Mieke Bal, *Narratology: Introduction to the Theory of Narrative* (Toronto: University of Toronto Press, 1985), p. 8.

15 The theory of markedness was first developed by linguists of the Prague School in relation to phonology but subsequently applied to all levels of linguistic analysis. For example, 'bitch' is the marked term and 'dog' is the unmarked term. Whereas 'bitch' is used only in relation to females, 'dog' is applicable to both males and females.

Chapter 8

The Museum as Information Utility

George F. MacDonald and Stephen Alsford

Traditionally, museums have focused their attentions on the past. Their preoccupation with the material remains of the past has made them object-orientated. This is reflected in the list of key functions of museums: to collect, preserve, study, exhibit, interpret; all are activities performed *on* museums' artifacts or specimens. This introverted focus has engendered the belief that artifactual collections are the raison d'être of museums, rather than a tool through which we learn, and teach, about heritage. This orientation towards artifacts rather than people is one reason why museums have acquired a popular image as forbidding institutions, musty storehouses of the relics of a dead past, amenable only to the intellectually or aesthetically elite.

Today there is a growing appreciation in the museum world that museums do not exist primarily to service their collections of material heritage, but rather to serve society by helping provide the knowledge its members need to survive and progress. Contemporary concerns, changes and challenges plaguing society on all fronts – cultural, technological, environmental – make it more important than ever that museums be responsive and relevant to the information needs of society. If museums fail to keep pace with a changing society, they may be perceived as redundant and be abandoned in favour of other types of information-providing institutions which have better adapted to the 'Information Society'.

It is too easy to relegate heritage to the past. It is really an integral part of our present. What we choose to preserve defines our communal identity, vital to social cohesion. We study yesterday to understand what we are today, and to supply information that helps us decide what to become tomorrow. In this ongoing process of shaping and reshaping culture, institutions that are memory-banks of heritage have a heavy responsibility to make accessible their information resources. Canada's new

Source: *Museum Management and Curatorship* vol. 10, 1991, pp. 305–11.

Museums Act (1990), for example, clearly expresses this responsibility of its national museums in its opening declaration:

> that the heritage of Canada and all its peoples is an important part of the world heritage and must be preserved for present and future generations and that each museum established by this Act (a) plays an essential role, individually and together with other museums and like institutions, in preserving and promoting the heritage of Canada and all its peoples throughout Canada and abroad and in contributing to the collective memory and sense of identity of all Canadians; and (b) is a source of inspiration, research, learning and entertainment that belongs to all Canadians and provides, in both official languages, a service that is essential to Canadian culture and available to all.[1]

One sign of maturity in a culture is the activity of gathering and systematizing information for use in decision-making. The benefit of information is to create a useful change in the state of knowledge in its recipient (although uncontrolled access to information may result in overload, which is counter-productive). In a democratic society decision-making relies on an informed citizenry. *Public* museums, like public libraries, were created because of a social understanding that knowledge is a public good and that public pools of information are necessary.[2] But it is not sufficient to be a repository of information. It is important for museums actively to use information to create understanding; or, to help their audiences exploit effectively the information resources in their self-directed quest for knowledge.

The present transition from Industrial Age to Information Age is prompting museums to re-evaluate their role. The centrality to that role of collections of original objects has been put to question by such institutions as:

• science centres and living history museums, more interested in processes than objects;
• children's museums, relying largely on replicas (at least in their public programmes);
• ecomuseums, emphasizing the totality of culture, not just its material expressions.

Efforts have been made to define a new role-paradigm by refining basic functions. One recent effort, for instance, formulated by an eminent museologist in Europe and supported by another in North America,[3] narrows them down to preservation, study and communication. However, this remains unhelpful in terms of bridging the gap between essentially competing interest groups within the museum world.[4]

It may be more helpful to examine the business of museums not from the perspective of functions, but from that of product. Certainly, as with any complex subject,[5] museums cannot be fully understood from any single perspective; they need to be thought about in a variety of ways, using diverse metaphors, analogies and analytical frameworks, all of which contribute to the complete picture. In terms of product, museums are (at the most fundamental level) concerned with information; and, by extension, with the knowledge shaped from informational entities, and ultimately the wisdom acquired from extensive and experience-enriched knowledge.

Museums are concerned with the generation, the perpetuation, the organization and the dissemination of information. To elaborate on these information-management activities in terms of traditional museum functions:

1   *Generation* of information results principally from the research activities of experts, as a product of the study of museum collections or the historical, cultural and natural contexts of items in the collections. It may, however, also result – intentionally or serendipitously – from such things as conservation activities, from the creation of replicas or the re-enactment of historical activities (and associated research activities sometimes termed 'experimental archaeology'), or from visitor feedback to public programmes.

2   *Perpetuation* of information most obviously results from conservation of collections; but dissemination of knowledge is also a perpetuation strategy. Preservation of heritage objects is not an end in itself, but serves to maximize (over time) the access to information encoded in them.

3   *Organization* involves establishing the relationships between discrete elements of information, bearing in mind that this involves the unavoidable intervention of subjectivity (both ethnocentric and idiocentric) and that information elements can interrelate in many different but nonetheless valid patterns. This function may express itself, for example, through classification systems used in collections management; or through interpretive activities, including the recontextualization of artifacts in a period-setting exhibit. In practice, generation and organization of knowledge often occur simultaneously, as researchers integrate new information into existing world-views.

4   *Dissemination* is achieved by creating access to information, which entails both making information readily available and ensuring that its users have the ability to comprehend it.[6] That access may be either museum-directed, such as through promotion, publications, exhibitions, and educational and interpretive programmes; or it may be client-directed, such as through research in the library, or remote searching of a museum database. It is important for museums to create an environment in which the audience is receptive to the information offered – this is an integral requirement for effective dissemination, and depends on a good understanding of audiences' wide-ranging needs, interests, tastes and learning styles.

These four functions are so interrelated and interdependent that it would be difficult to translate them directly into an organizational structure. Rather, they represent a unifying theory of operation, reflecting the information life-cycle and tying together the various individual departments within the museum. None of these functions can claim to be more important than the others, for all are vital to increasing human knowledge; any prioritization would only be the dictate of practical considerations in a given set of circumstances.

There are several advantages to thinking of the primary resource, or commodity, of the museum business as information, rather than as artifacts. One is that it validates the collecting and use of intangibles of culture (e.g. processes, oral history, mentifacts) and of replicas, without reducing the importance or value of material collections of original objects. Another is that it positions museums nicely to play a central role in the new age, in which information-based services are expected to be a key to economic prosperity and to social status – two things necessary, in the real world, to museums to ensure their effectiveness, if not their survival. A third advantage of a shift in orientation away from objects towards information is that it should make it easier (when formulating museums' missions, for instance) to balance the traditional functions of collection, preservation, research and display, with the newer rallying-flags of education and communication.

To illustrate this with the example of the authors' own institution, the Canadian Museum of Civilization, its mandated purpose is 'to increase ... knowledge and critical understanding of and appreciation and respect for human cultural achievements and human behaviour'.[7] The statement goes on to identify the function of building a collection of historical and cultural objects as simply one strategy necessary, but subsidiary, to achieving that purpose. The functions of collections research, conservation, exhibition, and so on, are to be similarly understood. They are the particular ways in which the Museum *manages* its purpose.

It must be stressed that an information-orientation approach to the role of museums in no way detracts from the importance of collections of material heritage. Artifacts remain a major *source* of information (and worthy of indefinite preservation for that reason), as well as one important vehicle for communicating information. For we must define 'information' broadly. It may be intellectual, aesthetic, sensory, spiritual or emotional in character; or, more likely, an experience involving some combination of these. Culture is learned as a bundle of 'messages', each bundle comprising various of these types of information. Culture is expressed not only through objects, but also through processes, ideas, feelings, personalities, and so on. The media of preservation and access have to reflect this diversity.[8]

Therefore, although artifacts remain museums' medium of specialization, a 'total media collections' approach is necessary: an acknowledgement that oral history, photographic and audiovisual materials, replicas, digital databases, re-enacted processes, live cultural performances and staff expertise are also important information resources that need to be managed. The relative merit of these various sources is not as important as the fact that they complement each other in communicating information. It follows from this that it is desirable to employ technologies capable of integrated information delivery, regardless of the format of information (audio, video, text, etc.). This does not refer exclusively to computerized technologies; it must be remembered that our everyday living environment is the most powerful 'technology' of multimedia information delivery.

Museums have been very active in the past in building collections of information resources. With the exception of their artifactual collections, they have not done so well in managing those resources. And certainly they have performed less effectively when it comes to disseminating the information amassed. They can no longer afford to build and maintain collections at the rate done in the past. But they *can* capitalize more thoroughly on the resources already built, thanks to the advent of capable modern technologies for mass communication. The marriage of computers and telecommunications could, ultimately, allow museums to become 'information utilities' (a metaphor calling to mind the ease of access to public utilities supplying electricity and water) available in every home. For a national museum, this offers the prospect of truly being able to reach a national audience.

Unfortunately, the lead in making use of the new electronic highways has been taken by the entertainment industry, a competitor with the museum world for the discretionary leisure time of the public. The power of television, film and video to inform, sway opinions and shape cultural consensus – now, at an international level – is enormous. They (together with other entertainment forms, such as pop music and computer games) are also raising public expectations for challenging content and fidelity of image and sound. Museums should also be concerned about whether theme parks may be having greater impact on the popular imagination than are museums, at least in North America – although EuroDisney looms large on the horizon. Messages communicated by the entertainment industry are often self-serving, not firmly rooted in reality, and yet transforming reality by reshaping popular consciousness of it.

This is something museums must combat, for their knowledge resources are grounded in the authentic material evidence of the past. We cannot outmatch our competitors in terms of scale; at least not until museums have formed a true resource-sharing community through effective networking. But we *can* outmatch them in terms of quality. The question is whether we can persuade the public to prefer our high-integrity information products to the products of institutions motivated primarily by profit. To do so, we will often need to adopt the tools and techniques those competitors have led the way in utilizing.

This is one of the reasons why many museums are now experimenting with entertainment forms in their public programmes. It is necessary to attract people whose recreational tastes have been conditioned by television and movies. Museums are also using live entertainment forms to provide dynamic ways of interpreting ideas, processes, traditions, and to increase the human element in interpretation. It would be wrong to conclude, however, that museums are in the entertainment business. The present debate over 'entertainment versus education' in museums can be put in perspective if we simply perceive them as two different ways of packaging information. Either form of packaging may be useful to a museum, for communication purposes, depending on the character of a particular audience (which includes its expectations). Entertainment in museums is not an end, but strictly a means, and we must beware of losing sight of this distinction.[9]

Education is closer to the mission of museums, but we should not think of our institutions as akin to schools. Museum attendance is purely discretionary, and the visitor experience largely self-directed and self-controlled. And schools deal with controlled, cumulative knowledge acquisition, whereas any museum presentation has to be able to communicate messages to viewers who may know nothing, a little or a great deal about the subject. Furthermore, in most cases museums cannot teach, they can only help their users learn. The tremendous diversity among museum audiences (actual or potential) makes this a difficult enough task. We must provide for visitors of different ages, different cultural backgrounds, different knowledge levels, different learning styles.

There are a number of particular challenges in the area of communication that museums will increasingly be forced to address. One relates to the ethics of representation. Within the interpretation offered by a museum, there needs to be made available not only the expert knowledge of its staff, but also alternative viewpoints – especially those of the cultures represented. In the past, museum interpretation has largely been based on the perspectives of scholars of western civilization. This is unacceptable in a culturally pluralistic society such as Canada, for example, is becoming. To serve such a society, museums must represent the viewpoints of all. These viewpoints may often be at odds with one another, but the differences will help people develop the tolerance for ambiguity and dissonance that is needed in a multicultural society.

At the same time, no single museum has a monopoly on truth nor can present a complete picture of the human condition; no more should we imagine that all heritage can be encompassed by museums. The museum world benefits from the large number of institutions and their diversity in character, a survival trait in the process of evolution of the institution. But this vast composite resource will never meet its full potential until museums find ways to share their information through joint venturing – notably the formation of networks.

A third challenge is to involve visitors more intimately in the process of interpretation, thereby helping them improve their own judgemental abilities. Conventionally, museums operate in a communicational mode: transmission of information to passive recipients. This is becoming unacceptable to leisure-seekers, who increasingly expect a participative role in shaping their experiences.[10] This is evidenced in the newer types of museums (mentioned above), in theme parks, in cultural tourism, and now even in broadcasting as interactive TV begins to appear. Participation is recognized as an aid to the learning process. It is easy to introduce interactivity at relatively superficial levels, but challenging to provide meaningful participation. Nonetheless, a conversational mode is what museums need to achieve: a transactional learning situation that is not simply a response to a stimulus, but a response that acts on the environment in a way that gives rise to further stimuli. This conversation may take place in the museum, or it could equally take place from a remote location, along the electronic highways already mentioned.[11]

Diversity is the key to a museum fulfilling its role as an information provider in the service of society. To accommodate the wide range of existing needs:

- Information must be provided in layers, of successively greater depth and detail. This is to ensure that all visitors can acquire *some* information from their museum experience, yet without suffering from information overload; and that those who wish may obtain as much information as they need – one layer of information should point users on to the next. It also helps satisfy the very different approaches required to introductory and advanced learning.[12] It is important for information to be on hand when it is needed, to prevent frustration of the spirit of inquiry.
- A comprehensive range of media must be used, to communicate to intellect, senses, emotions, etc. At the same time, emphasis should be on visual media, using images to communicate across the cultural barriers that verbal language imposes. Affective learning is still imperfectly understood and, consequently, inadequately provided for in museum programming; yet it may be in this realm, rather than that of cognitive learning, that museums are most effective.[13]

• A range of 'take-out' information products must be available. This would include TV transmission, text publications, audio and video cassettes, teleconferences, digital data downloadable from museum databases, laser discs and realia (e.g. craftworks sold through the boutique).

In an information institution the foundation for corporate success is effective management of information resources. This involves the recognition that information is both a product and a process, and that both aspects require managing. Museums have an important role to play in this time of significant change – a turning-point for our society, and perhaps for civilization as a whole. They must respond to the growing demand for understanding by making their information resources accessible to the public. This means utilizing all information and communication technologies now available. They must respond to people's need to cope with information overload by packaging information into meaningful bundles of knowledge. They must help people acquire the skills that will enable them to assume control of the interpretive process. And they must do all this using technologies in ways that capture and hold interest, rather than erect barriers to those who are technologically illiterate.

Museums that succeed in all this will find themselves indispensable and valued strands in the information fabric of tomorrow's society. That fabric requires two principal elements: a capacious memory and vehicles for communication. Together, memory and communication create cultural consciousness.

Notes

1 *Statutes of Canada*, 1990, 38 Eliz. 2, c.3, p. 1.
2 This is not to deny that the public museum owes something to the efforts of the socio-economically dominant class to inculcate the 'common man' with their values; C. Stapp, 'The Public Museum: A Review of the Literature', *Journal of Museum Education, xv*, 1990, p. 8.
3 P. van Mensch, 'Museology and museums', *ICOM News, xli*, 1988, pp. 5–10; S. Weil, 'Rethinking the Museum', *Museum News, lxix*, 1990, pp. 56–61.
4 On these competing interests see G. MacDonald and S. Alsford, *A Museum for the Global Village: the Canadian Museum of Civilization* (Hull, Quebec: Canadian Museum of Civilization, 1989), pp. 33–8.
5 R. Spiro et al., 'Cognitive Flexibility Theory: Advanced Knowledge Acquisition in Ill-structured Domains', *Tenth Annual Conference of the Cognitive Science Society* (Hillsdale, NJ: Erlbaum, 1988), pp. 377–80.
6 Thanks to their innate abilities, or to instruction provided by the museum, or to the way in which the information is presented.
7 *Statutes of Canada*, 1990, 38 Eliz. 2, c.3, p. 4.
8 MacDonald and Alsford, op. cit. note 4, pp. 60–2; G. MacDonald and S. Alsford, 'Future Horizons: the Information Age and Its Implications for Museums', paper presented at the conference *Museums and Information: New Technological Horizons*, Winnipeg, 2–4 May 1990; G. MacDonald, 'What Is Culture?', *Journal of Museum Education, xvi*, 1991, 10.

9 For further discussion on the roles of entertainment and education in museums, see S. Alsford and D. Parry, 'Interpretive Theatre: A Role in Museums', *Museum Management and Curatorship, 10*, 1991, pp. 8–23.

10 G. MacDonald and S. Alsford, 'Museums as Bridges to the Global Village', in *A Different Drummer: Readings in Anthropology with a Canadian Perspective* (Ottawa: Carleton University, 1989), p. 42.

11 MacDonald and Alsford, op. cit. note 4, pp. 51, 143, 149–50.

12 Spiro, op. cit. note 5, p. 375.

13 J. Bloom and A. Mintz, 'Museums and the Future of Education', *Journal of Museum Education, xv*, 1990, p. 13; L. Roberts, 'The Elusive Qualities of "Affect"', *Journal of Museum Education, xvi*, 1991, pp. 17–18.

Chapter 9

Museum Collections, Documentation, and Shifting Knowledge Paradigms

Fiona Cameron

Introduction

Despite recent technical advances in museum collections access, most notably on the World Wide Web, a number of key issues still remain. One of the most compelling ones first raised by Thomas and Mintz (1998: 2) concerns the question of data quality. The rate that museum data have been brought online has not been reciprocated by the critical evaluation of the actual significance or utility of the data.[1] The incongruence between this current lack and the potential for significant expansion via new technology also has invoked more fundamental questions about the types of information and the epistemological foundations of that knowledge.[2]

Media theorist Marshall McLuhan (1964) and more recently academic Paul Marty (1999) argued that information infrastructures can be viewed as organic, evolving with society or the organization they support, defining it as much as they are defined by it. Transposing this argument more specifically to a collections context and in the framework of the aforementioned issues, one might ask the following questions. How can documentation systems and practices evolve to meet the needs of contemporary knowledge paradigms and users? In what ways might they transform institutions and the way objects are understood and accessed? On the basis of these imperatives a sustained consideration beyond technological innovation, to pragmatic concerns arising from current acquisition and documentation practices and data quality is necessary. Coupled with this, a consolidated response is required to recent post-structuralist, postmodern epistemological, disciplinary, and museological debates about knowledge making and how these shifts relate to current collections documentation.

Source: *Collections – A Journal for Museum and Archive Professionals*, vol. 1, no. 3, 2005, pp. 243–259

In this paper I will draw on research findings from the *Knowledge Objects* project (an Australian Research Council funded Sesqui grant in partnership with the University of Sydney History Department and the Powerhouse Museum) to answer the afore-mentioned questions. This study offers fresh insights into ways that collections documentation might be reconceptualized to form new knowledge models in line with contemporary theoretical, pedagogic, and public access concerns. The findings were then used to formulate a novel and flexible multi-disciplinary knowledge template to give new documentation concepts a sustainable physical form. Our research also pointed to ways these templates might be integrated into existing collections databases as well as key areas for change in museum policy, staff roles, and the tasks of acquisition and documentation.

New knowledge models—the transformative process

The transformation of databases from documentation tools to effective and sustainable "knowledge environments" starts at the documentation level. Collections management databases are the primary means in which museums document their collections. And more importantly, these tools form the starting point that museums may define and communicate the significance and heritage value of objects.[3] Prominent museological scholar Gaynor Kavanagh (1990: 10) acknowledges that it is at the individual object records that conventional and totalizing practices take root. The manner in which an object is acquired and documented will, to a large extent, determine how current and future generations understand it. Kavanagh (1990: 63) argues albeit in terms of historical research that:

> The museum databank of objects and a range of other visual material and sound records needs to be understood from a different standpoint, as much more than the raw materials of the historian's craft, but as part, a remainder and a reminder, of cultural expression and social signification where material can have multiple layers of meaning.

If Kavanagh's comments, for example, are placed within a wider disciplinary and museum collections documentation context, it becomes necessary to revise current documentation structures in line with new knowledge as well as the attitudes museum staff members hold towards objects as material evidence. Documentation revision also must take account of the way digital technologies are and could potentially promote new knowledge making possibilities (Cameron 2003). Likewise, in the internet era where potential collections information becomes available to a wide range of potential users, their information needs must also form a basis for collections documentation revision.

At this juncture, an opportunity exists to embrace the opportunity for change.[4] Drawing on some preliminary observations from the *Knowledge Objects* project, the following considerations have been enumerated as critical to the transformative process.

1 Types of information required for in-house use and for diverse and targeted user groups and how these can be streamlined into the acquisition and documentation processes.
2 Contemporary knowledge making discourses and the possibilities they offer in meaning making around collections.
3 Current trends in learning theory.
4 New and emerging technologies and tools and the opportunities they have to offer in extending the interpretive potential of collections.
5 Ways existing data and investments in the digitization of materials can be reused and configured into new relationships.
6 A critical analysis of existing acquisition, interpretive, and documentation/classification paradigms, practices, and procedures and ways they can be adapted, modified, and streamlined to meet new information needs.
7 An examination of the broader information resources in museums and how they may contribute to collections data.
8 Ways to reconcile discipline-based documentation and interpretive practices.
9 A consideration of potential returns, such as the promotion of museums and their collections, increased accessibility and visitation to the physical site, and revenue generation.
10 Resource issues.

Technological considerations

In the digital era, knowledge about museum collections is now taking the form of a database of separate elements including media, images, sound, and texts that can be linked and navigated in a variety of ways. From a purely technological standpoint, the manner databases and narratives can work together and their potential discursive effects such as new relational paradigms enables users to link information in ways previously not possible, hence calling into question existing documentary structures. Additionally, the ability to store vast amounts of data, search, retrieve, and distribute information in space and to traverse trajectories of information in new ways sets the scene for a substantial revision of the way information is documented and linked. Furthermore, the potential to technologically liberate documentation from a standardized linear narrative descriptive format and to incorporate diverse media and create 3-D objects, visualizations, and simulations has major implications for the types of interpretive evidence gathered, recorded, digitized, and created around museum collections.

Museums and providers of collections management databases have responded to the technical possibilities digital technologies have to offer by exploring more effective ways to contextualize collections. The relational capacities of digital technologies have been harnessed in collection automation systems enabling objects to be contextualized with people, places, events, periods, classification, and multimedia content along with additional fields for the administration and description of collections.[5] Most museum websites now provide access to collections information and contextualize collections according to themes in the form of essays, quantitative data, and digital images.[6] Increasingly tools of navigation and searching employ data visualization models where contextual links and relevance relationships are shown between objects, subjects, and themes with text-based interpretive essays about the object's context, primary source materials, and media forms such as images, sound, digital video, 3-D objects, and movies.[7] These solutions, however, focus on context rather than the inherent plural meanings of collections. Information and multimedia, rather than sourced from databases, operate as a selection of items curated as an online exhibition via a web interface.

Therefore, the next challenge is to revisit the current epistemological foundations on which documentation is formulated and to consider how diverse cultural and theoretical ideas such as polysemic interpretive models (ones that recognize the inherent pluralistic meanings of objects) might revise documentation taking account of these technological potentialities.

Impact of post-structuralist and postmodern paradigms

Manual card systems and collections databases have traditionally functioned as internal documents, tailored to the needs of museum registrars and curators. Collections records favor descriptions, measurements, and taxonomies. These practices are rooted in nineteenth-century empiricist modes of thinking where a definitive meaning of an object was deemed to lie dormant in its physical form exposed through observation, description, and measurement. Once placed in classification sets, an interpretation of an object emerges, usurping other possible meanings. According to this empiricist tradition, documentation as a process and practice is viewed as the collation of self-evident data derived from the object as source rather than a subjective form of interpretation on the part of the curator as might be argued from a postmodernist's position.[8] Underlying this is the view that object descriptive data, the "cold hard facts" such as measurements and visual form, and meaning created through subsequent interpretive text, are two distinct fields.[9] That is, the former is objective and the latter is subjective in nature. It is from these material practices that current documentation procedures derive such as disciplinary classifications, lengthy descriptions of physical attributes, anonymous statements of significance, and provenance rather than so-called interpretive text. While material collections are no longer given privileged standing as definitive sources of knowledge, legacies of older empirical ways of thinking still reside in documentation practices. This, to a degree, determines and limits the possible meanings objects might derive in a contemporary knowledge context.

Contemporary post-structuralist paradigms in knowledge creation and understanding fundamentally challenge and undermine orthodox concepts about the truth-value of traditional forms of museum documentation. These approaches signify three broad theoretical positions (Lyotard 1984; Seely Brown and Duguid 2000). These are: the rejection of the existence of an inherent objective truth replaced instead by the belief in the arbitrariness of singular, authoritative interpretations; that any interpretation is seen as a construct by a given theorist/author; and that knowledge is a tradable commodity, that is not fixed or closed but constantly evolving and contextually specific.

The epistemological stance inherent in post-structuralism has important rami-fications in the area of museum object documentation. The provision of standard and universal descriptive categories for objects becomes an imposition of an arti-ficial order that fails to acknowledge the polysemy (intrinsic plurality of meaning) of objects. It calls into question the legitimacy of lengthy description as a means of collecting meaningful data about objects and the authority of museums to make statements about its collections. This approach questions the validity of all practices and methodologies that narrow down the frame of reference for object analysis and interpretation. Rather it supports a position that approaches objects from a variety of standpoints and promotes their multiple meanings.

Material culture has the potential to be interpreted in a variety of ways. Muse-ologist Eilean Hooper-Greenhill (1992: 7) draws attention to this when she writes: "a silver teaspoon made in the eighteenth century in Sheffield would be classified as 'Industrial Art' in Birmingham City Museum, 'Decorative Art' at Stoke-on-Trent, 'Silver' at the Victoria and Albert Museum, and 'Industry' at Kelham Island Museum in Sheffield." An object's meaning and its classification, is not self-evident or singular, but is imposed on the object depending on the position and aims of the museum. By naming objects according to prescribed and standardized descriptive fields, object documentation systems record the induction of objects into the museum contexts and thereby reduce their array of potential meanings down to one notion of signifi-cance. The rigid structures of acquisition, documentation practices, and object records currently in place in museums are ill-suited to new ways of seeing objects as polysemic entities. That is, objects subject to perpetual fluctuations of meaning and open to interdisciplinary interpretations.

This "new" discursive position and its potential for the epistemological rework-ing of the role of objects in a museum documentary context was most graphically illustrated in English historian Alun Munslow's critique of social historian Arthur Marwick's book, *The New Nature of History, Knowledge, Evidence and Language*.[10] Here Munslow rejects what he terms the "reconstructionist" approach to history, whereby historical sources are empirically identified, studied, and assembled to produce an understanding of what "actually" happened in the past.[11] In other words, the recon-structionist position, based on the premise of linear and objective historical knowl-edge, accepts the possibility that there is some direct correspondence between the "word" of the historian (the historical text) and the world being described.[12] The reconstructionist believes that the meaning of the past lies dormant in the sources, implying also that meaning is fixed, pre-determined and once activated by the histo-rian can only manifest itself in a single unalterable form. In the museum context, objects are seen as sources of various kinds of historical information and curators (and others) fill the role of historians. Therefore, the reconstructionist approach is reflected in documentation practices that emphasize physical description and other "verifiable" details such as date, maker, technique, style, and others, and one inter-pretation of an object presented as a truth statement.[13]

In attempting to reposition the role and uses of historical evidence in a context where historical inquiry no longer yields conclusive knowledge of the past, Munslow advocates the acceptance of an "epistemic relativist" approach to historical sources.[14] Epistemic relativism differs from what Munslow terms "metaphysical relativism."

The latter concept, first expressed by French philosopher Jacques Derrida posits that reality exists only in the mind of the individual, or that there is nothing outside the text. Munslow instead argues that epistemic relativism views knowledge of the "real" as derived through our ideas and concepts, including linguistic, spatial, cultural, and ideological compulsions.[15] As Munslow goes on to explain: "In acknowledging the sources and the weight of language as an ideologically drenched discourse, epistemic relativists do not deny there is no proximate truth in history but there is more than one way to get at it and, for that matter, represent it."[16]

Therefore, conclusive statements about objects and their use as objective "evidence" for past events are thrown into doubt. Given that object meanings from a post-structuralist/postmodern theoretical point of view are now seen as contextually specific, an object's assessment and hence its documentation should address questions such as who was involved with the object, how it was collected, who interpreted it and why, where the interpretation took place and so on.[17] Documentation must be viewed in a new way. First, the meaning and significance of an object or its history will always evade the curator to some extent. Second, meaning can never be objectified. And third, documentation must demonstrate a potential to represent a range of object meanings and relationships.[18]

Digital technologies are being harnessed to revise empiricist based forms of documentation through new discursive, relational possibilities, and the ability to store, search, and retrieve vast amounts of data and media. Technically these capabilities have the potential to emancipate museum objects from narrow cultural, disciplinary, and museum-based understandings afforded them through their relegation to particular cultural areas and institutions and to expose the nature of decision-making processes from which their meanings are ascribed. Much is yet to be done to truly engage polysemic models of interpretation. The authoring information for example, needs to engage users more actively in completing the cycle of knowledge making and expose the specific predilections that lie behind interpretive frameworks and texts.

Findings from user research undertaken as part of the *Themescaping Virtual Collections* research (Cameron 2003) supports this and suggests that the majority of user profiles take a position similar to Munslow's epistemic relativist stance. Museum collections are viewed as tools that provide interpretations at various levels and from different contextual points of view (Cameron 2003). Furthermore, users expressed a desire to exercise their democratic right to access information according to their own choices and be offered a range of opinions, explanations, resources and interpretations about museum collections (Cameron 2003). The majority of users interviewed do not accept an inherent inability to explain collections meanings but rather continue to seek authoritative and trustworthy information from museums according to a modernist paradigm albeit in a modified hyperlinked and authored form (Cameron 2003: 28). In other words, not all interpretations are seen as equal by users and museums must continue to provide reliable information based on scholarly research. Nonetheless, postmodernist fragmentation can be enjoyed through technical solutions such as mindmaps.[19] These, however, must be supported by a "knowable" framework such as chronologies and hierarchies of information in which objects can be placed and meanings made easily accessible (Cameron 2003: 26–8). Most users do not want to take full responsibility for the interpretive process.

Incorporating theoretical principles in practices and procedures

So how do we get collections documentation up to speed with current thinking, bearing in mind the potential digital technologies have to offer? Here museums are confronted with a difficult challenge. They need to provide a conceptual structure and order to disparate collections at a documentation level and acknowledge and utilize previous investments as well as engage with a growing community of users. The larger task is to bridge the gap between documentation practices and information needs that require the inclusion of modernist, post-structural, and postmodernist paradigms, and the particular social and cultural ideas posited by a diverse community of users. They need to provide authoritative information but also acknowledge the fragmentary, arbitrary, and plural nature of object interpretation. This process also needs to recognize shifts in relationships between museums and users and to allow greater interpretive freedom as a documentary practice. Given that potential user profiles are diverse and exhibit common but also divergent themes, should museums target specific audiences in terms of future acquisition and documentary practices? Whether this audience continues to be primarily curators and collection managers or includes the admission through documentation of the information needs of educators and a range of non-specialist users is a matter for individual consideration. This decision will be dependent on the mission, priorities, and resources individual institutions deem appropriate to bring to collections documentation reform. Herein, however, I will talk in terms of general documentary principles.

Our research identified three discursive principles that need to be built into collections documentation to address current theories around knowledge making and the specific information and interpretive needs of user groups. These include:

1   The role of objects as polysemic, that is, holding plural, cross-disciplinary, alternative and sometimes conflicting meanings.
2   An acknowledgement of the meaning of narratives and classifications systems as products of cultural, disciplinary, museum, and curatorial opinion.
3   In the current knowledge context where the belief in institutional authority, disciplinary privilege, and hierarchies becomes less persuasive, documentation also needs to acknowledge the role of users in the cycle of knowledge making.

Maximizing existing and enriched data

At the most basic level in the creation of new "knowledge environments," there needs to be a consideration through documentation of how information such as fielded data can be structured and coded in new ways. Equally important is the manner in which museums can maximize the use of enriched data through cross-linking and filtering to different collection records. This represents a strategy to improve the interpretive potential of collections and hence the creation of polysemic knowledge models and 3-D navigation and information spaces.

Beyond description

Recent documentation practices have witnessed a trend away from long descriptions to significance statements. Interestingly, the declining interest in description is related to a shift from a predominately empiricist documentation tradition based on the physicality of objects. Originally written to justify acquisitions to management, there needs to be a further consideration of how significance statements can be written in a compelling way for audiences. Curators need to consider the writing of text in the context of constructivist approaches to learning and to engage users in the cycle of knowledge making. This might, for example, include pointers to additional contextual sources, bibliographies, and media.

Addressing the "concreteness" of collections

The next task is to address issues around the concreteness of objects and their interpretations. Having said this, our research suggests that collections items and information must be considered as a growing and evolving body of knowledge rather than a definitive or quintessential set of facts. A science and technology curator at the Powerhouse Museum noted this point and stated that "there is the realization that while writing, a curator is creating an 'artifact' of that time, place and social context."[20] So here we need to present collections and information as temporarily situated expert opinions through authoring and dating.

Additionally we also need to instill a reflexive consciousness among curators regarding the limited legitimacy and lifespan of collections information as demonstrated by the apothecary and taxonomic paradigms mentioned in the previous sections.[21] A program of collections information revision and archiving needs to be instituted as part of the documentation process.

Exposing interpretive frameworks

A subsequent task is to expose the epistemological/disciplinary frameworks in which objects are interpreted, to explain the fact that object interpretations change and should no longer be presented as definitive accounts carrying the ultimate authority. Our research suggests that these postmodern principles could be shown through disclaimers, authored text, and linked curatorial essays about disciplinary contexts outlining the types of information privileged in each domain and how each contributes to our understanding of collections. Furthermore, exposing the nature of museum significance assessment procedures and links to museum collecting policies acknowledges the institutions' role in knowledge making.

Promoting plurality of meaning

Our research also suggests that museums need to capitalize on a plurality of meaning inherent in collection items, rather than favoring one interpretation. So how can these issues and array of influences be acknowledged and dealt with in documentation? Most basically this involves the rethinking of the relationships and meanings of collections in tandem with an understanding of the limitations of current approaches to knowledge making. The specific conceptual and disciplinary frameworks of art history, social history, science, decorative arts, anthropology, and the institutional tradition curators work within, as well as the individual standpoints of museum staff, determine the types of questions asked of objects. These establish the types of information documented and privileged in significance statements and the subsequent values and meanings ascribed to individual collection items, thereby narrowing their potential interpretive possibilities.

For example, a social historian may focus on the use, context, and the personal significance of an object to the owner or user. In contrast, a decorative arts curator may note its form, function, and material, how it fits into a chronological stylistic framework, the artist/maker, and its history of ownership. A technology curator on the other hand could look at the same object in terms of how it is manufactured, its degree of technological innovation, function, and how it works.

Our research also revealed the personal and idiosyncratic predilections, goals, and interests an individual curator may consciously and tacitly bring to bear on the analysis and documentation of objects.[22] Here the task of object interpretation is exposed as a dialogic and organic process where various influences come into play and intermingle.[23] One participant in the decorative arts focus group discussion at the Powerhouse Museum succinctly espoused the feelings of others by stating that "curators cast interpretations from different backgrounds and some objects have more to offer."[24]

Although many curators we interviewed were aware of the current discursive contexts of objects, appreciated the merits of other disciplinary interpretive frameworks, and experimented with integrating themes in exhibitions, this process has been slow to be applied to documentation. So how do we reconcile these information needs, revise the types of questions asked of collections, contribute to their broader understanding, and create a useful resource? These issues could be resolved through collaborations between departments/curators to discuss potential meanings and the significance of selected objects, and writing joint significance statements to expose a range of meanings and opinions across disciplinary areas. In procedural terms this involves pulling frameworks together while expanding the potential meanings of objects.

Our research also raised a very important point about the problem of "conceptual fit" between existing object meanings and classification schemes highlighting the difficulty of prescribing categories that can be applied universally (Cameron 2000). This was particularly obvious when we investigated issues around access to and the documentation of Maori and Aboriginal collections.[25] Currently institutions require the user to accept the institutional way of organizing information and the meanings ascribed to objects. Here is a strong case for the integration into documentation of alternative classification systems that acknowledge indigenous knowledge models.

Enabling a polysemic and shared interpretive approach

So how can a polysemic and shared interpretive approach be applied in documentation? Here a new polysemic knowledge model invites the opportunity to create categories and associated linkages through documentation that could potentially connect objects with a whole range of cultural, social, historical, technological, artistic, and disciplinary contexts. In conceptual terms, this involves the virtual layering of meanings and contexts of objects that can subsequently be configured and navigated in different ways in a live environment according to the individual interests of users. This could involve presenting information according to user profiles, age groups, and abilities as well as narrative and object-centered histories enabling multiple alternative interpretations (Cameron 2003). Links to related resources such as primary source materials, bibliographies, websites of current exhibitions, and a provision for user interpretations further elucidate knowledge making options. Establishing relationships between objects on the basis of extended fields and additional ontologies could form the basis of retrieval methods. However, developing concepts on how this metadata is to be handled and standardized will continue to be an important issue.

Extending thesauri, nomenclatures, and glossaries

Our research also revealed that problems of conceptual structure and naming within existing thesauri and nomenclatures need to be dealt with for documentation purposes. Furthermore, ensuring greater intellectual access to collections and enriched data means extending existing thesauri, nomenclatures and glossaries to reflect the plural meanings of objects. Most basically, this needs to occur during the documentation process in order to create a greater range of search and naming options thus contributing to and expanding interpretive options.

Use of non-text-based information

The need to address the emerging interest in the contextualization of objects and their non-textual representation in supporting a polysemic approach to collections interpretation emerged through both *Themescaping* and *Knowledge Objects* research. Specifically, user research suggests a trend away from detailed descriptions and primary text-based provenanced information to a greater use of non-text-based evidence such as video, audio, and 3-D simulations in supporting cinematic type experiences (Cameron 2003: 24). Here we need to consider how objects can be documented at acquisition, especially those deemed the most significant, in ways that capture a range of information. For example, this could include the digital recording of significance through comments by makers, users, and donors, the documentation and recording of the pre-museum contexts of objects, the digital rendering of objects in 3-D, and object movies.

Drawing on the wider information assets to best advantage

In Kevin Donovan's formative paper on the future of collections databases, he convincingly argued for the building of knowledge bases that draw together the wider information assets of a museum into a centralized resource.[26] Another important task is to consider how existing museum data can be put to more productive ends in the documentation and interpretive process. Research files, documents, recorded interviews, graphics, audio/visuals, publications, interactives, and educational materials are all currently held in separate files and collections. Furthermore, in the future all these components could be indexed, managed, and delivered by database tools while contributing to polysemic interpretive models such as relational thematic linkages, multimedia presentations, and rich research resources. The challenge of delivering multimedia within the context of constantly evolving digital platforms, however, will continue to have major implications for the ways in which collections information can be preserved, accessed, configured, and interpreted into the future.

Additionally, the emergence of more creative content environments, in particular 3-D visualizations and multimodal sensory experiences to which this material will contribute, are expected to become cheaper and more persuasive. In a collections context, this could potentially lead to the creation of complex cultural interpretations such as highly detailed and dynamic visualizations and navigation environments that have strong popular and pedagogic appeal for educators. As Scali and Tariffi (2001) argued, the rethinking of collection management and multimedia delivery systems to provide effective access to such multimedia content will have major implications on how collections information can be configured and elucidated.[27]

Linking practice to contemporary knowledge making

A shift from the predominant use of highly prescribed authored information, text-based descriptions, and significance statements to a greater inclusion of interpretive materials around selected significant objects will involve new curatorial roles. Curators may become more involved in bringing together and linking forms of evidence, for example, creating relationships between information and objects similar to an exhibitions paradigm. Likewise, the tasks of collection managers may witness a greater emphasis on creating and linking digital resources. Nonetheless as our research suggests, many users will continue to look to museum curators and collection managers to provide authoritative scholarly information in the form of authored significance statements, narrative-centered histories, and chronological frameworks.

Despite these content specifications, balancing both the need for modernist style texts with more fragmentary/subjective post-structuralist and postmodernist ones will together ensure a more open and inclusive approach to the ways these materials can be interpreted. This will give greater power to the user to create their own knowledge pathways and to make and "put up" their own interpretations in a kind of shared authorship. While this will undoubtedly require greater effort and resources in compiling each individual record, it will simultaneously allow a greater depth to knowledge woven around a given object, thereby maximizing its meaning potential.[28] One answer to the problem of workload is to institute a program of documentation where deemed significant objects get prior standing. Others, however, could be recorded according to a more simplistic polysemic template where hyperlinks in documentation are used as the primary tool in the creation of relationships and to link sources. Such practices correspond and embrace contemporary theoretical premises, that is, the recognition that objects are legitimately interpretable in a variety of ways.[29] This new way of curatorial thinking was aptly expressed by a participant in the science and technology focus group discussion; "as a curator, I would define myself as a 'knowledge broker:' we have to be aware of notions of pluralism and acknowledge the lack of singular authority of the museum or curator."[30]

Conclusion

The discussions in this paper attempt to go some way toward bridging the gap between theoretical deliberations that interpret museums and documentation processes from a distance and the practice and procedural preoccupations required by staff on a day-to-day basis.

The *Themescaping Virtual Collections* and the *Knowledge Objects* projects have revealed some possible directions for the next generation of online collections and documentation. It looks exciting but one of our greatest issues is the tension between the potential richness collections have to offer and museums as the relatively poorly resourced cultural institutions. This issue, first raised at the Digital Libraries Research for Access to Cultural and Scientific Resources meeting in Luxembourg in March 2000 (IST European Commission, 2000) will continue to be the single biggest defining matter in the future development of digital collections and knowledge environments.

From a broader discursive standpoint, the transformation of databases and documentation practices to meet these new needs and digital potentialities represents part of an ongoing institutional reframing process. Hilde Hein (2000) argues that objective knowledge and museums claims to it have been weakened by challenges to the empirical scientific genre, an epistemological position of which museums form a part. This decline in faith in a singular reality has instead been replaced by subjectivity and the condition of multiple realities (Hein 2000). Museum transformations have been rapid in some areas of operations such as programming through the inclusion of "other" voices in exhibitions and the growth in audience evaluation but documentation has lagged behind. Therefore, the revision of collections information to embrace user needs, current thinking, and the consequent transformation of the object from positively possessing one real meaning to one that is inherently polysemic is integral to the subsequent and on-going reconstruction of institutional identity, and modes of engagement with their constituents. Documentation, new acquisition processes, and digital media have the potential to reconstitute museum collections as sites for experiences, learning, knowledge making, and deconstruction, as well as inventory.

Bearing resources and the larger institutional transformative processes in mind, developing knowledge bases, and other potential futures such as interoperable libraries of collections and collaborative knowledge spaces can be viewed as an incremental process occurring through the establishment of a program of iterative development.[31]

One of our most fundamental strategic issues for the future, however, will be convincing management of the epistemological, educational, and marketing value of such initiatives and committing substantial resources to relevant projects.

Acknowledgements

This research was made possible by grants from the Australian Research Council. Special thanks goes to my colleagues, Sarah Kenderdine and Kevin Sumption, Powerhouse Museum and Bil Vernon, Vernon Systems Ltd, partner investigators on the *Themescaping Virtual Collections* project. I would also like to acknowledge Professor Stephen Garton, a fellow chief investigator, who has been a wonderful mentor and supporter. But most importantly I would like to express my gratitude to research assistant Helena Robinson who made an outstanding contribution to the *Knowledge Objects* project.

Notes

1   See H. Robinson and F. Cameron, 2003. 'Knowledge objects: Multidisciplinary approaches in museum collections documentation', unpublished manuscript. University of Sydney and Fiona Cameron, 2003. 'The next generation – Knowledge environments and digital collections', *Museums and the Web 2003 Conference*, 19–22 March, Charlotte, NC (http://www.archimuse. com/mw2003/papers/cameron/cameron.html).

2   Ibid.

3   H. Robinson and F. Cameron, 2003. 'Knowledge objects: Multidisciplinary approaches in museum collections documentation', unpublished manuscript, University of Sydney, 3.

4   Ibid.

5   Collection management systems that incorporate these features include KE Software, EMu (http://www.kesoftware.com/emu/index.html), Willoughby Associates (http://www.willo.com/mimsy_xg/default.asp), last accessed 3.15.04. Vernon Systems, Collection (http://www. vernonsystems.com), last accessed 3.15.04.

6   D. Peacock, J. Doolan and D. Ellis, 2004. 'Searching for Meaning. Not Just Records', *Museums and the Web 2004 Conference*, March 31–April 3, Arlington, VA/Washington DC (http://www. archimuse.com/mw2004/abstracts/prg_250000705.html), last accessed 8.4.04. Examples include the Metropolitan Museum of Art collections (http://www.metmuseum.org/works_of_Art), last accessed 3.15.04; J. Paul Getty Museum Collections (http://www.getty.edu/art/), last accessed 3.15.04; National Museum of Australia History browser (http://www.nma.gov.au), last accessed 3.15.04; Museum of Rural Life (http://www.ruralhistory.org/index.html), last accessed 1.15.04.

7   Examples include Revealing Things (http://www.si.edu/revealingthings), National Museum of American History, last accessed 7.15.03; Experience Music Project (http://www.emplive. com), last accessed 7.12.03; History Wired (http://histo rywired.si.edu/index.html), National Museum of American History, last accessed

7.15.03; Powerhouse Museum "Behind the Scenes" website (http://projects.power housemuseum.com/virtmus/), last accessed 8.4.04; National Museum of Australia History browser (http://www.nma.gov.au), last accessed 3.15.04; Hypermuseum (http://www.HyperMuseum.com), last accessed 1.15.04.

8 H. Robinson and F. Cameron, 2003. 'Knowledge objects: Multidisciplinary approaches in museum collections documentation', unpublished manuscript, University of Sydney, 24.

9 Ibid.

10 A. Munslow, Book Reviews, Institute of Historical Research, Reviews in History link, Discourse section: (http://www.history.ac.uk/reviews/discourse/index. html), last accessed 8.29.03.

11 Ibid.

12 Ibid, cited in H. Robinson and F. Cameron, 2003. 'Knowledge objects: Multidisciplinary approaches in museum collections documentation', unpublished manuscript, University of Sydney, 20.

13 Ibid.

14 A. Munslow, Book Reviews, Institute of Historical Research, Reviews in History link, Discourse section: (http://www.history.ac.uk/reviews/discourse/index. html), last accessed 8.29.03.

15 Ibid.

16 Ibid.

17 H. Robinson and F. Cameron, 2003. 'Knowledge objects: Multidisciplinary approaches in museum collections documentation', unpublished manuscript, University of Sydney, 21–23.

18 Ibid.

19 D. Adolsek and M. Freedman, 2001. 'Artifact as inspiration: Using existing collections and management systems to inform and create new narrative structures,' *Museums and the Web 2001 Conference*, 14–17 March, Seattle, WA, (http://www. archimuse.com/mw2001/papers/andolsek/undolsek.html), last accessed 7.14.03. Also see P. Gillard, 2002. 'Cruising through history wired', *Museums and the Web 2002 Conference*, 14–17 April, Boston, MA (http://www. archimuse.com/mw2002/ papers/gillard/gillard.html), last accessed 9.15.04.; P. Stuer, R. Meersman, and S. De Bruyne, 2001. 'The HyperMuseum theme generator system: Ontology-based internet support for the actual use of digital museum data for teaching and presentation,' *Museums and the Web 2001 Conference* 14–17 March, Seattle, WA (http://www. archimuse.com/mw2001/papers/stuer/stuer.html), last accessed 1.15.03.

20 H. Robinson and F. Cameron, 2003. 'Knowledge objects: Multidisciplinary approaches in museum collections documentation', unpublished manuscript, University of Sydney, 26.

21 Ibid: 23.

22 Ibid: 19.

23 Ibid.

24 Ibid: 36.

25 F. Cameron and S. Kenderdine, 2001. 'Themescaping virtual collections: Accessing and interpreting museum collections online', unpublished manuscript, University of Sydney and the Powerhouse Museum.

26 K. Donovan, 1998. 'The best of the intentions: Public access, the web & the evolution of museum automation', *Museums and the Web 1997 Conference*, 16–19 March,

Los Angeles, CA (http://www.archimuse.com/mw97/speak/donovan.htm), last accessed 7.15.03. Also see L. Sarasan and K. Donovan, 1998. 'The next step in museum automation: Staging encounters with remarkable things (the capture, management, distribution and presentation of cultural knowledge on-line)', *Occasional Papers on the Value and Use of Museum Information*, Willoughby Press (http://www.willo.com/text_frames/content/News/newarticles.htm), last accessed 7.15.03.; H. Besser, 1997. 'Integrating collections management information into online exhibits: The World Wide Web as a facilitator for linking 2 separate processes', *Museums and the Web 1997 Conference*, 16–19 March H. Besser, Los Angeles, CA (http://www.archimuse.com/mw97/speak/besser.htm), last accessed 7.15.03.; 1998. 'The transformation of the museum and the way it's perceived', in *The Wired Museum Emerging Technology and Changing Paradigms*, ed. K. Garmil-Jones. Washington DC: American Association of Museums, 153–170.

27   G. Scali and F. Tariffi, 2001. 'Bridging the collection management system multimedia exhibition divide: A new architecture for modular museum systems', *ICHIM Conference*, Milan, 3–7 September (http://www.archimuse.com/ichim2001/abstracts/prg_115000625.html), last accessed 7.12.03.

28   F. Cameron and S. Kenderdine, 2001. 'Themescaping virtual collections: Accessing and interpreting museum collections online', unpublished manuscript, University of Sydney and the Powerhouse Museum, 23.

29   Ibid.

30   H. Robinson and F. Cameron, 2003. 'Knowledge objects: Multidisciplinary approaches in museum collections documentation', unpublished manuscript, University of Sydney, 26.

31   M. Fleischmann, W. Strauss, G. Blome, J. Novak, and S. Paal, 2002. 'Netzspannung. org – A collaborative knowledge space for media art and technology', *Museums and the Web 2002 Conference*, 14–17 April, Boston, MA (http://www.archimuse.com/mw2002/papers/blome/blome.html), last accessed 1.14.04.

References

Cameron, F. R. 2000. 'Shaping Maori Histories and Identities: Collecting and Exhibiting Maori Material Culture at the Auckland and Canterbury Museums, 1850s to 1920s', Ph.D. thesis, Massey University, New Zealand.

Cameron, F. R. 2002. 'Wired collections – the next generation', *International Journal of Museum Management and Curatorship* 19 (3): 309–315.

Cameron, F. R. 2003. 'Digital futures I: Museum collections, digital technologies, and the cultural construction of knowledge', *Curator* 46(3): 325–339.

Hein, H. S. 2000. *The Museum in Transition: A Philosophical Perspective*. Washington DC and London: Smithsonian Institution Press.

Hooper-Greenhill, E. 1992. *Museums and the Shaping of Knowledge*. London: Routledge.

Kavanagh, G. 1990. *History Curatorship*. Leicester and London: Leicester University Press.

Lyotard, J. F. 1984. *The Postmodern Condition: A Report on Knowledge*. Trans. Geoff Bennington and Brian Massumi. Minneapolis, MN: University of Minnesota Press.

McLuhan, M. 1964. *Understanding Media: The Extensions of Man*. New York: McGraw-Hill.

Marwick, A. 2001. *The New Nature of History, Knowledge, Evidence and Language*. London: Palgrave.

Manovich, L. 2001. *The Language of New Media*. Cambridge, MA, and London: The MIT Press

Marty, P. F. 1999. 'Museum informatics and information infrastructures: Supporting collaboration across intra-museum boundaries,' *Archives and Museum Informatics* 13: 169–85.

Seely Brown, J. and P. Duguid 2000. *The Social Life of Information*. Boston: Harvard Business School.

Thomas, S. and A. Mintz 1998. *The Virtual and the Real – Media in Museums*. Washington, DC: American Association of Museums.

Chapter 10

Semantic Dissonance: do we need (and do we understand) the semantic web?

Ross Parry, Nick Poole and Jon Pratty

Collections and semantic thinking

Semantics have always been an integral part of museums. Just as the act of collecting objects into a singular physical site defines museums today and through history, so too does the ongoing act of making meaning with and between these objects. Through-out their (at least) five hundred year story, museums represent the coping strategy of countless historically and culturally differentiated communities to bring some degree of order to the world around them. Traditionally, museums bring fragments of society's knowledge and experience into a highly controlled environment, a closed system, within which order can then be found – or contrived. It has been the function of museums to find meaning within (or give meaning to) these highly orchestrated aggregated performances. Whether through narrative or systematics, genre or geography, the museum has sought to frame disparate objects with a rationalising discourse into a 'collection' or 'exhibition'. Using numbering, term lists, taxonomy or simply physical proximity, museums have deployed systems that have provided logic, a set of assumptions, and (invariably) a vocabulary to tame and explain their collections. This classificatory project (this syntax) and importantly, the semantics inextricably linked to it, are what has come to define the museum today and through history. Museums, in short, are places where, in a structured way, we give or reinforce meanings to things. This is museum semantics.

More recently (or, at least, in the last forty years) the automated and systematic processing of computer technology has come to support and augment this syntactical and semantic project. Unsurprisingly perhaps, when museums first began to

Source: *Museums and the Web 2008: Proceedings*, Toronto: Archives & Museum Informatics, 2008. http://www.archimuse.com/mw2008/papers/parry/parry.html.

explore the potential of computing it was specifically to the management and documentation of collections that they first turned (Vance 1973). In contrast to some highly localised, frequently personalised, at times idiosyncratic ordering systems that existed in museums, computing instead promised (indeed, required) a systematised and consistent treatment of collections. Computers could help generate (and, in fact, were dependent upon) a curatorial environment where the semantics of collections could be formalised and standardised. Moreover, the standard classificatory codes, data entry conventions, fixed fields and terminology control that the new automation was reliant upon came to resonate with the professional aspirations of the new managerialism that came to define the sector in the last quarter of the twentieth century. A professional museum was an ordered museum, and an ordered museum was a museum that used the new documentation – driven by standards and automation (Parry 2007). Within a generation (or two), therefore, the museum sector became familiar with the concept of a collection being organised and described in a highly structured and systemic way. Standardisation became orthodoxy. At least for classification and management purposes, semantics (the meanings associated with objects) became highly engineered.

However, in the last five years, this 'engineering' has been challenged by the new Web 2.0 environment. We are now perhaps all too familiar with the ways in which what was once an extensively broadcast model of centralised, specialised, institutional providers publishing flat online pages predicated upon agreed protocols and standards of collections management, has been supplanted by a much more diverse online cultural heritage ecology. This is the digital landscape where users become producers, where 'pages' are more transitory. This is a landscape characterised by syndication, where the Web (rather than in its old function as repository) becomes 'event' and communications space (Pratty 2006). (Or, to see it in Dickensian terms: this is a move from the Miss Havisham model to the Fagin model. The Miss Havisham model involves the museum sitting there in wedding dress waiting for people to turn up to the party, with cobwebs over the table, having gone to all this trouble, angry and bitter, destined to go up in flames. The Fagin model, on the other hand, is to be more cunning, to have lots of agents running around the city, slipping into all sorts of places, being discovered, not being discovered, moving things around, being exciting and, of course, being prepared to review the situation.) Significantly for our discussion here, this is a domain where meanings become more explicitly contested, where the diversity of online activity is matched by the diversity of interpretations and voices (Chun et al. 2006; Chan 2007); and it is here where the orthodox syntax and semantics of museum collections become both negotiable and negotiated.

Collections and semantic technologies

Although not always stated as such, technology (specifically computer technology) has had a conspicuous role to play in museum semantics. The early publications of the Museum Data Bank (headed by Robert Chenhall, and based at the University of Arkansas Museum) are testimony to how, even in the early 1970s, museum curators worried about how computer technology would reflect (or shape) the semantics of collections (Vance 1974). Likewise, the first generation of hierarchical database management systems that, in the UK, set the parameters on the MDA data model in the mid-1970s posed a series of questions for the development team on to what extent the terminology and data entered would need to be consistent and controlled (Roberts and Light 1984). The relational models and systems of the 1980s, and the more flexible standard units of information and documentation protocols that they prompted, saw computing, knowledge capture and documentation influence each other yet again, as demonstrated in the publication of MDA's SPECTRUM standard in the early 1990s (Nuttall 2000). Then later in the 1990s, and within the context of the Web, initiatives such as the European Union's 'Aquarelle' project yet again wrestled with how cultural heritage content might be made interoperable despite being contained within different semantic and syntactical systems and within different software and hardware platforms (Dawson 1998). In each case, museums had to reflect not just upon information retrieval, the harvesting of data and the interoperability of their systems, but also (fundamentally) upon how they made meaning with their collections. In each case, these were technologies that aimed to support and reflect museum semantics.

The unresolved semantic web

It is therefore into this deeper context of 'semantic technologies' that our recent engagements with the Semantic Web might usefully be seen. For five years now the museum sector has had its self-proclaimed 'primer' for understanding what might be the core building blocks of the Semantic Web (DigiCULT 2003). Subsequently, Seamus Ross (2006) articulated a clear and beguiling lexicon and outline of how the Semantic Web can be characterised for the culture heritage sector; namely, that it is participatory (cultural heritage and academic institutions can participate as well as students allowing for growing interconnections of knowledge); interactive (it is possible to trace different pathways, contribute to the process of knowledge development and learn by watching how others are adding to these interconnections); retentive (the Semantic Web has the property of retaining knowledge links and being functional so both people and machines can continue to use them in different ways); trans-disciplinary (in the cultural sector, not only do we think of content as being the curator's input, but we can also build up interconnections of knowledge stories that other people have and build those into other datasets in other cultural institutions); and trans-cultural (building in the cultural interconnections between, for example, Picasso's work, when heavily influenced by African art, and the pieces which influenced him, and other cultural activities that were going on at that time). During 2006 and 2007, the 'UK Museums and the Semantic Web' project funded by the AHRC also devoted considerable time to exploring the potentials and realities of these technologies for the sector. The objective of this series of workshops (the 'Semantic Web Thinktank' as it soon become known) was to identify the key challenges and opportunities that the Semantic Web presented for museums and galleries in the UK and to define how the culture sector should respond to them. The Thinktank brought together experts from a wide range of disciplines, including museum policy and management, cataloguing and computational science. Over nine months, twelve to fifteen semantic Web experts and museum professionals gathered in a series of closely documented meetings around the UK to explore ways forward for the sector into this more digitally connected future (http://culturalsemanticweb.wordpress.com/). But more recently still – and more tangibly – the sector has at last begun to glimpse localised, small-scale manifestations of semantic technologies being constructed and applied to real heritage content and contexts (Amin et al. 2007).

In each case, these projects continued to recognise the importance of metadata, turning data into meaningful objects sitting within intelligent semantic Web structures. However, as the number of initiatives working in this area grows, a number of recurring obstacles and questions continue to characterise (if not plague) the research and development landscape. At a very fundamental and practical level, as Ross (2006) observed so succinctly, Semantic Web projects continue to be hampered by a lack of standards, a lack of skills, a lack of investment, a lack of strong case studies, and the lack of immediate reward. As well as a series of technical questions (what role for RDF, XML, OWL or Topic Maps?), there remain conflicting visions of how the Semantic Web may play within the cultural heritage sector. Will (should?) the Semantic Web be a unified and collaborative venture within the sector? Or, is it more likely to be (and more likely to succeed as) a series of contained and localised systems and projects linked to a specified set of sites and resources? Likewise, will the ontologies upon which the Semantic Web is so reliant be 'universal', inviolate and few in number, or (in contrast) highly localised, variable, liquid and multiple? Is the Semantic Web for the heritage sector likely to grow from a coordinated sector-wide set of agreements, standards and joint initiatives? Or will the sector find itself responding to more user-generated ontologies and community-created solutions for intelligently discovering and searching heritage content?

Within these different versions of a semantic future for museums, there is at one extreme the vision of a hard 'Semantic Web', with prescribed and persistent ontologies predicated by the sector on existing collections standards (and perhaps term lists and thesauri) by the professional community of practice itself. On the other hand, there is a vision of a soft 'semantic Web', with user-defined (and likely more transitory and disparate) ontologies generated by different communities of interest outside of the institution. Both result in more efficient and intelligent resource discovery, but whereas the former appears to privilege an inward gaze towards more improved collections management, the latter looks instead outwards to how users outside the museum make their own meaning and search for and encounter digital cultural content online.

The aspirational semantic web

What is the aspiration for the Semantic Web? What would a semantic museum look like, and what problems would it solve? We may be able to find some indication in some of the innovative services and partnerships in which museums are currently engaged.

Recent work by Flickr in partnership with the Library of Congress (http://flickr.com/commons) illustrates the power and potential of working collaboratively with leading technology companies in developing semantic approaches. Using images from the Library of Congress collection as raw material, the popular photo-sharing service is enabling users to 'tag' images with their own descriptive metadata. In addition to providing semantically rich information, the project demonstrates the importance of bringing together content and platform in innovative ways. Politically and economically, this project represents an important step in the process of advocating a Semantic Web to the managers and funders of museum services. The culture sector is able to offer deep, rich contextual data and expertise in mediating and interpreting source materials. The private and commercial sectors are able to leverage technology, finance and market share to bring these cultural resources to a far greater audience than would otherwise be possible.

Experience tends to show that there is a cascade effect among the titans of the online world. The interest of Flickr in taxonomy and social classification may also prompt interest from companies such as Microsoft, Amazon or eBay, all of which have strongly vested interests in the successful implementation of semantics as part of service delivery. This cascade may just provide the momentum and technical research and development required to move the Semantic Web on from a conceptual framework to a concrete reality, something which the culture sector on its own is not in a position to achieve.

Most of the Internet's major companies are experimenting with tools, frameworks and systems which enable the user to interact not just with the information, but also at the level of the application itself. Platforms such as Google Base and Yahoo Pipes are encouraging a collaborative approach to experimentation and technical development. In this opening up of the development process, it is becoming increasingly feasible to embed true semantics into the base functionality of systems, and to expose these semantics to a massively distributed network. Above all, then, the semantic museum is likely to be one that is joined-up, integrated into and apparent within existing successful and large-scale consumer services. This, in itself, forms a compelling argument for museums to embrace semantics as a mechanism for reaching a vastly extended marketplace.

In the near future, the museum sector's response to the Semantic Web has to connect to current practice in the creation, management and delivery of digital content. In this context, the traditional standards-based museum digital approach will stand us in good stead. February 2008 discussions on the Museums Computer Group (UK) news list passionately exposed the long-running debate in British museums and galleries about good metadata practice and what it is for. Imagining the real possibility of a socially networked Web built from clusters of networked and semantically connected databases, then the long, long legacy of straight museum data with good URIs, consistent metadata and simple tagging are seen to provide a vitally stable infrastructure on which to build.

Another key development in the current generation of digital services is the erosion of the importance of 'place'. As the Web itself moves further towards distributed platforms and dynamic media, it seems likely that Web 'sites' will come to be replaced by Web 'services'. In this world of diffuse identities and services, persistent semantics – the ability to share meanings between platforms as well as records – will become the prime currency. With this likely scenario in mind, we should perhaps be considering the places and contexts where our digital cultural content might be found in future. Already we are familiar with search page results where particles of content or individual collection items are sometimes found. Already we may be familiar with massive numbers of one-page viewers of our sites, visitors attracted by search engines. Better quality search results must surely result in the centre of gravity of the online museum running away from the place of publishing towards remote published contexts, like blogs, search results pages, re-skinned or repurposed sites.

In this mid-term Semantic Web world, content needs to be self-describing, imbued with its own meaning and context. On your site it makes sense. When found in Google with a summary, it becomes puzzling. We know we need our content to be trusted, and we want our museum's name to be considered when the object or text is found in a search.

The disruptive semantic web

The genesis of the Semantic Web lies in a very specific technological context. The way it is presented, the jargon it has engendered and the solutions it promotes are strongly geared towards the technologist, and this places the entire momentum of its development at risk. The tendency to this point has been for the technologists to presume that the majority of people need not concern themselves with how the Semantic Web will function, but that they will simply benefit from the better, richer, more meaningful and intelligent experiences they will enjoy as a result. This view, however, contains a fundamental error. It is not possible to 'build' a Semantic Web, turn it on and enable people to use it. Instead, the development towards a semantically richer Web depends on the countless organisational and individual decisions made every day across the culture sector. It depends on the needs and expectations of the users of cultural services, and the extent to which semantic technologies and techniques can provide better service to meet them.

Whether one thinks of them as a sector, or an industry, or a public service, museums and related cultural organisations are part of a collective whole which maps in the mind of the ordinary user to the concept of 'museum'. Preparing museums for a Semantic future is a sector-wide issue which cuts across almost every area – from policy to standards, funding to professional practice. In this sense, the real challenge to pursuing a semantically rich cultural offer lies far away from technology. Effecting large-scale and permanent change across the museum sector depends on a variety of factors. From a top-down view, it depends on Government policy in areas such as technological innovation and social reform. These policy drivers inform both the strategic direction of the sector and, more important, the prioritisation of funding. From a bottom-up view, change depends on champions within organisations with the energy, commitment and management support to reset cultural values and attitudes. It depends on practitioners on the ground recognising and working to address the needs of the people who interact with their collections.

As it is currently presented, the potential of the Semantic Web for museums lacks this quality of immediacy and clarity. Although the high-level, long-term aim is clearly stated, Semantic Web discourse rapidly disintegrates into a multitude of candidate technologies and models, each of which independently lays claim to the orthodox definition of a truly semantic Web. Museums cannot dictate what the Semantic Web becomes: they can only participate in its development. If they are to achieve the change necessary to ensure that they are prepared for the Semantic Web, it will be necessary to lay claim to one particular view of what it is and how it works. If money is to be secured, standards changed and staff employed, then it will be necessary to parcel up the concept of a Semantic Web for museums and quite explicitly sell it – to Government, to agencies, to funders and to the profession.

Furthermore, if, over the last forty years, or even over the last ten years, we didn't have the time, resources, organisational commitment or systems in place to catalogue our collections, how is it that we think we will have any of these things to make the collections semantically rich? The answer, of course, is that we won't – and this presents a fundamental challenge to the ability of museums even to consider how to participate in a Semantic Web. If the vision for the development of a semantic museums sector is decoupled from the realities and practicalities of making it work, then it quite simply will not happen.

Nor does the development of the culture sector's response to the Semantic Web exist in isolation of the technical development which preceded it, and the current direction this work is taking. Building on the *Netful of Jewels* report (Keene et al. 1999), much of the past decade of technical development for UK museums has been occupied in pursuit of a vision founded on access and education. This vision depended on achieving a critical mass in the online publication of collections information. Broadcast models such as mass-digitisation and the provision of online access to museum catalogues were intended to achieve a ubiquity of cultural content that was embedded, coherent and fit for a variety of different purposes. In contrast, the policy focus of recent years has shifted towards making more active use of the capacity that is distributed across the sector. Instead of funding content creation per se, a new generation of funding streams is focusing on developing the infrastructure, standards and skills to aggregate content from multiple sources and to broker it to content platforms and services. The new vision is of a multi-faceted, domain-agnostic system that is capable of using any number of protocols to aggregate data from multiple sources, of repurposing that data, and of expressing it to many different services in structured ways.

As this policy agenda moves forward, however, it becomes increasingly exposed to the risk of diverging from the real, practical and on-the-ground business of managing a collection. The more the emphasis is placed on infrastructure and aggregation, the greater the danger that museums and practitioners will not be able to produce the content, the raw material with which to feed them. In this context, and inasmuch as it represents a next-generation challenge over and above the very real corporate challenges currently faced by cultural organisations, the Semantic Web may very well be a bridge too far. If museums are to become Semantic Web-ready, it will be necessary to divert these current developments to ensure that they address both the technical and the cultural challenges surrounding the delivery of semantically rich resources.

In the context of the Semantic Web, and indeed the more general trajectory of technological development in museums, the solution perhaps is prosaic but entirely necessary. Participating in the Semantic Web is no different, in practical terms, from participating in any other type of work. It requires skills and resources, it necessitates organisational and cultural change, and it requires clear practices and protocols. Although the potential of the Semantic Web is clearly transformative, the reality falls far short. In this sense, the progression towards a Semantic Web mirrors that of the development of Artificial Intelligence during the 1970s, 80s and 90s. The end goal is clear, but the path is anything but, and apparently promising approaches often yield very little progress. There is the sense, then, that the Semantic Web – tremendously powerful and promising though it may be – is a distraction from what should be the proper business of a museum in the digital age. Perhaps what is needed is clean and consistent data about objects, structured according to open standards and delivered through open architectures. Perhaps it is more important to develop the skills, both technical and managerial, to ensure that technology is well-planned and implemented, and that it delivers first and foremost against the core objectives of the organisation.

The dilemma of the semantic web

At the heart of the discourse about museums and the Semantic Web, then, lies a dilemma.

Intuitively, the imperative of the Semantic Web to connect meaning and object reflects the long-held imperative for museums to define, to classify and to present. There are approaches and models sitting alongside the development of a true Semantic Web which are clearly either parallel to or extensions of existing practices within museums. The Semantic Web also apparently has the potential to resolve some fundamental tensions which are currently inhibiting progress – such as the need to provide better-mediated search and discovery of resources via quasi-intelligent services.

At a conceptual level, therefore, it seems as though the development of semantic technologies and methodologies is the next best step towards a fully integrated, always-on, mediated and contextual online cultural offering. The dilemma faced by museums, however, hinges on the significant gap between the vision and the reality of the Semantic Web – a gap which critically undermines the ability of the sector to move forward in a clear and constructive way.

The whole online environment is experiencing a second generation that is characterised by rapid growth and equally rapid collapse. From this environment are emerging interesting and challenging models, some of which may point towards a more open and participative future. In the time since the first dotcom collapse in 2001, none of these models has had time to stabilise, to demonstrate its long term effectiveness. None of the Creative Industries has had time to learn about these new models, to test them out or to apply them in truly integrated ways to its services.

Museums are understandably driven to embrace new technologies which support the provision of better services to users. From the earliest days of computing and data manipulation, museums have found ways of harnessing technologies to achieve their aims. Where these technologies have succeeded, it has been because there is a natural and intuitive fit between the functionality of the technology and the requirements of the museum and its users.

The danger of the Semantic Web is that, unlike digitisation or cataloguing, it is not a coherent practice or set of practices. There is no coherent answer to the question, 'How do I do the Semantic Web?' and almost no information with which to make an informed decision about technologies, platforms, models and methodologies. Of course, most well-structured and standardised disciplines didn't start out as such, but the Semantic Web is proving uniquely resistant to specification and definition.

Achieving a constructive role for museums in the Semantic Web demands resources, and securing resources depends on the ability of the sector to express a clear and compelling case for investment. This case ultimately hinges on the extent to which semantics enables more people to reach better museum services. This is the bottom line towards which the Semantic Web for museums must be oriented, and without which it runs the risk of shattering into a thousand disconnected splinters.

As with everything else, the extent to which museums will be able to respond collectively and with confidence to the opportunities and challenges presented by the Semantic Web depends far more on politics, economics and people than it ever did on technology. After all the noise has died down, and the cutting edge of New Technology has moved on, it seems likely that the Semantic Web will prove to be, not our destination, but just another stop along the way.

Acknowledgements

This project was generously funded as part of the Arts and Humanities Research Council (UK) 'Research Workshops (Museums and Galleries)' scheme. Special thanks are due to the University of Cambridge, University of Glasgow, University of Leicester, University of Newcastle, 24 Hour Museum (Brighton) and the Victoria and Albert Museum (London) for hosting some of these discussions.

The authors are particularly grateful to all of the participants who formed the Semantic Web Thinktank. They were: Philip Adams, Senior Assistant Librarian (systems development) De Montfort University; Martin Bazley, e-learning consultant; Stephen Brown, Professor, De Montfort University; Robin Boast, deputy director; Museum of Arch. and Anth., Camb.; David Dawson, Digital Futures, MLA; Dylan Edgar, Scottish Museum Council; Jane Finnis, Director, 24 Hour Museum; Michael Freeman, Curator, Ceredigion Museum, Aberystwyth; Areti Galani, Lecturer, CCHS, University of Newcastle; David Gerrard, Web Developer, De Montfort University; Jeremy Keith, Clear Left Design Ltd.; Brian Kelly, UK Web Focus, UKOLN; Suzanne Keene, Lecturer, UCL; Richard Light, XML Consultant; Frances Lloyd-Baynes, Head of Records, V&A; Mike Lowndes, Interactive Media Manager, Natural History Museum; Lena Maculan, Digital Heritage Research Group, University of Leicester; Gordon Mckenna, Standards and Systems Manager, MDA; Mayra Ortiz-Williams, Digital Heritage Research Group, University of Leicester; Jeremy Ottevanger, Web Developer, Museum of London; Ross Parry, Digital Heritage Research Group, University of Leicester; Nick Poole, Director, MDA; Jon Pratty, Editor, 24 Hour Museum; Phill Purdy, Development Officer, Museums Library Archives Council; Mia Ridge, Database Developer, Museum of

London; Seamus Ross, Director of Humanities, Computing, University of Glasgow; Angelina Roussou, Researcher, Queensland Institute of Technology; Andy Sawyer, Museum Consultant, MWR Ltd.; Paul Shabajee, Research Fellow, University of Bristol/HP-Labs; Jennifer Trant, Partner and Principal Consultant, Archives and Museum Informatics, Canada; Alex Whitfield, Education Prog. Manager, British Library; Alison Wells, Doc. Assistant, Bristol City Museum and Art Gallery; Dan Zambonini, Technical Director, Box UK.

Bibliography

Amin, A., V. de Boer, L. Hardman et al. (2007) 'Searching and Annotating Virtual Heritage Collections with Semantic-Web Techniques'. In D. Bearman and J. Trant (eds), *Museums and the Web 2007: Proceedings*. Toronto: Archives & Museum Informatics, 2004. Consulted February 10, 2008. http://www.archimuse.com/mw2007/abstracts/prg_325000959.html.

Chan, S. (2007) 'Tagging and Searching: serendipity and museum collection databases'. In J. Trant and D. Bearman (eds), *Museums and the Web 2007: Proceedings*. Toronto: Archives & Museum Informatics, 2007. Consulted May 25, 2007. http://www.archimuse.com/mw2007/papers/chan/chan.html

Chun, S., R. Cherry, D. Hiwiller, J. Trant and B. Wyman (2006) 'Steve.museum: an ongoing experiment in social tagging, folksonomy, and museums'. In J. Trant and D. Bearman (eds), *Museums and the Web 2006: Proceedings*. Toronto: Archives & Museum Informatics. Consulted May 25, 2007. http://www.archimuse.com/mw2006/papers/wyman/wyman.html.

Dawson, D. (1998). 'Aquarelle – access to European Culture Heritage'. Museums Computer Group Newsletter, spring, 4–5.

DigiCULT (2003) 'Towards a Semantic Web for Heritage Resources: Thematic Issue 3'. DigiCULT project, Information Society Technologies Programme, European Commission. Available: http://www.digicult.info/downloads/ti3_high.pdf.

Fielding, R. T. (2000) 'Architectural Styles and the Design of Network-based Software Architectures'. University of California, Irvine. Consulted February 10, 2008. http://www.ics.uci.edu/~fielding/pubs/dissertation/top.htm.

International Standard, ISO 23950: 'Information Retrieval (Z39.50): Application Service Definition and Protocol Specification'. Consulted February 10, 2008. http://www.loc.gov/z3950/agency/.

Keene, S., B. Royan, D. Anderson (eds) (1999) 'A Netful of Jewels: New Museums in the Learning Age'. National Museum Directors Conference (NMDC). Consulted February 10, 2008. http://www.nationalmuseums.org.uk/images/publications/netful_of_jewels.pdf.

Merriman, N. (2007) 'A Sustainable Future for Collections'. In *Delivering Collections for the Future in the North West*, North West Museums, Libraries and Archives Council (MLA NW). Consulted February 10, 2008. http://www/mlanorthwest.org.uk/museumslibrariesarchives/museums/renaissancenw/collectionsforthefuture/

Nuttall, A. (2000) 'History of the MDA'. Internal unpublished report. Cambridge: MDA.

Open Archives Initiative Protocol for Metadata Harvesting. Consulted February 10, 2008. http://www.openarchives.org/OAI/openarchivesprotocol.html.

Parry, R. (2007) *Recording the Museum: Digital Heritage and the Technologies of Change*. London and New York: Routledge.

Pratty J. (2006) 'The inside out Web museum'. In J. Trant and D. Bearman (eds), *Museums and the Web 2006: Proceedings*, Toronto: Archives & Museum Informatics, 2006. Consulted February 10, 2008. http://www.archimuse.com/mw2006/papers/pratty/pratty.html.

Roberts, D.A. and R. Light (eds) (1984) 'Microcomputers in Museums'. MDA occasional paper 7. Duxford: Museum Documentation Association.

Ross, S. (2006) 'Semantic Web Thinktank: Workshop 1'. University of Glasgow, 13 October 2006. Consulted February 10, 2008. http://culturalsemanticweb.word press.com/workshop-reports.

Simple Object Access Protocol (SOAP) Consulted February 10 2008. http://www.w3schools.com/soap/default.asp.

Vance, D. (1973) *Computers in the Museum*. New York: IBM Corporation.

Vance, D. (1974) 'What are Data?' *Museum Data Bank Research Report no. 1*. New York: Museum Data Bank Committee.

Chapter 11

Building a Universal Digital Memory

Pierre Lévy

The culture of tomorrow

We are building a new civilization, a global society of networked knowledge. The development of communications, transportation and international trade has put us irreversibly on the road to global integration. Humanity, which up until relatively recently was largely rural, now lives within the meshes of a network of megalopolises. The rapid development of telecommunications and the spread of the universal digital network have forced us to radically rethink cultural data and to live in society in a way that is essentially different from the way our ancestors lived.

The inroads being made by cyberspace are accelerating: the slow development of telephone networks, the birth of electronics, the invention of the computer, followed by the personal computer, the interconnection of computers, the widespread digitization of communications, along with the development of wireless networks ... The Web did not even exist in 1992. Ten years on, hundreds of millions of people are browsing the Internet. The future will inevitably bring an increase in network capacity, not only in terms of data storage, but also processing power and bandwidth. There will be a proliferation of ways to access cyberspace, and they will become less and less expensive, with wireless access points everywhere. The more people interconnect, particularly in highly populated countries with a rich cultural heritage, like India, China, Brazil or Mexico, as well as in many Moslem cultures, whose heritage is ancient and refined. Cultures will encounter one another in the digital network.

The birth of cyberspace as a borderless interactive communications tool is opening a new form of *public space* on a new scale. Our messages converge and

Source: *Virtual Museum (of Canada): the next generation*, Canadian Heritage Information Network, 2005, pp. 55–62.

interact with one another on the undulating fabric of expanding hypertext. A meta city can be seen on the horizon of planetary culture.

The economy is becoming increasingly dependent on the development of knowledge. The management challenge we face is becoming increasingly complex in terms of the digital dataflows that supply and express our intermingled communities. An extension of existing trends would appear to point to the apparition of new forms of politics, economics and culture for the generations that will follow us. In the midst of uncertainty, a number of broad principles appear to be taking shape, for example, one that argues that ideas, knowledge and cultural heritage are what constitute the wealth of nations from now on.

The phenomenon of massive interconnection casts doubt, sometimes violently, on old ways of transmitting culture. The current wave, which is transforming symbolic life, is giving rise to fears, which are very understandable, of dissolution or loss of identity. At the same time, a multitude of personal and collective subjectivities can be found to an ever-expanding degree and in an increasingly professional manner on the internet, while a growing number of "virtual communities" are exploring new ways of *being together*, through digitized speech, images and music.

The responsibilities of memory institutions

People involved in culture, especially those whose mission is to transmit memory, have a great responsibility. The transmission of a meaningful heritage cannot be considered a deposit of dead things, with a simple instruction sheet or dogmas to be recited. In the everyday practice of receiving and transmitting culture, conservation, appreciation and development require personal research, and a headlong plunge, with all its attendant risks, into the depths of the heritage in question. Because the chains of transmission are alive, there is an obligation upon us to ask new questions in order to enlarge and develop the world of meanings transmitted to us.

The crucial problems addressed by traditional cultures must be rethought by each generation, whose responsibility it is to creatively regenerate the symbolic world that it will be passing on to future generations. More specifically, a generation finds itself confronted with *one* essential question, which is really a meta question, namely: "What is the essential problem facing us?" In other words, at what point must we rethink our traditions in as innovative and radical a manner as possible? Or to put it another way: What are we *most* responsible for?

Today, symbolic ecosystems of different cultures are being carried along in a movement towards growing convergence and interdependence. The new medium of interactive global communications is challenging the old rules of symbolic life. The trend towards globalization and computerization demands, *nolens volens*, that we find meaning in a future cultural unity for humanity. It is asking us to become a global interconnected society. Let us look at things as they are: the future of symbolic life must pass through a phase of universal memory that becomes our common cultural resource.

I am not speaking here of cyberspace as simply an *instrument* for transmitting our traditions as they stand. I am speaking of a global unified sphere of human culture that arises as a *problem*. Will we be able to find a way to establish some form of dynamic balance at a higher level of complexity, as our predecessors were able to do when major cultural mutations occurred? Will we have the courage to strive to make the most of our common heritage? Can we aim at a form of universal digital memory worthy of the great pluralist civilization, brought together as a result of a memory whose creation we can all contribute towards?

Rethinking archives

In order to meet this challenge, memory institutions need to take appropriate steps to deal with the new opportunities open to them. What we need in order to get people to stop thinking in earlier ways that involved very ancient technical limitations is a completely new way of thinking about archives. Once information has been digitized and indexed, it becomes possible to copy it and distribute it indefinitely at very low cost for every part of the network. As soon as the nature of digital information is understood, it becomes clear that no single location and no fixed visual form is involved. It can be everywhere and be used interactively in an infinite number of ways. It is virtually free from any limitations of physical space.

This means that it is now possible to make coherently available in cyberspace virtually all of the digital data stored and exhibited by all the nodes of the world network of museums and libraries. But this initial opportunity is only the physical and institutional portion of the redundancy possible in cyberspace. *Semantic redundancy* is more radical than that. Indeed, at the same time as technical constraints are removed, the loosening of inflexible symbolic codes and the introduction of an anthropological approach that has learned much about cultural diversity have blurred the distinctions that formerly applied in archival structures. There is no longer an *absolute* distinction between the "ordinary" and "that which is worthy of keeping", between the artist and the public, between visitors and those who mount exhibitions, between the critic and the public. As soon as a virtual community adopts a topic, an idea, or some form of heritage … packets of information automatically make it worth keeping. All human chronicles are interconnected by means of a proliferating worldwide conversation. Documents are linked by a dynamic and enormous hypertext that reflects movements in our writing, our links and the way we navigate.

Let us summarize a few of the more radical ways in which the traditional archive has been challenged in the twentieth century.

- First: all human activity can be an object of history and archaeology.
- Second: a cultural form of expression is legitimate as soon as it finds a community to preserve it.
- Third: the new place for the artist to display his works is the museum.

The universal digital memory of the future will have no trouble in incorporating these challenges. As reproduction costs virtually nothing, we can allow ourselves a proliferation of digital data in every form and use it and have access to it accordingly. It is henceforth possible to have as many points of view of universal memory as there are human communities. That is why I suggest conceiving the architectural future of information on the basis of a new "semantic perspective". It is called a perspective because the digital memory in question creates in cyberspace a *semantic mirror*, a virtual world that can be explored and whose function will be to reflect back to visitors the infinitely reproduced vision of their collective creation.

Museums and libraries can use available techniques to build an information architecture that is worthy of universal digital memory. We must therefore aim at an architecture of animated images that are flexible, transparent, distributed and open to collaborative efforts. In this program of work, the exhibition space for universal digital memory must organize a *way of creating a three-dimensional animated image* of the (human) memorable in which all virtual communities of visitors, authors and users can find one another and work together. For this, we can use the new opportunities made available through the *automatic projection of sharable three-dimensional virtual worlds* made possible by bandwidth and image synthesis software. These technical opportunities are already being used by people in the scientific community and by online games played by numerous participants in virtual worlds.

A new perspective

This mutation of our *understanding of meaning* can, I believe, benefit from a comparison with the mutation of our *understanding of the physical* as it occurred in Europe around the sixteenth century. The semantic perspective invented during the Renaissance was a revolution in the way people perceived. The perspective can be defined as the cultural construct through which space consists of different but symmetrical points of view. According to this structural definition, perspective was not something invented only for painting. It developed in relationships of equality among citizens, in the abstract shapes of geometry, and in physical relationships between the particles described by modern science. The challenging of our ethnocentricities by anthropology and the humanities have led us to such a perspective in the humanistic disciplines. But what is lacking in studies of humanity is a visualization of the objects under consideration in infinite three-dimensional space, something that would give it a complete perspective. That is why I suggest a potentially infinite virtual three-dimensional space in which each subject—object acts as a point of view that affects the very structure of exhibition space as a way of structuring universal digital memory. This would make it possible to have the point of view of each community united around a documentary heritage within the self-organized multitude of possible points of view. By making semantic space a form of perspective space, the memory institutions will create for each visitor a virtual representation of the *point of view of others*, which cannot be dissociated from the discovery of its own point of view.

Before implementing the program, a review of current semantic Web development would be useful. From a strictly technical standpoint, we know that the semantic Web being worked on today will make digital information more useful by providing flags or tags for the software agents that will search the network, making it possible to factor in the *meaning* of the documents and transactions in completing their tasks. Thanks to the semantic Web, it will be possible for universal digital memory data to be addressed and self-organized in terms of *meaning* and *practical uses* (if these two concepts mean different things, which – *pace* Peirce and Wittgenstein – I doubt). The semantic Web, as it stands today, is organized by a multitude of ontologies. This is only to be expected, because there must be many different ways of interpreting the world if a rich and productive collective intelligence is to thrive. And yet, if we want universal digital memory to adopt *a meaning-based addressing system*, we will have to be able to translate these many ontologies into a semantic architecture of memory that is coherent.

The adoption of a common language that can signal all possible perspectives of meaning is a precondition to the establishment of a universal digital memory. It is only if such a condition is met that a common digital memory will be able to coordinate and make intelligible the *relationships* between semantic zones that are structured by distinct local ontologies. The information architecture language that I am putting forward here meets this constraint in terms of a strategy for relationships because, as we shall see, its structure reflects a system of symmetrical relationships between different ontological points of view. Because it was developed in response to the geometric principles of reciprocal points of view, this *language of ideas* can meet the anthropological symmetry conditions required by a universal digital memory. But let us begin by asking what an idea is.

The language of ideas

The human species has opened up a new space, *an abstract space*, which reflects the evolution of the living. Articulated language made it possible for humanity to ask questions, tell stories and dialogue with one another. It made it possible for entities unknown to animal societies to develop: numbers, gods, laws, works of art, calendars, the adventure of technical developments and the whole world of culture. I use the term *ideas* to designate these complex forms that appear, reproduce or evolve only in the world of culture, in the meaningful space made possible by language. The sudden appearance of semantic space, in which ideas live, enabled human communities to move to the level of collective intelligence beyond hives, flocks, herds and packs because it created stronger, more flexible and more developmental competitive yet cooperative links than those that binds insects to ant colonies or monkeys to herds of baboons. What sets humanity apart is ideas. It is true that we are societies of animal organisms who came about as a result of biological evolution. But humanity is also the only environment in which *symbolic life* exists. Language is the threshold from which this second level of nature, made up of ecosystems of ideas – forms of spiritual hypertexts – lives in symbiosis with our communities of speaking primates. These ecosystems of ideas become more complex, wither, become more diverse and intermingle, giving rise to the societies that support them on the partly indeterminate road towards cultural evolution. Teilhard de Chardin used the word "Noosphere" to describe the world ecosystem of all the ideas that globalization and the development of forms of communication, culminating in cyberspace, are beginning to make a reality.

I suggested above that we could now consider the technical possibility of visualizing ecosystems of ideas in a *semantic mirror*: an animated three-dimensional simulation – complex, to be sure, but organized and coherent. Universal digital memory, which would result from the convergence of online museums and libraries, could help cultural expression proliferate for all publics in every direction of meaningful space by *putting on display the world of ideas in a filmic and interactive manner*.

What kind of ideas would we find in the virtual world that includes the interlaced multiplicity of memories? These would not exactly be platonic ideas. The founder of western philosophy described ideas as fixed, eternal and invisible to the senses. The ideas of our digital memory, on the other hand, are three-dimensional virtual subject–objects that can be explored by means of vision, touch and hearing, and that are developing within an ecosystem in which they live interdependently.

Digitong

Before launching into an exploration of this virtual world, a few words are in order about our choice of a *name* for our cinematographic information system. Digitong refers to a digital language, a visual language that semantically indexes information that cannot be "spoken" except through the computer network. The technical mediation of networked computers enables interlaced communities that "speak Digitong" to project a virtual three-dimensional world that reflects their meaningful relationships.

Ideas

Digitong computes the movement of ideas in three dimensions in an infinite and coherent virtual space in which spatial proximities reflect semantic proximities. The idea is here defined *officially* as the inseparable union of three interdependent dimensions of the same subject–object:

- a virtual community (the idea's intelligence);
- digital data processing (the idea's cognitive process);
- a constellation of symbolic images in digital memory (consciousness or self-representation of the idea).

Memes

Digitong can project a virtual world in which ideas absorb, transform and generate *multimedia information capsules*, which may be prepared by the online departments of museums and libraries. These packets of information are called "memes". The term was coined by Richard Dawkins, on the model of "gene", to designate the self-reproducing entity that circulates among human minds. I believe that Dawkins was on the right track in conceptualizing the cultural sphere as a form of ecology, and that is why I have adopted his term. But his meme only accounts for half of cognitive human ecology. To factor in the depth and complexity of the *semantic nature* of information, we cannot remain content with an equivalent to genes, as it is also necessary to have a (virtual) equivalent of organisms. In the universal digital memory structured by Digitong, ideas are precisely virtual organisms that absorb, process and disseminate memes. Ideas give *symbolic consistency* to human communities united by language, a consistency that memes alone could not account for.

Syntax and semantics

Digitong's syntax is basically a filmic or cinematographic function. It can use animated 3-D to represent a digital memory in which ideas exchange and transform memes. This syntax is intimately related to semantics, which provides a system of graphics coordinates that can project a potentially infinite virtual space – but precisely one that is addressable – in which ideas and memes interact. The geometric distances in the space engendered by this language represent *semantic distances*. The correspondence between semantic and geometric spaces is based on the two pillars of Digitong's information architecture: ideograms and an algorithm.

Ideograms

The role of Digitong ideograms is not to accurately translate the content of documents and digital transactions, but strictly to index or *address* them in semantic space. They can be thought of as a form of "postal codes" for universal memory.

Digitong ideograms are independent of language. They are constructed in accordance with a method that symmetrically divides the types of actions that structure human semantic space. These ideograms were inspired by *anthropological symmetry*, which makes it a satisfactory device for structuring universal memory. I call this symmetry *virtual perspective* because it deals accurately and symmetrically with the directions involved in meaning.

Digitong ideograms do not represent rigid concepts that behave like "categories" or sets that are hierarchically nested, and that separate the "inside" from the "outside". The range of ideograms provides a palette of the *qualities of actions* that are in a state of reciprocal and fractal warping in the ideas. Each ideogram is indexed by a number indicating the "semantic volume" assigned to the quality of the semantic action that it represents. As ideograms signal what might be called semantic colours or frequencies, the proportion and combination thereof can be continued indefinitely.

All memes that reside in memory, and that have been transformed and exchanged by ideas, are labelled by semantic codes. These codes invariably consist of an ordered sequence of volumes assigned to ideograms. Ideas can identify and process the memes through the use of codes that describe their semantic content. Ideas, in turn, can be found through reference to the semantic codes that express their activity and memory.

Ideograms represent *active operators* in the virtual world of memory:

- senders that allow the memes to identify themselves to the ideas they are heading to;
- antennas that enable ideas to receive and send memes;

- semantic switches that transform the information received by ideas into information that is transmitted;
- instruments that can help visitors navigate in semantic space.

Algorithmics

Because ideas are living things, their positions change as they go through their semantic navigations, and these changes restructure the space around them. The three-dimensional virtual space that expresses semantic distances is periodically recalculated on the basis of the codes assigned to ideas. Digitong algorithms construct universal space memory in accordance with an ongoing collective negotiation between ideas concerning their respective distances.

In addition to calculating a universal position for all ideas, Digitong algorithms project the *relative space* of each idea, along with its "field of vision" or its own universe. This is the ecological environment made up of *complementary ideas*, and with which the reference idea exchanges memes.

Furthermore, these algorithms spatially organise memes (depending on their semantic content) within ideas.

Analog semantic calculation

The ideas projected in 3-D by Digitong behave like analog processors of information contained within memes. As we mentioned, they have *semantic switches* that perform the transformation of memes received into memes transmitted. The table of switches for these semantic volumes at any given point in time provides a snapshot of an idea's position in *the space consisting of all possible semantic switching*. As it is impossible to represent such space, because its dimensions are infinite, the usefulness of Digitong algorithms rests on the ability to provide a three-dimensional navigable projection.

Moments, arks

Digitong's cinematographic perspective breaks down the movement of ideas into "fixed images" called *moments*. A moment in analog semantic processing by ideas can be analysed into: (1) receiving information, (2) transformation of the information received and (3) transmitting the information. Each moment projects a distinct image in three-dimensional space. Memes are stored in two *information arks* contained by the ideas at each moment along their path. One ark exhibits the memes that have been received and another the memes that have been transmitted. An archival architecture including arks seems appropriate at a time when there might be an informational deluge or flood.

Semes

The semantic transformation that is performed by an idea's moment is called a *seme*. The seme represents *a moment's action* in the form of the analog "program" followed by the idea when it transforms received memes into transmitted memes. At each moment, the seme indicates the specific refraction of an information flow effected by an idea. The seme itself is nothing more than the instantaneous trace of a semiotic act: the semantic navigation of an idea in an ecosystem of ideas. Moment after moment, the string of its meaningful actions helps to direct the semantic navigation of an idea.

Digitong matches up the meaning and the action. It is a language that processes meaning as a perspective of navigation in an infinite semantic space where no direction is privileged. Clear-headed thinkers from many traditions have noted the differential and relative nature of *meaning*, upon which it is much more difficult to reach agreement than for observables or logical–mathematical calculations. In keeping with this differential line of thought, Digitong identifies the semiotic act with a momentary *difference* between the faces of two ideogram configurations.

Information

The succession of an idea's moments projects the navigation of a community in semantic space. Digitong cinematographic approach makes it possible to visit the *semantic paths* of ideas that produce, exchange and use information. It also makes it possible to identify the information itself and place it in context. Indeed, memes, those multimedia capsules, are distributed redundantly within the information arks carried along by ideas and the memes are organized within the arks *in a contextual manner*, as a function of their semantic links.

Information represents everything that can have meaning or value for human beings: physical and technical resources, social roles, institutions, ideas, modes of organization, skills, knowledge, messages, images, music and symbols of all kinds. Virtual communities exchange and transform information within the universal digital memory network. The movement of information binds and separates: its fluctuating distribution structures semantic space. Together, ideas present a multitude of singular and interdependent moments of intelligence, with as many faces as the mirror of collective intelligence fractally reflects all aspects of meaning.

Space: visits, virtuality and distance

Introduction to Part Two

Ross Parry

PART ONE HELPED US TO SEE WAYS in which digital technologies have reorganised a core function of museums: the management of collections. Here, in Part Two, we now turn our attention to another of museums' defining characteristics: the visit. The following selection of articles and extracts (some previously published, some not, some written by academics, some by practitioners) all share a common interest in the idea of the museum as a venue and place. And all work to demonstrate – if with quite different approaches – how the space of the museum, and, more specifically, the idea of 'visiting', is troubled within an age where network connectivity and distance communication provide alternative channels through which audiences might consume cultural heritage.

Notice how Chapters 12, 13 and 17 all share a common intellectual reference point – André Malraux's concept of *Le muse imaginaire*. Translated in the English-speaking world as the 'museum without walls', Malraux's discussion was essentially a thesis on the impact of medium (the museum, the printed catalogue, photographic reproduction) on the meaning and future transformations of art. As is manifest here, this idea of technology liberating and reconfiguring the museum from its traditional modes of presentation has proved beguiling for many writers. The chapter by Erkki Huhtamo is a paper presented to a Nobel Symposium on 'Virtual Museums and public understanding of science and culture' in Stockholm, Sweden, in 2002. The author looks back to the avantgarde art movement of the early twentieth century in an attempt to historicise the notion of the 'virtual museum' and provocatively to suggest several of its artistic and design antecedents. Antonio Battro's paper (originally presented to the Xth World Federation Congress of Friends of Museums, Sydney, in 1999) uses Malraux more directly as a tool for identifying and acknowledging the transformative impact of new technology, such as the Web, on not just our notion of where a museum might be, but on the impact on visiting.

Chapters 14 and 15 then offer two (early) attempts to make sense of the notion of distance and virtual space – two concepts that seem, at first, to be at odds with the idea of a museum (singular, physical, aggregating). In the case of Chapter 15, it is useful to keep mindful of the context in which its author, Roland Jackson, was writing. The article, still relevant today, was originally delivered to a conference on 'contemporary science and technology in museums and science centres', held at the Science Museum, London, in 1996. Here, with the web revolution still in its first movement, before most museums had ventured online, we witness a museum practitioner attempting to identify and articulate the opportunities such computer-mediated communication could afford. Understandably, with still very little evidence to draw upon, Jackson is aware that his visions may be too 'risky' and bold. He is, after all, forming his judgements at a time prior to many of the developments (high-speed connectivity, rich multimedia content, social software, mobile content, semantics) that define the Web for us today. And yet, reading these early observations and predictions (on access, connectivity and collaboration) we see that the museum sector was, in fact, ready to recognise the Web's significance for exhibiting, for visiting, and the very notion of 'museum'.

Chapters 16 and 17 take us forward to some of the more museologically and technically challenging ways in which ideas of 'space' and 'visiting' have been pushed yet further. In their creative and explorative research project connecting on-site and off-site digital media, Galani and Chalmers question whether a sense of shared collective social experience could (or, indeed, should) exist between local and remote visitors to a exhibition space. Finally, Konstantinos Arvanitis considers a convergence between the idea of a 'post-museum' (after Hooper-Greenhill, that which extends beyond the traditional, institutional, physical museum), and the role of mobile phones (in allowing audiences to use everyday media to capture and share everyday meanings). And in doing so, looking outwards, beyond the walls of the museum, into the streets of the city beyond, Arvanitis takes our discussion, poignantly, back to Malraux.

Chapter 12

On the Origins of the Virtual Museum

Erkki Huhtamo

Through the dials of your Teleset you will share in the ownership of the world's great art treasures. (Frederick Kiesler)

Introduction: the notion of the virtual museum

The notion "virtual museum" has been evoked so often in cybercultural discourses that it has lost all of its novelty value. The list of websites purportedly falling under this category is long, and growing. A 2002 *Google* search for "virtual museum" brought up more than 141,000 hits; by January 2009, the figure had grown to over 1,190,000. Such a "category" is understandably extremely vague, accommodating entries that have little to do with each other regarding both their institutional status and their interpretation of the word museum. There are "virtual museums" that might more conveniently be classified as libraries or archives, although the cyberspace definitions of these are not absolutely clear-cut either. If "wired" virtual museums have a common denominator at all, it is a very general one, referring to almost any kind of collection of material (supposedly of "historical" or at least "cultural" value) put on general display on the Internet.

There is no doubt that the vogue for virtual museums received a powerful impetus from the emergence of the World Wide Web and particularly from its beginning transformation into a multimedia environment with the introduction of the Mosaic browser in 1993. Yet the idea did not originate with the WWW. The invention of the hypertext in the 1960s may, in the long term, have been a more decisive

Source: Nobel Symposium on 'Virtual Museums and public understanding of science and culture', Stockholm, Sweden, 2002.

influence, pointing out the possibility of creating huge non-linear data-architectures. Ted Nelson's "Xanadu" was an early description of the cultural implications of networked hypertext, which Nelson foresaw leading to the creation of an accumulating universal databank accessible from any node in the network.[1] A pioneering project investigating the implications of this idea for the museum institution was "The Museum Inside the Telephone Network", an exhibition organized in 1991 by the Project InterCommunication Center (ICC), founded by the Japanese telecom NTT.[2] The exhibition was only accessible to home users by means of the telephone, fax, and in a limited sense computer networking (the Internet was not yet available in Japan). It was meant as a model for a new kind of an "invisible" museum. Logically, it was followed up four years later by another ICC exhibition titled "The Museum Inside the Network" (1995). The "museum" had now been re-located into the Internet.[3]

In the early 1990s the possibilities of hypertext were applied to the creation of numerous CD-ROM-based virtual museums.[4] One of the first was Apple Computer's "Virtual Museum", a demonstration disc for Apple's proprietary Quick Time VR software shown at "Siggraph 92" in Chicago. By clicking the mouse the user was able to explore interactively a 3-D simulation of three interconnected museum spaces, one of which was a very conventional looking art museum gallery. Numerous commercial CD-ROM products, some of them highly successful at the time, but now almost totally forgotten, were conceived as virtual visits to existing art museums such as *Le Louvre* or the *Hermitage*.[5] These products rarely attempted to simulate in 3-D the physical space of the museum (with the exception of a CD-ROM about *Musée d'Orsay*, Paris). Rather, they deliberately limited their scope, highlighting some treasures from the collection and providing useful background information. For many users such CD-ROMs were supplements rather than substitutes for the physical museum. They were sold as souvenirs in the museum shops as part of their promotional machinery. In France, such CD-ROMs were also widely available through the FNAC chain of book and media stores. As products, they did little to question the legitimacy of the traditional museum institution. Many museum websites today continue this tradition, occasionally containing virtual galleries and other non-material elements that have no physical counterparts in the museum building. Whether straightforward museum websites merit the title "virtual museum" is open to debate.

As important as new software (hypercard, Quick Time VR, VRML) or new media (CD-ROM, the World Wide Web) were for the emergence of the virtual museum, the topic was also grounded in wider cultural issues. In recent years, we have seen a massive amount of academic writing about the museum as an institution. This received an impetus from a wave of postmodern theorizing about the impact of media on notions like authenticity and the original. With images and sounds reproduced in principle in unlimited numbers, and distributed, copied, mixed and manipulated at will by the media, the idea of temples dedicated to the cult of the authentic (or "auratic") objects seemed outdated to many. As prophesied by Walter Benjamin in 1936, the original was seen to be disappearing, replaced by an infinite number of copies.[6] The (media) reality itself was turning into an all-encompassing, albeit chaotic, museum available to anybody. Theorists and critics often felt they were standing, to quote the title of Douglas Crimp's well-known book, "on the museum's ruins".[7] This attitude was influenced by André Malraux's famous idea about the imaginary museum without walls, presented in 1947.[8] The main factor behind Malraux's questioning of the traditional role of the museum institution was the spreading of photography. The ever-present photographic reproductions of artworks made art accessible to audiences who would never have entered a museum. At the same time in the United States (but unknown to Malraux), Vannevar Bush was theorizing about the Memex, a new non-linear system of storing and retrieving data.[9] As is well known, Memex has been later recognized as the earliest model for hypertext. The ideas of Malraux and Bush combined take us to the gates of the virtual museum.

In this article, however, I will claim that the origins of the virtual museum can be taken even further back in time. A key factor in this respect is the emergence of exhibition design as a new medium within the avant-garde art movements of the early twentieth century. In their own ways artist-designers like László Moholy-Nagy, El Lissitzky, Herbert Bayer and Frederick Kiesler reacted to the challenges posed by new media technologies, like photography, film, and sound recording.[10] Aware of the need for radical changes in the concept and the roles of art, a radical re-thinking of the relationship between exhibition spaces, exhibits and spectators/visitors was needed. Besides redefining the public viewing contexts, the notion of "domestic picture galleries" was also raised and explored. Having a closer look at these experimental designs and their cultural backgrounds will help us understand better the design challenges facing the creators of virtual museums and galleries. One should also note that some of the issues explored by the avant-garde artists and designers of the first half of the twentieth century have been recently taken up by contemporary experimental media artists, working with installations and networked environments. Their works often raise issues like storage and erasure, memory and forgetting, revealing and hiding, the physical and the virtual. Some such works will be introduced and discussed in the final part of the article.

Exhibition design as a new medium

An important aspect of the explosion of art in the twentieth century was the introduction of new technological media from photography, film and sound reproduction to video, the computer and the Internet. The use of such media by artists contributed to the emergence of new aesthetic forms, such as the ready-made, the abstract or "absolute" film, the photomontage, mechanical or conceptual "bachelor machines", kinetic light displays, responsive cybernetic sculptures, video installations, interactive computer environments, and so on. From early on, the visionaries of the avant-garde felt that new media were changing the ways of perceiving and conceiving the world. This was clearly expressed by F.T. Marinetti, the leader of the Italian Futurists, in one of the *Futurist Manifestos*:

> Futurism is grounded in the complete renewal of human sensibility brought
> about by the great discoveries of science. Those people who today make use
> of the telegraph, the telephone, the phonograph, the train, the bicycle, the
> motorcycle, the automobile, the ocean liner, the dirigible, the aeroplane,

the cinema, the great newspaper (synthesis of a day in the world's life) do not realize that these various means of communication, transportation and information have a decisive influence on their psyches.[11]

Art based on such "discoveries" was obviously not easily compatible with existing cultural institutions and the ideologies on which they were grounded. As a consequence, an essential part of the avant-garde activity was the search for new ways of displaying art. The prevailing academic convention, still evident in the displays of early landmark avant-garde events such as the *Armory Show* in New York in 1913, used the gallery walls for framed paintings (often in several rows practically covering the wall), while free-standing sculptures on pedestals were distributed within the gallery space. The gallery was treated as a background, to be filled with significance by the artworks themselves. The nineteenth-century museum gallery could, however, hardly be treated as neutral, being the product of the overarching dominance of the bourgeois ideology as a cultural legitimating force. In reality, the museums and art galleries of the late nineteenth and early twentieth centuries were thoroughly permeated by connotations of cultural hierarchies and decorum (expressed in their stylistic eclecticism) that affected anything placed within their confines.[12] High cultural connotations were linked with the idea of the artwork as a cultural prestige object and, increasingly, as a financial investment.

For radical art, practices exposing the ideological camouflage of the exhibition space and re-configuring its elements were a major challenge. This might take the form of a calculated multi-sensory (and, anachronistically, multimedia) chaos of a Dadaist exhibition or it could be turned into a carefully orchestrated dialogue with established exhibition practices, as in the famous last exhibition of the Russian Futurists in Petrograd, 1915. Here the radical abstract compositions gained part of their revolutionary impact by having been arranged on the walls, as if substitutes for traditional paintings. *The Black Square* by Kasimir Malevich was placed in one of the upper corners of the room, a place traditionally reserved in Russian homes for the religious icon.[13] Marcel Duchamp's ready-mades also brought an element of ambiguity into the exhibition space. By placing banal everyday objects (often "prepared" by enigmatic linguistic puns inscribed on them) on display as artworks, Duchamp deliberately interfered with our relationships to objects, merging the banal tactility of a bicycle wheel or a urinal with the almost "sacred" untouchability of high art.

Groups like the Dadaists often abandoned the museum or the gallery altogether by re-defining art as a unique (and often deliberately scandalous) temporary "event".[14] Instead of denoting static objects for display and sale, art came to mean a process unfolding in a time and space and incorporating an element of surprise (or "indeterminacy", as defined later by John Cage). Such events could include time-based media, like film projections or playback of recorded sound. Yet, there were also artist-designers who made efforts to re-configure the gallery to correspond with the requirements of the new media, and also with the social and political realities of the time. Visionaries like László Moholy-Nagy, Frederick Kiesler, El Lissitzky and Herbert Bayer, saw exhibition design as a new medium, comparable to other new media (including electric light). Looking back in 1961, Herbert Bayer characterized exhibition design in words that may recall the Wagnerian notion of the *Gesamtkunst-werk*, but which at the same time anticipate future developments in the field of art and technology:

> Exhibition design has evolved as a new discipline, as an apex of all media and powers of communication and of collective efforts and effects. The combined means of visual communication constitutes a remarkable complexity: language as visible printing or as sound, pictures as symbols, paintings, and photographs, sculptural media, materials and surfaces, color, light, move-ment (of the display as well as the visitor), films, diagrams, and charts. The total application of all plastic and psychological means (more than anything else) makes exhibition design an intensified and new language.[15]

The key idea is integration. Here the exhibits are no longer seen as separate entities put on display in any space. Instead, they are considered integral elements of a total environment that envelops the visitors and encourages them into dynamic relation-ship with the space and all its dimensions and elements. The environment comprises different media and channels of communication. Instead of a passive spectator in front of static exhibits, the visitor is meant to turn into an active participant.

Activating the viewer

To achieve such goals, various strategies were developed. The space could be made more engaging by using reflective, optically flickering wall material that changed its nature depending on the visitor's movement through the space, as El Lissitzky did in his design for the "Abstract Cabinet" (Abstraktes Kabinett) commissioned by the *Landesmuseum* in Hannover in 1927–28. This idea in a sense anticipated Op-Art of the 1960s. El Lissitzky also placed some of the exhibits on sliding panels or rotating drums, which had to be physically manipulated by the visitors. El Lissitzky's comment on his achievement clearly anticipates the idea of interactive exhibition design: "If on previous occasions ... [the visitor] was lulled by the painting into a certain passivity, now our design should make the man active."[16]

Another strategy experimented with by the German architect and designer Fred-erick Kiesler in the 1920s, refused the convention of hanging exhibits on the walls. Influenced by Constructivism, Kiesler created an adaptable "L and T system" (*Leger und Träger*), which was first used at the "International Theatre Exhibition" in Vienna in 1924. The exhibition room was filled with a three-dimensional system of grid-like horizontal, vertical and diagonal supports, that were used to display images and other items. The visitors had to literally "immerse" themselves into the exhibition design and navigate amongst the architectural display "racks". The experience of the exhibi-tion was dependent on the routes and points of views chosen by each visitor. The walls of the gallery were left blank. The exhibition hall was on the way to becoming a non-linear data-space.[17] Related ideas were also explored by Moholy-Nagy and El Lissitzky. In his famous "Room one" for the "Film und Photo" exhibition in Berlin in 1929, Moholy-Nagy chose to display only photographic reproductions in different shapes and sizes without any captions to anchor their meanings, while El Lissitzky's contribution also contained special film-viewing machines.

An early example of multimedia exhibition design was Moholy-Nagy's *Raum der Gegenwart* (The Room of Our Time), commissioned by museum director Alexander Dorner for the Hannover *Landesmuseum* (begun in 1930). Moholy-Nagy included an ample selection of visual technologies: photography, film, reproductions of architecture, theater technique and design. In the center of the room he planned to place his *Lichtrequisit, or Licht-Raum Modulator* (Light Prop, Light-Space Modulator), a functioning machine creating variations of light and shadow.[18] Considered one of the precursors of kinetic art, *Light Prop* was a complex structure with machine-driven rotating metal plates and rods. By means of a push-button, the visitors could activate moving abstract light patterns that were projected on the walls and the ceiling. There were also photographic slide and film projections activated by other push buttons, although these never functioned satisfactorily due to technical problems.[19] Most importantly, the room contained no original works of art (with the exception of the *Light Prop*), only reproductions. Perhaps more than any other exhibition design from the early twentieth century, Moholy-Nagy's creation truly spoke "the language of new media". In its attention to the impact of the media on the notions of originality and authenticity, it anticipated Walter Benjamin's famous essay "The Work of Art in the Age of Mechanical Reproduction" (1936) by several years.

"Penny arcade without the pennies"

Moholy-Nagy's room has been considered a precursor to the famous exhibition designs Kiesler created for Peggy Guggenheim's Art of Our Century gallery in New York in 1942 (they remained in place until 1947). All the four galleries, although dedicated to different tendencies in modern art, emphasized the active role of the spectator. The designs refused to retreat to the background, enveloping both the artworks and the visitors. Kiesler later elaborated on his position in the *Second Manifesto of Correalism* he published in 1961:

> The traditional art object, be it a painting, a sculpture, or a piece of architecture, is no longer seen as an isolated entity but must be considered within the context of this expanding environment. The environment becomes equally as important as the object, if not more so, because the object breathes into the surrounding and also inhales the realities of the environment no matter in what space, close or wide apart, open air or indoor.[20]

Among the most well-known features of The Art of Our Century design were the horizontal rod-like wall mounts of the surrealist gallery. Each mount was holding an unframed (!) painting that could be manually swivelled by the spectator. The lights were continuously switched on and off, and recorded background noise was heard. In the abstract gallery the paintings and sculptures were held by bundles of strings stretched between the floor and the ceiling. Again, the artworks could be raised or lowered by hand. Perhaps the most exceptional solutions were those used in the "kinetic gallery", where works by Duchamp, André Breton and Paul Klee could be viewed by specially constructed viewer-activated "peep-show" devices. Breton's "poem object" was revealed from behind a shutter by means of a lever. The miniature objects from Duchamp's *La Bôite-en-valise* (a set of tiny replicas of Duchamp's most famous artworks in a carrying case; in itself an anticipation of the virtual museum) could be viewed by peering into a hole and simultaneously turning a large spiral-like wheel.[21]

Such "vision machines" could obviously be dismissed as mere trickery. Reviewers spoke about "a kind of artistic Coney island" or "a penny-arcade peep show without the pennies."[22] Quite clearly Kiesler was inspired by the well-known hand-cranked peep-show movie machines (like the *Mutoscope*) and other popular entertainment devices, just like Duchamp's "Roto-reliefs" had a relationship to nineteenth-century "proto-interactive" optical toys, like the phenakistiscope and the stereoscope.[23] Kiesler shared the Surrealists' fascination with "obsolete" machines and popular culture, but his interest in experimentation with visual technology went back further to his earliest efforts in theatre set design.[24] However, dismissing his creations as "a nostalgic return to individual perception at a time when the consumption of images had for a long time been a collective ritual" is clearly beside the point.[25] Although dominant at the time, the hegemonic position of the cinema as a ritual of mass media has since been challenged by a great variety of individual, interactive audiovisual experiences, from playing videogames and exploring educational science exhibits to surfing the Internet. Instead of seeing them as nostalgic, one might consider Kiesler's designs as remarkably forward looking, pointing towards the culture of interactivity.

Mary Anne Staniszewski's statement, according to which the international avant-garde's fascination with "viewer-activated gadgetry for installations [. . .] was no doubt linked to advances in technology and the growth of the mass media" needs to be specified.[26] The technology was used *against* collective consumption typical of mass media and *for* individualized and customized experiences. Kiesler's designs contested the taboo of touching the exhibits. This was especially poignant in the context of the academic art world, where the forbidden touch and the principle of "keeping distance" as a precondition of the aesthetic experience had long ago been established as timeless truths. The act of touching had been as if transposed (and almost "transfigured") from the fingertips to the remote "tactility" of the gaze.[27] Although it may indeed be true that "human history was cultivated through speech and the motions of fingers", in the ideology of the art world the "motions of fingers" had been strictly limited to the act of creation, and excluded from the acts of reception and consumption.[28] Creators like Duchamp and Kiesler were interested in bringing the "lost" dimension of tactility and with it a sense of "life" back to art.[29] This could be achieved, either by changing the nature of the art object itself (for example by "infecting" it with features from common everyday objects, including machines), or by changing the conditions within which art is perceived and consumed.

It should be noted, however, that until recently the established art world has not been very receptive to the kinds of designs Kiesler created. They have been doomed as an anomaly; excessive and disturbing, unnecessarily interfering with the artworks themselves. The dominant ideology behind art exhibition design has been the "empty room" of modernism, a neutral space that merely provides the necessary viewing context for the artworks, seen as autonomous in their essence. The modernist gallery is a space for meditation and interiority; in that sense it resembles a church. It could be claimed that the new principles of exhibition design first came to flourish outside the art world, at trade fairs, world fairs, amusement parks and science centers that were able to embrace the idea of interactive exhibits as a novelty without feeling the weight of tradition. Of the last mentioned, The *Palais de la Découverte* in Paris, opened just before WWII, and influenced by the educational ideas of Paul Valéry, is a good example. Many of the early interactive exhibits were targeted to children, which is understandable. The hands-on experience was seen as a necessary step in a child's development; manipulating interactive exhibits was a logical continuation to playing with toys; at the same time it was seen as unworthy of higher "cerebral" culture. Another target group for interactive exhibit design were the disabled; tactility was seen as a way of compensation for sensory deprivation (for blindness, for example).

The domestic pinacoteca

The exhibition projects analyzed so far introduced themes and motives that can be claimed to have prepared the way for future virtual museums in a number of ways. These include the idea of the gallery as a navigable non-linear database, the convergence of several different media and the visitor's/user's interactive and haptic relationship with the exhibits. On the other hand, although different from their pred-ecessors, all these exhibitions still took place within the material confines of a public exhibition. They involved physical movement through the space. In spite of the nature of the exhibits, visiting the gallery was still a collective experience. The exhibition was not only "location-based", it was also disconnected from the rest of the world. Against this background, it is interesting to note that artist–designers like Moholy-Nagy and Kiesler also envisioned new ways of displaying and consuming images in the home, thus attempting to supply the missing dimension of the virtual art museum – the domestic consumption of art at a distance.

As Didier Maleuvre has shown, the idea of turning the bourgeois home into a locus for pictures, even to a kind of private art museum, was an essential feature of the nineteenth-century bourgeois culture.[30] Beside paintings, many different types of "cheaper" images also penetrated the home, from chromolithographs to photographs. Innovators like Moholy-Nagy and Kiesler were aware of the increased visuality of the domestic interior. The real challenge was to classify and store this wealth of visual information and to marry it with the possibilities of the new media. Moholy-Nagy's classic Bauhaus-book *Painting Photography Film* (1925) contains a chapter entitled "Domestic Pinacoteca", in which the author presented in condensed form a great number of ideas about turning the home into a "picture gallery".[31] His ideas ranged from filing systems for traditional images (which would not be displayed all at once, but retrieved for viewing from a kind of "database" only when needed) and collec-tions of colored slides to hologram-like imaginary three-dimensional imaging systems which would not need a "direct plane of projection". Moholy-Nagy also anticipated the television, or what he called the "radio picture service", that he saw as an impor-tant future channel of visual information for the home.

A little later Kiesler envisioned a "Telemuseum" (1926), which may well have been influenced by Moholy-Nagy's description of the "Domestic Pinacoteca". Kiesler's design for the home was to have "walls for sensitized panels that would act as receiving surfaces for broadcasted pictures", and "built-in shrines for original masterpieces that will be concealed behind walls and revealed occasionally". When it comes to user interfaces, Kiesler imagined a kind of customized virtual museum. In a remarkable formulation he prophesized: "Through the dials of your Teleset you will share in the ownership of the world's great art treasures". He emphatically opposed the traditional display of paintings in the home: "The use of pictures as a permanent wall decoration will be discarded as practice." Although Kiesler never managed to build a complete version in time for the 1926 "Societé Anonyme" exhibition at the Brooklyn Museum, New York, a simplified version (described by some witnesses as a darkened gallery with push button interfaces that illuminated reproductions of classic artworks like *Mona Lisa*) was shown at the Anderson Galleries in 1927.[32]

There were other interesting efforts to re-define the relationship between art and new technology in the home, most of them fallen into oblivion. Among these are the "Luminars" and "Clavilux Juniors", produced in several different forms by the Danish-born Lumia-artist Thomas Wilfred in the United States from the late 1920s on.[33] Originally Wilfred created and performed moving light displays in public performances with instruments of his own design. In 1928 he began to adapt his ideas for home use, producing instruments that could present abstract moving color-light compositions, either on a screen or projecting them to the ceiling. Several of the models Wilfred produced had a remote control with a series of knobs, which allowed the viewer to change the light display interactively while sitting in his/her armchair gazing at the screen. Although Clavilux Junior provided no "radio picture service", it used "software", or changeable painted glass discs rotating inside the machine.[34] Although Wilfred's devices were never mass-produced, they were an early effort to introduce interactive art experiences to the home, replacing the static pictures on the walls with more dynamic and absorbing displays.

It would be interesting to investigate the media–archaeological background of Moholy-Nagy's, Kiesler's or Wilfred's domestic galleries and vision machines. In the interest of space, only a few preliminary remarks can be made here. It seems clear, however, that none of these ideas appeared out of nowhere. Since the mid-nineteenth century, a succession of new media technologies had entered the home. These included devices like the stereoscope, the phonograph, home movie equipment, and eventually the telephone and the radio (a novelty in the 1920s). The appearance of each of these technologies triggered great numbers of proposals for their possible uses, some of them realistic, some outright fantastic. There were many anticipations of the virtual museum. The phonograph was almost immediately seen as a way of storing the voices of remarkable personalities and creating an auditive museum of mankind. An interesting product was the dedicated filing cabinet for stereoscopic photographs marketed by large companies like Underwood & Underwood and Keystone.[35] These handsomely crafted cabinets were pieces of "database-furniture" for the domestic saloon. The companies also produced elaborate "travel systems", consisting of hundreds of numbered stereoviews, viewers, guidebooks and maps meant for "armchair travelling" within the home.[36] Consuming and storing stereoviews of famous art treasures was an essential aspect of such a domestic image bank. Almost as a premature echo of Moholy-Nagy's and Kiesler's suggestions, these images were not kept permanently on display. They were retrieved from the logically arranged databank only when needed.

Looking backward, many other historical precedents could be mentioned, including the habit of collecting and storing picture postcards of artworks and museum.[37] Looking forward, we could point out later media art projects that have raised and developed further the idea of the virtual museum. To mention just one example, the eminent Australian artist Jeffrey Shaw created an interactive work titled "The Virtual Museum" in 1990. Preceding the emergence of the World Wide Web, Shaw conceived his work as a gallery installation. The visitor sits on a motorized rotating platform, facing a large screen. By leaning in his/her chair sideways or forward/backward, the visitor controls both the rotation of the platform and his/her movements in the virtual world on the screen. The virtual world on the screen is an exact replica of the physical gallery space, with a difference: the visitor is able to penetrate through the virtual walls, discovering other galleries showing moving virtual sculptures and reliefs, works that could not exist in any normal museum. Shaw's installation evokes at the same time the earlier history of "armchair travelling" and the coming world of virtual museums. For Shaw, the virtual museum is a location that transcends the physical space, opening up new possibilities both for art and its display.[38] For him, merely replicating existing physical spaces does not make any sense. Last but not least, Shaw's work also shows that there is a line of development connecting interactive media art installations with the innovative exhibition design by Moholy-Nagy, Kiesler and others. So far, this has hardly been pointed out.[39]

Conclusion: challenges for virtual museum design

The aim of this article has been to shed new light on the design of virtual museums by looking at some of their anticipations in the fields of exhibition design and interactive media art. The article does not claim that these are the only factors that explain the nature and the emergence of the virtual museum as an institution. Even in the field of experimental art there are other phenomena that deserve to be investigated. An interesting starting point for this continued analysis is provided by Craig J. Saper's study *Networked Art*.[40] Saper explores the background of current electronic networking art practices by analyzing such overlooked phenomena as mail art networks and visual poetry as a communication system.

Based on the discussions in this article, the "historical" challenges for the creators of virtual museum can perhaps be best summed up as a series of questions:

- Public or private: should a virtual museum be addressed to the home user or the museum goer or both? How does this affect the design?
- What is the role of tactility? Can tele-tactility replace the physicality of touch?
- Push buttons and peep holes: are these still valid interfaces? What else is needed?

- How does one maintain user involvement without turning it into a goal in itself?
- What role does creating "a total atmosphere" play? Are there any alternatives?
- How does one make a distinction between a museum exhibit and an entertainment application?
- Is there a need for distancing the user, at least sometimes? When and under what conditions? For what purpose?
- Is there a limit to the "multisensory overload" in exhibition design? How many information channels can be added without causing confusion and miscommunication?
- How should physical museums relate to virtual ones? Can a virtual museum be merely a replica of the physical one, or should it be something radically different? What?
- Can all location-based exhibits be replaced by virtual ones? Is this a viable goal?
- How important is user interaction? Wouldn't it be good to try to do without it, at least sometimes? What would be the consequences of non-interactive virtual museum design?

As an institution, the digital and "wired" virtual museum is still at an early stage of its development. As a consequence, the key questions to ask will certainly change, and new ones will be added to the list. Much will depend on the development rate and the spreading of higher speed Internet connectivity to everyday consumers all around the planet. However, solving problems of routing and data-transfer is not everything. Our modes and routines of communicating and interfacing with multimedia databases are cultural, historical and ideological issues as well. Considering precedents from the non-digital eras – covering most of the history of mankind so far – should not be neglected.

Notes

This article is a slightly updated version of the lecture 'On the Origins of the Virtual Museum', given at the Nobel Symposium NS 120, Stockholm, Sweden, May 2002.

1 The idea of a global database or "world brain" was already presented in the early part of the twentieth century by H.G. Wells, who spoke about this idea in numerous lectures and articles. Wells saw microfilm as a possible medium for his project: "The time is close at hand when any student, in any part of the world, will be able to sit with his projector in his own study at his or her convenience to examine *any* book, *any* document, in an exact replica" (Wells' emphasis). It is tempting to replace "computer with Internet connection" to the projector. Wells' texts on the subject have been collected into the volume: H.G. Wells: *World Brain*, London: Adamantine Press, 1994 (quotation p. 116).

2 *InterCommunication '91 The Museum Inside The Telephone Network*, catalogue, edited by Urban Design Research Inc., Tokyo: NTT, 1991 (in Japanese/English). Most of the numerous works in the exhibition were contemporary projects. The ICC became a

physical institution as well, operating still (January 2009) at the Tokyo Opera City Tower in Western Shinjuku.

3 *InterCommunication '95 "on the Web": The Museum Inside The Network*, catalogue, edited by Junko Tachibana, Akira Takada and InterCommunication editorial office, Tokyo: NTT Publishing Co, 1995. Beside the Internet artworks, some broadband ISDN projects were presented.

4 Already earlier "virtual galleries" had been realized by 3-D computer graphics, for example, the videotape work *Luminaire* by John Sanborn and Dean Winkler (1985, running time: 6:54). The work was described as "a visual tribute to video artist Ed Emshwiller that includes a surreal space age landscape, digitally transformed dancers, and a central scene that traces the history of art through a computerized gallery". I would like to thank Professor Machiko Kusahara for informing me about this work. One of the earliest digital virtual museums within an actual museum was the Micro Gallery of the National Gallery in London. It was sponsored by American Express.

5 Among the most successful was *Louvre. Palais et Peintures*, realized by Montparnasse Multimédia and produced by the Reseaux des Musées nationaux in France. It sold many copies also in Japan, where it was translated and distributed by Fuji Television. According to Professor Machiko Kusahara, a leading multimedia specialist, the CD-ROM worked as a true virtual museum for many Japanese, who would never have been able to make a physical visit to the famous art museum (private conversation in Los Angeles, June 30, 2002).

6 Walter Benjamin: "The Work of Art in the Age of Mechanical Reproduction", translated by Harry Zohn, in *Illuminations*, Glasgow: Fontana/Collins, 1979, pp. 219–253.

7 Douglas Crimp: *On the Museum's Ruins*, Cambridge, MA: The MIT Press, 1993.

8 André Malraux: *Le Musée Imaginaire*, Paris: Gallimard, 1996 [orig. 1947].

9 Vannevar Bush: "As We May Think" (1945), in *Multimedia From Wagner to Virtual Reality*, edited by Randall Packer and Ken Jordan, New York: W.W. Norton, 2001, pp. 135–153.

10 For a very useful general account of exhibition projects by these and other pioneers, see the first chapter of Mary Anne Staniszewski: *The Power of Display. A History of Exhibition Installations at the Museum of Modern Art*, Cambridge, MA: The MIT Press, 1998, pp. 1–57.

11 F.T. Marinetti: "Destruction of Syntax/Imagination without strings/Words-in-Freedom", 1913, English translation online: http://www.unknown.nu/futurism/destruction.html (accessed January 17, 2009).

12 For a general treatment, see Roland Schaer: *L'invention des musées*, Paris: Découvertes Gallimard/Réunion des Musées nationaux, 1993.

13 See Kirk Varnedoe: *High & Low: Modern Art, Popular Culture*, New York: Museum of Modern Art. Distributed by H.N. Abrams, 1990.

14 About art "events", including those by the Dadaists, see *"Event" Arts and Art Events*, edited by Stephen C. Foster, Ann Arbor: UMI Research Press, 1988.

15 Herbert Bauer: "Aspects of Design of Exhibitions and Museums", 1961, cit. Staniszewski, op. cit., p. 3.

16 Staniszewski, op. cit., p. 20.

17 The idea of a kind of "proto-hypertext" was also present in Moholy-Nagy's "Filmváz: A nágyváros dinamikaja", a storyboard for an experimental documentary film first published in the Hungarian avant-garde journal *Ma* in the early 1920s and in revised

form in Moholy-Nagy's Bauhaus-book *Malerei Fotografie Film* (1925). Moholy-Nagy's storyboard tries to give form to a simultaneous, multi-sensory experience. It has been seen as a "graphic film", which could not have been realized by the linear film medium. Non-linear hypermedia and multimedia would probably have been the solutions Moholy-Nagy was looking for.

18 See Jack Burnham: *Beyond Modern Sculpture*, New York: George Braziller, 1968, pp. 291–292.

19 Staniszewski (op. cit, pp. 21–22) claims that the Light Prop was actually shown in Hannover. Lucia Moholy (Moholy-Nagy's first wife) claims that it was not shown publicly until an exhibition in Paris in 1930. Lucia Moholy also debates the nature of Licht Prop – is it sculpture or a machine, originally meant as an electric prop for experimental theatre? (Lucia Moholy: *Marginalien zu Moholy-Nagy Marginal Notes*, Krefeld: Scherpe Verlag, 1972, pp. 82–83.) The Light Prop is in the collection of the Busch-Reisinger Museum, Harvard, USA.

20 Cit. Staniszewski, op.cit., p. 8.

21 Herbert Bayer had already used the idea of the peep hole, although without any interactive mechanism, as part of his design for the Bauhaus 1919–38 exhibition at the Museum of Modern Art, 1938–39. Another peep hole can be found from the Exposition international du surrealisme (Galerie Maeght, Paris, 1947). A hole in the wall was used to see Duchamp's *Le Rayon vert* (The Green Ray). The work was installed by Kiesler according to Duchamp's instructions. The peep hole was also a central element of Duchamp's last major work Étant donnés (1946–66). See Dieter Daniels: "Points d'interférence entre Frederick Kiesler et Marcel Duchamp", in *Frederick Kiesler. Artiste-architecte*, edited by Chantal Béret, Paris: Éditions du Centre Pompidou, 1996, pp. 125–126. About the culture of peeping, see the author's "The Pleasures of the Peephole: An Archaeological Exploration of Peep Media", in *Book of Imaginary Media: Excavating the Dream of the Ultimate Communication Medium*, edited by Eric Kluitenberg, Rotterdam: NAi Publishers, 2006, pp. 74-155.

22 Cit. Lewis Kachur: *Displaying the Marvellous. Marcel Duchamp, Salvador Dali, and Surrealist Exhibition Installations*, Cambridge, MA: The MIT Press, 2001, p. 201.

23 This relationship was elaborated in the author's paper "The Avantgarde Goes to (Pre-)cinema, or Mr. Duchamp's Playtoy", read at the Excavating the Future conference, Goethe Institut, Prague, Dec. 3–5 2001. A version was published as "Mr. Duchamp's Playtoy, or Reflections on Marcel Duchamp's Relationship to Optical Science", in *Experiencing the Media: Assemblages and Cross-overs*, edited by Tanja Sihvonen and Pasi Väliaho, Turku (Finland): University of Turku. School of Art, Literature and Music, Media Studies, Series A, No 53, 2003, pp. 54-72. Interestingly, the connection between the Mutoscope and the idea of the virtual museum was made by a cartoonist in *Punch*, May 10, 1899. The cartoon showing a gentleman peeping into a Mutoscope and turning its crank, while other people in the background are seen observing wall-mounted paintings. The caption says: "Suggestion for the R.A. [Royal Academy]. A Mutoscope of the Pictures, for the use of visitors in hurry. The Royal Academy in five minutes." Reproduced in: Colin Harding and Simon Popple: *In the Kingdom of Shadows. A Companion to Early Cinema*, London: Cygnus Arts, 1996, p. 21.

24 Kiesler's first stage design was for Karel Capek's R.U.R. at the Theater am Kurfürstendamm in Berlin (1922). Its references to media included both a kind of large peepshow-like opening (provided with a large simulated camera shutter, one of Kiesler's "trademarks"), revealing a back-projected film, and a simulated

television screen – a very early anticipation of television. For more, see RoseLee Goldberg: *Performance. Live Art 1909 to the Present*, London: Thames and Hudson, 1979, pp. 75–76. Interestingly, Kiesler used the concept "Guckkastenbühne" (peepshow stage). See: Bruno Reichlin: "The City in Space", in *Frederick Kiesler. Artiste-architecte*, op. cit., p. 17. Kiesler returned to the theme of the peep hole with shutter in the "Screen-O-Scope" invented for the Guild Hall Cinema that he designed, New York, 1939. The Screen-O-Scope was an original high-tech replacement for the traditional theatre curtain.

25 Christoph Grunenberg: "Espaces spectaculaires: l'art de l'installation selon Frederick Kiesler", in *Frederick Kiesler. Artiste-architecte*, op. cit., p. 109.

26 Staniszewski, op. cit., p. 22.

27 About haptic or tactile vision, see Jacques Aumont: *The Image*, translated by Claire Pajackowska, London: BFI Publishing, 1994 (1990), pp. 77–78.

28 David Sudnow: *Pilgrim in the Microworld. Eye, Mind, and the Essence of Video Skill*, New York: Warner Books, 1983, p. 24.

29 In 1943 Duchamp and Kiesler collaborated on a project called "Twin-Touch-Test", which was published in the journal *VVV* (No 2–3, 1943). The idea was to have the readers move their hands pressed on a piece of actual wire fence (incorporated into a page of the journal), eyes closed. The reader was asked to describe one's sense of touch, and compete for five prizes that "will be given for the best solutions". See Yehuda Safran: "L'Angle de l'oeil. La Vision Machine de Frederick Kiesler", in *Frederick Kiesler. Artiste-architecte*, op. cit. p. 137. Duchamp also played with tactility by creating a foam model of a woman's breast for the cover of the exhibition catalogue *Le Surrélisme en 1947* (Gallerie Maeght, Paris, 1947) that he designed. The breast was accompanied by the exhortation "Prière de Toucher", Please Touch! A photo was taken in gallery about a nude female model with Duchamp's foam breast attached over her lower belly, standing next to Kiesler's "Totem des religions". (See reproduction in *Frederick Kiesler. Artiste-Architecte*, op. cit., p. 124.) About tactility and the history of art, see the author's "Twin-Touch-Test-Redux: Media Archaeological Approach to Art, Interactivity, and Tactility", in *MediaArtHistories*, edited by Oliver Grau, Cambridge, MA: The MIT Press, 2006, pp. 71-101.

30 Didier Maleuvre: *Museum Memories. History, Technology, Art*, Stanford: Stanford University Press, 1999, p. 115. The idea of home as a private museum was based on even longer historical traditions, particularly that of the curiosity cabinet. A wonderful example of the transition between these is Sir John Soane's Museum in London, still open to the public in much the same form as it was at the moment of its owner's death in 1837. See www.soane.org/ (accessed January 17, 2009).

31 László Moholy-Nagy: *Painting, Photography, Film*, translated by Janet Seligman, Cambridge, MA: The MIT Press, 1987, pp. 25–26 [orig. 1925].

32 Kiesler described the project in his book *Contemporary Art Applied to the Store and its Display*, New York: Brentano's, 1930. See: Staniszewski, op. cit., p. 313.

33 See Donna M. Stein: *Thomas Wilfred: Lumia. A Retrospective Exhibition*, Washington, D.C.: The Corcoran Gallery of Art, 1971, pp. 15–18.

34 I would like to thank the collector Dr Eugene Epstein of Los Angeles for an opportunity to examine the Clavilux Junior machines in his collection. There is also a well-preserved Clavilux Junior in the David Bermant Foundation collection, which its keepers have graciously allowed me to operate with my UCLA graduate students. See www.davidbermantfoundation.org/ (accessed January 17, 2009).

35 See *Points of View: The Stereograph in America — A Cultural History*, edited by Edward W. Earle, Rochester: The Visual Studies Workshop Press, 1979.

36 In his novel *Looking Backward 2000–1887* (1887) Edward Bellamy imagined the Boston of the year 2000. Among the wonders he imagined was a domestic "music room", which was connected by telephone lines to kind of pre-broadcasting music studios elsewhere in the city. The listener, who had to pay a fee for the service, could choose between four simultaneous channels. Although this is not a virtual museum, Bellamy's vision anticipates the idea of a permanent subscription-based, always available cultural service for domestic users. Edward Bellamy: *Looking Backward 2000–1887*, edited with an Introduction by Cecelia Tichi, Harmondsworth, Middlesex: Penguin Books, 1982, pp. 98–99.

37 Media artist George Legrady dealt with postcard culture, connecting it with contemporary networking practices, in his highly interesting CD-ROM-based artwork *Slippery Traces. The Postcard Trail*, published as part of the CD-ROM book combination *ArtIntact3*, Cantz Verlag and ZKM Karlsruhe, 1996.

38 The idea of the virtual museum both as an organizing principle and a metaphor has also been used by artists producing multimedia CD-ROMs. These include George Legrady's *An Anecdoted Archive from The Cold War* (1994–95), based on the ground plan of the Museum of the Workers' Movement (Munkásmozgalmi Museum) in Budapest. Another example is *Alice. An Interactive Museum* by Kuniyoshi Kaneko, Kazuhiko Kato and Haruhiko Shono (Japan: Toshiba EMI and Synergy, Inc., 1992).

39 For a general history of installation art, see Julie H. Reiss: *From Margin to Center. The Spaces of Installation Art,* Cambridge, MA: The MIT Press, 2001.

40 Craig J. Saper: *Networked Art,* Minneapolis: University of Minnesota Press, 2001.

Chapter 13

From Malraux's Imaginary Museum to the Virtual Museum

Antonio M. Battro

A romanesque crucifix was not originally a sculpture, Cimabue's Madonna was not a picture, nor was Phidias's Pallas Athena a statue. (p. 11)

Thus does André Malraux begin his *chef d'oeuvre* on the imaginary museum (Marlraux 1951). It deals with the transformation of a work of art, of how its meaning changes when exhibited in a museum. In a museum, a crucifix becomes a sculpture, an image of the Virgin is a picture, a sacred effigy a statue. Malraux deeply questions the ultimate meaning of this great transformation.

This he has done in more than 600 words of closely packed, penetrating and illuminating prose, with almost 500 illustrations mainly of photographs in black and white. The book was written almost half a century ago and conceived before the European war that so cruelly cut off millions of human lives, destroying and dispersing a significant portion of mankind's artistic heritage. It is a testimony to the turbulence of his time and, at the same time, a voice of hope. Malraux analyzes the new role of photographic reproduction in bringing to us the works of art of the whole world in a new format, on an accessible universal platform. This imaginary museum of Malraux's is not a volatile product of the imagination but a great world collection of images reproduced thanks to modern technology. We would now say it is both the product and a symptom of "globalization."

What Malraux predicted is at present coming true beyond his visionary expectations. As it is, digital technology has separated the photograph from its paper support, has promoted the expanded projection of high fidelity color images and, finally, has made the public independent of the exhibition hall, of the auditorium and the lecture room. We are witnessing a new transformation in the meaning of a work of art and

Source: Xth World Congress Friends of Museums, Sydney, September 13–18, 1999.

the birth of the virtual museum, a new kind of museum which is the product of the prodigious evolution of the imaginary museum. We shall try to show in what follows the articulation between both and the real museum.

The changing significance of the work of art in the museum

It is convenient to begin with Malraux's master description of the significance of a work of art and the function of the museum, which we can apply to all kinds of museums, whether real, imaginary or virtual.

> The role of museums in our relationship with works of art is so great that we have difficulty in thinking of museums as non-existent in those place where modern European civilization is, or was, unknown. This relationship has existed for us for scarcely two centuries. The nineteenth century lived off it and we continue to live off it, but we forget that museums have imposed on the viewer an absolutely new relationship with respect to the work of art. (pp. 11–12)

Malraux is writing of the twentieth-century museum but, as we shall see, we are certain that his ideas will continue to be valid in the twenty-first century. He refers to the transformation of the purpose or classical model of a work of art. In fact, museums in the western world,

> have contributed to freeing works of art from their expected performance, to change even portraits into pictures. Caesar's bust or the equestrian statue of Charles V are still Caesar and Charles V, yet the Duke of Olivares is only a Velazquez. What do we care about the identity of the man with the helmet, the man with the glove? They are Rembrandt and Titian. The portrait, especially, has ceased to be someone's portrait. (p. 12)

We could add that even the self-portrait of the painter has ceased to refer to his person. Let us take the case of the recent retrospective at the London National Gallery[1] where some thirty self-portraits of Rembrandt and numerous sketches and engravings were exhibited. They certainly show the passage of time in his long life, we are moved by their implacable realism or fantastic genius but, above all, those masterpieces imply a spiritual universe rather than their flesh and blood creator.

Malraux's central idea is that we are witnessing a "change of function" for the original artwork when we admire it in a museum. The fact that the artwork has been moved to an environment especially designed to show it off would of itself merit a more detailed analysis but we would be trespassing into the field of museum expertise, a fascinating field but one which takes us away from our subject. It is enough to observe that when faced with the "man in a golden helmet" the visitor bends down to read the name of the painter. He is interested in the attribution of the artwork. An unforgettable show took place in 1996 at the Metropolitan Museum of Art in New York on the subject of the many attributions given to Rembrandts at different times in the history of art. (von Sonnenburg 1995).

Almost six million people from all parts of the world visit the Louvre yearly: are they coming to see *The Gioconda* or a Leonardo da Vinci? Both the portrait of a beauty of Renaissance Florence and the genius of the artist will remain eternally linked for the present-day viewer, who is probably a greater admirer of the painting than of the lady's beauty. But this was not always so. In a contemporary description, an amateur visiting Fontainebleau relates: "There was also an oil painting of a certain lady from Lombardy (sic) a very beautiful woman, but to me not as beautiful as Madame Gualanda" (Cox-Rearick 1996). This admirer compared Lisa Gherardini dei Giocondo, wife of Francesco dei Giocondo, with Isabella Gualanda, a friend of Giuliano di Medici. His comment did not refer so much to Leonardo's painting but to the features of two very beautiful women. In this our amateur coincided with Leonardo's own commentary: "Can't you see that in human beauty it is the beauty of the face that amazes passers-by and not the richness of the adornments?" Moreover, in the catalogue of 1614 prepared by Sébastien Zamet, superintendent of the royal palace, item 78 is listed as "une joconde" (sic) with no mention of the painter! The subject of the painting at the time was more important than its creator. But the modern museum has produced a radical change in the history of art. As Malraux justly says,

> Until the XIX century, all works of art were the image of something that existed – or did not exist – before, prior to being works of art. Only to the eyes of the painter was the painting a painting; many times it was also poetry. And the museum suppressed from almost all portraits (even if only of a dream) almost all its models, at the same time that it forced works of art away from their function. (p. 12)

In a certain sense, the visitor to a museum enters an atelier empty of its models, there is no one posing, not a flower or a wine cup on the artist's table. There is only the painting as such and that is why it acquires new significance. When the painter's oeuvre enters the museum it is exhibited to the public in the context of a museum of "paintings" rather than of "pictures." The museum being open as well to a wider public not necessarily of experts or amateurs, has changed its function. In effect, the galleries of the great European collectors of the past – emperors, kings, popes, nobles, bankers, cardinals – were centers for a daily contact with beauty, for conversation, places for "sensual and intellectual delight." Francis I had copies of his exceptional collection of more than fifty masterpieces on exhibition in the royal baths at Fontainebleau for the enjoyment of his courtiers and guests. These treasures centuries later became the heritage of the Louvre Museum. What's more,

> The museum never knew a palladium, a saint, or Christ, or object of veneration, of similarity, of imagination, of decoration, of possession; only images of things, different from the things themselves, deriving from this difference its reason for being. (p. 12)

This is Malraux's central thesis. The museum has created an essential difference: the transmutation of an esthetic value. In a sense it is a transfiguration which leads to a confrontation of metamorphoses.

Before the existence of the museum,

The work of art had its associations: the gothic statue to the cathedral, the classic picture to contemporary decoration, but not to other works spiritually different. It was isolated from the rest for better appreciation. (p. 12)

The museum is a collection of pieces the unity of which is always in question. Only through an intellectual effort can we come close to art as different from each other as an African mask and a Renaissance painting. But both artworks are housed under the same roof in the great museums. We may well ask ourselves what is their common denominator, what is the fundamental fraternal relation between them that makes them members of the same family. It is an eternal question. Each age gives a different but always imperfect and incomplete answer.

Museums continue to be built, some collect more crowds and receive more visitors than entire cities. The ensemble of museums, large and small, important and not so important, exceeds all description. Their variety is incommensurable but all museums have in common one fact: the art they keep acquires a new life "because it is shared." Even where only one unique and isolated jewel is kept, as is the case of *The Burial of Count Orgaz* which although alone in the chapel of the Conception in the church of Santo Tomé in Toledo also participates, like a voice singing solo, in the fantastic concert offered by El Greco's city.

Mythology gave the name of Museum to the sacred home of the Muses of the arts and sciences: Erato, Euterpe, Calliope, Clio, Thalia, Melpomene, Terpsichore, Polymnia and Urania, daughters of Zeus and Mnemosyne. The virtual Museum also has its own muse. The new born is called *Dactylia*, she is the "digital Muse," with an infinity of fingers ... We mortals cannot begin to count her fingers and the art of all times incessantly honor her in pictures, sculptures, jewels and icons. All those digits pray, caress, embrace and play a game without end. It is the game of Dactylia, the divine beauty that illuminates the *virtual museum*.

Museum was also the name of the first "university" in the West: the Museum of Alexandria, founded by Ptolemy I Soter and by a Greek philosopher, Demetrius Phalerius (345–293 A.C.), a student of Theophrastus the great disciple of Aristoteles at the Lyceum in Athens (Pyenson 1999). The library of the museum, the celebrated Serapeium, was one of the wonders of classical antiquity. The museum was visited by geniuses such as Euclid, Eratosthenes and Archimedes. We should never forget that beauty and truth are essentially united not only in metaphysics but culturally. Malraux guides the discussion on museums to the root itself of the artistic act as one of human creation and revelation of its supreme mission.

To the "pleasure of looking," the succession of schools and their apparent contradictions contributed awareness of a passionate search to recreate the Universe vis-à-vis Creation. After all, the museum is one of the places that give the highest idea of man.

And the highest idea of mankind derives from man being in the image and likeness of his Creator. In man's intimate nature we find the spirit. We can now harvest its fruits because we know its origin.

The value of reproductions

The work of art has an admirable quality in that it invites reproduction. First of all, in the mind of the observer. But the mental process of recollection is not a copy but a reconstruction. The psychology of the twentieth century has made us aware of the subtle mechanisms for coding and decoding visual images, of the time scale involved in a short and transient memory or a long and a permanent one. Malraux questions the role of memory in many of his books, in particular in his *Antimémoires*. He is conscious of its limitations and deformations. That is why he analyzes with the greatest care the difference between the original work and its reproduction. We have forgotten, but the visitor to an European museum in 1900 had very few copies or engravings at his disposal and only black and white photographs. It was therefore not easy to establish comparisons. The geographic distance between museums was also a "mental distance." As Malraux so admirably states,

> the comparison of a picture in the Louvre with one in Madrid or Rome was between a picture and a thing remembered. (p. 14)

The cultivated visitor was a great traveler to the celebrated museums and the rich could buy engravings of the masterpieces and the others made do with photographs. All had to appeal to their memory, some took written notes or sketched a drawing. Artists, in their turn, went to the museums to copy from genius as part of their education and also as a source of income. There were copies for all tastes and pocketbooks. But, in truth, many reproductions were faulty and inadequate.

> One knew the Louvre (and only some sections at that) which we remembered as best we could. Now we have a greater number of significant works to remedy the weakness of our memory than are stored in the largest museum. (p. 14)

The situation continues to improve constantly thanks to new digital techniques for mass reproductions of the highest quality. Some of the great museums have projects for digital format reproductions, accessible via the internet, of the whole of their collections. Thus the Hermitage already has 2,000 works in a high-resolution digital format. Such reproductions constitute the enormous and magnificent heritage of the imaginary Museum which extends today to the virtual Museum, a museum that did not exist and was certainly unthinkable in the nineteenth century. At the end of this millennium, as Malraux said,

> an imaginary museum has opened that will push to extremes the incomplete confrontation imposed by real museums. In response to this, the fine arts require being printed. (p. 14)

What is that printing? The answer for Malraux's generation could only be photography. For us there is another answer, digital reproduction. To verify this we must now travel the road from the imaginary Museum to the virtual Museum. The concept of "virtual reality" was unknown in Malraux's time but it will be this virtual reality – and no other – that "will push to the extreme" our confrontation with the "original reality" of the work of art. "Art printing" for the twenty-first century will be decidedly "digital" and bits will replace the written word and pixels the grain of photography. The computer with its accessories and networking is the printer of the new digital era, of the new virtual culture.

A fictitious art

Malraux embodied in his own life how a written culture could be enriched by an image culture. He was one of the greatest writers of his time and in his illustrated books on art he took advantage, as few others, of the new culture of the graphic image. Besides, in an admirable decision he changed the appearance of French monuments. The façades of buildings in Paris were cleaned and what people saw was wonderfully transformed. He uncovered what had been hidden.

> The history of art for the last hundred years is the history of what can be photographed. (p. 28)

The imaginary Museum consists, in effect, of "mass reproductions" of works of art, in all forms and formats. But not only of this. Due to its peculiar dynamics reproduction in turn generates novel actions and attitudes with respect to the work of art. Malraux was aware of this paradox, of this feedback between reproduction and artistic creation.

> At the same time that photography offered artists a profusion of master-pieces, the artist's attitude to a work of art underwent a change. (p. 15)

In effect, the photograph was then a poor relative to an engraving. While the latter was used almost exclusively for acknowledged masterpieces, the photograph helped to popularize less important or forgotten works of art. But the constant progress and perfection of the tremendous photographic accumulation produced an unplanned fundamental change in artistic conception as such. Art was looked at in a different way. Specifically, photography made the most diverse objects equal, creating new families, suggesting new relationships and shared styles.

> A photograph in black and white relates the objects it represents wherever there is a connection. A tapestry, a miniature, a picture, a sculpture and a medieval vitraux, all very different objects, become related when repro-duced on the same page. They have lost their color, their material (sculpture some of its volume), their dimensions. They have lost specificity to their common style. (p. 18)

What happens when color, material, volume and even dimensions are lost? A repro-duction devoid of those essential attributes certainly cannot be like the original. It is a different work. But thanks to this loss it also gains something. And this is the secret of magic transmutation. It finds, says Malraux, its "style," in a very real sense it finds synchrony with other works that seemed unrelated to it. Malraux thus broaches complex subjects that today are in the domain of general linguistics. He restates the language proper to photographic reproduction, he alerts us to a syntaxis that exclusively addresses the relations between images, that abstracts their original sense. Van Gogh wrote to his brother Théo "we cannot do otherwise than make our pictures speak" (Plazy and del Moral). We should now, perhaps, build a new "grammar of style" to also be able to express ourselves in the field of graphic art reproductions.

One of the principal themes is the effect in reproduction of the altered scale of the work of art. So much so that fearing falsifications, many museums forbid a copy in the real size of the original. But this is a subject for lengthy analysis. The visual sciences teach us precisely the consequences of a loss of size constancy (and of color and shape). Malraux dared to pose this from the point of view of art.

> The development of reproduction also acts more subtly. In an album, in an art book, objects are mostly reproduced in a similar format. In fact, a stone Buddha twenty meters high is no more than four times as large as a Tanagra figurine … Scale is lost. (p. 18)

This is very important. In ordinary life, for example, when we see a car in the distance we still recognize it as such and it does not suddenly become to us a miniature or a toy car. Up to a certain distance the visual object "keeps" its size because our brain has developed mechanisms to preserve the scale of objects within certain limits. When we exceed those limits the result is a brutal and sudden alteration of our field of perception. When we lose scale there really occurs a "visual catastrophe." This happens to us, for example, when we fly up in an airplane or climb a very tall building. Up to a certain height we recognize buildings, trees and cars as familiar objects but over that limit, suddenly, the whole panorama becomes a miniature. We have "changed scale." The original size-preserving mechanisms no longer operate. Something similar occurs with photographic reproductions: it is possible to change, at will, the scale of objects. This manipulation of scale has very interesting consequences. In a certain sense the original artwork is enriched. It provides a new vision. For example,

> The art of the steppes was a subject for specialists, but when the bronze or gold plaques are shown on the same page above a roman bas-relief, they become bas-reliefs as well. Photographic reproduction frees them from the servitude of belonging to a minor art. (p. 20)

To show this, Malraux presents on the same page and in the same size a first-century Western Siberia depiction of an animal fight and the famous twelfth-century bas-relief in the Autun Cathedral showing Eve bending to pick the apple off the forbidden tree. The confrontation between a simple mythological scene in the steppes and a powerful evocation of Genesis, the first small in size, the second a large horizontal stone relief, is suggestive. The imaginary Museum is the ideal place to establish these unexpected relations, where style transcends form and matter. It has given place, says Malraux, to "fictitious art." The consequences of a simple photographic amplification or reduction are incalculable and sometimes open up new styles in art. When the scale of a work of art is "falsified," niches of new meaning may be discovered.

> Reproduction has made art fictitious (as happens with the novel where reality serves fiction) when it systematically falsifies the scale of objects and presents the figures on oriental seals and coins as if figures on columns, and amulets as statues. Furthermore, the unfinished execution resulting from the small size of the object becomes in the amplified photograph a large style, one with a modern accent. (p.22)

No one can doubt the value of photographic reproduction for the detailed study of a work of art. Moreover, it is frequently the only available means to fill in gaps in our historical knowledge. Many times large works have disappeared and we only have the testimony of the smaller ones. The style of these last makes us infer that of the major artworks when we use our imagination on the amplified photographs of the smaller surviving specimens. This is what Malraux has to say,

> Sometimes reproductions of minor artworks suggest certain grand styles that have disappeared, or that were possible. The number of great works of art prior to Christianity that have come down to us is insignificant compared with the number that have been lost. (p. 22)

In summary, the imaginary Museum of reproductions incites us to provoke the meta-morphosis of the original object, it invites us to discover and exhibit as a novelty that which was implicit in the art work but not apparent to the naked eye.

> The photo album isolates both to metamorphose (through enlargement) and for discovery (when it isolates a landscape in a Limbourg miniature) and so changes it into new art or for exhibition. (p. 25)

It sometimes allows us to better expose the artistic quality of a particular work of art.

> An art album on Oceania (Guiart 1963) in making us familiar with 200 sculptures reveals the quality of some of them. Familiarity with a large number of works of a same style determines the masterpieces of that style, because it forces us to understand the particular meaning of the style. (p. 17)

We come here to an issue of high educational value. For some time now the museums of the world summon multitudes with their famous "retrospective shows," which serve to appreciate a large number of original works usually dispersed or inaccessible. The imaginary Museum is eminently suited to this; as it is a "bespoke museum" as well as a "portable museum" with an infinite number of works of interest to us. Just as a musician can leaf through a score and enjoy the music without hearing it, in the same way a visitor to the imaginary Museum can visualize a reproduced artwork without actually seeing the original. In a luminous metaphor Paul Claudel used to say "close your eyes and you will see."

The musician and his score and the art lover and his reproduction "reconstruct" sound and visual images. In this capacity to reconstruct lies, precisely, one of the greatest contributions of the virtual Museum. We are dealing with a reconstruction that goes far beyond the photographic images of the imaginary Museum. Let us see some examples. There are few things as attractive as turning a Greek statue around on its pedestal. Some museums permit this, by nature the act of the sculptor in his studio or, in the case of an antique bowl, of the potter at his wheel. But it is not the usual thing. However, digital technology allows manipulating the art object without any risk. There are programs or applications that allow *rotating* a solid body in virtual space, including the shadings of dark and light. Many virtual Museums also offer the possibility of moving about, of walking through the rooms and contemplating the works of art one by one. New York's *Frick Collection* is one. Nothing is more appropriate to Malraux's imaginary museum than this leisurely visit.

But we can go even further in virtual space. As an implicit corollary of the theory of fictitious art, there are actually some virtual museums that have no existence in the real world! In digital jargon they are called web-only museums. These totally fictive museums have the peculiarity of inviting the visitor to a place that only exists on the web, although in the case of Montevideo's Virtual Museum the designers have invented a photomontage of a virtual building in a very well known park of that Uruguayan city. In these "only virtual museums" the visitor enters the simulated building, sees the billboards, decides what exhibition to see, climbs the stairs and contemplates art hung on virtual walls. An interesting exhibition of the Uruguayan painter Pedro Figari is shown in a virtual salon in the Montevideo Virtual Museum. And this poses an interesting question that duplicates the one on fictitious art. These works by Figari are reproductions of his original paintings, but they could well be mere "digital reconstructions" of perhaps non-existent works, hung on non-existent walls. Digital art will keep the matter permanently open to discussion. It is a new challenge which the digital culture brings to art and other fields.

Art forgeries are a problem central to modern museums, and can also become troublesome in virtual space. Malraux devotes several pages to the analysis of art forgeries and a detailed discussion of the work of Van Meegeren, the Vermeer forger. This celebrated forger presumed to rival Vermeer as an artist; he did not think of himself as an imitator but as a competitor, and that was his strange defense at his famous forgery trial, but his case was unusual. In general "the traditional forger (as Malraux says) does not try to compete with genius, he tries at most to imitate the manner or, in the case of anonymous artists, the style" (p. 369). We shall surely see many varieties of fictive art in this new digital culture, from pure forgery at one extreme, to the creation of art objects of impossible execution in real life but feasible in the world of digital make-believe.

Real and virtual visits

A visit to the virtual museum allows us in effect to carry out a series of instructive actions that exceed the limits of the mere photographic reproduction dear to Malraux. Viewing the computer screen one can walk down a gallery exhibiting artworks, close in on a particular one, zoom into the details and if necessary save that image and print a paper copy for personal use, and also obtain information on the work and the artist. In some cases one can participate as well in a guided virtual visit, eventually accompanied by *voice* and sounds.

It is worth stopping for a moment to consider some differences between a real visit and a virtual one. First of all, two different museums are concerned. In other words, photographic or digital reproductions are not original works but more or less successful replicas on different support systems. Leafing through an album of reproductions or visiting a website are significantly different acts from walking through a museum. The difference is obvious from all points of view, but nevertheless needs emphasizing. Malraux never thought of his imaginary museum as a substitute for a real one, but as a particular extension of the latter, with specific functions of artistic appreciation and historical research. The same occurs with virtual museums. A new door, inexistent in the past, has been opened to access the museum. But the visitor is also a special visitor, a *virtual one*. It is a different visit. Even many of these visitors are not human, but programs in search of information. In future these agents or robots may report to their "owner" that there is a particular exhibit or art piece worthy of a visit. There are millions of people today who use this digital door to visit museums, they are a new breed of remote visitors.

The lesson is that we must take good care of this new public. Access must be made easier. In the same way that ramps help invalids to move around a real museum, something analogous will be needed in the virtual museum. Systems have now been developed to make websites accessible to disabled users. It is advisable then that virtual museums take this need into account and eliminate barriers to virtual visiting, because we believe there is not sufficient awareness in this respect. In brief, we propose an act of solidarity by the art community: the *accessible* virtual museum.

We must also use this means to educate the occasional visitor. For example, "learning how to look at a picture" as is done by the Prado Museum, where every month a masterpiece is exhaustively analyzed on the internet. However, the subject of education exceeds the traditional museum program, guided visit or lecture. Today education has become one of the most important activities of a museum and takes multiple forms according to circumstance and place. The virtual museum has also opened up this *educational* niche with enormous success, helped by a great *academic* and *research* effort.

Finally, one of the most instructive comparisons is the relationship between the number of real visits and virtual ones per year.

The number of virtual visits to museums is in general less than the real visits, except for the equal number of visitors to the Washington National Gallery of Art. Perhaps the trend in time will be for virtual visits to become more frequent and even outnumber real ones.

This new cultural phenomenon has become an important field of museum activity. The process seems irreversible but we cannot forget that there are still many real museums that do not have a site on the internet. Some are working on it with international help, as is the case of St. Petersburg's Hermitage with one of the most elaborate sites in the world operated by IBM. Others have been satisfied with no more than a brochure on the net but the world's most important museums pay particular attention to these virtual visits and earmark large amounts of money and creative resources to maintain interest in their site. This virtual dimension is absolutely new. Malraux could not imagine anything like it, but surely, had he known it, he would have been one of its most enthusiastic supporters.

There is a collateral but equally important subject relative to genuine funding for the museum via the digital network. In some sites virtual visitors can shop long distance in the museum *shop* via the internet. For example, the MOMA's select *boutique* which offers reproductions, books, catalogues, CDs, sculpture and jewels is available to the remote visitor who can have his purchases mailed to his home and charged to his credit card. The economic contribution of this can be significant; we must not forget that some museums such as the Bilbao Guggenheim get as much income from their shops as from the visiting public. Certainly, with increasing expansion of the virtual visitor market via the internet this activity will become an important contribution to the museum's upkeep.

In summary, the virtual museum has ceased to be a simple reflection of the real one; it has developed a life of its own, no longer satisfied with informing and exhibiting but challenging to action and discovery. Let us see some examples. A friend of mine was interested in the *Tetragrammaton*, the "magic square" symbol widely used in Renaissance iconography. I remembered having seen it on a 4×4 number table hanging on a wall in Albrecht Dürer's famous engraving of 1514, *Melancholy*. I knew that Washington's National Gallery of Art kept a very valuable collection of Dürer's engravings and I found there a sufficiently clear copy showing the columns, lines and diagonals of the magic square in the engraving. I was pleasantly surprised to find dozens of Dürer engravings on show in the virtual museum and among them the one I sought. I quickly obtained a beautiful image of the work and zoomed in to the details of the inscription. Deciphering was difficult because some symbols were incomprehensible to me. Then I proceeded to a slow decoding on the basis of the arithmetical properties of the square. I remembered that the sum of the columns, diagonals and lines always gave the same number. Little by little, adding the numbers I managed, not without work, to decipher and consistently reach the number 34, another magic number. I completed the table correctly and sent it to my friend via the internet. All of this was done without leaving my house, thousands of kilometers away from Washington. Incidentally, this research certainly took me less time as a remote visitor than it would have as a real visitor.

Furthermore, in general, in a real museum not all its collections are on show and many will always remain inaccessible to the public due to their fragility. In the Chantilly Museum, where the *Très riches heures du Duc de Berry* is kept, there is a warning: "Your attention please! These works are so deteriorated that you can only see them on the internet!" Incidentally, here we see another very significant advantage of digital reproduction, when the original is inaccessible to the public because of its fragility and rarity.

On the other hand, in the same way that educational activities exist in real museums, so are they present in virtual museums. It is evident, in this sense, that Malraux's dream has come true. One notable example is the *QBIC (Query by Image Content)* program of the Hermitage Museum which lets us experiment with one of Malraux's most pleasant fancies, i.e., playing with visual associations to create style families. For example, the virtual visitor can select a color from a continuous spectrum and paint a variable band in a picture and entirely cover it in different colors. To try this out I chose only three, a certain blue, green and yellow shades in different proportions, that reminded me vaguely of the colors used by Matisse. To my surprised admiration there immediately appeared on the screen a series of paintings from the museum's collection, including two paintings by Matisse, *Woman on the Terrace* and *View of Colliure* which I never knew existed, besides other pictures by Derain, Signac, Manguin and Dupuis! In a way the QBIC program allowed me to recognize "the same palette" in this French style of the beginning of our century. The program also offers the possibility of selecting families of paintings by their forms.

The possibility of interacting at a distance with works of art is something fantastic but we must remember that this is only the beginning. There is a long way to go before esthetic pleasure can equal gazing at the original artwork. For the time being these are visual experiments in miniature, but it is not too venturesome to think that in a short time, comfortably seated in our homes, we will be able to contemplate our favorite works of art in their real size with a clarity even greater than the original, without protective glass or barriers standing in the way of some detail of interest to us. A successful effort has been made by the Toshiba Electronic Museum where the visitor can appreciate hundreds of works of art on high-fidelity digital screens that are transmitted, upon request, through a network, from an image database. However, we must acknowledge that we are a long way from perfection, that the usual images on our personal computer are far from being really attractive and if projected in actual size clarity is blurred and on the PC screen scale is irremediably lost.

Note

1   *Rembrandt by himself*. National Gallery. London. June–September 1999.

References

Cox-Rearick, J. *The Collections of Francis I: Royal Treasures*. New York: H. Abrams, 1996.

Guiart, J. *Océanie,* in *L'univers de formes*. Collection dirigée par André Malraux et Georges Salles. Paris: Gallimard, 1963.

Marlraux, André, *Le musée imaginaire,* in *Les voix du silence*. Paris: Nouvelle Revue Française, Gallimard, 1951 (*Museum Without Walls*, translation S. Gilbert and F. Price, London: Secker & Warburg, 1967).

Plazy, G. and del Moral, J. M., *Les chemins de Van Gogh*. Paris: Ed. du Chêne, 1997.

Pyenson, L. *Servants of Nature: A History of Scientific Institutions, Enterprises and Sensibilities*. New York: Norton, 1999.

von Sonnenburg, H. *Rembrandt / Not Rembrandt in the Metropolitan Museum of Art: Aspects of Connoisseurship*. (2 vol.) New York: Metropolitan Museum of Arts, 1995.

Chapter 14

Virtual Spaces and Museums

Andrea Bandelli

Communication technologies are changing the ways we use actual spaces – including museums. This research looks at some of the most common aspects of adding "virtual" components to traditional museum activities. Through some examples and observations, I conclude that while virtual resources do not necessarily undermine the social experience of the museum, at the same time, that they should be used with care.

When we talk about "virtual museums," we usually think of websites, electronic networks, and 3-D graphics. The debate about use of electronic tools inside museums began with the personal computer, which made it affordable to integrate electronic information into the museum setting, and intensified with the advent of the Internet, which makes it possible to access vast amounts of information regardless of where you are. But the adjective "virtual" takes on more significance if we associate it with the visitor's experience rather than just a specific technology or a way to represent reality.

Education – expanding the museum's social space

Sometimes the creation of a virtual space is clearly evident, and distinct from the conventional museum space. This is the case in several of the recent Internet-mediated partnerships between museums and schools. In addition to its usefulness in information-gathering and peer-to-peer communication, the network adds the possibility of exposing results of student projects to a wide audience, so that participants are challenged with publishing their work and making it understandable and relevant for viewers. It is this aspect of the network I will focus on, because this is most relevant for understanding how a virtual space may be connected with a museum.

Source: *Journal of Museum Education*, vol. 24, 1999, p. 20.

In 1994–96, I worked with the Laboratorio dell'Immaginario Scientifico (LIS) in Trieste, Italy, which at the time was the only Italian science center to have a website and an information network available to users in homes and schools. At LIS, we developed a series of educational activities on air pollution, recycling, drugs, and energy.[1] We asked students in several schools located in different parts of Italy and later all over Europe to work on these subjects and to use the network to exchange materials, keep in touch, and share resources. Initially, before their school had a computer and modem, students in Trieste came to the center to work. They arrived at 8 in the morning, and we had difficulty closing at 8 at night because they wanted to go on working. For as long as half a school year, small teams of students worked closely together, going to research institutes, contacting scientists, and gathering data. The learning experience was customized for every class, every teacher, and almost every working team.

One of the main outcomes of the three-year experiment was that the combination of "real" activities with "virtual" experiences proved to be seamless, with the science center playing a key role as gateway between the two contexts.[2] Teachers and classrooms, on their own, have in most cases been unable to create equally effective projects.[3]

In this case, a virtual space resulted from the possibility of acting in areas not limited by the physical constraints of the museum. For the museum, this meant working with groups of students and teachers from different areas, with activities that were very much a part of the community where the users resided. For the students, it meant working with other people, on activities the school could not afford, and then publishing the results to a broad and diverse public. For LIS, this work was much more than the usual outreach program: it meant not only working with communities that are culturally very different from Trieste, such as Naples and Bologna, but on topics such as recycling and drug addiction that are not easy subjects for field activities. While taking place in a "virtual" space, the work was a very real component of the science center, and one of the most important as well.

The most common critique of computers and the Internet is the sense of isolation they are supposed to bring, and the absence of contact with other people unmediated by the screen. On the contrary, as this experience shows, electronic networks are a tool that can extend the action range of the museum and the school and increase the social space.

Virtual spaces overlapping physical ones

Another important area where we can find a virtual museum is where the virtual context just overlaps the physical one, or better, where a new set of "rules" concerning social interaction, space, and time, is available to the visitors. This is easiest to think about in the case of art museums, where the distinction between "real" – original and unique works of art – and "virtual" is very clear. As we will see, the virtual museum in many cases is an environment superimposed on the real one, avoiding the constraints typical of physical environments.

It is reasonable to assume that visitors go to an art museum to see original works of art. Shows of copies, although not infrequent, do not register any considerable success, and art books, even those with beautiful, high-quality reproductions, are consulted mainly by scholars. The commonly accepted behavior from visitors is that social interaction occurs, with visitors quietly talking to each other or contemplating the objects. The object, painting, or artifact remains in the context of the gallery, usually thoughtfully placed next to other relevant ones.[4] One of the main characteristics of museums, thus, is that they are social spaces. In contrast, virtual spaces are often thought of as isolating and lacking in meaningful social contacts.

Now, let's think for a while about what happens when visitors walk through the galleries with audiotape guiding systems, headphones on their heads, following the story narrated by the tape. The interaction with other visitors is basically gone, or limited mostly to repeating the content of the tape to others who do not have it. There is no interaction with the narrator of the guide and his or her personal views. A "virtual" context is thus built, with its own, different rules of social behavior. Conversations are limited by several constraints: in time, because they interrupt the narration of the guide; in subject, because they are always initiated by the same stimuli coming from the narration; and in interactivity, because there is no reaction from the guide. Even in a gallery where real objects are present, then, the social context can be manipulated and changed using the appropriate technology. Headphone-based audioguides in effect build a new set of implicit rules and paths that visitors follow. Visitors are provided with some information, but their freedom to explore the museum is largely limited.

But there are also positive examples – including "computer rooms" like the MicroGallery at the National Gallery in London and the ARIA at the Rijksmuseum in Amsterdam – where the appropriate use of technology can result in enlarged opportunities for visitors. In both cases several computers give visitors the possibility of looking at paintings on the screen, finding out details and additional information, and creating their own tour through the museum, printing a floor map with all the objects they select. This is also a way to create a virtual context overlapping the physical one created by time, space, and objects in the museum.[5] So, a virtual environment does not have to be an artificial one, nor even a computer-mediated one.

Giving back control to the visitors

Just as many industrial virtual reality applications overcome the problem of acting in dangerous environments or performing destructive experiments, a "virtual museum" also can provide experiences that are not possible in the physical setting of the museum.

The first level of experience is one linked to information. Comprehensive background information is still hard to provide with the traditional media used by museums. It is not a question of which media to use; the problem lies in the different expectations, needs, and behaviors of the visitors. Offering a personalized system, which enables visitors to find information of varying levels of depth and accuracy, is the goal of the Actua system at the new Metropolis science center in Amsterdam.[6] The environment created by the computers in the Actua network is definitely a virtual one: the exhibits cease to be tools to engage processes and discoveries, and become portals to information grouped in categories like "Encyclopedia – facts and backgrounds," "Current issues and debates," and "Work and labor." The visitor is then helped to find his or her own personal interest in that exhibit: to find a job in a particular field, or to see how controversial issues such as pollution are discussed in the country. These processes are completely controlled by the visitor: using this system can be compared to walking through the museum, stopping at interesting spots. The system is not just a catalogue of existing information; rather, it takes advantage of the fact that contextual information can be available at the same time, and in the same place.

Another experience that is difficult to create in the physical domain is social inter-action between visitors, and especially between strangers. The new website of the Van Gogh Museum[7] will provide a function that I call a "catalyst" for starting conver-sations about the works of art. Even though still an experimental project, the aim of this website is to take advantage of actions that are easier in a virtual environment than in a physical one. In a museum, spontaneous conversations between individual visitors who do not know each other happen very seldom. The same two people on the Internet, however, can engage in a conversation much more easily, given the fact that all physical barriers disappear. Casual contacts can be initiated online, conversa-tions can arise, and a deeper understanding of the painting can occur.

There are of course some issues that need to be verified in the next future. The ease of social interaction online, for instance, has often resulted from an overly enthu-siastic response to the technology, which shifted the focus from the actual content of the conversation to the means of conducting it. I presume that as people become more accustomed to the technology, they will also re-create the social barriers to which we're now accustomed in using technologies like the telephone.

The social space: a parallel case – the short history of the cybercafé

Some five to six years ago there was an explosion in the phenomenon of cybercafés. After their initial success – especially in London, where the first European cybercafé, Cyberia, was located – the cybercafé rapidly became the "trendiest" place to be, the place to be "connected" and part of the digital age. Cybercafés blossomed every-where, and entire websites were devoted to listing and reviewing these places. But within just a few years, the situation changed. For one thing, communication devices became more readily available in homes, schools, and libraries. But more important, the café has an irreducible social function – as a place to sit in public, surrounded by people, and not isolated in a microworld. In the case of the cybercafé, technology changed the function of the space, but not for long – because the space was not simply a container; it had a function that could not be reproduced in another environment.

Space, thus, does not necessarily change its function simply because a new tech-nology is applied. Attempts to "rejuvenate" an existing space by adding computer components will not succeed, unless the technology can trigger a new function for that space.[8] At the same time, communication technologies do not necessarily need a special environment. In the city of Amsterdam, public Internet terminals are avail-able next to public phones in the streets. Communication technology doesn't need an incubator, a protected environment where it is decontextualized and given to the people.

The key to understanding the relationship between a virtual museum and a real one is thus to understand social actions in space and time, and the relevance of unique objects or reproducible ones and ways to experience them.

Conclusions

We are ready to move beyond the notion that virtual museums are just graphic representations of existing spaces. The appropriate application of communication technologies is to create virtual spaces – from the more "conceptual" ones like those of the Laboratorio dell'Imaginario Scientifico, to the more concrete ones like those of the Rijksmuseum that give access to a myriad of otherwise unavailable information – that become tools visitors can actively use.

Just as a museum has many functions – preservation, research, and display – in the same way, a virtual museum should also be rich and varied, not limited to a specific objective or target audience. The examples described, while still new, are moving in this direction, exploring ways that communication technologies can overcome the physical boundaries of the museum.

Notes

1   A description of these projects can be found in: "Linking schools through the network", presented at ECSITE conference, Amsterdam, 1994, and "Lessons from Laboratorio dell'Immaginario Scientifico", published in Informal Science, issue n. 20, p. 4 (Sept.–Oct. 1996), Washington, DC.
2   These ideas are expressed in the thesis "The knowledge agency", written by the author for the post-graduate master in communication of science, SISSA-ISAS, Trieste, 1996.
3   "Net Gains" – *Spectra*, the Museum Computer Network magazine, Winter 1996/97 issue (vol. 24, 2), pp. 30–33, Ottawa (co-written with James Bradburne).
4   For a critical description of how museums are traditionally structured, see P. Galluzzi, "Nuove tecnologie e funzione culturale dei musei", in *I formati della Memoria*, Giunti, Firenze, 1997.
5   A more detailed description of how our environments are being modified in the electronic age is in *City of Bits*, William J. Mitchell, 1995, MIT Press, Cambridge, MA.
6   For a description of the system and the way it is related to the activities in the science center, "Turning information into knowledge", in *Here and Now*, p. 181, Science Museum, London, 1996 (with James Bradburne).
7   http://www.vangoghmuseum.nl
8   A remarkable description of the social role of electronic communication, in places like cybercafés and other places, is in "Amsterdam's Brave New World", Matt Steinglass, *New York Times*, February 7, 1999.

Chapter 15

The Virtual Visit: towards a new concept for the electronic science centre

Roland Jackson

The vision

Where does the public find out about contemporary science and technology? Is it from magazines like *New Scientist* and *Scientific American*? From features in *Le Monde* or the *Independent* newspapers? Or perhaps from radio and television programmes? Almost certainly, science centres and museums play a relatively small part, so far. The advent of the Internet gives us the potential to make a much larger impact. Unlike magazines, newspapers and television programmes, the basis for our activities lies in the construction of relatively long-lasting exhibitions, supported and complemented by debates, discussions and other means of exchanging ideas and views.

Given their focus on exhibitions, science centres and museums now have a natural opportunity to lead the process of developing electronic exhibitions and the associated means of information exchange. Perhaps no other type of institution has the same clear potential niche or mission. Science centres and museums should be developing as nodal points in the access of the public to contemporary science and technology. They should be mixing thematic electronic exhibitions to immediate updates and live, online provision of information, mediating and guiding public access to the discoveries and issues of the day and to the people, views and concepts behind them. Whether it is the possibility of life on Mars, the vulcanology of Iceland, the safety of beef as a food or the progress and potential of the human genome project, electronic exhibitions created by science centres and museums ought to be the natural starting points for the public.

Source: Conference *Here and Now: improving the presentation of contemporary science and technology in museums and science centres*, Science Museum, London, 21–23 November, 1996. No longer available.

My proposal here is for a new paradigm to shape our work with the public towards this end.

The problems of prediction

The prediction of the impact, potential and development of electronic technologies is a risky business. Implicit in the followingt is the belief that global digital networking systems will change the nature of science centres and museums and their relationships with society, or at the very least with some parts of it. If I am completely wrong, I shall at least be in good company, as the following quotes demonstrate (even if they are apocryphal and probably taken out of context):

> I think there's a world market for maybe five computers.
>
> Thomas Watson, chairman of IBM, 1943

> There is no reason why anyone would want to have a computer in their home.
>
> Ken Olsen, president, chairman and founder of Digital Equipment Corporation, 1977

> 640K ought to be enough for anyone.
>
> Bill Gates, 1981

I conclude from those comments that one should err on the side of boldness.

Concepts and starting points

My emphasis is entirely on the Internet and related technologies, rather than with stand-alone systems and dedicated networks within science centres and museums or with specific digital products such as CD-ROMs.

The important features of the networking technologies is that they allow real-time and interactive access, by multiple simultaneous users, from (and to) any computer anywhere in the world that has a connection. All three parameters are significant. First, 'real-time and interactive access'. The virtual world is organic and can be up to date in a way that, for example, a book or a CD-ROM cannot be. Secondly, 'multiple simultaneous users'. Of course it is possible to have multiple-way phone conferences, and multiple access to local computer networks, but global networking adds a qualitatively different degree of scope and, in particular, of scale. Finally, 'any computer anywhere in the world'. This remote access is the real distinguishing feature of the global networks, allowing instant communication across and between different people, cultures and information sources.

Built on those three physical features of the system are the opportunities for the 'visitor' or online participant. These lie in three areas – *access to data and information*, *access to conferencing and discussion*, and access to what I shall define as *collaborative computing applications*.

Each of these will be examined in turn but, before that, it is necessary to consider the ways by which the public at large might make use of global networking technologies as they develop. For our purpose, that of presenting contemporary science and technology, three distinct groups of people are identifiable.

First, the not negligible group that will make little or no use of these technologies for leisure or even for general educational purposes. We might classify these people as technophobes, or simply recognise that they have different preferred styles of interacting and learning. Such people find the multimedia screen uni-dimensional (indeed not multimedia at all), lacking personal warmth and the reality of the physical world. I suspect this group is, and will remain, a large group, and will hopefully continue to flood into our real environments.

Secondly, the group of people who use the Internet as a library resource and as a means of exchanging views, but in the context of information largely structured by others. These are the people we can attract to our online exhibitions and conferences. We certainly do not yet know how large this group might be, how diverse, nor the details of the ways in which it uses our existing provision. There is a desperate need for more user research, given all the experimentation currently in process.

Thirdly, an emerging group of people who want to create new electronic worlds with others and including those who have an interest in shaping presentations of science and technology according to their own views and interests. The new technologies give us ways of empowering people at large to work creatively with like-minded enthusiasts to these ends, and I believe that science centres and museums should support, and indeed lead, this process. This group of people may be, and remain, small, but I would argue that we have a natural mission and responsibility to work with them given the overlap of their interest and expertise with ours and the their potential to generate with us a range of interesting perspectives for others to explore.

Access to data and information

This is perhaps the most obvious of the three broad areas of opportunity for online users. It is the logical extension of the CD-ROM-type database to become a multimedia, real-time, networked resource.

The Internet already gives access to a massive resource of scientific information in digital format (which could be described as a de facto distributed science information centre), made up of the millions of web pages produced by thousands of organisations, groups and individuals. Indexing facilities such as Yahoo, or search engines such as Lycos enable one to find information about almost any aspect of contemporary science and technology, even if the quality is variable. When I recently wanted to see for myself the evidence for possible life on Mars, following the analysis of the meteorite, the Science Museum's curator of space science pointed me to a web address containing the entire published paper.

Making use of this vast resource of data and information requires considerable initiative, commitment and existing knowledge on the part of the user. For the more casual online visitor it is important to provide more structured routes, and recommended highlights. Those online users with explicit educational objectives need a further range of suggestions and support. Much data and information can be presented interactively. The Franklin Science Museum's 'educational hotspots' page holds an interesting list of interactive exhibits, many with a direct relevance to contemporary science. Individual examples include the UK's own Bradford Robotic Telescope, available for the public to use over the Internet (there tends to be a waiting list!) and the San Francisco Exploratorium's on visual and aural perception. The stage beyond this is the development of more complex simulations – an example from around the world is the famous virtual frog dissection. With new software such as Java and Shockwave, the use of video and audio clips, and approaches to virtual reality such as Quick Time VR and VRML, all of which are already in use by science centres and museums, the potential is enormous. As yet, though, we have no idea how large the potential user group might be, how much it might pay and for what, nor enough research into the most effective design of presentations.

Conferencing and discussion

First, videoconferencing. If there is one virtual technology particularly suited to science centres and museums this must be it. It is an audio-visual, interactive medium. Imagine a member of staff walking round an exhibition carrying a camera and talking to a group of people in a remote school or community centre. The possibilities for visit planning, follow-up and indeed for special remote events are endless. Videoconferencing is difficult on the Internet at present, because of the problems of low bandwidths and speeds, but the situation is likely to improve. Even the existing CUSeeMe software is acceptable for some purposes now over the Internet, and as soon as genuine broadband networks are commonplace the opportunities will be much greater.

We have experimented with ISDN2 systems at the Science Museum. With this sort of bandwidth, a rapidly changing picture, such as would be obtained by walking around with a video camera, is of low quality. Working with schools in Scotland and in the Southampton area of southern England, scenarios such as a demonstration, interaction with a drama character and a question and answer session were set up, where most of the background is relatively static. That allows those parts of the image that do move, particularly the important human face, to be of reasonable quality and allows one to see the changing detail. The demonstration that was performed over the video link was entitled 'How does a telephone work?'. With close-up shots its was possible for people at the other end of the link to see all the relevant detail inside the mouthpiece and earphone as it was being demonstrated. We intend to install an ISDN6 system shortly, delivering images of higher quality and allowing the public to see directly into places of interest to the general public and schools such as space centres and computer research laboratories. Contemporary science and technology, and its practitioners, become accessible in real time to our visitors.

Secondly, e-mail conferencing. This may seem like going back in time to a more prosaic and wholly text-based application, because e-mail conferencing has been with us for many years. However, e-mail is far cheaper than videoconferencing, and more controllable. It is possible to collect, read and respond to messages at leisure, allowing more in-depth work.

The Science Museum has run three e-mail conferences to date, on the topics 'Do humans have a role in space?', 'Do we need more roads?' and 'IT – a help or hindrance to society?'. Each places a substantial number of students, of the order of 100, in direct contact with a range of experts in universities and research centres in the UK and further afield. We are gradually learning how to shape the discussion and make it a genuine dialogue rather than a series of questions and answers, however valuable that might be. As a means, particularly for schools, of engaging people in discussion about contemporary science and technology, this method continues to have much to offer.

Finally, a third example which is an innovative use of the Web. The Science Museum has been leading, in the UK, the concept of consensus conferences, including the first national consensus conference on the application of biotechnology to agriculture. The concept is that a group of lay people inform themselves about the issues, by reading and by interviewing expert witnesses, and come to recommendations about future developments. That idea has been extended to exploring the use of the World Wide Web for developing public understanding and the exchange of views on a variety of issues, and for consensus building. Users can express their views and vote on issues, in ways that immediately affect and update the web pages themselves, and read background information as appropriate.

Collaborative computing

This is where I believe that science centres have some radical options for the future. By 'collaborative computing' I mean people working together online to construct new electronic resources, including new online environments. I have in mind the construction of virtual spaces such as MOOs, with their increasingly graphic capabilities, and shared simulated 3-D workspaces. Essentially one is bringing together the use of the Internet and related systems to provide a massive resource of data and information and to enable real-time communication between multiple remote users, in ways that lead to people co-operatively constructing new cultural resources.

The electronic science centre of the future

The ease of creating web pages and the democratising (or, for some, anarchic) process that this makes possible, means that we now have the opportunity to invite the public at large, expert and non-expert, to help us create online science centres and museums. For perhaps the first time in history, the existence of the Internet enables us to put the development of such institutions, apart from their expensive physical realisation, directly into the hands of their communities and surrounding societies, rather than building them primarily as the product of a professional management. At the simplest level this can amount to institutions asking people to submit work, and then selecting and displaying it. The gallery of children's paintings displayed by the Israel Museum is an example of one type of this activity, but I am envisaging something rather more radical, in which real control is placed in the hands of the user.

Science centres and museums that wish to work with and reflect the views of their communities should deliberately encourage a co-operative endeavour with the interested public, within a generic but extremely flexible framework, that could rapidly produce a quite staggeringly large, comprehensive and varied series of products and perspectives.

Participants would collaborate to construct online exhibitions, discuss issues and debate with experts. They would create their own virtual worlds, simulations, libraries, and physical exhibits that could be operated remotely. The qualitative difference between this and the development of existing isolated resources by individuals, groups and organisations on the Internet would be that every participant was joining an integrated co-operative endeavour with the specific aim of creating online science centres and museums for themselves and for the interested public at large.

In this way each science centre and museum would remain a recognised centre of expertise and information, but also become a continuously developing societal construct. Quite apart from the point that I believe we should be doing this anyway, it is not likely to be long before groups come together to construct their own alternative electronic science centres. Individuals are already producing guides to specific museums such as the Louvre and the British Museum. Indeed, in time, the distinction between an electronic science centre and an electronic magazine may well collapse and merge into a new type of entity. Science centres and museums should lead and work with the process rather than simply react to such future developments.

How realistic is this vision? That depends on how bold science centre and museum directors are prepared to be, and to what extent these institutions are prepared to surrender some institutional control over content in order to give the public at large more space for expression.

Some facets of this vision are easier to realise in practice. For example, the principle described above can be applied more narrowly to the idea of inviting teachers to develop on the Web their own ideas, resources and experiences for using science centres and museums for a physical or online visit. The potential scale and richness of the resource that might be created can barely be imagined, and we shall be experimenting with the concept shortly at the Science Museum. Given that it is now possible to enable users to annotate web pages for subsequent readers, and that this may be supplemented by forums (like newsgroups or discussion lists), a rich, professional environment can readily be created. The Internet is a bottom-up system. No longer is it appropriate, if it ever was, for us to regard ourselves almost exclusively as the experts and the transmission of information as almost invariably one way, from us to the visitor. We have to adjust our ways of working, particularly in the electronic domain, and indeed our mind-set, to release the potential of these media for the benefit of all our online users and to create, with interested sections of society at large, the new generation of electronic science centres.

Chapter 16

Empowering the Remote Visitor: supporting social museum experiences among local and remote visitors

Areti Galani and Matthew Chalmers

Introduction

Museums have supported the design and implementation of a range of media, analogue and digital, which enhances the visitor experience for diverse audiences. Audio guides and touch screens have been in use in museums for some time now. Museum websites have also been widely implemented to attract new audiences, and support education and scholarship remotely. Beside museum professionals, sociologists also take the position that the museum's "enclosed nature and the well-defined role" renders it "a fertile ground for studying visitor behaviour and envisioning systems to enhance visitor experience" (vom Lehn et al. 2001) and therefore an "excellent location for testing ubiquitous systems" (Fleck et al. 2002). This concept of the museum as a test bed for technological innovation, or rather as a "media workshop" – a term coined by Thomas (Thomas 1998) – has given rise to extended technological experimentation in museum settings in the past few years. Projects such as HIPPIE (Oppermann et al. 1999) and Cooltown (Fleck et al. 2002) progressed from offering location-dependent information to visitors in the Museo Civico in Siena and the Exploratorium respectively, to additionally supporting recording and editing of parts of the experience for later reflection and sharing with friends and family. The Points of Departure project (Exploratorium 2001) in San Francisco Museum of Modern Art used PDAs and workstations to present videos of artists while creating the artworks on display in the gallery. Furthermore, the Sotto Voce electronic guidebook (Aoki et al. 2002) combined information delivery with sociality by supporting eavesdropping on one's friends' commentaries.

Source: Proceedings of 2nd International Conference of Museology, Mytilene, Greece, 2004, Athens: Kaleidoskopio, 2008.

Most of these applications, however, are designed to offer additional diverse and personalised information to individuals who already visit the museum. The choice of single-user technology and the emphasis on personalised information reflect, we believe, an assumption of the primacy of the physical experience and the belief that information is a primary function of a museum visit. In the museum studies literature, often the new media discussion focuses on the real–virtual divide (Mintz 1998) that treats remote visits as secondary or surrogate experiences to the physical ones, prioritising the unmediated experience of the museum object – "the real thing" – over the mediated experience via technology. Museum virtual presence, on the other hand, appears divided as to whether to provide genuine online visitor experiences or instead encourage and support physical visiting (Cunliffe et al. 2001). The result of the former approach is the design of radically distinctive online experiences that are accessible only to remote visitors, and in the opposite end, websites that resemble knowledge repositories more than museum experiences. Local and remote audiences appear segmented, and the connection between local and remote visitors has not been pursued, at least not in the context of a single synchronous visiting event.

Our research rather looks at the relation among local and remote visitors from the point of view of visitors' interaction. Instead of focusing on delivery of information in physical galleries, we investigate social interaction among friends in museums and how social conduct may blur the boundaries among local and remote, and may foster shared experiences for combined on-site and off-site audiences. We do not overlook information – rather, we treat it as a resource for interaction. We are interested in interpretation that is produced in the course of collaborative encounters among participants. In this way we wish to "regard new media, particularly the World Wide Web, as a resource that more closely resembles a museum visit than a museum collection" (Borysewicz 1998).

The next section elaborates on the notion of the museum visit as a social experience, particularly how social interaction often mediates and shapes the personal experience. That section is inspired by observational studies of non-educational groups of visitors in two cultural institutions in Glasgow, UK. We then discuss an excerpt from a mixed reality system that supported simultaneous visiting among local and remote members of groups of friends. Based on that knowledge, we argue that the categorisation of local and remote participants is not a straightforward cut. Instead, boundaries may be blurred with social conduct. Furthermore, we expand this discussion to issues regarding the status of the museum object in a mixed reality museum environment, the emergence of a mutually complementing physical and digital museum presence, and the practicalities of running and maintaining such environments.

Social experience

Museum visits are social events. Whether treated as educational activity or leisure activity, museum visiting is shaped by social contact in terms of both the visitor's intentions and the overall experience. In a pioneering research, Hood (Hood 1983) identified that "being with people" was highly valued among occasional visitors and non-visitors, and often a reason for people not to visit museums. Baxandall (Baxandall 1987) also noted that the bulk of art museum experience is not about "looking at pictures but about talking about looking at pictures", and the labels are a means of constructing the visitors dialogue about art. Falk and Dierking (Falk and Dierking 1992), following extensive visitor studies, defined social context as one of the three key elements that influence the way visitors experience museums and argued that learning in museums is necessarily socio-culturally mediated (Falk and Dierking 2000). A series of other visitor studies also looked at how social interaction might affect learning, and how social behaviour is expressed in museums, especially among family members. Although this type or research offers useful insights into the way that interpretation and learning are influenced by social interaction in museums, it offers little knowledge on how social interaction is realised throughout the visit. This is partly due to the research methods employed, for example interviews, focus groups and so forth, but also due a more historic orientation of traditional museum research towards the cognitive aspects of the museum experience.

Looking at social experience as it unfolds *in situ* is an approach that stems from the ethnographic tradition in social sciences. It has also become increasingly popular among exhibit and technology designers in the recent years. By looking in detail at what groups of visitors do in the galleries, we sought to understand the elements that make a museum visit involving a number of individuals into a shared museum experience. A deeper understanding of the social character of the museum visit may then offer useful insights to the design of technology that attempts to fill the space of social synchronous experiences among local and remote visitors. We observed non-educational groups of visitors in two cultural institutions in Glasgow. The first was the Mackintosh Interpretation Centre (Mack Room) in the Lighthouse, a gallery devoted to the life and work of the Glaswegian designer and architect, Charles Rennie Mackintosh. The second was the House for an Art Lover, effectively a historic house built and decorated on Mackintosh's designs. We followed people as they went around the room(s), we recorded overheard discussions and, in some cases, we video-recorded their visit.

Vom Lehn (vom Lehn 2002) also looked at the interactional aspect of social conduct in museums and identified the richness of interactions that happen in front of the exhibit. That research made obvious that the experience of artefacts is constantly negotiated and re-shaped by social conduct, and that detailed inspection of social interaction with and around museum exhibits may offer insights in the design of displays that encourage or enable social interaction. His research focused on the moments visitors spend in front of objects, although in the analysis of our data we noticed that social interaction does not only happen around and about displays but instead happens throughout the visit. The opening and closing of a visit, the pace of the visit and the way friends connect and combine displays, media, and routes throughout the museum environment are informed and influenced by social conduct. (Pace is discussed in more detail in Galani and Chalmers 2004.) Verbal and gestural activity informs the time people spend with the exhibits, their orientation and exploration of the exhibition content. Verbal and visual cues facilitate both direct interaction and peripheral awareness of one's friends while one balances personal engagement with the exhibition and social exchanges with friends.

Technology to support social interaction has been explored in other projects too, for example the Sotto Voce guidebook that we have already mentioned. It has also been explored by artistic installations like the Deus Oculi (Heath et al. 2002) and the Ghost Ship (Hindmarsh 2002) that attempted to stimulate social interaction among friends and strangers alike in an art exhibition. Furthermore, social interaction among remote-only museum visitors has been explored in the field of collaborative virtual environments such as the Virtual Leonardo project (Mirapaul 1999) and the virtual tour in the Van Gogh Museum. The connection between remote and local visitors has not been pursued with the exception of robot applications (Roussou et al. 2001) that offered guided tours to a mixture of local and remote audiences. In the *City* project, we explicitly aimed at studying both technological innovation and visitor experience with focus on social interaction.

The *City* system

The design of the *City* system was informed by the visitor studies described above, as well as by technical, theoretical and interaction design goals. The prototype explored covisiting among people who know each other and share an interest in museum visiting, but who may not always be able to visit together due to difficulties such as geographical separation. The *City* system was designed for a specific gallery: the Mack Room in The Lighthouse. The exhibition combines textual and graphical displays with authentic artefacts, and over twenty screens presenting video and interactive material to visitors.

The *City* system combined virtual environments (VE), hypermedia technology, hand-held devices and ultrasound positioning technology. It allowed at least three visitors, one on-site and two remote, to visit the Mack Room simultaneously. An ultrasound positioning system and a wireless communications network was installed in the Mack Room. The on-site visitor carried a PDA that was tracked via the ultrasonics. The hand-held displayed the ongoing positions of all three visitors on a map of the gallery. One off-site visitor used a web-only environment that comprised a standard web browser which also displayed the gallery map. The other off-site visitor used a first person, 3-D display with avatars representing the other visitors. All visitors shared an open audio channel, and wore headphones and microphones. The system also supported multimedia information for the off-site visitors only in the form of web pages that were dynamically presented upon movement in the map or VE. This automatic presentation schematically followed the spatial organisation of the exhibition, so that all three visitors could 'look' at the same display when in the corresponding location. In that respect, the system supported interaction around corresponding exhibits in the Mack Room and in digital form: 'hybrid exhibits' (Brown et al., 2003).

The visitors' experience

The user trials of the system took place in the Mack Room. The participants were recruited through poster advertisements as friends and museum-goers. Ten groups of three and two groups of two members participated. Each visiting experience lasted approximately one hour and comprised an explorative part and an activity-based part. In the first part, the members of each group were encouraged to familiarise themselves with the technology and explore the gallery according to their own interest. In the second part, they were given a mixture of open-ended and focused questions about Mackintosh's work, and were asked to come up with answers based on evidence from or experience of the exhibition. The group's activity and discussions were recorded, and a semi-structured interview followed each visit. The analytical treatment of the data was based on interaction analysis, which focuses on the moment-to-moment detailed observation of the participants' verbal and gestural activity. It was also informed by ethnomethodology, and particularly the notion of accountability (Garfinkel 1967). The excerpt considered in this section is taken from the exploratory part of the study.

Eric, Jo and Geisa are friends and colleagues. In the study, Eric was on-site, in the Mack Room, while Jo was visiting in the VE and Geisa was in the hypermedia environment. Geisa and Jo had earlier spotted the guest bedroom, designed by Mackintosh for 78 Derngate Street, and they had a chat about it. Eric, who was occupied on the other side of the room, overheard their discussion, checked his map and when he finished looking at the display he was examining, he started moving towards the area his friends were in. While Eric was moving towards the display, Jo moved away from it, and when they met up, Jo decided to follow him. This decision was verbalised but also acted upon. This is not an unusual behaviour in museums. Friends during their visit may attend different displays related to their own interest but remain peripherally aware of their friends' activity due to their proximity in the gallery or by retaining visual contact with them. This awareness is facilitated by visual cues and helps the members of the group to keep track of their friends, develop a shared visiting pace and also inform their own exploration. In the mixed reality environment, visual cues were limited in the display of the participants' position, hence movements of arrows or avatars on the map and the 3-D model. This limited cue, however, kept the on-site visitor aware of where his friends were and the rough location of the artefact in question; it was further confirmed verbally. Shared orientation towards the display involved several stages: the on-site visitor approached the area; the remote visitor gave a rough description of the artefact, which included its title, as mentioned on the available webpage, and a reference to group-specific knowledge, the location of the original artefact, in the Hunterian Art Gallery. After the orientation stage, the on-site visitor adopted a relaxed viewing position towards the display and the two visitors started talking – while being overheard by their friend – about the room decoration. Their discussion began with an aesthetic appreciation of the room and concluded with humorous comments about the potential effect of the decoration on one's mood. The latter, appeared to stem from Jo's personal experience but also Eric's knowledge of his friend's lifestyle and taste.

Discussion

The richness and topical coherence of visitors' interaction with each other and with the exhibition is the basis of our claim that local and remote museum visitors had a shared visit. In this co-visiting experience, the museum's remote presence was treated not strictly as an information space, used in isolation, but also as a social place to visit, enjoy and relate to others. The latter afforded a set of behaviours that, as we have shown, constitutes a social experience that shares several significant attributes of traditional museum co-visiting. The experience offered plentiful information and afforded rich interaction within a heterogeneous mix of media. This approach moves away from the traditional design focus on a single user's experience, towards multi-user interaction that treats the traditional and new media aspects of a museum as equally important elements of the museum experience (Galani 2003). Furthermore, it broadens design to address both personal and social aspects of the visit, and does not restrict the visitor to either one of these modes. It supports the individual's interpretation of artefacts and displays, which can be used as a resource for social interaction, and which in turn might inform and influence later individual interpretation.

Our work does not attempt to substitute or reproduce a visit to a traditional museum. It supports, however, a mixed reality museum visit that may cover needs and expectations that are not easily addressed by the traditional museum. Remote visitors, disenfranchised by geographical or other barriers, may interact with the layout and content of an exhibition and become immersed in exploration of and discussions about artefacts. Local visitors may also access information online, with the difference that they can use the contributions, experience and understanding of their remote friends.

This approach to remote access to museum environments creates new opportunities for museum experiences and exhibition design. It is not, however, unproblematic both in terms of technological implementation and museum practice. We would like to explore further the issues that arise from supporting socially interactive visits among local and remote participants, such as the collaborative production of interpretation through social interaction and how it is linked to the artefact as well as the empowerment of the remote visitor and the emergence of a mutually complementing physical and digital museum design. Additionally, we discuss some practical consideration regarding mixed reality environments and how they might fit with a museum's practices and priorities.

"Imagine ... waking up with a hangover!"

Studies of technology in museums, and especially of use of personal mobile devices, had shown that interaction with technology might inhibit social interaction (Walter 1996) as well as redirect the attention of the visitor from the museum artefacts to the information that is delivered on his/her device (vom Lehn and Heath 2003). Among the most reported disadvantages of such technologies is the decline of talk among visitors. On the contrary, in the mixed reality environment we observed a radical increase in talk among participants. For some of the off-site participants the experience was liberating: "I think it is fun though. I quite enjoyed the social engagement in that way, being able to talk about everything more and not feeling that you are disturbing ... not thinking about other users in the gallery. You know it's kind of liberating", and for others it was a good laugh: "I thought it was actually fun, and I thought it was a laugh; an easy pleasure."

In the relaxed manner of the visit we attribute the increased production of funny, unexpected and imaginative comments and reactions by the participants and the affective rather than scholarly approach to the available content. Co-visitors used and appropriated the available information to suit their shared knowledge and experiences. Although part of the conversation involved giving directions and instructions to one's friends regarding one's whereabouts, well reported museum behaviours were regularly observed: participants read aloud phrases from the exhibition text, communicated their own knowledge, made connections to their own everyday lives, expressed opinions and verbalised imaginative thoughts, like the phrase at the title of this section.

Furthermore, unlike the displacement of the object that is reported with mobile devices, in the mixed reality environment the constant focus of the attention was the displays and the environment. The hybrid character of the displays, which meant that the participants interacted with different presentations of the display according to their media, provoked extended discussions around the displays, initially in order to develop a shared understanding of what was available to each participant, to "translate" and "compare" it with each other, as one of the participants said, a process that "*gives a different kind of perspective*", then to discuss the content. Asymmetries in the presentation and the amount of content, afforded by the variety of the media, as well as the participants' eagerness to share, often sparked further investigation and exploration of content that was not accessible at the first glance. Furthermore, the attractiveness of displays in the different media was also variable resulting with people being prompted by their friends to see objects that they would have skipped otherwise. How asymmetries in the visiting environment functioned in interactional level is the topic of the next section.

"Oh I think it's bad from here!"

This phrase from the dialogue discussed earlier in the paper is at the heart of the discussion on new media and museums; one could argue that it verbalises the difference between "here" and "there": in the gallery and away from it, for the on-site visitor, and vice versa for off-site visitors. Mintz argued for this distinction by claiming that "a virtual visit to a museum is fundamentally a media experience, not a museum experience" (Mintz 1998). In our opinion, however, this distinction appears to stem from focusing on the individual media and their affordances instead of their use in context. We approach the sentence of this section's title by taking more account of the overall interaction between the two companions. We notice that the difference between the media and distinctions of "here" and "there" did not seem to impose problems in discussing the display and participating in the shared joke. On the contrary, and again using this dialogue as an example, the two friends used the displays at hand to initiate their discussion, and complemented it with their knowledge of each other's habits and tastes. The distance, the diversity of the environments and media did not inhibit their shared appreciation of the display. We suggest that a more fruitful way of looking at mixed reality environments in museums is to treat all media – new and old – as potentially equal resources in the course of interaction.

This concept is further supported by another point in the dialogue: the moment where the two friends decided to follow each other. Participants in the trials often followed each other in the course of their visit. Remote participants followed their local friends around; they also invited them to displays or suggested points of interest to them. Local participants invited their friends to come to where they were in the gallery, and shared recommendations on where to go next. Social conduct supported their interaction in and through physical and digital environments, and facilitated the blending of media and environments in one common activity. The participants appeared willing to follow their friends regardless of the media they were using, passing the "leading role" among them. Although one might expect the on-site exhibition to have primary impact on people's choices, we believe that participants often treated all environments as equal resources for interaction as long as they supported the activity at hand.

Furthermore, the support of social cues in the mixed reality environment created a sense of togetherness and engagement throughout the visit, which was highly valued by the participants in the debriefing interviews: "It would actually be nice to share opinions as you were looking rather than sat down and have a coffee afterwards to talk about what you've seen. A bit more engaged ...". We, however, feel that, in many cases, social interaction was favoured above individual engagement with the museum displays. In our initial studies of collocated visitors we had established that collaborative exploration of displays is based both on strong personal engagement and on social interaction. We believe that mixed reality environments, like the one presented in this paper, would benefit from focusing equally on attracting and sustaining personal engagement with the exhibition along with the support of group collaboration. One way of achieving this is by further exploring and exploiting the individual characteristics and affordances of each environment, for example by introducing complementary asymmetries in the quantity and type of information, e.g. having historical information about a painting presented to one person while another contributes technical information about its production. We believe that a design approach towards a diverse but mutually complementing physical and digital museum design would also fit with visitors' expectations as an off-site visitor said: "that would be really good. That's what I expected. I expected that I would have more text so I could look up and tell you more things than you would be able to get."

Practical considerations

We have discussed the social interaction among local and remote friends in a museum exhibition, and presented examples of both navigation around the exhibition and lively discussion around displays. In this section, our attention shifts to practical considerations regarding the application and maintenance of mixed reality technology in museum settings. Mixed reality environments may enhance visitor's experience but they also introduce practical challenges. This section explores two aspects of the challenge: the ecology of the museum environment and issues of maintenance and updating.

The remote participants, free of constraints usually imposed by the museum's sheer materiality as well as the corresponding social etiquette, were able to explore the displays and the environment in a highly individual manner. Technology enabled them to do things impossible by human standards, for instance passing through walls, as well as things incongruous with museum customs, such as racing each other. In the interviews, most of the remote participants mentioned this kind of freedom as one of the advantages of the experience. They were, however, aware of the fact that the person in the gallery was accountable for her behaviour not only among the members of the group but also other visitors. The unexpected navigation choices e.g. radical changes of direction, *impromptu* disruption of other visitors' field of view and so forth, was the most noticeable change in the visiting manner of the on-site participants. In the interviews, local visitors confirmed they did not feel intimidated by this freedom in the course of the trial, they expressed, however, concerns that it might be proved impractical in crowded exhibitions. Based on our experience with technology, we anticipate that subtler behaviours are usually developed as users become familiar with systems over longer or more regular periods of use. Nevertheless, the impact social interaction among on-site and off-site visitors might have on the navigational ecology of the gallery is worth revisiting.

Furthermore, hybrid exhibits that enable social interaction around and about displays also impose maintenance challenges to museums. Although asymmetries in the content appeared fruitful and often sparked further exploration, the hybrid character of the exhibits effectively means that changes in one environment should be reflected in the others so people can orientate themselves towards the same display. In our studies we found out that asymmetries in content were tolerated better by participants unlike asymmetries in the spatial representation, which almost unmistakably lead to confusion, disorientation and distrust of the technology. We emphasise that such asymmetries have to be carefully designed, just as any other exhibition feature would be. The cost and effort of creating and maintaining multiple media, and correspondences and asymmetries between them, suggest that mixed reality technologies may be especially suited to permanent exhibitions that do not change often or where changes are controlled and can be easily reflected in all modes of experience.

Conclusion

Technology in museums is not only about presenting information but also about supporting social interaction. The advent of wireless communications makes remote communication possible, but we have argued here that it may also be desirable since it can support social interaction that enriches exploration, appreciation and interpretation of collections. While there are undoubted costs of design and maintenance of new technologies and associated materials for display, we suggest that trends in computing and telephone technology will make such interaction possible among local and remote visitors. Such technology may, therefore, offer practical means to enhance the accessibility of collections and the educational activities of an institution.

References

Aoki, P. M., Grinter, R. E., et al. (2002) "Sotto Voce: Exploring the Interplay of Conversation and Mobile Audio Spaces", in *Proceedings of CHI 2002*, pp. 431–438.

Baxandall, M. (1987) *Patterns of Intention: On the Historical Explanation of Pictures*, Yale University Press, New Haven.

Borysewicz, S. (1998) "Networked Media: The Experience is Closer than You Think", *The Virtual and the Real: Media in the Museum*, A. Mintz, ed., American Association of Museums, Washington, pp. 103–117.

Brown, B., MacColl, I., et al. (2003) "Lessons from The Lighthouse: Collaboration in a shared mixed reality system", in *Proceedings of CHI 2003*, pp. 577–584.

Cunliffe, D., Kritou, E., et al. (2001) "Usability Evaluation for Museum Web Sites", *Museum Management and Curatorship*, 19(3): 229–252.

Exploratorium (2001) "Electronic Guidebook Forum", Exploratorium, San Francisco.

Falk, J. H., and Dierking, L. D. (1992) *The Museum Experience*, Whalesback Books, Washington, D.C.

Falk, J. H., and Dierking, L. D. (2000) *Learning from Museums: Visitor Experiences and the Making of Meaning*, Altamira Press, Walnut Creek.

Fleck, M., Frid, M., et al. (2002) "From Informing to Remembering: Ubiquitous Systems in Interactive Museums", *Pervasive Computing* (April–June), pp. 13–21.

Galani, A. (2003) "Mixed Reality Museum Visits: Using New Technologies to Support Co-visiting for Local and Remote Visitors", *Museological Review Extra, special issue*, 10: 1–15.

Galani, A., and Chalmers, M. (2004) "Production of Pace as Collaborative Activity", in *Extended Abstracts of CHI 2004*, pp. 1417–1420.

Garfinkel, H. (1967) *Studies in Ethnomethodology*, Polity Press, Cambridge.

Heath, C., Luff, P., et al. (2002) "Crafting Participation: Designing Ecologies, Configuring Experience", *Visual Communication*, 1(1): 9–33.

Hindmarsh, J. (2002) "Creating Assemblies: Aboard the *Ghost Ship*", in *Proceedings of CSCW 2002*.

Hood, M. G. (1983) "Staying Away: Why People Choose Not to Visit Museums", *Museum News*, 1983 (April), pp. 50–56.

Mintz, A. (1998) "Media and Museums: A Museum Perspective", *The Virtual and the Real: Media in the Museum*, A. Mintz, ed., American Association of Museums, Washington, pp. 19–35.

Mirapaul, M. (1999) "At this Virtual Museum, You can Bring a Date", *The New York Times on the Web*, http://www.nytimes.com.

Oppermann, R., Specht, M., et al. (1999) "Hippie: A Nomadic Information System", in *Proceedings of Handheld & Ubiquitous Computing*, pp. 330–333.

Roussou, M., Trahanias, P., et al. (2001) "Experiences from the Use of a Robotic Avatar in a Museum Setting", in *Proceedings of VAST01*, pp. 153–160.

Thomas, S. (1998) "Mediated Realities: A Media Perspective", *The Virtual and the Real: Media in the Museum*, A. Mintz, ed., American Association of Museums, Washington, pp. 1–17.

vom Lehn, D. (2002) "Exhibiting Interaction: Conduct and Participation in Museums and Galleries", Ph.D. Thesis, King's College, University of London, London.

vom Lehn, D., and Heath, C. (2003) "Displacing the Object: Mobile Technologies and Interpretive Resources", in *Proceedings of ICHIM 2003*.

vom Lehn, D., Heath, C., et al. (2001) "Exhibiting Interaction: Conduct of Collaboration in Museums and Galleries", *Symbolic Interaction*, 24(2): 189–216.

Walter, T. (1996) "From Museum to Morgue? Electronic Guides in Roman Bath", *Tourism Management*, 17(4): 241–245.

Chapter 17

Museums Outside Walls: mobile phones and the museum in the everyday

Konstantinos Arvanitis

Introduction

Ever since the Internet has been introduced into museums, it is often repeated that Andre Malraux's notion of the museum without walls (Malraux 1967) has met its best realisation. A 'museum without walls' stands for a museum that makes its information and knowledge available both to on-site and remote visitors. Accordingly, the Internet, along with related technological applications, has provided a materialisation of the above metaphor. As Antonio M. Battro says, 'we are witnessing a new transformation in the meaning of a work of art and the birth of the virtual museum, a new kind of museum which is the product of the prodigious evolution of the imaginary museum' (Battro 1999).

Museums have, also, included mobile media in their effort to create a 'museum without walls'. Beside the use of audio guides, PDAs and mobile phones inside galleries to enhance visitors' experience of collections, museums have, also, experimented with mobile media to enable remote access on museum information. Led by objectives such as outreach, dissemination of knowledge, access and social inclusion, museums are currently using mobile media as an alternative means to reproduce, distribute and popularise the museum content.

In other words, museums treat mobile media as vehicles to enter everyday life, by offering their users the opportunity to access the museum content remotely in their own space and time (at home, at work, or in leisure). No doubt, such an effort changes the occasional nature of the museum visit and transforms the museum information and knowledge into a portable commodity, available at any time and in any space. However, it does not take full advantage of the opportunities that mobile

Source: IADIS International Conference: Mobile Learning 2005, Qawra, Malta. Unpublished.

media may offer to museums. Drawing on excerpts from fieldwork, the research provided here discusses the role that mobile media may play in museums. It particularly focuses on the use of mobile media outside museums, rather than the in-gallery applications. On the basis of current museological developments and Michel de Certeau's perception of everyday life, this research suggests that mobile media can be used not only to bring museums into the everyday, but also to create a gateway for the everyday knowledge to enter museums.

'Museum without walls': mobile media and museums

Museums increasingly engage with the opportunities that mobile media may offer outside their walls. Mobile context-aware technology and GPS have already been used at an experimental level in cultural tourism to enable personalised learning (Cheverst et al. 2000) and co-visiting among users in different locations (Brown et al. 2005). Additionally, commercial products such as m-ToGuide (http://www.motorolatele. com/MOTOnow/) use mobile media to offer information to one's current location and personal interests. The purpose of such applications coincides partly with this conference's statement, that is, 'to develop ... understanding at the spot, just when it is needed ... so that ... learning moments happen when we are ready for it' (http://www.iadis.org/ml2005/). Such a perspective is in line with current museum practices that attempt to use both traditional and new means to take museum information and expertise out of the museum walls and into the everyday life of people. It, also, agrees with broadly accepted museological trends that emphasise the role of visitors' personal background and context in the process of meaning-making and learning in museums (Silvermann 1995; Falk and Dierking 2000).

Although the role of mobile media in museums is still under negotiation and development, the above-described applications neither take advantage of the full potential of mobile technology nor respond critically to current museological needs. In using mobile media as receivers and disseminators of museum information and knowledge, museums aim to extend their physical and conceptual presence. They create 'museum moments' away from the museum building, during which users can access the museum content remotely. Indeed, this agrees with the notion of the 'museum without walls', as already described. However, it does not contribute towards the enrichment of the idea of the museum.

Eilean Hooper-Greenhill has summarised the discussion around the evolving museum concept and has introduced the idea of the post-museum. In her book *Museums and the Interpretation of Visual Culture*, Hooper-Greenhill (2000) suggested that we move away from the modernist museum of the nineteenth century, which was imagined mainly as a building transmitting authoritative factual information through the means of exhibition, and experience the emerging of a new museum model, the post-museum. According to Hooper-Greenhill, the post-museum is a site of mutuality, where knowledge is constructed, rather than transmitted, through the account of multiple subjectivities and identities. In the post-museum the curator's voice is one voice among many others that are incorporated to create a constructive polyphony of views, experiences and values. Accordingly, the post-museum tries to involve the emotions and the imaginations of visitors. In the post-museum, the exhibition is only one form of museum communication, which is enriched with other communication means to fit with interpretations of objects and visitors' needs.

In the light of Hooper-Greenhill's concept of post-museum one might argue that current mobile museum applications repeat the one-way transmission of knowledge of the modern museum, rather than incorporating other voices, as suggested in the post-museum. Mobile media have been seen primarily as extensions of the museum content into the everyday environment. However, they could, also, be used in the opposite way: to bring the voices of the everyday into the museum.

The value of looking at everyday life and its knowledge has been acknowledged by sociological theory and in particular by Michel de Certeau. de Certeau (1988) argues that because of the 'everydayness' of daily life, people tend to give meanings to their surroundings in their own way, which may or may not agree with the meanings these surroundings are intended to have. However, this everyday knowledge should not be dismissed as trivial or of no use, because, in fact, it reveals the way we understand and interpret our everyday surroundings. Seen from this perspective, the everyday becomes extremely relevant to Hooper-Greenhill's idea of the post-museum and can provide a practical interpretation of her statement: 'the museum in the future may be imagined as a process or an experience. It is, however, not limited to its own walls, but moves a set of process into the spaces, the concerns and the ambitions of communities' (Hooper-Greenhill 2000:152).

Indeed, mobile media could provide the means to access and reveal the everyday. Been regarded as everyday technology, mobile media allow museums not only to create exceptional 'museum moments' in the everyday, but attempt to disclose the largely inaccessible everyday knowledge, that usually goes unnoticed. In other words, mobile media may make 'audible and visible' the knowledge and understandings that happen in the course of the everyday life. Respectively, the conference's question how 'institutionalised learning can benefit from mobile learning devices' can find – within the museum context – an answer by augmenting institutionalised museum knowledge with the ephemeral, everyday knowledge of its users. In accessing a range of understandings that belong to the ephemerality of everyday life, yet conveying deeper understandings and perceptions of material culture, museums may enhance the way they interpret material culture and provide richer experiences to both on-site and remote visitors.

'Museum outside walls': camera phones and the access of everyday life – an investigation

Towards the exploration of the potential of popular mobile media, to access, reveal and communicate the everyday knowledge to museums, a qualitative investigation involving camera phones was undertaken in Thessaloniki, Greece in summer 2004. Ten young residents of Thessaloniki (all university students) were invited to use their own camera phones to capture and communicate through MMS (Multimedia Messaging Service) the way they perceive and use three archaeological monuments that are part of the city's urban landscape.[1] The aim of this empirical study was to investigate to what extent camera phones can be used to access and reveal meanings that people make about archaeological monuments in their everyday life.

Camera phones were chosen because of their popularity among the Greek population (Giaglis and Vrehopoulos 2004). They are, also, becoming an everyday technology, 'compatible' with everyday life: camera phones are personal and portable and, therefore, they can 'follow' people's daily lives and enable an intuitive record of daily situations. They are, also, an increasingly affordable technology. Furthermore, no particular modification was required for the participants to use the camera phones. The latter was a crucial point in relation to the notion of the everyday life, as discussed earlier: that a common technology is used by common people to capture and reveal common interpretations.[2] The participants were not asked to send any particular number of messages in specific days. Instead, they were encouraged to send MMS messages only when their everyday routes were bringing them close to the monuments. Focus group and semi-structured interviews followed the initial study.

The analysis of the collected material suggests that MMS messages have revealed daily events, actions, behaviours or traces of the everyday, which influence the way people understand the monuments. MMS were used both to document an everyday behaviour or action and to express more repetitive understandings of the monuments.

One MMS pictured the arch of Galerius with a banner attached on the monument's protective fence. The banner is an invitation to an anti-racial festival in Thessaloniki. In this case, the participant chose to capture a temporary 'image' of the monument with a banner next to it. This MMS connects the ephemeral banner to the permanent monument, acknowledging this odd coexistence between the two in the space and time of everyday life. The text of the MMS emphasises that contradictory relation: it implies that the archaeological monument is not an appropriate place for a banner to be hanged, by acknowledging that the 'the fight for the rights is everywhere', even next to an archaeological monument. This MMS presents, then, the monument as the background of an activity not directly related to the monument's archaeological nature, revealing the extent that the monument is interweaved in the everyday life of the city. Another MMS shows part of the ruins of the ancient walls in Thessaloniki and a pedestrian bridge over them. The text of the MMS tells a short story of a daily situation: the difficulty of pedestrians to walk across the ruins in rainy days when mud covered the place. The participant sees the installation of the bridge in relation to this daily problem. It interprets the bridge over the ruins as a 'dry' pathway for passers-by, ignoring any issues of the ruins' protection and preservation that the bridge may serve. This underestimation of the preservation of the particular archaeological remains is further emphasised with the disregarding phrase 'the hell with these ruins'. This example shows a demystification of any cultural heritage values assigned to the monument in view of the problem it has created for the people's daily movement around the city. It seems, then, that in this context of everyday life, the ruins are primarily obstacles that need to be overcome.

Consequently, these two MMS messages have shown the reflexive role of the monuments: how they attract or discourage daily interactions and how daily routines overrule the monuments' distinct qualities. The MMS photos are not the 'postcard' photos or tourist pictures of archaeological monuments. They are a mirror of the everyday practice, which the monuments are part of. In everyday life, archaeological monuments are not primarily gazed at or admired for their direct connection to the past; instead, they are the scenery of everyday life. In addition, the MMS texts have added a personal interpretation to these collective daily images. As a result, the MMS have not only offered everyday meanings of the archaeological monuments, but also disclosed the reality of multiple and diverse interpretations of shared daily interactions with the monuments.

Furthermore, this everyday knowledge that usually goes unnoticed because of its familiarity, or underestimation, shows the appropriation of the monuments in the daily practices of the lived space. The MMS have acknowledged and communicated such everyday meanings of the monuments, offering potentially an enrichment of the traditional, archaeological knowledge that museums usually offer. In fact, such MMS messages are not just an enhancement of the museum's knowledge, but also a stimulus for people's learning process: It is worthwhile mentioning that the participants of the study got interested in the monuments by going through the process of creating a MMS message, as the follow-up focus groups have indicated. Their 'look' through the phone's camera, as well as the content of the text have stimulated their interest in the actual monuments: i.e. the monuments as part of the city's cultural heritage. Sending a MMS has activated the 'gaze' of the monuments that is, usually, 'deactivated' in the route of everyday life.

However, the use of the particular technology has presented some limitations. Although participants did not appear to have problems in acknowledging an everyday situation, they indicated that they felt uncomfortable in using the camera of their phone to capture an image of it. A sense of intrusion or embarrassment was identified in their responses regarding their experience of the project. Moreover, it was clear that limitations of the particular technology affected both the process of image capturing and the textual content of the MMS messages: poor image quality and restrictions in the number of characters per text message (no more than 70 characters) were identified as limitations. Further analysis of the data collected during the empirical study will reveal more about the use of camera phones to acknowledge and communicate the everyday meanings of the monuments. It is also anticipated that this research will contribute towards the understanding of the potential as well as the drawbacks of mobile media to connect museums and people through the context of everyday life.

Conclusion

Mobile media can, indeed, contribute to Malraux's 'museum without walls' by disseminating the museum knowledge outside the physical walls of the museum. However, this does not bring down the conceptual walls that museums have. By treating mobile media as 'couriers' of museum knowledge, rather than agents of a dialogic communication with users, museums contribute to further establishing their separation from the world outside their walls.

Drawing on the concepts of the post-museum and everyday life, as discussed in Hooper-Greenhill (2000) and Michel de Certeau (1988) and using examples from a qualitative investigation of the use of mobile phones, this research suggests that museums can use mobile media not just to leave their walls to enter the everyday, but also to disclose the everyday that usually goes unnoticed. The concept of 'post-museum' provides the necessary theoretical basis from a museological point of view, while the everyday nature of popular mobile devices, such as camera phones, can put theory into practice. The everyday is a site of multiplicity, where people's perceptions of their surroundings take the form of ephemeral knowledge. Mobile media could 'give a voice' to everyday life and enable museums to open up to the everyday of their users. In that respect, museums might be able to access the fabric of daily existence that makes people who they are, how they see and understand the world around them. If we cannot really have 'museums *without* walls', we can at least work towards 'museums *outside* walls'.

Acknowledgement

I am grateful to Anna Catalani and Areti Galani for their comments and suggestions on this paper.

Notes

1   The archaeological monuments were: the arch of Galerius (*c.* 304 AC), the ruins of Galerius' complex on Dimitrios Gounaris St. (*c.* 304 AC) and the ruins of the city walls on Melenikou street, all in Thessaloniki, Greece.

2   Projects, such as Urban Tapestries (http://urbantapestries.net/) and Annotate Space (www.annotatespace.com) deal as well with accessing and publishing multimedia content related to the everyday life of cities, but they use custom-made mobile devices, not yet widely available.

References

Annotate Space, www.annotatespace.com.

Battro, A. M., 1999. From Malraux's Imaginary Museum to the Virtual Museum. http://www.byd.com.ar/vm99sep.htm.

Brown, B., et al., 2005. Sharing the square: collaborative visiting in the city streets. *Proceedings of CHI 2005*. Portland, Oregon, USA.

Cheverst, K., et al., 2000. Developing a context aware electronic tourist guide: Some issues and experiences. *Proceedings of ACM CHI '00*. The Hague, The Netherlands, pp. 17–24.

de Certeau, M., 1988, *The Practice of Everyday Life* (trans. by Steven Rendall). University of California Press, Berkeley, Los Angeles.

Falk, J.H and Dierking, L.D., 2000. *Learning from Museums: Visitor Experiences and the Making of Meaning*. AltaMira Press, California.

Giaglis, G., and Vrehopoulos, M., 2004. *Worldwide Mobile Internet Survey, 3rd Round, Mobile Internet: Η Ελληνική Πραλματικότητα* [The Greek Reality]. Athens University of Economics and Business, Athens, Greece.

Hooper-Greenhill, E., 2000. *Museums and the Interpretation of Visual Culture*. Routledge, London and New York.

Malraux, A., 1967. *Museum Without Walls*. Secker and Warburg, London.

m-ToGuide. http://www.motorolatele.com/MOTOnow/.

Silverman, L. H., 1995. Visitor Meaning-Making in Museums for a New Age. *Curator*, Vol. 38, pp. 161–170.

Urban Tapestries, http://urbantapestries.net/.

Access: ability, usability and connectivity

Introduction to Part Three

Ross Parry

I N PART ONE AND PART TWO we have seen a number of ways in which digital media have made museum collections more accessible to their audiences. Whether through databases, websites or mobile media, or even the 'mixed realities' of Chapter 16, the previous discussions have illustrated technologies, developments and rationales that have characterised computing's impact on museum access.

On first reading, it would perhaps seem irrefutable that digital technology has provided the means for more efficient, intelligent and interoperable records management; for more blended and extended notions of on-site and off-site visiting experiences; and for more varied modes and opportunities of user participation and collaboration. Yet, as we shall now see, the mere presence of these technologies is not enough. A museum website may be *available*, but it is only *accessible* if users have the connectivity to it. Intra-gallery interactives and extra-gallery media may be on offer but they are only of use if their design facilitates usability. Collections databases may be outward-facing but they are only a genuine public resource if their content (in whatever rendition) is accessible to all users of all abilities. It is this responsibility of access to which Part Three now turns.

In Chapter 18, a former archaeologist at the National Museum of Kenya, Lorna Abungu writes as Executive Director of AFRICOM – the International Council of African Museums. The discussion (first published in *Museum International* in 2002) alerts us to the expanses of the 'digital divide' and the obstacles presented by the telecommunications infrastructures of many developing world nations. The paper provides a salutary reminder not only of the very different degrees of connectivity that can exist in different international contexts but also the assumptions that can all too easily pervade digital heritage literature. Abungu keeps us mindful of the critical importance of cultural context within any discussion of museum, technology and audience.

In Chapters 19 and 20, Kevin Carey adds yet further contexts, this time regarding disability and impairment. Both articles are previously unpublished; the first is based on a paper presented to the *UK Museums on the Web* national conference (in Leicester, 2004) convened by the Museums Computer Group, the second a re-evaluation written for this volume four years later. Carey begins by reflecting on Helen Petrie's work on how difficult it is for some users (disabled by poor design) to engage with websites, and makes a vociferous demand for 'just access' online. Notice, however, how four years later Carey's priorities for culture and disabled people have shifted. His 're-evaluation', as well as appearing more politicised (emphasising more strongly the legal question of equity and rights), sees the future less in the adherence simply to Web accessibility guidelines but rather in more creative use and exploration of 'digital plasticity' and the 'plurality of interface devices'. It is a call, in other words, for alternative rather than remedial media and provision.

In this way Carey shares a common point of view with the authors of Chapter 21 – Brian Kelly, Lawrie Phipps and Caro Howell. They, like Carey, make a case for a more holistic and circumspect approach to making museum media accessible to audiences of all abilities. Rather than slavishly making all online media compliant to the highest levels of accessibility, the authors make a case of some Web-based learning resources being judged in a wider context of institutional provision. In doing so they offer an alternative that might release museum website designers from strict compliance to accessibility minutiae, whilst still maintaining a strong commitment to Carey's 'just access'.

The final two chapters of Part Three explore further these themes of usability and design. Chapter 22, offers an insight into some of the issues confronted by many smaller museums in developing and maintaining a website. Since 2001, when the paper was originally published in *Museum Management and Curatorship*, the world of Web publishing has been transformed by freely available and highly flexible blogging tools as well as open source content management systems. But even if some of the challenges of coding and hosting may have recently been allayed for many smaller museums, Cunliffe, Kritou and Tudhope's article is still valuable in highlighting the limitations inherent in the non-professional Web development. In Chapter 23, Ranjit Makkuni presents one final influence on usability – *culture*. Originally presented at an international digital heritage conference (ICHIM), this paper suggests how an awareness of the aesthetics, history and culture of a nation can be reflected in its own chosen approach to digital development. It offers an image of 'culture conscious product design', where digital provision is imagined and engineered in a culturally specific and contingent way. A model of access built upon localisation and self-reflection, this is 'culturally rooted computing'.

Chapter 18

Access to Digital Heritage in Africa: bridging the digital divide

Lorna Abungu

Introduction

In most countries in Africa, museums were established during the colonial period and were modelled upon Western museums. This was understandable, as they were created by the colonialists themselves. Many museums exhibited cultural heritage (or ethnographic) objects and natural history specimens for a rich élite audience. Decades later, the African scene has changed: African countries are no longer ruled by colonial powers, and visitors to museums are not just the élite of society. This socio-political change and the emergence of New Information Communication Technologies (NICTs) in many African countries are, however, not yet adequately reflected in the museums. Many of the national museums are still clinging to the old style of exhibition (e.g. dusty objects hidden in glass cases), despite the changing needs of the African society that they now represent.

Changing needs

What is the role of a museum, especially in relation to the needs of the communities they represent? For an art museum in Europe, the role is very clearly defined. For museums in Africa, this is a question that was asked as far back as 1991. Museum professionals from the entire African continent met at a series of meetings in Benin, Ghana and Togo, organized by the International Council of Museums (ICOM). ICOM's president at the time was Alpha Oumar Konaré, until recently the president of Mali. At the meetings, Konaré very eloquently pointed out that it is now time 'to

Source: *Museum International*, vol. 54, no. 3, 2002, pp. 29–34.

eliminate the Western model for museums in Africa so that new methods for the preservation and promotion of Africa's cultural heritage can be allowed to flourish'. He
acknowledged, however, that this could not be done 'if the realms of education and
culture remain isolated from each other, as long as the population, especially in rural
areas, remains marginalized and even excluded' (ICOM, 1992).

As rural populations continue to be marginalized in many African countries, it
has become the responsibility of the museums to break down their walls and, quite
often, literally go out to the people. In the face of rapid globalization, museums in
Africa – despite limited financial and human resources – are trying to become more
socially relevant. They are increasingly trying to jump on the bandwagon to embrace
ICTs, and adapt them to the needs of the communities, so as to give them greater
access to their heritage.

Addressing the needs

No one will doubt that the basic priorities of most African governments are health
and education. Culture rarely gets the attention it deserves, and it is unfortunate that
it is not appreciated as the important tool it is for guiding national development policies. As more and more African museums are realizing that they can use the national
heritage to address social, economic and even political issues, culture may eventually
be accorded its rightful place in government priorities.

In South Africa, the Apartheid Museum, District Six Museum and the South
End Museum all address the atrocities of the Apartheid era, and serve as a common
ground for understanding the past. These 'new' African museums arose because of
the need from within the community to share their stories with each other and the
rest of the world. In Mali and Senegal, museums dedicated to the role of women in
society have emerged as powerful forces to address gender issues and raise awareness
of the role of women as the backbone of contemporary society. Specialized museums
for contemporary art, and even telecommunications, are emerging throughout the
continent, from Morocco to Mozambique.

The National Museums of Kenya and the National Museum of Mali are currently
undergoing major restructuring programmes that will result in increased exhibition
space and improved and modernized exhibitions.

These examples – as well as the establishment of organizations such as the
West African Museum Programme (WAMP) in Dakar, Senegal, and the International Council of African Museums (AFRICOM) in Nairobi, Kenya – clearly show
a determination by African museums to break away from the traditional Western
mould. With the emergence of these new museums aiming to be more relevant to
the communities they serve, also comes an attempt to embrace new technologies.

New technologies: facing the challenges

It is easy to talk about 'embracing new technologies', but the reality on the African
continent needs to be considered. A 1998 Nua Internet Survey showed that more

than half the Internet users worldwide are in the United States, despite the fact that the country makes up less than 5 per cent of the total world population. Surprisingly, by 1999, of the fifty-three African countries, fifty had direct Internet access (Black 1999); today, the figure may be slightly higher.

Yet while many African countries may have access, this does not mean that the population has access. On a continent where, in most countries, 80 per cent of the population live in rural areas, without running water or electricity, Internet access is but a dream. For those in towns who do have access to NICTs, Internet access can still be a hurdle (slow connections, expensive dial-up, etc.).

A major obstacle to African countries gaining access to digital information is the national telecommunications infrastructure. Even as developing countries are experiencing rapid extension and modernization of their telecommunications systems, most networks in Africa are analogue, and many sectors are highly unreliable, especially during rainy seasons. The Internet is dependent upon the quality of the underlying telecommunications infrastructure, and so the poor quality of the network still remains a basic impediment to rapid development in this area (Abungu et al. 1999). With such obstacles, how can Africans gain better access to digital information, and how can African museums help to bridge the 'Digital Divide'?

While the above is important, the obstacles to digital access are not only technical. There is also a psychological obstacle to New Information Communication Technologies. Within the heritage sector in Africa, many of the 'old guard' have refused to embrace NICTs due to a simple fear of change. Often, neither the benefits of NICTs are understood, nor their relevance to the heritage sector.

Bridging the gap

Africa's population can be estimated at almost 750 million; however, there are less than 20 million phone lines – fewer than in Manhattan or Tokyo. Of those lines, 80 per cent are in only six countries. In 1999 it was estimated that there were only 1 million Internet users on the entire African continent, compared with 10.5 million in the United Kingdom (Black 1999). With these statistics, the idea of bridging the 'Digital Divide' looks ever more difficult.

At the National Museums of Kenya (NMK), in Nairobi, the Computer Department has traditionally been used for data management for such mundane purposes as personnel and payroll records. When, in 1998, a few computer department staff utilized their self-taught HTML skills, Kenya's natural and cultural heritage made a splash on the World Wide Web. The NMK website (www.museums.or.ke) made a huge step in the region by putting Kenya's heritage on the world map. Now the entire world could share what hundreds of thousands of museum visitors see every year. Connected Kenyans throughout the country – however few – could also access their own digital heritage like others around the world.

The NMK's experience showed that African museums entering the twenty-first century must not only gear their efforts towards dynamic exhibitions, but must also keep abreast of new developments in technology. Among some of the latest technologies positively affecting museum operations globally are multimedia and communications. Many museums and museum associations around the world – even in Africa – are connected to the Internet, which has made the sharing and exchange of ideas and information much easier.

The Agence de la Francophonie, under the direction of the Director of the National Museum of Mali, produced a fascinating interactive CD-ROM that takes visitors on a virtual tour of the museum; it also guides them through the rich archaeological and cultural heritage of the country. A South African initiative joining several African countries, 'Culture Africa Network' (CAN), had the aim of developing an interactive cultural database for distribution on CD-ROM and on the Internet. While the project has stalled in some countries, Kenya's own subproject, 'Kenya-CAN' – which has received funding from the Ford Foundation – has resulted in a colourful, interactive and stimulating CD-ROM of Kenya's cultural heritage. The digital database has been further developed into a touch-screen module, which will soon be launched at the Nairobi Museum.

As African museums develop more community-oriented education programs and take these programs to the people, the potential to reach disadvantaged rural communities has increased. Dynamic, interactive education programs are being developed not only to teach the children, but to encourage them to think critically and analytically, and to introduce them to the reality of globalization. Efforts like these are indeed going some way in bridging the 'Digital Divide' and bringing access to digital heritage closer to the people.

Regional and international initiatives

While the actual facts and figures still place Africa at a disadvantage as concerns accessing digital information, there is a ray of hope. Many museums in Africa are facing up to the challenges of the twenty-first century: decreased government funding, low visitor statistics, stagnant exhibitions, high staff turnover, among others. Regional and international initiatives are helping African museums to face these challenges.

The International Council of Museums (ICOM) realized that the needs of African museums were particular. Its AFRICOM Programme was born as an outcome of the series of meetings in Benin, Ghana and Togo in November 1991. This was a very successful programme, and in 1999 the Constituent Assembly of AFRICOM convened in Lusaka, Zambia, and resolved to establish AFRICOM as a pan-African organization.

AFRICOM today is an international NGO registered by the Government of Kenya, with its headquarters in the capital city, Nairobi. AFRICOM in its new form seeks to contribute to the positive development of African societies by encouraging the role of museums as generators of culture and as agents of cultural cohesion. It aims to do this through developing projects that facilitate exchange and the sharing of experiences. By building an expansive network of museums and museum professionals, AFRICOM will be better placed to serve as a dynamic resource for cultural heritage on the continent.

In 1984, the Swedish National Committee of ICOM 'gave birth' to the Swedish–African Museum Programme (SAMP). Based in Stockholm, SAMP has, since its inception, been spearheading a unique programme of exchange and 'twinning' between African and Swedish museums. Among its achievements, the programme initiated a project to get more museums in Africa connected to the Internet.

Bodies such as AFRICOM, WAMP and SAMP – together with partners around the world – must continue to develop projects and seek funding to encourage and promote access to digital information on cultural heritage on the continent. Only in this way can the gap between the 'information rich' and the 'information poor' be filled.

Conclusion

This article has briefly discussed the origins of African museums and their development into the twenty-first century. At present, out of 357 known museums throughout the African continent (including the Indian Ocean islands), only seventy-five have – on an institutional level – at least basic Internet access for e-mail. While this shows an understanding of the need to embrace new technologies for the promotion of our national heritage, it also shows that more effort is needed to bridge the 'Digital Divide' in the heritage sector in Africa.

At a recent UNESCO initiative in preparation for the World Summit on the Information Society, participants stressed the important role that the non-governmental sector plays in the economic area, in education, in sciences, in culture and in the media and in the building up of the Information Society. A series of basic principles and resolutions – which aims to bridge the gap between 'information rich' and 'information poor' – were adopted and will hopefully be recognized at the World Summit in Geneva in 2003 and in Tunisia in 2004. The meeting clearly recognized the role of the heritage sector in Africa in advancing the Information Society and urged African governments to respect digital culture in all dimensions, and recognize and support the role of cultural organizations such as libraries, museums and archives as essential actors in the Information Society.

There are great obstacles to be overcome, but with growing awareness and respect for the 'Digital Revolution' in Africa, more people may soon be having improved access to digital information and therefore the digital heritage of the continent and the world at large.

References

Abungu, L., Monda, L., Ombachi, G. *Connectivity, Collaboration and Culture: Challenges of African Museums on the Web*. Paper presented at 'Museums and the Web', New Orleans, USA, 1999.

Black, J. Losing Ground Bit by Bit. *BBC News Online: Information Rich, Information Poor*, 1999.

ICOM (ed.). *What Museums for Africa: Heritage in the Future*. Paris. International Council of Museums, 1992.

UNESCO. Resolutions of the Meeting: 'Preparing the World Summit on the Information Society: Consultation with African Non-governmental Organizations'. Bamako, Mali, 26–27 May, 2002.

Chapter 19

My Dream of an Accessible Web Culture for Disabled People

Kevin Carey

Earlier this year when the e-Access Bulletin celebrated its fiftieth monthly issue it asked me to say how my ICT life had changed during the past four years. Sad to report, my PC and consumer electronics access had got worse, my difficulty with telephone access was static and only in the cookery department had my life improved with a talking microwave cooker and weighing scales. This is the context for any consideration of the Web. So when I use the word "Dream" in the title of my presentation I am talking literally; I don't mean long-term vision, I mean something as improbable as a dream.

In the context of a general access agenda I am not sold on the idea that because we can achieve interactivity we have to use it all the time. I think we need a much more purpose-driven, rational, market approach to information transactions with people. Very few of us produce more information than we consume; most of us only produce the kind of information that responds to questions and could be supplied through choosing 1–9 on a numeric keypad; so those who need a qwerty keyboard to produce information from scratch are not the norm round which everything should be designed. The book was not interactive; classical broadcasting, theatre, music performance, dance, are not interactive. So the first part of my vision, as opposed to my dream, is that we need to focus much more strongly on the new medium of digital broadcasting to meet the information needs of citizens. There are problems for me with the accessibility of remote controllers and tuners but these can be overcome relatively simply.

If we are sensible about why we need interactivity in citizen transactions, then we are much more likely to think clearly about our market; well, that is the theory. In fact web design is still in the hands of the aesthetes and the engineers; people even

Source: UK Museums and the Web Conference 2004, University of Leicester. Unpublished.

in large organisations rarely ask: "What is it for?" "Why do we need a website?" "Who will use it?"

You will hear how difficult it is for disabled people to access websites. I used to think that the problem lay with the economic or the demographic case. I no longer believe this. I do not think it much matters what demographic or economic case you make, those who build websites think they are an extension of the media industry; they do not trace their inheritance to the manufacture of graph paper, they are only a step away from television.

Rather than generalised problems, I want to concentrate on my own particular requirements and, again, ask yourselves whether it is me or the designers who are being unreasonable or unprofessional:

1 *Define taxonomy* carefully so that people can find things through simple, logical navigation.
2 To that end, use *the (7 + or − 2) rule* so that in complex arrays or searches there are no fewer than five and no more than nine elements.
3 If these first two have not been observed, it is vital to *enable cursor establishment from the keyboard*; without this, shopping, form filling and using key words in search boxes is impossible.
4 *Allow adjustability for* print font, size etc for metadata as well as data.
5 *Only use tables, frames* and other devices *for the purpose for which they were designed*.
6 Allow *exclusion of recurrent metadata*.
7 *Don't describe what you can link*.
8 *Balance aesthetics, purpose and end user requirements*.
9 *Do not slavishly digitise paper content*.
10 *Update or die*.

Here are some implications of what the more cryptic of these mean:

1 Taxonomy as a discipline is not usually combined with aesthetics but without it complex websites are useless.
2 I simply cannot imagine why such a well researched rule as (7 + or − 2) is ignored by people whose objective it is to help people to choose.
3 For people, such as blind people, who may find spatial navigation difficult, the use of keywords is essential but often a cursor cannot be established from a keyboard but requires a mouse.
4 Often you have to reach wonderfully accessible data through woodenly inaccessible metadata.
5 Often a screen reader will indicate a table with, say, five rows and four columns; you search methodically for the twenty elements but only find three. Why was the table used?
6 Most web pages have a mass of repeat data at the top of each page and sometimes new data is sandwiched between repeated data at the top and bottom; this makes using a screen reader very difficult.
7 Frequently, highly-skilled aesthetic designers write poor descriptions when good ones are readily available. If I wanted to describe the Mona Lisa, I would link to the appropriate page of the Louvre catalogue.

8 I frequently wonder whether sites were built for the pleasure of designers rather than the benefit of their organisations or users.

9 It is amazing how often digitisers just scan in a print document so that, for example, in form filling, the appropriate notes are not at the side of the operative box.

10 Updating is obvious.

So the second part of my vision, as opposed to my dream, is that:

- inter-sectoral teams of web designers will
- create sites focusing on corporate objectives and end users and
- user test sites on a representative sample of users.

I heard it said the other day that finding a representative sample of disabled people to test sites was difficult; my guess is that it's much easier if you offer to pay them. What justification is there for unemployed or poorly paid disabled people cross-subsidising government departments or major corporations. User testing should be incorporated into all estimates.

The third part of my vision is that people should get what they pay for. Again, the other day I heard someone say that accessibility might cost too much taxpayers' money; but he forgot that it is taxpayers like me who pay for the information to be created. I also pay for the products whose profits produce the funding for websites.

These three pieces of vision, then

- appropriate medium
- client- and user-centred design
- just access

are hardly controversial but they are as distant as a dream.

Why?

- People tend to travel into the future with their backs to the engine so, for example, they have not come to terms with the possibilities of digital television or broad band.
- Policy makers and marketing departments do not control the process which links their mission and vision to their media policies.
- Web design is classified as art not craft.
- Disabled people are marginal or invisible.

These are not technical but cultural problems. Our usual way for handling difficult cultural challenges is to legislate to change behaviour as a means to changing attitudes over a longer time period. To dream of statutes and court cases is an odd dream; but it's the only one I've got.

Chapter 20

My Dream of an Accessible Web Culture for Disabled People: a re-evaluation

Kevin Carey

When I went to visit the WELL Network[1] in 1990, Howard Rheingold and I disagreed about the culture and purposes of what turned out to be the World Wide Web: we agreed that it would be a paradise but his was for anarchists and mine for capitalists. Like all dichotomies – cursed be Plato! – this was false in terms of what has actually happened but it was nonetheless helpful in providing a framework for understanding what has happened. Thus, in the period of what we might call Web 1.0, the two paradises have operated in parallel and in the first decade of the twenty-first century that state is likely to continue with social networking (Web 2.0) operating in parallel with the migration of de-regulated television, both linear and on demand, to the internet. Yet I feel justified in thinking that I was more correct than Rheingold because the internet has not been immune from the general laws of competitive capitalism: enterprise designs novel products and distribution channels; and big fish eat small fish. Likewise, in spite of the plethora of digital photographs and emails sent across the planet and in spite of the blogosphere, the overall impression has been of a top-down phenomenon whereby enterprise promotes, government promulgates, the elite preaches and their counterparts consume, complete forms and carry on regardless. In the case of broadcasters and publishers this market dominance is understandable as, in contravention of Gresham's law, over two or three decades high quality material which commands repeat consumption will drive out mediocrity.

The direct result of this asymmetry, however, has been a gross failure in the education sector which has not so much spinelessly as unthinkingly (a peculiarly terrible indictment for the education sector) bought into the consumption paradigm, ignoring the warnings of Mr Micawber[2] and the forecasts of Alvin Toffler[3] that he who does not generate is lost. Inevitably, then, this consumption paradigm has had a

Source: Unpublished.

viral effect on public sector policy. Programmes in the mid-1990s to combat 'digital exclusion' or, later, to promote e-inclusion and 'social cohesion', focused almost entirely on the ability to access and process information. Thus, to take the particular case of disabled people experiencing problems with the internet, these were not articulated in such neutral terms as 'task completion' or 'peer equivalence' but were described in a purely consumer paradigm as 'accessibility' and 'usability'. Discussing these issues with politicians, one was therefore confronted with a peculiarly class-based paradox: whereas, on the one hand, computers were 'serious' and television was 'frivolous', interaction with the internet, on the other hand, was assumed to resemble the consumption of broadcasting. There was even a time in the late 1990s when the word 'interactive' meant the ability to choose between different strands of production, as if, to take the obvious example, analogue television could be defined as interactive because it had more than one channel.

This somewhat querulous introduction might seem to be irrelevant to the concerns of those wishing to make museums and art galleries as accessible as possible to the citizens who have paid for them because they are quintessentially institutions that operate like valves, distributing experience through a one-way channel but the key point here is that the top-down model, in emphasising accessing and processing, has also, as a form of intellectual collateral damage, determined not only what should be consumed but how it should be consumed. One of the reasons why convergence has been slower than the technical capacity to deliver it has been because of the analogue media silos that have persisted into the digital age. For instance, the UK government insists on almost monopolistic PC communication even though the people with whom it conducts most transactions, in aggregate and per capita, do now have a PC at home but can both read and send text messages; in Summer 2006 the number of people sending text messages passed the number using a home qwerty keyboard.[4]

It is one of the great curiosities of the digital age that it has become so attracted to Henry Ford's maxim that you can have any colour of car you like as long as it is black. The root cause of this authorial (I use the term 'author' to describe the original creator of a unique artefact) and publishing diktat is the self classification from the outset of web design as a branch of broadcasting but with a heavy aesthetic, as opposed, say, to a documentary, bias. This dual designation has served to militate against the very virtues of digital material (its general plasticity and its potential for separating style from content, thereby offering a high level of customisation) and the ranking of visual elegance over taxonomy and lexicographic clarity and consistency.

Allied with this producer self esteem there is a persistent, historical tendency to mystify the digital domain. The very first commercial mainframe computer, installed by Heinz, was rendered near useless because the engineers said they could not provide anything the sales team specified and, reciprocally, the sales team had no use for anything the engineers offered. A confusion has also arisen between the product as an end in itself, to be consumed in exchange for taxation or purchase in the case of broadcasting, and information as a means to sell products; thus the digital information designers have frequently become an obstacle to rather than a means of effective marketing. In such stand-offs the technology becomes an end in itself rather than a means to achieving a corporate objective and, at the customer interface it frequently means that the authorial intention is not clear. If a knitwear website is elegantly designed with an almost impossible ordering facility, the customer can be forgiven for believing that it is simply a showcase not a shop. At the same time, many people in marketing are not sure why they have information systems other than because their competitors have them. This frequently leads to 'portfolio' offerings that serve no corporate useful purpose but simply boost the self regard of the creator.

None of these issues will be resolved until our culture develops a new model for the 'ownership' of intellectual property. Retailing intellectual property is a relatively modern phenomenon (it is not insignificant that the father of copyright was censorship) and its protection was greatly facilitated by its production costs but is it the purpose of intellectual property rights to protect the capital investment required for production or simply to provide reasonable remuneration for the producer? If the primary purpose is the latter, then the protection required should be weakened as production costs fall. Further, because digital mass production can be undertaken by anyone, what controls should be placed on them by the author?

For our purposes, however, the more crucial question is that of the integrity of the product. Does the creator of digital content 'own' its integrity? Once the purchase price has been made, what control should the author have over what the consumer does with it? If I want to read an author in 16-point orange sans serif on black who only publishes in hard copy using Roman 12-point black on white, why should the author have a right to prevent me from creating and adapting a digital file of his work as long as I have bought the book? His defence might be that I am interfering with the integrity of his aesthetic but as long as he makes his work available in a public repository of 'read only' artefacts, his integrity is beyond challenge.

The issue of integrity, of insisting upon the fusion of style and content as if the context were still analogue, takes on a different complexion when the artefacts in question are the property of the public sector which owns very little (excepting donations of major works of art and the like not made in part payment of tax obligations) which has not been paid for out of taxation. How are we to balance the right of the author who has produced the work against that of the citizen on whose behalf the government has paid for it? As governments are increasingly subjecting themselves to non-discrimination legislation, to what extent can the author claim any special rights when work must be available to all citizens on a non-discriminatory basis?

These issues are no longer theoretical because of two major technological developments in user interface technology: intermedial transposition; and modular accessibility. The first, and more significant development allows content to be realised in different ways: utterance can be automatically transformed into text and vice versa; files of three-dimensional objects (CAD) can be realised with haptic feedback devices to produce virtual objects and with stereoscopic lithographic apparatus (SLA) to produce solid objects; and albeit with some difficulty, images can be specified precisely in formulae and no doubt that process will soon be reversible so that a scanning device can turn an image into formulae. Although the first and third are likely to be more economically significant, the second is of particular interest to the libraries and museums sector. Progress has been so rapid with SLA both in terms of improved resolution and in price reduction that the major obstacle is the digitisation of the specifications of artefacts; when laser three-dimensional measurement and SLA 'printing' are allied with copying technologies, it is easy to see how we will be able to mass produce sculpture. The lesser but still significant development, already commonplace in PCs, televisions and other consumer electronics devices, is the physical separation of information processors, controllers and output devices. At one end of the spectrum we have already become familiar with miniaturisation but we have not yet seen so many examples of gargantuanisation. Imagine the ability to take a small section of a Monet haystack and magnify it on a massive display screen. It is only a matter of time before we will also be able to use digital photography to deconstruct the layering of paint.

Taken together, digital plasticity, cheap copying, easier and more varied transposition and the plurality of user interface devices should finally see off the analogue exclusivity model except, of course, that professional protectionism will offer stiff resistance.

Notes

1   http://www.well.com/ – the WELL, a computer conferencing system.
2   Mr. Micawber in Dickens' *David Copperfield* 'Annual income twenty pounds, annual expenditure nineteen nineteen six, result happiness. Annual income twenty pounds, annual expenditure twenty pounds ought and six, result misery.'
3   Alvin Toffler (1980) *The Third Wave*. Bantam Books.
4   '44% of UK adults use text messaging on a daily basis, compared to 36% who use the internet'. Ed Richards, *Foreword* in CMR Ofcom Report, 14 August 2008. http://www.ofcom.org.uk/research/cm/cmr08/

Chapter 21

Implementing a Holistic Approach to E-Learning Accessibility

Brian Kelly, Lawrie Phipps and Caro Howell

About this paper

The importance of universal accessibility to web resources is widely acknowledged. W3C's Web Accessibility Initiative (WAI) has developed guidelines which
help to ensure that web resources can be accessed by people with disabilities. With
the Web providing the main delivery channel for e-learning resources it would appear
that the WAI guidelines should be a requirement for e-learning development. This
paper, however, puts the case for a wider perspective. There is a need to recognise
the limitations of WAI guidelines and implementation. In addition there is a need
to acknowledge that the IT sector has responded to demand for accessible digital
resources by providing accessible versions of proprietary formats and operating
systems. Finally there is a need to recognise that, just as IT has been used to provide
accessible simulations of inaccessible real world learning, so too can accessible real
world learning resources be used as a replacement for e-learning resources which
may be inaccessible.

The web accessibility initiative

The World Wide Web Consortium (W3C) (the body responsible for the coordination of developments to web standards) established the Web Accessibility Initiative
(WAI) with a remit to lead the Web to its full potential with a particular reference to

Source: *Exploring the Frontiers of E-Learning: borders, outposts and migration*, ALT-C 2005 12th
International Conference Research Proceedings, J. Cook and D. Whitelock (eds), Oxford:
ALT. http://www.ukoln.ac.uk/web-focus/papers/alt-c-2005/.

promoting a high degree of accessibility for people with disabilities. WAI has success-fully raised awareness of the importance of web accessibility and in developing guide-lines which help to ensure that web resources are accessible, with the Web Content Accessibility Guidelines, often referred to as WCAG (WAI 1999) being of particular relevance to developers of web resources.

Challenges in implementing WAI WCAG guidelines

Background to developments in the UK

In 2001 the UK Government introduced the Special Educational Needs and Disabil-ity Act (SENDA 2001), bringing the previously excluded elements of the education sector within the remit of existing anti-discrimination legislation. In the same year the JISC the (Joint Information Systems Committee) established the TechDis service with a remit for all aspects of technology and disability within education. Since 2001 the service has been working with other intermediaries to try and understand the ramifications of the legislation on, amongst other things, e-learning.

An excellent overview of the legislation highlighting many of the issues that would be affected by the legislation is given in Willder (2002). However, she concludes that until the legislation is tested it will be difficult to draw conclusions. Sloan (2002) suggests that there is little doubt that e-learning will be within the scope of UK legislation:

> it can be seen that there is likely to be a duty on higher and further educa-tion institutions to ensure that their online teaching resources and VLEs are provided in a form accessible to disabled students. Further, institutions will be expected to make 'reasonable adjustments' to overcome these problems and are unlikely to be able to justify continuing discrimination.

Over a period of four years the authors have been working together with academic staff and individuals working in the policy area to better understand how standards and guidelines fit together with UK legislation and how that then transposes onto the learning experience of a disabled student in the UK. In working with learning tech-nologists, disability staff and lecturers, the authors and others acknowledged in this paper have come to some interesting conclusions and challenges for those who are working in the field of accessibility.

This paper addresses some of these issues, discussing the work of standards organi-sations, exploring the nature of e-learning as both an isolated delivery method and a blended learning experience and how that can impact on disabled students. The paper concludes with a discussion of a holistic approach developed with involvement by several of the academic organisations involved in supporting e-learning and disability.

Experiences of implementing WAI WCAG guidelines

W3C WAI's success in developing accessibility guidelines has led to the need for tools which can be used to check for compliance with the guidelines. A variety of checking tools are now available, such as Bobby (Watchfire n.d.) and The WAVE (Webaim n.d.). Such tools have their limitations, as described by Ivory and Chevalier (2002) and Diaper and Worman (2003). However, they do have a valuable role to play if used in conjunction with manual checking of the accessibility of web resources.

A number of accessibility surveys have been carried out across the UK higher education community using an automated accessibility testing tool in order to profile the community and to gain an understanding of common accessibility problem areas.

A survey was carried out in August 2002 of the home page for over 160 UK university websites. The survey was carried out shortly before the SENDA legislation became law, which extended accessibility legislation to include the education sector. The survey revealed that about 57 per cent of the pages failed to comply with WCAG 1.0 guidelines (Kelly 2002).

The Disability Rights Commission (DRC) published a high profile report on the accessibility of 1,000 websites in the UK (DRC 2004). The survey revealed that 81 per cent of websites failed to meet minimum standards for disabled web access. At a related press conference it was noted that sites highlighted by the DRC as exemplars of good practice actually failed to meet the minimum WAI standards, even though they were identified as websites which disabled users found usable.

Discussion of findings

These findings seem depressing, particularly in light of the publicity given to the SENDA legislation across the community, the activities of support bodies such as TechDis and UKOLN and the level of awareness and support for WAI activities across the UK higher education sector.

The publication of the survey of the accessibility of UK university entry points led to interesting discussions on some of the difficulties of complying with the WAI WCAG guidelines and some concerns over the relevance of the guidelines. Areas of concern which have been raised are described by Kelly (2005b) and summarised in Table 21.1.

Table 21.1 WCAG implementation difficulties

Issue	Comments
Understanding and interpreting the guidelines	Guidelines can be difficult to understand and interpret consistently
Conflicts between accessibility and usability	Complying with accessibility guidelines may conflict with the website usability
Guidelines too theoretical	Some guidelines are felt to be too theoretical, promoting format not yet been widely deployed or accepted within the marketplace
Use of proprietary solutions	There is a need to make use of proprietary formats which provide an effective solution to users' needs
Other IT developments	The guidelines address only web standards and fail to acknowledge wider IT accessibility issues

Although implementation of the WCAG guidelines may not always be easy, it should be acknowledged that the guidelines have been developed in good faith, and that implementation of the guidelines can help to make web resources accessible. The over-ambitious nature of the guidelines has been observed in other areas: the initial version often seeks to address too many issues with subsequent versions having more realistic aims. It should be noted that WAI are currently developing WCAG 2.0 (WAI 2004), which may address some of these concerns, but not necessarily the concerns of those involved in developing e-learning resources.

A holistic approach

The need for a holistic approach

Much emphasis is now placed on accessibility in education; generally this has come to be synonymous with web accessibility or the accessibility of e-learning. However, to staff who are just starting out in educational development or using technology in a very iterative way with students the application of these standards and guidelines can be at best a discouragement or at worst damaging, preventing staff from exploring the potential of e-learning.

This approach also ignores a major facet of the educational experience: it is holistic. Students attend an institution and partake of a range of facilities and activities – some they will not relate to, others they will. Because a disabled student cannot access one type of assessment that happens to be delivered via a web browser, it does not mean they cannot instead do an oral examination in a one-to-one situation. The current accessibility paradigm places emphasis on total online access, or if materials cannot be made accessible, then providing an equivalent online experience. This can be damaging to the educational experience of attending an institution, ignoring the fact that institutions and their staff deploy a range of learning methods, some of which will suit all students; others will not. The only way to judge the accessibility of an institution is to assess it holistically and not judge it by a single method of delivery.

The components of a proposed holistic framework to support the development of e-learning resources are outlined below.

Usability issues

The Disability Rights Commission's report highlighted the importance of website usability for people with disabilities. The report pointed out that "45% of [the 585 accessibility and usability] problems were not a violation of any [WAI WCAG] Checkpoint and could therefore have been present on any WAI-conformant site regardless of rating". This point illustrates a limitation of the WAI WCAG guidelines. It should be self-evident that quality e-learning web resources should be usable and not just accessible. However, the strong emphasis given to accessibility, especially with concerns sometimes expressed that failure to comply with W3C WAI WCAG guidelines could lead to legal action, can lead to failure to give equal weight to usability issues.

Although it might appear desirable to include usability alongside accessibility, there is a need to be aware of potential conflicts. This may be partly due to poor support for web standards in browsers. In addition users may express preferences for e-learning resources in conflict with accessibility guidelines. The proprietary Flash format is widely used for the development of interactive e-learning resources and online games. Such resources may be accessible. The RNIB (Royal National Institute for the Blind), for example, has encouraged the development of accessible Flash resources. The RNIB also provide advice on the development of accessible Flash resources (RNIB n.d.). Although resources such as the RNIB Blind Date game may be usable and accessible, they would not appear to comply with the WAI WCAG guidelines as they make use of a proprietary file format.

Accessible e-learning or accessible learning?

In the holistic approach to accessible e-learning there is a need to provide accessible *learning* experiences, and not necessarily an accessible *e-learning* experience. This approach has parallels with the concept of *blended learning* rather than the more limited *e-learning* approach.

As an example, consider an e-learning environment which provides a highly interactive 3-D visualisation of a molecule. Such an environment is likely to be very difficult to make accessible to a visually impaired student or a student with impaired motor skills. Rather than seeking to develop an accessible version of such an environment (which, if possible to do, may prove costly, without any guarantee that the accessible equivalent will be usable by the student with disabilities), in such a case the teacher should consider the learning experience provided by the e-learning resources and seek to develop an alternative which provides an equivalent learning experience. In many cases it should be possible to find an acceptable equivalent learning experience, such as the resources used prior to the development of the e-learning resource (for example, a physical representation of a molecule).

This approach may also be used when a real-world learning experience is not accessible. For example, consider a field course for a geography student, which requires climbing a mountain or other terrain unsuited for a student in a wheelchair or with similar physical disabilities (this may include an overweight student or a heavy smoker who finds physical exertions difficult). A blinkered approach may seek to make the mountain accessible by using expensive all-terrain vehicles, building appropriate paths and ramps at key sites or, in the worst case scenario, cancelling the field trip for all students. A holistic approach allows the teacher to identify the learning experiences (such as the selection of appropriate sites to take water and soil samples) and seek equivalent learning experiences (perhaps providing the student with 3G phone technologies, videos, for use in selecting the sites, followed by discussion of the test results with other team members at base camp). This holistic approach to accessible learning has been accepted in a number of academic disciplines. For example the Virtual Field Course Web site (VFC n.d.) describes several approaches to support field studies for students with disabilities.

Accessible courses

This holistic approach encourages a more bird's eye view of the learning experience encountered by disabled students. The learning path that the student chooses to follow should be accessible while individual online components or learning objects may not. To provide another example, consider a blind student who wishes to take a degree in biochemistry. When choosing a course the student should be advised on course modules which the student's disability may make it difficult for the student to pass (such as options which may require a student to peer through a microscope and describe what they see). Although such courses may not be possible for a blind student to take, the department could seek to provide accessible alternative course options which would still allow the student to be awarded a degree.

Adapting to individual, local, political and cultural factors

The final components of the holistic framework for e-learning accessibility calls for an approach which takes into account individual needs and local cultural, political and social factors. Since accessibility is primarily about people and not about technologies the authors feel it is inappropriate to seek a universal solution. In seeking to provide accessible learning experiences it will be necessary to take into account the individual's specific needs, institutional factors, the subject discipline and the broader cultural and political factors.

Instead of aiming to provide an e-learning resource which is accessible to everyone this paper argues there can be advantages in providing resources which are tailored for the student's particular needs. An example of this approach is given in 'i-Map: a case study' below.

The holistic framework

The holistic framework for e-learning accessibility has been described elsewhere (Kelly 2005a).

Rather than relying purely on the WAI guidelines, the framework incorporates the guidelines as part of a broader approach to the provision of accessible e-learning resources. There is a need to address the usability of e-learning resources, the pedagogic aims of the e-learning resources, infrastructural and resources issues and to provide solutions which are appropriate to the needs of the framework. The authors feel that a quality assurance framework is needed to support this approach which will ensure that documented policies are provided and systematic procedures for ensuring compliance with the policies are implemented.

Discussion

It could be argued that this approach has limitations compared with the W3C WAI guidelines. The WAI guidelines can appear easier to implement as they provides a series of checklists. However, a checklist approach can, in fact, be counter-productive as it encourages developers to prioritise the objective areas which testing tools can easily report on.

Another limitation of this approach may be its lack of universality which is implicit in its inclusion of institutional and local factors. This criticism may, in fact, be regarded in some quarters as strength of the approach, as it does not seek to mandate a single global solution, but rather welcomes diversity and a learner-centric approach to e-learning.

Whilst this work has been discussed and revised at length at various workshops and conferences, there is still a need to develop the framework and to provide examples of how it could be applied in a variety of circumstances, including differing learning environments, students with a variety of disabilities, with the use of various technologies and in a variety of different organisations.

i-Map: a case study

As discussed in this paper, the ideal of an online education resource being 'accessible to all' is flawed, not just because different user needs require different approaches, but also because the content, format and pedagogy of every resource must be determined by the needs of its specific target audience. This is clearly illustrated when one considers the needs of people with sensory impairments accessing visual art online. Merely making the site accessible for screen readers is pointless if the visual concepts they narrate are incomprehensible to a congenitally blind person. Equally, a high resolution video clip translating audio or text into British Sign Language will be wasted if, as may be the case, the very language of art is alien to that person. Considering an impairment generically will not make a site 'fully accessible' since variants of that impairment may alter the shape of the resource; the needs of one variant may run counter to the needs of another. In the field of visual impairment one must consider whether the target user is blind or partially sighted, do they have any visual memory, are they an adult or child, what experience or knowledge of art do they currently have and what are they hoping to achieve from use of the resource? Each combination of variables will require a different approach to ensure accessibility and no single resource can meet the access needs of all these variables.

i-Map (Howell and Porter 2003) was developed for blind and partially sighted GCSE and A Level art pupils and their teachers. The aim of the project was to enable visually impaired students to critically and intellectually engage with the art of Matisse and Picasso, whilst providing their teachers with skills they could transfer to the study of other artists. The developers wanted i-Map to be a site that was not just technically accessible to these visually impaired users but also met their pedagogical needs. The developers were not concerned with the access needs of people with other impairments or with visually impaired people who had a sophisticated understanding of modern art.

The developers had no previous experience in this field and nor was there a clear precedent to follow. There was an early realisation that the accessibility guidelines provided only limited help when devising access to visual art on the Web. Testing

the site with blind users showed that technical accessibility does not equate to intellectual accessibility. Guidelines alone do not provide access to artworks – an ALT tag
merely names, does not explain an image. Sighted people are barely aware of how
much information is 'ocularcentric'. The Tate website, for example, provides a vast
range of texts and data about artworks and exhibitions that a blind user can technically navigate, but most of this information is intellectually inaccessible.

The original prototype attempted to meet the needs of both blind and partially
sighted people in a single screen. Although functional, it was clumsy, overly complicated to use and meant that blind users had to contend with functions and content
that applied only to partially sighted users and *vice versa*. As a result the site was split,
with an animated version for partially sighted people, a text only version supported
by raised drawings for people with no useful sight and a gateway that made explicit
the intended users for each. When tested by a blind web expert at the RNIB, no
design faults were observed.

Every aspect of i-Map is designed to meet the specific needs of the targeted audience. Most obvious were the decisions concerning language. First, the writing style
took into account the difficulty of absorbing information delivered by a screen reader.
A monotonous, deadpan voice that lacks cadence and emphasis needs sentence structures to be short and simple, while information must be delivered systematically,
chronologically and incrementally if meaning is to be clear. This commitment to
clarity also meant that i-Map's texts are very long, which suits visually impaired
people who are used to listening attentively and prefer detailed explanations to hasty
summations. Other examples include moving navigation links to the foot of the page
to avoid endless repetition, having different methodologies of deconstruction tailored
to the artwork in question, ensuring that careful attention to a detail was not immediately followed by a much wider view since dramatic leaps in scale are confusing,
not removing ambiguity if that would alter the integrity of the artwork, but instead
explaining how and why this was the artist's intension. Finally there was a need to
contend with 'real life' demands such as maintaining continuity with the design of the
Tate site as a whole, or negotiating with sponsors for the removal of logos and strap
lines in the body of the site so that textual continuity wasn't disrupted.

So although guidelines are essential for mapping out the landscape of web accessibility, they can become problematic once content moves beyond basic information. Dedicated interpretation and education resources are by their nature exclusive,
be they for primary school children with learning difficulties, families with a deaf
member or congenitally blind artists.

The need for a holistic approach

An article (Sitemorse 2005) published by the accessibility auditing software company
Sitemorse has generated heated debate over the relative merits of automated accessibility checking versus manual testing. The article describes the findings of an automated
analysis carried out by Sitemorse across the websites of various disability organisations within the UK including the RNIB, RNID, the Disability Rights Commission,
etc. The arguments over the relevance of the findings clearly demonstrates a lack of

consensus and illustrates the difficulties that even national disability organisations find in complying with even basic WAI WCAG guidelines.

However, the article failed to provide a solution to these conflicts. In this paper a framework has been described which does provide a resolution to this impasse. The framework is applicable to a learning context but is also well-suited to the provision of informational resources, such as those provided by disability organisations (who are targeting specific audiences) mentioned in the Sitemorse article.

Implementing holistic accessibility – building on a quality assurance framework

How might the holistic framework described in this paper be applied more widely to the development of e-learning resources? The JISC development programme funds a wide range of e-learning initiatives across the higher and further education sector. From 2002–2004 JISC funded the QA Focus project to develop a quality assurance (QA) framework which would help ensure wide accessibility and interoperability of project deliverables. The QA framework which was developed rejected the notion of formal compliance testing with standards as inappropriate for the JISC development community. Instead the framework requires projects to document their decisions on the standards and guidelines to be used and to implement systematic procedures to ensure these policy decisions were implemented correctly (Kelly et al. 2003).

The authors feel that this approach is well suited to addressing the accessibility of project deliverables. In submissions projects could be expected to describe how they will ensure their project deliverables will be widely accessible, but not necessarily mandate compliance with a particular WAI WCAG compliance level or, alternatively, require compliance with, say, WAI WCAG A, but allow projects to explain non-compliance. It may be legitimate in certain circumstances (e.g. deliberate selection of proprietary formats such as Flash to develop an e-learning resource) but not allowable in others (e.g. with information resources). A template which could apply to future programme calls is illustrated below:

Purposes of project deliverables:	Summarise the high-level purposes of project deliverables.
Policies on accessibility of project deliverables:	State your policies on the accessibility of project deliverables.
Compliance checking procedures:	Describes the procedures you will deploy which will ensure that the project deliverables comply with your policies.
Difficulties:	Describe any difficulties you envisage in implementing your policies.
Strategies for addressing deliverables:	Describe possible approaches for addressing the difficulties.

We can see how this could be applied from an example described at a conference in which a speaker described a range of applications of web technologies within a public library setting. The example of providing an online game developed using Flash was given. In response to a question concerning the accessibility of the game, the speaker responded that, although the game had proved popular, it would probably have to be removed once accessibility legislation became law. In response to a question about the purpose of the game, it emerged that the high-level purpose was to entertain children while their parents browse books in the library. Applying the holistic framework it can be seen that rather than seeking to develop an accessible version of the game, it would be perfectly legitimate to provide an alternative such as building blocks or a bouncy castle to entertain the children. This would have the additional benefit in not having to treat children who could not use Flash due to their disabilities in a special fashion; rather this approach provides an alterative resource for all children.

Conclusions

This paper argues that although the W3C WAI guidelines for content accessibility are valuable, they should not be regarded as the only set of criteria which developers of e-learning resources need to consider. Not only is there a need to address a wider set of issues than those addressed in the WAI guidelines, there are also other factors which need to be addressed, some of which may conflict with WAI guidelines. In addition there is a need to place the learner at the centre of the development process. This approach focuses on the broad learning outcomes and recognises that inaccessible e-learning resources may be deployed provided that disabled learners are still able to demonstrate the required learning outcomes in a way that does not disadvantage them or their non-disabled peers.

The authors acknowledge that, in some quarters, these ideas might be regarded as controversial, especially in organisations which have defined e-learning accessibility policies solely using the WAI guidelines. It is also recognised that there is still an on-going debate to be held. The authors welcome comments and input to this debate.

References

Diaper, D. and Worman, L. (2003) Two Falls out of Three in the Automated Accessibility Assessment of World Wide Web Sites: A-Prompt v. Bobby. Conference paper presented at the 17th Annual Human–Computer Interaction Conference (HCI 2003), Bath, UK, Sept. 8–12, 2003. Johnson, P. and Palanque, P. (eds) *People and Computers XVII*. Springer-Verlag. Retrieved 18 May 2005 from http://dec.bournemouth.ac.uk/staff/ddiaper/dan_access.html.

DRC (2004) Formal Investigation Report: Web Accessibility. Retrieved 21 January 2005 from http://www.drc-gb.org/publicationsandreports/report.asp.

Howell, C. and Porter, D. (2003) Re-assessing Practice: Visual Art, Visually Impaired People and the Web. Museums and the Web 2003 Conference. Retrieved 18 May 2005 from http://www.archimuse.com/mw2003/papers/howell/howell.html.

Ivory, M. and Chevalier, A. (2002) A Study of Automated Web Site Evaluation Tools. Technical Report UW-CSE-02-10-01, University of Washington, Department of Computer Science and Engineering. Retrieved 18 May 2005 from http://ubit. ischool.washington.edu/pubs/tr02/toolstudy.pdf.

Kelly, B. (2002) An Accessibility Analysis Of UK University Entry Points, *Ariadne* 33, Sept. 2002. Retrieved 18 May 2005 from http://www.ariadne.ac.uk/issue33/ webwatch/.

Kelly, B., Guy, M. and James, H. (2003) Developing A Quality Culture For Digital Library Programme, *Informatica* 27 (3), Oct. 2003. ISSN 0350–5596. Retrieved 18 May 2005 from http://www.ukoln.ac.uk/qa-focus/documents/papers/eunis-2003/.

Kelly, B., Phipps, L. and Swift, E. (2005a) Developing A Holistic Approach For E-Learning Accessibility, *Canadian Journal of Learning and Technology* 30 (3). Retrieved 18 May 2005 from http://www.ukoln.ac.uk/qa-focus/papers/cjtl-2004/.

Kelly, B., Sloan, D., Phipps, L., Petrie, H. and Hamilton, F. (2005b) Forcing Standardization or Accommodating Diversity? A Framework for Applying the WCAG in the Real World, *Proceedings of the 2005 International Cross-Disciplinary Workshop on Web Accessibility (W4A)*. ISBN: 1-59593-036-1. Retrieved 18 May 2005 from http://www.ukoln. ac.uk/web-focus/papers/w4a-2005/.

RNIB (n.d.) Web Access Centre. Retrieved 18 May 2005 from RNIB website: http:// www.rnib.org.uk/xpedio/groups/public/documents/publicwebsite/public_ macromediafl ash.hcsp.

SENDA (2001) Special Educational Needs and Disability Act 2001, HMSO. Retrieved 18 May 2005 from http://www.hmso.gov.uk/acts/acts2001/20010010.htm.

Sitemorse (2005) Confusion Reigns Over Website Accessibility Compliance. Retrieved 18 May 2005 from SiteMorse website: http://www.business2www.com/news. html?id=1217547344.

Sloan, M. (2002) E-Learning and Legislation. Retrieved 18 May 2005 from TechDis website: http://www.techdis.ac.uk/resources/msloan02.html.

VFC (n.d.) The Virtual Field Course. Retrieved 18 May 2005 from University of Leicester website: http://www.geog.le.ac.uk/vfc/education/.

WAI (1999) Web Content Accessibility Guidelines 1.0, W3C Recommendation 5-May-1999. Retrieved 18 May 2005 from W3C website: http://www.w3.org/TR/ WCAG10/.

WAI (2004) Web Content Accessibility Guidelines 2.0. W3C Working Draft 19 November 2004. Retrieved 18 May 2005 from W3C website: http://www.w3.org/TR/ WCAG20/.

Watchfire (n.d.) Welcome to Bobby WorldWide. Retrieved 18 May 2005 from Watchfire website: http://bobby.watchfire.com/.

Webaim (n.d.) WAVE 3.0 Web Accessibility Versatile Evaluator. Retrieved 18 May 2005 from http://wave.webaim.org/.

Willder, B. (2002) 'Disability legislation: implications for learning technologists in the UK,' in *Access All Areas: Disability, Technology and Learning*, Phipps, L., Sutherland, A. and Seale, J. (ed.) ALT/JISC/TechDis. pp. 6–9.

Chapter 22

Usability Evaluation for Museum Websites

Daniel Cunliffe, Efmorphia Kritou and Douglas Tudhope

This case study concerns the resource-limited evaluation of a website providing information about an annual review journal, *The New Review of Multimedia and Hypermedia* (NRHM 2000). It is a relatively small site, consisting of approximately 160 pages, mainly paper abstracts. According to Oono (1998), museum websites are likely to contain only a small number of pages, 28.8 per cent having less than twenty pages and almost half having less than fifty pages. No formal development model was used for the site though Bevan (1998) was taken as an informal guide. The development of the site was completed without any formal user input, relying on the intuitions of the information providers and competitive analysis (Nielsen 1993) of existing websites to provide user needs models. A summative evaluation of the site was then performed using a combination of evaluation methods selected according to the following factors (Kritou 1998):

- Time was limited due to organisational constraints, since the evaluations would run for approximately two weeks, the methods selected would have to provide results within that time.
- The users of the website were spread across the globe.
- The most common tasks of the users needed to be tested.
- The evaluation team consisted of one inexperienced person, and there was no access to specialist HCI testing facilities or equipment.

These factors have much in common with those of the non-professional museum web development environment. Four evaluation techniques were selected: direct observation of usability tests, log analysis, online questionnaire, and heuristic evalu-

Source: *Museum Management and Curatorship*, vol. 19, no. 3, 2001, pp. 229–252.

ation. The following sections discuss the findings from the investigation, identifying the potential benefits and limitations of the different methods with reference to the museum context.

Direct observation

Within the constraints of the evaluation, the gathering of a test group of real users proved problematic. In order to perform an evaluation with the five 'proxy users' who were available, a set of six task scenarios was constructed; each task scenario presented a specific task (Kritou 1998):

> Assume that you are an author who wants to submit a paper and looks for an appropriate journal. You have found the NRHM Web-Site. Find out what topics can be submitted in the next issue and the guidelines for submitting a paper to this journal.

During the evaluation subjects were encouraged to 'think aloud', a video camera was used to record the users' utterances and on-screen behaviour. The evaluator also completed an observer's notebook during the evaluation. Ideally, direct observation will record the behaviour of the visitor performing natural tasks, in a natural context and under natural motivation. Museums have experience of observing visitors in exhibition areas. These observations may include subjective interpretation of facial expression, body language, snatches of conversation and interaction among group members, typically resulting in very rich descriptions and codings of visitor behaviour, 'small boy (6) seems awestruck by sounds/colors but soon fidgets as watches … The girl doing computer is quite relaxed, interested' (Hilke et al. 1988). When considering direct observation of virtual visitors the situation is more complex – it is typically not possible to observe virtual visitors in their natural context of use, which might be their home or office. The recording of virtual visitor behaviour in log files is one way this can be achieved and is discussed in Log Analysis. Generally direct observation of virtual visitors is carried out under the following limitations.

The context of use may be artificial

Typically direct observations will be carried out under controlled circumstances in a specially prepared room. In some cases observation subjects are asked to imagine that they are in a particular environment, Hardman (1989) reporting on the evaluation of Glasgow Online kiosk writes 'All the observations were carried out in an office, and readers were asked to imagine that they were currently at Queen Street Station, one of the main-line stations in central Glasgow'. The NRHM observations were performed in the subjects' offices to provide a reasonably natural context. Even where the actual context of use is broadly similar to the observation situation, the visitor may behave differently in the knowledge that they are being observed – the 'Hawthorn effect'.

The tasks the subject carries out may be artificial

Typically the observation subject will be provided with a set of tasks they must carry out. Often these tasks are based on the developers' perceptions of what constitute typical user tasks. One method for reducing the potential for bias in the creation of tasks is to involve users in their creation (Erskine et al. 1997). It is also worth conducting a pilot test of the tasks themselves, for example in the NRHM evaluation a pilot test identified an ambiguity in one of the task scenarios. Heinecke (1995) suggests that the goals and intentions of 'point of information' system users in museums may be highly individualistic and that it is necessary to observe users in order to understand their goals. There is no reason to suppose that this will not also be true on the Web. The tasks will generally focus on information finding rather than browsing, as Hardman (1989) observes, 'No observation looked at how readers would use the information available for browsing, since it would be very difficult to keep track of readers' goals and whether they had reached them or not.' Since browsing is a natural behaviour on the web, and one which a museum website would seek to encourage, this is an important limitation of such task-based observations. One interesting observation made during the NRHM evaluation was that a number of the subjects started the tasks by general browsing around the site. It may be that strict adherence to information finding tasks places an artificial restriction on their interactions and that browsing behaviour should be incorporated within the observations.

The motivation for the subject conducting the task may be artificial

Differences in motivation between real users with real information needs and observation subjects with artificial motivations may result in misleading findings (Hardman 1989). In the NRHM observations the evaluator reported that some of the test subjects experienced problems because they had not paid attention to the task requirements, perhaps reflecting lack of motivation when completing artificial tasks.

The observation subjects may not actually be part of the virtual visitor population

In the NRHM evaluation few typical users were available, so use was made of 'proxy' users, raising doubts as to the validity of the behaviours observed. Also some of the reported problems appeared to be due to lack of familiarity with the domain rather than actual usability problems. In some cases distinguishing between the two may not be easy.

Reassuring users

During a direct observation, as in a physical visitor observation, there are a variety of data which could be collected. This is influenced to an extent by the facilities and staff available, balanced against the need not to intimidate the observation subjects. A very practical concern is the need to reassure users that they are not the focus of the evaluation but rather the system and that should they feel uncomfortable they may stop at any time.

Think-aloud protocol

A think-aloud protocol can be used with direct observation, and in the NRHM evaluation a video camera was used to record the on-screen behaviour and spoken comments of observation subjects. This proved useful in understanding *why* the subject had or had not performed a particular action. However, all bar one of the subjects were uncomfortable with the thinking-aloud protocol and reported that it interfered with execution of the tasks.

Video

The use of a video camera to capture the subjects' on-screen behaviour can be useful for creating an accurate and impartial record of that behaviour (see, for example, Cleary 2000). The audio track can also be used to record a subjects' thinking-aloud, providing easy synchronisation with the on-screen behaviour. Whilst subjects are often uncomfortable in front of a camera, a camera directed at the screen is perceived as being less threatening. In the NRHM evaluation video analysis proved time consuming, but did enable the observer to identify things which might otherwise have been missed. Retrospective testing (Nielsen 1993), in which the test subjects comment on the recorded session, might be used as a way of reducing analysis time.

Observer's note book

The observer's note book can be used to record a number of different events. Borda et al. (1999) use observation sheets which attempt to generate a rich description, requiring the observer to 'Describe step by step how visitor navigates and holds interest' and record "What do they say or ask each other/you?' There are issues involved with gathering rich descriptions including accurate recording, subjective interpretation, and subjective recording. In the NRHM evaluation the notebook was used to record the time taken for each task, whether the task was completed, whether the test subject followed the optimal path (see below) and the subject's affective state. In retrospect, the observer's notebook required the evaluator to take down too many details during evaluations.

Optimal path

One event which was recorded by the observer in the NRHM evaluation (see also Badre and Jacobs 1999) was deviance from the optimal path when completing a task – that is the path involving the fewest link traversals. It is important to consider whether this is an appropriate measure for a browsing activity, even when the subject is performing an information finding task. Adherence to an optimum path could indicate a failure to engage with the content being passed through.

Time to complete

It is often tempting to record the time taken to complete a task or set of tasks during a direct observation. Indeed, during the NRHM evaluation, the time to complete a task was recorded. What is less clear is *why* this data would be useful. First, the time taken to complete a task is only of value if there exists some other experimental condition, or some absolute performance target with which to compare it. Secondly, in an environment which is intended to facilitate browsing, the time taken to complete a task becomes relatively unimportant. Where the application is essentially an information retrieval task, speed of task completion may be more relevant. Given that speed of downloading is an issue for web users, this may be a factor which could be assessed in an observation, but typically the experimental conditions do not replicate network traffic, caching, speed of the server under load, and so on.

Interviews

Direct observation is often combined with an interview or questionnaire (see, for example, Borda et al. 1999; Cleary 2000). The NRHM direct observations were followed by a short interview during which the subjects were encouraged to comment generally on their experience and to express their subjective satisfaction. Where a task was not completed the subject was asked if they had expected to find the information elsewhere. If subjects appeared unsatisfied when they had completed a task, they were asked if they were expecting to find more or different information. The interviews identified several missed opportunities in terms of not meeting user expectations and were able to generate suggestions for improvement. All the subjects had previous experience using the Web and were familiar with the sorts of facilities which can be provided. It is not clear whether the feedback from more naive web users would be so informative. The interviews also provided positive comments which confirmed the appropriateness of some design decisions.

Direct observation sessions can be performed reasonably quickly, depending on the nature of the tasks and whether or not an interview is performed. They are also relatively cheap, if observation subjects and access to computer facilities can be located cost free, the only real cost is the evaluator's time. Video cameras are commonly available, but are not essential for direct observation methods. Direct observation is ideally a method which uses real users and real tasks – real usability problems can be identified with only a small number of test subjects. The method is reusable and can be used to test initial concepts, prototypes and completed systems. The tasks and scenarios generated to support direct observation can also be used to guide inspection methods, see below in 'Heuristic evaluation'.

Log analysis

Several museum developers have stressed the importance of gathering web statistics through log analysis (for example, Streten 2000). The automatic collection and analysis of access logs appears to be a close analogy to observing visitors in an exhibition area, potentially gathering important information about real users and real patterns of use within a site and avoiding the problems of artificiality faced by direct observation. Heinecke (1995) suggests that methods such as direct observation and interviews are not cost effective for museums, and favours log analysis as a cheap approach. The NRHM evaluation collected web access logs over a period of sixteen days. In addition to simple 'hits per page' information, the evaluator was interested in trying to characterise particular patterns of use. This identified a number of problems with log analysis.

Difficulties in identifying visitors and defining sessions

A session refers to the set of activities performed by a single visitor during a single visit to the site. However, web log information identifies the originator of a request for a file by the IP address of the requesting computer. IP addresses are not necessarily unique to a person and may not be unique to a particular computer. This means that, unless there is a controlled experimental environment, it is not possible to generate a record of visitor activity over several sessions as it is impossible to be sure that sessions with the same IP address were conducted by the same user. It is also necessary to determine how long a period of inactivity will be taken to indicate the end of a session. The 'timeout' period for a website will generally be longer than that of an interactive, for example, 20 minutes in the NRHM evaluation. There are problems in determining the duration of the timeout period. When a different visitor accesses from the same IP address within 20 minutes of a previous visitor's session finishing, the two sessions will be treated as a single session by a single visitor. On the other hand, if a visitor pauses on a single page for more than 20 minutes, perhaps because the content is particularly interesting or complicated, then their subsequent activity will form a separate session and will not be attributed to the same visitor. It is also not possible to determine when a group of visitors is sharing a machine during a session.

Caching

The caching of web pages is a part of the normal working of the Internet. However, if visitors retrieve cached pages rather than retrieving them from the server, the log of accesses no longer contains a full record of a visitor session.

Limited range of data captured

Compared to the rich descriptions generated during the observation of visitors in an exhibition area, in the logging of interactions with an interactive or kiosk, or during some direct observations, the data gathered in a typical web log is relatively poor.

Essentially it comprises the IP address of the requesting computer, the file requested, and the time that the request was made. Some useful indicative data may be gathered, regarding hits on specific pages, country of origin of requests, requests for download-able files, and so on. Streten (2000) suggests that log files are useful for analysing the most popular entry and exit points and paths through site.

In the NRHM logs it was possible to identify some patterns of behaviour which seemed to confirm the patterns of use hypothesised during the site development. However, given the problems with the log data and the subjective nature of their interpretation as user behaviours, it proved difficult to draw any definite conclusions. The analysis of the data is non-trivial and it is difficult to identify specific usability problems from the analysis of logs alone. The difficulties in mapping from *what the user did* to *why the user did it* are significant. Streten (2000) found that some assumptions made on the basis of access analysis were not backed up by questioning users and recommends that log analysis needs to be augmented by qualitative evidence about the user experience. Shneiderman et al. (1989) suggest that observation and interviews be used in addi-tion to log analysis to gather information about problems and potential solutions. For further discussion of the issues surrounding log analysis, see Berthon et al. (1997), Bertot et al. (1997) and Drott (1998).

In order to generate sufficient data for analysis, logging must run for some time depending on the number of visitors to the site. The logging can be run continuously with data analysis performed at regular intervals. The analysis of the data can be performed quickly if only simple information is required. More complex analysis of user behaviour is more time consuming. Comparison of data over the long term can be used to capture the dynamic changes in user behaviour over time.

Online questionnaire and feedback

Questionnaires are often used in visitor studies, and their familiarity suggests they would make an ideal tool for museum web developers. In the NRHM evaluation an online questionnaire was created containing questions to gather three types of information: demographic information, technical information, and visit informa-tion. Demographic information included occupation, age, locality and Internet expe-rience. Technical information included the type of browser used and the speed of their Internet connection. As the intended audience was expected to be technically literate, this type of question was appropriate. Where the users are technically naive they may not know the answers to them, potentially leading to non-completion of the questionnaire, guessed answers, or missing data. Visit information included the number of times the user had visited the site, their purpose in visiting the site, the page they entered the site on, pages they visited, how useful they found the pages they visited and which pages they bookmarked. These questions were intended to build up a more detailed picture of user behaviour. Users were also asked to rate their general satisfaction with the site and were offered the opportunity make any general comments. The questionnaire was linked to prominently from the NRHM homepage and email sent to various mailing lists.

The two major concerns with online questionnaires and similar feedback mechanisms are the self-selecting nature of the sample and the response rate required to draw reliable conclusions. For the NRHM evaluation, if the total number of visitors is determined by unique IP address (assuming that each distinct IP address is a distinct visitor and that multiple sessions from the same IP address are the same visitor), then the responses represent approximately 5.9 per cent response rate. However, if the number of visitors is determined by unique sessions (assuming that each distinct session is a distinct visitor, even where the IP address is the same), the responses represent only 2.3 per cent. The true figure is likely to fall somewhere between the two extremes. This low response rate is not unusual for web-based questionnaires. Nordbotten (2000) reports a response rate of 4 per cent and Thomas and Paterson (1998) report 2 per cent. The importance of the absolute number of responses must also be considered, since the 2 per cent response rate reported by Thomas and Paterson was made up of 215 responses, whereas the 4 per cent reported by Nordbotten was made up of only five. In the NRHM evaluation there were only five responses, and it was considered impossible to draw reliable conclusions from the results. It is possible that this low response rate was in part due to the timing of the questionnaire, as it was run for only a short time in August, a month when many of the target audience would have been on holiday.

Other difficulties with online questionnaires are discussed by Zhang (1999), and some useful design pointers can be found in Feinberg and Johnson (1998). Borland and Wongse-Sanit (1997) use both an online comments form and an email feedback link but question their value: 'In general unsolicited comments have not been particularly useful as an assessment tool. ... Many send us very nice comments and a few have found typographical errors that we missed.' Such feedback may also be useful for detecting broken links within a site. One possible way to encourage completion of a questionnaire is to offer some form of inducement. Kiernan (1998, cited in Chadwick and Boverie, 1999) reports a 70 per cent response rate to an online survey conducted by NASA when a free photograph was offered as an inducement. The problem with this approach is that it may simply change the nature of the self-selecting sample and people may visit the site simply to complete the questionnaire and receive the inducement. Questionnaires and feedback are relatively cheap methods, ideally suited to the maintenance stage of the development, though procedures must be put in place to deal with a continuous stream of responses. In the case of a questionnaire it may be beneficial to keep it online for a limited period, rather than run it continuously. The NRHM experience suggests that the timing of the release of a limited period questionnaire may have an impact on the response rate.

Heuristic evaluation

An alternative to testing with users is to use methods that do not require users. Inspection-based methods are a class of usability evaluation method which involve a systematic (but not necessarily exhaustive) comparison of a prototype or final design against a pre-determined set of criteria or guidelines (see Nielsen and Mack, 1994 for a detailed discussion). These methods typically require a degree of informed judgement on the part of the evaluator. The use of inspection methods in museum web development is not widely reported in the literature, possibly because of concerns over the expense involved in using trained evaluators (Heinecke 1995). However, Nielsen (1993) suggests that whilst evaluators should *ideally* have experience in performing such evaluations, useful results can be achieved by non-experts. It is likely that many developers are performing informal inspections but do not judge them worthy of reporting (for an exception see Hoff 2000). Museum developments may benefit from a wider appreciation of inspection methods which will enable them to be placed on a more rigorous footing. More generally, inspection methods tend to be popular within web development. Some of them require less formal training than other methods, they can be used throughout the development process, they do not require test users or specialist facilities, and they find a large number of usability problems (Sears 1997). Concerns have, however, been raised regarding the number of false usability problems, i.e. those that actual users would not perceive as problems, which such methods identify (Bailey et al. 1992, cited in Gray and Salzman 1998).

There are a variety of inspection methods, using different types of guidelines, some involving scenarios of use. For heuristic evaluation, for example, Nielsen (1993) recommends using around ten high level heuristics. The effective use of high level, abstract heuristics, such as 'Speak the users' language' (Nielsen 1993) requires a degree of professional judgement. Less experienced evaluators may find a larger, more detailed set of guidelines more appropriate. HCI research has produced a number of sets of high level heuristics (for example, Nielsen 1994) and low level guidelines (for example, Smith and Mosier 1986; Brown 1998). More specialised sets of evaluation criteria also exist, for example, CIDOC have developed a set of 'Multimedia Evaluation Criteria' (CIDOC 1997) and Barker and King (1993) have developed an evaluation check list and supporting notes for the evaluation of interactive multimedia courseware. However, the direct application of a set of guidelines to websites is not always appropriate or sufficient. Even where an existing set of guidelines seems well suited to an application, for example the Campbell and Wells (1996) criteria for museum website homepages, the appropriateness of the guidelines for the *specific* site being evaluated must be considered. Levi and Conrad (1996) present an informative case study of the heuristic evaluation of a website.

Systematic Usability Evaluation (SUE) is an inspection-based method which has been applied to museum websites (Garzotto et al. 1995, 1998; Garzotto and Matera 1997). In the inspection phase SUE uses a set of specific abstract tasks which codify the inspection patterns and behaviours of experienced evaluators in a form that can be applied by non-expert evaluators. It also integrates inspection methods with empirical user testing in order to verify the results of the inspection, thus reducing false usability problems. Whilst the philosophy of the approach is to support novice inspections, currently SUE involves a preparatory phase requiring the use of a formal hypermedia model, typically not appropriate for non-expert evaluators. However, work is ongoing and the aim is to develop a method which yields high levels of inter-evaluator consistency.

In the NRHM evaluation a heuristic evaluation was performed by an untrained evaluator, using a small set of high-level heuristics judged to be appropriate to the site. The evaluator reviewed a number of well-established principles of usability and website design in order to derive a set of eight high level heuristics. Each heuristic was described by a heading (shown below) and a short paragraph highlighting key concerns. The evaluator then performed a comprehensive page by page inspection of the entire site.

1   Consistency and conformance to standards.
2   Recognition and predictability.
3   Web pages should stand alone.
4   Flexibility and efficiency of use.
5   Effectiveness.
6   Readability.
7   Every page should express one topic or concept.
8   Consider the global audience.

Generally, inspection methods should be carried out by a number of evaluators, and for heuristic evaluation Nielsen (1993) suggests about five and at least three. The use of fewer evaluators raises a number of issues, including subjectivity in the selection of heuristics, subjectivity in the application of heuristics, and the possibility of usability problems being missed.

The time taken to apply an inspection method depends on the approach taken and the number of pages inspected. One way of addressing this is to use key user scenarios to guide a heuristic walkthrough and to identify which usability problems are likely to have the most impact on users. The use of scenarios to guide heuristic evaluation may also reduce the number of false usability problems identified. Other approaches to reducing the number of pages which need to be inspected are to focus on key pages (Nielsen 1998a) e.g. download pages, registration pages, product purchase pages, or to identify repeated page templates and inspect only one of each type.

Comparison

In the NRHM evaluation a total of twenty-two potential usability problems were identified by the evaluation methods used: one by the questionnaire, two from log analysis, twelve from direct observation, and thirteen from heuristic evaluation (see Table 22.1).

Table 22.1 NRHM comparison of evaluation methods

Description of the problem	HE	DO	LA	OQ
Search facilities are not efficient enough	x	x	x	x
Index is not consistent across the website	x	x	x	
'Return to top' is not used consistently	x			
There are four broken links in the website	x			
There is no Help facility	x			
Search facility not visible instantly/Grouping of links not effective		x		
Instructions to Authors link not available next to each submission theme		x		

Description of the problem	HE	DO	LA	OQ
A Volume page in Hypermedia Journal doesn't link back to the Volume	x			
Pages don't provide the creator, date of creation, update and copyright	x			
The title (in <TITLE> tag) is not always representative of the website	x			
In a small screen the Home Page is too long	x			
As the website gets larger the Index will be very long		x		
The layout is too simple and not inviting		x		
Hypermedia Journal not visible in Volume Contents in a small screen	x			
The distinction between the two journals is not emphasised enough	x	x		
The author's address is not available when clicking on his name		x		
The difference between Editors and Editorial Board is not explained		x		
Subscription information is insufficient		x		
The list of papers under an author's name is not numbered		x		
The purpose of the website is not stated	x			
The 'no abstract available' message causes confusion	x			
There are no instructions on how to get a full paper		x		

(HE=Heuristic Evaluation, DO=Direct Observation, LA=Log Analysis, OQ=Online Questionnaire).

The usability problem identified by the online questionnaire 'Search facilities are not efficient enough' was contained as a general comment rather than in answer to a specific question. The two usability problems identified by log analysis – 'Search facilities are not efficient enough' and 'Index is not consistent across the website' – relied heavily on the evaluators' subjective interpretation. Questionnaires can also be useful for determining whether a site is meeting the general needs of its users and whether they are satisfied with the experience. This suggests that their major role may be in the long-term development and maintenance of a site.

There was relatively little overlap between the usability problems identified by direct observation and those identified by heuristic evaluation. Direct observation proved useful in identifying usability problems relating to user needs: 'There are no instructions on how to get a full paper'; and the user's subjective impression: 'The layout is too simple and not inviting'. The usability problems identified by direct observation include some probable false positives such as 'The difference between Editors and Editorial Board is not explained'. This is due to using proxy users as test subjects rather than real users. It is also possible that the use of proxy users resulted in some false negatives: they may have missed usability problems which real users would have encountered. This emphasises the benefits of including real users in the evaluation process.

Heuristic evaluation identified the largest number of potential usability problems, and generally identified problems which were not detected in the direct observations, such as '*Return to top* is not used consistently'. Some of the problems identified, such as 'The *no abstract available* message causes confusion' were rare and localised and were only found because the inspection was comprehensive. If a scenario-based inspection had been performed, it is unlikely that they would have been discovered. The heuristic evaluation also identified potential false positives, such as 'There is no

Help facility'. This reflects the difficulty and potential subjectivity in selecting and applying appropriate heuristics.

The purpose in identifying usability problems is that they can then be rectified. However, in many cases it may not be cost effective to rectify all the problems which have been identified. In order to make an informed choice, some form of severity ranking is necessary (Nielsen 1999b). Often this involves ranking by, and agreement between experienced evaluators. Methods for placing this on a systematic footing, so that non-expert evaluators can perform this activity effectively, have yet to be developed.

There are a number of other evaluation methods which can be used. Borland and Wongse-Sanit (1997) use online focus groups who respond to detailed questions about various aspects of site. They also monitor contributions to an email discussion group of people interested in the topic area and have occasionally sent questionnaires to the list, though still with a disappointing response rate. For other methods and more general discussion refer to HCI texts dealing with evaluation issues (for example, Nielsen 1993; Shneiderman 1998). There is also a large quantity of useful information available on the Web. Instone (2000) maintains 'Usable Web' a searchable, categorised collection of over 1000 links to web resources focusing on usability and the Web.

Bibliography

Alsford, S. (1997) From pilot to program: organizing content creation as a web site grows. In *Proceedings of Museums and the Web '97*, Los Angeles, USA, 1997. Also available via www.archimuse.com/ (consulted 24 August 2000).

Badre, A. and Jacobs, A. (1999) Usability, aesthetics and efficiency: an evaluation in a multimedia environment. In *Proceedings IEEE Multimedia Systems, ICMCS'99*, Florence, Italy, 1999: 103–106.

Barker, P. and King, T. (1993) Evaluating interactive multimedia courseware – a methodology. *Computers in Education*, 21(4): 307–319.

BCMA (1996) Report on cultural heritage institution marketing on the internets. Report by BC Museums Association (Dogwood Regional Network) and the Canada–BC Agreement on Culture and Communications, 1996. Available at www.museumassn. bc.ca/report.html (consulted 24 August 2000).

Berthon, P., Pitt, L. and Prendergast, G. (1997) Visits, hits, caching and counting on the world wide web: old wine in new bottles? *Internet Research: Electronic Networking Applications and Policy*, 7(1): 5–8.

Bertot, J., McClure, C., Moen, W. and Rubin, J. (1997) Web usage statistics: measurement issues and analytical techniques. *Government Information Quarterly*, 14(4): 373–395.

Besser, H. (1995) Multimedia and networks teach about museums. In *Multimedia Computing and Museums – Selected Papers from ICHIM'95 and MCN'95*, ed. D. Bearman, Archives and Museum Informatics, Pittsburgh, PA, pp. 124–140.

Bevan, N. (1998) Usability issues in web site design (version 3, April 1998). Available via www.usability.serco.com/netscape/index.html (consulted 24 August 2000).

Booth, B. (1998a) Information for visitors to cultural attraction? *Journal of Information Science*, 24(5): 291–303.

Booth, B. (1998b) Understanding the information needs of visitors to museums. *Museum Management and Curatorship*, 17(2): 139–157.

Borda, A., Romans, J. and Payne, J. (1999) *Evaluation of Prototype Exhiblets*. Science Museum Report, London: Science Museum, 1999.

Borland, C. and Wongse-Sanit, N. (1997) ArtsEdNet: assessing an arts education web site. In *Proceedings of Museums and the Web '97*, Los Angeles, USA, 1997. Also available via www.archimuse.com/ (consulted 24 August 2000).

Bowen, J. (1999) Time for renovations: a survey of museum web sites. In *Proceedings of Museums and the Web '99*, New Orleans, USA, 1999. Also available via www.archimuse.com/ (consulted 24 August 2000).

Bowen, J. (2000) The website of the UK museum of the year, 1999. In *Proceedings of Museums and the Web '00*, Minneapolis, USA, 2000. Also available via www.arhimuse.com/ (consulted 24 August 2000).

Bowen, J., Bennett, J. and Johnson, J. (1998) Virtual visits to virtual museums. In *Proceedings of Museums and the Web '98*, Toronto, Canada, 1998. Also available via www.archimuse.com/ (consulted 24 August 2000).

Brown, C. (1998) *Human–Computer Interface Design Guidelines*. Intellect Books, Bristol.

Campbell, H. and Wells, M. (1996) Assessment of museum world wide web home page format. *Visitor Studies: Theory, Research and Practice*, 9: 216–226.

Chadwick, J. and Boverie, P. (1999) A survey of characteristics and patterns of behaviour in visitors to a museum web site. In *Proceedings of Museums and the Web '99*, New Orleans, USA, 1999. Also available via www.archimuse.com/ (consulted 24 August 2000).

CIDOC (1997) Multimedia evaluation criteria. ICOM CIDOC Draft Report, 1997. Available at www.archimuse.com/papers/cidoc/cidoc.mmwg.eval.crit.html (consulted 24 August 2000).

Cleary, Y. (2000) An examination of the impact of subjective cultural issues on the usability of a localized web site – the Louvre museum web site. In *Proceedings of Museums and the Web '00*, Minneapolis, USA, 2000. Also available via www.archimuse.com/ (consulted 24 August 2000).

Cunliffe, D. (2000) Developing usable web sites – a review and model. *Internet Research: Electronic Networking Applications and Policy*, 10(4): 295–307.

Cunliffe, D., Taylor, C. and Tudhope, D. (1997) Query-based navigation in semantically indexed hypermedia. In *Proceedings 8th ACM Conference on Hypertext – Hypertext '97*, 1997: 87–95.

Dawson, D. and McKenna, G. (1998) MDA survey of information technology in museums 1998. *MDA Information*, 4(1). Available at www.mdocassn.demon.co.uk/info41.htm (consulted 24 August 2000).

Day, A. (1997) A model for monitoring web site effectiveness. *Internet Research: Electronic Net-working Applications and Policy*, 7(2): 109–115.

Drennan, C., Nash, C. and Bonaventura, P. (1998) The web as art space, museum and forum in Tumblong. In *Proceedings 4th International Conference on Virtual Systems and Multimedia, VSMM 98*. Gifu, Japan, 1998: 275–280.

Drott, M. (1998) Using web server logs to improve site design. In *Proceedings ACM SIGDOC '98*, Quebec, Canada, 1998: 43–50.

Economou, M. (1998) The evaluation of museum multimedia applications: lessons from research, *Museum Management and Curatorship*, 17(2): 173–187.

Erskine, L., Carter-Tod, D. and Burton, J. (1997) Dialogical techniques for the design of web sites. *International Journal of Human–Computer Studies*, 47: 169–195.

Feinberg, S. and Johnson, P. (1998) Designing and developing surveys on WWW sites. In *Proceedings 6th ACM Annual Conference on Computer Documentation*, 1998, pp. 38–42.

Flemming, J. (1998) *Web Navigation: Designing the user experience*. O'Reilly, Sebastopol, CA.

Futers, K. (1997) Tell me what you want, what you really, really want: a look at internet user need. In *EVA'97 Conference*, 1997. Available at www.open.gov.uk/mdocassn/eva-kf.htm (consulted 24 August 2000).

Gammon, B. (1999) Visitor's use of computer exhibits: general findings from 5 years of watching visitors getting it wrong. Science Museum, Wellcome Wing Exhibition Development Report, London, 1999. Also available in *Informal Learning Review*, 38 September/October 1999.

Garzotto, F., Mainetti, L. and Paolini, P. (1995) User interaction styles in museum hypermedia. In *Multimedia computing and museums – selected papers from ICHIM'95 and MCN'95*, D. Bearman (ed.), Archives and Museum Informatics, Pittsburgh, PA, pp. 217–234.

Garzotto, F. and Matera, M. (1997) A systematic method for hypermedia usability inspection. *The New Review of Hypermedia and Multimedia*, 3: 39–65.

Garzotto, F., Matera, M. and Paolini, P. (1998) To use or not to use? Evaluating usability of museum web sites. In *Proceedings of Museums and the Web '98*, Toronto, Canada, 1998. Also available via www.archimuse.com/ (consulted 24 August 2000).

Gray, W. and Salzman, M. (1998) Damaged merchandise? A review of experiments that compare usability evaluation methods. *Human–Computer Interaction*, 13: 203–261.

Haapalainen, R. (1999) Revising the Finnish National Gallery's web pages. In *Proceedings of Museums and the Web '99*, New Orleans, USA, 1999. Also available via <www.archimuse.com/> (consulted 24 August 2000).

Hardman, L. (1989) Evaluating the usability of the Glasgow online hypertext. *Hypermedia*, 1(1): 34–63.

Heinecke, A. (1995) Evaluation of hypermedia systems in museums. In *Multimedia Computing and Museums – Selected Papers from ICHIM'95 and MCN'95*, ed. D. Bearman, Archives and Museum Informatics, Pittsburgh, PA, pp. 67–78.

Hertzum, M. (1998) A review of museum web sites: in search of user-centred design. *Archives and Museum Informatics*, 12: 127–138.

Hilke, D., Hennings, E. and Springuel, M. (1988) The impact of interactive computer software on visitors' experiences: a case study. *International Laboratory for Visitor Studies Review*, 1(1): 34–49.

Hoff, K. (2000) The small museum web site: a case study of the web site development and strategy in a small art museum. In *Proceedings of Museums and the Web '00*, Minneapolis, USA, 2000. Also available via www.archimuse.com/ (consulted 24 August 2000).

Instone, K. (2000) Usable Web. www.usableweb.com/ (consulted 24 August 2000).

James, S. (1997) Museum web page survey result. MSc Dissertation (Toronto: Department of Museum Studies, University of Toronto).

Kritou, E. (1998) A case study of web usability evaluation. MSc Dissertation (Pontypridd: School of Computing, University of Glamorgan, 1998).

Levi, M. and Conrad, F. (1996) A heuristic evaluation of a world wide web prototype, *ACM Interactions*, III. 4 July and August 1996: 50–61.

Lowe, D. and Hall, W. (1999) *Hypermedia and the Web: An Engineering Approach*. Wiley, Chichester.

Lu, M. and Yeung, W. (1998) A framework for effective commercial web application development. *Internet Research: Electronic Networking Applications and Policy*, 8 (2): 166–173.

Morrison, I. (1998) SCRAN and its users. *The New Review of Hypermedia and Multimedia*, 4: 255–260.

Murugesan, S. (1999) Web engineering. *ACM SIGWEB Newsletter*, 8 (3): 28–32.

Nielsen, J. (1993) *Usability Engineering*. AP Professional, London.

Nielsen, J. (1994) Heuristic evaluation. In *Usability Inspection Methods*, J. Nielsen and R. Mack (eds), John Wiley & Sons, Chichester, pp. 25–62.

Nielsen, J. (1998a) Cost of user testing a website. *Alertbox*, May 3, 1998, www.useit.com/alertbox/980503.html (consulted 24 August 2000).

Nielsen, J. (1998b) Failure of corporate websites. *Alertbox*, October 18, 1998, www.useit.com/alertbox/981018.html (consulted 24 August 2000).

Nielsen, J. (1999) User interface directions for the web. *Communications of the ACM*, 42 (1): 65–72.

Nielsen, J. (1999b) Severity ratings in heuristic evaluation. www.useit.com/papers/heuristic/severityrating.html (consulted 24 August 2000).

Nielsen, J. (2000a) useit.com: Jakob Nielsen's Website, www.useit.com (consulted 24 August 2000).

Nielsen, J. (2000b) *Designing Web Usability: The Practice of Simplicity*. New Riders, Indianapolis, LA.

Nielsen, J. and Mack, R. (1994) *Usability Inspection Methods*. John Wiley & Sons, Chichester.

Nordbotten, J. (2000) Entering through the side door – a usage analysis of a web presentation. In *Proceedings of Museums and the Web '00*, Minneapolis, USA, 2000. Also available via www.archimuse.com/ (consulted 24 August 2000).

NRHM (2000) The new review of hypermedia and multimedia. www.comp.glam.ac.uk/NRHM/ (consulted 24 August 2000).

Oono, S. (1998) The world wide museum survey on the web. Internet Museum, Japan, 1998. www.museum.or.jp/IM—english/f-survey.html (consulted 24 August 2000).

Pierroux, P. (1999) *Art in Networks: Information and Communication Technology in Art Museums*. Department of Media and Communication Technical Report, Oslo: University of Oslo, 1999. Also available at www.media.uio.no/internettiendring/publikasjoner/tekst/Pierroux/02Contents.html (consulted 24 August 2000).

Quinn, C. (1998) Why are we here? In *Proceedings of Museums and the Web '98*, Toronto, Canada, 1998. Also available via www.archimuse.com/ (consulted 24 August 2000).

Rees, J. (1998) On the subject of intellectual property rights (IPR), including copyright – a help and a hindrance to cultural heritage? *The New Review of Hypermedia and Multimedia*, 4: 215–244.

Reynolds, R. (1997) Museums and the internet: what purpose should the information supplied by museums on the world wide web serve? MSc Dissertation (Leicester: Department of Museum Studies, Leicester University).

Rosenfeld, L. and Morville, P. (1998) *Information Architecture for the World Wide Web*. O'Reilly, Sebastopol, CA.

Schweibenz, W. (1998) The 'virtual museum': new perspectives for museums to present objects and information using the internet as a knowledge base and communication system. In *Proceedings of ISI'98*, Internationalen Symposiums für Informationswissenschaft, Prague, 1998.

Sears, A. (1997) Heuristic walkthroughs: finding the problems without the noise. *International Journal of Human–Computer Interaction*, 9 (3): 213–234.

Shneiderman, B. (1998) *Designing the User Interface*. Addison Wesley, Reading, MA.

Shneiderman, B., Brethauer, D., Plaisant, C. and Potter, R. (1989) Evaluating three museum installations of a hypertext system. *Journal of the American Society for Information Science*, 40 (3): 172–182.

Smith, S. and Mosier, J. (1986) Guidelines for designing user interface software. Mitre Corporation Report MTR-9420. Mitre Corporation, 1986.

Sphaera (1999) Real visits and virtual visits. *The Newsletter of the Museum of the History of Science*, Oxford, issue 10, Autumn, available at www.mhs.ox.ac.uk/sphaera/index.htm?issue10/articl10 (consulted 24 August 2000).

Streten, K. (2000) Honoured guests – towards a visitor centred web experience. In *Proceedings of Museums and the Web '00*, Minneapolis, USA, 2000. Also available via www.archimuse.com/ (consulted 24 August 2000).

Teather, L. (1998) A museum is a museum is a museum ... or is it?: exploring museology and the web. In *Proceedings of Museums and the Web '98*, Toronto, Canada, 1998. Also available via www.archimuse.com/ (consulted 24 August 2000).

Teather, L. and Wilhelm, K. (1999) Web musing: evaluating museums on the web from learning theory to methodology. In *Proceedings of Museums and the Web '99*, New Orleans, USA, 1999. Also available via www.archimuse.com/ (consulted 24 August 2000).

Thomas, N. and Paterson, I. (1998) Science museum web site assessment. Research Report, Solomon Business Research, 1998. www.nmsi.ac.uk/eval/index.htm (consulted 24 August 2000).

Tinkler, M. and Freedman, M. (1998) Online exhibitions: a philosophy of design and technological implementation. In *Proceedings of Museums and the Web '98*, Toronto, Canada, 1998. Also available via www.archimuse.com/ (consulted 24 August 2000).

Trant, J. (1999) When all you've got is 'the real thing': Museums and authenticity in the networked world. *Archives and Museum Informatics*, 12 (2): 107–125.

Zhang, Y. (1999) Using the internet for survey research: a case study. *Journal of the American Society for Information Science*, 51 (1): 57–68.

Chapter 23

Culture as a Driver of Innovation

Ranjit Makkuni

Introduction

Over the past eighteen years, through a series of technology exhibits of traditional culture shown in museums, we have explored new forms of dissemination of culture through multimedia technology, but also how cultural domains can shape new interface technology. The projects aim to preserve, disseminate, and re-interpret the world's traditional knowledge using digital tools, but the contribution goes beyond just museum applications. They create an interesting space of culture-conscious product design for "the rest of us", the four billion people lying on the wrong side of the digital divide.

The work encompasses three themes as follows.

Re-questioning the interface

The present form of the PC consisting of TV display of screen, keyboard and mouse is based on a 30-year-old invention of the optical mouse. While the hardware form of the PC (keyboard, mouse) and software form (button pushing, windows, point and click) has stabilized over time and has created rich genres of multimedia documents, it is clear that this form needs to be re-questioned as paradigms of information access move from personal computing to ubiquitous, mobile and physical and tactile computing.

Source: ICHIM, Paris, Archives & Museum Informatics Europe, 2003.

Culturally rooted computing

Over the past decade there has been an increasing interest in bringing computing to developing cultures, and within these cultures bringing computing to untapped markets in rural areas. Since rural areas of the world represent the last remaining areas of living, "analog" cultures in the world, i.e., cultures that rely on hand-based skills, our work seeks to integrate traditional knowledge, hand-skills and body-friendly design in new interface technology and learning applications.

We present here three examples that explore culturally rooted computing which shows how interaction with the cultural domain can help in the re-design of the form of the computer itself. It is our hope that "culture" doesn't remain only within the confines of museum walls, but becomes an important driver for the design of richer computing interfaces.

The Crossing Project

The term "Crossing" is related to the Sanskrit term for a pilgrimage site, i.e., pilgrimage site as a crossing point into a space of learning, refection and transformation (see Makkuni 2003). The Crossing Project has created a physical/virtual multimedia exhibit shown in Bombay, New Delhi, New York and Linz that allowed learners to connect to the living knowledge traditions of Banaras, India, a pilgrimage site by the river Ganges, and a 2000-year-old centre of learning. The technologies invented illustrate a new form of body-friendly, culture-friendly, tangible interfaces into digital content.

The Crossing Project brought together futuristic, mobile, multimedia technology and archetypal content, dealing with one of the world's most ancient living cultures, Banaras. With respect to technology, it questioned the very form of a computing system and the Graphical User Interface paradigm, which has served as the substrate of modern computing systems for thirty years; (see Wellner 1993; Ishii and Ullmer 1997; Want et al. 1998). The Crossing technology presents alternate paradigms of information access, integrating the hand and the body in the act of computer-based communication and learning. With respect to content, it brought to focus a traditional society's notion of eco-cosmic connections through mobile, multimedia technology-based connections. With respect to design, it incorporated the expressions of traditional arts and crafts in the design of expressive information delivery devices.

The exhibit created forty-one installations that illustrated alternatives to users interacting with a computing workstation form – consisting of keyboard, mouse and display. These included the users' touching, turning, and tilting of interface objects to access learning content.

Vrindavan Physical–Virtual Authoring Tools

Physical–virtual authoring tools

The Crossing Project was disseminated principally as a museum exhibit. However, its contribution extend to fields of product design and user interaction paradigms. In the

Vrindavan Physical–Virtual Authoring Tools Project, we extend the tactile physical icons concept developed by the Crossing Project to explore continuous authoring activities using physical and virtual media. In doing so, we examine how physical interactions with computing representations present us with a new medium for creative expression. At the higher level, the development of such interfaces could be applicable to cultures where keyboard and mouse paradigms may not make sense.

The Vrindavan content domain

The Vrindavan Project explores new forms of physical–virtual authoring tools, in which children can compose multimedia representations using physical icons as well as virtual multimedia.

To explore the new media, we worked with the children from Vrindavan, a culturally rich city in North India. The city of Vrindavan, the domain of research, is a site of sacred geography, and has been for many hundreds of years associated with the mythology and legends of the cowherd god Krishna, and his consort, Radha. Since places in Vrindavan are physical embodiments of mythology, the city becomes a living document enacting ancient mythology.

Workshops

A series of experiments in visual and tangible multimedia composition allowed village children to understand examples of form and composition in modern multimedia. Second, a series of experiments in "representation" allowed these children to represent concepts, calendars and develop storyboards, and to plan and execute a multimedia presentation.

Work process

Children huddle around a shared representational and display space when composing work in traditional media, working together on clay icons, seeing and interacting with each other socially, observing each other's tools and the emerging forms of the shared emergent artifact. This is in contrast to most modern workstations, which function as individual workspaces with no provision for social sharing or for people to access shared representations of the "collective" or the "sense of periphery of the collective".

Physical and virtual authoring medium

Inspired by the form of a huddled group of children around a shared work and presentation space, we recreated a computational display and interface where a group of children could huddle together around a shared representation (a combined display screen and interface) and use tools to compose a multimedia presentation using physical tactile and digital multimedia. We call this process 'PV' – physical and virtual authoring. The size of the display allows a group of seven to eight children to work together around a shared surface and compose a map of their city. Children see each other around a shared display, share each other's tools, while display also functions as an interface. Children can place physical objects on the surface to affect the state of the presentation, so that an interface action and the resulting display-update occur on the same surface.

Composition tools and process

We used this new display and interface media to allow children to compose a map of their city, Vrindavan. Vrindavan is a city of temples and gardens, with mythological stories associated with physical spaces. The map of the city consists of roads, temples, trees, and gardens. Children make up the map by composing roads, positioning temples and trees, and associating different elements on the map with associated video links. The links play back videos composed by the children. In total, the selection of images, arrangement of images on a map, and the creation of links to points in the map roughly allows the child to create a reasonably complex multimedia document.

Personalization of transportation technology in Asia

A wide spectrum of public transportation is used in Asia, such as rickshaws and taxis. These functional modes of transportation that serve millions of people are adorned by communities who personalize them with their own narratives. In essence, the technologies that would otherwise homogenize the users thrive as platforms for cultural expression.

Communities of users personalize their vehicles to different degrees of ornamentation. The resulting array of graphics, textures, patterns, motifs, paintings, embossing, composite materials, talismans, quotes and decorative accessories present us with an amazing variety of anonymous artists and their indigenous art. This culture of ornamentation sustains street artists, who work with different styles of vehicle personalization, such as hand painting, poster art, paper cutting, audio mixing and accessory art.

One can delight in the diverse ways in which different communities collectively express their identities. This study focuses on vehicular graphic art as a point of departure to explore how the need to ornament is fundamental to Asian cultures. Since global companies are becoming interested in the dissemination and accessibility of ICT for emerging economies, this study in particular provokes one to understand the process of personalization so that future products and services respect this fundamental cultural need. This study infers that culturally rooted technology is a means to increasing accessibility of ICT in emerging economies.

In this era of globalization, we therefore deduce that technologies that provide for personalization can enable cultures to preserve their identities.

Conclusion

These projects present us with beautiful examples of how technology that "ceases" to be just a "technology" becomes an extension and experience of identity of a community. Engagement with such cultural content provoked innovation at fundamental levels of user interfaces as well as highlighted designers' awareness for ornamentation, customization and personalization. The rich technologies described here actually become a valuable benchmark and set an important design value towards the design of culturally appropriate computing in developing and developed nations.

References

Ishii, H., Ullmer, B., 1997. "Tangible bits: towards seamless interfaces between people, bits and atoms," Conference on Human Factors and Computing Systems, Conference Proceedings on Human Factors in Computing Systems, Atlanta, ACM Press, New York.

Want, R., Fishkin, K., Gujar, A., Harrison, B., 1998. "Bridging Physical and Virtual Worlds with Electronic Tags," Xerox PARC report, submitted to CHI 99.

Wellner, P., 1993 "Interacting with paper on the Digital Desk", Communication of ACM, July 1993.

Makkuni, R., 2003. "The Crossing", Exhibit Catalogue, Sacred World Foundation, San Francisco.

Interpretation: communication, interactivity and learning

Introduction to Part Four

Ross Parry

DIGITAL MEDIA (LIKE ANY MEDIA) is anything but a neutral vessel. Instead of passively and objectively carrying and migrating content, digital technology contributes its own sets of connotations and inferences for the user. Consequently, to decide to convey an idea using a computer is also to decide (implicitly) to cast this idea within another set of meanings associated with computing. In short – *if it is not too evident to say so* – digital media becomes part of the message. So what are these consequences of communicating via digital technology? How is reading and interacting with a computer different to other media? And what do we know about how museum audiences, in particular, react to digital interfaces and computer-based experiences? It is to these themes that Part Four now looks.

We begin (in Chapter 24) with an often-quoted article by Peter Walsh. Originally published in the journal *Archives and Museum Informatics*, this paper highlights the question of authorship and authority online. Written at the moment when most museums were just starting their journeys on the Internet, Walsh's article helped set in motion a series of debates and lines of enquiry about how a distributed network medium, such as the Web, might impact on the way a museum communicated with its audiences. In the challenges and opportunities it highlights, here is a discussion anticipating the debates around user-generated content, audience participation, and the rise of the heritage 'prosumer' (the producer–consumer) online – discussions that would come to characterise so much Web development and activity in the years to follow.

Chapters 25 and 26 move our attention specifically to the role of digital media within learning. In an article originally published in Scott Paris' edited volume *Perspectives on Object-centered Learning in Museums*, Olivia Frost helpfully takes us back to some fundamental principles, identifying the attributes and functions of the 'digital object' and the impact of these on the dynamics of learning. What emerges is that a digital resource may not carry the physicality and uniqueness of its material 'original', but its other traits (of manipulation, multiplication, migration) endow it with other possibilities for the communicating museum. Then, in a paper taken from the journal *Computers in Entertainment*, Maria Roussou draws confidently from technological practice and pedagogical theory, to triangulate play, learning and media. As with Frost, Roussou demonstrates the defining role digital technology plays within such interactions, as well as the value of theory (and deeper intellectualising and evidencing) of museums' deployment of digital media in the support of learning.

By way of contrast to the 'potentials' and 'opportunities' trialed to this point, the last two chapters (27 and 28) ground us back into some of the realities and practicalities of technology-based interactions in the museum. For instance, it is revealing to read the optimism of Frost alongside the empiricism of Heath and vom Lehn. Here the authors' observation-based research signals a more problematic role for digital media. Their findings are of in-gallery media interactivity coming at the cost of social interaction, where visitor co-operation and collaboration is potentially impoverished. Equally, it is revealing to consider the theory-informed discourse of Roussou's chapter alongside the pragmatism of Ben Gammon in Chapter 28. In a paper originally published in *The Informal Learning Review*, Gammon candidly shares with his professional peers what his team at the Science Museum, London, learned from testing computer interactive exhibits from, as he calls it, 'mostly bitter experience'. As we hear this frank perspective of an honest and generous practitioner (especially when heard alongside the other voices in this section), we are struck by the inseparability of grounded theory and reflective practice within digital heritage.

Chapter 24

The Web and the Unassailable Voice

Peter Walsh

Let me begin with a passage from *Mr. Wilson's Cabinet of Wonder*, Lawrence Weschler's book on the Museum of Jurassic Technology. Weschler is describing the audio commentaries that accompany the exhibits in this strange, postmodern museum in Venice, CA. "The voice in the receiver," Weschler writes, "the same voice as in all the other receivers, it may occur to you, is in fact the same, bland, slightly unctuous voice you've heard in every museum slide show or Acoustiguide tour or PBS nature special you've ever endured: the reassuringly measured voice of unassailable institutional authority."

This Unassailable Voice has, for many decades, been an essential part of the museum experience. It is a tone and attitude that pervades museum labels, brochures, exhibitions, catalogues, the guided tour, audio-visual presentations, and now websites. For the most part, it is both impersonal and disembodied: it is usually not a true human voice, connected to a real identity and personality, but a bureaucratic composite, in some ways closer to an IRS form than a living art historian or scientist.

The tone or accent of the Voice varies, of course, from institution to institution. I am writing here primarily from the point of view of the art museum, which is the kind I know best. I have been involved with many kinds of museums, however, including natural history museums and a zoo. The art museum accent can be particularly aloof and other kinds of museums speak with a cozier tone. Still, I think some variant of the Voice is nearly universal in the museum world.

Those of us who actually work in museums, of course, realize that the Unassailable Voice is a myth. Like the floating head and thundering words of the Wizard of Oz, the Unassailable Voice is created by smoke and high-tech projections, designed to hide most of the human activity and frailties behind it.

Source: *Archives and Museum Informatics*, vol. 11, no. 2, 1997, pp. 77–85.

The typical interpretive art museum label, for example, is the work of a group of educators, editors, scholars, and administrators who not infrequently disagree. Even the simple line "attributed to" can, in a museum label, conceal fierce behind-the-scenes debates over the nature of the art object it purports to describe.

The words of the Unassailable Voice, for all its apparent unflappable confidence, often represent a series of compromises: compromises between the views of different experts or compromises between simple, understandable, and apparently fixed explanations on the one hand and, on the other hand, the complex and ever-changing, but richer and truer, accounts of reality. These complex and hidden accounts, however, are the ones historians and scientists actually grapple with every day of their professional lives.

Thus the Unassailable Voice has the flattened, vaguely evasive tone of a text created by committee. The voice itself often doesn't even believe or understand what it says. Sometimes borrowed from a professional presenter or actor, the voice merely mouths words of a disembodied, anonymous authority. In most cases, this authority is not the property of a single person but a group.

As you may have guessed by now, in my opinion, the Unassailable Voice is not an entirely benevolent presence in the museum. It tends to enhance the slightly patronizing, intimidating atmosphere found particularly in larger institutions, some-times aided and abetted by their monumental architecture. This institutional atmos-phere keeps some people out of museums altogether and vaguely irritates others. In its attempts to smooth over and conceal the complex and often contentious intellec-tual processes that really go into creating a museum, the string pullers behind the Unassailable Voice often edit out some of the most interesting and compelling parts of what a museum truly is.

The most deplorable side effect of the Unassailable Voice, the one that means that it often must be endured rather than enjoyed, is that it tends to make people feel ignorant, and thus alienates them from the entire experience of the museum. This result, however unintended, should not come as a surprise. After all, in normal life, the know-it-all who speaks in a polished, endless monologue and has no interest in the ideas and opinions of others is not so much admired as he is considered a bore.

In their first forays into the World Wide Web, many art museums have, in effect, tried to carry that Unassailable Voice into a new technology. Museum sites are grad-ually standardizing themselves around a formula that essentially duplicates a collec-tion of familiar museum products: the floor plan, the exhibition catalogue, the label, the Acoustiguide, the docent tour, and the audio-visual presentation. All of these are built around variations on the Unassailable Voice, whose message is, on a subcon-scious level at least, that museums have the knowledge and then benevolently dole it out to the comparatively ignorant public.

Will this approach work in this new medium of cyberspace? I suspect not. The very nature of the Web, I think, works against it.

In fact, in many ways the Web is the opposite of the Unassailable Voice. Where the Voice exudes reason and order, the Web is chaotic. Despite recent attempts to regulate it, there are no cops in the Internet. Unlike other forms of media, which require the coordination of large amounts of money and people to work, the Web is, in theory at least, open to everyone with access to a computer and a modem.[1] The

Web has no particular organization, no hierarchy, no catalogue numbers. Thus the Web is like a vast library without librarians, a library that accepts any book or manuscript that anyone brings to it, puts it on its shelves, and circulates it at random.

The Unassailable Voice is the projection of timeless authority, uncorrupted by fashion, commercialism, or the relentless pace of modern life. The Web, however, is a faddish new medium and is constantly changing. What it is this afternoon it will not be tonight or tomorrow morning. In this it defies virtually all the usual guidelines of verifying and checking knowledge: it cannot be rationally footnoted or checked as a reference, nor can its results always be easily repeated.

No one can predict at this point where the Web is going and what it will be a few months or years from now. It is already vast and growing constantly. It is a vast, trackless space of extraordinarily diverse information which no one can map or fully understand. It is a virtual frontier that is growing far faster than explorers can advance toward it. Is its value to society primarily as an information source or as communication? Can it be made to turn a profit? Will it stay the preserve of a small elite or will it develop into a true mass medium as television did in the 1950s, with all the pluses and minuses that that suggests?

Moreover, the Web is becoming increasingly commercial, and profit motives are gradually infecting the information there. As Brian Hecht wrote recently in *The New Republic*, "Growing numbers of Web sites conveniently ignore the old 'separation of church and state' that divides editorial from advertising in quality print publications."[2] Even some museum websites are now commercially supported and include advertising, which increasingly is the main financial support of the Web in general. The line between fact and ad is regularly bent and obscured in many websites, more so than has traditionally been true of, for example, newspapers and broadcast news, where it is usually easier to tell what is news and what is a commercial.

Most importantly, the Web is an environment where fact and fiction blend and meld. As Brian Hecht points out, on the Web, "it is impossible to know where information comes from, who has paid for it, whether it is reliable and whether you will ever be able to find it again. A student looking for information on the Internet about, say, World War II, cannot know whether a given 'page' has been posted by a legitimate historian or by a Holocaust revisionist."[3]

In a recent story about misinformation in *The New Yorker*, Burt Andersen points out that the very accessibility of the Web has its downside. On the Web, he writes, "not only is every citizen entitled to his or her opinion but he or she is entitled to deliver it instantaneously, studded with chunks of fake information, to the whole world. With a computer and a phone line, anyone can become his own publisher/commentator/reporter/anchor, dispatching to everyone everywhere credible-looking opinions, facts, and 'facts' via the Internet. . . . Thanks to the Web, amateurism and spuriousness no longer need look amateurish or spurious."[4]

Until someone invents a system of authentication parallel to the ones that have grown up around print media, the tendency of the Web to always put "fact" between quotes will continue.[5] Even when such systems are in place, however, the suspicion of spuriousness will likely cast a shadow over every website, no matter how reputable its name and purported origin; it is simply too easy, on the Web, to mimic the gloss of institutional authority. Early surfers of museum websites will recall, for example, that the original "Louvre Museum" website had nothing to do with the famous Paris institution: it was created entirely by a French computer engineer. For some time, it was the only Louvre website and, despite its disclaimers, undoubtedly misled many visitors into believing it was official.

For many, foraging the Web for knowledge, in its present immature state, can be a hazardous experience. The current search engines do not discriminate the gems from the dregs. For example, when I searched the Web recently for information on the Pyramids of Giza, the very first site the search engine turned up was an authoritative-looking site with impressive diagrams and quotations from prominent Egyptologists and PBS programs.

Only by penetrating to the very bottom of this site and moving to its author's homepage[6] do you realize it is put together by a gentleman from Georgia, depicted in a ten-gallon hat, who also offers information on such subjects as the I Ching as conveyer of genetic code, parallel universes, the extraterrestrial entities known as the "massless lightcone beings of the luminous dharmata," and the nature of time as "a holographic interference pattern". This website concludes with the assurance that "the internet is the most effect way ever devised for ideas to be communicated among humans. You might even regard ideas as life forms living on a human-internet substrate."

In fact, mystical prophecies about a hidden Hall of Records at Giza and New Age theories about pyramid power and the extraterrestrial origins of ancient civilizations predominate in websites about ancient Egypt. The same is true of other popular subjects. Many such websites seem to occupy an odd, unfocused realm between fact, fantasy, and satire. Some of the strangest sites can also be some of the most fascinating and most difficult to interpret.

As I said above, I believe the qualities of World Wide Web I have just described make it fundamentally hostile to the Unassailable Voice. The tone of institutional authority that has been the essential medium of museums for decades will not easily cross the barriers of modems and HTML where all authority yields to a kind of electronic leveling.

This is not to say that museums won't try, aren't trying, the transition. It is not to say that they might not create the illusion of a successful transition. But I believe it does mean that museums must find a new voice for the Web, one that does not rely on blind faith and Oz-like illusion to authenticate its authority. It is no longer possible or responsible to present "facts" over the Web without first admitting the medium's vulnerability to falsehood and distortion. On the Web, everyone is the Wizard of Oz.

This state of affairs may be difficult for many museum officials to swallow. Museums have relied so long on the Unassailable Voice and its barrage of invulnerable facts that it has become part of their identity. It has thus become difficult for them to imagine other paths to knowledge.

As they learn more about the Web's tendency to meld facts and authority, some museum officials will undoubtedly try to shut out the Web altogether. This will not solve the problem, of course, as new technologies have a way of making their presence felt everywhere, almost like a force of nature. It is also not desirable, as I think that the World Wide Web has a great potential, one not yet fully exploited, of changing the partly falsified monologue most museums carry on with the world into an infinitely richer and truer dialogue. It will mean abandoning or greatly modifying the tone of the Unassailable Voice, but, as I have already suggested, the Voice itself is not always a welcome or positive presence for everyone.

What might a museum website look like without the Unassailable Voice? Let me suggest three basic principles that might guide it. The core idea behind these principles is that the medium should be used for what it can do that other media cannot do: it should not merely duplicate what has traditionally, and probably more effectively, been done in print.

First, the museum site should always be built with the assumption of change and provisionality. The Web is constantly changing and is never complete. Museums, although they tend to ignore this, are the same. Not only do the exhibits and the physical plant of the museum change, its collections change, and, more importantly, its understanding of the meaning of those collections changes. Unlike the catalogue card for a book, the information about an object in a museum collection is constantly being revised. Art works are reattributed to new artists, X-rays reveal other images below the surface of a painting. Scientific specimens in a natural history museum are constantly being reclassified and the significance of, say, a fossil jaw from the Jurassic, may change abruptly with new information, a new discovery, or a new theory. Museums, although they try hard not to admit it, are in a constant state of revolution.

The Web has a great potential for reflecting this process of change and reevaluation because it can so easily be updated and modified. A physical exhibition takes months and years to organize and present. Information on the Web can be changed in a few minutes. New scientific developments can be documented as they happen. For example, images of the recently discovered cave paintings in the Ardeche region of France were transmitted around the world within a few days the discovery, thanks to the Web.

Exhibitions and other temporary phenomena in art museums can similarly be quickly mounted and presented to the world. The Dia Art Foundation in New York, for example, uses its website to present artist installations that physically exist at its various exhibition sites. Museums could also use the Web to present an exhibition as it is developed, or to present day-by-day reports of an object as it is studied by a group of scholars and scientists.

Exploiting the temporary and provisional nature of information on the Web in this way has another important benefit: it shifts the relationship between the Web and facts, which can easily be falsified there. By changing the nature of truth from the fixed state of the Unassailable Voice to a process over time, which is far closer to what really happens with the development of knowledge, the Web can build a process of self-validation. If the steps in the process of building information are logical and hang together, they will tend to be self-validating. They will also teach a far more powerful lesson on the nature of information: that it is subject to a constant process of challenge and checking against other information. This is a lesson that needs to be taught about our entire system of knowledge in this electronic age.

Second, the Web should exploit its powerful ability to be interactive. Not long ago, I came across a message that asked for advice about dealing with the "problem" of questions coming into a museum website from its public. Apart from the logistics, I would suggest, this is not a problem but an enormous opportunity.

Museums have traditionally ignored an important aspect of communication: that communication is not a monologue, but a dialogue. In order for true communication to exist, information must pass from both sides, like a conversation, so that each side can check and question the message.

Museums are almost unique among educational institutions in that they still are using a one-sided method of communication. This is unlike the relationship between a teacher and his students, for example, which is two-way: the teacher presenting information, the students responding with questions; the teacher testing how the information comes across with exams, the students responding with answers; the student making the information their own with papers and projects, the teacher evaluating how effectively that information has been absorbed.

Museums largely by-pass this feedback approach. As a result, they lose an enormous amount of information about their visitors and their likes and dislikes, information that any business would consider invaluable and essential for its survival. Such an ivory tower approach has often left museums out of touch with their public, and, I think, left them vulnerable and unprepared to deal with the wave of controversies that have engulfed public funding for museums in recent years. As any successful business knows, constant two-way responsive communication with your clients is a prime way to build trust and confidence, and to give yourself a margin of tolerance should problems arise.

With only a monologue between them and the public, museums are also less likely to adjust ineffective methods of communication and can miscommunicate on a grand scale. Let me use a small example from my own museum, the Davis Museum and Cultural Center, which is on the campus of Wellesley College. When the Museum was built three years ago, a small gallery off a much larger gallery of twentieth-century art was set aside for Wellesley's small but choice collection of African art. This was, in fact, the first art museum gallery in the Greater Boston area devoted to African art.

African-American students on the campus, however, interpreted this gallery differently. They saw the African collection's separation as segregation, and the gallery's relatively small size not as a reflection of the size of the collection but a judgment on the importance of African art relative to Western art. In other words, they saw the entire arrangement as yet another racially based narrative of exclusion and implied inferiority – a message that, needless to say, the museum never intended to communicate.[7]

I believe this sort of unfortunate and unintended miscommunication takes place every day in museums for the very reason that there has, until now, been no easy way to check up on how the words of the Unassailable Voice are actually coming across in the world. The Web's interactive capabilities can change that dramatically. For example, in a special project designed by a Davis Museum intern, the Web and the campus computer network are being used to help plan the exhibit of an Ashanti seat soon to be given to the Davis Museum collection. Through the network, students, scholars, and curators will discuss the meaning of the object and the extent to which it was shaped or reinterpreted by European imperialism in Africa. A special web page will present the object, perhaps in the context of other art works, and will feature a more elaborate written discussion about how best to display the work and explain its meaning. Eventually, this discussion will help shape how the Ashanti seat is shown in the museum.

Third, museums should exploit the Web's ability to look below the surface, to present the layers of knowledge that museums have not previously been able to show the public. Because of its ability to organize large amounts of information in a relatively compact area, the Web opens up possibilities that the simple, and necessarily deeply abridged, museum label can never do.

For example, in collaboration with Professor of Classics Miranda Marvin, we created a special label project on our museum website and on a computer installation in the Davis Museum's classical galleries. The project used more than a century of research on a single object in the collection: a classical sculpture sometimes known as the "Wellesley Athlete," to explore the gap between what is known about an art object by museum officials and scholars and what is typically presented to the museum's visitors.

Professor Marvin named this project "Truth in Advertising" because she believes most museum labels for classical sculpture are out of date and deeply misleading. In the "Truth in Advertising" website, visitors were able to click on phrases of the original label for the Wellesley Athlete to learn more about the research and scholarly attitudes behind each term. In the process, they could explore how museum labels can distort and even conceal the truth about an art object and its history.

Projects like "Truth in Advertising" are only a small foray into what I see is the great potential of the on-going collaboration between museums and the World Wide Web.[8] This collaboration, properly directed, can not only bring the wealth of museums to a far wider audience, it can help replace the traditional "Unassailable Voice" with one that is kinder, gentler, less pompous, more interesting, and, ultimately, far more inspiring.

Marshall McLuhan, whose long neglected ideas seem to have taken on new significance in the era of the World Wide Web,[9] emphasized that new media can only be understood through the transformations they bring to society; the content of these new media he saw as camouflaging their true effects. In a 1974 interview, McLuhan summarized his position: "If we understand the revolutionary transformations caused by new media, we can anticipate and control them; but if we continue in our self-induced subliminal trance, we will be their slaves."[10]

I have hinted, in this paper, at the sort of transformations that the dramatic increase in access to and interactivity of the World Wide Web are causing and explained why I think they render the old, content-based Unassailable Voice obsolete. Ironically, I think museums – institutions heavily invested in the past – are potentially in a good position both to understand these future transformations and make good use of them. In doing this, museums can also take leadership in shaping the Web to benefit the advancement of knowledge around the world.

Notes

1   Although access to the Web is doubtless subject to the same class, race, and educational barriers presented by other media, the threshold seems to have been

dramatically lowered with the advent of the Web. I have seen Internet-connected computers in small towns in New Hampshire and have heard Australians describe traveling computer centers that ply the outback settlements. Recent projects involving community access to the Web, proposed FCC rulings, and Bill Gates' recently announced major gift to facilitate computer access promise to vastly widen that access. As with so many other aspects of the Web, the long-term implications of this huge and unprecedented increase in the ability of everyone to reach everyone else on the planet are as yet unclear.

2 Brian Hecht, "Net Loss," *The New Republic*, February 17, 1997, p. 16.

3 Hecht, loc. cit., p. 15.

4 Kurt Anderson, "The Age of Unreason," *The New Yorker*, February 3, 1997.

5 Several ideas have already been put forward for "branding" or "authenticating" websites in various ways. Jane Sledge of the Getty Information Institute has suggested that museum sites might include an "AAM" accredited museum logo linked to a place on a website managed by the American Association of Museums. No matter what system is devised, I would argue that the Web's subversion of the norms of authority separate it fundamentally from what makes the Unassailable Voice possible: the assumption of truth based on what amounts to tone and delivery rather than substance.

6 Currently located at gallaxy.cau.edu/tsmith/TShome.html, after a previous location on the Web was "taken over" by the wizard Mordred.

7 It might be argued here, as one of my readers pointed out, that *intention* is an ambiguous term in this context: that, as contemporary social critics often argue, the inherent racism of Western institutions leads it to subconsciously present a continuous narrative of Western superiority no matter what their stated aims might be. The epistemology of institutional racism is a gigantic and complex topic too large to address in this paper. Suffice it to say, at this point, that the Davis Museum's conscious efforts were to be as culturally sensitive and politically correct as possible. Despite these efforts, however, the communication was otherwise.

8 Perhaps prompted by the issues automatically raised by the use of new technologies like the Internet, museums have already begun to examine some of the assumptions underlying the Unassailable Voice. Jane Sledge has outlined some of the results in a paper on the "Points of View" project of the Getty Information Institute and the Consortium for the Computer Interchange of Museum Information. Ms. Sledge's paper was presented at the 1995 ICHIM Conference and is available in the conference proceedings.

9 Coincidentally, the last thing I wrote before beginning work on this paper was a review of the new book on Marshall McLuhan which I quote below. Oddly, McLuhan's observations often seem to apply even more directly to the wired and digitized 1990s than they did to the 1960s, when he made them.

10 Paul Benedetti and Nancy DeHart (eds), *Forward through the Rearview Mirror: Reflections On and By Marshall McLuhan* (Cambridge, MA: MIT Press, 1997), p. 198.

Chapter 25

When the Object is Digital: properties of digital surrogate objects and implications for learning

Olivia C. Frost

Digital communities and their impact on individual and shared learning

Personal computers and access to the World Wide Web are now becoming a prevalent part of our everyday lives at school, work, and home. Costs of computing are making such access more affordable, and advances in usability of computers and programs are making it easier for ordinary citizens to use increasingly sophisticated and powerful technology. In light of these developments, and the rapid proliferation of information systems that overcome barriers of place and time, the access to information objects becomes less and less dependent on where we are, who we are, and at what point in the day we use information. At the same time, although digital technologies can broaden the reach and exchange of information and ideas, there are differences in income, education status, race and ethnicity, and/or geographic region that can have broad impacts on access (National Telecommunications Infrastructure Administration 2000).

The use of digital information can bring with it profound changes in the way in which we interact with others in society. At the same time that digital technologies make it easier for us to have access to information on an individual, and even anonymous level, these technologies give us the power to extend our reach and join or even form new communities. With the capability of disseminating information both instantly and to an infinitely large and diverse set of recipients, users can create audiences for their communication. In Galston's view (1999), the Internet makes it possible to combine individual autonomy and social ties. The ability to exchange

Source: *Perspectives on Object-centered Learning in Museums*, Scott G. Paris (ed.), Mahwah, NJ: Lawrence Erlbaum Associates, Inc., 2002 pp. 79–94.

information and opinions with others of shared interests is a powerful force in Internet communities.

Viewing materials online can be both socially enriching and isolating. The Internet can foster community, but it can also facilitate individual, one-on-one engagement between people and the information objects found on their computers, leaving out the intermediary. This direct interaction with information makes it easier to connect to resources at our own convenience, providing we have appropriate means of access to computers and connectivity. However, there are value-added benefits that an intermediary can provide that may be lost if the learner goes directly to the resources and by-passes the assistance of the librarian or museum intermediary. The personalized help that a librarian or school media specialist can bring to an information search is usually lost to the learner in online visits to libraries. Although online versions of resources can also provide their own powerful personalized assistance, this may be lost if learners lack awareness of these tools or lack the skills to take advantage of them. In visiting a museum website, the learner may lose the benefit provided by the museum guide who serves as an intermediary to bring context, personalization, and similar assistance to help enrich the understanding of museum objects. In considering the role of mediation in determining experience with objects, Hapgood and Palinscar (2002) observe that "[w]hether and how one experiences objects is a function of the interplay of the characteristics of the object, the knowledge and dispositions that one brings to the viewing, and the context in which one views the object" and argue the need for providing viewers with different lenses that they can apply to their experiences with objects.

Given the relatively anonymous context in which information creation and use occurs, those who create information resources may have little idea of who uses the information they distribute, where these users are, and under what circumstances or for what purposes the information is being used. Because people are often alone when they use their computers, the experience is individual and one-on-one with their computers, rather than a shared experience with a live group. The experience becomes in some ways more personalized, with the ability of the online tools to deliver custom-tailored information. At the same time, the experience can be devoid of the shared appreciation taking place with others at a physical museums, for example, or enriched through online interaction with others who may have viewed the same object. Rowe (2002) points out that a significant percentage of museum goers visit as part of a group, with group activity and meaning-making developing in socially mediated ways.

Some museums offer online access to digital objects at the physical museum site. This offers the museums visitor the opportunity to interact with virtual and actual objects, and to benefit from a shared experience with a group as well as individually, particularly as computer use by groups is not unusual in museums (Chadwick 1992). Falk and Dierking (1992) explored the role of social context in a museum experience and noted differences between the experience of individuals and those visiting as a group (Falk and Dierking 1998), and a study by Chadwick (1999) looked at differences in behavior between individuals and groups visiting a museum website. In his online questionnaire surveying visitors to a museum website, Chadwick found that nearly 30 per cent of respondents were visiting the museum as part of a group. The study revealed differences between groups and individuals while visiting the museum. For example, groups were likely to visit more pages during an online visit than individuals and were also more likely to be engaged in browsing behaviors, whereas individual visitors engaged in more directed searches.

For young learners working independently on their computers, the experience can be both enriching in the way it provides freedom of access to new kinds of information and limiting in its absence of guidance and context, and with the new technologies come both opportunities and challenges. Opportunities arise as online connections make resources accessible to an infinite array of audiences, and sophisticated finding tools enable novice users to locate materials by chance or by design. Because of this, there is a far greater likelihood that materials that were previously in the domain of groups privileged by education, social connection, mobility, or resources will now be accessible to much wider audiences. Accordingly, there is the potential for breaking down social and age boundaries as well as interesting possibilities for exchanges across cultures, generations, and geographic boundaries. The ability to co-locate disparate groups can enrich the audience appreciation base of an object. As a result, objects in museums, archives, and libraries are now accessible to viewers around the globe. Repositories such as archival collections, a type of material previously off-limits to all but a few scholarly users, can now in effect be in the public domain when made accessible through the Internet. Accessibility to an infinitely broad and rich set or original materials can vastly increase the availability of primary resources available to learners.

Among the challenges of online access is the fact that broad access may come with its own intellectual constraints. For example, the understanding and appreciation of objects may assume a knowledge base shared by scholarly communities and other groups with specialized expertise. Access to objects and information about them is available to both novice and expert users alike; however, the impact of the object may diminish significantly without the surrounding background necessary to understand its origins. This heightens the need for contextual resources to accompany the object. For example, sites that are enriched with material explaining the significance of a photographic exhibit can make it easier for viewers to understand more fully the importance of these materials, or engage viewers in a way that can enable them to relate what they have seen to their own experience (Frost 1999). Increasingly, archivists have become more engaged in helping develop online primary resources for incorporation into K-12 classrooms (Gilliland-Swetland et al. 1999). Learners can have access to a rich array of archival resources available online, such as the National Archives Digital Classroom and the Learning Page of the Library of Congress' American Memory Project sites. With widely available access to these kinds of online materials, young learners can observe and participate on a much more level playing field. Broadening the access can increase the audience base for an information object and thus dramatically affect the potential of its social impact.

A major force in the dynamic of digital communities results from the ability of users to become creators as well as consumers of information objects. The self-publishing aspects of digital communication now make it possible for a wide and diverse set of users to create and distribute their works. Even relatively inexperienced computer users are able to create multimedia collages of sound, images, moving pictures, and text, and with hypertext linkages, users can place a document in a contextual setting. In using digital representations of objects, learners can go well beyond the mere viewing of an object to create their own objects or information de novo or as an extension or augmentation of an original artifact they have found. For example, learners can locate an artifact on the Internet and then provide context for it by identifying background and paths to related works and information. Another potential is to provide a new version of the artifact, for example, a drawing inspired by an original art work or a poem inspired by a piece of sculpture. The ability of new technologies to facilitate collaborative work also makes possible the opportunity for participatory creation.

Because digital information objects can be so easily altered, extended, and otherwise manipulated, a user may decide to add context to a work, reconfigure it, and use it for a different purpose. For example, a high school learner may take an image from a museum website and incorporate it into a report, combining it with music clips and video images retrieved online, as well as with text from an online encyclopedia and links to related sites. With the capability that new technologies offer to combine works of different media and to bring together images, sound, text, and software programs to create new material, such creations are increasingly common. As a result, concepts of ownership of ideas and intellectual property become increasingly complex in the creation and use of digital information. Teaching information literacy in the use of these tools will require that we go beyond the technical use of these tools. Equally important is the recognition of what it means to be an informed information citizen when it comes to concepts of intellectual property and ownership of ideas and content, as learners take existing original contents and use them as building blocks of a new creation. In new information environments, it becomes critical to understand how to use information objects in a responsible way that recognizes principles of intellectual ownership. This is especially important in view of cultural forces that have tended to make it socially acceptable to share and copy information found on the World Wide Web.

In the new digital environment, our understanding of fair use may be challenged. As educators, we, like others, are likely to make extensive use of content from other sources in our teaching. We may want to alter content to suit curricular goals and also share that content with our students, as well as with other teachers and learners. The traditions of access to information and freedom of expression are prevalent in educational institutions and the repositories, such as libraries, that serve them. For the classroom teacher and museum educator, familiar assumptions regarding appropriate use of intellectual property may no longer be valid in a digital environment. In a classroom, a teacher may assume, when he or she copies the work of others to create a lesson plan, that this is "fair use" and serves a social good. However, this may change when technologies with "anytime/anyplace" properties make it possible for us to use educational materials in locales outside the classroom, for example, if we distribute a lesson plan using a personal website, or include materials for educational use in a resource to be published for commercial profit. These considerations make it difficult to relegate certain kinds of appropriate uses to specific contexts (National Research Council 2000). The challenge will be to identify and interpret a complex and changing environment of intellectual property in the digital environment while exploiting the capabilities of digital technologies to make information relevant and meaningful through personalization and contextualization.

Navigation and intellectual access to objects

Brown (2000) asserted that:

> [t]the new information literacy, beyond text and image, is one of informa-
> tion navigation. The real literacy of tomorrow entails the ability to be your
> own personal reference librarian – to know how to navigate through confus-
> ing, complex information spaces and feel comfortable doing so. "Naviga-
> tion" may well be the main form of literacy for the 21st century. (p. 14)

Navigating information space in an environment where information grows exponen-
tially and is no longer contained in neat boundaries becomes a major obstacle in
gaining intellectual access to information objects. At the same time, new information tools can facilitate information discovery and can also bring us more directly
into contact with representations of images and other objects. Previously, searches
in the library card catalog retrieved only surrogate descriptions of a book, image, or
information object. Now, online searches can retrieve not only the descriptions about
information, such as index terms and annotations, but also the information object
itself. Full-text retrieval of texts and retrieval of image and sound documents are
now readily accessible. Learners now have easier access to reproductions of primary
resources, rather than relying on descriptions.

Intellectual access to information objects is also immensely facilitated through
the power of hyperlinking. In looking up information on a given topic, a user may
consult the library online card catalog to help find materials on a particular subject,
or may use the catalog to locate a book or a representation of an object by its title or
artist. A different, and at times more powerful, means of search is to identify a document that is close to our interests, and find what works have been linked to or from
this document, a process similar to scanning a known document for its footnotes or
consulting a citation index. With the Web, however, there is a far easier and more
powerful means of finding items related to documents identified as being of interest.
Hyperlinking in today's Internet environment takes on additional dimensions in that
it allows the user to determine and create the links, thus resulting in connections
that indexers and catalogers may never have dreamed of. In this way, users of the
site are no longer relying solely on the links established by traditional and relatively
static knowledge structures such as the Dewey Decimal Classification. Instead of or
in addition to this, users are creating their own networks of connections, making
hypertext links to provide their own connections to information and objects, as they
identify and link related sites. At the same time, networks of links can become a
maze, and it is all too easy for viewers to lose their way along the information path.
In going from link to link, and from one reference point to another, it is often difficult for users to remember the starting point of the search and the points along the
way. Navigating effectively among related links and information spaces becomes an
important skill.

Another powerful capability of computer searching for objects is the facilitation
of browsing. Whereas search engines require a user to submit specific terms and
thus assume a certain knowledge of the subject before a search can begin, there is a

wide array of browsing tools that make it easier for the novice to navigate a search through unfamiliar territory or abstract concepts. Many users may have a relatively unformed notion of what they are looking for, for example, how strength and pride are conveyed in art. Their browsing may be based on the assumption that "I'll know it when I see it." In browse mode, a user may look through a set of items and, on finding one of interest, may say to the system, "Give me more like that!" As a result, the browse mode does not require the user to initiate the query with a specific search term, but it does require the user to have some idea in mind of where to start and what collections will be browsed. One of the primary attraction of browsing is that it allows users to recognize what is interesting rather than formulating a precise information query in advance.

The power of browsing has particular implications for the discovery of image objects, inasmuch as a pictorial image is able to present itself in its own medium of expression and thus has the potential to allow users to employ their cognitive abilities to scan image content within sets of images to retrieve desired information. Browsing has an added advantage of helping users navigate without prior knowledge of subject content (Kwasnik 1992), and has the unique advantage as "a simple and convivial form of access to information sources, particularly for occasional and inexpert users" (Bawden 1993: 72.). For those lacking special expertise in a subject area, this has particular relevance.

Frost's research investigated users' preferences for retrieving image data. Focus group interviews were conducted with art history faculty and museum curators, as well as with student and faculty who were not specialists in art history. The study found that whereas specialists preferred a direct search, generalists or novice users used browsing as their preferred mode. However, both specialists and novice searchers found each mode to play a role depending on information need, and found value in a system combining both browse and direct search. For example, generalist or novice users in focus groups noted the advantages gained by browsing when the user was not able to articulate a known item search or when the priority was on ideas. One generalist in the focus group pointed out the benefits of browsing if the name of an artist or title was not known:

> If you're looking for paintings or drawings or something specific by a specific artist, you might not actually know the painting by its title, you might only know it by how you've seen it. Like I know quite a few paintings from like older periods where I would have no idea what the name is, I only know the artist, I only know what they look like. (Frost et al. 2000: 307)

Respondents in the focus groups also emphasized the distinct discovery appeal afforded by online browsing, and its ability to lead to new lines of thought that might stimulate the imagination. One art history specialist noted that, "My kids sit on the computer and they just look and see what's out there, they just go from image to image, just to see what's in there" (Frost et al. 2000: 298).

The power of serendipity in browsing often leads people to continue to search, even when they have already found what they are looking for. One art history specialist observed, "Even if you found what you wanted, or close to what you wanted, you're not likely, if you're human, to be satisfied with that, anyway. You're gonna browse anyway, just to see if there might be something a little bit better" (Frost et al. 2000: 298).

Whether a user chooses to browse or search often depends on the purpose of the search. An art specialist explained how the nature of a search task determined his use of the browse or search mode:

> When I would search or when I would browse would depend on what I was looking for. If I'm looking for something colorful or something flashy, then I might browse a set of images and see one that strikes my eye and hopefully they'd be nicely arranged into different thumbnails. But if I'm looking for something specific, say I was writing a paper on Monet, and I wanted to put one of Monet's pictures in, I would want to be able to get to a Monet specifically and do that. (Frost et al. 2000: 298)

Although navigation is important, authentication and validation of digital objects are also critical skills for effectives use of digital information objects. When an object or unit of information resides in a collection, that collection serves a filtering or sanctioning role. When we visit a museum, the curators of the collection have brought to bear considerable expertise in selection and organization of the objects that are available for public view. Librarian selectors, museum curators, archival appraisers, and publishers can offer value by bringing to their collections an evaluative component that assumes that the artifacts or objects represented have been carefully selected from a broader universe of objects on the basis of their quality, fit, or other criteria. With the autonomous dimension of self-publishing on the Internet, users may not have the assurance that what they are viewing represents the best of a genre. When visiting a website, a viewer may not know whether that resource is authentic or whether it has been evaluated.

Problems of authentication can also emerge when a user employs highly powerful and sophisticated search engines to retrieve small pieces of information out of context. A search query may result in identifying an individual page, but when this individual page is retrieved outside of the context of the entire document, learners may miss out on important background information; for example, when a student retrieves a page from a website, she may not realize that the site was created by amateurs rather than museum experts. Another important feature of digital information literacy worth recognizing is that objects can be distorted or provide misleading information, losing the quality and accuracy of the original. Whereas the physical artifact remains more or less constant, there is the potential for changing its digital representation.

In a distributed information environment, computer-assisted search mechanisms such as web crawlers, while powerful, can also be manipulated by creators of web pages as well as by the designers of retrieval systems. Lynch cautioned that little technology is available that allows an indexing crawler to determine whether indexing data can be believed or whether it is simply attached to a web page in an attempt to shape the outcome of the indexing process. He stressed the need for users to understand the behavior of retrieval systems, so that users can recognize why a given result was retrieved, and observed that "[a]lmost nobody understands why they get the results that they do from a search engine; they just deal with the results that they do get" (Lynch 2001: 17).

The potential for deception and misuse of information in Internet communities increases the importance of mechanisms for evaluation and judgment. When we find information in a networked environment, we may know little about its creators or the circumstances of its creation. When we ourselves create and distribute information, we have little idea of who uses the information we distribute, under what circumstances, or for what purposes. Building mechanisms that allow us to decide which information can be trusted and is authoritative is an important skill that must be learned for effective Internet use.

Conclusion

Digital technologies can offer a wide array of learning opportunities in the discovery, representation, dissemination, and use of information objects. Learners now have access to an immense and diverse universe of objects, and can build on these objects to create new information resources and creations. Avenues for sharing information hold the potential for exchange and interaction with other learners as well as with a broadened community. The wealth of opportunities also calls for a new digital literacy that provides skills for exploiting the potential of tools for effective information discovery, recognition of appropriate use of other's intellectual property, and appreciation of the strengths and limitations of digital representations so that they can enhance, not replace, the real world experience of an object. With access to digital collections of local museums, learners can develop background knowledge needed to understand the exhibits, and pursue their own inquiries over time. This provides an opportunity for students to develop and enhance their own understanding and appreciation of objects, to create their own objects, and to share and showcase their own creativity and understanding with a wider audience.

Objects in their original format have characteristics that make the viewing of an original artifact a quite different experience from the viewing of a representation. There is undoubtedly no replacement for the experience of viewing an object in its original form and setting. However, digital representations, while they provide an inferior viewing experience in some ways, have their own advantages unique to digital information formats. Information in digital form can reach far wider audiences, can be accessible in anywhere/anytime modalities, and can provide contextual information that can enrich and inform the viewing experience. The two formats need not compete with each other. Indeed, the power of digital technologies can be used to stimulate interest in a broad array of viewers and result in greater levels of engagement with the real objects in museums.

Bibliography

Bawden, D. (1993) Browsing: Theory and practice. *Perspectives in Information Management,* 3, 71–85.

Bearman, D., and Trant, J. (1998, June) Authenticity of digital resources: Towards a statement of requirements in the research process. *D-Lib Magazine*. Available: http://www.dlib.org/dlib/june98/06bearman.html (2001, January 28).

Brown, J.S. (2000, March/April) Growing up digital: How the web changes work, education, and the ways people learn. *Change*, March/April, 11–20.

Chadwick, J. C. (1992) The development of a museum multimedia program. *Journal of Educational Multimedia and Hypermedia, 1*, 331–340.

——. (1999) A survey of characteristics and patterns of behavior in visitors to a museum web site. In D. Bearman and J. Trant (eds) *Museums and the Web 1999: Selected Papers from an International Conference*. Archives and Museum Informatics. Available: http://www.archimuse.com/mw99/papers/chadwick/chadwick.html (2001, January 28).

Davis, D. (2000, September 24) The virtual museum, imperfect but promising, *The New York Times*, pp. 1, 32.

Falk, J. H., and Dierking, L. D. (1992) *The Museum Experience*. Washington, DC: Whalesback.

Falk, J. H., and Dierking, L. D. (1998) Understanding free-choice learning: A review of the research and its application to museum web sites. In D. Bearman and J. Trant (eds) *Museums and the Web 98 Proceedings* (CD-ROM). Archives and Museums Informatics. Available: http://www. archimuse.com/mw98/papers/dierking/dierking_paper.html (2001, January 28).

Frost, C. O. (1999) Cultural heritage outreach and museum/school partnerships: Initiatives at the School of Information, University of Michigan. In D. Bearman and J. Trant (eds), *Museums and the Web 1999: Selected Papers from an International Conference*. Archives and Museum Informatics, 223–229. Available: http://www.archimuse.com/mw99/papers/frost.html (2001, January 28).

Frost, C.O., Taylor, B., Noakes, A., Markel, S., and Drabenstott, K. M. (2000) Browse and search patterns in a digital image database. *Information Retrieval, 1*, 287–313.

Galston, W.A. (1999) (How) does the Internet affect community? Some speculations in search of evidence. Available: www.ksg.harvard.edu/visions/galston.htm (2001, January 28).

Gilliland-Swetland, A.J., Kafai, Y.B., and Landis, W.E. (1999) Integrating primary sources into the elementary school classroom: A case study of teachers' perspectives. *Archivaria, 48*, 89–116.

Greenman, C. (2000) Museum goers get a virtual hands-on experience, *The New York Times*, September 14, p. D9.

Hapgood, S.E., and Palinscar, A.S. (2002) Fostering an investigatory stance. In S.G. Paris (ed.), *Perspectives on Object-centred Learning in Museums*. Mahwah, NJ: Lawrence Erlbaum Associates.

Hindle, B. (1978) How much is a piece of the true cross worth? In I.M.G. Quimby (ed.), *Material Culture and the Study of American Life*. New York: W.W. Norton, pp. 5–20.

Jones, L. S. (1990) *Art Information: Research Methods and Resources* (3rd ed.). Dubuque, IA: Kendall/Hunt.

Keim, A. (2000) Discovering dinosaurs on 2 CD-ROMs. *The New York Times*, September 14, p. D9.

Kwasnik, B. H. (1992) The functional components of browsing. *Annual Review of OCLC Research July 1991–July 1992*, 53–56.

Library of Congress. *American Memory Project*. Available: http://lcweb2.loc.gov/ammem/ndlpedu/index.html (2001, January 28).

Lynch, C. A. (2001). When documents deceive: Trust and provenance as new factors for information retrieval in a trangled web. *Journal of the American Society for Information Science and Technology 52*, 12–17.

Mirapaul, M. (2001). Museum tries mounting its latest show in cyberspace. *The New York Times*, January 8, p. B2.

National Archives Digital Classroom. Available: http://www.nara.gov/education/ (2001, January 28).

National Research Council (2000) Committee on Intellectual Property Rights and Emerging Information Infrastructure. *The digital dilemma: Intellectual property in the information age*. Available: http://books.nap.edu/html/digital_dilemma/ (2001, January 28).

National Telecommunications Infrastructure Administration (2000) Falling through the net: Toward digital inclusion. Available: http://www.ntia.doc.gov/ntiahome/digitaldivide/ (2001, January 28).

Osborne, H. (ed.) (1970) *The Oxford Companion to Art*. Oxford: The Clarendon Press.

Research Libraries Group (1996) *Preserving Digital Information. Report of the Task Force on Archiving of Digital Information*. Commissioned by the Research Libraries Group and the Commission for Preservation and Access. Available: http://www.rig.org/ArchTF/tfadl. objects.htm (2001, January 28).

Rowe, S. (2002) The role of objects in active, distributed meaning-making. In S.G. Paris (ed.), *Perspectives on Object-centred Learning in Museums*. Mahwah, NJ: Lawrence Erlbaum Associates.

Taylor, B. L. (2000) The effect of surrogation on viewer response to expressional qualities in works of art. Unpublished doctoral dissertation, University of Michigan, School of Information.

Thompson, C. (1982) Why do you need to see the original painting anyway? *Visual Resources, 2*: 21–36.

Chapter 26

Learning by Doing and Learning Through Play: an exploration of interactivity in virtual environments for children

Maria Roussou

Introduction

Virtual reality (VR), the three-dimensional multisensory, immersive, and interactive digital environment, has triggered public imagination as the technology that will dominate the way our work, education, and leisure are delivered in the future. To date, VR installations and applications have been the main concern of the scientific visualization communities, and of certain industrial research and development projects. However, in the past few years, there has been a proliferation of VR installations (in the form of exhibits) and VR applications (in the form of "experiences") available and accessible to the public.

The entertainment market, traditionally concerned with the creation of spectacles and, more recently, multisensory experiences, was one of the first to embrace current achievements in VR, in order to advance the "art of experience" both through gaming machines and location-based entertainment. Other public settings, such as museums and informal educational institutions, generally hesitant in adopting cutting-edge digital technologies, are now considering various forms of VR to attract and motivate visitors, but also to ultimately deliver their educational agenda more effectively. Recent success stories that exemplify the "edutainment"[1] venue include the Hayden Planetarium's 400-seat all-digital dome system at the American Museum of Natural History in New York,[2] the Glasgow Science Centre's immersive Virtual Science Theatre,[3] the VR Theatre in Korea (the largest immersive and interactive theater in the world) (Park et al. 2002), or the cubic immersive (CAVE®-like) displays installed permanently at "unusual" museums such as the Ars Electronica Center in Austria,[4] the ICC in Japan[5] or the Foundation of the Hellenic World in

Source: *Computers in Entertainment*, vol. 2, no. 1, 2004, pp. 1–23.

Greece (Gaitatzes et al. 2000). Although these are high-cost semi- or fully immersive installations with interactive capabilities, it may not be long before appropriated scaled-down versions make their way into the schools and eventually into the home. The most notable example of an immersive system in such an everyday context is described in Johnson et al. (2001), which discusses the issues and reports the results of a project involving the multiyear deployment of an immersive VR display in an elementary school for science education.

Consequently, VR application development has increased its range of practice while advancing the techniques and art of constructing immersive worlds. On the other hand, techniques for developing interactivity, the process with which users act upon and even modify virtual worlds, are relatively unexplored. However, as the plethora of interactive systems of all kinds indicates, our culture, formerly one of immersive ideals is now a culture more concerned with interactivity (Ryan 2000). Indeed, in every new application directed to the public, from computer games to educational software, interactivity is widely advertised, primarily for its recreational potential but also for its significance for learning. This is even more prominent in the case of virtual reality, since interactivity is largely seen as one of the medium's essential properties.

In our research we explore interactivity as an essential yet complex property of virtual reality environments, in its effects on leisure and learning. Examples of immersive virtual reality worlds for children, with particular attention to the role and nature of interactivity, are discussed. We also make an effort to place interactivity in a broader context, together with an exploration of its relationship to learning through activity and learning through play, but also through storytelling, immersion, realism, and illusion.

But what exactly is interactivity?

There is certainly an appeal in interactivity, shown by the attention the word has received in the media over the last several years. But despite great interest, there appears to be no consensus on what interactivity actually means and represents, to the point where the word has become confusing. What exactly is interactivity? What is the goal of interactivity? Is there one kind or many different types of interactivity? These questions alone illustrate the complexity and multidimensionality of the concept. *The Oxford English Dictionary* defines interaction as reciprocal action, action or influence of persons or things on each other. To interact is to act reciprocally, to act on each other, to act together or toward others or with others. Reciprocity can take place between people, people and machines, people and software, or even machines and machines. With respect to human–computer environments, interactivity can have many meanings, depending on whether the context is operational, mechanical, or practical (in which case its study involves the HCI and interface design fields), educational, social/communicational, artistic, or recreational.

On an operational level, interactivity has been defined as the function of input required by the user while responding to the computer and the nature of the system's response to the input action (Sims 1997). Steuer (1992) regards interactivity as the degree to which users of a medium can influence the form or content of the mediated environment. However, this definition does not entail any form of response; a drastic and profound influence on an environment can be to turn it off, which involves no reciprocal action from the environment, and is generally not considered an interactive capability. Talin (1998) is more specific in distinguishing an interactive digital environment (such as a computer game) from a less interactive system (like a VCR), in that the more interactive system adapts to the user's actions and allows varied degrees of freedom (more control over factors like time, space, "plot", etc). In general, and due to the vague use of the term, interactivity is often confused with the ability to merely move a joystick or click on a mouse (Murray 1997).

In the context of public exhibits where emphasis is on a more social and affective perspective, Adams and Moussouri (2002) define the interactive experience as that which can actively involve the visitor physically, intellectually, emotionally, and/or socially. Ryan claims that an interactive medium opens its world after the user has made a significant intellectual and emotional investment (Ryan 2000). Artists who have explored interactivity in their digital installations define the interactive experience as an active form of engagement (Rokeby 1998). This connection between interactivity and engagement is also explored later in the context of games and play.

Finally, much of the above comes together in an educational context. There is general agreement among many educational technologists about the need for interactivity in learning. Barker considers interactivity in learning as "a necessary and fundamental mechanism for knowledge acquisition and the development of both cognitive and physical skills" (Barker 1994; Sims 1997). G.R. Amthor's argument that people retain about 20 per cent of what they hear; 40 per cent of what they see and hear; and 75 per cent of what they see, hear, and do (Amthor 1992) is cited widely in the literature to back up this belief (as is P.R. Halmos: "I hear, I forget; I see, I remember; I do, I understand").

Interactivity is generally seen as an intrinsic feature of educational practice in the sense of social communication, but also as an inherent property of any interactive multimedia or virtual reality environment that promises physical and sensory, in addition to mental, activity and response. This belief derives from a more general view that characterizes learning as a process of making meaning through personally constructed or socially co-constructed knowledge (Jonassen 2000).

Learning through activity

Current thinking about how learning takes place emphasizes the constructivist approach, which argues that learners must actively "construct" knowledge by drawing it out of experiences that have meaning and importance to them (Dewey 1966). Participants in an activity construct their own knowledge by testing ideas and concepts based on prior knowledge and experience, applying them to a new situation, and integrating the new knowledge with pre-existing intellectual constructs; a process familiar to us from real-world situations. The individual continually constructs hypotheses, and thereby attempts to generate knowledge that must ultimately be pieced together.

Current education practices in both formal (i.e., schools) and informal (i.e., museums) settings have advanced constructivist theories in the design of curricula and exhibits. Due to their practical experience with interactivity, schools and museums can assert that understanding is gradually built up, step-by-step, through active involvement (DeVries and Kohlberg 1987). A substantial body of literature backs this approach to learning: Dewey argued that education depends on action (Dewey 1966). Piaget, known for his theory on the psychological development of children, believed in the role of action in development and the notion that children develop cognitive structure through action and spontaneous activity (Piaget 1973; DeVries and Kohlberg 1987). Seymour Papert calls for further refinement of constructivist theory, by focusing on the involvement of the student in the actual design, construction, and erection of "external" products or artefacts (Papert 1980). The reason for using raw data, primary sources, physical, and interactive materials in the real world is to help learners generate the abstractions that bind phenomena together. Papert and his colleagues coined the word "constructionism" to describe the knowledge-construction process that arises from the physical creation of objects.

Related principles apply to the discourse on activity theory (Nardi 1996), which adds a social aspect to constructivism by arguing that everyday practice is full of dynamic, context-dependent problems in need of tools to support high-level human activity. In activity theory it is assumed that consciousness and activity are inseparable: we cannot separate knowledge of something from our interactions with that something. In other words, knowledge that is integrated with an activity cannot be considered outside the context in which it was constructed (Jonassen 2000).

Most of these theories reflect student-centered learning practices, which have recently emerged to counter behaviorist and cognitive learning models. The shift from highly guided knowledge transfer to the more open-ended, activity-based, social learning process is also appropriated in the development of educational technology, namely in the way new media resources are formed to support new teaching and learning methods. A substantial body of literature in the learning sciences has been used to support interactive learning systems, both theoretically and practically. This is particularly true for constructivism, which has emerged in the last decade as an alternate pedagogy closely related to advances in educational technology, as reflected in the plethora of computer-based software that draws on constructivist premises. It has turned into a trend, and supplies technologists with the theoretical foundations to support development of open, informal, and virtual learning environments.

Museums have embraced these ideas by acting on them, primarily with the development of "hands-on" exhibits that can be touched and manipulated (one of the most famous being the Exploratorium[6] in San Francisco where users participate in hands-on scientific experiments). Moreover, as museums become more open and involved with interactive technologies, their conception of the audience as active participants or maybe even creators of the work also emerges. Paradoxically the creation of interactive experiences begins to converge with the entertainment industry's push to develop edutainment-style exhibitions. An all-encompassing "active experience" has become key, in the sense of an "expanded metacinema," to borrow P. Greenaway's term. While Greenaway (a film director) refers to cinema, he suggests integrating all manner of sophisticated cultural languages into a three-dimensional form with "stimulus for all five senses." Here the viewer does not sit passively, but can create his or her own timeframe for viewing objects and can (as good as) touch the objects he or she is viewing, and certainly have a more physical/virtual relationship with them (Pascoe 1997). This can easily be adapted to a museum experience; and while museum audiences may not expect the sensorial richness of Greenaway's vision, they do expect the museum to provide a stimulating experience that, at the end of the day, will include a bit of its educational authority too.

In summary, many of the ideas rooted in activity theory, constructivism or theories of motivation and engagement can be directly related to the concept of interactivity. Constructivism is adopted as the basic driving force in the development of highly interactive and participatory environments, where the user is able to modify, build, appropriate elements, test ideas, and actively engage in problem-solving and critical thinking. These views have influenced the development of interactive and virtual learning environments, which seem to tie in well with the "learning by doing" and "hands-on" practices of modern museums. And since virtual reality technologies provide a wide range of possibilities for this kind of interactivity and support for active participation in the formation of the content, they become well suited, powerful media for use by schools, museums and edutainment centers.

Learning through play

When it comes to children, the essential characteristics of the methods described above are that they inspire children and appeal to their spontaneity. Piaget's constructivism is rooted in stimulating *interest, initiative, experimentation, discovery, play*, and *imagination* as fundamental to the development of a child's capacity to learn (Piaget 1973). Play, in particular, can unite imagination and intellect in more than one way, and help children discover things at their own pace and in their own way.

Undoubtedly, play is a child's favourite activity, so the belief that learning occurs more readily in an environment of fun, challenge, and variety may seem obvious. However, concern has been raised regarding the drawbacks of learning through play, especially if learning is made to be "too much fun." According to this view, the goal is not to create fun-only environments but to create meaningful tasks, so that students take learning seriously and learn to do difficult tasks. Kay makes the distinction between soft fun (when the environment does most of the things for you) and hard fun (playing a musical instrument as opposed to listening to it) that encourage children to "stretch and grow."[7] According to Kay, soft fun is a very big industry; critics of edutainment centers use a similar argument to point out the shortcomings of edutainment models when they try to incorporate educational (or at least the impression of educational) elements in their productions.

Nevertheless, the non-formal learning world encourages the designers of its programs to focus around play, discovery, and engagement. Science and children's museums that are not bound by national standards and state-imposed curricula have freely embraced these ideas and use play as one of their principal learning tools. Many examples exist of hands-on exhibits that engage all the senses and of inventive methods that encourage children to speculate, manipulate, experiment, and imagine, inspiring them to discover and learn. Even art museums, traditionally more concerned with institutional credibility, include physical or web-based playgrounds for their young audiences as part of their outreach programs. The formal education curricula have also come to recognize play as an essential activity in a child's development.

This high value attributed to play as a component of learning subsides when it comes to computers and play. Computers and play automatically brings to mind the computer game industry, which, in public consciousness, excludes education and learning. Educational software design has attempted to include many of the tricks that characterize game design, such as the goal-directed nature of most games, ability to personalize the experience, advancement of complexity over time, etc., but has failed to equal the appeal and excitement that computer games bring to children. Hence, the division between tools for learning, represented by instructional or educational software, and tools for fun, represented by computer games, still holds.

Nevertheless, the rapid growth and popularity of games has triggered increasing interest among researchers, and a number of studies have been carried out as a result. Several theories tie the learning possibilities provided by games to motivation and engagement. Perhaps the best known is the work of Malone and Lepper, which considers games as providers of intrinsic motivations for learning (Malone and Lepper 1987). The first four kinds of intrinsic motivations (challenge, curiosity, control, and fantasy) may be present in any learning situation, even those that involve only one person. The other elements of intrinsic motivation (competition, cooperation, and recognition) are categorized as interpersonal motivations, since they rely on the existence of other players. In some cases, these elements come together (as in projects where children assume the role of game designers (Kafai 1999)). Interactivity can also be considered an intrinsic property of game design. Games hold the users' attention via interactive features, whether these are intended to advance the story or allow the development and exploration of social interactions and relationships (as in multiuser games).

Based on the above, we could argue that a strong connection binds *interactivity, engagement*, and *learning*. Together, they can form the foundation for the development of a successful virtual reality environment: an interactive VR "play space," which allows children to engage in creative and constructive play, and achieve the ideal blend of educational and recreational value. Successful examples, such as the KidsRoom project (Bobick et al. 1999) serve as excellent demonstrations of this model where the spontaneity and collaborative nature of real-world physical play come together in a fantasy story. Although the KidsRoom project was not designed as an educational project with explicit learning goals, and technically speaking has no virtual reality component, its combination of narrative, play, and both individual and group activity opens up vast pedagogical and educational possibilities.

In the following sections, we will first look at some of the issues concerning interactivity in virtual reality and then review a number of VR environments created in different educational contexts or for different purposes. In all of the reviewed examples, the ideas of interactivity, engagement, and learning are approached in a variety of ways.

The nature of interactivity in virtual reality

Many believe that interactivity is a *raison d'être* for a virtual reality world, one of its most important properties. Today's virtual reality interfaces and applications are designed with an awareness of interactivity by providing a means for the user to literally feel placed in the scene and be actively engaged with the surrounding environment. The development of larger projection-based systems such as CAVE® is one of the better examples in this direction. The more natural physical set-up of a CAVE-type display (typically a room rather than a device), the relatively non-intrusive display hardware (no helmets to wear, no isolation from the surrounding physical environment), and its relative multiuser support (while one user experiences total virtual reality in controlling the viewpoint and the interaction device, a number of others can "share" this experience at the same time) show promise as a VR setting for development of recreational/learning environments. On the other hand, the use of these systems in public settings continues to come with a number of practical problems. Apart from the obvious drawbacks of high cost and high maintenance, they suffer from a number of usability problems that inevitably impact their potential for interactivity: the displays must be designed to withstand breakage, short attention spans, greasy fingers, and large numbers of visitors of all ages; the special glasses are expensive and can break easily, as they do not fit everyone; they must also be cleaned after each use; the same applies to interaction devices, which must be ergonomically designed with rugged cables and visible buttons (preferably, color-coded). High-throughput 3-D theatres, such as IMAX®, have been successful in overcoming some of these problems by creating custom-based solutions. But this is not necessarily feasible for smaller-sized, lower-budget venues. Nevertheless, high-tech attractions such as the DisneyQuest™ theme parks (the first to provide sophisticated interactive VR productions to a large public) have paved the way for careful engineering of interactivity, on both an interface and an applications level (Pausch et al 1998; Schell and Shochet 2001).

But assuming that technology and usability problems will be overcome by the continuous development of new and better hardware (and that market demand will drive development) let us focus on the nature of interactivity with respect to the user of a virtual environment. In the context of VR, interactivity is usually identified with the ability to choose a course within the virtual environment and to freely navigate in it. Spatial navigation with a joystick-like device is the most common "interactive" activity, equivalent to pointing and clicking with a mouse in a 2-D environment. The user can explore from multiple points of view, fly, and go through walls, but cannot intervene in or modify the environment. The majority of architectural and cultural heritage virtual worlds have been designed on this principle.

There are two main problems with this. First, how can more than one user share the same experience at the same time with the same level of control? On a technical level, viewer-centered perspective and single-person tracked devices exclude the simultaneous participation of a group of people. Second, in terms of interactivity, a distinction must be made between mere navigation in a virtual space (or even examination of a virtual object from different viewpoints) and active participation by the user in what happens in it. Most VR applications made for the public advertise interactivity widely, when what this really translates to is the ability to explore and perceive a virtual world from different viewpoints. Cultural VR experiences, for instance, have become synonymous with passive walks through realistic (technology permitting) recreations of architectural worlds, in which the user is allowed little more than the choice of where to go and what to see.

Active participation means placing the user in a central active role with the ability to modify the environment. This complicates the conventional pattern of user versus creator of an interactive experience. The user assumes the role of both actor and audience (Laurel 1993), while the creator must understand how to manipulate the audience into becoming an actor (Anstey 1998). The creators/authors of artistic virtual reality have been the ones to experiment most with the idea of user as active participant in the virtual experience. The four examples of CAVE-based virtual reality artworks below have been involved in this kind of exploration. Although their approaches and forms vary greatly, interactivity, or its absence, serves as a key element in the experience of virtual reality, in a way that affects the user's engagement, sense of presence, and development of the narrative. For example, Benayoun's *World Skin*[8] places the visitor in a very powerful position. Armed with a single interaction device (a tracked camera), visitors are positioned in a 3-D land of war where they embark on a photographic safari. In this war landscape, every camera-click extinguishes a fragment of the virtual world; each photograph replaces a fragment from the virtual world with blank white space. The world falls victim to the viewer's glance, and everyone is involved in its disappearance. Technically, the interaction is limited to the simple click of a button. Conceptually, the system's response to this simple action is a complex sequence of social, political, and moral associations.

Fischnaller's *Multi Mega Book*[9] is a virtual reality piece that juxtaposes two periods in human history, the Renaissance and the electronic age. An idealized Renaissance city, including famous buildings such as the Duomo in Florence, an animated 3-D representation of da Vinci's Last Supper, Gutenberg's printing press, and a fictional digital city, form the different parts of the world that the user is able to navigate and freely explore. An animated virtual character, a kind of tour guide, draws the user into the different spaces by moving about the virtual space and positioning itself at various points of interest. The user may choose to follow the "tour guide" or ignore it. Mitologies,[10] a virtual reality artwork with an approach similar to the *Multi Mega Book*, is an attempt to adapt traditional narrative content and structure to a virtual experience. The film-like structure was selected both for its familiarity to viewers and as a mode of expression. The narrative draws inspiration from a pool of mythological and medieval literary and artistic sources, and takes an approach that almost intentionally ignores interactivity. The thematic content is loosely based on the Cretan myth of the Minotaur, the Apocalypse, or Revelations, of St. John, Dante's Inferno, Durer's woodcuts after the Apocalypse, and Borges' Library of Babel. Music from Wagner's *Der Ring Des Nibelungen* is used as a motif to structure the narrative. The work explores the enigmatic relationships among these sources and captures them in a *mise-en-scene* rooted in the illusion-like narrative tradition of other media, such as cinema. Although created and exhibited on a virtual reality platform that allowed for a high degree of interactivity, in most cases the audience of Mitologies had no control. The cinematic narrative form preserves itself through the continuous slow pace and progression from one scene to the next. The virtual journey through a labyrinth presents its visitors with a narrow range of choices, yet all choices are in essence illusory, as they ultimately lead to the same final confrontation with the Minotaur, the fall through a trap door, and the return to the boat where the experience began, thus completing a circular journey (Roussos and Bizri 1998).

On the other hand, *The Thing* (Anstey et al. 2000) engages the user in interactivity through constant "conversation" with a virtual character rich in changing emotional states. The work is structured in three acts in order to take advantage of narrative tools like pacing, surprise, and movement through time. For the story to progress, the user must engage in activities and respond to the character's requests by dancing, moving, selecting objects, or performing actions. *The Thing* provides us with an example where interactivity is closely intertwined with narrative. In this case, storytelling serves as a driving force for a highly interactive experience, and, vice versa, interaction between real and virtual characters, plot, and emotion becomes central to the form of the story.

The approaches to virtual reality taken above are situated at opposite ends of the interactivity–immersion spectrum. *Mitologies* employs high-quality, visually complex scenes that take advantage of the immersive qualities of the medium at the expense of interactivity. Its cinematic form is familiar and safe. It does not allow much exploration and does not require much activity on the part of the user (thus also eliminating the need to train the user). Similarly, the *Multi Mega Book* makes a strong impression on the user with its stunning visual form, in an environment with no apparent story or goal. The user is encouraged to explore by following the virtual character, which follows its own course and is not responsive to the user's presence in the virtual environment. On the antithetical side, *The Thing* bases all of its power on interactivity by maintaining a simple visual and aesthetic form. Visuals are used to set the scene rather than define the artistic process, while the constant demand for interaction between the participant and the virtual character helps the participant to almost entirely ignore the surroundings. Despite this fact, the participant's discourse with the "Thing" becomes so involved that a strong sense of presence is also achieved. Similarly, *World Skin* achieves a strong sense of presence without, however, using the default interaction capabilities of the given VR system or any sophisticated interaction engine. The interface and activity are so simplified that interaction is taken to another, more conceptual, level, perhaps even one that is realized after the virtual experience has ended.

In all the examples above, the creators have engaged in a sophisticated engineering of interactions, or more precisely, in engineering the illusion of interaction. No matter what choices the user makes, whatever the attempts to modify the world or cause a response, the final result is derived from a set of predefined options, predetermined by the creator. Further examples that demonstrate mastery of what Schell refers to as "indirect control" (Schell 2003), include the DisneyQuest virtual reality attractions of Aladdin, Hercules, and the more recent adventure of the Pirates of the Caribbean (Schell and Shochet 2001). In all these cases, visitors assume the roles of central characters in the story and, for the duration of their experience, believe they control the progress of the story, which is rapidly building to a climax, when in fact every aspect of the experience has been carefully and intelligently planned in advance. Although none of these examples were created as learning environments for children, the underlying principles serve as different human–virtual system models to draw from when designing interactive VR experiences for learning.

Virtual learning environments

Virtual reality continues to be regarded as an emerging field, especially when it comes to its actual use in artistic, educational, and cultural contexts. Virtual learning environments, due to the use of high-end equipment and to the dispersed and non-standard ways in which applications are developed, are limited to projects with special funding, such as academic and research environments. The projects mentioned below were for the most part intended for children, and only in structured experiments. Many of the early VR projects for children were developed especially for head-mounted display systems (HMDs), while later projects began to explore the use of the physical space along with the virtual by employing projection-based or even mobile technologies.

Whatever the output medium, a large part of educational research has focused on science education, like the ScienceSpace projects, which set out to explore motion, electrostatic forces, and other physics concepts. The initial, formative evaluation reports on learners' engagement with, surprise at, and understanding of the alternative representations of the concepts in the ScienceSpace world.[11] In these projects, other than navigation and pick-and-place activity, the world was not dynamically altered by the learner's participation. Similarly, the Computer Museum in Boston created and tested a VR exhibit on cell biology. The Human Interface Technology Laboratory (HITL)[12] at the University of Washington is one of the early educational seedbeds for VR, with projects such as the Virtual Reality Roving Vehicle (VRRV), Water on Tap, and summer camp programs in VR for students. The VRRV and summer camp projects focus on "world-building," where students conceive and create the objects of their own virtual worlds, by using 3-D modeling software on desktop computers. Although this sounds like a highly interactive process, it is focused only on the process involved in creating a virtual world, rather than interacting with one. The actual immersive experience is limited to a short visit of the predesigned virtual worlds (4 to 10-minute VR experiences). The concept that virtual reality is a process and not a product is important, but may not take advantage of VR's potential educational benefits and may not justify its use. One of the reasons students are not more actively involved with the actual virtual experience within the virtual reality system is that the systems used by these projects (HMDs) are not flexible enough to allow more than one participant at a time. The VRRV project attempts to overcome such restrictions in an interesting way, that is, by travelling to schools and giving students (in grades 4 to 12) the possibility of experiencing VR, although still one at a time and for a short time.

Immersive projection-based VR displays, such as the CAVE®, the curved screen displays, and the single-screen immersive desks, are freed from the limitations of HMDs (unwieldy hardware, single-user participation, short and infrequent immersive experiences), but not the limitations of size and cost. Although these systems have been used successfully in scientific visualization, development of CAVE applications for education has been almost nonexistent. CitySpace,[13] a project in which children build their own virtual cities, was one of the early attempts demonstrated in CAVE®.

However, as in VRRV, the children's modeling activity was emphasized prior to incorporating the models into the virtual worlds. Although the tasks resemble highly constructivist physical play, a significant amount of guidance is required before simultaneous construction of mental models along with the physical ones can take place (Sherman and Craig 2003).

The NICE (Narrative-based, Immersive, Constructionist/Collaborative Environments) project, an interactive virtual learning environment for young children, was one of the first educational VR applications designed and developed for CAVE (Roussos et al. 1999, 1997; Sherman and Craig 2003). In NICE, children could collaboratively plant a garden and construct stories as a result of their activities. NICE served as a test bed for exploring virtual reality as a learning medium, focusing on informal education and domains with social content. As its acronym suggests, the NICE project embraced the constructivist approach to learning, combined with collaboration through telepresence, interactive "tools" that helped children to cultivate a virtual garden, and the development of a final story.

Lessons learned from the NICE project, helped to focus and form the design of the Round Earth project (Johnson et al. 1999). The Round Earth project investigates how virtual reality can be used to teach young children that the earth is a sphere when their everyday experiences tell them it is flat. VR is used as part of a larger strategy to create an alternative cognitive starting point where this concept can be established before it is brought into contact with the learner's past experiences. Further projects focused on investigating the effectiveness of virtual environments as simulated data collection environments for children engaged in inquiry-based science activities. Ongoing work to move this effort out of the lab and into schools with an ImmersaDesk™ and other more consumer-driven technologies reflects a trend to finally take VR learning endeavors out of the laboratories and into the real world of the formal education system (Kafai 1995).

Both quantitative and qualitative studies for most of the projects above were not able to report much on children's conceptual learning in the virtual environments. However, most studies confirm a high level of enjoyment, especially compared to other media. In studies comparing immersive VR to two-dimensional desktop or even video instruction, the immersive users enjoyed their experience the most and reported the most desire to continue learning about the subject. Interactivity, here identified with control over the environment, scored as the most significant component of the virtual environments. Giving a child control meant that the child tended to be more engaged with the educational content and to learn more (Roussos et al. 1999).

These qualitative findings indicate that interactivity may be a defining component in a successful outcome of a virtual learning environment, and certainly call for further examination. Unlike the art projects mentioned previously, most educational virtual world projects have done little to explore interactivity, and, in most cases, used the default interactive capabilities provided by the technology. At best, these efforts resulted in glorified multiple-choice systems, making "choice" the fundamental means of expression for the user. This kind of interactivity may not be the kind to foster conceptual learning, at least in the constructivist sense; however, this remains to be examined.

Virtual learning environments in the context of a public space

As mentioned throughout this paper, museums continue to accept virtual reality technology in both theory and practice, due to the new possibilities it offers science, art history education, and cultural heritage representations. Museums, as the main authorities on cultural content, are adapting more and more interactive hands-on techniques and (those that can) virtual technologies for use in exhibitions and public programs.

At the Foundation of the Hellenic World (FHW), a cultural heritage institution in Athens, Greece, virtual reality is used both as an educational/recreational tool and as an instrument for historic research, simulation, and reconstruction. The FHW develops its own cultural and educational virtual reality programs that are shown to the public in the cultural center's two immersive VR exhibits/theaters: the *Magic Screen* (an ImmersaDesk™) and the *Kivotos* (a CAVE-like cubic immersive display for up to ten people). The VR exhibits have been open to the public since 1999, and are the most popular attraction at the museum, with over 200,000 visitors, most of whom are students visiting the Center with their schools.

The programs range from highly detailed reconstructions of ancient cities that can be experienced as they were in antiquity to interactive educational programs that require active visitor participation (Gaitatzes et al. 2000). The three-dimensional reconstructions, including the site of ancient Olympia and the city of ancient Miletus, were created with all the clichés of a passive virtual experience, but served as major attractors to the public. From all practical points of view, the 12-minute virtual tour (controlled by a museum guide) provides enough time to visit the virtual site without demanding anything from the visitors. This is enough to create and preserve a lasting impression on adult visitors (who, for the most part, do not wish to take on a more active role), but falls short of children's expectations, both on the engagement level (the novelty wears off quickly) and the conceptual level (they do go to a museum expecting something creative and challenging after all).

The more interactive projects are also the most demanding in terms of human resources and time. Due to limitations of the VR equipment (single-viewer perspective and one interaction device), and for the programs to provide their full educational potential, students must take turns interacting while specially trained museum educators coordinate the experience. Due to these difficulties, the interactive programs are not attractive to museums on a cost-benefit basis. However, the more interactive projects are the more interesting ones from an informal educational perspective.

Olympic Pottery Puzzles is one of the first programs developed on the basis of a simple idea: children assume the roles of archeologists who must piece together ceramic shards in order to restore ancient vases. Each vase depicts images of athletes taking part in Olympic games. By assembling pieces of the broken pottery, the renderings depicted on the front of the reconstructed vases come to life with 2-D and 3-D animation, rewarding the user for successfully completing the task. Through a very familiar and engaging learning-by-doing process, children learn about the process of restoration and details about ancient sports, athletes, and the Olympic games.

Similarly, *EUREKA!!! Stories from Archimedes* is a series of interactive "exercises" developed to complement an exhibition on ancient Greek mathematics. The program is based on Archimedes, one of the most important figures in ancient and medieval science. Through interactive virtual experiments, visitors of all ages can come to understand some of the most famous of Archimedes' discoveries, such as the method for measuring the volume of a sphere, the principle of hydrostatics (our well-known EUREKA!), the invention of the water screw (a device to manipulate water levels for irrigation and drainage), and stories about burning mirrors and the iron hand or claw, both used to destroy Roman ships.

In the more involved interaction scenario of the *Magical Wardrobe* program, young users can select a garment from a set of virtual costumes, each from a different period of Hellenic history, and by "wearing" it, be transported to the corresponding time period. Once in this fairytale land of colorful scenery and virtual characters, the task is to search for costumes and accessories to help the virtual people of that time to prepare for a celebration. This process of searching for, discovering, and identifying different costumes, fosters inquiry that can lead to knowledge of the cultural, sociological, and political importance of costume at the time.

Finally, perhaps the most involved "constructivist" activity is an integral part of the design of the *Workshop of Phedias in Olympia*. This interactive virtual experience places young visitors in the workshop of the sculptor Phedias in ancient Olympia, in an accurate reconstruction of the famous statue of Zeus (one of the seven wonders of the ancient world), among the sculptor's tools and materials. According to the "scenario," young visitors take on the role of the sculptor's helpers, who actively participate in the creation of the huge statue by means of virtual tools.

Through this activity, the museum hopes to give students a sense of the creative process involved in making an ancient Greek sculpture, about the tools, the materials, and procedures, but also an opportunity to learn about ancient Olympia and the Olympic games.

A number of other interactive productions follow the same motif: for example, "Discovering Liquid Gold" where visitors interact with a reconstructed traditional mill to make olive oil. All productions have an embedded sense of narrative. In some programs it appears in a more literal and obvious form through recorded or "live" narration, while in others, it is implied in the interaction with the virtual environment and in the completion of tasks with a concrete goal.

Does the use of interactivity with the public make sense?

The use of interactivity in projects, like those above, has proved to be a strong public attractant, one that can redefine the relationships among the audience, the virtual experience, the context, and the real purpose of the experience. Whether it's the novelty of interactive technology and virtual reality exhibits or the compelling nature of the applications themselves, visitors go to experience the new and cutting edge, even if the themes of the virtual reality content remain relatively unchanged. At the same time, most people do not understand how to deal with interactive computer-based environments, let alone with interactivity in immersive and, in many cases, complex virtual worlds. The virtual experience can be disorienting, unnatural, and difficult to be part of, even if the technology is as simple and natural as current development allows. Furthermore, the interactive part of most public experiences is inevitably controlled, structured, and brief. All this generates added complexity for "experience creators" who must design by synthesizing many different and sometimes conflicting parameters, including commercial considerations such as providing extra novelty, accommodating an increasing range of experience, and enhancing the visitor demographic.

The immediate implication, which can be drawn from the artistic, educational, and museum virtual reality examples in this research, is the common belief that the effectiveness of a virtual environment with a high degree of interactivity is substantially better than where there is no interactivity. Likewise, the learning and learning technology communities believe that the need for interactivity is indisputable. However, little systematic research is available to substantiate this assumption in the context of VR, and, to date, no clear evidence exists that interactive VR applications can bring "added value" to learning, especially for children. Hence, a central question emerges: Does interactivity, as an essential property of the virtual reality medium, aid in the learning goals that the context set out to achieve? And if indeed this can be proven, then how should interactivity be designed into the virtual experience in order to enhance learning? Numerous observations of adults, single viewers, groups, novice and even expert users in the leisure-based and informal education VR worlds, indicate that interactivity is a major attractor, but may not be what matters to visitors after all. It is certainly significant as a vehicle to suspend disbelief and provide stimulating experiences, but perhaps not much more (Pausch et al. 1998; Anstey 1998). However, this may differ in the case of children. It is our belief that when combining learning and leisure for children, interactivity is essential, not as another tool but as the central model around which the experience should be structured. In this sense, it requires careful study, as the relationships among interactivity, learning, and all the other pieces of the "experience" puzzle are unavoidably complicated, and cannot be isolated from the plethora of contextual issues that surround it

These contextual issues become even more complex in the case of museums. Museums "tell stories" through the collection, informed selection, and meaningful display of artifacts and the use of explanatory visual and narrative motifs in their exhibits and in the spaces between exhibits. This interpretative process is at the heart of the museum as an unassailable institutional authority, and remains the most significant factor that differentiates museums as informal education spaces from theme parks. In other words, authenticity is both an effect that exhibit makers strive to achieve and an experience that audiences come to expect from museums. It is crucial for museums to preserve this context of knowledge and credibility while providing memorable experiences that keep visitors coming back. Thus, the introduction of virtual technologies in museums runs up against a number of issues: among others, the physical context of the public space, support for the conceptual and aesthetic standards of the exhibition and its learning goals, and functionality and accessibility for its intended audience.

Interactivity in a museum VR exhibit has the challenge of preserving a balance among the following: accuracy, educational efficacy, high motivational and engagement levels, quality visitor experience, and seamless, natural, and customized modes of interaction. Ultimately, it must be designed to encourage visitors to question what they experience and to engage in "contradiction, confusion, and multiplicity of representations" (Pascoe 1997) inherent in the display of museum content, while at the same time avoiding the danger of a confusing and fragmented experience.

The entertainment world has devised many tricks to provide structure and tight control in its productions. The most common trick is the use of stories and characters with human-like behaviors and simulation of a perceptual, cognitive, and emotional level that can produce a predictable and consistent visitor response. The use of intelligent agents in virtual environments presents a similar attempt to simulate human qualities and create the illusion of a responsive environment. Characters in virtual worlds draw on codes heavily used and tested by the masters of fantasy and entertainment experiences. Their task is to deliver anthropomorphism, embodiment, and believability to a virtual experience. However, technical limitations have so far not allowed the development of agents intelligent enough to respond to the human users' wealth of emotional states and improvisational behaviors or the construction of meaningful interactive experience. In some cases, limitations in developing intelligent characters for virtual worlds are overcome by the use of avatars or actors; that is, virtual representations of real people. In the *NICE* project, intelligent agents were originally conceived to act as mentors, by helping students to complete tasks, as well as by being fun characters that keep interest alive and help progress the story. In NICE, the construction of the environment was designed to foster collaboration between remotely located users. Through the use of avatars, geographically separated learners are simultaneously present in the virtual environment. The ability to connect with learners at distant locations, enhanced by visual, gestural, and verbal interactions, was employed to develop unique interactive experiences for both students and educators. Initial research indicated that current technical developments were not advanced enough to construct "intelligent" agents that could respond to the needs of students from different locations. By replacing the agents with avatars of (real) people, teachers or parents were able to participate either as members of the groups or disguised as characters in the environment. This allowed teachers to mentor the children in person, to guide parts of the activity from "behind the scenes," and to help shape more interesting and engaging experiences.[14]

The cultural heritage institution mentioned above adopted a similar method, one that complements virtual experience with the power of human mediation. The role of the museum educator, guide, or facilitator is critical in structuring the interactive experience so that children can build bridges between different perspectives and gain a deeper understanding of the content. Furthermore, the use of museum educators as guides in the virtual experience not only helps "externalize" the learning concepts built into the experience but promises the development of a unique "show" every time. Thus, museums can maintain the potential for multiple, different experiences that respond to visitor needs rather than a single, repetitive, identical experience. Different people employ different processes and have different comfort levels with the technology. The multiplicity of approaches also means that the visitor experience depends on the skills of the educator/guide, in the sense that even unpredictable external reasons ("having a bad day") can change the quality of the experience dramatically, making it inconsistent. These processes are reflected in forming the visitor experience and the methods of structuring the interactive experience to encourage new forms of interactivity. The interaction varies with the guides' preferences and capabilities: some may choose to keep exclusive control of the interface and others to share the controller among all visitors; some prefer to direct the experience, others to suggest possible courses of action; some encourage interaction, while others prefer a more structured experience; some use the experience as a way to generate questions from the visitors, others as a vehicle for dramatic improvisation and magic. This is the ultimate interactive process, facilitated by the virtual environment, but contextualized and completed by humans. It is an almost ideal-world scenario of personalized, customized learning and entertainment, if it doesn't stumble on the economics of a continuously increasing competition between the entertainment industry and the museum world.

The question, whether intended or not, evoked by this limited review of virtual reality asks whether, before we speak of interactive virtual worlds for educating children, we can develop a whole new mindset? A mindset that takes into account interactivity as a central design component, one that explores the role of the child/learner/visitor/participant as an essential part of the experience, and regards interactivity, constructive play, motivation, engagement, and learning as interconnected.

Prevailing trends in education and leisure show an evolution of convergence, an evolution of museums as spaces with more attractive digital applications, and leisure centers as models of attraction with an enhanced educational flavor. Interactivity has great potential to unite these trends and become the basis for VR experiences that are engaging and educational at the same time. The exploration of the complex relationship among interactivity, learning, and the virtual reality medium should continue in order to provide insights as to how people interact in virtual environments and how interactivity should be designed to achieve meaningful leisure and learning experiences. A better understanding of the design and engineering of interactivity can lead to the design of better interaction methodologies to support formal and informal educational and entertainment contexts.

Notes

1 The term "edutainment" is indicative of a growing competition between the entertainment and informal education worlds in attracting visitors. Although it was coined by the computer industry about ten years ago, the term has also been adopted by the family entertainment industry in an attempt to "add depth" to exhibits that were made for pure recreation, and thus did not enjoy the credibility inherent to museum educational efforts or educational CD-ROMs. However, as museums and science centers become more popular family destinations and compete in the leisure marketplace, the word reflects an interesting convergence.

2 The American Museum of Natural History, Hayden Planetarium, New York, http://www.amnh.org/rose/ haydenplanetarium.html (link last visited: June 2003).

3 Glasgow Science Centre, Virtual Science Theatre, http://www.gsc.org.uk/gsc/vst.htm (link last visited: June 2003).

4 The CAVE® at the Ars Electronica Center, Linz, Austria, http://www.aec.at/ (link last visited: June 2003).

5 NTT InterCommunication Center, Tokyo, Japan, http://www.ntticc.or.jp/index_e.html (link last visited: June 2003).

6 Exploratorium http://www.exploratorium.org. Additionally, most science and technology centers adopt the same model (see www.astc.org for a list of such museums and centers).

7 See the interview with Alan Kay in *Government Technology Magazine*, Feb. 1998; http://www.govtech.net/magazine/visions/feb98vision/kay.phtml.

8 Benayoun, M.: *World Skin*. In the catalog of Ars Electronica Festival 98, Linz, Austria (1998).

9 Fischnaller, F. and Singh, Y.: *Multi Mega Book*. In the catalog of Ars Electronica Festival 97, Linz, Austria (1997).

10 Mitologies, http://www.evl.uic.edu/mitologies/.

11 Information on the ScienceSpace projects can be found in publications by Chris Dede, Marilyn Salzman, and Bowen R. Loftin.

12 See http://www.hitl.washington.edu/ for publications related to the HITL's VR projects.

13 CitySpace, Visual Proceedings of ACM SIGGRAPH 95, p.142.

14 The technique of using a human to simulate the intelligent component of a system is widely known in the HCI field as the Wizard of Oz (WoZ) technique. The teachers, in this case, interacted with the children in a way that made them believe that they were interacting with the virtual characters, not with real people.

References

Adams, M. and Moussouri, T. 2002. The interactive experience: Linking research and practice. In *Proceedings of International Conference on Interactive Learning in Museums of Art and Design* (London, 2002). Victoria and Albert Museum.

Amthor, G. R. 1992. Multimedia In education: An introduction. *Int. Business Mag.* (1992).

Anstey, J. 1998. Are you waving or drowning? *Art, Interaction, Manipulation and Complexity. Leonardo Electronic Almanac* 6 (11).

Anstey, J., Pape, D., and Sandin, D. 2000. Building a VR narrative. In *Proceedings of the SPIE Conference on Stereoscopic Displays and Virtual Reality Systems VII* (The Engineering Reality of Virtual Reality 2000). Vol. 3957.

Barker, P. 1994. Designing interactive learning. In *Design and Production of Multimedia and Simulation-based Learning Material*. T. de Jong and L. Sarti, eds. Kluwer Academic, Dordrecht.

Bobick, A., Intille, S., Davis, J., Baird, F., Pinhanez, C., Campbell, L., Ivanov, Y., Schutte, A., and Wilson, A. 1999. The KidsRoom: A perceptually-based interactive immersive story environment. *Presence* 8 (4): 367–391.

DeVries, R. and Kohlberg, L. 1987. *Programs of Early Education: The Constructivist View*. Longman, New York.

Dewey, J. 1966. *Democracy and Education*. Free Press, New York.

Gaitatzes, A., Christopoulos, D., Voulgari, A., and Roussou, M. 2000. Hellenic cultural heritage through immersive virtual archaeology. In *Proceedings of the 6th International Conference on Virtual Systems and Multimedia* (Japan, 2000).

Johnson, A., Moher, T., Ohlsson, S., and Gillingham, M. 1999. Bridging strategies for VR-based learning. In *Proceedings of CHI '99* (Pittsburgh, PA, 1999).

Johnson, A., Moher, T., Ohlsson, S., and Leigh, J. 2001. Exploring multiple representations in elementary school science education. In *Proceedings of the IEEE VR* (2001), 201–208.

Jonassen, D. 2000. *Learning as Activity*. AECT.

Kafai, Y. 1999. Children as designers, testers, and evaluators of educational software. In *The Design of Children's Technology*. A. Druin, ed. Morgan Kaufmann.

Kafai, Y. 1995. *Minds in Play: Computer Game Design as a Context for Children's Learning*. Hillsdale, NJ: Lawrence Erlbaum.

Laurel, B. 1993. *Computers as Theatre*. Addison-Wesley, Reading, MA.

Malone, T. W. and Lepper, M. R. 1987. Making learning fun: A taxonomy of intrinsic motivations for learning. In *Aptitude, Learning, and Instruction: Cognitive and Affective Process Analyses*. R. Snow and M. Farr, eds. Lawrence Erlbaum, Hillsdale, NJ.

Murray, J. H. 1997. *Hamlet on the Holodeck*. Free Press.

Nardi, B.A. 1996. *Context and Consciousness: Activity Theory and Human–Computer Interaction*. MIT Press, Cambridge, MA.

Papert, S. 1980. *Mindstorms: Children, Computers, and Powerful Ideas*. Basic Books, New York.

Park, C., Ko, H., Kim, I-J., Ahn, S.C., Kwon, Y-M., and Kim, H-G. 2002. The making of Kyongju VR theatre. In *Proceedings of IEEE VR 2002 Conference*, 249–251.

Pascoe, D. 1997. *Peter Greenaway: Museums and Moving Images*. Reaktion Books, London.

Pausch, R., Snoddy, J., Taylor, R., Watson, S., and Haseltine, E. 1998. Disney's *Aladdin*: First steps toward storytelling in virtual reality. In *Digital Illusion: Entertaining the Future with High Technology*. C. Dodsworth, Jr., ed. Addison-Wesley, Reading, MA, 357–372.

Piaget, J. 1973. *To Understand is to Invent: The Future of Education*. Grossman, New York.

Rokeby, D. 1998. The construction of experience: Interface as content. In *Digital Illusion: Entertaining the Future with High Technology*. C. Dodsworth, Jr., ed. Addison-Wesley, Reading, MA, 27–47.

Roussos, M. and Bizri, H. M. 1998. Mitologies: Medieval labyrinth narratives in virtual reality. In *Proceedings of the 1st International Conference on Virtual Worlds* (Paris, 1998), 373–383.

Roussos, M., Johnson, A., Leigh, J., Vasilakis, C., Barnes, C., and Moher, T. 1997. NICE: Combining constructionism, narrative, and collaboration in a virtual learning environment. *ACM Trans. Comput. Graph.* SIGGRAPH, 62–63.

Roussos, M., Johnson, A., Moher, T., Leigh, J., Vasilakis, C., and Barnes, C. 1999. Learning and building together in an immersive virtual world. *Presence 8* (3): 247–263.

Ryan, M. 2000. *Narrative as Virtual Reality*. The Johns Hopkins University Press.

Schell, J. 2003. Understanding entertainment: story and gameplay are one. In *The Human–Computer Interaction Handbook*. J. A. Jacko and A. Sears, eds. Lawrence Erlbaum, Ch. 43.

Schell, J. and Shochet, J. 2001. Designing interactive theme park rides. *IEEE Computer Graphics and Applications*. (July-Aug.), 11–13.

Sideris, A. and Roussou, M. 2001. Making a new world out of an old one: In search of a common language for archaeological immersive VR representation. In *Proceedings of the 8th International Conference on Virtual Systems and Multimedia* (VSMM, 2002), 31–42.

Sims, R. 1997. Interactivity: A forgotten art? Instructional Technology Research Online, http://intro.base.org/docs/interact/.

Sherman, W. and Craig, A. 2003. *Understanding Virtual Reality: Interface Application and Design*. Morgan Kaufmann.

Steuer, J. 1992. Defining virtual reality: Dimensions determining telepresence. *Journal of Communication 42* (2): 73–93.

Talin. 1998. Real interactivity in interactive entertainment. In *Digital Illusion: Entertaining the Future with High Technology*. C. Dodsworth, Jr., ed. Addison-Wesley, Reading, PA, 151–159.

Chapter 27

Interactivity and Collaboration: new forms of participation in museums, galleries and science centres

Christian Heath and Dirk vom Lehn

Introduction

It is increasingly recognised that social interaction, interaction between visitors, is critical to how we experience museums and galleries (cf. Falk and Dierking 1992; Hein 1998). We often visit museums with others – whether friends, family, peers or colleagues – and even when we visit a museum alone we are sensitive to the behaviour of others. Our own research and studies by others reveal the ways in which social interaction has a pervasive influence on what we choose to look at, how we approach exhibits, the ways in which we explore and examine particular objects and artefacts and undoubtedly the conclusions we draw (cf. Bradburne 2000; Heath and vom Lehn 2004; Leinhardt et al. 2002; vom Lehn et al. 2001). Our aesthetic and practical experience of exhibits and exhibitions in museums and galleries emerges in and through our talk and interaction with others, be they people we are with or others who just happen to be in the same space.

This growing recognition of the importance of social interaction in museums and galleries can be seen as part of a broader trend, a trend that is increasingly placing 'interactivity' at the heart of the agenda, not only in science museums and science centres but also increasingly in the arts – and not just the contemporary arts (Dinkla 1995; Huennekens 1997; Schulze 2001). This developing commitment to 'interactivity' is being driven by a range of concerns and considerations. It may be worthwhile mentioning just one or two. In education, for example, there is a burgeoning body of research in the social and cognitive sciences that demonstrates the importance of social interaction in learning and the ways in which knowledge and skills are gained

Source: *The Proceedings of Interactive Learning in Museums of Art and Design*, Morna Hinton (ed.), London: Victoria and Albert Museum, 2003.

in practical situations in and through the communication between people whether children or adults (cf. Lave 1988; Rogoff et al. 2001). This growing emphasis on the situated, interactional and informal character of learning gives museums and galleries, it is argued, a unique opportunity to contribute to education. It is suggested that 'interactives' provide important resources in engaging people in exhibits and more generally exhibitions in museums and galleries (cf. Marty and Jones 2007; Thomas and Mintz 1998).

The importance of 'interactivity' in museums and galleries, and of the very term 'interactivity', has been profoundly influenced by the remarkable developments in communication and information technologies that have emerged over the past couple of decades. The widespread and seemingly successful deployment of digital technologies in the workplace, the home and, increasingly, the public arena has encouraged museum managers, curators and educationalists to explore ways in which information technology can enhance our experience of and in exhibitions (Cheverst et al. 2000; Spasojevic and Kindberg 2001; Exploratorium 2001; Aoki et al. 2002). Quite understandably, science museums and science centres, such as the Wellcome Wing in London, Explore@Bristol, the Glasgow Science Centre, the Exploratorium in San Francisco and many others have led the way in creating new forms of 'interactive' experience, but increasingly there is a growing commitment to exploring how these new technologies can enhance our access to and experience of more traditional objects and collections, not simply through the 'Web', but actually at the exhibit face itself. Indeed, 'interactivity' is seen as an important resource in enhancing interpretation and creating new forms of engagement with museum collections.

These developments, allied to a political agenda that makes museums and galleries increasingly accountable in terms of the visitor numbers and their social background, combine to give 'interactivity' an institutional significance that increasingly pervades the development and redevelopment of exhibits, exhibitions, galleries and museums. Surprisingly, however, the actual 'interactivity' that arises within museums and galleries with and around these new forms of exhibit and exhibition, remains largely unexplored. We know little of the effect of these new 'interactives' on how people behave, let alone about their effect on how people understand and learn. Indeed, our own research suggests that in some cases, while enhancing an individual's experience, 'interactives' – in particular those relying on computing and information technologies – may inadvertently undermine co-participation and collaboration that can arise with and around exhibits in museums and galleries. There is a danger that we confuse 'interactivity' with social interaction and collaboration.

We would like to illustrate and discuss here some of these issues with reference to examples drawn from science centres as well as art galleries and museums. In the first part we will begin by discussing some of the difficulties that arise when people encounter and examine computer-based 'interactives' and then go on to discuss a number of more 'low-tech' exhibits and information displays. In particular, we will draw on one or two examples from the new British Galleries at the V&A, which have an impressive range of 'interactives'. The observations are drawn from extensive video-based field studies we have undertaken over the past few years in a range of museums, galleries and science centres, including Explore@Bristol, the Science Museum London, the V&A, the Courtauld Institute, Nottingham Castle Museum and the Musée des Beaux-Arts, Rouen. The approach draws on our wide-ranging studies of technology and interaction in complex organisational environments (Heath and Luff 2000).

Prescribing interaction

One of the difficulties with 'interactivity' is that it tends to reflect a particular model of human interaction that is not primarily concerned with interaction between people. The model is implicitly, and sometimes explicitly, drawn from computer science or at least from the ways in which people are thought to interact with computer systems. It is a model that pervades the design of computing technology, ranging from simple workstations through to complex systems, and it is a model with a long history in Artificial Intelligence and Human Computer Interaction (Dreyfus 1992; Suchman 2006). There is not the space to discuss the approach in detail, but it is worth mentioning one or two points. The model places the individual and the individual's interaction with the artefact or system at the heart of the agenda. It assumes that activities derive from plans and goals, and that actions are organised in terms of rules that determine patterns or sequences of conduct to allow those goals to be achieved. The execution of action involves complex cognitive processing through which the individual develops representations of the system, for example, and enacts the appropriate sequence of conduct. Many computer-based systems are based implicitly on this approach to human interaction and ironically, perhaps, it was computer systems and their operation that provided the basis to the model in first instance, not unlike the ways in which the telephone exchange became a model of the mind in the 1930s.

It is perhaps worth briefly considering the use of one or two examples of seemingly successful 'interactives' that embody this model. The exhibits are part of exhibitions in two well-known science centres, Explore@Bristol and the Wellcome Wing of the Science Museum in London.

The Word Skills exhibit at Explore@Bristol, for example, is designed to test the word skills of visitors. It consists of a conventional 19" active screen monitor placed in a large free-standing casing, with a seat for visitors directly in front. Interaction with the exhibit takes place through touching the screen. The system presents visitors with a series of tests that become progressively more difficult as they proceed through a series of successive topics and issues. At the end of the exercise each visitor is given a score. Completing the sequence of actions and achieving a score can take up to ten minutes, and at busy times in the museum this causes some difficulties.

The 'interaction' is primarily designed for a single user who undertakes a series of actions in response to pre-specified questions or puzzles posed by the system. Interaction with the system is structured through a series of two-part 'actions': system action – user response and so on. Each of these sequences of system–user action allows the visitor to progress towards the achievement of the particular goal, which is explicitly presented at the beginning: 'Test Your Word Skills'.

The illustration shows that the individual user is often accompanied both by members of his/her own group and by others visitors waiting their turn. Their physi-

cal arrangement and orientation is quite interesting and reflects the limited participation available to others within the surrounding ecology of the exhibit. Those who
are waiting their turn, become *partial witnesses* to the actions of the user. They have
limited access to the information presented on the screen (by virtue of the size of text
and the position of the user) and cannot necessarily see the actions in which he/she
engages. Given that in some cases visitors may have to queue for five minutes or so
one can understand why they become a little restless and occasionally agitated.

Even for those visitors accompanying the user there is limited opportunity to
co-participate in the activity. First, the progressive sequence of actions and the goal
of the overall individual score undermine both the ability and the value of a co-
participant contributing to the test. Second, the display and input technology restricts
a co-participant's access to the system's operation. In many cases, those accompanying a visitor simply wait and watch what he/she is doing. In cases where others do try
to collaborate, we find numerous examples of the principal user becoming irritated
and in some cases trying to push their eager co-participant away.

It is worthwhile considering a rather different kind of exhibit: one that involves
having a photograph taken, which is then digitally transformed to make the visitor
appear as if he/she has changed sex or age. The exhibit forms part of 'Who Am I' a
section of the Wellcome Wing at the Science Museum.

The exhibit is housed in a large amoeba-like structure, nicknamed a 'bloid',
which contains one or two other exhibits positioned at some distance. Once again
it consists of a conventional 19" touch-screen monitor. The operation of the system
consists of a series of actions specified by the system to enable the user to select
the sex in question, to align his/her face correctly to the camera placed above the
monitor, and to take the photograph at the right moment. At the beginning of the
sequence the system makes clear to the user the purpose of the exhibit.

The system is designed to enable a single user to have his/her photograph taken
and transformed. In many cases the user is accompanied by others, again including
both members of their own group of visitors and others waiting to use the exhibit.
Unlike Word Skills however, the involvement of others does not necessarily undermine the overall goal of the exhibit, and people enjoy seeing pictures of each other
after they have 'changed sex'. There is, therefore, some collaboration both in operating the system and in appreciating the results.

The system is rather difficult to use. In particular, users have difficulty in aligning
themselves to the camera and it is not unusual to find them making several attempts
to produce an appropriate image. The collaboration of others largely consists of a
friend or members of the family trying to help the principal user operate the system
and adopt the correct alignment. Sadly, once the picture is taken there may be little
time to appreciate the results, since others may be gathering near the exhibit and the
results are visible only on the screen. The collaboration of others is limited not only
by the organisation of the sequence of actions prescribed by the system, but also by
the size of the screen and the surrounding casing, so that only one accompanying
adult at a time can satisfactorily see what is on screen and help the principal user.
Indeed, it is interesting to note that even families with young children often have to
split up, with the father and one child, for example, attempting to operate the system
while the mother and a second child stand back and wait.

In one sense therefore, the Sex Change exhibit encourages collaboration and in terms of one of the conventional criteria for measuring success in museums and galleries, namely 'dwell time', people do indeed spend extended periods of time at the exhibit, as they do with the Word Skills exhibit at Explore@Bristol. The character of the collaboration, the social interaction prompted by the exhibit, however, raises some serious questions about whether the exhibit is as successful as we might like to believe. It also raises doubts as to the usefulness of conventional measures such as 'dwell time'. When we look at what happens when people use the exhibit, we find that in many cases users spend a substantial proportion of their time attempting to operate the exhibit in the way intended and that collaboration is often limited to one person helping the other to follow the instructions, the prescribed sequence of actions. 'Dwell time' becomes extended further not by virtue of participants discussing the end result, the transformed image and its implications for our perception of sex characteristics and conventions, but rather by participants having to make several attempts to produce an image that is clear enough to be able to see the user in the guise of the opposite sex. The collaboration that the exhibit produces is therefore largely concerned with trying to operate the exhibit rather than discussing, or even appreciating, sex characteristics.

Word Skills and Sex Change are not unusual computer-based exhibits. They both use basic information system and conventional hardware. They embody many of the features of the conventional computer-based interactive exhibits found in science centres, museums and galleries. The forms of interaction and collaboration they engender are also not unusual. Like many other computer-based 'interactive' exhibits, they are designed for one principal user, who interacts individually with the system to achieve a particular goal. The interaction with the system is scaffolded to elicit successive single actions from the user in response to 'moves' by the system, whether in the form of instructions, questions or some other prompt. The organisation of the 'interaction', a series of two-part sequences of action is designed for, and favours, a single respondent. The organisation is not dissimilar to a series of questions and answers in a conversation, such as an interview, which can provide little opportunity for the respondent to initiate action and which biases the interaction towards the same respondent (cf. Sacks 1992, 1974; Schegloff 2007). The conventional input and display technologies used in these exhibits also undermine the collaboration of others by restricting the ability of people gathered at the exhibit to see the screen, to see the principal user's operation of the system and to select items or moves on the screen itself. Like conventional PCs and workstations, on which these exhibits are based, these types of computer-based exhibit are designed for single users, people on their own interacting with the system to accomplish a particular task. The collaboration of others is restricted in large part to watching the principal user as he/she 'interacts' with the system and occasionally helping or interjecting comments.

None of this is to suggest that visitors do not use, or do not attempt to use, these exhibits for more complex forms of collaboration; indeed they do, sometimes successfully. Moreover, when the opportunity arises and they have worked out how to use the system, visitors will take turns in using the exhibit and compare and contrast their performance and results. In fact, not unlike some games in amusement arcades, some of these computer-based exhibits are specifically designed to encourage comparison and competition between users. Unfortunately, however, despite their commitment to 'interactivity' in many cases, computer-based exhibits support relatively limited forms of co-participation and collaboration. In many cases it consists of little more than helping to operate the system or interjecting answers or solutions to a puzzle, often to the frustration of the principal user. The fact that something like 70 per cent of people visit museums and galleries with other people makes this something of a disadvantage.

'Interactives' and social interaction

Unfortunately, perhaps, the term 'interactive' is used to encompass a broad range of exhibits and artefacts, only some of which are based on information and communication technologies. Increasingly, the term is used to include a range of materials and even teaching packages that are designed to enhance interpretation, discussion and learning. Even if we adopt a relatively narrow focus and simply include objects and artefacts that involve an 'interaction', for example by being manipulated, the term still encompasses a rich variety of devices, exhibits and techniques. Even within this more narrow definition, the new British Galleries at the V&A include a variety of 'interactives', ranging from models of the Crystal Palace to gauntlets that may be worn by visitors, from short video programmes describing particular objects through to fragments of porcelain that may be touched and felt. We have undertaken fieldwork and video recording in the British Galleries of people using a number of these 'interactives', and it may be interesting to consider briefly one or two examples.

At the outset it should be said that the different 'interactives' engender very different forms of interaction with the object and social interaction between people with, through and around the object. They facilitate very different actions and activities and provide very different opportunities for exploration, investigation and discussion. For example, when people assemble the Crystal Palace we find a strict division of labour where each visitor builds sections independently and as they complete different parts attempt to merge them together. Talk between visitors arises mainly during the integration of the different parts and at the beginning and end of the assembly process. In contrast, when trying on the corset, one participant becomes an assistant helping and receiving instructions from the other ('tighter, tighter') until the hiatus where they both appreciate the result. Assembling the model eighteenth-century chair is different again; it necessitates intense real-time co-ordination and collaboration, where the participants' contributions are tightly synchronised; few succeed in assembling the complete chair, yet it serves to engender much discussion and comment. Very different activities and forms of participation are involved in the completion of these various tasks and one would suspect the implications for learning are very different.

It is worth mentioning that, despite the apparent success of these interactives, there is no significant evidence to suggest that visitors connect the activities they undertake with the interactives to the original object(s) that they are designed to illuminate. The two interactives described are physically separated from their relevant objects and visitors do not necessarily, for example, go from the interactive to the object or vice versa. In the case of the chair this was not the intention. When the British Galleries opened, there was a real eighteenth-century chair mounted on the wall above the activity, but this had to be removed because it was too vulnerable. It is intended to put an image of the real chair there, as has been done with the corset and crinoline. Physical separation may not necessarily matter, but if the interactives are designed to illuminate particular objects, then we need to explore ways in which we can encourage visitors to make systematic connections.

Most of the interactives in the British Galleries are in fact next to the relevant objects and the relationship between the activity and the object would appear to be obvious. However, even in these cases visitors do not necessarily explore or even discover the connection.

Discovering connections

In the seventeenth-century section of the new British Galleries there is a display case containing examples of ceramics, both British and Chinese. Below the case are a series of pieces of pottery and porcelain for visitors to handle, including British and Chinese examples.

The handling activity provides visitors with a puzzle: to feel and distinguish between the pieces and relate them to the examples within the display case itself. When groups visit the exhibit there is once again an interesting division of labour. One person will read the label out loud while their co-participant will touch and feel the ceramic pieces. As he/she touches the pieces the visitor will often say aloud how the different frag-ments feel, providing comment and criticism, and discussing the relative merits of the different types of ceramic. Remarkably, it is not unusual for only one of the visitors actually to feel the samples, while the co-participant will read out the labels and listen to the spoken response to the pieces, without necessarily feeling the fragments for him/ herself. Even though the two participants are together, their use of the interactive and their actual experience of the exhibit is thus very different.

The fragments and accompanying labels are designed to provide visitors with a tactile sense of the different types of ceramic displayed in the case above. Despite some stylistic similarities, there is indeed striking contrast between the tactile qualities of the different pieces, in particular the English and Chinese. In some instances, however, if only occasionally, visitors in groups fail to make the connection between the fragments for handling and the relevant objects in the display case above. For example, visitors will touch and feel the pieces and examine the objects in the case but fail to relate the two and sometimes remain puzzled as to the purpose of the fragments. On occasions, not infrequently after the pieces have been touched, one of the visitors will discover the accompanying information and retrospectively establish the connection and, if they are still available, touch the handling pieces again. However, the accompanying information often remains undiscovered, especially by visitors who approach the exhibit from the right rather than the left. This may be because the information introducing the activity is to the left of the fragments, although text about individual pieces is next to the relevant shard. Visitors often leave the display without ever making the connection between the fragments and the objects in the display case.

So even where the interactive is placed in immediate juxtaposition to the objects in question, and accompanying information is provided to enable one to make connections, visitors do not necessarily discover the relationship. The very purpose of the interactive – to enable visitors to look at the objects in the case with a deeper understanding of their physical qualities – passes unnoticed.

There are a number of other interesting issues concerning the use of the interactive at the seventeenth-century ceramics display. The direction from which visitors arrive at the display has an important bearing on whether they touch the fragments and whether they are able to discover what they are for and how they relate to the objects in the case. The arrangement of objects, fragments and accompanying textual information appears to presuppose a particular pattern of navigation from visitors, arriving at the left facing the case and progressing to the right. In fact, the team were well aware that visitors do not follow predetermined routes, but the difficulties of fitting the interactive within a constrained space have militated against this knowledge. Not infrequently visitors arrive from the right and as a consequence not only fail to discover the information that will allow them to make sense of the display but actually progress through the wrong sequence of actions. The problem is how to position text with objects in a confined area in such a way that it is immediately accessible, regardless of the direction of approach.

The difficulties are exacerbated when the section is crowded. Even if visitors approach from the appropriate direction, it is not always possible to progress through the appropriate sequence of actions, because other visitors restrict access to particular objects or to the fragments. Most interesting, perhaps, is the very different experiences that people within groups gain from the exhibit. In such cases there is a wide range of possibilities, for example, as to who actually touches the piece, who reads the labels, the order in which the objects are viewed and the connections made. This 'asymmetry' in the action and interaction that arises around the exhibit is critical to the experience gained, and it is perhaps a mistake to believe, even when people look at an exhibit or display together, that what they learn is equal or 'shared'. These asymmetries in how people use and experience exhibits when they are with others raises important issues about the design of interactives and in particular about designing interactives to support and enhance collaboration.

Creating audiences

The British Galleries also include digital interactives, which are designed to enhance the visitors' experience of a particular object or exhibit. One type of digital interactive consists of a screen that plays a short video illustrating the design and function of a particular piece. One example is based in the nineteenth-century galleries. It shows a short film, lasting about two minutes, which demonstrates the operation of a washstand designed by William Burges and illustrates various features of its design. The film consists of a series of interconnected but continuous parts that focus on particular aspects of the piece. Each of these parts includes one or two subtitles summarising a particular feature; for example, 'the bowl is emptied into the container underneath'. The monitor is placed on a low stand to the right of the Burges washstand. The film is begun by touching the screen and continues without interruption to the end.

There is, of course, some variation in whether and how people use the interactive, and this can be profoundly influenced by the presence and behaviour of others who happen to be in the same area. For example, it is not unusual when the gallery is relatively crowded for visitors to glance at the Burges piece and, seeing people watching the video, simply to move on rather than wait. Alternatively, if there are one or two people looking at the piece itself, or if they approach from the right rather than the left, visitors will not infrequently watch the video before looking at the object itself. More importantly, however, the video itself can and does become a substitute for the original object, the Burges washstand. It is not unusual for visitors to view the video, occasionally glancing at the exhibit, and then, as the film comes to end, to look at the piece very briefly before moving on. Of course, this may be influenced by the presence of others, but it is also due to the quality of the film, which allows the visitor to see details that are difficult to view on the object itself and gives a sense of how the exhibit operates that is not available in the gallery display. In one sense, therefore, the video undoubtedly extends 'dwell time' at this area of the gallery. The fact that visitors spend time watching the film without necessarily examining the object may not be important, but it once again points to the rather delicate, if not tenuous, relationship between interactives and the objects whose interpretation and exploration they are designed to enhance.

The short film itself does not necessarily serve to encourage or engender discussion and collaboration between visitors in groups. It is not unusual for visitors when watching a film together to fall silent, to become members of an audience, if only temporarily. Interestingly, we have found a parallel shift in the character of participation when children doing an exercise together in the classroom turn from looking at a book together to watching a CD on the computer. Visitors will make brief comments and occasionally glance at the exhibit itself, but to a large extent their co-participation is limited to a mutual alignment towards the film.

This may not be surprising. The narrative structure of the film and its uninterrupted flow to completion limits the opportunities for visitors simultaneously to look at the object or converse with each other. If visitors do look up and examine the piece for more than a second or so, then they may well miss the next part of the film, which demonstrates or illustrates some aspect of the exhibit. Similarly, if visitors exchange more than a brief comment, then their talk soon becomes unrelated to the material they are viewing on screen. Moreover, any comments that are made encourage the co-participant to turn and look at some feature of the exhibit itself; yet, if they respond appropriately, they are likely to miss the next part of the film.

Visitors go to some lengths in an attempt to co-participate in simultaneously watching the video and looking at the exhibit. Once again we find examples of a division of labour emerging, where one visitor will watch the video and speak the subtitles as they appear, while his/her partner inspects the actual piece. Rather sadly, however, these forms of collaboration often lead to difficulties since the visitor viewing the piece will demand his/her partner's attention in examining some feature of the washstand, while the partner attempts to continue to watch the film. Unfortunately perhaps, the structure and pace of the film provides limited opportunities for simultaneous participation in examining the exhibit, watching the video and discussing the object in question. When visitors do attempt to use the film to create a more collaborative examination of the exhibit, for example by selectively speaking the subtitles to a partner, tensions arise between the interaction of the visitors and the structure and demands of the film. As in the case discussed here, there is a delicate process of negotiation through which the visitors attempt to establish and maintain a common focus of involvement that interleaves the film with the exhibit, but within moments a fragmentation generally arises or the second person simply joins his/her partner and watches the video.

None of this is to suggest that the accompanying films are not interesting and informative. In the case of the Burges exhibit the film dramatically illustrates aesthetic and functional aspects of the washstand that would be difficult, if not impossible, to describe in a label or even in accompanying pictures. However, the location, length and structure of the film have a significant impact on the ways in which visitors inspect and experience the original washstand and, more broadly, the ecology of participation and interaction that arises within the area of the exhibit itself. The film engenders particular forms of participation and can temporarily transform visitors into an audience, undermining their ability to explore and discuss the piece collaboratively. The relationship between viewing the film and inspecting the object is highly dependent on the presence and actions of others within the same space and even on the direction from which the visitor approaches this particular area of the displays. However, unlike a conventional label, which provides resources for comment and discussion and the collaborative inspection of the exhibit, the film does not necessarily remain subservient to the object it is illustrating and, rather than engendering discussion, it can transform the visitor into a more passive participant while removing the necessity to examine the object.

Rethinking 'interaction'

The term 'interactive' is misleading. It encompasses an extraordinary range of tools, technologies and techniques, objects and artefacts that are designed to create 'interactivity' in museums and galleries. It includes sophisticated information systems that prescribe complex forms of interaction between the user and the exhibit through to 'low-tech' artefacts designed to enhance visitors' understanding of particular objects. Different 'interactives' engender very different forms of interaction and provide highly variable opportunities for co-participation and collaboration. As yet we know little of the conduct and collaboration that different 'interactives' afford, still less of the ways in which they might contribute to learning.

The term 'interactivity' suggests active participation, human action creatively articulated not only with regard to an object, artefact or system but in response to an active, potentially intelligent and intentional agent. Unfortunately 'interactivity' is conflated with human social interaction. However, 'interactives' are rarely designed to support or enhance social interaction; rather, in most cases they are principally concerned to provide individual users with the ability to operate or manipulate a system or object. In the case of exhibits based on information and communication systems these operations can be relatively complex and engage the user in a lengthy series of structured action and activity prescribed by the particular 'interactive'. The design and development of 'interactive' and new exhibitions, including a number of major projects over the past few years, continue to prioritise the individual user, often at the expense of co-participation and collaboration. The fact that visitors are seldom on their own and that the object, artefact or system may well be used in inter-action with others is not infrequently disregarded. There are important exceptions, and it is interesting to note that these often involve 'low-tech' objects and artefacts and are designed to necessitate co-operation and collaboration. With the develop-ment of more technically sophisticated 'interactives', when the presence of others is taken into account, their participation is often limited to the role of spectator or witness, an accompanying visitor(s) who, it is believed, will watch their friends or partners and then engage in the particular activity itself. The 'myth of the individual user', as Jo Graham suggests, continues to pervade the design and development of 'interactives' in museums and galleries – a general reflection perhaps not only of the provenance of the term, but more worryingly, of the prevailing curatorial and educa-tional concept of the visitor.

It is hardly surprising that 'interactives' meet with varying success when deployed in museums and galleries. Their actual use rarely appears to reflect the ideas and assumptions that informed their original purpose and design. In prioritis-ing the individual visitor rather than the social and interactional circumstances in which the 'interactive' will be used and seen, a complex array of issues and factors come into play that profoundly affect the visitor's encounter with and discovery of the exhibit(s) or artefact. These are largely disregarded in the design and deploy-ment of the 'interactive' and yet have a critical affect on its ability to function and engage. Visitors do whatever they can with many 'interactives' and show remark-able ingenuity in using them to support forms of social interaction and collabora-tion that they were never intended to support. More disturbing, perhaps, is that, despite their apparent success in terms of conventional measures such as 'dwell time', the forms and quality of interaction and collaboration that arise with and around the exhibit would do little to please the objects' original designers or the curatorial staff.

One of the more interesting issues that arises when one considers the incongru-ity between the design of the 'interactive' and the conduct and interaction that arise when it is actually deployed has a bearing on the growing concern with learning and education in museums and galleries. Many interactives have been driven in part by the learning agenda in museums and galleries and yet if the interaction that they give rise to is somewhat at odds with the original design, then it perhaps raises problems concerning the motivation and validity of the concept behind the interactive. Learn-ing may well take place, but not necessarily in the way predicted and as yet, given how little we know of the interaction that interactives produce, we are hardly in a position to make an informed judgement.

Surprisingly, perhaps, curators and museum managers have long been aware of their inability to prescribe how visitors explore and experience objects and exhibitions. In his introduction to *A Grand Design* Malcolm Baker suggests, for example:

While guidebooks may suggest what a visitor should look at, and even the route that he or she should follow – and the meanings that the single individual might read into the objects encountered along the way – will only rarely coincide with the strategic thinking of the Museum's planners. How a visitor interacts with artworks and their settings is determined by personal needs, associations, biases, and fantasies rather than by institutional recommendations. In considering this history – that of response to, and reception of, the collections – the issue is not with the Museum defined by its official aims and aspirations, but with how it is reconstituted in the individual imagination.

(Baker 1997: 18–19)

In the case of many 'interactives' these difficulties become exacerbated. The 'interactive' is designed to facilitate particular forms of conduct and experience and relies on visitors using the exhibit or artefact in particular ways. The 'interactive' may even necessitate the visitor interrelating objects and making connections between exhibits that are not necessarily located together. Unfortunately, however, visitors do not necessarily respond in the ways we imagine or hope, and circumstances may arise that make it difficult if not impossible for them to undertake the pattern of action required by the 'interactive'. Even if we reflect on one of the more seemingly straightforward assumption entailed in many 'interactives' and exhibitions – that visitors will normally follow particular navigation paths and thereby be in a position to undertake the relevant actions in the appropriate sequential order – we can see how easily such an assumption may be undermined simply by virtue of the number of visitors or different pace or direction in which they pass through the galleries. These and many more considerations besides are important factors in designing exhibitions and need to be placed high on the agenda when we are developing 'interactives'.

In designing and developing for museum and galleries we have to reshape the ways in which we think of and conceptualise the visitor, to break away from the individualistic model that continues to pervade 'interactives' and the very idea of 'interactivity'. Unless we place the social and interactional at the heart of agenda we will continue to be disappointed by the unanticipated ways in which people use our 'interactives' and disappointed when we examine their conduct and experience, let alone learning. The lone visitor wandering through galleries and achieving a pure aesthetic or scientific encounter with objects is largely a myth, despite the wishes of certain curators in more contemporary spaces. The presence and conduct of others have a profound impact on what we see and do, and on the opportunities that arise for exploration, investigation and learning. 'Interactives' are encountered and used with regard to the conduct and interaction of others, just as 'interactives' have a profound affect on the opportunities and organisation of conduct that arises within the domain, the perceptual range, of the exhibit and its surrounding context. Social interaction in museums and galleries is highly contingent and reveals complex and variable forms of participation and collaboration. Our discovery and experience of the museum arises in and through this interaction and, if they are to meet with success, our 'interactives' have to be sensitive to, and designed with respect for, the social interaction that will inevitably inform their use.

One final point: despite the substantial body of research concerned with visitor behaviour and the growing interest in 'interactivity' in museums and galleries, we still know relatively little about how people respond to exhibits in museums and galleries and interact with and around the objects and artefacts they contain. Save for a few important exceptions, conduct and social interaction at the exhibit face remain unexplored territory and yet provide the foundation, the very basis, for people's experience of, and learning in, museums and galleries. It seems critical therefore that in developing new forms of exhibit and exhibition that are designed to enhance learning and interaction we need a more thorough understanding of how visitors behave in museums and galleries and of the ways in which their behaviour is prompted and affected by social interaction with others. Without this understanding it is unlikely that the hopes, principles and ideas that underlie the development of new forms of interactivity will be reflected in the actual response and conduct of visitors.

Postscript

Since the conference at the Victoria and Albert Museum in 2002, where a version of this research was originally presented, technology and with it museum exhibitions have changed significantly. For example, a number of museums of art provide visitors with mobile information devices such as Personal Digital Assistants (PDA) as well as touch-screen systems to enhance engagement with exhibits and in science museums and science centres there has been an increasing commitment to creating installations that encourage and facilitate co-participation and collaboration. A number of these developments have ameliorated some of the difficulties that arose with certain forms of 'interactive' and provided new forms of engagement. Yet an undercurrent of 'interactivity', of individual interacting with a system still pervades some of these developments. So, for example, despite the enormous potential of mobile technologies, including PDAs, to enhance the museum visit, aside from a few important exceptions, (Aoki et al. 2002; Woodruff et al. 2001), it can prove difficult to share, exchange and discuss the information thereby inadvertently undermining co-participation and collaboration. It is worth noting however, in recent years we have witnessed the emergence of a number of innovative installations and exhibitions including, for example, the new Energy galleries at the Science Museum in London (Meisner et al. 2007), the Ename Museum in Greece (Pujol and Economou 2007), the Exploratorium in San Francisco (Humphrey and Gutwill 2005), the Tate Britain's exhibition of "Constables Landscapes" (vom Lehn et al. 2007) that have facilitated highly distinctive forms of co-participation and collaboration. With these and other exemplars, coupled with rethinking the very idea of interactivity, we can undoubtedly create exciting, challenging and innovative exhibits and exhibitions that not only enhance interaction collaboration but also form the foundation to engagement and learning.

Acknowledgements

We would like to thank James Bradburne, Richard Glassborow, Gail Durbin and Morna Hinton and others who participated in the conference for their comments on an earlier version of this paper, and Ben Gammon and Malcolm Baker for helping to stimulate and facilitate the programme of research of which this paper is part. We would also like to thank Paul Luff, Jon Hindmarsh, Ella Tallyn, Jo Graham, Kathy Sykes, Sarah Stallard, Dinah Casson, Sarah Hyde and others for their ideas and insightful comments concerning the issues discussed in this paper. The paper is based on projects funded by the AHRC (AR17441) and the project "Design for Interaction and Collaboration" funded by the ESRC PACCIT Programme (#L328253030).

Bibliography

Aoki, Paul M. et al. 2002. 'Sotto Voce: Exploring the Interplay of Conversation and Mobile Audio Spaces', pp. 431-438 in *CHI 2002*. Minneapolis: ACM-Press.

Baker, Malcolm (co-editor Brenda Richards). 1997. *A Grand Design: The Art of the Victoria and Albert Museum*. London: V&A, with the Baltimore Museum of Art.

Bradburne, James M. 2000. *Interaction in Museums. Observing Supporting Learning*. Libri Books on Demand.

Cheverst, Keith, Nigel Davies, Keith Mitchell, Adrian Friday, and Christos Efstratiou. 2000. 'Developing a Context-aware Electronic tourist Guide: Some Issues and Experiences', pp. 17-24 in *CHI 2000*. The Hague, Amsterdam: ACM.

Dinkla, Soeke. 1995. *Pioniere Interaktiver Kunst von 1970 bis heute*. Hamburg: Cantz Verlag.

Dreyfus, Hubert L. 1992. *What Computers Still Can't Do: A Critique of Artifical Reason*. Cambridge, MA: The MIT Press.

Exploratorium. 2001. 'Electronic Guidebook Forum.' http://www.exploratorium.edu/guidebook/forum/.

Falk, John, and Lynn Dierking. 1992. *The Museum Experience*. Washington.

Heath, Christian, and Dirk vom Lehn. 2004. 'Configuring Reception: (Dis-)Regarding the "Spectator" in Museums and Galleries', *Theory, Culture & Society* 21: 43–65.

Heath, Christian, and Paul Luff, 2000. *Technology in Action*. Cambridge: Cambridge University Press.

Hein, George. 1998. *Learning in the Museum*. Cambridge, MA.

Huennekens, A. 1997. *Der bewegte Betrachter. Theorien der interaktiven Medienkunst*. Köln.

Humphrey, Thomas, and Joshua Gutwill. 2005. *Fostering Active Prolonged Engagement*. San Francisco, CA: The Exploratorium.

Lave, Jean. 1988. *Cognition in Practice: Mind, Mathematics and Culture in Everyday Life*. Cambridge: Cambridge University Press.

Leinhardt, G., K. Crowley, and K. Knutson. 2002. *Learning Conversations in Museums*. Mahwah, NJ: LEA.

Marty, Paul F., and Katherine B. Jones. 2007. *Museum Informatics: People, Information, and Technology in Museums*. Routledge.

Meisner, Robin et al. 2007. 'Exhibiting Performance: Co-participation in Science Centres and Museums', *International Journal of Science Education* 29: 1531–1555.

Pujol, Laia Tost, and Maria Economou. 2007. 'Exploring the suitability of Virtual Reality interactivity for exhibitions through an integrated evaluation: the case of the Ename Museum', *Online International Museology Journal* 4: 84–97.

Rogoff, Barbara, Carolyn Goodman Turkanis, and Leslee Bartlett. 2001. *Learning Together: Children and Adults in a School Community*. New York: OUP.

Sacks, Harvey. 1974. 'A Simplest Systematics For The Organization Of Turn-taking For Conversation', *Language. Journal Of The Linguistic Society Of America* 50: 696–735.

Sacks, Harvey. 1992. 'Button-Button Who's Got the Button', pp. 363-369 in *Lectures on Conversation*. Part III, Lecture 13. Blackwells.

Schegloff, Emanuel A. 2007. *Sequence Organization in Interaction. A Primer in Conversation Analysis. Volume 1*. Cambridge: Cambridge University Press.

Schulze, Claudia. 2001. *Multimedia in Museen. Standpunkte und Aspekte interaktiver digitaler Systeme im Ausstellungsbereich*. Deutscher Universitäts-Verlag.

Spasojevic, Mirjana, and Tim Kindberg. 2001. *A Study of an Augmented Museum Experience*. Hewlett Packard.

Suchman, Lucy. 2006. *Human and Machine Reconfigurations: Plans and Situated Actions*. 2nd ed. Cambridge: Cambridge University Press.

Thomas, Selma, and Ann Mintz. 1998. *The Virtual and the Real: Media in the Museum*. Washington, DC: American Association of Museums.

vom Lehn, Dirk, and Christian Heath. 2005. 'Accounting for New Technology in Museums', *International Journal of Arts Management* 7: 11–21.

vom Lehn, Dirk, Christian Heath, and Jon Hindmarsh. 2001. 'Exhibiting Interaction: Conduct and Collaboration in Museums and Galleries', *Symbolic Interaction* 24: 189–216.

vom Lehn, Dirk, Jon Hindmarsh, Paul Luff, and Christian Heath. 2007. 'Engaging Constable: revealing art with new technology', pp. 1485–1494 in *Conference on Human Factors in Computing Systems (CHI)*. San Jose: ACM.

Woodruff, A., P. M. Aoki, A. Hurst, and M. H. Szymanski. 2001. 'Electronic Guidebooks and Visitor Attention', pp. 437-454. in *Proc. 6th Int'l Cultural Heritage Informatics Meeting*, Milan, Italy.

Chapter 28

Visitors' Use of Computer Exhibits: findings from five gruelling years of watching visitors getting it wrong

Ben Gammon

General comments

Computer screen-based interactives can be robust and very effective exhibits. They are extremely popular with visitors, especially children, although not to the exclusion of other forms of exhibitory.

Visitors are not techno-phobic

We have detected little or no evidence of technophobia among visitors. Indeed the usage of computers among visitors – at work, home or school – is very high at around 80–90 per cent, well above the national average (circa 1999). Almost three-quarters of the visitors questioned had at least some experience of using networked computers. Visitors also seem much more comfortable with qwerty rather than alphabetical keyboards, again indicating familiarity with computers.

In fact we tend to find techno-fatigue rather than techno-phobia among some (but only some) of the adult visitors.

Visitors are not stupid. These days they are not going to be amazed simply by a touch-screen full of words. They are expecting something exciting, colourful, challenging, with graphics, sound, movement.

Source: *The Informal Learning Review*, 1112-a, 1999.

Use sound

Wherever possible use sound in the exhibit. Not only does this attract visitors but it also helps to indicate when: a button has been activated; an answer is right or wrong; a mistake has been made. Sound can also add humour to an exhibit.

There is no clear 'average' time that visitors spend at computer exhibits

Visitors will spend anywhere from 30 seconds to 40 minutes or more on computer exhibits. The time they spend is determined mainly by the quality of the content and screen layout, whether or not seating is provided and how crowded and uncomfortable the gallery is where the exhibit is located. Providing seating can dramatically increase the amount of time someone will spend at an exhibit.

Restart buttons always cause problems

Visitors often mistake them as 'next' or 'previous page' buttons. If they have spent 5 minutes getting into the game and then accidentally get returned to the start, they are unlikely to try again. On other occasions other visitors (e.g. siblings waiting to have a turn on the exhibit) repeatedly reach across and press the restart button to stop the other person from getting into the game or simply to see what will happen. There isn't really any need for a restart button. It is far better to have a time-out option where the computer returns to the screen-saver if nobody touches the interface for x minutes (determined by evaluation). Whether you use a restart button or a time-out option, you should always have a warning screen appear before the computer returns to the start asking visitors whether they really want to finish the game.

The three modes of computer use

Visitors at computer exhibits tend to exhibit three modes of behaviour: purposeful use – people carefully and thoughtfully searching though the software looking for something specific; exploratory – people flicking through pages looking carefully to find out what is there; playing – people (usually children) rapidly moving through the different screens at random to see what happens.

Help buttons seem to receive little usage

Visitors often misinterpret the function of help buttons – believing that it will provide very specific help about a particular question in a game or very general information about how to use computers. It seems that visitors have bad experiences of help buttons from word processing and other commercial software packages. When they see a help button, they expect to find something equally dire – so don't expect most visitors to open the help screens. If there are vital instructions to be conveyed they must appear on other screens as well.

Text on screen

30–60 words per screen

As a rule we try and restrict the amount of text to around 30–60 words per screen. If you need more words, put them on a following screen with a next or more button.

Avoid using scroll-bars

Where possible avoid using scroll-bars as visitors often miss or ignore these and so fail to see the hidden portions of the screen. If you can't fit it all on a screen, put it on a following page.

Design the interface so visitors have to stop and read

If they possibly can, visitors will race past text or spoken instructions and go straight into the game (this is especially true of children). Of course this often means that they then cannot work out what to do. Therefore, if there is a particular set of instructions that visitors must read or hear then design the interface so they have to stop and read/listen. For example, if you have some spoken instructions don't allow visitors to move on to the next section until the instructions have finished. If they are written instructions don't have the 'next' button appear for a minute or so, to 'force' visitors to search through the text to find out what to do next.

Create incentives for visitors to read text

It's unlikely that visitors will read reams of text before starting a game or selecting an answer. It's like getting a new board game for Christmas – you don't want to spend hours reading the instruction book, you just want to get on and play the game. As a rule we've found visitors are much more likely to read text while they are engaged in a task or after they have answered a question, to find out how well they did or why they got the answer wrong. One option is to present visitors with what appears to be an easy question which they get wrong. There is then a powerful incentive to read the text to find out why. Another option is to make explanatory text look like instructions. Visitors are slightly more likely to read instructions than explanatory text as there is a stronger imperative and a clear pay-off for them.

Important instructions must appear in the central portion of the screen

We've also consistently found that visitors ignore any text that appears in the top third of the screen and sometimes things that appear at the sides of the screen as well. This is found both with horizontal screens and with screens mounted at an angle.

Therefore, important instructions must appear in the central portion of the screen and ideally should clearly stand out from the background. Subtle changes of text on the screen will probably be missed so make changes blatant.

The screen is much more interesting than any printed text

It is difficult to get visitors to see external instructions or directions (i.e. label text) because they tend to immediately focus on the computer screen. The computer screen is vastly more interesting than any printed text around the screen.

Target audiences for your exhibit?

Layer the activities so children can gain something from the exhibit while more interested visitors can delve deeper

Children will be attracted to any computer exhibit. In the past, exhibit developers have naively assumed that they can target computer exhibits at an adult audience through the design and content of the screens. Children still use these exhibits seemly working upon the assumption that if they press the screen enough times they will eventually find something they can do. This means that the computers are still being used by children, but that they gain little or nothing from the interaction. It is better to accept that whatever you do, children will form part of your target audience, and layer the information/complexity of the activities so that children can gain something from the exhibit while more interested or knowledgeable visitors can delve deeper.

Ensure that three or so people can group comfortably around the computer screen

Computer exhibits are often used by small groups of visitors rather than individuals – not surprising given that only 18 per cent of Science Museum visitors are lone visitors. Ensure that three or so people can group comfortably around the computer screen. They will do this anyway, so you may as well make them welcome. And if you are providing seating, give visitors more than one seat or a bench of some sorts.

Touch-screens

Touch-screens are still the most common form of computer interface we use at the Science Museum and are likely to remain so for the foreseeable future.

Touch-screens have proved to be highly effective, robust and easy to use. In fact these days visitors seem to assume that *any* TV monitor (or even surfaces on which an image is projected) are touch sensitive. This can be rather problematic because things may be changing on the screen as they touch it leading visitors to assume that they are causing this to happen.

Problems

Main problems with touch-screens centre around visitors not being able to identify active areas, the active areas being too small to be easily activated and the computer responding too slowly.

Active area design

As a rule the active areas on a touch-screen should be brightly coloured and clearly stand out from the background screen. But watch out for screen design that use red buttons on green or vice versa, 8 per cent of the male population and 0.1 per cent of the female population are red–green colour blind and may not be able to see the difference. Smaller numbers of people are blue–yellow colour blind.

Visitors often assume that any picture, or anything that moves, is an active area so it is best to make these the active areas or respond in some fashion. Visitors assume that touch-screens are pressure sensitive and when they touch an inactive area of the screen and nothing happens, they simply assume that they haven't hit it hard enough/ often enough.

Active area size

The active areas should be at least 1 cm square. One mistake that occurs occasionally is where people load software designed for a keyboard and mouse interface onto a touch-screen. This is always a disaster since the active areas are far too small even for a child's finger, although they would be fine with a mouse and cursor. If you are using Web-Sites or other software design for conventional interfaces, you will need to use a tracker-ball or some form of mouse.

Touch-screen action

Unlike conventional buttons, touch-screen provide no tactile feedback so visitors often fail to realise when they have activated the computer. The touch-screen should, therefore be set on 'mouse-down' i.e. active as soon as touched and not require the user to remove their finger from the screen. The computer should respond to touch within 1 second. Failure to do this will result in visitors ramming their fingers with increasing force into the screen assuming that the touch-screen is pressure sensitive and therefore that the button has not activated because they have not pressed it hard enough. When touched buttons should appear to depress, change colour and produce a clearly audible sound.

Active area location on screen

Another common problem is caused by overlapping active areas on adjacent screens. Visitors often accidentally double touch an active area inadvertently activating the button on the next screen, stacking commands and so jumping on to the third screen. This can be solved by ensuring that no active area on adjacent pages occupy the same parts of the screen. Alternatively, and more effectively, we ensure that once a button has been activated the screen becomes inactive for a few seconds. This gives the computer time to react and means that even if the visitor does press the screen again by mistake they don't shoot pass this next screen.

Remember that buttons need to be clearly and unambiguously labelled so that visitors can work out what they are suppose to do. This requires careful formative evaluation.

Visitor assumptions about buttons

Visitors seem to assume that the function of any button is to start an action or sequence of actions i.e. they press it and expect something then to happen automatically. Problems arise when the active areas actually are tools that the visitor must select and then move the cursor/tool over the screen e.g. to paint or colour and area. Visitors are often observed to click on the tool and then wait, expecting something to happen.

One of the problems with touch-screens is that they can only be used by one person at a time. If you try to touch the screen in more than one place at a time, either the computer does not respond or it activates a button that lies in between the two points of contact. This means that if two people try to use the touch-screen simultaneously they will have serious problems getting the computer to respond properly.

Touch-screens are not very good when you need to use 'click and drag' functions.

Touch-screens for young children

Very young children (under 7 years) have problems operating touch-screens when the active areas are small and close together. Young children have considerable difficulty touching the screen with just one finger. Often they use their whole hand. Therefore touch-screens designed specifically for young children must have active areas that are large (3–4 cm sq.) and well spaced.

Other forms of interface

Although touch-screens represent the bulk of the computer interfaces we currently use, we are now looking at using different forms of interface as well. Also there are an increasing number of computer based exhibits that do not even use a screen to display the output. So far we have only evaluated some of these but here are some initial thoughts.

Most of the principles of good touch-screen design apply to other interfaces. The computer should respond to an input within 1 second; active areas on screen should be large and prominent; buttons should be clearly and unambiguously labelled; non-tactile buttons need to respond on mouse-down.

Tracker-ball and push buttons

These generally seem to be easy for visitors to use and are reasonably robust. They also allow you to use smaller active areas. They can present maintenance problems of dirt getting trapped under/around the ball.

Be sure the tracker-ball and button are not the same colour as the surface they are mounted on. It looks slick, but it makes the ball difficult to find. Also, many tracker-balls come in the same colour as the control unit they are mounted in, but it has been found that it is much easier for visitors to locate them if the colours of the ball and control unit contrast. Black-on-black tracker-ball/control units are especially well camouflaged, as computers are often located in indirectly lit spaces to prevent screen glare.

The movement of the tracker-ball should match the movement of the cursor on the screen i.e. moving the ball forward should move the cursor up; moving it left should move the cursor leftwards and so on. We have come across tracker-balls that work the other way around – basically these are computer mice that have been turned upside down. And do they confuse visitors!

The cursor needs to be prominent and must not become lost in the background screen design or disappear off the edge of the screen.

A tracker-ball control is not the same as a computer mouse. Tracker-balls are not good interfaces for click and drag functions where the user has to hold the button down while they move the ball. Due to the design of most tracker-balls this would prove to be a very awkward manoeuvre. Also moving the ball is not the same as moving the whole mouse – there is not the same mapping of the action onto the outcome. Ideally the tracker-ball would simply move the cursor to select active areas or to apply a tool to an area of the screen.

Light beams

We've found these to work well provided visitors can clearly see where to break the light beam and can see the image of the beam on their hands. This interface allows you to have multiple users at the same time although this then causes serious problems where visitors don't know who is causing what to happen so is not actually a good idea.

Infra-red beams

These are disastrous, because visitors cannot see where the beams are, nor can they see when they have broken the beams. This means that they fail to activate the computer when they are supposed to and activate it by mistake when they shouldn't.

Touch sensors fixed to the inside of glass display cases

These seem to work surprisingly well as long as there is a clear physical link between the sensors and the computer screen (e.g. a big cable) so visitors realise what these are and to which exhibit they are linked. The sensors need to be set so that they are continuously 'polled' to see if someone is touching them. Visitors often place their hands over the sensor and leave it there until something happens on the screen. The problem is that the sensor may be inactive when the visitor first places their hand over it. If the sensor is set to look for a change, then it will not respond until the visitor removes their hand and replaces it again.

The sensor technology must be robust as visitors often pressed the sensors repeatedly and with considerable force. The sensors should be set to activate on mouse-down.

Touch sensors should be labelled so that visual reference can be made to them on the screen. Sensors should be grouped close together so that they are in-line-of-sight for the user and can be easily reached by children or wheel-chair users. Ideally the array of sensors should cover an area of no more than about 1.5 metres.

Sensors should be within the visual field of someone looking at the screen while standing within easy reach of the sensors.

It is vital that there is a high quality of sound output so that visitors can follow the instructions.

Keyboards

We have found that both qwerty and alphabetical keyboards work well with visitors. Qwerty keyboards are easier for visitors who are familiar with computers, while alphabetical keyboards work better with young children. But to be honest the difference is slight.

Mechanical keyboards (as opposed to keyboards on touch-screens) have robustness problems and need to be reinforced and protected from liquid spills.

We have tried a wide variety of keyboard designs and none of them are perfect. It is best to find a design that can be easily customised so that redundant keys can be removed and special keys added.

Keyboards that do not provide any tactile feedback – i.e. where the keys do not move – need to generate a sound when each key is pressed. These keyboards should be on mouse-down setting.

The keyboard also needs to have arrow buttons (or similar functions) so that visitors can move the cursor within the text and delete mistakes they have previously made. Visitors find it very frustrating when they have to delete whole lines of text just to remove one small typo in the first line.

Electronic pens

Electronic pens with moving parts have proved not to be robust enough to survive even the briefest of exposes to visitors. Electronic pens with no moving parts have proved to be much more reliable.

Electronic pen systems that involve writing directly on the screen have proved to be much more effective than systems that involve writing on a separate tablet.

Visitors can sometimes mistake electronic pen systems as some form of children's 'electro-sketch' or drawing activity rather than a serious exhibit aimed at adults *and* children.

The quality of people's handwriting when using the electronic pen can also lead adults to assume that only children have previously used the exhibit.

Fingerprint scanners

These can be highly effective methods of logging on to a network of computer exhibits so that each exhibit can recognise the visitor and store information about them. However, specific problems have been identified:

- Children often forget which finger they have used previously, or do not realise that they need to use the same finger each time.
- Children tend to press just the tip of their finger onto the scanner rather than laying their hand flat and placing the whole of their finger tip across the sensor.
- One approach is to use an outline hand-print with the sensor at the tip of the first finger. This acts as an effective prompt to visitors to position their hand correctly and to use the same finger each time. The hand-print should be child-sized as children tend to align their hands with the bottom edge of the hand-print rather than the finger tips.
- The sensor itself can have problems logging on and/or recognising small fingerprints from children below the age of 9/10 years.
- Showing visitors the image of their fingerprint from the scanner on the computer screen is enormously helpful. Visitors can then see how to adjust the position of their finger to get a better image and can judge when they are pressing too lightly or too hard on the scanner.
- Visitors often assume that they need to keep their finger on the scanner throughout their interaction with the exhibit and need to be told when to remove it.

Video cameras

Visitors often find it difficult to position themselves in front of a video camera because what is shown on the screen is not a mirror image. Visitors often move in the wrong direction or move too far one way or the other.

One possible solution is to present visitors with a mirror image rather than a conventional video image.

Another problem is where visitors are asked to position themselves in front of a video camera and then have to lean forward to press a button to capture their image. This means that they are not in the correct position when the camera takes their picture.

One solution is to design the exhibit to be more like a commercial photo-booth where visitors press a button which starts a count-down at the end of which the camera takes their picture. This means that visitors have a few seconds to position themselves and hopefully are stationary when their image is captured.

Remember: visitors do weird things

We once developed a series of linked computer exhibits which included a video-phone. Visitors were supposed to play a game and when someone arrived at another terminal, phone them up and have a chat. The telephone was made to look and operate like a conventional phone because, we reasoned, people would know how to use it. However, we forgot that the meaning visitors attach to a phone in a museum setting is very different to the meaning they attach to a phone in a work or home environment. What actually happens is that as soon as a visitor approaches a terminal they picked up the telephone handset and jammed it under their chin. Even though they can clearly see the loudspeaker in front of them and surely can hear that the audio output is coming from the speaker and not the telephone, they still hold on to the handset. What this means is that the terminal is permanently engaged all the time and no one at another terminal can phone them.

The underlying reason seems to be that when a visitor sees a telephone handset in a museum environment, they assume that by picking it up they will hear a commentary. Obviously they would not go into someone's office or home and pick-up the telephone but then they would be in a different environment with a different set of rules and expectations.

Object: authenticity, authority and trust

Introduction to Part Five

Ross Parry

H ISTORICALLY, MUSEUMS HAVE BEEN about material things. After several centuries of collecting and displaying physical objects, curatorial practice has largely been predisposed to the solidity of collections and exhibitions. Up to the digital age, the museum was ostensibly a project in practically apprehending and spatially rendering cultural heritage. Consequently, digitality presented something of an anomaly to the profession; at once in tune with the institution's instinct to research and accrue information and to present knowledge compellingly; yet, a departure from the tangibility that had defined the venue, visit and vocation of the museum. This dilemma has pivoted around questions of authenticity and trust. How, after all, could a digital resource – so easily edited, so easily reticulated, so easily reproduced – be authoritative? And did audiences expect more than just digital simulacra within an institution established upon genuineness and originality? Taking the notion of 'the object' as its focus, Part Five traces the parameters of these debates around authenticity, virtuality and the museum – debates that take us to the core of digital heritage.

The six chapters presented here evidence a curatorial, technological, directorial, conservational and artistic engagement with questions of digital trust and authenticity. Our discussion begins with extracts from Klaus Müller's short article on 'Museums and Virtuality' that first appeared in the journal *Curator*. Müller suggests not just a more positive definition of 'virtuality' (one that does more than labour on the distinctions between digital and non-digital), but also that museum exhibition practice is, in actuality, an exercise in virtuality. Jennifer Trant produces an equally constructive reading of virtuality in Chapter 30. Perceptively, she identifies a role for the museum online built upon (rather than eroded by) questions of trust. Trant helps us to see that in the vastness of the Web, amidst the white noise of mass comment, and the uncertainties of unmediated content, there is a role (a vital role perhaps) for the trusted guide and the steward of authenticated content. Not startled by virtuality, Trant is therefore confident about how, online, museums can offer interpretations of authentic material culture to, as she puts it, 'a generation comfortable in an immaterial world'. In Chapter 31, Clifford Lynch's concern is less museums' authenticating voice online, but rather the authentication of digital resources themselves. Acting as a prism on the intellectual and practical dimensions to conceiving 'digital information objects' as authentic, Lynch's paper skilfully separates a series of terms ('integrity', 'essence', 'provenance') and techniques (watermarking, digital signatures) that make up an evolving system of trust, identity and authentication for the online cultural environment.

Together Trant and Lynch ought to provide the reassurance sought by a museum director such as Marc Pachter (in Chapter 32). His chapter is an extract from a keynote address to an MDA annual congress. In his speech he reminds a conference hall of curators, academics, collection managers and information professionals of the ritualistic and spiritual dimension to museum visiting and being proximate to authentic museum objects. Pachter parks the information society alongside museums' role as 'emotional, physical enhancers of meaning'. For Pachter (like Trant), 'the electronic will draw us more to the physical'.

The last two chapters of Part Five (both discussions from specialist symposia) open the door to two key implications of this complementary and augmenting role for digitisation within the material traditions of the museum: digital preservation; and digital curation. In Chapter 33, Peter Lyman and Howard Besser warn us of disappearing digital culture heritage – that is, the elements of our contemporary and past cultures that are in digital form. Contrasting the persistence of 'atoms' and 'bits', their concern is for how digital content can become 'inaccessible', 'unreadable' or even 'obsolete' as a result of media deterioration and advances in information technology. Looking at the authors' arguments from the vantage point of the cultural heritage sector, it brings into focus a series of questions on what responsibility museums, libraries and archives have (as collecting organisations and mirrors of our world) for actively acquiring and preserving digital content. The final chapter is a transcript of Matthew Gansallo's contribution to an International Seminar at BALTIC (the centre for contemporary arts in Gateshead, UK). Speaking as Senior Research Fellow for Tate's National Programmes, Gansallo shares the experience of commissioning and curating web-based art. Revealingly, his monologue exposes the new thought processes and work patterns that an organisation such as Tate had to go through as they entered a new mode of online curation. Not only did the institution need to find new ways of developing encounters with artists, but its existing curatorial, educational and marketing teams had to adjust and accommodate another format of art and an alternative channel of exhibition. We read here of an institution, confronted with new modes of (digital) curation, renegotiating fundamental curatorial matters of 'ownership, acquisition, procurement, collection, archiving and provenance'.

Chapter 29

Museums and Virtuality

Klaus Müller

Introduction

Leonardo da Vinci's *Last Supper* is one of the great paintings of European art. Housed in the Santa Maria delle Grazie church in Milan, visitors can see it only in small groups, under tightly controlled conditions, which include a limited time-slot and prior reservations. At least, that's the theory. In today's world, the *Last Supper* has become a virtual painting, because few people ever really get to view it. You can visit the charming church of Santa Maria, but then the staff will tell you that you can make a reservation only by phone. If you call, the line is always busy. So there you are, in the middle of Milan, but da Vinci is as far away as ever. The air pollution we all generate has driven the painting into seclusion.

An ever-growing part of our cultural heritage is stored in museum archives and repositories, where visitors can neither see nor access it. Such conditions contradict a museum's mission to "represent the world's natural and cultural commonwealth" (as stated in the AAM *Code of Ethics for Museums*). In their efforts to preserve cultural heritage, museums are also placing it under lock and key. How often do visitors visit a museum to see a particular painting or artifact, only to find it not on display? In a library, at least, we can request to see and study the desired object; rarely is that possible in museums. But through the Web, a museum can now provide public access to its entire collection.

Digital heritage projects have stored images of countless artifacts in collections databases. Despite such considerable efforts, few museums have fully embraced the diverse possibilities of having an unlimited space for display and communication. While other industries have expanded and reconfigured their business on the Web in

Source: *Curator*, vol. 45, no. 1, 2002, pp. 21–33.

recent years (or were forced to do so), museums have approached it with a mixture of caution and distance. In 1998, a survey of museums worldwide (by the Internet Museum) indicated how slowly museums ventured into online development. Fully 53.7 percent indicated that they launched their websites in 1995 or after; 70 percent were spending less than $1,000 per year on the Web (not including personnel costs); and 57 percent had one-person web departments. (See the bibliography for the URL for this survey and all the sites referred to in this article.)

However, *The Status of Technology and Digitization in the Nation's Museums and Libraries* (IMLS 2002) indicates that a rapid change has occurred in American museums. According to the report, all large museums in this country now have websites, followed by 93 percent of medium-sized and 41 percent of small museums. Fifteen percent of those without a website plan to add one in the coming year, and a majority of all American museums cited a need for additional funding (79 percent) and staff with greater expertise (63 percent) for their web-based projects.

Many museum websites offer rudimentary information regarding location, hours, and services and general descriptions of collections. But are museums carrying their missions to the Web? It is the digitization of collections that dominates the digital profile of most museums (and the IMLS report shows that museums consider access to collections to be the main goal of digitization). Virtual collaborations with visitors or other museums, digital content development, handheld devices and wireless applications, distance learning, and interactive communication with online visitors may lead eventually to a broader role for museums. But that has not yet been achieved. Despite heavy investments in digital heritage programs, museums are still struggling to find the connection between the *reality* of an artifact and its *virtual* representation.

Notions of virtuality usually have a technological basis. Digitization hereby refers to the transfer of existing information and the reproduction of physical objects in an electronic form. In such an understanding, virtual appears as the opposite of real. But do virtual reproductions simply mimic their real counterparts? Digitization is more than a reproduction technique. Virtuality comes from the Latin *virtus*, which has several meanings, including excellence, strength, power, and (in its plural form) mighty works. The word describes a modus of participation or potentiality. In this sense, virtual objects can be seen as illuminating the potential meanings of art and other objects. Virtual exhibitions and digital museum environments contextualize objects through narratives and links. Thus, virtuality should be understood as a complex cultural interpretation of objects that forces us to rethink the tangible and intangible imprints of our cultural history.

Museums' relationships with virtuality

Virtuality in on-site museums

Debates about whether museums are about objects or ideas seldom focus on the relevance of virtuality to the museum experience. When museums define themselves as showcases of material objects that visitors can experience on-location, the virtual display mode of the Web appears to be a distortion of this encounter. The most discussed museum endeavors in recent years – the Guggenheim in Bilbao, the Tate Modern in London, the Jewish Museum in Berlin – all seem to underline the singular quality of space and spatial experience for an understanding of art and material culture. Many visitors see museums as civic spaces (and, at times, even sacred spaces), and this perception also reflects the power of the museum as a physical site. That may contribute to the remarkable expectations that many visitors have of museums – that they should present impartial and truthful voices.

In a world where experiences are increasingly produced, translated, or shaped by media, the museum often seems to be the only place to find the "authentic." The public has chosen museums over schools, universities, and the media as the "most trusted cultural institutions" (Rosenzweig and Thelen 1998), but is this perhaps because visitors (mis)understand – or are (mis)led – to understand the artifacts as such impartial material witnesses?

Artifacts may tell a story, but they do so within the curatorial and architectural framework created by the museum display. That is why "virtuality" is a fundamental exhibiting practice. The integration of objects into museum collections removes and alienates the object from its "authentic" (original, historical, physical, emotional) context and places it in a new and virtual "museum order." New meanings are imposed on the artifact, ranging from its captions to its placement in the show. The artifact's physical presence within its new curatorial context is the basis of the "museum experience" that engages our visitors.

Of course, there is a difference between real objects displayed in an on-site museum and their virtual reproductions in an online environment. But the dichotomy between real and virtual is misleading and obscures their commonalities, simplifying the multiple meanings objects acquire through cultural history.

Placing virtual reproductions on a website is similar to moving an object from its authentic context into the museum environment. Just as a museum collection redefines the value and meaning of a newly acquired artifact, the digital environment changes an object's frame of reference once again. Museums have long been expert at framing objects in ever-new contexts, and the Web is just one of them.

The translation of museum objects into electronic representations renders both gains and losses. The much-praised social and civic space in which the object is experienced is lost. The digital reproduction appears foremost as visual (or aural) information, similar to a document. Although in galleries visitors experience the objects in a spatial order, they usually cannot touch the objects. Virtual programs eliminate the physical dimension altogether as well as the momentum created by the object's physical presence (after all, bytes have no aura). But the digital copy can offer new venues for contextualizing the object and investigating its informational layers as well as interactive options for exploring its characteristics and history.

In recent years, many museums have moved from object-centered to story-centered exhibitions, while still maintaining the importance of the real object experience. That is one reason why museums rarely display reproductions. However, they often use technology and media to enhance the visitor experience. Lighting dramatizes the object's presence; audio tours narrate its stories; and video productions offer historical overviews. Quality installations identify all of these things as valuable exhibit components. Similarly, the object's digital counterpart identifies it as an important part of our heritage; the quality of its presentation influences our comprehension; and virtual exhibitions and collection highlights recount its history. Removed from a physical space, however, the digital experience might encourage a more rational reception of the artifact on display.

Today's debates on virtuality recall those on art and reproduction technologies that took place in the first part of the twentieth century. As early as 1934, philosopher Walter Benjamin wrote in *The Work of Art in the Age of Mechanical Reproduction*: "[T]he technique of reproduction detaches the reproduced object from the domain of tradition. By making reproductions it substitutes a plurality of copies for a unique existence." Benjamin's dictum, that art looses its aura and immediacy of experience through the possibility of its mechanical reproduction (its reproducibility), was written during the newly emerging development of mass culture, (e.g. film), and at the time of radical attacks on "authentic art" by artists themselves, as in Dada or Surrealism.

Benjamin's influential thesis was much quoted in the debate of "The Work of Art in the Age of Digital Reproduction" (Baudrillard et al. 1988). Praised by some for his sharp analysis of pre-modern art in a time of technological change, Benjamin is seen by others as a nostalgic apologist for a singular, elitist experience of art. "It's worse when we insist – as Walter Benjamin insisted," notes one critic, "on the sacred 'aura' of the original. You must stand in front of the *Mona Lisa* or else. You can't fall in love with her reproduction, no, no no – that's masturbation" (Davis 1995). But Benjamin wanted neither to go back in time nor to embrace technological progress for its own sake. Rather, he was exploring the impact of mass reproduction on our perception of art. The digitization of artifacts and their worldwide accessibility, via the Web, alters this perception again. The transformation from the physical domain to the digital has blurred the distinction between authentic and virtual: they increasingly overlap.

Virtuality and cultural heritage

In the coming years, more and more museums will place digitized information on the Web. Digital heritage programs ensure integrated access to collections and materials held in memory institutions such as museums, libraries, and archives. They are guided by professional organizations around the world, including the National Initiative for a Networked Cultural Heritage (NINCH), in the U.S., Australian Museums On-line (AMOL), the Canadian Heritage Information Network (CHIN), and the Digital Heritage Initiative of the European Commission, among others. Library catalogue and database standards have often been used as models for these works-in-progress. The sheer volume of digitized collections that audiences will be able to access is unprecedented, and will lead to significant changes in how we look at, consume, and interpret cultural artifacts.

For example, in the mid-1990s, AMOL was developed as the main gateway to Australian museums and galleries. The portal is supported as a collaborative project by the country's national and local governments and the museum sector. After several pilots, the website was launched in 1998; it now has collection descriptions of more than 400,000 objects and images from nearly 1,100 Australian museums. Recognized in the 2002 *Best of the Web* competition as the best Museum Professional's Site, AMOL has set standards for digital collaborations among museums and for digital outreach to both museum professionals and audiences. Its website also features discussion forums, online journals, news items, and stories about objects and collections.

In 1995, under the guidance of the French Ministry of Culture, the French museum database, *Joconde*, began to make collections accessible through digitized reproductions on the Web. In 2001, more than 132,000 images from seventy-five museum collections could be searched. And the number of users is growing, from 52,000 hits in 1999 to 335,000 in 2001. Similar national (and European Community-supported) digital heritage initiatives are underway in most other European countries, often supported by substantial funds. In early 2002, for example, the U.K. New Opportunities Fund announced the creation of a £50-million (approximately $73 million) fund for the digitization of Britain's national heritage. This European subsidy system has its advantages. Smaller museums, which often lack resources for technology, benefit from national initiatives that support digitization and website development and give them a place in national museum portals, central points for both museum professionals and audiences. But there is a downside to these national initiatives: they can inhibit museums from defining their own needs and unique visions.

In contrast, American museums have been forced to find funding for their own technological expansions, though many have received logistical help from the former Getty Information Institute and NINCH. In addition, the aforementioned IMLS report lists many examples of digitization efforts that led to regional and/or collection-based cooperation among museums, libraries, archives, and historical societies, including research, training, technical support, and shared databases open for public access. But overall American museums have had to develop and define their own institutional and programmatic goals for potential funders. (Naturally, smaller museums, having less branding power, have struggled to attract such funding.) The digital profile that many American museums developed and the know-how for finding non-government sponsors for technology are rarely found in the European museum field. The effects of economic liberalization and changing governance models make this a pressing dilemma for many European museums.

Reproductions, replicas, and authenticity

What is a reproduction and how can it help us to understand our culture? Does the fact that an original work of art is digitally reproducible enhance or diminish its value? Three brief examples may be helpful to illuminate these questions.

Reproduction is nearly as old as the artistic process and often has been accepted as an original craft or even an artistic act. Today's conventional notion of its inferiority to the original work disregards cultural history. Much of what we know about Greek culture comes from Roman reproductions. And the fifteenth- and sixteenth-century Renaissance of Greek and Roman antiquity was guided by replicas of the Roman copies. Reproductions have long shaped our perceptions about the "classical age." As such, the original Greek works represent only one, often undocumented layer of this history.

Early twentieth-century art questioned the excessive value given to "original" art works. Duchamp's "ready-mades" – mass-produced objects displayed as art – attacked traditional notions of "uniqueness" and "authenticity." Various artists emulated his radical gesture throughout twentieth-century art. Nevertheless, "authenticity" survived, and the cultural industry adapted and exploited its notion of originality. Today, museums offer replicas of Duchamp's ready-mades, produced in limited editions with his permission.

Finally, late nineteenth- and early twentieth-century reproduction technologies, such as photography and film, were met initially with disdain, characterized as mechanical enterprises, mere forms of documentation or entertainment. But in time, they became art forms in their own right. Now technology has brought us yet another dilemma. Digital and digitized photography and film now surpass a polarized "original" versus "copy" categorization. Whereas analogue duplication still leads to a loss of a "generation" (as one coined the quality loss within each reproduction cycle), digital reproductions of photography and film seem identical with the original: What is what? In the case of the digital copy, degradation exists only on a theoretical, imperceptible level. The lines between "originals" and "copies" have been blurred and partially eliminated.

A mix of original and reproduced works informs much of our current knowledge of cultural history. The moment of intense encounter with a work of art or a historical artifact can have a long-lasting influence on our emotional curiosity and our quest for knowledge. But, often, love for art and culture is nurtured by reproductions: book and catalogue illustrations; postcards; posters, and now, thumbnails. Shouldn't museums find ways to use both the precious original and its precious reproductions?

While the singularity and presence of the artifact fades in its duplication, most of its informational layers stay intact. Education and understanding of culture is based on this information and not exclusively on the emphatic experience of the objects' presence. The object's materiality is translated into a sequence of zeros and ones. This transfer permits digital-advanced investigations and tests. Art-historical comparative research is greatly enhanced by the accessibility of digital copies. It is not the quality of the reproduction that constitutes the challenge of digitization but its quantity. Museums might be able to ensure access to databases of thousands or millions of images, but how do they help their online visitors wade through such an overwhelming amount of data?

Exhibiting cultures online

Like libraries, museums collect, preserve, and provide access. In addition, their mission requires that they interpret and exhibit the unique objects entrusted to them. Thus far, this aspect of the museum's mission has not made its way to the Web. At least temporarily, digitization has changed the profile of museums from information interpreters to information providers. How can museums translate their curatorial expertise to the digital environment and encourage visitors to interact with artifacts online?

I would like to suggest seven features necessary for the development of online exhibitions: space, time, links, storytelling, interactivity, production values and accessibility.

Space

An online show creates a two-dimensional display (comparable to film or television). The social and physical experience of space is reduced to the intimate interaction between the user and the monitor. It is an intimate and partially isolated space (comparable to reading a book), but it allows access from any connected computer worldwide. Online exhibitions are no longer regional, but speak to a global audience. Digital advanced viewing can challenge and expand our perception of works of art. The virtual display removes objects from the referential frame of a traditional museum space. Virtual museum "spaces" can take on any shape they want, but they lack the conventional authority and emotion a museum building evokes.

Time

Online exhibitions are defined by the time that visitors need to access them. This is a technological notion of time, counted in seconds and bandwidth. But these sites only close when the server is down. Otherwise, visitors can come and go whenever they want, without communicating with staff or other visitors, or waiting until the ticket office opens. Within such a space, users easily loose track of time while surfing. However, web time is easily organized according to the user's individual needs: visitors can engage for a limited time, interrupt and mark the virtual show for a later return. Similar to a book, they decide when to open the page.

Links

Surfing illuminates the language of the Web as a series of windows (or frames) and links. An online show speaks through a montage of images, sound, text, and design and the navigation of its pages. Although books have trained us to perceive information in a linear way, online exhibitions could lead to multilayered exhibition structures in on-site museums that combine textual and visual information or sound with moving images. But the Web is an enervated medium, a cabinet of wonders and curiosities. Everything is just a click away. A visit to a virtual space might not be as intentional as a visit to the physical museum, where visitors wander dutifully through the galleries, even if they are not enchanted. Web semiotics encourage rapid decisions, and museums are challenged to make their voices heard within this new environment.

Storytelling

Of the thousands of digitized museum images in existence, only a small percentage of them are immediately compelling or engaging. Most digital reproductions only gain depth when they are presented as part of a larger story. Multimedia can lead to a diversity of voices in an exhibition, whether on site or online. Storytelling creates a sense of space the Web deeply needs.

Interactivity

The information age has increased our access to resources in an unprecedented way. In future years, digital heritage programs will place hundreds of thousands of images and other data on the Web, altering our visual memory and cultural perception in unknown ways. The information age also has changed the way we acquire information. As information becomes more and more accessible, hierarchical communication makes less and less sense.

Online exhibitions must find ways of nurturing interactivity and facilitating access by including such options as nonlinear but transparent navigation of informational resources; behind-the-scenes examinations of curatorial work; and open communication via e-mail and guest books. Such increased access might lead to a change from the current emphasis on the composition and arrangement of artifacts to an open and interactive approach that permits visitors to become commentators, contributors, or even co-producers.

Production values

The development of data standards and the digitization of artifacts continue to be costly enterprises. Online exhibitions, however, can benefit from the groundwork that others have done. Online curators do not have to worry about shipping, installation, conservation, or insurance issues. Working with digitized information is cheaper, faster, and more flexible. And the low production costs of online shows make them good tools for small and large museums to re-define and innovate themselves.

Accessibility

Online accessibility of museum resources, either through exhibitions or collections, is the main incentive of digital heritage programs. The Web Accessibility Initiative (WAI), part of the World Wide Web consortium, developed guidelines to ensure that online environments do not create limitations for people with disabilities. Braille interfaces, transcripts of audio and video content, consistent navigation mechanisms, and screen magnifiers are typical enhancements. Of course, a transparent design improves a website's usability for all visitors.

Simulated spaces, virtual realities

Some objects and environments are too fragile for people to visit. Simulated spaces, ranging from simple online tours to virtual reality (VR) installations, can recreate cultural heritage artifacts that physical visits might jeopardize and/or destroy. VR installations engage the user through an array of interactive devices – gloves, headsets, motion detectors, animated images – in a computer-generated environment. Segments of virtual reality technology are already in use in many areas, such as entertainment, architecture, medicine, and engineering. Just like film and theater, VR applications broaden the way we perceive the world. However, in a VR environment the visitor becomes part of the virtual world and can change it through his actions. VR allows a person to use her mind, eyes, and hands to enter a place she may have otherwise only visited in her imagination. A few mainstream museums have used VR applications, mostly as online tours of their on-site galler-ies. In children's museums, however, VR is old news. Following the lead of their video-game savvy visitors, many youth museums already have implemented VR applications into their shows.

VR also allows us to go to places that are off limits to visitors because they are being restored or renovated or because they no longer exist. The recent (and disputed) restoration of the Giotto fresco cycle of 100 biblical scenes in the Scrovegni Chapel in Padua, commissioned some 700 years ago, used the most advanced tech-niques. But now only twenty-five people at a time can visit the fresco, and each group is allowed no more than 15 minutes. Although the entire chapel was scanned during the approximately $1.8-million restoration, the digitized images have not been used – with the exception of an online panorama – to offset the limitations placed on visitors. Like the Scrovegni Chapel, other sites face the dangers of pollu-tion and temperature fluctuations caused by visitors. The cave paintings of Lascaux and Chauvet-Pont-d'Arc, the latter "commissioned' approximately 31,000 years ago, can tolerate only virtual visits. Only scientists are allowed to study the actual caves and must follow strict protocols.

Online panoramas and tours are, of course, very rudimentary forms of simula-tion. Archeological excavation sites like the Belgian Ename open-air museum use digital imagery to visualize a Benedictine abbey that dominated life in the Flemish Ardennes from 1063 to 1795. On-site kiosks transmit virtual reconstructions of the successive structures that stood on the spot and superimpose them on the excavated foundations. Thus, a visit to the open-air museum becomes like time travel, enabling visitors to envision how the original structures appeared. Of course, turning to simu-lated spaces may blur the lines between museums and theme parks and speed up the "Disneyfication" of culture. This largely depends on the level of historical research and accuracy used for such simulations. But the desire to attract greater public support and visitation is already encouraging archeological sites, and some museums, to use virtual reconstruction as one tool.

Thinking about museums from the perspective of the Internet

Whereas in the above sections virtuality is discussed from a museum perspective and appears as an expansion of classical museum functions and objectives into the net, it can be explored from a different perspective, that of the Internet. Can the digital trans-formation lead to new forms of museology and new relationships between museums and their visitors? There are many open questions and good reasons to speculate.

A museum defines itself through its collection. But once information about that collection is transferred into a database, does it matter where the database originates or where it is accessed? How important is museum identity in a digital world, and how can it be sustained? Furthermore, although the ownership of intellectual prop-erty on the Internet is still being debated, it seems clear that many web users do not concern themselves with the provenance of their downloads. What does this mean for museums?

From an Internet perspective, many of our habitual definitions are no longer self-evident. Museums no longer necessarily require buildings. With the DCS/Digital

Cellular System or the GSM/Global System for Mobile Communications, they could be readable landscapes – a status currently being planned by the Identity Factory South-east in the South of the Netherlands. Standing in the middle of a Dutch landscape, we may learn about its often-invisible historical layers through artifacts that once came from this landscape, but in time were taken out of context and placed in diverse museum collections. Now, we at least can see their digital replicas close to their original "home."

Wireless applications will change our perceptions of museums as restricted spaces and return artifacts (in their digitized version) to their "authentic" provenance. The Nuovo Museo Elettronico (NUME) in Bologna has turned the old part of the city into a virtual museum by developing a three-dimensional historical model that allows a visitor to walk through 1,000 years of Bologna's history. In both projects, visitors do not go to an actual museum, but they visit an environment that becomes readable, through a PAD device, a website, or a virtual theater. However, it is too early to know whether this and other similar experiments will lead to successful hybrid spaces in museums that allow visitors to move between real and virtual sensory experiences. It might very well be that they share the limited success of earlier 3-D experiments such as stereoscopic photography, 3-D movies or holographic images.

Does virtual cooperation between museums alter the notion of a traditional museum space? "Crossfade," a curated virtual space exploring sound as an artistic medium, was developed through the virtual cooperation of four institutions: the Goethe-Institute in San Francisco; the Walker Art Center in Minneapolis; the San Francisco Museum of Modern Art; and ZKM (Center for Art and Media) in Karlsruhe, Germany. Accessible through the websites of all four partner institutions, the work-in-progress has developed its own identity. Once a user bookmarks it as a favorite, "Crossfade" departs from its institutional origins. How can a museum define its space in a digital environment without becoming fragmented or transitory? How often do we find things on the Net and then cannot remember where we first saw them?

While established museums are moving cautiously to the Net, new museums are often going the other way and starting their initiatives with a website. The Gay Museum and the International Museum of Women are just two examples; both institutions challenge our ideas of how to develop a museum and its audience. It is still too early to predict if exclusively virtual museums will be successful. In fact, there are no standards for measuring success in a digital environment, although research into online visitors and evaluations of their experiences are the focus of the "What Clicks?" study of the Minneapolis Institute of Arts and a two-year survey by Soren and Lemelin, among others.

Less than ten years ago most of us did not have e-mail. Less than five years ago most museums did not have a website. Both now are seen as essential and integral tools for museums. Increasingly, a merger of the real and the virtual is characterizing contemporary life. The digital transformation of museums is challenging traditional ideas of what they are about. Digital objects, online visitors, and virtual communication are redefining the museum, both online and on site. I predict that museums will continue to reinvent themselves in the virtual world, to ensure that they fulfill their mission to help people explore culture, memory and identity in the twenty-first century.

Acknowledgments

The author expresses his sincere thanks to Selma Thomas and Jane Lusaka for their wonderful support and help with this article.

Selected bibliography

Bandelli, Andrea. 1999. "Virtual Spaces and Museums." *Journal of Museum Education*, 24 (1 and 2).

Baudrillard, Jean, Stuart Hall, and Paul Virilio. 1988. "The Work of Art in the Electronic Age." *Block* 14.

Benjamin, Walter. 1968. *Illuminations*. Trans. Harry Zohn. Ed. Hannah Arendt. New York: Schocken Books.

Bowen, Jonathan. Virtual Visits to Virtual Museums, www.archimuse.com/mw98/papers/bowen/bowen_paper.html.

Bronner, Stephen. Reclaiming the Fragments: On the Messianic Materialism of Walter Benjamin, www.uta.edu/huma/illuminations/bron3a.htm.

Castells, Manuel. 2001. *The Internet Galaxy: Reflections on the Internet, Business, and Society*. Oxford: Oxford University Press.

MacDonald, George, and Stephen Alsford. 1997. "The Digital Museum," in *The Wired Museum: Emerging Technology and Changing Paradigms*. Ed. Katherine Jones-Garmil. Washington D. C.: American Association of Museums.

Davis, Ben. 1994. "Digital Museums." *Aperture* (Fall).

Davis, Douglas. 1995. "The Work of Art in the Age of Digital Reproduction (An Evolving Thesis: 1991–1995)." *Leonardo*. 28 (5): 381–386.

Himanen, Pekka. 2001. *The Hacker Ethic and the Spirit of the Information Age*. New York: Random House.

Johnson, Steven. 1977. *Interface Culture*. San Francisco: Basic Books.

Kenderdine, Sarah. 1998. Inside the Meta-Center: A Wonder Cabinet. http://amol.org.au/downloads/about_amol/cabinet_of_wonder.doc (June).

Mannoni, Bruno. 1996. "Bringing Museums On Line," in *Communications of the ACM* (June). www.mygale.org/~mannoni/cacm.htm.

Rosenzweig, Roy, and David Thelen. 1998. *The Presence of the Past: Popular Uses of History in American Life*. New York: Columbia University Press.

Schlesinger, Marissa. 1997 "Digital Information and the Future of Museums," *Spectra* 24 (4): 17–20.

Schweibenz, Werner. 1998. The 'Virtual Museum': New Perspectives For Museums to Present Objects and Information Using the Internet as a Knowledge Base and Communication System, www.phil.uni-sb.de/fr/infowiss/projekte/virtualmuseum/virtual_museum_ISI98.htm.

Soren, B. J., and N. Lemelin. *Cyberpals: A Look at On-line Museum Visitor Experiences*. The Imperial Oil Centre for Science, Mathematics and Technology Education, OISE/UT, University of Toronto, unpublished manuscript.

Chapter 30

When All You've Got is 'The Real Thing': museums and authenticity in the networked world

Jennifer Trant

Introduction

It resonates with a generation, that famous advertising campaign for Coca Cola ending with the tag line, that provides the title for this paper: "It's the Real Thing". This is a phrase that has come to be a part of contemporary culture, giving titles to Doris Lessing and Tom Stoppard[1] among others. Its assertion of reality over appearance has given me pause as I looked at the question of museums and authenticity. Coke's "Real Thing" campaign sits in opposition to the challenge of "The Pepsi Generation" – an exercise in positioning a new product as an alternative to an established and institutionalized nineteenth-century beverage. It seems that the cultural heritage communities' current concerns with "authenticity" and "quality" arise from a similar challenge: museums are deluged with an onslaught of interpretations of culture from an incredible number of sources, and forced into an awareness that they are no longer the sole interpreters of their collections. At the same time, cultural heritage institutions are being challenged to incorporate other voices and other experiences into their interpretations of history and culture, and have begun to rethink traditional interpretive strategies to be more inclusive.

This crisis is coming to a head in a new digital landscape, where the traditional roles of author, editor, publisher, distributor and consumer of information have dramatically altered. When authors are creators and anyone can be a publisher, what is the place and role of cultural heritage institutions? Where and how can they find their niche, as relevant players in the digital world?

Source: *Archives and Museum Informatics*, vol. 12, 1998, pp. 107–125.

Architecture and authenticity

In networked space, users are without the traditional visual and spatial vocabulary of communication. Museums find themselves unable to rely upon the semiotics of a century of museological symbols that have enabled them, in public buildings and spaces, to create the aura of authenticity and rarification cultivated to communicate the uniqueness of each of artifacts, and the seriousness of the educational experience. Rightly, museums have been criticized for this approach, and the redesign of museum spaces has become more open and welcoming.[2] But, no doubt partly because this tradition as exhibiting institutions has shaped museums' sense of the intellectual categorization of the objects that they interpret, many institutions have modeled their networked spaces on their physical spaces.

One example of this spatially dictated organization of information can be found in the website of The Metropolitan Museum of Art (MMA), in New York. Here, the "map" of the collections is drawn from the map of the museum that a visitor picks up from the information desk, after she's climbed the long stone staircase and walked between the fluted columns. While the opening page of the website tries to communicate this experience, the picture of the happy, assembled throngs on the steps of the MMA that is found on their website doesn't create the sense of anticipation and the feeling "something important" is about to happen, that comes from climbing those stairs, and the stairs inside that lead to the second floor painting galleries.

As compelling as it may be to rely on the physical nature of the museum to convey its weight and presence, such metaphors are often less than successful at communicating either content or context in the 640 × 480 pixel world.[3] The spatial organization of the galleries may or often may not reflect a logical sequence or progression, and can be confusing and haphazard when seen without the physical context of the building. Why, for example, does this map say that Nineteenth Century European Paintings are *between* Islamic Art, and Twentieth Century Art, but that there is *little connection* between European painting and Nineteenth Century painting? Maps of physical spaces don't always transpose into maps of information spaces.

Museums often gave into the temptation, in an information space without maps, to transpose the physical world onto this new medium. But the intellectual inferences made based on graphic proximity in schematic diagrams are not those of the relative physical positioning of navigational maps.[4] Transposing physical navigation into conceptual space risks introducing errors in interpretation, as well as failure to communicate clearly. Despite this danger, museums' collective sense of the importance of their physical nature has given rise to many architecturally driven website structures. Institutions are hanging onto their pediments and porticoes as talismans of the aura of authenticity that they symbolize.

Museums without walls, or buildings either ...

Unfortunately, it is the dematerialization of networked information space that has given rise to some of the greatest concerns in the museum world. Nicolas Pioch created Le Web Louvre, since metamorphosed into le web museum (sunsite.unc.edu/wm/), without the involvement of Le Louvre. le web museum is perhaps the most well known and widely consulted of a plethora of 'personal museums'. These range from the "Art Galaxy" maintained by Massoud Malek, Professor of Mathematics and Computer Science at California State University, Hayward, to the professionally presented texas.net Museum of Art maintained by Mark Harden.

On the one hand, this personal interest and enthusiasm could be seen as a positive force, to be directed and channeled by museums in their online programming. But the disregard for copyright and intellectual property law – despite the occasional presence of disclaimers that the sites are being created for personal and educational use – and the appropriation of published materials without acknowledgment, is worrisome; the appropriation of symbols may pose more of a challenge, as they could be considered misleading.

Perhaps more significantly, these sites exist without reference to the reality that they represent. Reproductions of works of art are most often online without any indication of their original size, position, or placement. The hangings of virtual galleries are often impossible: the *Mona Lisa*, a Canaletto, and a Mary Cassatt drypoint are all almost the same size in the Art Galaxy.

Often manipulated or altered images are included without reference to the original. In the Art Galaxy's Gallery of Illusions, a series of well known paintings are manipulated so that the red and blue color spaces are offset slightly.

While it is possible to find a more faithful reproduction of Mary Cassatt's *Boating Party* elsewhere on this site (and many other places on the Internet, including the National Gallery of Art), there is no link between "the real thing" and this manipulation. Nor does the author of the site provide any details about the individual work, its size or its location. The only background provided is a brief biography of the artist. Obviously, these images were created with a thesis in mind, for much care was taken in altering the original visual representation of this work of art. But this point is not clear from this website. While Malek isn't making a claim to be "the real thing" – indeed he's asserting an illusion – he also isn't accurately representing the original work of art, either. Whatever the goal of this alteration, its evocative power would be strengthened by a link to a faithful reproduction.

Don't fence me in

On their own, and taken as individual instances, these small-scale, simply virtual galleries should not cause a great deal of concern for museums. In fact, museums have something to learn from the many personalized museum-like installations that are appearing on the Web, for they point out a need to interpret and contextualize works in an individualized space. As Peter Walsh has reminded us, the Web can provide museums with an alternative to the "Unassailable Voice" of museum authority.[5] Walsh rightly points out that the Web provides an opportunity to stop speaking in the voice of the all-knowing narrator, familiar to all of us from Acoustiguide™ tours or Educational Television, and to incorporate multiple perspectives and visitor feedback into interpretive programs.

Losing some historical baggage might not be a bad thing for museums as they re-create themselves on the Web, but how are people supposed to identify the *real thing*? Where does the museum's traditional role as custodian and interpreter of cultural heritage fit in the highly diversified information frontier? How can museums best use the web to communicate, and accommodate diverging points of view, without sacrificing educational and interpretive goals, or compromising the moral rights of the artists whose works are in care? Disorientation is often the prime sentiment of a web surfer. Museums have an opportunity to provide a touchstone.

Provide a good foundation

The key to a good museum site, and what sets it apart from many of the sites of individual art enthusiasts, is the depth and breadth of the content that museums can provide. Reproductions of Mary Cassatt's *Boating Party* can be found at the Art Galaxy site,[6] in the Web Museum,[7] as part of Mark Harden's Artichive[8] and on a number of other personal home pages. What sets apart the exploration of the painting at the National Gallery of Art is the interpretation and context provided.

A main page introduces the painting,[9] and provides links to a number of other types of information: a full screen image, a number of details, a detailed bibliography, exhibition history, provenance (including links to other works from the Chester Dale Collection), and the location where the work hangs in the Gallery. In addition to this somewhat scholarly art historical information, the work is placed in the context of a tour of the work of "Mary Cassatt and Auguste Renoir", that explores both artists' interest in scenes of everyday life.

The work comes alive, however, in the narration by Phillip Conisbee, Curator of French paintings at the National Gallery of Art, available in an audio clip. He relates the painting compositionally to the Japanese woodblock prints that had such an influence on Cassatt. Pointing out the high horizon line and the angled forms that flow out of the frame, his reference to this visual precedent prompts a query of the NGA collection for examples – one that unfortunately yielded an unsatisfactory result, because the information given in the narrative was not precise enough to inform a meaningful database query. A link to a known work would have been more helpful.

Another significant point in Conisbee's analysis is also lost: a narrative reference to Manet's *Boating*, now in the collection of The Metropolitan Museum of Art, is unaccompanied by an image, or any means to follow up the relationship between these painters or their work. In both cases, the limitations of one medium – either print or audio – have provided false boundaries in a new multimedia space. Rather than leading to richer detail to explore, both leave the visitor intrigued but unsatisfied.

It becomes clear that access to "the real thing" includes the ability to demonstrate its physicality (through view of brushstrokes, for example). Close proximity also enables the development of knowledge about a work, that, when communicated in meaningful way, sets the museum site apart from others. Some aspects of the museum's interpretation of "the real thing" become discernible in the sea of images because of the context that surrounds it. But the "realness" in detail and context is not dependent upon the "thingness" that is granted by custody of the original work itself.

A scholar with good reference works to hand could construct a similar inter-woven narrative about this Mary Cassatt painting.

Museums are learning, however, to explore the "thingness" or artefactuality of the works in their care. They can build up knowledge of the physical makeup of works of art through interpretive installations about their conservation or restoration, and through the distribution of images that show a work from multiple points of view, or in different lighting conditions. Detailed knowledge about the actual construction of a work is one of the keys to establishing its authenticity. In a paper on "The Future of the Past: Archaeology and Anthropology on the Web", John Hoopes posits that "virtual reality might face stiff competition from virtual tours of reality"[10] if museums made remote sensing devices, microscopes, and gallery cameras available to their networked visitors. The Exploratorium in San Francisco (www.exploratorium.org) has also used the Web successfully to make the large small (and bring the Hubble Space Telescope Service Mission to the floor of their exhibit space), and to make the small, large (through an online cow's eye dissection).

Build bridges and pathways

Providing experiences in museums that can't be had elsewhere is one way to draw visitors into cultural heritage websites. Building museum-to-museum connections ensures that the web that a visitor then follows is one of trusted and authentic links. It should be possible for an individual interested in an artistic theme or personage, to move between the websites of collecting and research institutions, learning more about the works in each collection, and building a sense of meaning and context from their inter-relationships.

However, with museums' traditional focus on specific collections, this remains one of the weakest points in museum websites. What is needed are vehicles that enable visitors to traverse a cultural information space, and to find information about themes, artists, time periods, without necessarily limiting their results to single collections. As much as this may run counter to traditional instincts to keep museums visitors 'within the walls', it is critical for the creation of meaningful pathways into and through digital cultural heritage collections. Finding things on the Web is as much about the links one follows as the place one starts. If cultural heritage institutions are not building richly interconnected spaces that reflect the concerns of visitors – person, place, time, subject, theme – then they risk having visitors bypass carefully structured sites, to use the unstructured word-based search engines as a finding aid instead.

The risk of a majority of users relying on network search engines as their point of departure is great – for the majority of museum information available *through* the Web is not actually *on* the Web. Instead, detailed databases of museum content are available through search interfaces. While this approach provides a much more flexible way to deliver dynamic content and manage a growing site, databased information delivery does not mesh with the "web crawling" robots that construct Hotbot, Lycos, alta Vista, WebCrawler, or Excite – to name just a few of the existing search engines.

As a result, museum information loses pride of place to the more thematically oriented personal galleries. A search for information about an artist, such as Mary Cassatt, will produce significantly more "hits" from private pages than from museums themselves.[11]

Conclusions

Writing about the approach taken to the development of the new CD *Voices & Images of California Art* Peter Samis of the San Francisco Museum of Modern Art said:

> I know our program was a departure from the standard collection-based museum CD-ROM/multimedia experience, and our decision to focus narrowly in great depth – with more than an hour's worth of assets devoted to each of only eight artists – was a bit risky. As a result, we left many important artists and works out of our first multimedia publication, and included many works and resources that are not even in the museum's holdings. But it seems to be working: a group of teachers has designed a curriculum based on the CD that cuts across subject areas (and even encourages uniting them in inter-teacher collaborations) ... [this is] fertile ground for us as museum educators: giving our audiences the tools to construct their own meanings, which include, but are far from exhausted by, those that we ourselves might attribute to the works in our care.[12]

Museums need to find a way to move the knowledge they hold of art and culture out beyond their walls, and into a new set of spaces. Networked information space is the natural place of discourse for the next generation; chat rooms are as comfortable as the mall was to the generation previously, and the coffeehouse to the one before that. If cultural heritage institutions are to ensure that these network experiences are based on reality as much as on virtual reality, they have to make their collections and the way they communicate about them accessible and relevant.

Authenticity has its roots in trust. To develop a trust in cultural information resources in the generation now being educated, museums must encourage users to expect a challenging, interesting and enjoyable experience, and enable them to make critical judgments about the meaning of the world around them, as reflected in the unique works of art and artifacts in museum collections. Perhaps it's not about having "The Real Thing" at all, but about having "The Right Stuff". Museums are seeing others with access to information about their collections work re-present them in ways that are personally meaningful. Museums need to find a way to set their sites apart. The challenge is to set museums' sights on the development of a new set of symbols, a new vocabulary that allows museum collections to speak in a narrative and/or interconnected (hyper) information space, constructed by and for the visitor. Using new networked information tools, cultural heritage institutions could weave a web of new realities and interpretations, that communicates the magic of the material past to a generation comfortable in an immaterial world.

Notes

1 Tom Stoppard, *The Real Thing*, 1984 and Dorris Lessing, *The Real Thing, Stories and Sketches*, HarperCollins, 1992.

2 See Eilean Hooper-Greenhill, *Museums and the Shaping of Knowledge*, London and New York: Routledge, 1992, p. 202 for a discussion of the transformation of museum lobbies from resembling prisons to resembling hotel lobbies, in a chapter entitled "A useful past for the present".

3 I'm grateful to one of the reviewers of this article for pointing out that architectural and spatial metaphors are often used with great success in computer games. One good example from the cultural heritage field is *Versailles 1685: a game of intrigue at the court of Louis XIV* from the Réunion des Musés Nationaux. However, I contend that the metaphor of a built environment fails as a communication device if the digital experience simply models the physical one. There are too many physical constraints of 'reality' that do not correspond to the cognitive connections that we wish to communicate for a rendered 3-D space to be satisfactory by itself. We find ourselves wanting more, wishing to move from physical to categorical space, for example, by following the relationships between a painting on a wall that are *not* those of proximity in the exhibition gallery.

4 Much new work is now going on regarding the interpretation of complex information spaces. For example, Dynamic Diagrams has mapped the Mystic Seaport site, using its Mapa software. See www.mystic.org and www.dynamicdiagrams.com.

5 Peter Walsh, "The Web and the Unassailable Voice" *Archives and Museum Informatics: the cultural heritage informatics quarterly* Vol. 11, no 2, reprinted in *Museums and the Web 97: Selected Papers*, Pittsburgh, PA: Archives & Museum Informatics, 1997, pp. 69–76.

6 See www.mcs.csuhayward.edu/~malek/Artfolder/cassat9.htm (Sept. 1997), identified only as *The Boating Party*, and reproduced as a JPEG, www.mcs.cushayward.edu/~malek/cassat9.jpg (Sept. 1997) of 699 × 540 pixels.

7 See sunsite.unc.edu/louvre/paint/auth/cassatt/ (Sept. 1997) identified as The Boating Party/1893–1894 (130 kb); Oil on canvas, 90.2 × 117.5 cm (35½ × 46¼ in); National Gallery of Art, Washington and accompanied by a thumbnail image and a JPEG, sunsite.unc.edu/louvre/paint/auth/cassatt/boating.jpg (Sept. 1997) of 1042 × 786 pixels.

8 See www.artchive.com/artchive/C/cassatt.html (Aug. 1998), identified as CASSATT, Mary/The Boating Party/1893–1894/Oil on canvas/90.2 × 117.5 cm (35½ × 46¼ in.) and accompanied by a JPEG boating.jpg (1042 × 786 pixels) (Aug. 1998).

9 See www.nga.gov/cgi-bin/pinfo?Object=46286+0+none (Sept. 1997) where the work is identified as "Mary Cassatt/American, 1844–1926/The Boating Party, 1893/1894/oil on canvas, 0.900 × 1.173 m (35⁷⁄₁₆ × 46⅛ in.)/Chester Dale Collection/1963.10.94" and accompanied by a thumbnail image (190 × 172 pixels).

10 John Hoopes, "The Future of the Past: Archaeology and Anthropology on the Web," *Museums and the Web 97: Selected Papers*, Pittsburgh: PA, Archives & Museum Informatics, 1997, pp. 279–292, reprinted from *Archives and Museum Informatics; a cultural heritage informatics quarterly*, vol. 11, no. 2, 1997.

11 Searches made during the preparation of this paper, on popular artists' names such as Cassatt and Seurat, rarely produced a museum site in the top ten results from any

of the search engines. Although replicating specific searches is impossible, given the dynamic nature of the Web and its discovery tools, it is possible to regularly reproduce similar results. The CIMI Dublin Core Testbed Project, which may address some of these issues, was announced in early 1998 after this paper was given: see www.cimi.org.

12 From a posting by Peter Samis, Program Manager, Interactive Educational Technologies, San Francisco Museum of Modern Art, to museum–ed@pfreedom.mtn.org, 18 Jun, 1997, with the title "RE: Interpretation & Constructivist approaches".

Chapter 31

Authenticity and Integrity in the Digital Environment: an exploratory analysis of the central role of trust

Clifford Lynch

Introduction

This research seeks to illuminate several issues surrounding the ideas of authenticity, integrity, and provenance in the networked information environment. Its perspective is pragmatic and computational, rather than philosophical. Authenticity and integrity are in fact deep and controversial philosophical ideas that are linked in complex ways to our conceptual views of documents and artifacts and their legal, social, cultural, and historical contexts and roles. (See Bearman and Trant (1998) for an excellent introduction to these issues.)

In the digital environment, as Larry Lessig (1999) has recently emphasized, computer code is operationalizing and codifying ideas and principles that, historically, have been fuzzy or subjective, or that have been based on situational legal or social constructs. Authenticity and integrity are two of the key arenas where computational technology connects with philosophy and social constructs. One goal of this research is to help distinguish between what can be done in code and what must be left for human and social judgment in areas related to authenticity and integrity.

Gustavus Simmons wrote a paper in the 1980s with the memorable title "Secure Communications in the Presence of Pervasive Deceit." The contents of the paper are not relevant here, but the phrase "pervasive deceit" has stuck in my mind because I believe it perfectly captures the concerns and fears that many people are voicing about information on the Internet. There seems to be a sense that digital information needs to be held to a higher standard for authenticity and integrity than has printed information. In other words, many people feel that in an environment characterized

Source: *Authenticity in a Digital Environment*, Council on Library and Information Resources (ed.) Washington, DC: Council on Library and Information Resources, 2000.

by pervasive deceit, it will be necessary to provide verifiable proof for claims related to authorship and integrity that would usually be taken at face value in the physical world. For example, although forgeries are always a concern in the art world, one seldom hears concerns about (apparently) mass-produced physical goods – books, journal issues, audio CDs – being undetected and undetectable fakes.[1]

This distrust of the immaterial world of digital information has forced us to closely and rigorously examine definitions of authenticity and integrity – definitions that we have historically been rather glib about – using the requirements for verifiable proofs as a benchmark. As this research will demonstrate, authenticity and integrity, when held to this standard, are elusive properties. It is much easier to devise abstract definitions than testable ones. When we try to define integrity and authenticity with precision and rigor, the definitions recurse into a wilderness of mirrors, of questions about trust and identity in the networked information world.

While there is widespread distrust of the digital environment, there also seems to be considerable faith and optimism about the potential for information technology to address concerns about authenticity and integrity. Those unfamiliar with the details of cryptographic technology assume the magical arsenal of this technology has solved the problems of certifying authorship and integrity. Moreover, there seems to be an assumption that the solutions are not deployed yet because of some perverse reluctance to implement the necessary tools and infrastructure.[2] This research will take a critical view of these cryptographic technologies. It will try to distinguish between the problems that cryptographic technologies can and cannot solve and how they relate to the development of infrastructure services. There seems to have been surprisingly little examination of these questions; this is itself surprising.

Before attempting to define integrity or authenticity, it is worth trying to gain an intuitive sense of how the digital environment differs from the physical world of information-bearing artifacts ("meatspace," as some now call it). The archetypal situation is this: We have an object and a collection of assertions about it. The assertions may be internal, as in a claim of authorship or date and place of publication on the title page of a book, or external, represented in metadata that accompany the object, perhaps provided by third parties. We want to ask questions about the integrity of the object: Has the object been changed since its creation, and, if so, has this altered the fundamental essence of the object? (This can include asking these questions about accompanying assertions, either embedded in the object or embodied in accompanying metadata). Further, we want to ask questions about the authenticity of the object: If its integrity is intact, are the assertions that cluster around the object (including those embedded within it, if any) true or false?

How do we begin to answer these questions in meatspace? There are only a few fundamental approaches.

- We examine the provenance of the object (for example, the documentation of the chain of custody) and the extent to which we trust and believe this documentation as well as the extent to which we trust the custodians themselves.
- We perform a forensic and diplomatic examination of the object (both its content and its artifactual form) to ensure that its characteristics and content are consistent with the claims made about it and the record of its provenance.

- We rely on signatures and seals that are attached to the object or the claims that come with it, or both, and evaluate their forensics and diplomatics and their consistency with claims and provenance.
- For mass-produced and distributed (i.e., published) objects, we compare the object in hand with other versions (copies) of the object that may be available (which, in turn, means also assessing the integrity and provenance of these other versions or copies).

In the digital environment, there are few forensics or diplomatics,[3] other than the forensics and diplomatics of content itself. We cannot evaluate inks, papers, binding technology, and similar physical characteristics.[4] We can note, just as with a physical work, that an essay allegedly written in 1997 that makes detailed references to events and publications from 1999 is either remarkably prescient or incorrectly dated. There are limited forensics of availability, and they mainly provide negative information. For example, if a document claims to have been written in 1998 and we have copies of it that were deposited on various servers in 1997 (and we trust the claims of the servers that the material was in fact deposited in 1997), we can build a case that it was first distributed *no later than* 1997, regardless of the date contained in the object. Nevertheless, this does not tell us when the document was written.

The fundamental concept of publication in the digital environment – the dissemination of a large number of copies to arbitrary interested parties that are subsequently autonomously managed and maintained – has come under great stress from numerous factors in the networked information environment. These factors include, for example, the move from sale to licensing, limited distribution, making copies public for viewing without giving viewers permission to maintain the copies, and technical protection systems (National Research Council 2000). While the basic principle of broad distribution and subsequent autonomous management of copies remains valid and useful as a base of evidence against which to test the authenticity of documents in question, the availability of relevant and trustworthy copies may be limited in the digital environment, and assessing the copies is likely to be more difficult. Moreover, the forensics and diplomatics of evaluating seals and signatures, and documentation of provenance, become much more formal and computational. It is difficult to say whether digital seals and signatures are more or less compelling in the digital world than in the analog world, but their characters unquestionably change. Finally, provenance and chains of custody in the digital world begin to reflect our evaluation of archives and custodians as implementers and operators of "trusted systems" that enforce the integrity and provenance records of objects entrusted to them.

At some level, authenticity and integrity are mechanical characteristics of digital objects; they do not speak to deeper questions of whether the contents of a digital document are accurate or truthful when judged objectively. An authentic document may faithfully transmit complete falsehoods. There is a hierarchy of assessment in operation: forensics, diplomatics, intellectual analyses of consistency and plausibility, and evaluations of truthfulness and accuracy. Our concern here is with the lower levels of this hierarchy (i.e., forensics and diplomatics as they are reconceived in the digital environment) but we must recognize that conclusive evaluations at the higher levels may also provide evidence that is relevant to lower-level assessment.

Exploring definitions and defining terms: digital objects, integrity, and authenticity

The nature of digital information objects

Before we can discuss integrity and authenticity, we must examine the objects to which we apply these characterizations.

Most commonly, computer scientists are concerned with digital objects that are defined as a set of sequences of bits. One can then ask computationally based questions about whether one has the correct set of sequences of bits, such as whether the digital object in one's possession is the same as that which some entity published under a specific identifier at a specific point in time. However, this is a simplistic notion. There are additional factors to consider.

Bits are not directly apprehended by the human sensory apparatus – they are never truly artifacts. Instead, they are rendered, executed, performed, and presented to people by hardware and software systems that interpret them. The question is how sophisticated these environmental hardware and software systems are and how integral they are to the understanding of the bits. In some cases, the focus is purely on the bits: numeric data files, or sensor outputs, for example, that are manipulated by computational or visualization programs. Documentary objects are characterized primarily by their bits (think of simple ASCII text), but the craft of publishing begins to make a sensory presentation of this collection of bits – to turn content into experience. Text, marked up in HTML and displayed through a web browser, takes on a sensory dimension; the words that make up the text being rendered no longer tell the whole story. Digital objects that are performed – music, video, images that are rendered on screen – incorporate a stronger sensory component. Issues of interaction with the human sensory system – psychoacoustics, quality of reproduction, visual artifacts, and the like – become more important. The bits may be the same across space and time, but because of differences in the hardware and software used by recipients, the experience of viewing them may vary substantially. This raises questions about how to define and measure authenticity and integrity. In the most extreme case, we have objects that are rendered experientially – video games, virtual reality walk-throughs, and similar interactive works – where the focus shifts from the bits that constitute the digital object to the behavior of the rendering system, or at least to the interaction between the digital object and the rendering system.

Thus, we might think about a hierarchy of digital objects that could be expressed as follows:

> (Interactive) experiential works
> Sensory presentations
> Documents
> Data

As we move up the hierarchy, from data to experiential works, the questions about the integrity and authenticity of the digital objects become more complex and perhaps more subjective; they address experience rather than documentary content (Lynch 2000). This research will focus on the lower part of the digital object hierarchy. The upper part is poorly understood and today is addressed only in a limited way; for example, through discussions about emulation as a preservation strategy (Rothenberg 1999, 1995). It seems conceivable that one could extend some of the observations and assertions discussed later in this research to the more experiential works by performing computations on the output of the renderings rather than on the objects themselves. However, this approach is fraught with problems involving canonical representations of the user interface (which, in the most complex cases, involves interaction and not just presentation) and agreeing on what constitutes the authentic experience of the work.

In meatspace, we cheerfully extend the notion of authenticity to much more than objects – in fact, we explicitly apply it to the experiential sphere, speaking of an "authentic" performance of a baroque concerto or an "authentic" Hawaiian luau. To the extent that we can make the extension and expansion of the use of authenticity as a characteristic precise within the framework and terminology of this research, these statements seem to parallel statements about integrity of what in the digital environment could be viewed as experiential works, or performance.

Even as we struggle with definitions and tests of integrity and authenticity for intellectual works in the digital environment, we are seeing new classes of digital objects – for example, e-cash and digital bearer bonds – that explicitly involve and rely upon stylized and precise manipulation of provenance, authenticity, identity and anonymity, and integrity within a specific trust framework and infrastructure. While these fit somewhere between data and documents in the digital object hierarchy, they are interesting because they derive their meaning and significance from their explicit interaction with frameworks of integrity, authenticity, provenance, and trust.

Canonicalization and (computational) essence

Often, we seek to discuss the essence of a work rather than the exact set of sequences of bits that may represent it in a specific context; we are concerned with integrity and authenticity as they apply to this essence, rather than to the literal bits. Discussions of essence become more problematic as we move up the digital object hierarchy. However, even at the lower levels of data and documents, we encounter a troublesome imprecision that is a barrier to making definitions operational computationally when we move beyond the literal definition of precisely equivalent sets of sequences of bits. Those approaching the question from a literary or documentary perspective cast the issue in a palette of grays: there are series (not necessarily a strict hierarchy; at best a partial ordering) of intellectual abstractions of a document that capture its essence at various levels, and the key problem is whether this abstract essence is retained. The abstraction may involve words, layout, typography, or even the feel of the pages. Are hardcover and paperback editions of a book equivalent? Does equivalence depend on whether the pagination is identical? Elsewhere, I have proposed *canonicalization* as a method of making such abstractions precise (Lynch 1999). The fundamental point of canonicalization as an organizing principle is that it defines *computational algorithms* (called "canonicalizations") that can be used to extract the "essence" of documents according to various definitions of what constitutes that essence. If we have such computational procedures for extracting the essence of digital objects, we can then compare digital objects through the prism of that definition of essence. We can also make assertions that involve abstract representations of this essence, rather than more specific (and presumably haphazard) representations that incorporate extraneous characteristics.

The hard problem, of course, is precisely defining and achieving a consensus about the right canonicalization algorithm, or algorithms, for a given context.

Integrity

When we say that a digital object has "integrity," we mean that it has not been corrupted over time or in transit; in other words, that we have in hand the same set of sequences of bits that came into existence when the object was created. The introduction of appropriate canonicalization algorithms allows us to consider the integrity of various abstractions of the object, rather than of the literal bits that make it up, and to operationalize this discussion of abstractions into equality of sets of sequences of bits produced by the canonicalization algorithm.

When we seek to test the integrity of an object, however, we encounter paradoxes and puzzles. One way to test integrity is to compare the object in hand with a copy that is known to be "true."[5] Yet, if we have a secure channel to a known true copy, we can simply take a duplicate of the known true copy. We do not need to worry about the accuracy of the copy in hand, unless the point of the exercise is to ensure that the copy in hand is correct – for example, to detect an attempt at fraud, rather than to be sure that we have a correct copy. These are subtly different questions.[6]

If we do not have secure access to an independently maintained, known true copy of the object (or at least a digest surrogate), then our testing of integrity is limited to internal consistency checking. If the object is accompanied by an authenticated ("digitally signed") digest, we can check whether the object is consistent with the digest (and thus whether its integrity has been maintained) by recomputing the digest from the object in hand and then comparing it with the authenticated digest. But our confidence in the integrity of the object is only as good as our confidence in the authenticity and integrity of the digest. We have only changed the locus of the question to say that *if* the digest is authentic and accurate, then we can trust the integrity of the object. Verifying integrity is no different from verifying the authenticity of a claim that "the correct message digest for this object is M" without assigning a name to the object. The linkage between claim and object is done by association and context – by keeping the claim bound with the object, perhaps within the scope of a trusted processing system such as an object repository.

In the digital environment, we also commonly encounter the issue of what might be termed "situational" integrity, i.e., the integrity of derivative works. Consider questions such as "Is this an accurate transcript?", "Is this a correct translation?", or "Is this the best possible version given a specific set of constraints on display capability?" Here we are raising a pair of questions: one about the integrity of a base object, and another about the correctness of a computation or other transformation applied to the object. (To be comprehensive, we must also consider the integrity of the result of the computation or transformation after it has been produced.) This usually boils down to trust in the source or provider of the computation or transformation, and thus to a question of authentication of source or of validity, integrity, and correctness of code.

Authenticity

Validating authenticity entails verifying claims that are associated with an object — in effect, verifying that an object is indeed what it claims to be, or what it is claimed to be (by external metadata). For example, an object may claim to be created on a given date, to be authored by a specific person, or to be the object that corresponds with a name or identifier assigned by some organization. Some claims may be more mechanistic and indirect than others. For example, a claim that "This object was deposited in a given repository by an entity holding this public/private key pair at this time" might be used as evidence to support authorship or precedence in discovery. Typically, claims are linked to an object in such a way that they include, at least implicitly, a verification of integrity of the object about which claims are made. Rather than simply speaking of the (implied) object accompanying the claim (under the assumption that the correct object will be kept with the claims, and that the object management environment will ensure the integrity of the object) one may include a message digest (and any necessary information about canonicalization algorithms to be applied prior to computing the digest) as part of the metadata assertion that embodies the claim.

It is important to note that tests of authenticity deal only with specific claims (for example, "did X author this document?") and not with open-ended inquiry ("Who wrote it?"). Validating the authenticity of an object is more limited than is an open-ended inquiry into its nature and provenance.

There are two basic strategies for testing a claim. The first is to believe the claim because we can verify its integrity and authenticate its source, and because we choose to trust the source. In other words, we validate the claim that "A is the author of the object with digest X" by first verifying the integrity of the object relative to the claim (that it has digest X), and then by checking that the claim is authenticated (i.e., digitally signed) by a trusted entity (T). The heart of the problem is ensuring that we are certain who T really is, and that T really makes or warrants the claim. The second strategy is what we might call "independent verification" of the claim. For example, if there is a national author registry that we trust, we might verify that the data in the author registry are consistent with the claim of authorship. In both cases, however, validating a claim that is associated with an object ultimately means nothing more or less than making the decision to trust some entity that makes or warrants the claim.

Several final points about authenticity merit attention. First, trust in the maker or warrantor of a claim is not necessarily binary; in the real world, we deal with levels of confidence or degrees of trust. Second, many claims may accompany an object; in evaluating different claims, we may assign them differing degrees of confidence or trust. Thus, it does not necessarily make sense to speak about checking the authenticity of an object as if it were a simple true-or-false test – a computation that produces a one or a zero. It may be more constructive to think about checking authenticity as a process of examining and assigning confidence to a collection of claims. Finally, claims may be interdependent. For example, an object may be accompanied by claims that "This is the object with identifier N," and "The object with identifier N was authored by A" (the second claim, of course, is independent of the document itself, in some sense). Perhaps more interesting, in an archival context, would be claims that "This object was derived from the object with message digest M by a specific reformatting process" and "The object with message digest M was authored by A." (See Lynch 1999 for a more detailed discussion of this case.)

Comparing integrity and authenticity

It is an interesting, and possibly surprising, conclusion that in the digital environment, tests of integrity can be viewed as just special cases and byproducts of evaluations of authenticity. Part of this comes from the perspective of the environment of "pervasive deceit" and the idea that checking integrity of an object means comparing it with some precisely identified and rigorously vetted "original version" or "authoritative copy." In fact, much of the checking for integrity in the physical world is not about ferreting out pervasive deceit and malice, but rather about accepting artifacts for roughly what they seem to be on face value and then looking for evidence of damage or corruption (i.e., torn-out pages or redacted text). For this kind of integrity checking, a message digest that accompanies a digital object as metadata serves as an effective mechanism to ensure that the object has not been damaged or corrupted. This is true even if the message digest is not supported by an elaborate signature chain and trust assessment, but only by a general level of confidence in the computational context in which the objects are being stored and transmitted. In the digital environment, there is a tendency to down-play the need for this kind of integrity checking in favor of stronger measures that combine authenticity claims with integrity checks.

The role of copies

David Levy argues that all digital objects are copies; this echoes the findings of the National Research Council Committee on Intellectual Property in the Emerging Information Infrastructure that use – reading, for example – implies the making of copies (National Research Council 2000). If we accept this view, authenticity can be viewed as an assessment that we make about something in the present – something that we have in hand – relative to claims about the past (predecessor copies). The persistent question is whether a given object X has the same properties as object Y. There is no "original." This is particularly relevant when we are dealing with dynamic objects such as databases, where an economy of copies is meaningless. In such cases, there is no question of authenticity through comparison with other copies; there is only trust or lack of trust in the location and delivery processes and, perhaps, in the archival custodial chain.

Provenance

The term *provenance* comes up often in discussions of authenticity and integrity. Provenance, broadly speaking, is documentation about the origin, characteristics, and history of an object; its chain of custody; and its relationship to other objects. The final point is particularly important. There are two ways to think about a digital object that is created by changing the format of an older object that has been validated according to some specific canonicalization algorithm. We might think about a single object the provenance of which includes a particular transformation, or we might think about multiple objects that are related through provenance documentation. Thus, provenance is not simply metadata about an object – it can also be metadata that describe the relationships between objects. Because provenance also includes claims about objects, it is part of the authentication and trust infrastructures and frameworks.

I do not believe that we have a clear understanding of (and surely not consensus about) where provenance data should be maintained in the digital environment, or by what agencies. Indeed, it is not clear to what extent the record of provenance exists independently and permanently, as opposed to being assembled when needed from various pools of metadata that may be maintained by various systems in association with the digital objects that they manage. We also lack well-developed metadata element sets and interchange structures for documenting provenance. It seems possible that the Dublin Core, augmented by semantics for signing metadata assertions, might form a foundation for this, although attributes such as relationship would need to be extended to allow for very precise vocabularies to describe algorithmically based derivations of objects from other objects (or transformations of objects). We would probably also need to incorporate metadata assertions that allow an entity to record claims such as "Object X is equivalent to object Y under canonicalization C."

Watermarks, authenticity, and integrity

In the most general sense, watermarking can be viewed as an attempt to ensure that a set of claims is inseparably bound to a digital object and thus can be assumed to travel with the object: one does not have to trust transport and storage systems to correctly perform this function. The most common use of watermarks today is to help protect intellectual property by attaching a copyright claim (and possibly an object-specific serial number to allow tracing of individual copies) to an object. Software exists to scan public websites for objects that contain watermarks and to notify the rights holders about where these objects have been found. A serial number, if present, helps the rights holder not only identify the presence of a possibly illegal copy but also determine where it came from. Various trusted system-based architectures for the control of copyrighted works have also been proposed that use watermarking (for example, the Secure Digital Music Initiative 2000). The idea is that devices will refuse to play, print, or otherwise process digital objects if the appropriate watermarks are not present.[7] The desirable properties of watermarks include being very hard to remove computationally (at least without knowledge of the private key as well as the algorithm used to generate the watermark) and being resilient under various alterations that may be applied to the watermarked file (lossy compression, for example, or image cropping). The development of effective watermarking systems is currently a very active area of research.[8]

From the perspective of authenticity and integrity, watermarks present several problems. First, they deliberately and systematically corrupt the objects to which they are applied, in much the same way that techniques such as lossy compression do. Fingerprints (individualized watermarks) are particularly bad in this regard since they defeat comparisons among copies as a way of establishing authenticity – indeed this is exactly what they are designed to do, to make each copy unique and traceable. Applying a watermark to a digital object means changing bits within the object, but in such a way that they change the perception of the object only slightly. Thus, finding and verifying a watermark in a digital object give us only weak evidence of its integrity. In fact, the very presence of the watermark means that integrity has been compromised at some level, unless we are willing to accept the watermarked version of the object as the actual authoritative one – an image or sound recording that includes some data that allegedly does not much change our perception of the object. If a watermark can easily be stripped out of an object (a bad watermark design, but perhaps characteristic of watermarking systems that try to minimize corruption), then the absence of such a watermark does not tell us much about the possible corruption of other parts of the object.

A second problem is that some watermarking systems do not emphasize preventing the creation of fake watermarks; they are concerned primarily with the preservation of legitimate watermarks as evidence of ownership or status of the watermarked object. To use watermarking to address authenticity issues, it seems likely that one would need to use it simply as a means of embedding a claim in an object, under the assumption that the claim would then have to be separately verifiable (for example, by being digitally signed).

To summarize: if one obtains a digital object that contains a watermark, particularly if that watermark contains separately verifiable claims, it can provide useful evidence about the provenance and characteristics of the object, including good reasons to assume that it is a systematically and deliberately corrupted version of a predecessor digital object that one may or may not have access to or be able to locate. The watermark may have some value in forensic examination of digital objects, but it does not seem to be a good tool for the *management* of digital objects within a controlled environment such as an archive or repository system that is concerned with object integrity. It seems more appropriate to require that the environment take responsibility for maintaining linkages and associations between metadata (claims) and the objects themselves. Watermarks are more appropriate for an uncontrolled public distribution environment where integrity is just one variable in a complex set of trade-offs about the management and protection of content.

Semantics of digital signatures

One serious shortcoming of current cryptographic technology has to do with the semantics of digital signatures – or, more precisely, the lack thereof. In fairness, many cryptographers are not concerned with replicating the higher levels of semantics that accompany the use of signatures in the physical world. They regard these issues as the responsibility of an applications environment that uses digital signatures as a tool or supporting mechanism. But wherever we assign responsibility for establishing a system of semantics, the need for such semantics is very real, and I believe that many people outside the cryptographic community have been misled by their assumptions about the word *signature*. They do not understand that the semantics problem is still largely unaddressed.

At its core, a digital signature is a mechanical, computational process. Some entity in possession of a public/private key pair was willing to perform a computation on a set of data using this key pair, which permits someone who knows the public key of the key pair to verify that the data were known to and computed upon by an entity that held the key pair. A digital signature amounts to nothing more than this. Notice that any digital data can be signed – not just documents or their digests, but also assertions about documents. The interface between digital signature processing and documents is extremely complex, questions about the semantics of signatures aside. The reader is invited to explore the work of the joint Worldwide Web Consortium/Internet Engineering Task Force on digital signatures for XML documents (1998) to get a sense of how issues such as canonicalization come into play here.

The use of digital signature in conjunction with a public key infrastructure (PKI) offers a little more.[9] People can choose to trust the procedures of a PKI to do the following kinds of things:

- To verify, according to published policies, a user's right to an "identity" and to subsequently document the binding between that identity and a public/private key pair. Verification policies vary widely, from taking someone's word in an e-mail message to demanding witnesses, extensive documentation such as passports and birth certificates, personal interviews, and other proof. In essence, one can trust the PKI service to provide the public key that corresponds to an identity. The identity can be either a name ("John Smith") or a role ("Chief Financial Officer of X Corporation"). Attributes can also be bound to the identity.
- To provide a means for determining when a key pair/identity binding has been compromised, expired, or revoked and should no longer be considered valid.

Compare this mechanistic view of signatures with the rich and diverse semantics of signatures in the real world. A signature might mean that the signer

- authored the document;
- witnessed the document and other signatures on it;
- believes that the document is correct;
- has seen, or received, the document;
- approves the actions proposed in the document; or
- agrees to the document.

There are questions not only about the meaning of signatures but also about their scope. In some situations, for example, documents are signed or initialed on every page; in others, a signature witnesses only another signature, not the entire document. Questions of scope become complex in a digital world, particularly as signed objects undergo transformations over time (because of reformatting, for example). Considerable research is needed in these areas.

Digital signatures alone can neither differentiate among the possible semantics outlined earlier, nor provide direct evidence of any one of them. In other words, there is no reasonable "default" meaning that can be given to a signature computation. Such signatures can tell us that a set of bits has been computed upon, and, in conjunction with a PKI, they can tell us who performed that computation. We clearly need a mechanism for expressing semantics of signatures that can be used in conjunction with the actual computational signature mechanism – a vocabulary for expressing the meaning of a signature in relationship to a digital object (or, in fact, a set of digital objects that might include other signed assertions).

One can imagine defining such a vocabulary and interchange syntax for the management and preservation of digital objects – for a community of archives and cultural heritage organizations, for example. But there is another problem that has not been well explored, to my knowledge. It is likely that we will see the development of one or more "public" vocabularies for commerce and contracting, and perhaps additional ones for the registry and management of intellectual property. These vocabularies might vary among nations, or even among states in a nation such as the United States, where much contracting is governed by state law.[10] In addition, we will almost certainly see the development of organization-specific "internal" vocabularies in support of institutional processes. Many of the initial claims about objects will likely be expressed in one of these other vocabularies rather than the vocabularies of the cultural heritage communities; consequently, we will face complex problems of mapping and interpreting vocabularies. We will also face the problems of trying to interpret vocabularies that may belong to organizations that no longer exist or vocabularies in which usage has changed over time, perhaps in poorly documented ways.

The roles of identity and trust

Virtually all determination of authenticity or integrity in the digital environment ultimately depends on trust. We verify the source of claims about digital objects or, more generally, claims about sets of digital objects and other claims, and, on the basis of that source, assign a level of belief or trust to the claims. As a second, more intellectual form of analysis, we can consider the consistency of claims, and then further consider these claims in light of other contextual knowledge and common sense. For example, an object that claims to have been authored in 2003 by someone who died in 2001 would reasonably raise questions, even if all of the signatures verify. We can draw precious few conclusions from objects standing alone, except by applying this kind of broader intellectual analysis. As we have seen, ensuring the validity of linkages between claims and the objects about which those claims make assertions is an important question. The question becomes even more difficult when we recognize that both objects and sets of claims evolve independently and at different rates, because of maintenance processes such as reformatting or the expiration of key pairs and the issuance of new ones.

Ultimately, trust plays a central role, yet it is elusive. Signatures can allow us to trust a claim if we trust the holder of a key pair, and a public key infrastructure can allow us to know the identity (name) of the holder of a key pair if we trust the operator of the PKI. If we know the name of the entity we trust, we can thus use the PKI to determine its public key and use that to verify signatures that the entity has made. We can establish the link between identity and keys directly (we can directly obtain, through some secure method, the public key from a trusted entity) or through informal intermediaries (we can securely obtain the key from someone we know and trust, as is done in the Pretty Good Privacy (PGP) system) (Zimmermann 1995).

It is important to recognize that trust is not necessarily an absolute, but often a subjective probability that we assign case by case. The probability of trustworthiness may be higher for some PKIs than for others, because of their policies for establishing identity. Moreover, we may establish higher levels of trust based on identities that we have directly confirmed ourselves than on those confirmed by others. Considerable research is being done on methods that people could use to define rules about how they assign trust and belief. These rules can drive computations for a calculus of trust in evaluating claims within the context of a set of known keys and identities and PKI services that maintain identities. An interesting question, which I do not think we are close to being able to answer, is whether there will be a community consensus on trust assignment rules within the cultural heritage community, or whether we will see many, wildly differing, choices about when to establish trust.

We also need an extensive inquiry into the nature of identity in the digital world as it relates to authenticity questions such as claims of authorship. Consider just a few points here. Identity in the digital world means that someone has agreed to trust an association between a name and a key pair, because he or she has directly verified it or trusts an intermediary, such as a PKI, that records such an association. Control of an identity, however, can be mechanically transferred or shared by the simple act of the owner of a key pair sharing that key pair with some other entity. We have to trust not only the identity but also the behavior of the owner of that identity.

If we are to trust a claim of authorship, whom do we expect to sign it? The author? The publisher? A registry such as the copyright office, which would more likely sign a claim stating that the author has registered the object and claimed authorship?

Identity is more than simply a name. We frequently find anonymous or pseudonymous authorship; how are these identities created and named? We have works of corporate authorship, including the notion of "official" works that are created through deliberate corporate acts and that represent policy or statements with legal implications. In this case, the signatory may be someone with a specific role or office within a corporation (an officer of the corporation or the corporate secretary, for example). These may be very volatile in an era of endless mergers and acquisitions, as well as occasional bankruptcies. Finally, we have various ad-hoc groups that come together to author works; these groups may be unwilling or unable to create digital identities within the trust and identity infrastructure (consider, for example, artistic, revolutionary, or terrorist manifestos).

We know little about how identity management systems operate over very long periods. Imagine a digital object that is released from an archive in 2100 for the first time – an object that had been sealed since its deposit in 2000. A group of experts is trying to assess the claims associated with the object. One scenario is that all claims were verified upon deposit, and the archive has recorded that verification; the experts then trust the archive to have correctly maintained the object since its deposit and to have appropriately verified the claims. A second scenario is that the group of experts chooses to re-verify the claims. This may take them into an elaborate exploration of the historical evolution of policies of certificate authorities and public key infrastructure operators that have long since vanished, of histories of key assignment and expiration, and perhaps even of the evolution of our understanding of the vulnerabilities of cryptographic algorithms themselves. This suggests that our ability to manage and understand authenticity and integrity over long periods of time will require us to manage and preserve documentation about the evolution of the trust and identity management infrastructure that supports the assertions and evaluation of authenticity and integrity. This, in turn, raises the concern that relying on services and infrastructure that are being established primarily to support relatively short-term commercial activities may be problematic. At a minimum, it suggests that we may need to begin a discussion about the archival requirements for such services if they are to support the long-term management of our cultural and intellectual heritage.

Authorship is just one example of the difficulties involved in "literary" signature semantics. Consider the problem of assigning publication dates as another example. Every publisher has different standards and thus different semantics.

Conclusions

In an attempt to explore the central roles of trust and identity in addressing authenticity and integrity for digital objects, this research points to a wide-ranging series of questions. It identifies the need to begin considering standardization efforts in areas such as signing metadata claims and the semantics of digital signatures to support authenticity and integrity.

But a set of more basic issues about infrastructure development and large-scale deployment also needs to be carefully considered. A great deal of technology and infrastructure now being deployed will be useful in managing integrity and authenticity over time. However, these developments are being driven by commercial requirements with short time horizons in areas such as authentication, electronic commerce, electronic contracting, and management and control of digital intellectual property. The good news is that there is a huge economic base in these areas that will underwrite the development of infrastructure and drive deployment. To the extent that we can share this work to manage cultural and intellectual heritage, we need to worry only about how to pay to use it for these applications, not about how to underwrite its development. Even there, however, we need to think about who will pay to establish the necessary identities and key pairs and to apply them to create the appropriate claims that will accompany digital objects. The less-good news is that we need to be sure that the infrastructure and deployed technology base actually meet the needs of very long-term management of digital objects. To take one example, knowing the authorship of a work is still important, even after all the rights to the work have entered the public domain. It is essential that institutions concerned with the management and preservation of cultural and intellectual heritage engage, participate in, and continue to critically analyze the development of the evolving systems for implementing trust, identity, and attribution in the digital environment.

Notes

1   Confusingly, however, we have the appearance of perfect forgeries (at least in terms of content; the packaging is often substandard) of digital goods in the form of pirate audio CDs, DVDs, and software CD-ROMs. In these cases, the purpose is not usually intellectual fraud so much as commercial fraud through piracy. One might argue that these copies have integrity (they are, after all, bitwise equivalent); however, their authenticity is dubious, or at least needs to be proved by comparison with copies that have a provenance that can be documented. Another case that bears consideration and helps refine our thinking is the bootleg or "gray-market" recording – perhaps an audio CD of a live performance of a well-known band, released without the authorization of the performers and not on their usual record label. This does not stop the recording from being authentic and accurate, albeit unauthorized. The performers may or may not be willing to vouch for the authenticity of the recording; alternatively, one may have to rely on the evidence of the content (i.e., nobody else sounds like that) and, possibly, metadata provided by a third party that potentially has its own provenance.

2   It would be useful to better understand why there has not been a greater effort to deploy these capabilities, even though they have substantial limitations. Contributing factors undoubtedly include export controls and other government regulations on cryptography, both in the United States and elsewhere; legal and liability issues involved in an infrastructure that addresses authentication and identity; and social and cultural concerns about privacy, accountability, and related topics. Patent issues are a particular problem. It is hard to develop infrastructure, widely deployed standards, and critical mass when key elements are tied up by patents. With the recent insane proliferation of patents on software methods, algorithms, business models, and the like, uncertainty about patent issues is also a serious barrier to deployment. All of these have been well covered in the literature and the press. What has been less well examined is the lack of clear, well-established economic models to support systems of authentication and integrity management. To put it bluntly, it is not clear who is willing to pay for the substantial development, deployment, and operation of such a system. While many people say they are worried about authenticity and integrity in a digital environment, it is not clear that they are willing to pay the increased costs to effectively address these concerns.

3   It is worth carefully examining the forensic clues available when evaluating a digital object as an artifact. Today, many of them seem trivial, but as our history with digital technology grows longer, understanding them will likely become a specialized body

of expertise. Examples include character codes, file formats, and formats of embedded fonts, all of which can help at least place the earliest time that a digital object could be created, and perhaps even provide evidence to argue that it was unlikely to have been created after a certain time. For an object that has undergone format conversions over time as part of its preservation, these forensic clues help only in the evaluation of the record of provenance.

4 For digital objects created by digitizing physical artifacts, if we can identify and obtain access to the source physical artifact, we can apply well-established forensic and diplomatic analysis practices to the source object.

5 As soon as we begin to speak of copies, however, we need to be very careful. Unless we know the location of the copy through some external (contextual) information, we run the risk of confusing authenticity and integrity. For example, if we have an object that includes a claim that "the identifier of this object is N" and we simply go looking for copies of objects with identifier N on a server that we trust, and then securely compare the object in hand with one of these copies, what we have really done is simply to trust the server to make statements about the assignment of the identifier N and then confirmed we had an accurate copy of the object with that identifier in hand. The key difference is between trusting the server to keep a true copy of an object in a known place and trusting the server to vouch for the assignment of an identifier to an object.

6 One thing that we can do with cryptographic technology – specifically, digest algorithms – is to test whether two copies of an object are identical without actually exchanging the object. This is important in contexts where economics and intellectual property come into play. For example, a publisher that is offering copies of a digital document for license can also offer a verification service, where the holder of a copy of a digital object can verify its integrity without having to purchase access to a new copy. Or, two institutions, each of which holds a copy of a digital object but does not have rights to share it with another institution, can verify that they hold the same object. Digest algorithms are also useful for efficiency purposes, because they avoid the need to transmit copies of what may be very large objects in order to test integrity. We should note that digest algorithms are *probabilistic* statements, however; the algorithms are designed to make it very unlikely that two different objects (particularly two similar but distinct documents) will have the same digest.

7 This is not a universally accepted definition of a digital watermark. The term is also used to refer to other things, such as modifications to images that allow them to be viewed on-screen with only moderate degradation but that produce very visible and unsightly artifacts when the image is printed. The description here characterizes what I believe to be the most commonly used definition of the technology. Sometimes "watermark" is reserved for a "universal" encoding hidden in all copies of a digital object that are distributed by a given source (for example, containing an object identifier) and the term "fingerprint" is reserved for watermarks that are copy-specific, that is personalized to given recipients (containing a serial number or the recipient's identifier). The fingerprint individualizes an object to a version associated with a specific recipient.

8 See, for example, the proceedings of the series of conferences on Information Hiding (Anderson 1996, Aucsmith 1998, Pfitzmann 2000). See also proceedings from the first, second, and third international conferences on financial cryptography (Hirschfeld 1997, Hirschfeld 1998, Franklin 1999).

9 See, for example, Ford and Baum 1997; Feghhi and Williams 1999.
10 In the United States, some of this is likely to be determined by how quickly federal law regarding digital signatures is established and by the extent to which federal law preempts developing state laws. Changes to the Uniform Commercial Code will likely play a role. See http://washofc.epic.org/crypto/dss/ for information on a variety of material on current legislative and standards developments related to digital signatures.

References

Anderson, Ross, ed. 1996. Information Hiding: First International Workshop, Cambridge, U.K., May 30–June 1, 1996, proceedings. *Lecture Notes in Computer Science*, vol. 1174. Berlin and New York: Springer.

Aucsmith, David, ed. 1998. Information Hiding: Second International Workshop, Portland, Oregon, U.S.A., April 14–17 1998, proceedings. *Lecture Notes in Computer Science*, vol. 1525. Berlin and New York: Springer.

Bearman, David, and Jennifer Trant. 1998. Authenticity of Digital Resources: Towards a Statement of Requirements in the Research Process, *D-Lib Magazine* (June). Available from http://www.dlib.org/dlib/june98/06bearman.html.

Duranti, Luciana. 1998. *Diplomatics: New Uses for an Old Science*. Lanham, MD: Scarecrow Press.

Hirschfeld, Rafael, ed. 1997. Financial Cryptography: First International Conference, Anguilla, British West Indies, February 24–28, 1997, proceedings. *Lecture Notes in Computer Science*, vol. 1318. Berlin and New York: Springer.

Hirschfeld, Rafael, ed. 1998. Financial Cryptography: Second International Conference, Anguilla, British West Indies, February 23–25, 1988, proceedings. *Lecture Notes in Computer Science*, vol. 1465. Berlin and New York: Springer.

Feghhi, Jalal, and Peter Williams. 1999. *Digital Certificates: Applied Internet Security*. Reading, MA: Addison Wesley.

Ford, Warwick, and Michael S. Baum. 1997. *Secure Electronic Commerce: Building the Infrastructure for Digital Signatures and Encryption*. Upper Saddle River, NJ: Prentice Hall.

Franklin, Matthew, ed. 1999. Financial Cryptography: Third International Conference, Anguilla, British West Indies, February 22–25, 1999, proceedings. *Lecture Notes in Computer Science*, vol. 1648. Berlin and New York: Springer.

Lessig, Lawrence. 1999. *Code and Other Laws of Cyberspace*. New York: Basic Books.

Lynch, Clifford. 2000. "Experiential Documents and the Technologies of Remembrance," in *I in the Sky: Visions of the Information Future*, edited by Alison Scammell. London: Library Association Publishing.

Lynch, Clifford. 1999. Canonicalization: A Fundamental Tool to Facilitate Preservation and Management of Digital Information, *D-Lib Magazine* 5(9) (September). Available from http://www.dlib.org/dlib/september99/09lynch.html.

National Research Council. 2000. *The Digital Dilemma: Intellectual Property in the Information Infrastructure*. Washington, DC: National Academy Press.

Pfitzmann, Andreas, ed. 2000. Information Hiding: Third International Workshop, Dresden, Germany, September 29–October 1, 1999, proceedings. *Lecture Notes in Computer Science*, vol. 1768. Berlin and New York: Springer.

Rothenberg, Jeff. 1999. *Avoiding Technological Quicksand: Finding a Viable Technical Foundation for Digital Preservation*. Washington, DC, Council on Library and Information Resources. Available from http://www.clir.org.

Rothenberg, Jeff. 1995. Ensuring the Longevity of Digital Documents. *Scientific American* 272 (1): 24–9.

Secure Digital Music Initiative. 2000. Available from http://www.sdmi.org.

Worldwide Web Consortium/Internet Engineering Task Force on Digital Signatures for XML Documents. 1998. Digital Signature Initiative. Available from http://www.w3.org/DSig.

Zimmerman, Philip R. 1995. *The Official PGP User's Guide*. Cambridge, MA: MIT Press.

Chapter 32

Why Museums Matter

Marc Pachter

A uthenticity only becomes a significant, emotional, almost transcendent idea in an age of artifice, in an age where replication, bastardisation, cheapening of all sorts of things is possible. There are wonderful aspects to all of this, mass availability of things and on and on. I don't mean to condemn our age for its ability to replicate or to produce qualities of fantasy in entertainment and so forth. I'm only saying that the age has not allowed for other attributes that we've actually become quite hungry for, so authenticity, which might have been a given in the pre-industrial world, and simply was what was, has become now a kind of holy concept with museums becoming places of the authentic. Again, this won't be a radical idea to you, it's simply making it an emotional fact – not just an intellectual fact – that I am conveying as an argument. So authenticity becomes one of those transcendent values.

Originality, which again may have seemed initially a sort of snobbishness about things, has become something that we need to nurture and treasure more and more: the question of something having a unique quality in its nature, being the first of it; the actual painting by; the whatever. What's interesting is that I can't make this argument, except at an emotional level, because when I think about it, and this was actually something I read about in an interesting book by Stephen Weil called *Making Museums Matter* – and that's where I took my title but he's less optimistic than I am as I think they do and I don't make a question about it – in which he brought up a fascinating point made at a conference he had attended about nanotechnology.

Nanotechnology in the twenty-first century will be the technology which will be, sort of, the equivalent of cloning human beings for inanimate objects. More and more we will have the capacity to replicate, to the last molecule, any object we have. Now, we're some years away from being able to do that, but it is absolutely on the

Source: *Common Threads*, MDA Conference, 2002.

cards. So, let us look at that with regard to a painting or an object in our collections. Will the fact that everyone will be able to have a Mona Lisa that in every element replicates the construction of the original painting matter to our sense of the holiness, and again I use these words in an unembarrassed way, of the original Mona Lisa? It's a fair question for the future but my argument is that, yes, the object will still have a particular quality of value that we will respond to in our imaginations and our spirits, independent of the perfectly replicated. The perfectly replicated will simply lead us to revere technology – or at least be impressed by it – but it will not lead to the flight of imagination and meaning that the original was. Now you may dispute that, but I invite you to think about it, and to think about it as the age becomes more and more capable of replication and what it means to the original. Museums will be more and more important in this world, not less and less important, I would argue.

However, I'm making a curious argument for historicism as the resonance of our collections increasingly in the future far more than either their scientific value for knowledge or their artistic quality in terms of the particular brush strokes, if you will, invested in them, because if, in fact, we can perfectly replicate in the future, can we not learn as much or more from those kinds of objects than from the original objects? Again, an open question – I simply present it to you – but we will never be able to have objects that are witnesses to history, to their creation and to the history and the overlapping experience of time. That's why, for me, whether it is painting or a scientific or historic object, they are all in a way, and, again, I use this word deliberately to be provocative, it's not a word I really use very often but in the end the relic will become the most important reason for objects to exist. So, again, you'll see me constantly referring to the terminology of religion but not the particular state of it. It is the emotions that gather around those kinds of responses. So we will have the resonance of the object.

We also have, I would argue, the triumph of the physical in the museum and it becomes more and more important, the physical, which in the year before the electronic, was a given. It was the only reality and it now becomes one version of reality because the virtual is not, from my point of view, a false reality. It is another reality, it is another way of going across time and space and learning and so forth, but it has made us increasingly, I argue, enamoured of the physical. I think more and more people are coming to physical places, not only museums – museums do this in a particular way – but physical places as a relief from the non-physical existence that they have in the electronic world. So museums need to more and more be conscious of their physicality, not only their objects and how they're placed, but in the presentation of those objects and the physical spaces in which people exist. This is why I believe that the architecture of museums has come back to being the signal architecture of our day. Why have museums become the cathedrals of our time? It's because it is the definition of a physical space in which the physical is made transcendent in the best of the architectural work. We looked at many examples of this but when you enter those spaces you enter dimension; you enter the experience of light in a certain way; and you enter this very tangible universe which, rather than seeming limited and material because all the things that the material world provides us can be provided in all the objects of replication we have in the electronic information world and so forth, is the material made spiritual. Again, in a secular age what the cathedral did.

These are experiences that I argue are not only necessary for society, but that in fact society has been brutalised by, by de-emphasising without necessarily having to, if you are secular yourself, relapse into religion. This is not an argument for religion, it's not an argument against it either, but the fact of the matter about religion, at least in our western societies, is that it no longer has that unifying collective transcendent experience available to communities. By virtue of that we must find those experiences elsewhere if we are to cohere as communities in a context of higher aspiration, not just the everyday world. So we have turned to museums as places of this.

Now there are versions of this in the other arts: there's a term that may cause you to groan or may cause you to marvel at its aptness, but in the performing arts world there is more and more a discussion of the phrase *liveness*, which is their version of why people come to concerts, come to plays, come to festivals, when they could literally get it at home in their television set, on their stereo equipment and so forth. It's not the music, it's not the play – that is available to them in countless other ways in the twenty-first century. It is the physical, social, transformational, emotional, coming together and responding at the moment in a personal way to a series of possibilities. That is why people go to concerts and if you despair of people in the future going to museums – you may not, the numbers are quite good these days, but I'm trying to explain why they're quite good – you only have to look at generations, beginning with my own. We call ourselves the boomer generation, and we're certainly the first rock and roll generation in America. These are not generations that have avoided assembling, that have, because of the record, not gone to the rock concert – they have been drawn even more towards it.

So the electronic will draw us more to the physical, the replicated will draw us more to the original, and we just need to be unembarrassed in our announcement of these qualities of availability in our precincts. You may not want to call them sacred precincts, you can use another terminology but you have to use words, I believe in our world, that link us to this higher emotional reality that we represent. We represent the original; we represent the authentic; we represent the physical; we represent the historical and, again, the historical is understood as the passage of time. We are witnesses and I'm very struck by the fact that increasingly certain kinds of museums, mostly museums of social purpose explicitly, in their own articulation, are willing to call themselves witnesses. The Holocaust Museum in Washington, which is an amazing combination of the understanding of the physical – of course it's a particular narrative of social purpose and its use of objects is very discreet and profound: its using them well, not using lots of them, that is the point of that brilliant presentation – is a museum of witness. There's another museum in America I would refer to in this context – The Tenement Museum in New York – which is really quite spectacular in trying to convey a sense of what poverty was like in New York at a particular point. I believe all museums in the future are places of witness and, again, I'm using religious terms or even, you could argue, judicial terms without intending them to be specifically with regard to religion. I'm simply speaking continually of the emotions evoked by those words. So witnessing becomes increasingly important.

My own museum, one of the two I'm in charge of at the moment, The National Museum of American History, is doing an exhibit on 9/11, as we refer to it, which I'm returning to open. The title of it *Bearing Witness to History* is quite interesting, because it's very radical for that museum. What is either modest, or immodest in that title, I haven't decided which it is, is the fact that we have not claimed knowledge about the event. This is not an interpretation of what led to it, or what the consequences might be. We are humbled for one thing by the fact that we have no idea what will happen as a result of it and so forth, and normally a history museum would decide not to do an exhibit at all – it would be defined as premature – because we have not digested it into knowledge. However, the museum felt an emotional responsibility to create a neutral, authentic zone of witnessing where not only images of the event, accounts of it, responses to it, and confusions about it would be allowed, but allowed in a place that gave people the space, literally, to think either privately or publicly about those events. This to me is a twenty-first-century way of doing an exhibit that is aware of what the public requires of museums. The idea for doing it occurred to me when I saw reported in the New York papers – and, again, it's not a competition with religion, it's just the secular framework for these feelings – that after 9/11 people fled to museums in New York far more than churches. This is why I make that point not to be competitive but just to underscore this fact. They actually went to museums as places to be and they went to them not to learn about 9/11, they didn't go to them even to learn about the particular exhibits or collections on view, they went to spaces consecrated to longer term purposes and values and that's where they felt, if you will, safe, if not in the literal sense then in the emotional sense. So, I propose to you that museums are more and more asked to do this by the public, and are actually more and more consciously or unconsciously providing these services. I only argue that the lapse happens at the level of awareness that we are doing this and the kind of either embarrassment about this fact or, worse, a sense that this is a distraction from our real purpose.

Chapter 33

Defining the Problem of Our Vanishing Memory: background, current status, models for resolution

Peter Lyman and Howard Besser

Introduction

Digital information saturates most aspects of everyday life: from international financial markets to the grocery checkout counter; from children's mental picture of dinosaurs to Voyager's computer-generated images of the solar system; from databases mapping the locations of toxic dumps to those tracking our retirement funds. What if the digital information with which we manage our lives and institutions were to disappear? What kind of picture of life in the late twentieth century could the historians of the future uncover, if the only lasting record of our time were printed on paper?

In fact, our digital cultural heritage is disappearing, almost as fast as it is recorded. Atoms, as in ink on paper, tend to persist. Digital records tend to become inaccessible, rendered unreadable by media deterioration, or obsolete by the pace of innovation in information technology. Consider the following.

Most computers have electronic clocks which will not allow them – or the data, images, and information they contain – to operate past the year 1999. Were this to happen, the twenty-first century, predicted to be the age of information, would begin with the loss of most of its digital memory, and with it the recent history of science and technology, the information records of government and corporations, popular culture and the digital arts.

Electronic mail and document files, which constitute the informal life of nearly every organization, can disappear when a hard disk crashes.

Source: *Time and Bits: managing digital continuity*, Margaret MacLean and Ben H. Davis (eds) Los Angeles: Getty Conservation Institution, Getty Information Institute and The Long Now Foundation, 1998, pp. 11–20.

How, then, can we create a historical record of our digital cultural heritage, like that created by libraries and archives for print, and by museums for artifacts? Are digital signals destined to be a kind of oral culture, living only as long as they are remembered and repeated? What can be done to preserve our digital cultural heritage?

Principal issues in digital preservation

In the development of every new communication medium, there is a moment of realization that the origins of a new era or culture are being lost, and should be saved. This was true of paper, of film and photography, of early radio and television, of sound recording, and now of digital works.

The long-term preservation of information in digital form requires not only technical solutions and new organizational strategies, but also the building of a new culture that values and supports the survival of bits over time. This requires that a diverse community of experts – computer scientists, archivists, social scientists, artists, lawyers, and politicians – collaborate to ensure the preservation of a new kind of cultural heritage, the digital document. We can identify four themes where key issues must be addressed at the start.

- technical profile
- socio-economic factors
- organizational contexts
- legal constraints.

Aspects of the problem

File formats are still being developed without regard for their incompatibility. "Refreshing," or copying files from an old storage medium onto a newer, more commonplace one, is often done as a matter of course. Unfortunately, this addresses only one aspect of the problem: the physical medium. It fails to address the key issue of file formats. A few years ago, many of us had to transfer files from 5-inch to 3-inch diskettes; some files are likely to have been in WordStar or VisiCalc. Such files would be completely unreadable by today's software, which often cannot even decipher files created by older versions of the same programs.

Increasingly, the value of documents lies in their linked relationship to other resources. The Task Force on Archiving Digital Information suggested that physical strata and file format problems might be handled through either emulation strategies or migration strategies, which continually move data into new formats that work with contemporary applications. Such strategies may be more effective if coupled with attempts to "exercise" digital documents periodically; using them is one method to make sure that they will continue to be usable. But these strategies become more problematic as we move to information environments that are not fully contained within a limited space. These strategies can work well with models based upon single files or discrete groups of files, but become more difficult to follow when the boundaries of an information environment are unclear or very large. Backing up a website or down-loading a website to a non-networked laptop requires a range of decisions on how much of the website is gathered up. What does one choose to move? Only a particu-lar hierarchy of their own files? Or some of the files that are linked to? And if so, how deep does one follow the links? As information environments become larger and more interconnected, can we develop strategies to save these?

Many documents have embedded within them a very useful kind of interactivity. In addi-tion to the problem of saving a given work within its more general context, there is also the problem of saving the various behaviors of a work, and making sure that these persist over time. For instance, a "digital book" might incorporate behaviors that let the user jump from a table of contents to a given chapter, or from a section of text to the accompanying footnote. We need to find ways not only to make the text persist over time and into new display environments, but also to make the appropri-ate behaviors persist somehow as well.

Short-term solutions cause long-term problems. Another key set of issues revolves around longevity problems that may be provoked by attempts to fix more immediate problems like those involving delivery, storage, and commerce. Much work in recent years has focused on altering file formats in order to solve immediate problems. Compression schemes have been developed to ease storage and delivery problems. Encryption schemes and container architectures have been developed to enhance digital commerce. Many of these file alterations use proprietary schemes and do not adhere to widely accepted standards. These alterations add an extra level of complex-ity to viewing a file, one that may not work well in future information environments that look radically different from those of today. While some of us may have faith that fifty years from now we'll have the tools to display an ordinary Microsoft Word file from today, the ability to display an encrypted Word file (or one wrapped in a Digibox or a Cryptalope) is likely to be problematic.

Should commercial, proprietary concerns legally override the obligation of copying for the sake of preservation? Copyright establishes a time-delimited right to distribute the original expressions of an idea, balanced by some public rights such as Fair Use. Copyright laws now also permit copying for the purpose of preservation of printed records, although in practical terms the right to preservation copying is clearest when potential historical interest outweighs economic value. Given the creation of secondary markets for intellectual property in new media, however, there is consid-erable political pressure to extend the length of copyright, and a growing practice of protecting intellectual property through contract (e.g., licensing instead of selling, and particularly, "shrink wrap" licenses) that do not grant preservation rights, or may reduce the right to use materials that have been preserved.

Broad strategies for preservation

A number of different approaches are now emerging to deal with some or all of these problems, and most of these do not exclude the other approaches. Since impor-tant experiments and prototypes are emerging from sectors that often do not easily exchange information with each other — hardware manufacturers, software designers and vendors, academic computer scientists, archivists and librarians, and publishers – information is still difficult to obtain.

Save everything. The Internet Archive follows the approach of trying to save most of what is on the public Web in time slices governed by how long it takes their web crawlers to copy everything they are seeking (currently approximately two full slices per month). Internet Archive, a non-profit organization, uses a data archive developed by Alexa Internet, which generates income from access to "lost" files and data mining. Long-term questions involve how well this will scale as the Internet continues its explosive growth, strategies for making sure these extensive backups will persist over time, by evolving copyright regimes and liabilities, and whether decisions that have been made about what not to save (i.e., the potential liability of archiving, such as pornographic material under legislation like the Communications Decency Act, or protected or inaccessible sites, etc.) may have long-term historical implications.

Employ tested strategies for refreshing documents and data. The practice of moving bits to a new physical storage medium is well understood by those who maintain backup files of large quantities of data. Most large organizations with mainframe computers understand the technical and economic issues involved in periodic movement of data to new physical strata, and in storage of that strata over time. But this strategy does not take into account the problem that the file formats which are continuously refreshed may not be readable by future applications (the "WordStar problem").

Stay abreast of developing strategies for data migration. We know very little about the process of refreshing, while at the same time moving to new, more accessible file formats. We know even less about what it takes to create emulation software. We need to begin to understand the technical issues and costs involved in following these kind of strategies.

Consider the data "exercising" strategies that meet your needs. The idea that continual community use of a digital object will make it persist over time is a very powerful one, but this is something that we don't yet understand very well. We can imagine that members of the public will continuously convert popular works into forms viewable in newer environments. But we know little about how this will affect any guarantee of the integrity of these works, or how this strategy will affect less popular works. We need further work on the likely impacts of these strategies.

Think ahead, and assume responsibility for the long term. Innovators within the archives and records management community have begun stressing "life-cycle management," wherein information professionals become involved with documents as early as possible in the document's life in order to best ensure that that document will persist over time. This paradigm (which differs from the late-stage interventionist model that has characterized much previous preservation work) has been applied particularly to collections of electronic records.

Specific suggestions for use in the short term

Until a viable holistic approach emerges, what should we do to ensure that our works will persist as long as possible into the future? In the long run, both print and digital preservation strategies are best sustained by the definition of technical standards, but standards evolve from "best practices," which are currently evolving in the following areas.

Save in the most common file formats. The more files that exist in a given format, the more likely that file converters or emulators will be written for that format (because of economies of scale). Conversely, files stored in less common formats will face more obstacles being viewed in future environments.

Avoid compression wherever possible. Future viewing environments will not necessarily know how to decompress current compression formats. When compression is necessary, use the most common compression formats.

For image capture, use standard color bars and scales. Color bars and scales within an image can be effective in rebalancing color and in classifying image size for future viewing environments.

Keep a log of processes and changes to the digital object. Many seemingly innocuous things we do to a digital object may have significance for future viewing environments. Keeping a record of processes and changes done to an object, and the tools used, should ease adjustments to future environments.

Save as much metadata as possible. When we create or alter a digital object, we usually have much greater access to information about that object than at any other point in its life cycle. Because we know so little about future viewing environments, we don't know which of the seemingly innocuous bits of metadata may later prove important to those environments. Embedded metadata will allow future users and applications to know what type of digital object this is, what file format, what will be needed to emulate a viewer for this file, etc. The more information we can save, the more likely we will be able to provide future generations with a "key" for unlocking the contents of whole classes of data. This is the Rosetta Stone strategy.

Exploring existing models of effective preservation

The wealth of practical expertise developed in the preservation and conservation of the traditional media for our cultural heritage has much to offer to the challenges relating to digital heritage. Although bits and atoms have very different technical profiles and social contexts, the progress made in the management of the acidic paper crisis and in conservation of works of art is the best guide available with which to explore strategies for preserving digital documents. This case has resulted in some lessons that might be usefully applied to the current situation.

The case of acid paper

The rapid expansion of the use of paper records in the nineteenth century, and the need for inexpensive materials for mass production techniques, led to the widespread use of wood-based, acidic paper which quickly oxidized and turned brittle. This economical and technical decision had unanticipated and alarming long-term consequences for the persistence of the written record. A number of preservation strategies which were required to address the problems caused by these decisions might serve as instructive models for managing digital documents.

- The commercial firms had to redesign their technology for paper production.
- Articulating the tradeoff between costs and durability of the paper medium raised the consciousness of publishers to make better decisions about the long-term cost and value of information through its entire life cycle.
- Librarians now monitor and manage storage conditions (especially humidity and heat) that speed the rate of decay of paper. They regulate the use of brittle books, and are trained to intervene with repairs and conservation.
- Materials and conservation science have developed new techniques for large-scale de-acidification to preserve important and vulnerable documents.
- The information content of vulnerable paper documents is often saved by their conversion to microfilm or digital media.

In sum, the strength of the strategies that have been developed to preserve paper documents is that paper is relatively well integrated into organizational frameworks of various kinds, and managed by professional librarians and archivists who are aware of the problem and trained to manage it; and, given the persistence of the medium, the fundamental strategy is educational – documenting the conditions and practices that reinforce the essential stability of the medium.

The weakness of the preservation strategy for paper is that awareness of the problem often becomes apparent at the end of the information life cycle, when there is relatively little economic incentive or organized social interest to solve it. "Preservation," then, is not a systemic solution, and for this reason it is unlikely to attract new technology. While all of the strategies for preservation of paper are useful models for enhancing the persistence of digital documents, given the pace of technical innovation it is still possible to redesign the medium itself to enable the persistence of bits over time, if the technology community becomes aware that its work constitutes a cultural heritage which is disappearing. As printed documents lose their market value, the methodology for preserving them may shift to "access," that is, minimizing the potential costs involved in finding and using a document. The access rationale often leads to the digitizing of digital documents, both to preserve the original from the wear and tear of use, and to make it possible to use a document without travel.

To test this link between preservation and access, the non-profit initiative Journal Storage Project (JSTOR) was created by the Mellon Foundation as a national digital archive of back issues of scholarly journals (see http://www.jstor.org). Instead of focusing on the technical issues, JSTOR's approach is through the economic model. Its mission is to explore the possibility that individual institutions would agree to fund a national digital archive dedicated to preservation and access of rarely used but potentially important journals, in place of local copies of the same journals which require ongoing space and maintenance costs.

The important differences between atoms and bits in preservation

However instructive the lessons of paper preservation may be, bits and atoms are very different information media, which will require very different preservation strategies. Without intervention, the default condition of paper is persistence; the default condition of electronic signals is interruption. The characteristic persistence of digital documents is suggested by the term "memory," a term which simultaneously manages to suggest both the persistence of memory and the possibility of forgetting. Recognizing the principal differences between paper-based and digital documents is a critical element in their long-term protection.

As signals, the persistence of a digital document is dependent upon the nature of the artifacts that it may inhabit at any given point in time. In active memory (RAM), it is dependent upon the presence of electricity. Stored on a ferro-magnetic medium (disk or tape) or optical medium (CD or other), it may well outlast the operating system which is required to access it, but in any case neither medium is rated to last as long as fifty years even in ideal conditions. While new physical media (such as glass substrate optical disks) may be engineered to last longer, a more critical problem is that the file formats in which digital documents are encoded will not be readable by future systems unless proactive measures are taken to make them persist. Suggestions to address this include periodic migration from system to system as quickly as the process of innovation demands, or periodic creation of emulation software to make these documents accessible on future systems.

Both the form and the content of knowledge in digital forms are still being continuously reinvented through a process of technical innovation; thus digital documents present a continuous problem of obsolescence, not only in their form but in their content as well. This obsolescence is both technical and economic, in that there must be continuous and active technical investment to preserve digital documents.

Organizations dependent upon digital records, such as corporations and governments, need straightforward risk management strategies for "refreshing" digital documents, focused upon minimizing the vulnerability of the media upon which they are stored, and upon moving data from one system to another. (Corporate data processing centers, university computing centers, and other mainframe-based organizations understand issues of backup and refreshment of data, but don't necessarily understand the implications of real migration, particularly for more complex digital documents, or digital information within software environments that are still evolving rapidly and thus creating subtle kinds of obsolescence.)

Unlike print, which has had 500 years to create institutional contexts, digital documents are still in the early stages of innovation. Typically, in the first phase of innovation a new technology will imitate an older one; thus digitized documents are created from printed originals as a means to create new value by expanded access. But new social and organizational contexts made possible by digital documents are still emerging, only suggested by terms like "virtual community" and "distance education." In this sense, the organizational contexts which are responsible for digital documents remain to be defined and founded.

Who is responsible?

There are serious questions as to who will take responsibility for making digital information persist over time. In the world of printed publications, owners of intellectual property rights generally do not take on this role, but cede it to libraries. In the digital world, legal, technical, and economic factors may preclude libraries from doing this. Even if the legal and technical issues are overcome for libraries (or if content owners decide to manage persistence over time themselves), we may need to develop social and legal mechanisms for "rescuing" digital information when the organization in charge of making it persist no longer has the resources or will to do so. We also need to deal with the issue of how many copies of anything digital we need to save; published material persists in part because of redundant saving of the items.

In the debates about the forms that intellectual property might take in dealing with digital documents, such as the Commerce Department's Report of the Working Group on Intellectual Property Rights (September 1995) and subsequent proposed legislation, there is tension between two principles. On the one hand, it is often granted that preservation is a legitimate public good which should have special status in the law; on the other, the concept of public good is being replaced by the commodification of digital knowledge in order to create the electronic marketplace.

In the print world, the space between is occupied by the doctrine of Fair Use, which exempts educational and preservationist activities from copyright. In the digital world, there is as yet no Fair Use; indeed the White Paper rejects the concept as an unfair subsidy of education by publishers. Thus, for example, the paper on digital preservation commissioned by the Research Libraries Group and the Commission on Preservation and Access suggests that "certified archives" may have to be more like time capsules than archives or libraries: that is, removed from public access until their contents had come into the public domain with the end of copyright, whenever that might be.

The obvious question is: Given this withdrawal from use, what incentive would exist to fund such an archive? Further, it is increasingly likely that digital documents will not be governed by an intellectual property regime at all, but will be protected either by technological means ("Cryptalopes," digital boxes) which would make them even more difficult to preserve, or by licensing mechanisms under the Uniform Commercial Code section IIB (e.g., "shrinkwrap" licenses). One dimension of the creation of methodologies for the preservation of digital documents, then, must be participation in the ongoing legislation, litigation, and treaty negotiations which are shaping the intellectual property regime within which digital documents will be managed and preserved.

As in every other dimension of the information revolution, our thinking about the persistence of digital memories tends to be trapped inside the cultural habits of an industrial age. Thus we speak of the twenty-first century using metaphors of the nineteenth century: information "highways," "digital libraries," "electronic publishing." The problem of preservation or persistence of digital documents, "time and bits," might best be solved by changing the rules and adopting new visions and metaphors that would both reflect and redefine the way we think about information.

Chapter 34

Curating New Media

Matthew Gansallo

I'm going to speak about the encounters I had to overcome while I was commissioning and curating artists for the Tate website in November of 1999. I studied fine art and have curated some shows with paintings and sculptures; moved on to installation and public art. I also worked in responsive architecture (using light and walls to confuse the users of certain buildings as though they were falling into a well or walking into a wall and so forth). That was one of the remits I had with technology before working as a Senior Research Fellow at the Tate.

Under the aegis of the Tate National Programmes, in November 1999 I was asked to curate and commission art for the newly designed Tate website and the initial motive for these commissions was to coincide with the opening of Tate Modern in the spring of 2000. The commissions didn't quite make it for the opening of Tate Modern for various reasons. One being that the commissioned artists did not want their works to be swamped by all the press and the glory of Tate Modern and for their works to become a side issue. I will begin by explaining how I commissioned the artists, and also about the departments at the Tate that helped in the process of curating. When I say they helped, it was in the sense that I had to make them realise that this wasn't a side issue and that they had to take the commissions seriously, with regards to press, development and marketing. A lot of work had to be done in these areas.

The first Tate online projects commission went live with the work of Harwood@ Mongrel on 26 June 2000 and the work of Simon Patterson on 12 July 2000. My main concern was how these commissions would be perceived as art in the way contemporary art museums like the Tate define and present art. Another concern was to investigate artists working with Internet technology, with the virtual, that

Source: *Curating New Media*, Third BALTIC International Seminar 10–12 May 2001, Sarah Cook, Beryl Graham and Sarah Martin (eds), Gateshead: BALTIC, 2002, pp. 61–72.

can be presented within the physical spaces of contemporary art museums, without just introducing a couple of PCs and a workstation into a small, stuffy room within a gallery (because that was the initial idea from some quarters). I was also trying to look at viewing the works of different artists that would put a question to and perhaps clarify web-art, web-design and art on the Web. I was trying to define those three strands: what is web-art? What is art on the Web and what are the boundaries we can find between web graphics and web-art – or web design graphics and web-art? I'm not saying that I've come up with any definite answers, but this was one of the starting points for investigation and research for these commissions, which lead us to the ZKM in Karlsruhe in February 2000.

We went to ZKM to look at how these works of a computer and Internet dimension had been curated in a physical space, because we were thinking of doing the work in a similar way to what Julian Stallabrass has done (in 'Art and Money Online') – putting Net-art in a physical space. But really the remit was 'how do we use the Tate website to inform and investigate certain artists and artworks?' So there was this idea of having the work strictly online, but the possibilities of also having it in a physical space in Tate Modern or Tate Britain.

I prepared some questions, so that when we look at the work you will probably be able to tell me if these questions have been addressed:

- How can web-artists raise the profile of the autonomous artistic project vis-à-vis heavily marketed entertainment products and are there any examples?
- What forms of synergy can be tapped to create ambitious web-based art?
- Is it possible to genuinely bring together spheres of e-commerce and the fine art economy to create web-art? Any examples?
- Has digital art created a particular type of visual dialogue among users on the Net?
- Has this created an art Net-community that can be termed a movement or school?
- In web-art is it possible to know and recognise the difference between social communication and symbolic representation?
- What are traditional web-art functions?
- Are there important relations between web-art and video art and other multi-media forms?
- What is absolutely specific to what makes web-art a form in its own right?
- How can an environment of ongoing process and human interaction, which has been at the core of the development of artistic projects related to the Internet, be represented and presented in the museum project?
- How do you encourage interaction in both the gallery and online environment?
- Many artists have been interested in the Internet precisely because it has a decentralised power-base and falls outside existing networks of institutions and their legitimising structures. If this is still the case, how does an institution like the Tate take up a role?

Well, it was well worth the trip to ZKM and by the time we got back we were all as confused as ever! However, there was one thing I was sure about, which was that this work, whatever form it took, was going to be online. We also looked at work that with a few more applications could sit in the physical gallery or museum space without having too much conflict. So after looking at quite a lot of work on the Web and trying to define which was design and which wasn't (according to what museums say and do) I commissioned two artists because their work was the closest to the rhetoric of viewing and engaging with all sorts of coded symbols to challenge and give insight into different images, conceptions and other issues to do with the production of contemporary art and the history of art. Those two artists were Simon Patterson and Graham Harwood – or Harwood@Mongrel, as he prefers to be called.

Simon Patterson's current work explored the use of colour, perception and language and also his personal reinterpretation of fixed observations of charts and coded information systems. Simon Patterson has never used computers before to inform his work, but his work has a relation to some technological reference and the interfaces of technology. If you know anything about Simon Patterson's work, you probably know the piece *The Great Bear* (1992), in which he challenged the London tube map by changing all the stations into names of philosophers, actors and other famous figures. When I approached Simon Patterson, I said 'What do you think about this? Let's discuss your ideas.' He said he would really like to give it a go and said he believed he was from the school of, 'Oh, I can't touch new media because I've been swamped up by all these galleries and new media is an area that I never ever thought I would go into.' I said, 'Well, give it a go and if it goes wrong, don't blame me!'

Then I met with Harwood@Mongrel whose work has really been engaged with computers from the outset and he's also a programmer who can make that demarcation between being a programmer and creating what we term and what we view as art, in the museum and gallery world. One of Harwood's works is called *The Rehearsal of Memory* and is in the permanent collection of the Pompidou Centre in Paris. This was one of the works he showed me, which was created using the personalities of the inmates of Ashford Maximum Security Hospital. This work explored, through the use of technology, the peeling off of certain parts of an inmate's body, which revealed their personalities in relation to their convictions. You'd click on an image – maybe a hand or face – and it would peel through and you would hear their voices, what they had done and how they were convicted.

I approached the artists and said 'First, show me your current work', which we discussed and 'How would you approach creating work for the Tate website?'

In keeping with what was termed the 'Net-community' and their language, and complementing the contemporary art museum language of criticism within art history, I also commissioned Matthew Fuller, a lecturer, writer and critic of new media to write texts on the emergence of this new type of Net-art and on the completed works of both artists. The title of Harwood@Mongrel's work is *Uncomfortable Proximity* and the title of Simon Patterson's work is *La Match de Couleur*. The title of Matthew Fuller's critical text online is: one, an introduction to online art titled *Art Meet Net – Net Meet Art*; two, *Bridge the Pieces* for *Uncomfortable Proximity*; and three, *The Systematic Arrangement of the Senseless* for *La Match de Couleur*.

I will leave it to the audience when viewing the works to judge if the commissions have addressed some of the questions I presented earlier. But what both artists have done is to recontextualise and recombine the Tate website, especially the Harwood@ Mongrel work, which explores the relationship between new media, Internet art and museum institutions and its traditions. It gives the impression of hacking the Tate website and keeping with the current concerns of Internet technology, viruses, hacking, etc. Whereby Simon's work takes over the entire screen of the computer, Harwood's work sits behind it and pops up when the computer is being shut down, as a way of asserting its presence.

Harwood@Mongrel has taken the Tate website and rewritten the history of the Tate from a personal point of view. What he did was take a digital camera around Tate Britain after six o'clock when the galleries were shut, photographing the works of J. M. Turner, and made a collage of them and put links in them. Believe me, some curators were not very happy with that, with this chap roaming around the place after hours with a digital camera, while they were about to do some serious work. Harwood's take on this was that he was linking the history of Tate Britain – in the sense that he was peeling off the fabric and revealing what the Tate used to be – with what it has become, as well as mixing it with his family history and his take on how certain institutions have now been converted into institutions of culture (Tate Modern in the Bankside Power Station building, for example). Collating the collection, putting it on the Web and putting it within all the pages of the official Tate website, so that the audience will read another history, written by Graham Harwood.

I just want to compare this with the 'mongrelised' site, which is now known as Tate-Mongrel. What Mongrel has actually done is to give the impression that he has hacked into the site and confused everybody. The idea is that the art is created in the reading of these pieces, when you read them and find out that it isn't really the Tate's official website, but something completely different.

For the Tate website, Simon was keen to explore the use of sound, colour and the coded information systems of the Internet. Simon Patterson's work presents colours together with their hexi-decimal equivalent, which are matched with every team that has ever played in the French Football League, with the results being read by Eugene Sacromano of Radio France. You have to click on a colour to start. Simon was also interested in the waiting and the expectation of the computer and the Internet: when you click on something and you wait for something to come up. So it started with this series of colour shots. It will slowly begin to change and will make an announcement to each colour of the football league [website plays]. When I click on this, it does not go back to the Home Page and this was the initial intention of Simon's work, in the sense that he wanted to trap you here and so you have to go through all the colour charts before you can escape. So Simon's work and this idea of trapping the viewer and getting into the maze of colours, came about through various meetings with the artist.

I will explain the curatorial process through the departments that had to begin to engage with this work as an exhibition in itself, rather than just something that was happening on the Tate Web with computers.

As the commissions were going ahead, I had to have a lot of meetings with differ-ent departments to enable the curating of the work – and I think that's where the 'curating' lay in doing this work, doing it strictly online. The marketing depart-ment is in effect the manager of the Tate website, and since a lot of information and marketing is done through its website, you can understand the amount of problems that I caused the marketing manager because of Simon's work, and in particular Harwood's work – because of its controversial angle and the artists' personal take on the Tate history.

The Harwood work was meant to drop in to the Tate website after every fifth hit to the site, so that after every fifth hit you would get the Mongrel site popping up right in front, confusing whoever is using it, making them say 'What's happening here? Is someone hacking through or what?' They would have to find their way all through the Web to find out this is a work of art, or there would be something that the viewers come across that might say 'This is a work of art', and then they could go back to the real Tate site. The marketing department hit the roof: 'We did not spend all this money and time creating the Tate website to give information about our exhibitions and collections for you to come and start confusing our guests with every fifth hit seeing just the Mongrel work. It's not going to work!' I said, 'Well, let's deal!' and that is where we started.

The marketing staff were very concerned that Mongrel was confusing their work – I can understand their point. They said. 'It is all well and good as a work of art but we don't want our hitters to just hit and disappear because we want to speak about a collection, we want to speak about information on exhibitions and education programmes.' However, Mongrel maintained that the art in his work – this particular work – was made when the hitter was confused by the hacked Tate website, thinking it is the real one and then figuring out that it was not. For him, that was the interaction and where the art lay. I spoke with Simon who also said that he wanted to trap viewers in the maze of colours, so you can't escape unless you find out what you're doing. Simon also maintained that his art for the Tate website was to trap the audience in this maze of colour and language and they have to go through everything before they can get out of the site, allowing them to engage with the work.

As I said, the marketing department maintained that this would lose potential customers and it became my job to create a clarity between the work – the art – and the business of marketing. So this had to be carefully managed and, in a way, carefully curated. It had to be carefully managed to create a confusion then a realisation, which was what Harwood's work was about, and the erasure then replacement, which is what Simon Patterson's work was about. A decision had to be made whether to curate a demarcation and clarification of when the art starts and ends, or an interruption of the Tate website by the works, bearing in mind the needs of the artist and the needs of the audience of the website. While I was busy discussing this about Harwood's work, Simon then decided that he also wanted his work to drop in at every sixth hit!

From the outset I explained to the Exhibition, the Education and the National Programmes teams that I was commissioning artists to work as if we were actually commissioning artists who were creating physical or object-related work for one of the galleries of the Tate. So the artists have the right to present their ideas and their work without any interference whatsoever from people telling them what art is and what they should and shouldn't do. But in this case, it was relatively different and this is where we all learnt how to create a balance – and that was the curatorial challenge. That is what we're now seeing on the Tate's Arts Project Online.

So instead of the drop-in – after numerous meetings with the artists about how it could feed into the Tate website, the visual space – it was decided the Mongrel work would prop-up the Tate website, so when you try to click on it, the Mongrel work pops up. Instead of the trap in the maze of colour, the viewer can escape by a click to the bottom of Simon Patterson's work and return to the Tate Home Page.

So Harwood@Mongrel's work was in effect mongrelised to create that demarcation. If you came onto the site, these little details [Slide: putting the Mongrel tag on top of other visual elements and logos] were some aspects of what we had to discuss between the artists and myself, and this is where the curating lay. There were a certain number of pages that had to be mongrelised and we had to discuss the best possible way to do that. On every single page, everything was a mongrelised version – Supporters, Sponsorship, Corporate Involvement.

There is also, at the Tate, a Development Department, which deals with sponsors. The Development Department was concerned about the names of the sponsors and individuals who support the organisation appearing on the Mongrel/Tate website, and whether or not they would find it offensive. The Development Department were worried that the controversial nature of the Tate-Mongrel site would not attract new sponsors for future exhibition programmes and might make existing sponsors withdraw their sponsorship of future events and exhibitions. In view of this I had to come up with an idea. So letters had to be written to all the sponsors that appear – The Millennium Project, BT, The Guardian, The Observer and so forth – asking if they had any objection to their logos appearing on the Tate-Mongrel site, as it does on the Tate home website. All the companies, organisations and individuals Sandy Nairne and I wrote to said that they did not mind if their logos appeared on the Tate-Mongrel site. However, a few did write back saying they would object if their logos were not included on the Mongrel site! So we thought 'Oh, they are interested in art', so that was quite good.

There was also a question about pay. How much should artists who are commissioned to make works online, through a link, get paid? Will they be doing any work? We [the Tate] have programmers who are doing the programming, and they are just creating an idea that we are going to program in – so how much can the artist be paid? That was another interesting conversation. However, I am pleased to say that payments to the artists invited to produce work was in tandem with others supplying work for temporary exhibitions at organisations and national museums like the Tate Gallery.

Another interesting thing that we had to go through was that art projects online reviewed the standard contract Tate prepares for artists and raised new issues and laws of copyright. For the first time in many years, Tate contracts with artists had to change to accommodate this type of out-of-line commission. Other issues were addressed such as ownership, acquisition, procurement, collection, archiving and provenance – how do you collect and archive such a work? How long will the work be live on the Tate Web? If the artists have the permission to show the work on another website, when still on the Tate website, does this mean that they have a contract for one year? Taking into account the nature of the Internet and its communicative ease and access, all these had to be worked into the contracts for the artists.

So these were the issues I had to encounter in the curatorial process. I am, however, encouraged that the Tate has taken a bold, positive step in this sector of contemporary art and has, in effect, created a platform for more research, experiments and dialogue in museum curating and presenting new media. We were quite aggressive in advertising these works within the marketing, press and promotions departments because, just to take a question that came up from the audience, we didn't want the artists to say that artworks were going out that no one knew about. In the museum context, there are still quite a lot of questions about how new media art is promoted. How does it get marketed and how do people get to know about it? That's still a very fuzzy area for a lot art critics and museum press professionals. How on earth do we begin to write about it and write PR stuff that will get people interested? The fact is that a lot of these departments do not consider this a form of art, so the most important thing is to understand that it is not just about the curating, but it is also about the business of publicising this work and getting the right press, the right critical language, the right critical dialogue and then developing it.

Contemporary art museums of the future will exhibit the virtual and the real alongside one another, crossing and overlapping each other's boundaries, creating an amazing visual and interactive experience within and without walls. It is therefore inevitable that museum architecture will have to change to accommodate the ever-growing advance and innovation in technology. I believe this will enhance the way we use, view and live with new media as part of our cultural consumption.

Delivery: production, evaluation and sustainability

Introduction to Part Six

Ross Parry

To this point, Parts One to Five have considered a number of key facets of museum practice, and the presence of digital media within each. In these previous enquiries into information, space, access, interpretation and objects, we have been able to construct a series of historical contexts and theoretical frameworks through which to understand the place and consequences of digital technology in the museum. In each discussion our emphasis has tended to be on context, rationale and issues. Stressing adoption and impact, much has been said here, therefore, about the motivation and initiation of museum computing.

So what about the realities of *production?* A museum may have reconciled the idea of having 'digital objects' in its collections, but how does it actually approach that process of digitisation? An informed case may have been made by an exhibition team for the use of in-gallery digital interactives, but how is this multimedia practically tested, evaluated and maintained? Similarly, an institution might have made a strategic commitment to the Web, but how is this obligation sustained? What, in other words, does it take to deliver digital media in the museum? It is these practical and managerial questions of workflow, planning and production to which Part Six now looks.

Much like in previous sections, the following five chapters present the work of academics, museum professionals and technologists. Just as before, the articles and extracts here cut across the literature available, including excerpts from professional manuals, agency reports and scholarly papers. The first two chapters (both drawn from handbooks aimed at practitioners) provide indispensible clarity on project management. In Chapter 35, taken from the MDA's guide to *Managing New Technology Projects in Museums and Galleries*, Matthew Stiff demystifies project initiation, distilling the process down to a series of accessible questions and workable checklists. Likewise, in Chapter 36, by prudently balancing 'purpose' with 'source' and 'technology', Paul Conway puts in our hand a simple (yet powerful) tool for decision making in digitisation projects. Notably, sharing a 'textbook' tone, both authors write with the confidence of a sector now familiar with digital production. In a sense, both extracts are indicative of the extent to which computing has become part of the profession's standard manual of best practice. This, in a sense, is digital heritage as orthodoxy rather than advocacy.

The next two chapters turn our attention, if in different ways, to evaluation. The authors of Chapters 37 and 38 both think about targeting digital resources for specific audiences and both extol the importance of extensive evaluation, yet the scale, focus and tone of each is very different: Maria Economou's paper represents the results of a PhD thesis, whereas Frank Colson and Jean Colson's account is the honest summations of two academics on a major government-funded national project on which they had a leading role; Economou's subject is in-gallery media, the other authors instead focus on the Web; Economou is positive about her clear, listed findings and the impact these might have on honing evaluation techniques for future projects, Colson and Colson instead are more circumspect and discursive about reflecting upon the complex intellectual, institutional and political risks involved in producing (in this case) a landmark online resource for a museum. Read together, both chapters parade the decisions producers of multimedia content make when targeting rich content to museum audiences.

Colson and Colson's story of how the Science Museum built a website as considerable and as involved as 'Making the Modern World' also reminds us of another (our final) dimension to production: *sustainability*. After all, it is one matter to co-ordinate the collections, the narratives, the curatorial teams, the educationalists, the web designers, the evaluating schools, not to mention the funding and critical path of production. It is, however, something else to maintain a digital resource of this scale and this visibility. The challenge for the Science Museum and 'Making the Modern World' was as much, it seems, about its enduring use, re-use and possible re-invention, as it was about its initial purpose and design. What, in other words, happens in the longer term to a website of this size and substance – indeed, of any digital resource? What life span can such digital assets have? And how can museums maintain and sustain the functionality and value of such resources? Chapter 39, the final chapter of this section, sees an information management consultant and former president of the Museum Computer Network expose some of these realities of digital sustainability. In an extract from her survey produced for the Council on Library and Information Resources, Diane Zorich reports, revealingly, on how successful (or not) cultural heritage organisations across the US have been at sustaining their digital resources. The picture (perhaps ironical for a sector predicated upon its ability to preserve) is of many institutions still finding proven ways to preserve and sustain digital resources as consistently as the other objects of which they are custodians.

Chapter 35

Managing New Technology Projects in Museums and Galleries

Matthew Stiff

Understanding your organisation

It may seem patronising, if not downright insulting, to suggest that you take the trouble at the outset of a project to consider what it is that your organisation actually does. I can only say that it is worth the time and effort because it helps to establish a business case for any development you have in mind. It provides a chance to review your museum or gallery in the context of all its business functions. This will include managing, displaying and interpreting the collections and supporting information, managing sites and services, supporting the admissions and retailing functions, accounts and payroll management, marketing, and implementing the general communications infrastructure required to support these and many more activities commonly found in cultural institutions.

A re-examination of your business is particularly useful in the following two scenarios:

- You have a clear idea of your ICT project but need to examine how it fits in with the overall aims and objectives of your museum. This will include where your project sits in the list of priorities when considering use of finite resources.
- You know that something needs to be done but have no idea what is required or where to concentrate your effort. In this scenario a re-examination of your organisation should help to focus on the weaker aspects of your operation, highlighting areas in which effort should be focused. In this case, the answers may not necessarily lie in the use of ICT.

Source: *Managing New Technology Projects in Museums and Galleries,* Cambridge: MDA, 2002 pp. 13–25.

In conducting a review of the mission of your museum or gallery, revisit your Forward Plan and reassess it taking into account your current situation and concentrating on the following questions:

- What is the mission of your museum? – What are its collecting policy, target audiences, educational and social remit?
- How do you currently go about fulfilling this mission? – How is the collection interpreted and developed, target audience reached, educational and social remit fulfilled?
- How do you want to develop your mission? – What are the opportunities and threats facing the organisation; how might this mission be adapted or developed to meet the future?

Conducting a SWOT analysis (constructing a list of the Strengths, Weaknesses, Opportunities and Threats faced by your museum) is a simple way of focusing on these issues.

The first of the two scenarios described is most likely to emerge to address a perceived opportunity. The second is more likely to require the development of a project in order to provide a solution to a threat. In terms of your business, however, it is important to realise that whether a project is established in response to an opportunity or a threat, it will inevitably result in change.

Museums and galleries cannot measure the benefits of investment in ICT in quite the same way that businesses do. Where the processes involved are similar it is not a problem: investment in retailing or accounts software and hardware will produce measurable benefits in the same way as in the commercial sector. Similarly, collections management systems improve efficiency in much the same way as stock-control systems. Registrars and collections managers are able to respond to queries more quickly and effectively. However, the greatest growth area in the use of ICT in museums is in audience communication and here it will mainly translate itself into an improved visitor experience. The only way of measuring this is in terms of retention and growth of visitor numbers and qualitative feedback.

Benchmarking is a useful technique to use in any examination of your museum and its activities. This involves comparing the performance of your organisation against other similar organisations. This should be based on measurable criteria and will allow you to judge your levels of service, not just to your visitors but also to your staff. Benchmarking will help you to highlight areas of weakness in your organisation and may suggest ways in which new technology can be applied to improve standards.

When you have revisited the core activities of your organisation, you will be better placed to consider the possible applications of new technologies. You should not limit your thinking to the needs of current users: consider non-users too. How can you cater for their needs and increase their level of interest? Whatever you do, however, there are some fundamental basics you must bear in mind in the planning process:

- Users make or break systems. It is no good taking a management decision to implement new systems or practices without getting the users to support these changes. This is simpler when involving members of staff in the selection of a collections management system. It becomes more complex when trying to assess levels of satisfaction and interest from members of the public towards a gallery interactive. As for online resources, obtaining and interpreting useful information is even more problematic. Although it is possible to analyse the paths taken by an individual through a website, the anonymity of this medium makes it difficult to obtain accurate demographic information or to assess the quality of the visitor experience.

• Successful projects are based on shared responsibility. Make sure that everyone is properly represented in the management of the project. Trustees should publicly state their support, senior managers should commit themselves to the project and the end-users should be properly involved. If the end-users are museum visitors, make sure that you include people from outside your museum to represent their interests and provide objective feedback.

Understanding your organisation

Check list

☐ Does your museum have a mission statement and a set of published objectives?
☐ Does your museum have an up-to-date Forward Plan?
☐ Does your museum have an ICT strategy?
☐ Does the ICT strategy relate directly to the Forward Plan?
☐ Are arrangements in place to benchmark performance so that improvements can be measured?
☐ Do you regularly review projects to insure that they have delivered the promised contributions towards the Forward Plan?
☐ Do your plans allow for modification in order to respond to new opportunities and threats?

Look out for... .

• Lack of relevance of the project to the strategic aims of your museum or gallery.
• Lack of agreement between project managers and users over the way the proposed project fits in with your museum's objectives and Forward Plan.
• Failure to share responsibility for the project.

• Users of new systems cannot be expected to use them without adequate training. This cannot be treated as an afterthought. It should be built into the planning process from the outset.
• Plan for the future. The world of new technologies is rapidly changing. In particular, huge strides are being made, both in museums and in the broader public

sector, in the development of standards and guidelines. It is important to adopt a flexible approach to planning and implementing your project. Otherwise there is a danger that changes taking place while it is being developed will render it obsolete.

It is not enough to try to take into account the interests of as many people as possible in your review of your business. You need to ensure that they are actively involved in this process and that it is not merely tokenism. The end result should be a shared vision, not necessarily to everyone's liking but recognised as an accurate statement of your museum's mission, addressing the key issues and proposing the best overall approach. It is worth remembering that the biggest risk to a project is likely to be the reactions of people to changes in their working patterns and environment. This will be minimised if members of staff and users of the new system are fully involved in the process and have shared ownership of the project. By definition this means shared ownership of the risk as well as the potential success.

Stimulating ideas

It is worth remembering that it is usually better to be the second person to do something than the first. There is always something to be learned from the experience of others. There is much to be said in favour of facilitated group sessions when trying to develop answers to particular problems. These can involve members of staff, trustees, volunteers, friends, regular visitors or other key stakeholders. The important thing is to try to impose some structure on discussion. Try to focus thinking around the following groups of questions:

- Who are you doing this project for? What is your target audience?
- Why are you doing it? What is it for?
- What will be the end result? What will it look like?
- How will you know if you have succeeded? What are the measurable performance indicators?

The answers to these questions should be captured and written up. They will form the basis of any future documentation for the project and will help to focus thinking. We have already seen that projects spring from opportunities and/or threats and result in change. Many people find change threatening so it is important to minimise anxieties in order to promote creative exploration of issues.

Other ways of stimulating ideas include looking at what other organisations in similar situations to yours have done. Many museums and galleries will be only too pleased to share their successes with you. Unfortunately, somewhat fewer are willing to own up to their failures. By asking careful questions, however, it should be possible to gauge the suitability of a solution to your needs. Try not to limit yourself to other museums, however. For business applications you can look across all sectors for ideas. The commercial "heritage" sector has also brought innovations, some of which may be applicable within your organisation. The secret to success is to maintain an open mind, document what you see and carefully evaluate any systems you may wish to consider.

Once again, whatever ideas emerge, ask the questions outlined above in order to ensure that you have fully explored the rationale behind any proposed project.

Stimulating ideas

Check list

- ☐ Have you talked to similar organisations to your own?
- ☐ Have you looked at what the "heritage" sector is doing?
- ☐ Have you involved all staff and stakeholders in your museum?
- ☐ Have you documented the results of your discussions and research?

Remember

Structure your sessions to focus on key questions required in the planning process.

Specifying requirements

Specifying requirements is a two-stage process resulting in two distinct documents. One should address the business requirements of the proposed project and the other the functional requirements. Analysing and expressing business and functional requirements and developing specifications are skilled processes and you may wish to think about obtaining external assistance. There may be some merit in including the development of the functional specification within the contract with your chosen technical supplier. Often such organisations will be able to bring extensive experience and expertise to the table. Alternatively, you may prefer to use an independent consultant who knows the cultural sector. Whoever you use it is very important to ensure that they have a sound understanding of your business needs and a proven track record in undertaking this type of analysis. It is also important to beware of technical suppliers leading you towards adopting their own preferred approach rather than the one that is right for your individual requirements.

Business requirements specification: "Why is this project or system needed?"

When embarking on a new project it is important to start off by clearly stating what the business requirements are. These should be expressed in non-technical terms. For example, it may be that your overall objective is to procure a collections management system for the museum to enable you to keep track of objects in the collection, handle loans and record contextual information. It is very easy to link this to the aims and objectives of your museum as expressed in your organisation's Forward Plan. It should also be linked directly to your analysis of your business needs and should support your ICT strategy.

It is important to begin by describing as clearly as possible the requirements of your new system. Use your understanding of what is technically feasible but try to avoid suggesting or ruling out particular solutions to your needs. Keep your options open so that all possibilities can be considered and their relative merits properly weighed. Try to establish clearly measurable success criteria at this stage. They will help you to assess possible solutions to your particular needs and will also ensure that the successful delivery of these solutions can be properly measured.

Functional requirements specification: "What should this project or system be capable of doing?"

Having defined the business requirements of your project you will need to use them to create a functional specification for the proposed system. These are usually highly structured documents and many project-management methodologies will provide templates for their construction. Alternatively, if you are working in a larger museum or organisation you may find that you already have guidelines for constructing such documents. The functional specification should state very clearly what the system should do (be it a gallery interactive, an environmental monitoring system or a ticketing system). It should also provide a clear basis for evaluating the system to guide testing and acceptance phases of the project. Above all it should show the degree of correlation between the business requirements and what is technically achievable. At this stage you may find that you need to undertake a feasibility study to determine the extent of any mismatch. Alternatively, you may find that your project requires a prototyping stage in order to elicit more information about what is and is not possible. Finally, you may find that the gap between what is required and what is feasible is too great (for reasons of complexity, resources or technicality) and that the only thing that can be done is to stop the project. It is better to do so at this phase rather than later in the process when expectations have been raised and resources committed.

It is important not to confuse highly structured for highly detailed. There may be a tendency to over-specify systems in terms of both functionality and the detail in which that functionality is expressed. This results in built-in inflexibility and often fails to capitalise on the skills and expertise of the chosen suppliers. Finally, it is important to recognise that no specifications, be they business requirements or functional requirements, will be complete. It is inevitable that during the course of your project you will develop new ideas, recognise new opportunities and be forced to respond to changes in circumstance. Flexibility will enable you to anticipate and plan for such changes as you proceed. Be aware, however, of the possible impact on others involved in the project. Suppliers in particular may not be able to respond with the same degree of flexibility.

Writing a project brief

The information gathered in the last two sections can be brought together to start forming the basis of a document often called a project brief. Different approaches to project management will produce different names and formats for such documents. PRINCE2 (Projects in Controlled Environments, Version 2) provides templates for all key documents and would expect the following to be addressed in the brief:

- A clear statement of purpose for the document.
- Background to the project.
- A definition of the project including:
  - Objectives – what the project hopes to achieve.
  - Scope – what will be included in the project.
  - Outline of deliverables and desired outcomes.
  - Exclusions – what is not included (to avoid possible confusion and manage expectations).
  - Constraints – aspects such as time, money, resources etc.
  - Interfaces – other projects or programmes likely to be affected.
- The business case including the reasoning behind the chosen solution.
- A listing of the customer's quality expectations.
- A listing of acceptance criteria.
- A listing of known risks.
- An outline project plan.

You may not be in a position to provide all of this information at this stage, but remember that project documentation grows and develops along with the project itself. The final version of the project brief will be much more detailed than the first.

Specifying requirements

Check list

☐ Have you involved all stakeholders in specifying system or product requirements?

☐ Do your requirements fulfil the needs of the users?

☐ Do your requirements fulfil the needs of managers?

☐ Is the final responsibility for the business and functional requirements specifications shared among stakeholders?

☐ Are the business and functional requirements specifications compatible?

☐ Do your requirements specify compatibility with existing systems, software and/or hardware?

☐ Are the specifications flexible enough to be able to adapt to changing requirements?

> **Remember**
>
> Avoid setting your project in stone. ICT projects need to be able to adapt quickly to changes in technology and to new opportunities. The important thing is to be able to plan these changes, not find them working their way into the project unexpectedly.

Identifying the type of project

Different types of project require different approaches. Put bluntly, what kind of monster are you dealing with? Knowing the kind of project that you are facing is very important to its successful management as it will help you to assemble the required skills and expertise. It will also help you to take difficult decisions, including recognising when something is beyond your ability to manage. It will also help you to examine ways of turning a complex project into something easier. It is not just a question of examining the project itself. It has to be considered within the context of your broader ICT strategy, taking into account its impact on existing systems. Simple projects may become more complex if they have a knock-on effect on other areas of your museum's activities. Risk will rise along with the complexity of the project: simple projects are low risk; complex projects are high risk.

Simple ICT projects

Broadly speaking a simple ICT project will focus on one area of activity such as identifying and purchasing accounting software or procuring an environmental monitoring system. It should be based on an off-the-shelf solution with minimal changes or configuration requirements. There should be no dependencies on other ICT projects being implemented at your museum and should not involve changes to the type of hardware commonly used or to your operating system (this need not be true of something like an environmental monitoring system if it is running off a dedicated computer and is provided as part of a package). The proposed system should not affect more than one area of your museum's business (e.g. collections management or education) and should complement, or require only minor modifications to, the existing business processes. Above all, your organisation must have experience in managing this type of project. A successful simple project will demonstrate careful planning and adherence to that planning during its execution. It will resist attempts to add complexity or deviate from the project plan and timetable and will meet the original specification. This means that it is possible to assess the capabilities of the system and its suitability for the intended purpose.

When is a simple ICT project not a simple ICT project?

ICT projects are fickle beasts and have a habit of changing into something nasty when least expected. This is particularly true if you are inexperienced and your initial assessment of the situation turns out to have been wrong. So, what should you look out for? A simple ICT project may be becoming complex if:

- You are beginning to fall behind schedule.
- You find yourself redefining your requirements.
- You discover that new partners are required.
- You discover that new consultants or suppliers are required.
- Your "off the shelf solution" begins to require significant changes or enhancements rather than configuration of the normal features.
- Your supplier begins to ask for more money because of increasing demands outside the original contract.

Complex ICT projects

It sounds obvious, but a project is complex when it is not simple! Basically a project is complex if it involves more than one business area, more than two suppliers, major changes to hardware as well as software or requires a bespoke system to be developed. Typical complex ICT systems include new collections management systems, new computer networks requiring changes to both software and hardware, retailing systems or building management systems. The key focus has to be on minimising the complexity and thereby reducing the risk.

Simplifying complexity

Assuming that you have already produced a clear business requirements document (see section 'understanding your organisation') the next thing to do is to turn your big problem into lots of smaller, easier ones. Identifying clearly defined modules or work packages (a term used in EC-funded projects) is the key to this. By concentrating on discrete units of work it is possible to quantify risk more easily and assign responsibility for the delivery of individual components. Each module should have its own resources, methodology and outputs. You will also need to have a highly skilled and experienced project manager, skilled task managers, experienced suppliers and sound procedures for monitoring progress, quality and risk. Occasionally a project will be so innovative that risk is difficult to quantify. Under such circumstances it is worth considering developing prototypes or models in order to gather more information before going on to develop the full system. This is also an approach that can be adopted to assess user interest.

If you are working with more than two contractors, you may wish to consider allocating responsibility to a single prime contractor. This will then make it the responsibility of that contractor to select and manage the subcontractors. In reality many ICT suppliers have already developed such relationships. For example, companies specialising in the development of databases often work with design houses when bidding for contracts to produce websites. When contractors are familiar with each other's working practices the risks are considerably reduced.

The risks to complex ICT projects are not dissimilar to those affecting simple ones (only on a much bigger scale). The key thing is to be brutally honest with yourself. Ask the difficult questions. Is support still there at the highest level for this project? Are the users still committed?

Identifying the type of project

Check list

☐ Have you ascertained the type of project?
☐ Have you done all that you can to minimise risks?
☐ Are trustees, senior managers and users still committed to the project?

Remember

A new technology project is only simple if it represents a low risk to your museum: Even simple projects can fail!

Chapter 36

Rationale for Digitization and Preservation

Paul Conway

Introduction

In *Motel of the Mysteries*, illustrator David Macaulay (1979) speculates about how people 2,000 years from now might interpret the cultural significance of a low-budget roadside motel, Toot 'n C'mon, buried intact under junk mail and pollution. Beyond being a wry satire on the science of archeology, the book is a clever reminder of the danger of trying to interpret the past without documentary evidence. A *Do Not Disturb* sign becomes a sacred seal "placed upon the handle of the great outer door by the necropolis officials following the closing of the tomb." A charge card becomes "a portable shrine which was to be carried through life and into eternal life." A television represents "the essence of religious communication." Archeologists and historians know that the impulses to record and to keep are practically a part of our human nature. Truth is embedded in the symbols and artifacts that we create and then keep by choice or by accident. And yet, as the twenty-first century dawns, we find ourselves potentially confronting the dilemma of Howard Carson, Macaulay's amateur digger: a vast void of knowledge filled by myth and speculation. Information in digital form, the newest currency of our world, is more fragile than the fragments of papyrus found buried with the pharaohs.

Digital imaging is 'hot.' Major daily newspapers devote entire sections on emerging trends in digital technology. Notwithstanding the results of recent surveys of the Web showing that the overall proportion (83%) of Internet content is commercial in character and that only six percent is educational or informational, the perception persists that everything of value is becoming digital or created in that form.

Source: *Handbook for Digital Projects: A Management Tool for Preservation and Access*, Maxine K. Sitts (ed.), Massachusetts: Northeast Document Conservation Center, Andover, 2000.

Digital images are indeed becoming commonplace in libraries and archives. The quality of digital image products can be spectacular. There is little doubt that quality will improve as the technology matures. Organizations are rearranging budgets, raising money, and anticipating income streams to make digital projects happen. Can any institution – library, archives, historical society, or museum – afford to squander this investment? Without serious effort to ensure long-term access to today's digital image files, however, the risk of loss is tremendous.

Preservation is not just for the world of paper. We know that digital imaging technology, in and of itself, provides no easy answers to the preservation question. Indeed, simply defining what preservation means in the digital imaging environment is a challenge. Responding to the insight that such a definition might provide is harder still. The digital world poses significant challenges to, but does not eliminate the need for, responsible, effective preservation activity (Waters and Garrett 1996).

Advantages of digital access

Digital imaging technology offers distinctive advantages to institutions with impressive collections of scholarly resources. Information content can be delivered directly to the reader without human intervention. Information content in digital form can be retrieved by readers remotely, although such delivery may tax the capabilities of even the most sophisticated projection equipment and networks. Digital image quality is extraordinary and is improving constantly. It is now possible to represent almost any type of traditional research material with such visual quality that reference to the original materials is unnecessary for most, if not all, purposes. The power of full-text searching and sophisticated, cross-collection indexing affords readers the opportunity to make new uses of traditional research resources. Newly developed system interfaces (the look and feel of the computer screen) combined with new ways to deliver manageable portions of large image data files promise to revolutionize the ways in which research materials are used for teaching and learning. It is no wonder that there is a nearly overwhelming rush to jump on the digital bandwagon.

Risks of digital imaging projects

Pressures from all fronts to digitize traditional research materials carry distinctive risks. The required investment for digital image conversion is tremendous – possibly dollars for each and every page or frame converted. Digital imaging technologies require tremendous capital investment for underlying support systems in an environment of flat or marginally increasing budgets. Digital image conversion, in an operational environment, requires a deep and long-standing institutional commitment to traditional preservation, the full integration of the technology into information management procedures and processes, and significant leadership in developing appropriate definitions and standards for digital preservation.

The risk of loss is high – far higher than in most other programs and activities carried out in a cultural institution. The nearly constant swirl of product development that fuels our perceptions of change raises the stakes higher still. When a library, archives, historical society, museum, or any other cultural organization with a preservation mandate stops experimenting with digital technology and decides to use it to improve services or transform operations, that institution has embarked down the preservation path.

What digital imaging is not

In the past few years, significant progress has been made to define the terms and outline a research agenda for preserving digital information that was either "born digital" or transformed to digital from traditional sources. "Digital preservation refers to the various methods of keeping digital materials alive into the future," according to a recent statement from the Council on Library and Information Resources (Waters November/December 1998). Digital preservation typically centers on the choice of interim storage media, the life expectancy of a digital imaging system, and the expectation to migrate the digital files to future systems while maintaining both the full functionality and the integrity of the original digital system. PBS recently aired the film *Into the Future*, which graphically portrayed the problem of digital information and speculated widely on the consequences of inaction, all the while offering precious few ideas of what to do about the dilemma.

It may be premature for most of us to worry about preserving digital objects until we have figured out how to make digital products that are worth preserving. Digital imaging technologies create an entirely new form of information from traditional documents. Digital imaging technology is not simply another reformatting option in the preservation tool kit. Digital imaging involves transforming the very concept of format, not simply creating a faithful reproduction of a book, document, photograph, or map on a different medium. The power of digital enhancement, the possibilities for structured indexes, and the mathematics of compression and communication together fundamentally alter the concept of preservation in the digital world. These transformations, along with the new possibilities they place on information professionals, force us to transform library and archival services and programs in turn.

Preservation in the digital world

The essence of traditional preservation management is resource allocation. People, money, and materials must be acquired, organized, and put to work to prevent deterioration or renew the usability of selected groups of materials. Preservation largely is concerned with the evidence embedded in a nearly endless variety of forms and formats. Things are preserved so that they can be used for all kinds of purposes, scholarly and otherwise.

People with the responsibility to do so have determined that some small portion of the vast sea of information, structured as collections of documents, books, collections, and other things, has research value as evidence well beyond the time and way intended by those who created or published it (Buckland 1991). This distinction between the value of the information content (usually text and illustration) and the value of the evidence embedded in the artifact is at the heart of a decision-making process that is itself central to the effective management of both traditional and digital library materials.

In the digital world, preservation is the creation of digital products worth maintaining over time.

Each of these words carries weight.

- IS. Preservation is a reality and not merely a metaphor for or symbol of access.
- CREATION. The time to be concerned about the long-term persistence of digital products is when a system is designed and before digital conversion has begun.
- PRODUCTS. A digital product has its own identity and exists within a market economy. It is not necessary to sell or license a digital product for the product to have an identity within a community of end-users.
- WORTH. The work to design and create a digital product adds value to the information contained in the documents that serve as sources. The value added to a digital product must ultimately result in a product that is an essential and vital capital resource to the institution that has chosen to create it in the first place.
- MAINTAINING. The persistence of digital products requires careful attention to the maintenance of content (the bits and bytes) functionality (how the bits work in a system).
- OVER TIME. Preservation in the digital world is not absolute, but depends instead on the continuing transformative impact of the digital product on the information work of end-users.

It is impossible to come to terms with the responsibilities inherent in creating digital products without distinguishing between acquiring digital imaging technologies to solve a particular problem and adopting them as an information management strategy. Acquiring an imaging system to enhance access to library and archives materials is as simple as choosing the combination of off-the-shelf scanners, computers, and monitors that meets immediate functional specifications. Hundreds of cultural organizations already have invested in or are planning to purchase digital image conversion systems and experiment with their capabilities. Innumerable pilot projects have shown how much more challenging it is to digitize scholarly resources than the modern office correspondence and case files that drove the technology two decades ago. In time, most of these small-scale, pilot projects will fade away quietly – and the initial investment will be lost – as the costs of maintaining these systems become apparent, as vendors go out of business, and as patrons become more accustomed to remote-access image databases and the latest bells and whistles.

Administrators who have responsibility for selecting systems for converting materials with long-term value also bear responsibility for preserving their investment in the product. This commitment is a continuing one – decisions about preservation cannot be deferred in the hope that technological solutions will emerge like a medieval knight in shining armor. An appraisal of the present value of a book, a manuscript collection, or a series of photographs in its original format is the necessary point of departure for making a judgment about preservation of the digital image version. The mere potential of increased access to a digitized collection does not add value to an underutilized collection. Similarly, the powerful capabilities of a relational index cannot compensate for a collection of documents whose structure, relationships, and intellectual content are poorly understood. Random access is not a magic potion for effective collection management.

Relationships among purpose, source, and technology

The key to a successful conversion project or ongoing program lies in a thorough understanding of the relationships among three concepts. These concepts are (1) the characteristics of the source material being converted, (2) the capabilities of the technology used to accomplish the digital conversion, and (3) the purposes or uses to which the digital end product will be put.

The preservation purposes of the digital product

It is possible to distinguish among three distinctive but not mutually exclusive preservation applications of digital technologies, defined in part by the possible purposes that the products may serve for end-users.

Protect Originals. The most common application of digital technologies in an archive or library is digital copies that can be used for ready reference in lieu of casual browsing through the original sources. Preservation goals are met because physical access to the original documents is limited. Examples include image reference files of photograph, clipping, or vertical files that permit the identification of individual items requiring closer study. The original order of the collection, or a book, may be frozen much like microfilm sets images in a linear array. This preservation use of the technology has become a compelling force motivating archives and libraries to experiment with hardware and software capabilities.

Represent Originals. A digital system could be built that represents the information content of the original sources in such detail that the system can be used to fulfill most, if not all, of the research and learning potential of the original documents. High-resolution systems that strive for comprehensive and complete content and seek to obtain full information capture, based on emerging standards and best practices, fit this definition. Systems of this intermediate level of quality open new avenues of research and use and could have a transformative effect on the service missions of those who create the products.

Transcend Originals. In a very small but increasing number of applications, digital imaging holds the promise of generating a product that can be used for purposes that are impossible to achieve with the original sources. This category includes imaging that uses special lighting to draw out details obscured by age, use, and environmental damage; imaging that makes use of specialized photographic intermediates; or imaging of such high resolution that the study of artifactual characteristics is possible. This category also includes digital imaging products that incorporate searchable full text (marked up or raw). Additionally, digital products that draw together, organize, and enhance access to widely dispersed research materials may have transcendental impact on the people who use them.

Each of these preservation applications places separate but increasingly rigorous demands on digital technologies. In each case, the use of an intermediate film or paper copy to facilitate the scanning process may or may not be necessary or advisable. Finally, the disposition of original sources (including undertaking preservation treatments before or after conversion) is a matter quite separate from the decision to undertake digital conversion. Ultimately, the purpose of digital image products is determined by the uses to which they will be put, while preservation of original source documents must be determined by their specific preservation needs.

The characteristics of source materials being converted

A major challenge in choosing paths from analog to digital is obtaining an in-depth understanding of the particular characteristics of the collections or the individual items being converted (Robinson 1993). The most important characteristics are:

* format of the source (including size of object, its structure, and its physical condition)
* physical condition and its impact on the ability of the item to be handled during the conversion process
* visual characteristics (including the centrality of text versus illustration)
* color as an essential carrier of information content
* level of detail (including the size and style of typefaces, the type of illustrative content, and the overall range of tonal values).

Beyond these specific characteristics, the degree of visual and physical similarity among the individual items in a given collection can have a significant impact on the cost, quality, and complexity of the conversion project.

The capabilities of scanning technology

The third key to building a viable digital product is the measurement of the capabilities of the digital imaging hardware/software system in relation to the source documents and the purposes of the product. Digital conversion systems vary widely in capability and cost. Rigorous mechanical and electrical engineering plays a big role in the design and manufacture of specialized conversion tools. Many products are optimized for the conversion of a single type of document. All conversion tools have limitations in terms of the size of source documents they can handle with a given level of digital resolution. Although the adage, "You get what you pay for" typically applies in the acquisition of conversion hardware, there is no substitute for careful and thorough testing and benchmarking of conversion systems (Besser and Trant 1995).

The expected uses of the product may drive the choice of technological applications, but the opposite is not necessarily true. It is important to recognize that standards and best practices that support digital product development should not be driven by the present limitations of digital image capture, display, and output. Matters such as the limited resolution of today's display screens and projection devices, the limited bandwidth of wide and local area networks, and the limitations of resolution and tone reproduction in printers should not determine the quality thresholds of image system design.

The relationships among source characteristics, technology capabilities, and the purposes of the end product bear upon the definitions of quality, cost, and access. In the area of quality, for example, an input source with particular characteristics, the limitations or costs of scanning technology at a given point, and the expected uses of the product interact to set the threshold requirements for image quality. Similarly, the expected purposes of the digital product and the characteristics of the source interact with imaging technology capabilities to determine the cost of creating the product with the intended purpose. The same is true for access, where the intellectual complexity of the source documents and the specification for the ways in which the image product will be used to interact with the sophistication (or lack of it) of the hardware and software tools for building metadata files and other associated indexes.

Transformation of preservation principles

In the past two decades, a consensus has emerged within a community of practitioners about a set of fundamental principles that should govern the management of available resources in a mature preservation program. The principles of preservation in the digital world are the same as those of the analog world, and, in essence, define the priorities for extending the useful life of information resources. These concepts are longevity, choice, quality, integrity, and accessibility.

Preservation in the digital world is one of the central leadership issues of our day. It is the shared responsibility of many people in many institutions fulfilling many roles. An understanding of the impact of this role differentiation on digital preservation action is crucial. Role differentiation helps archivists and librarians – acting as digital product developers – know when to control their use of digital technologies, when they need to influence trends, and when they need to relinquish any expectation for either control or influence.

The transformation of longevity

The central concern in traditional preservation practice is the media upon which information is stored. The top priority is extending the life of paper, film, and magnetic tape by stabilizing their structures and limiting the ability of internal and external factors to cause deterioration. The focus on external factors has led to specifications for proper environmental controls, care and handling guidelines, and disaster recovery procedures. Progress on efforts to control or mitigate the internal factors of deterioration has resulted in alkaline paper standards, archival quality microfilm, mass deacidification, and more rugged magnetic media. And yet, now that archivists and librarians have defined the issues surrounding the life expectancy of storage media, the very concept of permanence that has driven the search for "archival" media is fading as a meaningful intellectual construct for preservation (O'Toole 1989).

Preservation in the digital context has little concern for the longevity of optical disks and newer, more fragile storage media. The viability of digital image files depends far more on the life expectancy of the access system – a chain only as strong as its weakest component. Today's optical media most likely will far outlast the capability of systems to retrieve and interpret the data stored on them. Since it can never be known for certain when a system cannot be maintained or supported by a vendor, product developers must anticipate that valuable image data, indexes, and software will be migrated in their professional lifetimes to future generations of the technology.

Digital project managers can exercise a large measure of control over the longevity of digital image data through the careful selection, handling, and storage of rugged, well-tested storage media. They can influence the life expectancy of the information by making sure that local budgetary commitments are made consistently at an appropriate level. Ultimately, they have no control over the evolution of the imaging marketplace, especially corporate research and development activities that have a tremendous impact on the life expectancy of the digital systems created today.

The transformation of choice

Choice is selection. Preservation adds value through the process of selection. Choice involves defining value, recognizing it in something, and then deciding to address its preservation needs in the way most appropriate to that value. Over decades the act of preservation has evolved from saving material from oblivion and assembling it in secure buildings to more sophisticated assessing of condition and value on already-collected materials. Preservation selection has largely been driven by the need to stretch limited resources in as wise a fashion as possible, resulting in the dictum that "no item shall be preserved twice." The net result is a growing virtual special collection of items preserved with a variety of techniques, most notably by reformatting on microfilm. Selection is perhaps the most difficult of undertakings precisely because it is static and conceived by practitioners as either completely divorced from present use or completely driven by demand.

Selection in the digital world is not a choice made once and for all near the end of an item's life cycle, but rather is an ongoing process intimately connected to the active use of the digital files (Hazen et al. 1998). The value judgments applied when making a decision to convert documents from paper or film to digital images are valid only within the context of the original system. It is a rare collection of digital files, indeed, that can justify the cost of a comprehensive migration strategy without factoring in the larger intellectual context of related digital files stored elsewhere and their combined uses for teaching and learning.

Even while recognizing that selection decisions cannot be made autonomously or in a vacuum, librarians and archivists can choose which books, articles, photographs, film, and other materials are converted from paper or film into digital image form. Influence over the continuing value of digital image files is largely vested in the right to decide when it is time to migrate image data to a future storage and access system and when a digital file has outlived its usefulness to the institution charged with preserving it. What digital product developers cannot control is the impact of their ongoing value judgments on the abilities of readers to find and use information in digital form. Unused digital products might as well not exist; they certainly will not survive for long as mere artifacts of the conversion process.

The transformation of quality

Maximizing the quality of all work performed is such an important maxim in the preservation field that few people state this fundamental principle directly. Instead, the preservation literature dictates high quality outcomes by specifying standards for treatment options, reformatting processes, and preventive measures. The commitment to quality standards – do it once, do it right – permeates all preservation activity, including library binding standards, archival microfilm creation guidelines, conservation treatment procedures, the choice of supplies and materials, and a low tolerance for error. The evolution of preservation microfilming as a central strategy for the bulk of brittle library materials has placed the quality of the medium and the quality of the visual image on an equal plane. In the pursuit of quality microfilm, compromise on visual truth and archival stability is dictated largely by the characteristics of the item chosen for preservation.

Quality in the digital world, on the other hand, is conditioned significantly by the limitations of capture and display technology. Digital conversion places less emphasis on obtaining a faithful reproduction of the original in favor of finding the best representation of the original with a given technology. Mechanisms and techniques for judging the quality of digital reproductions are different and more sophisticated than those for assessing microfilm or photocopy reproductions (Kenney and Chapman 1996). Additionally, the primary goal of preservation quality is to capture as much intellectual and visual content as is technically possible and then present that content to end-users in ways most appropriate to their needs.

The image market has subsumed the principle of maximum quality to the "solution" that finds the minimum level of quality acceptable to today's system users. Digital product developers must reclaim image quality as the heart and soul of preservation. This means maximizing the amount of data captured in the digital scanning process, documenting image enhancement techniques, and specifying file compression routines that do not result in the loss of data during telecommunication. The control of digital quality standards is possible now, just as it is for microfilm. However, librarians and archivists can only influence the development of standards for data compression, communication, display, and output. Improvements in the technical capabilities of image conversion hardware and software are in the hands of the imaging industry.

The transformation of integrity

The concept of integrity has two dimensions in the traditional preservation context – physical and intellectual – both of which concern the nature of the evidence contained in the document. Physical integrity largely concerns the item as artifact. It plays out most directly in the conservation studio, where skilled bench staff use water-soluble glues, age-old hand-binding techniques, and high quality materials to protect historical evidence of use, past conservation treatments, and intended or unintended changes to the structure of the item. The preservation of intellectual integrity is based upon concern for evidence of a different sort. The authenticity, or truthfulness, of the information content of an item, maintained through documentation of both prov-enance – the chain of ownership – and treatment, where appropriate, is at the heart of intellectual integrity. Beyond the history of an item is concern for protecting and documenting the relationships among items in a collection. In traditional preserva-tion practice, the concepts of quality and integrity reinforce each other.

In the digital world, maintaining the physical integrity of a digital image file has far less to do with the media than with the loss of information when a file is created origi-nally, then compressed mathematically, stored in various formats, and sent across a network. In the domain of intellectual integrity, structural indexes and data descrip-tions traditionally published with an item as tables of contents or prepared as discrete finding aids or bibliographic records must be inextricably linked and preserved along with the digital image files themselves. Preserving intellectual integrity also involves authentication procedures, like audit trails, that make sure files are not altered inten-tionally or accidentally (Duranti 1995). Ultimately, the digital world fundamentally transforms traditional preservation principles from guaranteeing the physical integ-rity of the object to specifying the creation of the object whose intellectual integrity is its primary characteristic.

Librarians and archivists can exercise control over the integrity of digital image files by authenticating access procedures and documenting successive modifications to a given digital record. They can also create and maintain structural indexes and bibliographic linkages within well-developed and well-understood database stand-ards. Digital product developers also have a role to play in influencing the develop-ment of metadata interchange standards including the tools and techniques that will allow structured, documented, and standardized information about data files and databases to be shared across platforms, systems, and international boundaries. It is vain to think, however, that librarians and archivists are anything but bystanders observing the rapid development of network protocols, bandwidth, or the data secu-rity techniques that are essential to the persistence of digital objects over time.

The transformation of access

In the fifty years that preservation has been emerging as a professional specialty in libraries and archives, the preservation and access responsibilities of an archive or library have often been in tension. "While preservation is a primary goal or respon-sibility, an equally compelling mandate – access and use – sets up a classic conflict that must be arbitrated by the custodians and caretakers of archival records," states a fundamental textbook in the field (Ritzenthaler, 1993). The intimate relationship between preservation and access has changed in ways that mirror the technological environment of cultural institutions.

Preservation OR Access. In the early years of modern archival agencies – prior to World War II – preservation simply meant collecting. The sheer act of pulling a collection of manuscripts from a barn, a basement, or a parking garage and placing it intact in a dry building with locks on the door fulfilled the fundamental preservation mandate of the institution. In this regard preservation and access are mutually exclusive activities. Use exposes a collection to risk of theft, damage, or misuse of either content or object. The safest way to ensure that a book lasts for a long time is to lock it up or make a copy for use.

Preservation AND Access. Modern preservation management strategies posit that preservation and access are mutually reinforcing ideas. Preservation action is taken on an item so that it may be used. In this view, creating a preservation copy on microfilm of a deteriorated book without making it possible to find the film is a waste of money. In the world of preservation AND access, however, it is theoretically possible to fulfill a preservation need without solving access problems. Conversely, access to scholarly materials can be guaranteed for a very long period, indeed, without taking any concrete preservation action on them.

Preservation IS Access. Librarians and archivists concerned about the preservation of electronic records sometimes view the two concepts as cause and effect. The act of preserving makes access possible. Equating preservation with access, however, implies that preservation is defined by availability, when indeed this construct may be getting it backwards. Preservation is no more access than access is preservation. Simply refocusing the preservation issue on access oversimplifies the preservation issues by suggesting that access is the engine of preservation without addressing the nature of the thing being preserved.

Preservation OF Access. In the digital world, preservation is the action and access is the thing – the act of preserving access. A more accurate construct simply states "preserve accessibility." When transformed in this way, a whole new series of complexities arises. Preserve access to what? The answer suggested in this chapter is: a high quality, high value, well-protected, and fully integrated digital product that is derived from but independent of original source documents. The content, structure, and integrity of the digital product assume center stage – and the ability of a machine to transport and display this product becomes an assumed end result of the preservation action rather than its primary goal.

Control over accessibility, especially the capacity of the system to export digital image files (and associated indexes) to future generations of the technology, can be exercised in part through prudent purchases of only nonproprietary hardware and software components. In the present environment, true plug-and-play components are more widely available. The financial commitment by librarians and archivists is one of the only incentives that vendors have to adopt open system architectures or at least provide better documentation on the inner workings of their systems. Additionally, librarians and archivists can influence vendors and manufacturers to provide new equipment that is backward compatible with existing systems. This capability assists image file system migration in the same way that today's word processing software allows access to documents created with earlier versions. Much as they might wish otherwise, digital product developers have little or no control over the life expectancy of a given digital image system and the decision to abandon that system.

Conclusion

Fifty years ago, one of the foremost and persistent advocates for quality library bookbinding put his finger on the centrality of preservation to the mission of modern research libraries and archives. Preservation, wrote Pelham Barr in his most frequently cited work, "as responsible custody, is the only library function which should be continuously at work twenty-four hours a day. It is the only function which should be concerned with every piece of material in the library from the moment the selector becomes aware of its existence to the day it is discarded" (Barr, 1946). Barr's allusion to the lifecycle of information sources is timeless. Today the concept is at the center of information management theory and practice, including specifications for the disposition of government archives, the management of book collections, and the maintenance of large-scale information technology systems. Responsible custody circumscribes preservation in the digital world as well, where the creation of digital products worth maintaining over time is the measure of success. The idea of responsible custody should govern actions as we build digital products vested with the value of intellectual endeavors.

Summary of key principles and points

- Define clear boundaries for a digital conversion project, particularly the end point.
- Brainstorm: in nontechnical terms, state the desired outcomes for the source materials and the functional requirements for the digital reproductions.
- Justify why digital, rather than analog, reproduction is necessary.
  - Describe the audiences and their needs.
  - Describe the things that digital copies will do that analog copies cannot.
- Project a lifespan for the digital reproductions.
- Plan: write a project plan, budget, timeline, and other planning documents.
- Budget and plan workflow based upon the results of scanning and cataloging a representative sample of material.
- Budget (time, if not dollars) for training.
- Implement: coordinate simultaneous or overlapping workflows.
- Segregate materials into batches for conversion and quality control.
- Write documentation during the project.
- Report on the lessons learned, particularly the failures and blind alleys: help yourself and your colleagues to learn from your mistakes.

Bibliography

Barr, Pelham. "Book Conservation and University Library Administration," *College & Research Libraries* 7 (July 1946): 218–19.

Besser, Howard and Jennifer Trant. *Introduction to Imaging: Issues in Constructing an Image Database*. Santa Monica: Getty Art History Information Program, 1995. *http://www.gii.getty.edu/intro_imaging/*

Buckland, Michael K. "Information as Thing," *Journal of the American Society for Information Science 42* (June 1991): 351–60.

Conway, Paul. *Preservation in the Digital World.* Washington, DC: Commission on Preservation and Access, March 1996. *http://www.clir.org/cpa/reports/conway2/*

Digital Imaging Technology for Preservation. Proceedings from an RLG Symposium Held March 17 and 18, 1994. Nancy E. Elkington, ed. Mountain View, CA: Research Libraries Group, 1994.

Duranti, Luciana. *The Preservation of the Integrity of Electronic Records*. School of Library, Archival, and Information Studies, University of British Columbia, 1994–97. *http://www.slais.ubc.ca/users/duranti/intro.htm*

———. "Reliability and Authenticity. The Concepts and Their Implications." *Archivaria 39* (Spring 1995): 5–10.

Ester, Michael. *Digital Image Collections: Issues and Practice*. Washington, DC: Commission on Preservation and Access, 1996.

Frey, Franziska. "Digital Imaging for Photographic Collections: Foundations for Technical Standards." *RLG DigiNews 1* (3), December 15, 1997. *http://www.rlg.org/preserv/diginews/*

Graham, Peter S. "Requirements for the Digital Research Library." *College & Research Libraries 56* (July 1995): 331–39.

Hazen, Dan, Jeffrey Horrell, and Jan Merrill-Oldham. *Selecting Research Collections for Digitization.* Washington, DC: Council on Library and Information Resources, 1998. *http://www.clir.org/pubs/reports/hazen/pub74.html*

Kenney, Anne R. and Stephen Chapman. *Digital Imaging for Libraries and Archives*. Ithaca, NY: Dept. of Preservation and Conservation, Cornell University Library, 1996.

Levy, David M. "Heroic Measures: Reflections on the Possibility and Purpose of Digital Preservation." *Proceedings of the Third ACM Conference on Digital Libraries*, 1998, p. 152–61. *http://www.acm.org/pubs/citations/proceedings/dl/276675/p152-levy/*

Lynch, Clifford. "The Integrity of Digital Information: Mechanics and Definitional Issues." *Journal of the American Society for Information Science 45* (December 1994): 737–44.

Macaulay, David. *Motel of the Mysteries*. Boston: Houghton Mifflin, 1979.

Mohlhenrich, Janice. *Preservation of Electronic Formats: Electronic Formats for Preservation*. Fort Atkinson, WI: Highsmith, 1993.

O'Toole, James M. "On the Idea of Permanence." *American Archivist 52* (Winter 1989): 10–25.

Reilly, James M. and Franziska A. Frey. *Recommendations for the Evaluation of Digital Images Produced from Photographic, Microphotographic, and Various Paper Formats*. Report to the Library of Congress National Digital Library Project. Rochester, NY: Image Permanence Institute, May 1996. *http://memory.loc.gov/ammem/ipirpt.html*

Ritzenthaler, Mary Lynn. *Preserving Archives and Manuscripts*. Chicago: Society of American Archivists, 1993, p.1.

Robinson, Peter. *The Digitization of Primary Textual Sources*. Office for Humanities Communication Publication, no. 4. Oxford: Oxford University Computing Services, 1993.

Rothenberg, Jeff. "Ensuring the Longevity of Digital Documents." *Scientific American 272* (January 1995): 42–47.

Smith, Abby. *The Future of the Past: Preservation in American Research Libraries*. Washington, DC: Council on Library and Information Resources, 1999. *http://www/clir.org/ pubs/reports/pub82/pub82text.html*

———. *Why Digitize?* Washington, DC: Council on Library and Information Resources, 1999. *http://www.clir.org/pubs/reports/pub80-smith/pub80.html*

Van Bogart, John W. *Magnetic Tape Storage and Handling: A Guide for Libraries and Archives*. Washington, DC: Commission on Preservation and Access, 1995.

Waters, Donald J. "What Are Digital Libraries?" *CLIR Issues 4* (July/August 1998). *http:// www.clir.org/pubs/issues/issues04.html*

———. "Digital Preservation?" *CLIR Issues 6* (November/December 1998): 1. *http://www. clir.org/pubs/issues/issues.html*

Waters, Donald and John Garrett. *Preserving Digital Information: Report of the Task Force on Archiving of Digital Information*. Washington, DC: Research Libraries Group and Commission on Preservation and Access, May 1996. *http://www.rlg.org/ArchTF/*

Chapter 37

'Speaking for Themselves': new media and 'Making the Modern World'

Frank Colson and Jean Colson

Introduction: publishing history in an immature media[1]

The new media is still an immature one. Although ubiquitous since its inception in 1993–94, read by millions, and part of all our daily lives, there is still no clearly established canon that exists for high quality academic but public digital publication that uses it. The absence of such a canon should not provide a reason for disengagement. For the involvement of historians with electronic media since the 1960s has meant that a great deal of preparatory work has been undertaken to establish and publish 'authoritative sources' in a scholarly manner yet engaging to the public. With authority comes trust and it is only upon trust, in the quality of 'sources', 'writing' and 'voice', can powerful public history be broadcast. The major task of those who worked on 'Making the Modern World' was to guarantee the authority of all sources, including museum objects the digital surrogates of which were to be incorporated into publication.

In 2000–2001 colleagues at the UK Science Museum, mwr.ltd, a small new media company, and Peter Symonds College, a 16–19 teaching institution, successfully sought resources from private and public funds. They would collaborate so as to create an online version of the Museum's highly successful 'Making the Modern World' exhibition that had opened in 2000. The team that emerged, in which the authors of this paper played a role, envisaged something quite different from the exhibition, and the various print publications that had already been created. The aim was to provide an interpretation of the history of technology in such a stimulating and authoritative way as to fire the imaginations of the millions of readers and viewers whom might access to the internet. In particular they wanted to broaden the

Source: Paper presented to various events. Unpublished.

experience of students aged 14–19 so as to bring the history of science and technology centre stage, emphasizing the pervasiveness of its influence across a wide range of disciplines, and in our everyday lives. Influence was seen in its widest possible sense, so that the publication could contribute to an understanding of contemporary British political and intellectual history, as much as the impact of medical technologies, or the mobile phone. While it had taken many years to conceive, the ensuing publication itself took only two years to develop and publish. At the same time it combined the professional expertise of a very large group of colleagues. The discussion is a sober reflection of the experience of two of those most closely involved from the project in embryo to its official publication in June 2004.

What was this common experience of the Science Museum, mwr and Peter Symonds College? First, all were accustomed to immersing their audience, whether reader, viewer, user, or student in discussion. Secondly, all knew how to argue, discuss and debate information without being either gimmicky or 'gamesey'. All three had experimented with 3-D, TV-led and traditional games metaphors. These metaphors have often proved to be difficult to implement. Whether in a gallery, classroom or laboratory maintaining fealty to the source, deploying such source in the context of its contribution to our 'everyday lives' was seen as key to capturing and retaining the attention of the audience. All three partners took seriously Henry Ford's reported remark that 'history which excluded the tools of everyday life was bunk' and that history which is 'written in the things that our people have made and used' is a beautiful foil for teaching and publication in a range of subjects. The consortium could boast of decades of such experience, often working with successive cohorts of students to deploy primary sources some of which were truly massive in scale.[2]

For the Museum this digital publication is the result of almost ten years' labour as it sought to deploy its incomparable collection of 'world firsts' in innovation in such a way that their sheer authenticity since 'the shock of the real' can fascinate the audience of the future. The digital publication idealized as early as 1993 built upon a landmark exhibition that housed some 2000 artifacts, and was known through two popular print publications. As the gallery was built in 1996–2000 these artifacts were deployed in four linear exhibitions in the heart of the old Museum. Each artifact had its own internal narrative, which justified its inclusion in the exhibit as a whole because, Andrew Nahum and his colleagues argued:

> The history we will construct, with its clocks, locks, sewer pipes, machine guns and contraceptives is just as authentic an account of 'how we got to where we are now' as the political history of kings and presidents, parliaments and revolutions.[3]

Every component of the four linear exhibitions, parallel narratives, was intensely critiqued by its curators, graphic designers, and architects. In a daring feat of expression the sweeping vista of the whole exhibition moves through 250 years in little more than 100 yards. It deploys two-dimensional pictorial and archive material alongside the museum objects to speak to each age since each is a story. The culmination of these stories is a reflection on the 'Age of Ambivalence' which portrays a troubling future in which high technology coexists with a fractured, violently dislocated social organization. This future contrasts vividly with the hum of everyday life, where the objects we use everyday have undergone extraordinary revolutions and re-inventions, continuously permeating our lives yet often retaining a surprising continuity of form.

The experience of mwr in the deployment of sources ranks large on any scale, and curators from the Science Museum had expressed an interest in the work undertaken by its founders for almost a decade before joint work began on the digital publication. By early 1994 the Museum was working with mwr's founders, then at the University of Southampton to explore the potential of story telling using hypermedia story telling techniques. A prototype digital architecture was subsequently commissioned by the Museum in 1998.[4]

Clearly, the collaboration that occurred between a powerful and authoritative entity the Science Museum which had full control of authentic and authoritative sources and the prospect of their exploitation via multiple narratives would be very strong. The story would be dramatic. It would be firmly based on a variety of facsimile sources, with very clear indication of editorial intervention since the 'dramatic reconstructions' in 'Making the Modern World' are essentially just platforms for further interpretation.[5]

The contribution of an experienced and well-regarded teaching institution was absolutely crucial to ensure the publication responded to the needs of education professionals and achieved a substantial audience. This was important for the schools and junior colleges since they followed similar curricula, preparing students for university-entrance examinations. They did not suffer from the 'not invented here' syndrome typical of so many universities. Peter Symonds College in Winchester is renowned for the quality of its teaching, the scholarly, dedicated and enlightened approach of its teachers, and their continuing role in the pursuit of 'best practice' at all levels of teaching, both nationally and internationally. The decade-long experimental collaboration between the founders of mwr and leading teachers in Peter Symonds was vital in order to bring a thorough understanding of the changing student and teacher environment of the 1990s into a publication which would endure over the next decades.

By the mid-1990s, it had became abundantly clear that any institution that attempted to blend the best of traditional and new methods in teaching the 16 and over cohorts in the UK had to deal with six challenges. The first was both technical and intellectual as their students were increasingly influenced by the 'instant gratification' offered by early generations of computer games. The second was the academic one which occurred as students responded to the narrower and narrower testing that was demanded by the authorities and buried their heads in the narrow and binary explanations offered by textbooks. The third was social, since large numbers of students were walking through Peter Symonds' doors 'who lacked the range of study skills let alone the supportive milieu at one time thought appropriate to the courses on offer. The fourth, which was psychological, emerged more slowly with the growing understanding by teachers of the idea that many varieties of learners existed and needed to be catered for. A further and fifth challenge was administrative. It was caused by the welter of confusing and potentially deadly top-down driven institutional changes that occurred at the time.

The sixth and final challenge, one faced by all in the teaching profession, was potentially far more serious. Students were now far more sceptical of the benefits conveyed by scientific endeavour and increasingly cynical of the links between big science and the corporate sector. This meant that sources for teachers from Peter Symonds College had to be deployed with adequate supporting materials so that they could be smoothly related to whatever subject the teacher addressed. At the same time, these sources and the subject had to be presented by the teacher who was engaging the student in a 'conversational' manner. The impact of post-modernity on all our teaching institutions around the globe has been such that 'received wisdom' is, in fact, no longer received, and 'celebrities' have replaced heroes. The deeply populist shift from 'sage on the stage' to 'guide by your side' is invariably problematic for any institution wholly devoted to rapidly teaching hurried cohorts of students.

It was therefore vital for the teachers at Peter Symonds, that the '*moral authority*' of the source must be evident. This '*moral authority*' had to be tempered by an individual teacher's decades of understanding of the ways in which a source could be most effectively presented. It was imperative that the publication itself was worked up to delight, intrigue, and encourage students to use their scarcest resource – time – in the most effective manner. The College demanded that *scenes* and *stories* be deployed across a variety of disciplines. History had to be deployed as aid to the public understanding of the wealth of experience that is science. Ten years' collaboration and decades of man-hours during the early 1990s encouraged mwr and teachers at Peter Symonds to develop a number of approaches that informed '*Making the Modern World*'. This collaboration resulted in the development of a family of interactive publications not just deployed in the classroom, but equally useful to the general reader. At the same time senior teachers had worked on ways in which the moral authority of the teacher could be enhanced by using specific tools. This experience although it was limited to a very narrow range of students, was vital to the '*Making the Modern World*'. The teaching packages produced at Southampton in the early 1990s and by mwr in the years before '*Making the Modern World*' were the anvils on which editorial and source issues could be forged. They provided ways in which the more flexible presentation tools of the web could be articulated and employed for a variety of learners.[6]

To achieve this aim '*Making the Modern World*' would be produced using appropriate and granular methodologies re-interpreted for the purpose. These production methodologies had to firmly indicate points of decision and indicate those contributing to such decisions. Production methodologies had to be developed while keeping intellectual quality and reach within a clear framework. This was vital so that the substantial act of interpretation was set before its varied audiences and would retain its inherent power. If compromise had to occur it had to be worked through and the grounds clearly delineated. New arrangements had to outlined, made clear and agreed by all concerned. Nothing was undertaken simply because it was: '*technically feasible*', '*corporate policy*', fascinating to one individual or simply the '*mode of the month*'. Once commissioned the publication project would be sovereign. Well-hewn evaluation procedures would ensure that the end-users were well-served.[7]

The '*shock of the real*' provided the catalyst for effective collaboration. Challenges were posed by the sheer scale involved in attempting to deploy these magnificent materials into home and classroom in the expectation that they would attract debate. During the early 1990s the consortium emerged in embryonic form during a time of extraordinary growth in student numbers. All involved in the consortium understood that the learning in 'Making the Modern World' was deeply embedded in the tacit knowledge of our everyday lives. New knowledge acquired on a daily basis by scientific endeavour would enter popular discourse.

Observers such as Trigger and Katz have observed that the encouragement of discourse is not simply a question of available resources. It has been made more difficult as a consequence of the impact of new communications and knowledge of the digital revolution on our learned communities. Katz highlights the fact that much of the malaise of the academic world, the 'democratic deficit', of the universities stems from the relentless narrow commercialism of the very media in which we intend to publish. This is not unrelated to the 'democratic deficit' experienced by the society in which our students live and which scholars seek to address. It was clear that with only twenty-four months from conception to publication the consortium required every last millimetre of their combined experience and capabilities to 'interpret' their vast resources to complete their task.[8]

'Defiant Modernism': the scene and the source[9]

Four stories are housed in the theme of 'Defiant Modernism' and they illustrate the thrust of 'Making the Modern World' as a whole. They deployed sources: whether audio, video, printed source facsimile, image and text, or any combination of these, in a manner that makes them a powerful 'bridge' between elements of the publication. They powerfully illustrate the 'grand perspectives' the interplay of 'risk', 'people', 'icons' and 'everyday life'.[10] These stories illustrate the concern of the consortium to deploy new media to its best advantage not intending to replicate the metaphor of the book, movie, TV show, library archive or museum metaphor. The theme called 'Defiant Modernism' depicts this period as perhaps the last in which technology, progress and the Enlightenment models of rationality appeared to operate synchronously. Hence the people who lived during this period

> envisaged a powerful role for science under conditions of total war in high-level war planning, in operating the national economy and even in developing the national diet. As a result the new subject of 'operational research' (OR), which became a vital element in Allied planning and in eventual victory.[11]

The Initial Design Specification, an administrative document, conveyed this sense of totality and outlined the ways in which the intellectual thrust of 'Making the Modern World' could be carried forward. It built upon earlier technical work, developed at Southampton, to outline the notion of the 'Scene' as an integral part of the story. The Scene united views of the objects deemed as 'iconic', texts and static images with the ultimate goal that they would subsequently become 'mined' by stories, activities and through an informal narrative give way naturally to the 'learning modules'. These '*learning modules*' were designed to be superficially more linear in their approach in contrast to the Rich Media Scenes which are standalone '*learning objects*'.[12]

The '*scene*' is arguably the fundamental component in the success of '*Making the Modern World*'. Each '*scene*' provides not just access to a wide range of sources (film, photograph, text) but considerable possibilities for entering into the larger debates existing within the entire dataset. It provides an instance of how several debates can overlay and intersect each other. The V2 rocket Rich Media Scene provides a useful example. It is only possible to understand the importance of the missile by situating it within a specific context: the bombing of Peenemunde (the German missile base). This occurred during the development of the V2, both slave workers and research staff were killed and missiles destroyed. This event is discussed in a '*dramatic recon-struction*' of a meeting between Churchill, his scientific advisor, Lord Cherwell and Dr. R.V. Jones (head of the MI6 team). It is possible that, as a result, the V-bombing of London was delayed by three months, with consequent impact on the course of the war in Western Europe. The *scene* empowers the reader to branch off via an informal narrative logically either into another larger story entitled '*The Space Race*', or to consider the accompanying evidence (through *Ingenious*, the accompanying Museum site), or move to '*Projectiles*'.[13] In essence the reader can either follow a discus-sion and activity which enables an understanding of the mathematics of rocketry or examine a survey of the personalities and '*iconic objects*' involved. In all of these *scenes* accent is placed on presentation of sources *in natura*, in an implied narrative. In '*The Space Race*' several forms of evidence are presented as the background to Kennedy's commitment for the US to put a man on the moon before the end of the 1960s. The implications of that commitment are clearly articulated as are the relationships between evidence and interpretation, event and context, cause and effect. The learn-ing module on '*gravity*' which accompanies '*The Space Race*' encapsulates the essential pragmatism of science:[14]

> While Einstein's theory superseded that of Newton's and radically changed the way we think about the universe, the theoretical model adopted by NASA for its mission to the Moon was based on Newton's ideas. Essen-tially, relativistic ideas become important when we are looking at objects travelling at very high velocities relative to the speed of light. For NASA's purposes, Newton's laws worked well enough.
>
> Rocket technology was developed during the Second World War, by the Nazis in particular. The German scientist Wernher von Braun (1912–77), who led the team of German scientists that developed the V2 rocket, was employed after the war by the United States to develop its rocket programme. He and his team were the chief architects of the Saturn V rockets used for the Apollo missions.[15]

The *scenes* were articulated in the later revision of the Content Specification. The *scenes* play a crucial role in managing the interplay between public imagining, high politics, technological change and human agency which frame work in the sciences. In classic cinematic fashion they juxtapose image, text, narrative. The development of the *scene* was far more than just a pragmatic response to the practical problems faced by the consortium. They permitted the '*authoritative*' sources to be utilized rather than being presented merely to illustrate points. In terms of experience the *scenes* built upon the earlier research at Southampton and the fund of knowledge that could be articulated. Flexibly deployed they could be deeply enmeshed with the stories and the overall theme of the publication, informing editorial practice so that the reader of a story would never become 'lost in cyberspace' or would feel constrained to one specific narrative.[16]

Lessons learned: the enduring challenge of publishing in the new media

We now know that '*Making the Modern World*' offers explanations of the evolution of scientific endeavors from 1750 to 2000 in a manner that has been accessible to a global audience. However, this audience is neither influenced nor guided by academic concerns. The Public History will be publicly crafted. It is now clear, that the student audience was not the only part of the population that was fascinated by this publication. It was important that we understood that '*Making the Modern World*' was created within a new and obviously immature medium. One in which a healthy blend of the academic, the pragmatic and commercial was the key to a successful publication. To be controversial and popular with regard to the source and script, without being '*populist*' was also an imperative.

It is ironic that '*fitness for purpose*', first worked up as part of database development by historians using software in the early 1980s, has endured as a cardinal principle. Data should never be shoe-horned into software. This principle has been reinforced in scholarly terms by literary critics such as Jerome McGann, John Unsworth, and most powerfully, by the work of the Dutch historian Georg Welling. They are all correct in stating that best practice humanities computing, such as that of '*Making the Modern World*', must provide for the modelling of multiple views but must actively engage the reader in the process of reading and reflection.

To achieve the interactivity required for teaching that explains relationships and goes beyond mere depiction, and is highly creative, the authors of '*Making the Modern World*' have had to be obsessed with maintaining clarity of meaning and 'fitness for purpose'. Good communication demanded no less. '*Fitness for purpose*' profoundly influenced the creation of the massive editorial collateral necessary to achieve the interactivity and reach of this large project. In addition to the academic imperative, the editorial guides developed to be used by all concerned had to draw upon many editorial traditions. They had to draw on commercial and advertising media practices, canons of graphic design and the experience of working with major online news providers such as the BBC and UK national press. All this had to occur in conjunction with the academic canons evolved by the Museum and the pedagogical experience of both Peter Symonds and the mwr teams. '*Fitness for Purpose*' clearly overcame the design and technical dogmatism of today's 'information age'.[17]

Even wider considerations have always existed. If the audience data is closely examined it is evident that '*Making the Modern World*' has successfully delivered several interpretations of a vital area of Western History to a global audience via the various media which are appropriate to the task in hand. '*Making the Modern World*' has delivered these interpretations to a global audience. The highly-informed polymath approach of the curators and the pragmatics of the classroom presentation inevitably privileged original interpretations of a very high order. This approach exemplified the use of digital technology outside the narrow world of librarians, archivists and editors in the service of self-aware reflection and interpretation for which the new media is best suited. What remains fascinating is that in New Media, '*context*' and '*source*', the historian's specific concerns, remain '*king*'.

Key lessons have been learnt. Firstly, the structures employed to create and build a publication of this scale are the results of a sustained feat of intellectual modelling. This modelling extends across a range of disciplines and draws heavily from the Arts and Social Sciences. This intellectual modelling is highly disciplined, demanding, not at all a game for academics. At a pragmatic level, if the navigation of this huge resource works well – and clearly, to a large extent, it has worked well – it is because the designers' brief faithfully reflected that intellectual modelling. Intellectual risk that always threatens coherence was mitigated by the participation of the partners in modelling the argument of the exhibition. The implication of this was impressive. It meant that once funding was secured the project employed a flexible but controlled approach to project governance. This ensured that the '*Making the Modern World*' was delivered on time, to budget and specification. Earlier work was always available and used for reference during the many reviews of the specification that occurred during the life-cycle of the production. In this way coherence was maintained.

Secondly, the sponsoring consortium has to be prepared to take the huge risks involved in ceding a carefully circumscribed autonomy to the project so that it could take on a life of its own. For the most serious project risk was the academic and civil service propensity for micromanagement simply because one hundred and forty-seven people were involved. To call '*Making the Modern World*' a work of art is perhaps to go too far: but inasmuch as the meaningful deployment of colour, shape, sound and text – and a sense of narrative, of story telling – bring pleasure, its production involved an act of creation and artistic inspiration. This is absolutely not the remit of bureaucrats or would-be academic politicians.

On the third point, the creation of such a large-scale interactive publication resembles the construction of an aircraft and therefore demands project management of a very high order. No room exists for a latter-day Cecil B. DeMille-style director because at the turn of the twenty-first century and operating with vastly more complex technologies and the rigors of accountability which pervade a public–private partnership the directors of such projects must be consensus builders. This is also crucial since the range of technologies which are deployed is simply too great for any one person to comprehend.

Finally, major publication projects must be grown organically using such project management and core competences as are fit for purpose. There is no reason why they cannot grow within a consortium. Production workshops should be carefully deployed through the production process so as to bring scattered components together at well-specified instances. '*Making the Modern World*' developed the notion of a '*story*' with its integral '*scenes*' as core to a web of annotated sources. The stories and their respective scenes should be created and used by individual scholars who should collaborate closely with production houses and institutions such as libraries and archives who are able to provide validated digital surrogates.

Notes

1 The URL for the publication is www.makingthemodernworld.org An early draft of the paper was first read to the H-Net 'editorial workshop' held in January 8th 2005 on the occasion of the AHA Conference at Seattle. The authors would like to acknowledge the comments of that meeting, especially those of Marilyn Levine and Peter Kupfner. The authors would especially acknowledge the detailed comment and powerful contributions of Martyn Farrows and Andrew Sawyer of mwr.ltd, Ian Shaw of mwrinfosecurity ltd., also those of Robert Bud, Andrew Nahum, and Ben Russell, of the Science Museum.

   Thanks also to Marigene Allison, without whose hospitality and unfailing support, on board 'Eye on the Sky' in Sausalito and on the 'Île de quatre esprits' on Lac Archambault, we could not have stolen the time to piece together the experience of 'Making the Modern World'.

2 Nahum, p. 71. on the making of the landmark exhibition in the 1990s.

3 R. Bud et.al. 'Introduction' in *Inventing the Modern World*, Science Museum (London: Dorling Kindersley, 2000).

4 Commissioned from one of the authors, Jean Colson.

5 Digital objects as presaged in "The Real Thing? Visuality, Virtuality, Reality" by Ross Parry. "The Attack on the President of Brazil: Rio de Janeiro, 5th November 1897: The Narration of the Moment" by Frank Colson. "The Comprehension of the Image. Power and the Dutch Republic, 1588: Narrative as Hierarchy and Linearity" by Andrew Sawyer. "Chicago 1919: Collaboration in Exploration" by Jean Colson: subsequently reworked and published in 'Cutting-off the King's Head': Images and the (Dis)Location of Power http://www.kalkmalerier.dk/congress/default.html A. Bolvig and P. Lindley (eds) *History and Images Towards a New Iconology*. Brepols, 2003 pp. 187–209. Bos and Welling neatly summarized the dilemma for those involved in computing in the humanities. They had to be designers as well as software engineers with an acute sense of the needs of the humanities since commercial suppliers were highly unlikely to develop the sophisticated tools required for the task. 'The significance of user-interfaces for historical software.' "The Art of Communication: Grazer Grundwissenshachfteliche [1995]. 24pp.

6 J.N. Hare, 'The College and the Outside World: A Case Study.' Posted: 28th June, 2002 www.psc.ac.uk. Many of the teaching packages developed in Southampton were subsequently published by Primary Source Media, 1994, and distributed worldwide. HTML versions (major re-editions) were broadcast by www.angliacampus.com 2000. The most influential was John Hare, 'Dissolution of the Monasteries. A case study from Hampshire, 1536–1540.' which can be viewed from www.mwr.biz/portfolio.html. A bespoke package – 'How to read a document' is published by the National Archives http://eden.learningcurve.pro.gov.uk and is an instantiation of the use of sources in the UK classroom

7 PRINCE2, which stands for Projects in Controlled Environments (Version 2), was the project management method covering the organization, management and control of projects. PRINCE2 was first developed by the Central Computer and Telecom-

munications Agency (CCTA) now part of the Office of Government Commerce
(OGC) in 1989 as a UK Government standard for IT project management. It is
highly granular and was adapted for use on multimedia projects by mwr.ltd. Its intui-
tive methodology enables the Project Board to firmly allocate responsibility, manage
risk and provide authors with clear directions. mwr's use of Prince2 to deliver
Making the Modern World' to quality, time and budget was praised by the ISB itself
(ISB Conference Report – November, 2003). The publication itself was based on
Open Systems architecture (Linux), instantiating XML–XSL. The Editorial Steering
Group, which advised the Project Board rejected both 3-D and televisual approaches
as too cumbersome for effective classroom delivery; it advocated a solution which
wove in timelines. These were neither hard-wired nor based on specific architec-
tures. This ensured that interpretation was not ontologically driven.

8 Politicians, inveterate practitioners of the short-term fix slither around and see these
issues as merely concerned with cash resources. They miss the point. 'What we want to
do is to see a sustained improvement in the quality of what is available for young people'
(Steven Twigg, Minister of State, Department of Education, Speech of 2 December
2004 to Heads of VI Form Colleges). But what does 'available' mean if timescales which
have been dictated by political consideration are far too short for reflective learning?
As Kenneth Minogue has recently argued in 'Journalism: Power without responsibility' *The New Criterion*, 23 (6), February 2005, politicians like Twigg seem incapable of
raising their sights beyond those of 'rolling news', a media that seeks instant gratification rather than reflection. Trigger (p. 79) argues that in order to counter the spread
of 'half truths' in today's pulsating plethora of communications. 'it is imperative to try
to educate people in ways that will help them evaluate and synthesize knowledge more
critically and comprehensively'. In other words reflect. Katz puts his finger on the other
side of the issue, 'It may also be the case that the theoretical complexity of the knowledge currently generated by research universities is too inaccessible to large numbers
of citizens outside the academy. That is true in the sciences and the humanities and the
social sciences, though it may well be that the tradition of high-level popularization of
scientific thought is healthier than in the social sciences and humanities. There is a sense
in which the modalities for communicating with the public are less vibrant than they
used to be. If so, that is probably as much a factor of the dominance of highly commer-
cialized new media as it is of the unwillingness or inability of academics to translate
their work for the general public. And the current crisis – economic and intellectual –
in serious publishing is surely another sign of the same phenomenon.'

9 'Defiant Modernism', the term, was first used by Robert Bud, in his article, 'Peni-
cillin and the new Elizabethans', *British Journal for the History of Science*, 31 (110)
(September 1998): 305–33, p. 312. The term was subsequently used in *Inventing
the Modern World* (2000) published by the museum as a complement to the original
Exhibition.

10 http://www.makingthemodernworld.org.uk/. The home page is a carousel whereby
a number of images are deployed to indicate the 'grand themes'. Each is accompanied
by a caption to indicate the component of the publication which enlarges upon it.

11 http://www.makingthemodernworld.org.uk/stories/defiant_modernism/01.
ST.03/?scene=3. 'Tots and Quots'.

12 The Initial Design Specification process document was compiled from notes of meetings and workshops with editors and authors by Jon Weinbren, Director of 'Imaginary'. The idea of the 'scene' is as ancient as classical Greece but it emerged in early

discussions amongst members of the Editorial Steering Group as a means of 'bridging' image and text. It was developed in part from student projects produced as a part of the offering of J. Colson's course 'Questioning The Image' in Southampton (1989–96); fleshed out in the digital architecture outlined by Jean Colson for the Science Museum in early 1998. The Initial Design Specification enabled the two creative teams (curators and teachers with mwr advisors) to bridge their respective approaches via a reference to the image and an acceptance of its iconicity. The Steering Group accepted the conceptual structure proposed by the Specification as well as the instantiation of images in 'flash' procedures rather than 3-D. Detailed briefing of creative teams could then concentrate on the production of three prototype 'stories' with their component 'scenes' to allow for 'bridging' to the 'learning modules', which were produced in parallel. The experience of the prototypes was distilled into the Content Specification, a further process-management document completed in consultation with the Editorial Steering Group by one of the authors of this paper. 'Fitness for purpose' was the criterion which informed the pragmatic technical solutions. The results of the evaluation were fed in to the overall Content Specification.

Process was monitored to PRINCE2 requirements by the Project Board which was chaired by Robert Bud. The Project Board monitors performance and project risk: attended by funders, partners and executives. It answered to the Executive who in this case was the Science Museum, who answered for partners to the Ministry of Culture, then to the Treasury/Cabinet Office ISB team which was led by Mike Thornton. This team reported directly to Cabinet Office/Treasury via the Chief Secretary to the Treasury, Paul Boateng. The need to use Rich Media Scenes standalone was seen as a means of introducing teachers to digital media by the Further Education Resources for Learning which favours an electic approach to learning, http://ferl. becta.org.uk/display.cfm?page=1, 'Given the growing awareness of student learning styles and inclusivity, online learning offers real opportunities to offer students a variety of differentiated learning experiences with minimal bureaucracy'. The trials of stories and scenes in Peter Symonds College and a mirror site were organized by the Audience evaluator team and the results incorporated into the work by the members of the ESG.

13 From the Home Page. 'Ingenious is a new website that brings together images and viewpoints to create insights into science and culture. It weaves unusual and thought-provoking connections between people, innovations and ideas. Drawing on the resources of NMSI, the site contains over 30,000 images which are used to illustrate over 30 different subjects, topics and debates.' http://www.ingenious.org.uk

14 http://www.makingthemodernworld.org.uk/learning_modules/maths/06. TU.02/. Available via 'related materials' http://www.makingthemodernworld.org. uk/stories/defiant_modernism/05.ST.07/?scene=3.

15 http://www.makingthemodernworld.org.uk/learning_modules/maths/06. TU.02/?section=7.

16 Hall, W. and Colson, F. (1991) 'Multimedia teaching with Microcosm-HiDES: Viceroy Mountbatten and the partition of India', *History and Computing*, 3 (2): 89–98. The Yugoslavian Civil War dataset was begun in 1989 by Jean and Frank Colson, see 'The application of interactive videodisc to the teaching of history'. Leverhulme Trust Grant mlt\fl800x. Report, January 1995. In both cases the advantages of open hypermedia structures were explored as a way of providing various readings of the

documentation. These structures are ones in which links are separately stored. They are not embedded in the source.

17 Jerome McGann, *Radiant Textuality: literature after the world wide web* (New York and Basingstoke, Hampshire: Palgrave Macmillan, 2001) makes the point elegantly. 'Digital technology has remained instrumental in serving the technical and pre-critical occupations of librarians and archivists and editors. But the general field of humanities education and scholarship will not take the use of digital technology seriously until one demonstrates how its tools improve the ways we explore and explain aesthetic works—until, that is, they expand our interpretational procedures'. His position is echoed in John Unsworth's telling phrase 'the more room a resource offers for the exercise of independent imagination and curiosity, the more substantially well thought-out, well-designed, and well-produced a resource it must be' is implied in 'What is humanities computing and what is it not?' (8 November 2002) his lecture published in http://computerphilologie.uni-muenchen.de/jg02/unsworth.html. They do not appear to be aware of Georg Welling's seminal work on the Amsterdam Port (Pallgeld) a model of 'best practice' in computational history. Utilizing the Pallgeld data he argues that the struggle between Napoleon and England was global, commercial and military and not just merely 'continental', with the Americas playing a major role. The Appendix is an excellent example of data modelling. It presents the data and enables colleagues to 'read' and work with it. Work with it is precisely the model later suggested by Unsworth as 'best practice'. Revised in 2002 it is a splendid antidote to the euro-centric, even anglo-centric bias of so much work on the economic history of that period. Welling's *'The Prize of Neutrality. Trade relations between Amsterdam and North America 1771–1817. A study in computational history* (Hilversum 1998). The data are contained in the Appendix, published online in http://odur.let.rug.nl/~welling/paalgeld/appendix.html. In a previous work, Welling discusses the implications of his view for interface development with Bert Bos, 'The significance of user-interfaces for historical software'. In: Gerhard Jaritz, Ingo H. Kropac and Peter Teibenbacher (eds), *The Art of Communication*. Grazer Grundwissenschaftliche Forschungen, (Graz 1995), pp. 223–237.

Chapter 38

The Evaluation of Museum Multimedia Applications: lessons from research

Maria Economou

Introduction

In museums and exhibitions, the use of interactive multimedia applications continues to spread, and now that the technological problems of the early experimental
years have largely been solved, curators and educators are focusing more on the audience's needs and the quality of the interactive experience (Bearman 1995). Although
the museum community is becoming increasingly aware of the need to evaluate
multimedia displays (McNamara 1986; Raphling 1994; Dierking and Falk 1998), it
is surprising and disappointing that to date very few systematic, in-depth evaluation
studies are publicly available. This research first describes briefly the results obtained
from a study which examined the effectiveness of a multimedia application created
for exhibition interpretation, and then it examines the lessons to be learned from this
project and refers to their wider implications for those involved in the design and
evaluation of museum multimedia. The study was part of doctoral research carried
out at the University of Oxford, funded by a scholarship from the Lambrakis Research
Foundation, Athens. It focused on the design and evaluation of a prototype gallery
interactive developed for the presentation of an important archaeological site, the
classical Greek colony of Euesperides in North Africa. This was a component of the
temporary exhibition on the archaeology of Euesperides which was organized by the
Ashmolean Museum, Oxford, and shown at the Museum of Oxford in autumn 1995.
The Euesperides program combined the fragmented information derived from the
excavation of the site – near modern Benghazi in Libya (Vickers et al. 1994) – with
the historical background of the city (Economou 1993), and set out to interpret the
objects on display.

Source: *Museum Management and Curatorship*, vol. 17, no. 2, 1998, pp. 173–187.

The project followed all the standard stages of a multimedia production for a museum exhibition: (a) Research on the content of the application; (b) Collection of the material; (c) Multimedia design and programming (Economou, 1995); (d) Formative evaluation; (e) Integration in a museum exhibition; (f) Summative evaluation of the program's effectiveness (Economou 1996, 1997); (g) Study of the long-term effect on visitors; and (h) Impact on museum staff. More specifically, the areas investigated were:

1   the potential of multimedia for presenting the results from an excavation and thus improving the public understanding of archaeology;
2   the way formative evaluation assisted and influenced the design of the application;
3   who used the program in the exhibition (and who did not);
4   the way those visitors used the multimedia application;
5   the learning outcomes and emotional impact of the program (immediate and long-term);
6   the effect of the presence of the computer program on the way visitors explored the exhibition.

Methodology

Throughout its design, the Euesperides prototype was tested with a variety of users including schoolchildren, adults, the Education Guides of the Ashmolean Museum, graduate students, and curators. Formative evaluation followed two main approaches: (i) informal sessions observing the users' interaction with the prototype and recording their reactions and comments while they were encouraged to 'think aloud'; and (ii) more structured evaluation, where the users were asked to fill in a questionnaire after using the program. Summative evaluation constituted the main focus of the study and employed six different methods: observation (sample 117) and interviews with users (sample 75) and non-users (sample 59) of the multimedia program, computer interaction logging (361 valid logs of a total of 446), self-administered questionnaires (qualitative information, self-selected sample), analysis of comments in the visitors book (qualitative information, self-selected sample), mail survey with computer users five to six months after their visit to the exhibition (38 letters received), and interviews with museum staff. The combination of a variety of methods allowed the comparison of findings and the examination of different aspects of the museum interactive experience (Economou 1997).

Findings

Overall, the results obtained from the evaluation of the Euesperides prototype were positive about the use of the program both as an independent interpretative device and as a component of the exhibition. However, any generalization must be treated with caution. Like all cultural multimedia products, the Euesperides program was created and used within a unique environment and the results of the study must be considered in this context. Nevertheless, some of the findings have broader applicability and the valuable lessons learned from the Euesperides study would benefit any museum professional considering the use of multimedia technology for public presentation.

Formative evaluation

The experience from the Euesperides project demonstrated the valuable role of formative evaluation and confirmed the importance of testing with the users. Even when informal and with a small sample, formative evaluation offered useful feedback about the program's content, language, navigation, and the intuitiveness of the interface, before too much effort and resources had been expended. User input throughout the design process led to several changes (for example, in the basic structure of the prototype, the titling of certain features, and the addition of sound buttons for the pronunciation of difficult words). It also helped to define the profile and needs of different user groups.

The computer program as an interpretative device

The computer program functioned successfully as a presentation and interpretation medium. It offered background information about the largely unknown ancient city of Euesperides, contextualized the artefacts on display, and explained their importance today. One of the most attractive features of the program was its interactive character. Several users commented on the fact that they could choose what they wanted to see, explore different paths, and control navigation. This was an interesting finding, particularly since in this experimental and low-cost prototype the level of interactivity was actually rather limited. In the event, the computer program turned out to be one of the most popular exhibits in the gallery, receiving the highest number of visitors (40 per cent of the 117 tracked visitors) and the highest number of repeat visits of all exhibits (eight of thirty-two repeat visits). Additionally, visitors spent more time with the computer program (3.75 minutes mean) than with any other exhibit (1.3 minutes with exhibit in the second ranking). The novelty of the technology appears to have played an important part in this, attracting visitors with no prior knowledge of or interest in the subject. It is likely that this element will become less important in attracting visitors to specific museum displays as the use of computers continues to penetrate all aspects of our lives (Department of Trade and Industry 1997). The success of the computer program might also be related to the fact that some of the other exhibits were supported by limited or unattractive explanatory material, whereas the objects certainly required some explanation if their meaning was to be understood and the exhibition layout may have been confusing to some.

Several months after their visit, most respondents to the mail survey were able to recall many details of their experience. Visitors remembered not only what they had done and felt during their visit, but could also describe what the exhibition and the program had been about, what they had contained, and the thoughts that these had triggered. Their answers suggest that the visit to the exhibition, and particularly the interaction with the computer program, was memorable and had had a lasting impact. Nevertheless, it was interesting to observe that almost 20 per cent of users interviewed could not describe correctly what the program was about even after three minutes' interaction. In order to understand the subject and main ideas of the program, users apparently needed to invest more than a few minutes. This was particularly true for casual visitors who had come upon the exhibition unprepared and without any particular interest in the subject matter. The results might be related to the complexity and design of the program. It is also possible that for a portion of the audience, the *process* of using a touch-screen computer was the prime attraction during the initial period of interaction, while attention to the subject matter and understanding of it began to be established only after a few minutes' use.

All these findings indicate that in the setting of an exhibition the multimedia program is a very powerful medium with considerable potential for communicating ideas. But they also raise issues about its relationship with the other, more traditional media used in the exhibition, and in particular with the real artefacts. How did the virtual affect the real, especially in this situation, where they were placed in the same room? This important issue is discussed below.

The computer program as a component of the exhibition

In direct contrast to the fears of many museum professionals, the results of the Euesperides study indicated that the computer's presence in the exhibition generally enhanced the visitors' experience. For a large section of users the computer interactive contributed considerably to their enjoyment (73 per cent of seventy-five users interviewed) and understanding of the display (57 to 62 per cent of users interviewed). Similar comments were mentioned in the post-exhibition mail survey. A female visitor in her forties, for example, wrote:

> The program provided a useful tool which enabled not only myself, but also my six-year-old son, to gain much more from the exhibition than would otherwise have been the case. . . .We . . . felt that being able to use the computer greatly increased our enjoyment and understanding.

Several users mentioned in the interviews that the program made things clearer, put them into perspective, and motivated them to go back and look at the objects again, though over a quarter of the tracked visitors were simply using the exhibition space as a corridor on their way out and a slightly smaller group (19 per cent) would have probably used the exhibition in the same way, but stopped instead to sample the interactive program. As a couple of visitors mentioned specifically in their letters, the computer program was what had attracted them to the display and without which they would probably not have stopped to look at the exhibition at all. Almost half of this group then stayed longer to look at the objects on display, but only after using the program.

Visitors invested substantial amounts of time interacting with the computer, more than with any other individual exhibit, though it was interesting to observe that the time visitors spent at the computer did not affect adversely the time they spent in the rest of the gallery. Computer users spent over seven minutes longer in the gallery than non-users. Even when the time at the computer is deducted, the remaining time they spent in the gallery (4.8 minutes mean, 2.1 minutes median time) is still considerably higher than the time spent by non-users (Table 38.1). This confirms that the computer program encouraged visitors to explore and engage with the rest of the exhibits. Furthermore, interaction with the computer program helped several users learn about specific themes related to the exhibition. That learning was related to the acquisition of factual information, but it also involved the consolidation of previous knowledge, the raising of questions, and the development of an awareness of the way in which archaeologists work and the types of evidence they exploit to extract information about the past.

Table 38.1 Comparison of time spent in the gallery between computer users and non-users (sample: 117)

	Mean time with computer	Mean time – rest of exhibition
1 Computer Users	3.7 minutes	4.8 minutes
2 Non-users	–	1.5 minutes

At the same time, the program sometimes also overshadowed, at least temporarily, the rest of the displays. Several visitors were absorbed in the Euesperides prototype *while* using it, but some of them would explore the exhibition *afterwards*. Few visitors (eight of 117 observed), however, returned to the computer kiosk after looking at the objects. This indicates that the program was not successful in making direct links with the specific objects on display. One reason for this can be attributed to the late preparation of the exhibition's layout and choice of specific objects to be displayed, which in turn did not allow for the design of more explicit links between the information presented on-screen and the exhibition cases. But even without this practical limitation, the absorbing power of the computer screen made difficult the successful integration of the interactive program with the surrounding static displays.

Who used the program?

The specific profile of users and non-users of the Euesperides program might be related to a number of factors, such as the type of exhibition, the specific museum, or its admission policy. What is of general interest is that the computer program appealed to all age and gender combinations. Female and male visitors were equally likely to use it, even when the ratio of male/female visitors is taken into account. This is in contrast to the findings of most museum multimedia evaluations. With the exception of two other studies (Hilke et al. 1988; Allison and Gwaltney 1991), most evaluations of computer interactives in museum settings showed a predominance of male users (Sharpe 1983; Doering et al. 1989; Menninger 1991; McManus 1993;

Giusti 1994a, b). Furthermore, female users of the Euesperides program tended to spend longer with the program. Children under age 11 represent the largest age group of computer users, almost a quarter of the total number of users (394 valid interaction logs). This confirms the commonly held belief that these programs are popular with a young audience. However, the program was also used by visitors over 55 years old (19 per cent). Unlike most similar studies (Sharpe 1983; Doering et al. 1989; Allison and Gwaltney 1991; Giusti 1994a), more than half of the computer users were over 25.

Both results relating to the gender and the age of computer users are not surprising, if we consider the penetration of information technology into all sections of society. It is useful to take into account the results of a study of 5,000 households and 1,300 businesses in the United Kingdom, the United States of America, Japan, Germany, and France commissioned by the United Kingdom Department of Trade and Industry in 1997. This showed that 'across all the benchmark countries ownership and usage of information and communication technologies is growing' (Department of Trade and Industry 1997: 127). Currently the consumer penetration of hardware and infrastructure (39 per cent) is substantially lower than that of business (94 per cent) (Department of Trade and Industry 1997: 17). The expansion of information technology in the business sector is, however, likely to have a growing impact on the general population. Of those who use computers outside the home, 33 per cent of their time at either work, school, or college is taken up in front of a computer screen. Considering these general changes in society, we can anticipate that museum visitors will be increasingly familiar with computers. Interestingly, however, the Euesperides program was also used by a considerable number of visitors with very little (7 per cent) or no previous experience (16 per cent) of their use, whereas a very small number of visitors who did not use the program were opposed to the use of computers in museums in general, not finding them useful and preferring the 'real thing'.

How was the program used?

While most users found this program easy to use, there were, in general, several indications that its usability could have been improved. Because the program presented a large amount of information, including a complex set of links, it did not always succeed in maintaining ease of use. Furthermore, the introduction of an evaluation screen after only a few minutes' use of the application appeared to disrupt communication. This was programmed to appear after three minutes' use of the program and asked about ease of use and satisfaction with the level of information provided. It also asked users to select one or more adjectives from a list provided describing the program. Although the answers which visitors gave to the on-screen questions offered useful feedback, the way this evaluation screen was introduced in the Euesperides prototype disoriented and confused many users.

Visitors' gender, age, and group composition were also reflected in their behaviour and interaction with the computer at the exhibition on Euesperides. Almost 60 per cent of 117 tracked visitors used the computer in groups of two or more, which was in accordance with the findings of other studies (Doering et al. 1989; Menninger 1991; McManus 1993; Giusti 1994b). Most users created unique paths through the application, taking advantage of the options offered, but some general trends emerged. The analysis of the interaction logs indicated that the most popular type of navigation of all age groups was linear (36 per cent of the 391 valid logs). It appears that older visitors in particular were more likely to explore the program in a linear fashion. Younger visitors (under 18), on the other hand, showed a greater tendency to navigate randomly and explore several areas superficially. It cannot be excluded that more extensive general use of programs and systems designed in a hypertext way, such as those available on the World Wide Web, might gradually encourage non-linear ways of thinking and exploring.

Recommendations for similar projects

These findings, as well as the general experience gained from the study, can be interpreted in a wider museum context. The implications of the results and the lessons learned are presented below in the form of guidelines for enthusiasts, professionals, and institutions working in the area of cultural multimedia.

Guidelines for user interface design

User interface design is an important part of multimedia production; a badly designed interface will make the program difficult to use and can negate impressive and rich content.

- Formative testing of the interface is vital and should be undertaken at several stages during the design of the program. This can be carried out informally with a small number of visitors or potential users.
- The application should be programmed so that it forgives users' mistakes and offers feedback about the various operations. For example, users should be warned about images which will take a long time to appear on-screen.
- Public information systems addressing a wide audience of mixed abilities and computer experience should be kept very simple. This is often difficult to reconcile with depth and complexity of content.
- Interactive programs should include some form of concept map or index, providing an indication of how much material has been included and the best way to access it quickly. This is important, because, as compared to traditional media, multimedia programs do not offer a clear indication of what is there to explore.
- When providing additional information for the more interested users, it is more effective to offer it in layers, keeping the interface simple and intuitive. Broad-ranging and information-rich applications require even more attention to evaluation, the structuring and layering of information, and the provision of concept maps, indexes, clear navigation and searching tools. These would prevent new users becoming intimidated by cluttered screens and, at the same time, they allow more interested visitors to navigate easily in greater depth.

- Important messages and content information need to be repeated in different ways throughout the interactive program and not be concentrated in the first few screens alone because visitors are likely to spend the first few minutes exploring the interface of the application and not pay particular attention to the subject content. For this reason, the main interactive features, buttons, and special effects will work more effectively when presented in the beginning, so that users can experience them and become familiar with their functions.

- If the function of navigation buttons is not immediately clear, there should be a part of the program set aside for users to test and learn what all the buttons do. The names for buttons should be chosen carefully so as to offer a clear indication of their function, especially for the benefit of users not familiar with computer terminology. Adding titles to button icons will assist communication.

- Metaphors from the real world can be used very effectively to communicate messages (e.g. the metaphor of a library or a book shelf for organizing literary sources or bibliography, and the floorplan of a gallery or museum for connecting and grouping images of different objects). Badly chosen or ill-implemented metaphors, however, can have the opposite effect. The use of metaphors must be considered carefully and tested with the users, whereas designers should also remain aware that some metaphors might have a short life-span.

- Quizzes and games can be incorporated in the application, since they are attractive to both young and old visitors. These can be used to make links to information presented in the program and repeat in a playful way messages presented previously.

- The use of sound must be thought out very carefully in a public gallery, because it can be disruptive. Used sparingly, however, it can reinforce actions and offer useful feedback to users, e.g. to indicate when an operation has been successfully completed. In some cases, it can also offer information which cannot be provided otherwise, e.g. the pronunciation of specific words.

- The use of video is demanding on software and hardware, as well as requiring special programming and design skills. It should be used only when it offers additional information which cannot be communicated in other ways, and it should always be provided with an 'escape' option.

- When introducing an electronic evaluation form into the program, great care needs to be exercised over its implementation, because it can disrupt communication seriously and disorientate users. Formative testing can explore whether introducing it as a game, making it optional or voluntary, offering a warning, or placing it at the end of the interaction, will have a positive effect. If used, it should always be accompanied by an easy 'escape' route, because users may be intensely irritated by their main exploration being interrupted by an invitation to evaluate what they have seen.

- It is very effective to program the system so that it records information about individual users' profiles, their type of navigation and the choices made. Apart from its usefulness for evaluation, this information can then be used by the program to present customized information in accordance with that user's profile and history of interaction.

Guidelines for navigation through multimedia programs

- The concept map or index provided should have active links to all the items listed so that these can be accessed directly. In addition, it is more effective when it indicates the user's present position, past moves, and available paths.
- Linear navigation through the program should be supported, as a number of visitors are likely to prefer it. Designers should always provide a form of 'Next' and 'Back' buttons and also consider providing an electronic 'guided tour'.
- At the same time, they should exploit the power of the medium and provide, at least in parts, a more flexible, open structure with multiple associative links and alternative ways of navigating for the benefit of more adventurous users or for those who have already become familiar with the application. A variety of options and navigation styles should be provided (though without sacrificing ease of use), so as to cater for the diverse audiences of museums and the wide range of learning styles.
- When hypertext links are provided, they should be very carefully thought out. Designers should consider providing a warning to users about where the active link is likely to take them, as they can easily become confused and disorientated when navigating in this fashion.

Guidelines for museums considering multimedia production: 1. Before becoming involved with multimedia

- The Euesperides project made it clear that multimedia design is a laborious, time-consuming, and demanding task. Even with a low-cost, experimental application the investment of time and effort was still considerable. In that particular case, all the design and production work for it was included in a grant-assisted research project and it was possible to obtain additional sponsorship for part of the computer equipment used in the exhibition. In most cases, however, multimedia production involves considerable costs. When moving images and video are included these costs can rise dramatically, and they are factors which museums or relevant bodies need to take into serious consideration before embarking on any multimedia project.
- Until today the financial success of a cultural CD-ROM has been very rare (Herszberg 1997). Naturally, it needs to be taken into consideration that CD-ROMs can be physically detached and used outside the museum in different contexts from the multimedia program studied here. Furthermore, this research study did not deal with the commercial viability of museum multimedia products. Museums planning to enter the field of electronic publishing and multimedia production, should first consider carefully their preliminary feasibility and marketing studies.

Guidelines for museums: 2. Collecting the material

- Museum staff planning to undertake similar experiments should not underestimate the time and effort involved in collecting the material and researching the content. Several aspects of multimedia production (from programming to user interface design) can be successfully undertaken outside the museum by specialists collaborating with the staff, but deciding about the content of the application and selecting the relevant material requires the experience and knowledge of curators, collection managers, or other subject specialists. For this reason, it may be more efficient to select as the subject of the program an area which has already been well researched and published, with an abundance of good quality material. Plenty of time should be allowed in the planning for evaluating the available material and for assessing its potential for communicating messages, aesthetic value, suitability for digitization, educational impact, and relevance to the national curriculum.

- If considering the inclusion of material drawn from outside the museum or organization, additional time – together with appropriate financial provision – needs to be allowed for communications with external institutions or individuals and for negotiating copyright issues. Contributors and rights need to be acknowledged in the program and the relevant objects, media, or information must be presented accurately.

- The level of information which the proposed multimedia applications will provide should be carefully considered. In the case of the Euesperides project, the majority of visitors were satisfied with a program which included a wealth of information and covered a broad range of topics. Although in other circumstances extended coverage of several topics might not be appropriate, the use of expensive hardware and software for applications with limited range and shallow level of information, in general, does not take full advantage of multimedia's potential or address a wide spectrum of the public. Interactive applications often inspire heightened interest and curiosity, which they should then be able to satisfy.

- Capturing cultural information and its meaning on computers is a very complex process, as the simple acquisition of data – the mass of detailed information – does not in itself convey the content. In most cases, the current utilization of information technology presents data rather than the information content, and thus fails to enlighten or teach anything. Museum professionals, especially curators and collection managers, need to understand what the users want to see – for what they are asking. We need to overcome our fascination with the technology and the mass of data which we can process with computers, and we must not fail to recognize that 'the reduction of information humans necessarily do without technical help, is not only a loss, but a deep intellectual process to find out what is relevant, what is worth being taught, what we should learn' (Doerr 1996). On the other hand, the free association of data through a computer screen can potentially assist in a synthesis of cultural puzzles, and the construction of a holistic picture from rudimentary fragments of information.

- When preparing the content, it is useful for museum staff to keep in mind that visitors are very interested in information about people and their lives and are often assisted by the personalization of otherwise bare facts. Additionally, humour, when used with discretion in a particular application, can be a very powerful and effective way to communicate ideas.

Guidelines for museums: 3. During the design process

- The design of cultural multimedia is inherently an act of interpretation and communication. Even when multimedia production is commissioned outside, the museum staff must be closely involved so as to ensure that the choices made are those of their institution and that the messages communicated are those intended.
- There is a danger of multimedia programs being presented as absolute truth or the only authoritative interpretation. The technology can be used, instead, in a more powerful and liberating way to make available alternative views, set out dispassionately fascinating problems, and admit doubt and uncertainty when it exists.
- The design of multimedia is a very creative process, requiring imagination and a wide range of skills. Although for practical reasons all production stages of the Euesperides program had to be carried out by one person, it became very clear throughout the design process that these programs should ideally be the product of team work. For the design of successful educational and interpretative applications a balance needs to be struck between the technical requirements, the artistic presentation, and the content. It is debatable who can best meet the requirements asked of this new type of multi-talented professional. In my personal opinion, for any successful undertaking in cultural multimedia, it is necessary for both museum professionals and subject specialists to have an understanding of the technology and an ability to reach a public beyond their peers, and for the computer experts to be enthusiastic about museums and understand their educational role and special character.
- For many museums the decision to use interactive multimedia involves creating partnerships with other museums, universities, and cultural organizations, as well as interacting with the commercial world of production companies and technology consultants, often in different countries. This tendency will probably increase in the future, and can prove very useful, but only so long as humanists and museum staff keep an open mind about the benefits to be derived from the new technology, together with a dose of healthy scepticism about the exaggerated claims made of it and wariness of the pitfalls involved. Keeping in touch with new developments, accumulated experience, constant research, and careful evaluation can help them to make informed decisions.
- A larger body of knowledge needs to be built up before we can generalize about the characteristics of users of museum computer interactives. The profile of the users of the Euesperides prototype indicated that the common belief about the attraction of the medium being mainly for young children and male computer enthusiasts is not always confirmed by real research and observation, and any decision to incorporate interactive programs in an exhibition does not necessarily exclude a large section of its audience.
- It is important not to design these programs in a gender-specific way. The Euesperides study showed that female and male visitors were equally likely to use the computer program. The expansion of the use of computers in society is diminishing any differences in their use and exposure as between the sexes. Designers of

multimedia programs need to be careful that the language, metaphors, and icons used are not excluding female users.

Guidelines for museums: 4. Integrating multimedia in the exhibition

• The attraction of interactivity should not be underestimated when preparing exhibitions, especially when this is implemented at an advanced level, with a system which encourages user input, offers customized information according to the characteristics of different users, and incorporates computer simulation and role-playing metaphors. This human–computer mode of communication, endowed with the ability for visitors to select from a rich store of material which particularly interests them, and choose the way it is presented, is one of the particular features of multimedia which cannot be offered by more traditional means of museum presentation.

• The use of intuitive and user-friendly interface devices and hardware which reduce any technophobic predilections of visitors is likely to provide better communication to the real information content, even if the first few minutes of interaction have to be devoted to exploring the interface.

• Despite the attraction of the medium, the average time visitors will spend with a multimedia program in a public gallery is still likely to be under 10 minutes. In the case of the Euesperides project, it was between 3.7 and 7.7 minutes on average (2.2 to 5.6 minutes median time). Having said that, it cannot be excluded that a more advanced computer program, or a topic more attractive and accessible to a wide audience, might significantly increase the period of interaction.

• Multimedia applications have particular strengths for archaeological displays. Their ability to provide an idea of the original context of the objects on display, as well as an explanation of archaeological work itself, were particularly attractive to the public in the exhibition on Euesperides. Visitors greatly appreciate graphics, photographs and video-clips of where and how the objects were found; visual information on other archaeological features which cannot be displayed in the gallery, such as buildings, earth works, and town plans; information on how these were made and used, e.g. how pottery or bronze statues were made; reconstructions and models prepared by the excavators, alternative interpretations; and explanations of concepts like stratigraphy and the grid method. Interactivity can also be used to invite active participation by the users, by placing them, on-screen, in the excavator's role in a simulated archaeological trench. Some of these ideas are applicable to other museum presentation methods as well, but multimedia can combine these features in a particularly effective way.

• The ability of the system to accommodate group interaction needs to be seriously considered. Museum professionals need to investigate the rapid developments of the technology in this direction (wall-size displays, 'slave' monitors, hand-held devices, visitor-aware interfaces) and the possibilities for extending the human–computer communication to include more than one visitor and thus accommodate the social character of the museum experience.

- Exhibition designers face a particularly demanding task when designing programs which expect visitors to observe or relate the physical exhibits *simultaneously* with what is displayed on screen. Extensive planning and testing is necessary for this direct linking to succeed.
- The computer should not be chosen as the sole medium for communicating messages. There will always be a section of the public, even if it is small, which is not attracted to computer programs and disapproves of their use in exhibitions. Exhibition designers should also strive to provide computer-free spaces for undistracted recollection, contemplation or discussion.

After the opening of the exhibition: the importance of summative evaluation

In any evaluation study the identification of appropriate criteria is vital. Although these always depend on the scope and purpose of the specific study and the aims of the multimedia program, it is important to combine criteria about:

- the user interface and presentation;
- the structure and navigation;
- the programming;
- the content;
- the integration with exhibition/museum display; and
- overall impressions and effect on visitors.

The experience gained from this project has also been helpful for evaluating the evaluation tools. Used on their own, none of them would have offered sufficient evidence for understanding the complex experience of the museum visit and how it is affected by the presence of the computer station. In combination, however, they illuminated different aspects of a multi-faceted phenomenon. For any museum evaluation the choice of specific methodological techniques depends on the questions to be investigated. What can be suggested in general, however, is that a combination of different methods should be used when evaluating the effectiveness of these programs in cultural and educational settings. The experience from the Euesperides project has highlighted the importance of conducting evaluation research of this type in the natural environment, or if this is not practicable, in a naturalistic environment, closely resembling that in which the application will finally be placed. In-depth evaluation studies of cultural multimedia need to take into account the specific character and atmosphere of the museum or exhibition under study, as well as the physical, social, and personal contexts of its visitors, since all these factors affect the way in which visitors will interact with the computer program (Falk and Dierking 1992).

Beyond Euesperides: a wider perspective of museum multimedia

The findings of this study have shown that one type of computer interactive attracted and engaged visitors in Oxford and enhanced their experience of the specific archaeological exhibition. Under different conditions, in a different setting, and with different material, multimedia interactives might not have been appropriate or effective. Before making the decision to use multimedia interactives, museums need to consider carefully whether this medium is the one best suited to the task in hand, taking into account the technical, financial, aesthetic, and pedagogical implications.

Multimedia applications are just another tool for presenting and interpreting objects and ideas. Museum professionals need to become familiar with its strengths and weaknesses, so as to control uncritical enthusiasm as well as technophobic resistance. In any museum presentation, the emphasis has to be on the message, not the medium. However, the experience from the Euesperides project and other findings are showing that the power and attraction of the medium are very impressive and can in certain circumstances be effective in attracting visitors to receive the message successfully.

Despite the constant activity and developments of the last decade, the potential of this technology in the cultural sector has not yet been fully realized, and the emphasis should be directed towards deeper understanding and research. The leading role needs to be given to the museums and humanities sector, rather than to computer science which can only play a supporting role in this path of exploration of how culture is perceived through a computer screen. Closer collaboration between content specialists, program designers and educators can play an important role in this direction. Furthermore, systematic testing and rigorous investigation, as the Euesperides research study has shown, can help to make interactive multimedia effective interpretation tools which enrich the experience of museum audiences, both real and 'virtual'. I hope that the findings and observations generated here will be of general use in the creation of powerful and attractive applications that assist the understanding of objects and the communication of ideas.

References

Allison, D.K. and Gwaltney, T. (1991) How people use electronic interactives: information age – people, information and technology. In *Proceedings of the First International Conference on Hypermedia and Interactivity in Museums (ICHIM '91)*, ed. D. Bearman, pp. 62–73. Archives and Museum Informatics, Pittsburgh, PA.

Bearman, D. (1995) Hands-on: a snapshot of the evolution of interactive multimedia. In *Hands on Hypermedia and Interactivity in Museums, Vol. 2. ICHIM '95/MCN '95 (2)*, ed. D. Bearman, pp. i–ii. (Conference Proceedings). Archives and Museum Informatics, Pittsburgh, PA.

Department of Trade and Industry (UK) (1997) *Moving into the Information Society: an International Benchmarking Study*. Report commissioned from Spectrum Strategy Consultants.

Dierking, L.D. and Falk, J.H. (1998) Audience and accessibility. In *The Virtual and the Real: Media in the Museum*, eds. S. Thomas and A. Mintz, pp. 57–70. American Association of Museums, Washington, DC.

Doering, Z.D., Pawluklewicz, J.D. and Bohling, K. (1989) *The Caribou Connection: Will People Stop, Look, and Question?* Smithsonian Institution, Washington, DC.

Doerr, M. (1996) In *Forum (ICHIM '95)*, Dallas, C. (moderator). Participants: Costis Dallas, Martin Doerr, Maria Economou, Spyros Michailidis, Xavier Perrot, Mitos, 3: 27–34 (in Greek).

Economou, M. (1993) Euesperides: a devastated site – a challenge for multimedia presentation. *Electronic Antiquity*, 1(4), ftp://FTP.utas.edu.au/departments/classics/antiquity/1,4-September1993/(04)Articles/

Economou, M. (1995) Quest for the golden apples of the Hesperides: Hypermedia design for an archaeological exhibition. In *Multimedia Computing and Museums – Selected Papers from the Third International Conference on Hypermedia and Interactivity in Museums (ICHIM '95/MCN '95)*, ed. D. Bearman, pp. 248–266. Archives and Museum Informatics, Pittsburgh, PA.

Economou, M. (1996) Designing and evaluating a museum multimedia application: The Euesperides project in Oxford. *Spectra*, 23 (4): 18–23.

Economou, M. (1997) The evaluation of a multimedia application for gallery interpretation – the Euesperides Project in Oxford, ICHIM '97. (Conference Proceedings) Paris, 3–5 September 1997. Archives and Museum Informatics, Pittsburgh, PA. pp. 46–54.

Falk, J.H. and Dierking, L.D. (1992) *The Museum Experience*. Whalesback Books, Washington, DC.

Giusti, E. (1994a) *Electronic Newspaper Evaluation*. American Museum of Natural History, 15 February.

Giusti, E. (1994b) *Hall of Human Biology and Evolution: Summative Evaluation*. American Museum of Natural History, 3 March.

Herszberg, L. (1997) *Le marché Des Produits Multimédia, ICHIM '97*. pp. 13–17 (Conference Proceedings) Paris, 3–5 September 1997. Archives & Museum Informatics, Pittsburgh, PA.

Hilke, D.D., Hennings, E. and Springuel, M. (1988) The impact of interactive computer software on visitors' experiences: a case study. *ILVS Review*, 1 (1): 34–49.

McManus, P. (1993) A survey of visitors' reactions to the interactive video programme 'Collectors in the South Pacific'. In *Gallery 33: A Visitor Study*, ed. J. Peirson Jones, pp. 74–114. Birmingham Museums and Art Gallery, Birmingham.

McNamara, P. (1986) Computers everywhere – but what happened to the research? *The Journal of Museum Education: Roundtable Reports*, 11 (1): 21–24.

Menninger, M. (1991) *An Evaluation Study of the Interactive Videodisc Program on Illuminated Manuscripts*. The J. Paul Getty Museum, May.

Raphling, B. (1994) An 'ideal' way to evaluate interactive computer programs. *Current Trends in Audience Research and Evaluation*, 8: 44–48.

Sharpe, E. (1983). *Touch-Screen Computers – an Experimental Orientation Device at the National Museum of American History*. Office of Public and Academic Programs, National Museum of American History, Smithsonian Institution.

Vickers, M., Gill, D. and Economou, M. (1994) Euesperides: the rescue of an excavation. *Libyan Studies*, 25: 125–136.

Chapter 39

A Survey on Digital Cultural Heritage Initiatives and Their Sustainability Concerns

Diane M. Zorich

Sustainability issues

Survey participants were asked about issues they faced in "achieving and maintaining sustainability" for their organizations or programs. While the questions were asked separately to draw out distinctions between becoming sustainable and continuing to remain so, it soon became apparent that there were no such distinctions. The issues discussed in response to both questions overlapped considerably. Furthermore, many of the organizations participating in this survey have not yet reached a sustainable state (as one interviewee quipped, they "have hovered on the brink of sustainability" since their founding), making questions about "maintaining sustainability" irrelevant. For these reasons, issues that compromise "achieving and maintaining sustainability" are presented here as one. They are presented in the order of frequency in which they were cited.

The economy

The current economic downturn was a near-universal lament among survey participants. It is affecting all areas of these organizations' operations: endowment value (and income) is decreasing; memberships are declining as a result of budget cutbacks at member institutions; dues cannot be increased because members are feeling a financial pinch; enrollments in revenue-generating programs such as conferences and workshops are lower; and fund raising is more difficult because foundation endowments

Source: *A Survey on Digital Cultural Heritage Initiatives and Their Sustainability Concerns*, Washington DC: Council on Library and Information Resources, 2003, pp. 22–32.

are doing poorly and corporations are tightening their belts. Participants detected a "cooling" in all markets, but felt it was especially acute in the education sector.

Digital cultural heritage initiatives (DCHIs) that are collaborative or consortial ventures noted that large organizations, which are usually the stalwart members of these projects, can no longer participate as readily as they did in the past. Many felt that new consortial projects are going to be very difficult to start up at this time. DCHIs transitioning from startups to established projects are also finding it is a risky time to change business models to reflect their more mature organizational status.

Another sobering effect of the economic downturn is its impact on creative endeavors in the digital cultural heritage arena. Collaborative efforts to produce networked, community-wide cultural resources have stopped dead in their tracks, and few new efforts are being initiated. Moreover, new program development *within* DCHIs has slowed substantially. Some organizations are holding back because they are concerned about launching a new program in uncertain fiscal times, while others have sustained across-the-board budget cuts that make new program development impossible (except at the expense of an existing program). The apparent moratorium on new digital projects will affect research and development in humanities computing and will slow the pace of placing cultural content online. The long-term impact of this is difficult to determine, but it comes at an inopportune moment – namely, a time when more people are looking for, and expecting to find, scholarly and cultural information online.

Funding and foundations

Many survey participants expressed concern about the effect that the current market situation will have over the next several years, even if the economy improves overnight. Many of the DCHIs felt they could "ride out" one bad year, but they would find it very difficult to continue if the economic downturn continued. In anticipation of a hard road ahead, DCHIs that rely heavily on foundation support are exploring ways to diversify their funding base, although many admit they are not certain how to do this. Income diversification takes time; substantial planning must be done before one can reap results. DCHIs that have not yet started planning are particularly at risk.

Other factors are at work in the funding arena. Chief among these is an alarming trend among foundations to discontinue their arts programs. These changes mean less foundation support is on the horizon, even when the economic climate improves. Some survey participants felt this trend was a clarion call to the community to start proactively "growing" future funders who could make up for this loss.

Survey participants were critical of foundation funding strategies. They noted, for example, that foundations are very willing to give seed money for projects but unwilling to provide general operating support to sustain those projects once they are up and running. Foundations were also taken to task for being collections-driven, rather than user-driven, in their funding. They were thought to be "behind the curve" in understanding digital humanities projects and needs. The time between submitting a proposal and receiving a grant was deemed too long for digital projects. Respondents commented that this lag, which is particularly long with federal grants, precluded organizations from responding to an emerging digital initiative in a timely fashion.

Finally, there was a concern that DCHIs that rely heavily on grant support often find themselves being driven by where the money is rather than by their own strategic plans. While acknowledging the realities of grant and foundation funding, respondents stressed that DCHIs must strike a balance between funders' priorities and their own. In the end, foundation support, despite its uncertainties and demands, is a critical part of DCHIs' long-term plans, because the DCHIs own constituencies (particularly artists or scholars) can never be expected to support these initiatives on their own.

Operationalizing digital initiatives in cultural institutions

After funding and economic issues, the next perceived threat to sustainability was the failure of cultural organizations to treat digital cultural heritage projects as a permanent part of their overall institutional operations. There is a prevailing sense that cultural institutions rush toward digital project development without considering the burdens these projects will place on budgets, staff, and time. Digital initiatives are treated as "special projects" rather than as long-term programs. This shortsightedness leads to inadequate financial resources, the lack of a long-term plan for sustainability, and huge burdens on existing staff.

DCHIs have now existed for a decade or longer, and their prevalence is challenging institutional perceptions and management. Unfortunately, there are few signs that cultural institutions are making the necessary adjustments. Responding to fiscal pressures induced by the current economy, cultural institutions are ignoring the larger problem of how to properly manage digital projects. They are cutting back on training funds at a time when training is more critical than ever, and they are pressuring their staffs to take on digital projects without any additional resources.

Of particular concern was the burden these projects are placing on staff members who struggle to carry out their ongoing responsibilities while taking on demanding new ones. The ramifications of overwhelming workloads are being felt even outside individual institutions. For example, one DCHI representative noted that the organization's volunteer base was dwindling and blamed it directly on the local digital projects that its members now must administer in addition to their previous responsibilities. As a result of these growing demands, these members can no longer offer their time and expertise to their profession. In effect, digital projects are rendering professional colleagues less available to offer assistance at the very time when that assistance is more critical than ever because cultural institutions themselves are not providing it.

Clarifying organizational missions and domains

There is general agreement that the time is ripe for DCHIs to reassess and clarify their missions. The cultural community as a whole has become more engaged and knowledgeable about these projects, and DCHIs need to consider how they can best serve the community today. The Association for Computing in the Humanities (ACH), for example, has found that its mission – to encourage and support humanities computing – is not as critical as it once was, now that humanities computing is more prevalent. Consequently, ACH is reassessing its mission to more accurately address the contribution it can make in today's digital landscape.

The proliferation of DCHIs has led to considerable overlap in the missions of various organizations and created confusion in the cultural community. Several participants are finding that potential members, when considering where to place their limited resources, now ask how their organization differs from "organization XYZ." One interviewee disappointingly noted that his DCHI was now defining itself less by its mission and more by how it compares and contrasts with other groups. This situation makes it increasingly difficult for the DCHI to articulate its unique offerings and not stray from its intended purpose.

There also was a sense that the missions of some DCHIs are not fully developed or have not been adequately translated into objectives. As a result, too many DCHIs lurch from idea to idea without guiding principles. They emerge with great passion, but are unrealistic about their capability and capacity in terms of staff and economics. Some culling of these DCHIs was felt to be appropriate; however, this action will be difficult to undertake, because "passion" often persuades members and funders to keep assisting a DCHI as it struggles from one program to the next. One interviewee felt that stopgaps were needed to allow unsuccessful DCHIs to cease operations in a dignified manner; otherwise, these projects might linger for years, draining resources to no avail.

DCHIs also expressed concern about how they can explore new opportunities without losing focus and straying from their mission. Many new opportunities are moving precariously close to commercial ventures, jeopardizing the DCHIs' nonprofit purpose and status.

Finally, organizations that deal peripherally with DCHI issues wonder how they can enter the arena more directly. What niche can they fill? Without knowing "who does what" in the current environment, one institution expressed hesitancy in delving into this area because it was uncertain about the role it could play and the contributions it could make.

Standards, practices, and preservation

There are many community-wide standards issues that affect sustainability. Initiatives that rely on museum collections note that one of their greatest sustainability problems is rooted in the heterogeneous recording practices that plague the museum community. These different practices translate into huge editing and integration costs when trying to bring museum information into a digital library. Such costs cannot be minimized until the museum community reconciles its myriad local practices through content description and documentation standards.

Standards issues hamper other digital projects as well. The electronic publishing community is struggling with standards for e-books, numbering schemas for online books, and metadata and file format standards. Until these issues are resolved, projects currently under way risk obsolescence or require frequent, costly migrations.

A concern that crosscuts all sectors was the lack of digital preservation standards and policies, particularly the uncertainty about long-term preservation and archiving strategies for digital products. Preservation and archiving efforts are seen as dispersed, leading one participant to suggest that an "archiving czar" is needed to lead a coordinated effort in this area. At a local level, DCHIs are clearly becoming overwhelmed with archiving their digital resources, finding the time, storage space, and procedures and migration efforts extremely costly. No electronic archiving budgets exist for these projects; many DCHIs did not realize the costs would be so great as to require one.

Increasingly, DCHIs are looking at external sources for long-term preservation and archiving of their resources, realizing they cannot continue to do this on their own. But who should be the trusted repository? Libraries and publishers were the most frequently cited candidates, and DCHIs are hoping that these organizations will collect and sustain humanities computing projects once they reach a certain established state. The Institute for Advanced Technology in the Humanities (IATH) has taken a proactive stance on this front, initiating discussions with the University of Virginia Libraries and Press to examine how to collect and sustain born-digital humanities resources.

On a policy level, the lack of knowledge management policies and procedures in cultural institutions was cited as a threat to sustainability for any digital resource. In the absence of such policies, digital resources grow into unwieldy projects that are costly to manage.

Business models

DCHIs lack proven, sustainable business models. Despite a great deal of experimentation, no one is certain which models work. Even a model that appears successful in one circumstance may not work in another equivalent situation. For example, the decentralized model used by the CDP (Colorado Digitization Project) was rejected by H-Net, which started out with a distributed model but soon found that it needed a centralized system to ensure a technology hub for new projects, to control the technology infrastructure, and to streamline administration.

DCHIs faulted many business models for their failure to provide access to capital for the development of new projects. With no surplus funds to use for research and development, anything outside "business as usual" is not possible. Current business models also do not provide for funding of ongoing investment areas, such as electronic archiving.

Finally, there was a sense that the collaborative model for problem solving was becoming less viable for DCHIs in today's economic climate. No one is certain what the price point for this model is. How much are people willing to contribute to solve a problem collaboratively? DCHIs and their members consistently underestimate the costs of large-scale collaborative projects; as a result, collaborations unravel before any results can be achieved or find themselves scrambling for funding late in the process.

Growing pains

Transitional phases for DCHIs, such as when they are moving from startup or experimental projects to maturing programs, are periods of intense stress and high risk. A maturing program needs to develop a structure to permanently oversee and house its activities and to formalize governance for this new structure. Identifying the right structure and moving the organization into it is, as one interviewee described it, a "delicate task." It involves radically changing the way one does business while taking care not to alienate those who supported or nurtured the initiative to its current state.

Scale of growth is another issue. Some DCHIs rapidly exceed the resources their parent organizations can be expected to provide. H-Net is a vivid illustration of this: it is searching for a way to keep access available to all its digital content, which is growing at a phenomenal rate. Increased storage capacity, programming, and frequent migrations are necessary, and all three needs are very costly. Even H-Net's stable university environment cannot be expected to sustain this expanding resource. Alternative models of funding will need to be sought.

The growth phases of DCHIs and the costs at various stages of that growth have yet to be studied in depth. IATH has observed that its scholarly projects have a distinct life span that requires different resources (for example, funding and staff) and activities (for example, grant writing, planning, implementation) at different times. Each IATH project takes about six to eight years to become viable. At that point, the digital project needs to be turned over to another entity for continued sustainability and persistence as a scholarly resource. Further study is required to determine whether other digital projects follow this pattern.

The online intellectual property miasma

The issue of access to intellectual property (IP) is a formidable problem, especially for DCHIs that incorporate sound or images in their digital resources. Some DCHIs, such as AMICO (Art Museum Image Consortium), have worked out unique licensing arrangements with artists' rights agencies, but for many DCHIs the problems are more complicated. The prevailing sentiment among image rights holders is to license electronic rights to image resources on a renewable basis, but this presents an untenable situation for DCHIs. They cannot administer thousands of different licenses and, more broadly, they question what nonperpetual licenses mean for persistence in a resource where images are integrally tied to text.

A case in point is the archiving of image-laden publications in electronic archives. Prime among these are art and art history journals, art history doctoral dissertations, monographs, and *catalogues raisonnés*. At the time when these works were published in print, the publishers may or may not have cleared permission for electronic format archiving. Depending on the format of the archive and the copyright status of the images, rights may be in question. Authors, publishers, and archives now face the daunting task of assessing what new rights may need to be obtained – and, worse, they may need to track down all the original rights holders for both the artworks and the photographs of the artworks. In addition, if rights must be cleared, either the publisher or the electronic archive needs to consider how it will administer thousands of unique license arrangements, many with term limits and recurring costs built in. Few nonprofit organizations (publishers, museums, archives, authors) can manage a workload of this kind, yet having the images embedded in the text in the electronic archive is critical to art historical scholarship and to accurate archiving of the discipline's publications.

Another IP question arises with ownership of resources developed by a consortial group of volunteers. Who, for example, owns the IP in a digital standard that was developed by a community of volunteers? And what happens when that standard work moves into a formal initiative, where it becomes that initiative's primary asset? Few, if any, volunteer consortial initiatives have considered the IP implications or addressed them at the outset via formal written agreements. As a result, when these projects mature to the point where the initiative must be formalized, IP issues come to the fore and prove to be a significant impediment to the transition process. The TEI-C (Text Encoding Initiative Consortium) faced this predicament as it moved from a loose coalition of scholarly organizations and editors to a membership-only initiative whose primary asset is the TEI Guidelines.

Internal tensions

DCHIs housed in a larger parent organization report a constant tension between DCHIs and their parent institutions. Sometimes the tension is caused by the parent's apparent lack of interest in the special needs of the DCHI. Or there may be a lack of clarity about the role of the DCHI within the parent organization and with any of its affiliate units. At other times, the tension stems from competition over programs (the DCHI being but one of several programs within the parent organization), resource allocation, or financial management.

In large, established DCHIs, the tensions may crop up from the organization's own agenda. An interviewee from one DCHI cited a persistent pull between its dual roles as a provider of goods and services and as a collaborative venue or facilitator. Another source of tension is differences of opinion among board members or among the membership. These disagreements often arise when an organization debates whether it is the right time to move from volunteer to professional management. Finally, organizations experience internal tensions when determining asset allocation – what one interviewee described as "the constant question of where is the best place to put our financial resources."

For DCHIs whose core mission is the development of a scholarly resource, there were concerns about inevitable staff changes and what they mean for the initiative and its position within the parent organization. It is difficult to reconstitute the intellectual experience that brings digital scholarly resources together, and when a key staff member leaves, the dynamics of the project and its political position in a larger program may alter dramatically.

Increasing competition

The value of digital content is creating competition for DCHIs in both commercial and nonprofit venues. The commercial sector is realizing that even old content made available online can be valuable, and many feel it will not be long before commercial ventures directly compete with existing DCHI offerings. Within the nonprofit cultural community, some individuals noted that larger and better-financed nonprofits already are competing with smaller DCHIs.

The increase in numbers of DCHIs was seen as another form of competition. DCHIs that function as "umbrella organizations" for a particular cultural sector are finding that increasing numbers of smaller, single-purpose groups are now competing with them for members. Again, there was the call for culling and, where appropriate, integration of some of these groups. One interviewee, in discussing the proliferation of DCHIs, noted that the community is now in a "collaborative age of single-purpose groups."

Competition also comes from the ever-increasing number of freely available online resources. In such an information-rich environment, the value of any particular DCHI product is likely to be diluted.

Uncertain market needs

Many DCHIs burst on the scene with no knowledge of user interest levels or of what it would take to enlist collaborators and partners. They often found that their targeted constituency and partners were wary about the validity and benefit of their project or product. Publishers were cautious about participating in DCHIs involving electronic publishing because the intellectual property and economics of the endeavor were uncertain. Scholars were hesitant about creating born-digital monographs because their value in a tenure evaluation was unknown. Museums were slow to participate in standards collaborations or union database projects because they required the investment of huge amounts of resources but offered no immediate or near-term benefit.

Hand-in-hand with uncertain interest levels was an absence of knowledge about user needs. Many projects found their usage was much less than anticipated. Even now, most DCHIs feel that no one really understands what users want, despite a recent increase in studies of user needs.

International issues

As North American DCHIs grow, a few are entering the international arena, where they are confronted with new sustainability concerns. The most difficult issue is the various legal regimes that must be addressed when moving to an international stage. TEI-C, for example, discovered that the U.S. nonprofit model it wished to operate under had no equivalent in the European Union (EU). Consequently, in order for TEI-C to establish itself as a legal international organization, the group's bylaws and constitution had to be debated, rewritten, and vetted by international lawyers.

There are also philosophical differences between European and U.S./Canadian cultural organizations that pose problems for a DCHI wishing to conduct business in the EU. European museums, for example, have no tradition or precedent for paying for services that are not mandated by their government's cultural ministries. These ministries feel that any digital resource developed with even a partial contribution of public funds should be available free of charge. The European cultural community was described as "having an aversion to revenue generation," which makes it hard for North American DCHIs whose business models include this income source to make inroads in this community.

Board development

Some survey participants felt that DCHIs need to recruit more corporate board members, because such individuals can bring resources to these organizations that membership-based boards cannot. These individuals were not advocating for all-corporate boards, but rather boards that had some corporate representation. They saw this as a way of cultivating leaders in corporate America who could support their endeavors and as one strategy to "grow" funders at a time when the fund-raising horizon looks bleak.

Clarifying digital cultural heritage's value to society

DCHIs feel they have not clearly articulated their purposes and goals to the public. The often arcane and abstract nature of their projects makes it difficult to present them in a way that is compelling to a nonspecialist. Many believe this failure is directly responsible for the relatively poor attention these projects command in the funding world. An interviewee knowledgeable about the funding arena estimated that less than 13 percent of all funding in the United States is designated for the cultural sector, and funding targeted toward digital cultural heritage represents only a fraction of this amount.

One reason cited for the inability of DCHIs to demonstrate the importance of their efforts was the absence of supporting metrics that prove the value of their resources to a broader public. Another reason was that DCHIs fail to promote their efforts outside their own narrow community of users.

Straddling two worlds

Some DCHIs felt that lack of holistic thinking about the digital world created a broad impediment to sustainability. The prevailing mind-set was described as "paper first, digital second." While all DCHIs are hampered by the need to straddle the analog and digital worlds, these two worlds have distinctly different needs, and cultural organizations were accused of planning the digital through an analog lens.

Costs of technology resources

DCHIs routinely underestimated the costs and work involved in developing and maintaining technology resources. They are confronted with a pressing need for more capital for technology maintenance and growth.

Leadership changes

A few DCHIs felt leadership turnover presented significant problems in membership retention. If an institutional member had a newly appointed chief executive officer whose agenda did not match that of the DCHI, the institution would withdraw or fail to renew its membership. Others were less concerned about this issue, feeling it was a zero-sum proposition, because new leaders were just as likely to bring potential members to the DCHI as they were to take them away.

Hazards of being "first on the block"

The DCHIs that were among the earliest in their discipline to develop a digital cultural product or program often followed a circuitous path in the development and implementation of these projects. They "had to make it up as they went along," experimenting constantly and failing frequently. Inexperience with starting and managing digital projects led to redundancy and wrong choices that often complicated the DCHIs' efforts to achieve sustainability.

The political landscape

The current political climate was portrayed as unfavorable to the digital world and cultural heritage. One participant noted that the priorities of the current presidential administration make it hard to get national attention for any sort for cultural activities, and felt that this state of affairs would not change until a new administration was in place. Another pointed out that federal grant agencies are at constant risk of changes to their agendas because of administration politics and appointments, which makes for an unstable federal funding environment and uncertain support of cultural heritage initiatives.

Becoming a sustainable organization

Several DCHIs whose fiscal and programmatic health is stable or thriving offered their ideas on the critical components for sustainability in any organization. Key among these was the belief that all digital projects or programs should have well-defined, discrete objectives with measurable goals that can be used to determine success. For many, this takes the form of a separate business plan for every project undertaken.

Timing was a second critical factor. Developing a product or program when the market or community shows high interest and demand minimizes the risky proposition of trying to drum up support or sell the idea. Survey participants offered examples of organizations or projects with good ideas but bad timing; in most cases, the problem was the proverbial circumstance of being "ahead of one's time."

Continual organizational reassessment – defined as review, self-critique, and realignment – was deemed critical to ensuring that DCHIs deliver value over time. The core issues of these initiatives need to be "reengaged" over and over again to address new needs, demands, technology changes, and audiences. Failure to do this means a DCHI will eventually fall out of step with the evolution and changes in its environment.

Futures: priorities, approaches and aspirations

Introduction to Part Seven

Ross Parry

A TEMPTATION WHEN WRITING on modern technology is to stray into the precincts of futurology. The culture of computing in particular appears inextricably drawn to the future. Digital media (presenting itself both as a synecdoche of contemporariness, and a glimpse of tomorrow) can quickly fix an author's eye to the horizon – sometimes at the expense of historicisation or even reflective practice. In being drawn into asking *what will happen next*, the risk is to forget to ask (perhaps more answerable) questions of *why do we have this technology* and *how are we using it*. For this reason, much of the attention in this volume so far has been grounded intentionally in current practice and past experience.

Therefore, to finish our discussion, the last part of this volume acknowledges the role that some of these forward-facing discourses can have on this subject. At their least helpful, such discussions can be speculative musings. Yet, at their most valuable and incisive, this writing can be both inspiring and influential – setting priorities and defining aspirations. The following chapters thus offer four perspectives on the future of digital heritage: philosophical; professional; strategic; and academic.

Tomislav Šola (in Chapter 40) imagines a new concept of museum (the 'total museum') that draws its inspiration from, and is intellectually underpinned by, the presence of digital technology. Here, more than just a tool, computing becomes a function and fundamental logic of the museum. Then, in Chapter 41, Manuel Castells challenges the international community of museum professionals to rise to the opportunities of an age defined by its valuing of information and information exchange. Here is a vision (a responsibility even) of museums as 'cultural connectors' for society, an institution potentially transformed by the agency and architecture of networked computing and multimedia. More cautiously and critically, Simon Knell (in Chapter 42) critiques some of the proposed future digital landscapes sponsored by governments. In a dissection of a number of key reports and strategy documents produced by the European Union, Knell extracts (and questions) assumptions about the role museums might have within a networked society. Surprisingly, the concepts Knell discovers appear to belong to an older, rather than a new, paradigm of collecting and museums. His worry is that the vision on offer is perhaps not visionary enough.

Fittingly, for a volume that as a whole has attempted to frame a new area of study, the final chapter then steps back and considers the subject of digital heritage itself. It charts the 'cultural turn' (the adoption of a raft of theoretical frameworks from cultural studies and sociology) within the subject of museum computing at the end of the twentieth-century, and the emergence of a more intellectually mature, more self-aware, and (in terms of its research funding and curricula) more formalised subject calling itself 'digital heritage'. The article calls for more subtle models of change and agency, as well as more nuanced debate – distancing itself from earlier discussions characterised by the binary nature of their advocate and sceptic discourse. It is a vision of an academically credible, methodologically robust and internationally visible subject area. A vision – indeed – epitomised in the collection of preceding chapters, and in the presence of this volume as a whole.

Chapter 40

Making the Total Museum Possible

Tomislav Šola

1. The practice and theory of IT (information technology) offer the final chance to form the general theory of heritage care and communication. This rising discipline derives its logical existence from the zone of resonances where museology, librarianship, and archives and records management meet.

Museology, or museum studies, as this theoretical body is called outside continental Europe, has gained the status of a scientific discipline from being a recognized subject at various universities. It is doubtful, however, whether it could endure the strains and affirm itself as a stable value. It is being created under the pressure of the century-long "status nascendi" of museology. It would be hard to imagine any science being formed upon the single institutional sector, upon the logic and detail of the museum working process. Its structure could hardly claim more than the status of a theory to a certain practice, which, indeed, might be its current position. Underlying science makes a true profession possible, being essential in creating its mission and its precise place among the various institutional mechanisms of society. Museology is no longer able to nurse ambitions that it is supposed to satisfy. Destined to the fight on the wrong ground it has to retreat to a theory describing the history, methods and procedures of a single although expanding institution. The same will happen to librarianship and archival studies.

The nature and the logic of IT apply so well to the entirety of the cultural heritage concept and the totality of heritage that its influence will have crucial consequences upon its further development. Each of the above-mentioned disciplines (their names and relations still rather diversely dealt with at different universities) has its own theoretical field with aspirations of reaching the coherence and standard of a science.

Source: *Essays on Museums and Their Theory*, Helsinki: Finish Museums Association, 1997, pp. 268–275.

In spite of a great effort the results are disputable, as all of them tend to stay firmly attached to the particularity of their related practices. The logic of the new technologies, including telematics and hypermedia, suggest, however, that there might be a higher level of possible resonances, of overlapping of interests where the central concept is heritage, and where practices still may differ, but leaving the common denominator obvious. What we should talk about is the totality of the human experience – the ways to select it, and convey it to the users of today (and tomorrow). The ethical implications (what and to whom) are so great that we rightly have the feeling of touching the very essence of human society.

What we seem to be finding there is a multidisciplinary body of knowledge being formed at the intersection between areas of interest of many disciplines, the zone where they all collect, analyse, store and distribute the collective memory as the complex human experience. The immense importance of simple questions like what, why, by whom, in whose name, for whom and, partly, how, is important as the answers tell us who we are and what we might become. Never before IT was this area of multidisciplinary resonance so obvious and so ready to be turned into a positive fact. Apart from accumulating a vast weight of messages, it creates this necessity to perceive memory as the raw material of wisdom, dictating the creation of a scientific discipline "in charge" of a huge field of heritage.

2. The IT call for new cohesion in the heritage field, networking and commonality of interests that might make those institutions a stronger partner in the social contract.

The museums in Europe, and to some extent in the States, will be facing a still stronger pressure on the part of the different levels of the administration, to give more for less, the introduction of performance indicators and the value-for-money approach being only obvious parts of the new requirements. An increasing pressure is coming from the corporate sector too, as they find this area an extremely subtle way of ensuring their place in people's minds. Museums and kindred institutions are social mechanisms and agents of the social contract in which their place is more or less clearly defined. But since society is a complex entity, larger and more subtle than the state, it may or may not be served by its own mechanisms to their full extent. Through IT museums, libraries and archives get a new powerful mechanism in their hands to explore their enormous potential and to achieve a subtle and unprecedented presence in the individual environment. Their mission defines the quality of their presence whereas their means define its reach. Using the immense capacity of IT is part of their responsibility towards the society that pays them.

The appearance of the heritage industry and heritage-oriented entertainment with its increasing need for credibility will call for new alliances, at least at the level of information sharing. Quite indirectly, the new technologies induce new motives for stronger connections between institutions, requiring sharing capacities and expenses. In some cases, be it the creation of a complex programme or its distribution, the new technologies involve physical linkages among the institutions involved. This, in its turn, might or even should produce unity of the profession under the same mission of bringing the quality experience needed for survival of identities from the past.

The inherited and developing diversity of institutions will, thanks to the possibility of virtual, informatic networking, become an integrated resource for data, information and messages. An informatic network obviates the necessity of physical changes to institutions as it adds a new level to their performance (through their cumulative capacity). Community and cohesion may just be a way to approach the challenge of the age of synthesis we are entering. It is quite curious that IT reinforces the point more clearly than any theoretical or practical proposal has so far. Synthesis is more than cross-reference and a practical tool for research or meaningful presentation. It is the way out of the labyrinth of specialized area of knowledge and an end to the incessant manipulation of laymen's interests.

What was obvious only at the level of knowing the positions of these traditional practical and theoretical areas, i.e. the shared interests in general, now becomes part of their survival model. Hypermedia bring the logic which forms their common basis and becomes the new language for them to share. At the very beginning of its syntax there was MacLuhan's warning that the new language would change the vision of the world – again the global concept that cannot be but shared.

3. IT: changing the professional mind, or new means for old ways of thinking? Can museums, archives and libraries remain the same?

Much too often one sees that new media, adding so enormously to the performance capacities of individuals and institutions, suffer from misuse. Neither the logic of their appearance nor the nature of the expression they suggest and contain is understood or applied according to the specific circumstances of different institutions. Seeing that new medium invested with the same traditional logic and the same philosophy as before is rather disappointing. In many situations, particularly in the countries lagging behind the main current of development, the new technologies are a symbolic appropriation of these developments or a disguise in a vain endeavour to follow the dynamic of change at least at the formal level. Thus they are repeating the same old practice using new means. If no research is practised in a certain institution, then having an information base created for that purpose is a waste of money or misguided priorities.

There is also a viability level for any technology, below which no investment pays off. Many museum collections are still manageable in a traditional way, unless they form part of an informatic network. The informatization of an unorganized whole cannot but contribute to chaos or existing divisions, making it less manageable and just an easy prey to ever-newer software and hardware packages. This is happening in most countries of the world and, again, especially in those that have little experience in new technologies. The whole of Eastern Europe suffers from the effect of this "short-cut philosophy", seeing technology as the content, not the tool. It was the same with the invention of museums. Once the physical remnants of disappearing culture were placed in the glass cases, the culture was proclaimed saved, only museological reformists realizing that the level and quality of involvement in the real life of its users are the measure of their effectiveness.

The new technologies are still much too incomprehensible to the majority of professionals, as they have trouble of going beyond the form and method. One should not blame producers of IT for not being able to induce enough understanding as they rarely know the subtleties of the museum mission. The profession itself has difficulties with that same understanding, thus endangering its own survival in the face of rising competition. We have still to wait for understanding of how to use, explore and advance IT, improving its own performance and influencing the development of the technologies themselves. The experiments, however, are extremely encouraging.

IT has become a legitimate part of what was formerly a closed institutional circle. The database is the virtual storage of a museum, a virtual library or archive, a source of information one can use in many ways from scientific research to enjoyment. It would be bad if IT imposed on and subordinated the traditional institutions to mere resources for its expansion. We should avoid the imposition of this new possibility, envisaging it rather as a missing part of the whole. An original object can convey itself best if encircled by an informatic aura, thus enabling the full use of its potential. The medium *is* the message, as McLuhan would claim, and no institution from the field of heritage will remain the same. New alliances will be formed for at least two reasons: first, they will be needed as a consequence of the logic of IT that unites their forces, and, secondly, they will have to defend themselves from the rising competition, be it the institutionalized IT or heritage-based entertainment.

4. Will IT transform the present heritage occupations into true professions? May we hope that a new amalgamated, integrated mega-profession will emerge if we recognize the new philosophy introduced by the informatics, hypermedia and inter-activity approach?

There seem to be enough arguments to claim that none of the jobs we know in the heritage field, be it the experts working in museums or the staff of heritage attractions, represent a true profession but an occupation. Even in museums, particularly in some countries of Europe, not to mention the undeveloped world, professional workers represent a scattered army, not even a guild. On the other hand the spreading configuration of heritage-based institutions and actions (besides archives and libraries) still functions very much as separate fields or even institutions. They all have difficulties in recognizing the sameness of their interests nor can they recognize their common mission in society. The new technologies already help museums to build a specific medium, one that obviously merges them with other institutions from the field of heritage care and communication, thus opening the possibility of one day forming a mega-profession consisting of a huge network composed of once completely separated institutional sectors. The logic of holistic, integral and multidisciplinary information, as suggested by IT, with complex, active messages must broaden professional concern and bring into its daily practice the consciousness of unity through the mission. The mission, defined upon moral principles and ethical choice, is the first condition for having a profession, which then becomes a powerful partner in any endeavour, able to acquire its autonomy and self-determination, able to act correctively upon society.

This mega-profession will not be traditionally organized and described but will represent a pulsating unity of common interest. The important thing is that we start to speak the same language, that we recognize what the quality of our product is, who our true bosses are and what the ultimate reason for our existence is.

The major task of this professional phalanx would be to ensure autonomy of action, so that financing does not directly influence the institutional philosophy and practical outcome.

5. Do we finally see the outlines of the total museum, the true cybernetic museum – an invention for the next millennium?

With hypermedia, telematics and the interactivity, all traditional limitations must fall, making possible museums without walls, curators outside museums, museum action and museum objects *in situ* and in use. The museum should be the way of appreciating the environment not only in its time–space but also its spiritual dimension. With the possibility of moving freely in the information space of the past and present (as the past in process), the utopia of the total museum comes closer and we advance towards the museum as part of everyday behaviour. Museums existed before they were turned into institutions and the amazing capacity of IT will bring back some of that completeness. To conserve, classify, combine and use memory is something humans always did. Having an endangered identity and wishing to reconstruct it, they needed, at one stage of history, extensions of their abilities. The museum was an answer. The global museum which dispenses any form of knowledge and the liberty to combine it in ever-new meanings is still better.

It is not only data or information but powerful sources of messages and knowledge that constitute the new configuration of responsibility. Dispensing such a powerful backup of stored knowledge and scientifically analysed experience will allow new museums to correct and interfere by offering their users insight and choice. Their subtle role, the role as a counter-active mechanism of society will increasingly demonstrate their cybernetic quality, making them one of the guiding mechanisms of modern society. This neurotic world, exposed to constant aggression, where power and greed have more and more sophisticated ways of oppression, desperately needs concerted action by all agents of society towards harmony and balance.

The heritage institutions, even when offering delectation more than knowledge, do help modern man to comprehend the past and present, to adjust to the changing reality by understanding its nature. IT places a powerful means in the hands of those whose implied mission is betterment of the world. It is towards this objective that we could imagine institutions using their autonomous status and the capacity for interpreting the powerful information storages they contain. What they should produce is information and knowledge, but also much more than that: *wisdom* is the logical consequence of their creative selection.

The total museum is a possibility very much helped in its feasibility by the existence of IT and the trans-institutional logic it implies. Informatic networking makes it still more obvious that a certain territory has to be appropriately covered by institutions, their extensions, outposts and regular actions. A clear professional philosophy, and a counter-active strategy as a regulatory mechanism of the given society/community allows the vision of a network of heritage action units as physical evidence of the cybernetic mission of heritage itself. The more we elaborate the subtle structure of the collective memory and make it accessible, the less we deal with institutions and more with conscience and way of living. Thus we may achieve the sensitivity needed for sustainable development and quality survival. Heritage institutions, be it museums or anything else, should find fulfilment in their role by constant deinstitutionalization, transforming themselves into patterns of altered behaviour. The omnipresent "museum" is perpetually recreated by the widespread new sensibility and awareness.

The total museum is thus created in cyberspace and in its counterpart of the human mind. The seeming virtuality of both aspects of this museum should not cause concern as it does not exclude traditional museum procedure. If correctly under-stood, hypermedia are pushing museums towards a profounder understanding of their proper nature, giving them simultaneously powerful means to cure most of the vices accumulated during the last century or two of their existence. Understanding of IT should break through most of the limits and barriers that made the museums' triumph in the last decades extremely fragile. The boom of museums proves only that the solution for endangered identities was sought with a weak partner. Given a chance, it offered the usual but more expensive product. Successful institutional survival may be found in the new marriage of the perplexed museum aristocrat and self-assured, entrepreneurial *bourgeoise* of IT. Knowing the groom well one feels tempted to ask the bride for merciful and compassionate understanding.

Chapter 41

Museums in the Information Era: cultural connectors of time and space

Manuel Castells

My aim here is to situate museums in the context of the cultural and technological changes of the information era.

It goes without saying that museums can be virtual, present on and through the Internet. It is obvious also that the Internet is a major means of communication and expression in our lives and in all areas of society, just as it is obvious that museums form a part of this. Virtual museums are more and more common, and the articulation between the real and the virtual, the physical and the symbolic is increasingly developing new cultural hybrids that generate the renewal of cultural communication in the world, using new forms of information and communications technology.

Consequently, I am not telling you anything particularly new, and you know these phenomena better than I do. That is why, when we talk nowadays about the partial virtuality of museums, we are doing nothing but confirming the technological and cultural practice which is becoming the rule – and not the exception – in the world of museums today.

My aim is to concentrate on a more fundamental issue: what capacity do museums have to intervene in the significant cultural contradiction that is emerging in the information era? This contradiction consists of the current alternative between, on the one hand, technological creativity and global cultural communication and, on the other hand, a strong tendency towards the individualisation of messages, the fragmentation of societies and a lack of shared codes of communication between particular identities. Put differently, on the one hand we see a network society, a society of hyper-communication emerging and on the other we see a rupture of communication between particular identities. If this situation continues, it could mean the end of society, for society is, first and foremost, a system of communication, plural and

Source: *ICOM News*, special issue vol. 54, no. 3, 2001, pp 4–7.

conflictual. If we do not communicate, we cannot live together, and if we cannot live together, there is no more society.

In homage to my original Cartesian training, I will first define the museum and culture, and then broach conceptually three features which I believe contribute to the division between global and individual communication. The development of cultural forms through the new electronic communications systems and the constitution of an electronic hypertext that leads to the fragmentation of sense, constitute the first feature. The emergence of a new type of temporality, that I call atemporal time, is the second feature. Lastly, the emergence of a new type of space, the space of flows that opposes and isolates the local from the global constitutes the third point. After analysing these three features and the problems raised by the new communications systems, I will present some examples of museological practice, to illustrate these ideas and the new role of museums in this cultural and technological context.

First, museums are cultural institutions, that is, systems for the storage, processing and transmission of potentially interactive cultural messages, in and for a determined social context. As for the term *culture*, I use it in the classical sociological and anthropological sense of a system of values and beliefs that inform the behaviour of people and that are articulated and expressed through social institutions.

The electronic hypertext and the fragmentation of sense

Let us now analyse the transformation of the technological systems through which cultural communication occurs and the emergence of a new type of culture that I call *real virtuality*. The basis of my empirical analysis is that a new system of communication is being organised in our societies, mainly through a multimedia system itself based on an electronic communications system. In other words, all means of communication can be linked up through the Internet, which makes for the socialisation of communication. The essential elements in the cultural expression of our society and its cultural experience are transmitted and linked up through an electronic hypertext in which figure television, radio, Internet, audio-visual systems, etc.

I call this culture *real virtuality* – not virtual reality as one usually says – because the concept of virtual reality implies that, on the one hand, there is a reality which is the truth, the reality which we live and, on the other hand, a virtual reality which is the reality of communication media and Internet, which we do not live. However, we receive most of our codes of cultural communication by electronic means. Much of our imaginary and our political and social practices are conditioned and organised by and through the electronic communications system. Consequently, a fundamental element, or even *the* fundamental element, of our society's cultural communication and transmission is carried out through this electronic hypertext. This is our reality and, consequently, reality is virtual and culture is a culture of real virtuality.

Here I would like to rectify a thesis developed in my book on the information era, to stress that different means of communication are not converging in the electronic system, they each retain their own specificity and particular form of expression: radio remains radio, television remains television and the Internet does not integrate everything.

The Internet has the effect of enabling us to connect selectively with different forms of cultural expression and different electronic communications systems and to assemble – according to what each of us desires, thinks or feels – different elements of this communications system, such that the hypertext lives in each of us. From these fragments we construct a specific and personalised communication system where elements from television, radio, Internet, the press and all other kinds of cultural expression cohabit. Thus, for every project we have, the Internet enables us to create a customised and internalised hypertext, whether we are an individual, a group or a culture.

Since every subject, whether individual or collective, constructs their own hypertext, there ensues a fragmentation of sense. Since each of us has his or her own text, the question becomes: how does this text communicate and articulate with the other texts produced by other subjects or cultures? How is communicability guaranteed? How can communicable codes exist? It is the same old problem in a new technological context: how can the communicability of cultural codes be assured in the context of the fragmentation of sense and cultural expression?

Generally, throughout history and even today, it is through shared experience that we learn to communicate and to translate our different systems of communication into each other: we live together, we understand what the other wants to say and we deduce codes of communication from this shared experience. However, we are in a situation where there is not only this fragmented, personalised hypertext, but social developments as a whole are tending towards the generalised individualisation of our lives, our social practices and our work, the fragmentation of social groups, and the generalisation of a private individualised perception separated from the common references of society – whether this concerns the crisis of political legitimation or our capacity to choose within mass communications systems. For, as we all know, mass communication belongs to the past and nowadays each of us selects his or her own communication systems. So, since shared experience is less and less shared, and we live in a society structurally destined to an ever-increasing individualisation of communication processes, we are witnessing the fragmentation of communication systems and of the codes of cultural communication existing between different individual and collective subjects.

Communication protocols and art

A possible response to this would be the search for what I call *cultural communication protocols*, an expression based on the computing term, *communication protocol*, that is to say, the system's capacity to translate from one code to another. What are these cultural communication protocols? History shows us the fundamental importance of the protocols that allow us to pass from one culture to another through the community, through human experience. It appears that art (in all its expressions) plays a key role in these protocols. Art has always been a tool for building bridges between people from different countries, cultures, of different gender, of different social class, ethnic group or position of power. Art has always been a protocol of communication capable of restoring the unity of human experience beyond oppression, differences and conflicts. The paintings that show powerful people in their human misery, the sculptures that represent oppressed people in their human dignity, the bridges that link the beauty of our environment with the inner hell of our psychology – as in Van Gogh's landscapes – are all mediating forms of expression that go beyond the inevitable suffering of life in order to express happiness, the meanings and feelings that unite us, and which make this planet, beyond its atrocities and conflicts, a shared one. More than ever, this is the role that art must play in a culture like ours, characterised structurally and technologically by the fragmentation of sense and the potential lack of codes of communication, a culture in which, paradoxically, the multiplicity of cultural expressions in reality decreases the capacity to share sense and, hence, to communicate.

The lack of communication and of common codes of communication is, in reality, a direct cause of alienation, in the specific sense that the other, the *alter*, becomes an expression of what cannot be communicated and, therefore, of what is not human, in a world where everyone speaks a different language based on a personalised hypertext, in a world of broken mirrors, made of texts that cannot be communicated. In this world, art, without having any institutionally assigned role, without trying to do anything special, but by the mere fact of being art, can become a communication protocol and a tool for social reconstruction. Art as an hybrid expression of physical and virtual materials in the present and the future can become an essential element in the building of bridges between the Net and the self. So this is my first point concerning the tendency to fragmentation and the possibility of reconstituting codes of communication.

Atemporal time and the time of the museum

The second element is the transformation of time. Culture and cultural expression are produced materially through an articulation in space developed through time. This development in time and space is how systems of cultural codes are constituted. What happens when time disintegrates and space is globalised?

Time disintegrates through the emergence in our society of what I call *atemporal time*. As we know, time, like everything else, is relative – both in society and in nature. The time of the industrial era, chronological time, sequential time, is disappearing in social practice. It is disappearing in two ways simultaneously: the compression of time and the destruction of time sequences due to this compression. This happens, for example, on the global financial markets that try to suppress time or reduce it to fractions of a second in order to perform huge investments and accelerate the movement of capital. Another example of time compression: developed countries with high levels of technology attempt to reduce the time-span of wars – which were previously of 100 years, then 100 months and more recently of 100 days or even 100 hours – using technological systems that inflict devastating damage to the enemy in just a few hours.

Time is compressed, it disappears, and this is why everything is accelerated. But how can we say that time is disappearing when we cannot stop looking at our watch? The reason is that we try to pack more and more activity into the same time-span. Consequently, we behave as the financial markets do, compressing time because we believe we have the technological ability to do so. Time then goes faster, but this acceleration is in fact a race to make chronology itself disappear through altering temporal sequences: instead of going from one to two, then to three and four, time goes directly from one to five and can then come back to two, breaking the sequence and hence chronological time as we know it. This break in temporal sequences is evident in society through such features as the disappearance of the concept of life stages. There is no longer childhood, adolescence, maturity, older people, each with their specific activities. At present, the sequence of people's lives is being totally transformed as regards what we can do at any specific time. For example, we can have children at different ages, in different ways, using different techniques and involving different relations between the sexes. Similarly, the professional career is no longer sequential and predictable. The time when one would be hired by a company and would progressively climb the ladder until retirement – a retirement as one would wish it – is a thing of the past. The life-cycle rhythm – whether biological or professional – has been profoundly transformed. The rhythm of cultural transmission takes place in an electronic atemporal hypertext in which history, the past and the present are all mixed together in the same sequence. That is why, when we destroy temporal sequences in our perception of culture, we also destroy chronological time. In other words, post-modern culture is a constant effort to make collages out of different cultural forms and different historical times that, consequently, break the cultural historical sequence.

This is the structural tendency which, from the subject's point of view, gives rise to a plurality of temporalities which each individual constructs. Time is not imposed on us; on the contrary, we build our own perception of time. But when historical and sequential perspectives are lost, the temporalities of each one of us become incommunicable. We therefore end up facing another gap: communication is out of step with the perception of time. Here again, communication protocols can be envisaged in our society, and museums can play a role in this.

Museums are repositories of temporality. They constitute an accumulated historical tradition or a projection into the future. They are thus an archive of human time, lived or to be lived, an archive of the future. Re-establishing temporalities in a long-term perspective is fundamental to a society in which communication, technological systems and social structures converge to destroy time by suppressing or compressing it, or arbitrarily altering time sequences. For instance, in the San Francisco area, where I lived for twenty-two years, a group of friends – Stewart Brand among them – has created the *Long Now Foundation* in an effort to re-establish the concept of millenary time. They have built a millenary clock with a hand which moves forwards every year and which chimes every one hundred years – and even more so every thousand years – and which is programmed for ten thousand years. A time museum, a library and a seminar series have been set up around this clock, to reintegrate into our society which destroys time, the perspective of where we come from, where we are going and the confirmation that we are indeed a millenary species. This is a direct, rather than metaphorical, example of the role that museological structures have to play. The big challenge is how to articulate the archives of the present and the projections of the future within the living experience of the present. For if there is no articulation here, and museums are merely archives and projections, they lose contact with life. They are mausoleums of culture and not means of communication. Hence museums, as reminders of temporality, must be capable of articulating living culture, the practice of the present, with cultural heritage, not only as far as art is concerned but also as regards human experience.

The space of flows and the built environment

I come now to my third point, which concerns the appearance of a new dominant space, which I call in my research the *space of flows*. It is the space in which the major activities of our society take place. For example, financial activity is carried out in physical places such as the stock exchanges of Madrid, Barcelona, Paris, Frankfurt, the City of London and Wall Street, where information is processed. But all these stock markets are connected through an electronic system, which is where decisions are really taken, money circulates and investments are really made.

All major economic and cultural activities are carried out through this connection between different places in the world. These places, along with others, form part of a space, a single hyper-space organised in electronic communication flows and rapid transport systems which join these places into a real network. These places are far more connected to this system than to their immediate environment, as the expression "Tokyo global city" suggests. Similarly, the main universities of the world are connected through an electronic communications system and therefore constitute elements of a global metacampus where science and technology are really concentrated. All the activities which are centrally and strategically important in our societies arise in this space of flows, whereas it is in the space of places, the space we have always known, the space of physical closeness that identity is constituted and experience expressed. This space will either become isolated and a refuge for particularisms or it will be subordinated to whatever occurs in that other hyper-space.

This situation issues in a dissociation between, on the one hand, global, cosmopolitan culture, based on the dominant networks of the space of flows, and, on the other hand, multiple, local identities based on particular codes drawn from local experience. As the archived tradition, for instance the museological tradition, becomes increasingly cosmopolitan, particular identities are forced to become standardised in order to circulate globally as commodities. But these specific identities do not recognise themselves in the global culture. Hence museum culture is divided between the culture of a global elite and, on the other hand, the affirmation of specific signs of identity. From this point of view, museums, far from being communication protocols, could emphasise this cultural affirmation which is incommunicable outside of its own system of reference and, consequently, could increase the cultural fragmentation of societies in our globalised world (leading to an opposition between network museums and museums of identity).

As regards spatial structures themselves, a new form of urbanisation has emerged. The information era and new technologies have not dissolved cities, as futurologists forecasted. On the contrary, we are in the most intensive phase of urbanisation known to human history. Over 50 per cent of the world's population is currently urban. The phenomenon is gaining momentum and it is predicted that, in approximately twenty-five years, two-thirds of humankind will live in cities. Cities will be of a new kind: they will be megacities, huge undifferentiated spatial extensions of nameless urban developments, juxtaposed agglomerations of different functions – residential spaces, shopping malls – situated along communication routes, motorways in North or South America, and increasingly rapid trains in Europe. In this extended urban space, there are, on the one hand, significant urban cultural centres and, on the other, vast stretches of territory without identity, nameless conurbations. Museums, which are powerful symbolic cultural institutions, tend to be associated with the dominant, central and significant space (even if there are also museums on the outskirts of cities – but these are in the minority). The problem we face is knowing to what extent museums can become architectural and urban forms capable of restoring signs of spatial identity to an undifferentiated conurbation. How and in what form can museums – not solely as contents but also as "containers" – become a new expression of the urban monument in a world desperately lacking in monuments, that is to say, in signs of spatial identity?

This transformation of space and this separation between the space of flows and the space of places leads to another fragmentation. On the one hand, global elites are integrated into a common system of reference and into a common system of communication while, on the other hand, local societies fragment into individual projects and specific communities. In order to overcome this separation between the articulated global dimension and the disarticulated local one, public spaces in cities have become essential elements for coexistence. These public spaces could be based around cultural institutions such as, among others, museums, whose role in the reconstruction of public space is increasingly important, as is evident today in various cities around the world.

Museums, cultural connectors of time and space

Essentially, then, how can compatible codes of communication – or, in my vocabulary, communication protocols – be created, and what form should they take, in a network society where communication is fragmented in the electronic hypertext, and where temporalities and forms of spatial coexistence are also fragmented? Can museums act as communication protocols in this society so lacking in communication? For the multidimensional transformations brought about by technology in the information era have led to connections being made on the global level and disconnection on the local, the destruction of a common temporal horizon and the emergence of a culture of virtual reality organised in an electronic hypertext, whose fragments are recombined individually into texts that are almost incommunicable. Our societies oscillate between instrumental hyper-communication and lack of expressive communication, between global cacophony and local individualisation.

In this context, museums can become communication protocols between different identities, by communicating art, science and human experience; and they can set themselves up as connectors of different temporalities, translating them into a common synchrony while maintaining a historical perspective. Lastly, they can connect up the global and local dimensions of identity, space and local society.

However, not every museum can do this. Only those which are capable of articulating virtual flows in a specific place – for communication and culture are global and virtual, but also require spatial markers; those which are capable of synthesising art, human experience and technology, creating new technological forms of communication protocols; those which are open to society and hence are not only archives but also educational and interactive institutions, which are anchored in a specific historical identity while also being open to present and future multicultural currents. Lastly, together with other cultural institutions, museums must be able to become not only repositories of heritage but also spaces of cultural innovation and centres of experimentation. One could say that they should play the same role in the field of cultural innovation as hospitals are currently playing in medical research.

The following are three new museums that are good examples – not models, for I am not in a position to judge – of the roles museums can play. The first is the Guggenheim Museum in Bilbao, Spain, that has contributed to the urban regeneration of a city and a society in crisis, as well as constructing a bridge between a strong local cultural identity and modernisation projects which have a global reference. The second museum is the New Tate Gallery in London, with its openness and its mix of temporalities, in other words, its capacity to link the present, the past and the future within a multicultural initiative.

The third museum, the San José Tech Museum, California, to which I am personally attached, re-establishes the connection between technology and culture. This museum, set in Silicon Valley, has succeeded in integrating state-of-the-art research and high-tech systems into the educative and leisure functions of the museum, in an environment where technological development raises fear and scepticism. This connection between technology and society is achieved, on the one hand, by the constant incorporation of technological innovations and, on the other, by involving children, since they are more open to innovation than adults and can transmit this capacity to communicate to society as a whole. This museum is also committed to exploring the global problems of humanity, particularly through awarding prizes, such as the technological innovation prize which rewards the most useful innovation for the good of humankind.

In conclusion, museums can become mausoleums of historical culture reserved for the pleasure of a global elite or they can respond to the challenge and become cultural connectors for a society which no longer knows how to communicate. In other words, museums can remain – as Josep Ramoneda, Director of the Barcelona Centre for Contemporary Culture put it – "museum pieces", or they can reinvent themselves as communication protocols for a new humankind.

Chapter 42

The Shape of Things to Come: museums in the technological landscape

Simon J. Knell

Introduction

Since the mid-1980s, museum directors have understood that the key to their success lies in how well they manage change within their organisations. The large political and economic swings of the final decades of that century demonstrated to museums in many parts of the world that they had no assurance of a future unless they could demonstrate strong and cost-effective, socially and politically endorsed, benefit. The history of museums demonstrates that this has always been so: the combination of precarious museum funding and continual change has led to erratic fortunes (Knell 1996, 2000, 2001, 2004).[1] Yet every generation has held optimistic beliefs about the future: 'We may fairly presume, that the most liberal support will be given to an Institution, so well calculated to promote the credit and advantage of the town, and the intellectual improvement of its inhabitants, not only in the present day but in future ages' (Whitby Literary and Philosophical Society 1826). In the present age, one such vision comes to us from Europe.[2] It pictures a world altered by technologies, but within which museums have a new and critical role. It is a vision worthy of closer attention as this future is destined to engulf us all, and with its cultural diversity, social complexity, established heritage and not inconsiderable investment in technological research, Europe's concerns and experiences are likely to be widely shared. It also provides an opportunity to ask questions about how a sector of society formulates a vision of the future, what makes this vision plausible and useful, and then what history tells us about its likelihood of coming to fruition.

Source: *Museum and Society*, vol. 1, no. 3, 2003, 132–146.

When culture becomes information

Museums, we are told by the European Commission (EC), are at a point of transition: a 'technology-driven mutation' in the evolution of 'cultural heritage institutions' will redefine the sector and blur institutional boundaries. As Bernard Smith, the Commission's Head of the Preservation and Enhancement of Cultural Heritage Unit, remarks:

> Europe's cultural and memory institutions are facing very rapid and dramatic transformations. These transformations are not only due to the use of increasingly sophisticated technologies, which becomes obsolete more and more rapidly, but also due to a re-examination of the role of modern public institutions in today's society and the related fast changing user demands. These trends affect all the functions of the modern cultural institution, from collection management and scholarly study through restoration and preservation to providing new forms of universal and dynamic access to their holdings. (European Commission 2002a: 6)

A revolution is at hand. The future of museums is, so it seems from these European developments, beginning to be shaped by the visionary apparatus of technocrats; by computer scientists who have, in the recent tradition of museum operation, been servants of the museum mission. The opportunities provided by technology have developed so rapidly and become so pervasive that these workers are beginning to emerge from their backroom documentation projects to join up with academic researchers from leading university computer science departments, in order to construct a roadmap that will take museums into the future.[3] Congregating around the flag of the Commission, these technologists are the inspiration and lifeblood of DigiCULT, the 'digital preservation and cultural content' domain of Europe's Information Society Technologies (IST) research programme. And their great achievement to date is in making cultural concerns a distinct component in this major research programme.[4]

Europe's wake-up call to the technological revolution, and its implications for world commerce, came with the publication of US Information Infrastructure Task Force's (USIIFT) *National Information Infrastructure: Agenda for Action* in September 1993. Vice President Al Gore had first backed the idea of an Information Superhighway in technology reforms introduced in 1991. In the intervening years there had been much lobbying to extend the Internet beyond the bounds of the research, defence and education communities (Malhotra et al. 1995). *Agenda for Action* did just this, and within months Gore and Secretary of Commerce, Ron Brown, were championing major communications reforms. Europe's own vision appeared in the following June, *Europe and the Global Information Society* (European Commission 2002a: 23; European Council 1994). The EC began to fund ICT research immediately, and this evolved through a number of subsequent research 'Frameworks' to become the multi-billion Euro IST programme, which acquired a keen interest in culture from 1998 (Fifth Framework). Further impetus came from the European Council meeting in Lisbon in 2000. Here a commitment was made to develop a 'knowledge-based economy' and in that year the action plan *eEurope 2002: An Information Society for All* was published, recommending action on coordination, sustainability and the enhancement of digital content. A move closer to realising this plan came with a meeting of experts the following year. This resulted in the 'Lund Principles' for the coordination of digitisation programmes (European Council 2001; European Commission 2002a: 44). On both sides of the Atlantic the drive was for economic prosperity and competitiveness, and consequently the private sector and marketplace have a significant developmental role. It is now a subject of global concern: the United Nations will begin a two-phase World Summit on the Information Society (WSIS) in Geneva in December 2003.[5]

Clearly, it is believed that an increasingly pervasive 'information society' will fundamentally alter everyday practices, and perhaps change the position of museums in society. With digitisation becoming the new watchword for access and preservation, the future for museums appears to be one of new spaces, new collections and new audiences, and rather different risks and opportunities. To prepare the sector for this future, the EC commissioned a 324 page report, *Technological Landscapes for Tomorrow's Cultural Economy: Unlocking the Value of Cultural Heritage* (European Commission 2002a), which suggests how the sector might confront this information revolution. However, to understand this vision and its implications for museums, one needs to look to earlier research which drew up a more holistic picture of the knowledge-based, information-driven, technological landscape that is destined to become the backdrop to European life. It was developed by the IST Advisory Group (ISTAG) and conceived of a world of 'Ambient Intelligence' (AmI):[6]

> People are surrounded by intelligent intuitive interfaces that are embedded in all kinds of objects and an environment that is capable of recognising and responding to the presence of different individuals in a seamless, unobtrusive and often invisible way. (Ducatel et al. 2001: 1)

In this world, the invented character Dimitrios is wearing a digital avatar of himself – a 'D-Me' or 'Digital Me' – which gathers data, and helps with communication and decision making. In some of the interactions the D-Me acts independently and multilingually, leaving the real Dimitrios to get on with his life (Ducatel et al. 2001: 5, 32–7). To create this kind of scenario, ISTAG considered the way technologies were developing but placed particular emphasis on human practices and needs. Technological innovation suggested that three major breakpoints lay on the road ahead: the standardisation of interfaces, which is already well advanced; developments in fuzzy matching techniques to spur on a massive growth in artificial intelligence applications; and the transition of technologies to nanoscale.

This big picture of a possible technological future has helped shape the major programme of technological (IST) research funded through the Sixth Framework, which began in 2003. Cultural heritage is a small but important 'plug-in' providing real-world content and context, and in a reflexive way this relationship is also projecting a vision of what our technologically mutated museums might look like. Perhaps unsurprisingly, the future lies not in the invention of the 'eMuseum' – a new type of museum to sit alongside ecomuseums, rural life museums, and so on – but in a reconceiving of the museum itself in a new world of opportunity. The challenge for the sector is huge, not just in terms of adapting or participating, but because notions of repository, evidence, authenticity, authority, preservation and access will have to change. This future may push museums more centrally into our lives or it could unleash yet more new competition into areas that were once the preserve of museums. Cultural assets (collections and sites) will continue to be key to our lives but in what form? Can digital heritage really replace the real and if so how? The World Wide Web has already blurred the boundary between exhibition and publication, and widespread museum digitisation programmes seem to push museums closer to becoming libraries. Is the distinctive role of museums challenged by this future? Will museums be reconceived, hybridised or merely altered?

A roadmap of the present for the future

Technological Landscapes, the authors tell us, is 'a roadmap for action in the years to come ... a reasonable view of how the cultural landscape will unfold' (European Commission 2002a: 31). As such it presents a linear vision in which 'cultural heritage institutions' are destined to engage with a succession of new technologies. Since billions of Euros are being put into making the ISTAG vision, or something like it, a reality, the roadmap is better described as an architectural blueprint, a plan for conducting a campaign to make it so. But the very notion of a roadmap for the sector raises all kinds of questions about the contemporary world which shapes these visions, for although it talks in the language of the future this map is very much made from components of the present; inevitably, it addresses contemporary concerns and needs, as it cannot know future ones. It is also a plan built on the political power of education and technology in modern society. It must also make assumptions about the values of culture (though it is admirably aware of how these have changed in the last ten years) and how they can be enhanced by technology; but clearly the technological drive which is implicit in this document is beyond question, since this is the very motive for the report. There are aspirations here which are reminiscent of those of nearly two centuries ago when the modern museum movement was founded:

> Today, the volume of material to be digitised is the most pressing digitisation issue, and related to that, the need to select. With growing scale, the nature of object digitisation changes considerably and poses problems to cultural institutions that are not yet solved, such as mass digitisation, integration of metadata at the point of digitisation, the internal transfer and storage of huge amounts of data and, of course, the exploding costs related to all these tasks. Volume and scale of future digitisation highlight the need for automated processes and integration of object digitisation into the overall workflow within cultural heritage institutions. (European Commission 2002a: 16)

There is a sense of urgency and imperative here which has the hallmarks of an early nineteenth-century manifesto to build a collection and a museum. These earlier museum makers had no experience of large-scale collecting or of what a museum might become and could only learn the realities after they had built their vision.

Modern digital collection makers seem to have the same relationship to their project. Initially, the museum founders saw the collecting programme as being as finite as the natural world, and collected against a specific and evolving intellectual framework. Indeed, they too were creating a pervasive new technology, offering previously unseen access to ordered knowledge built upon the act of gathering. The technological leap was no less remarkable:

> Eminent metropolitan geologists, such as Roderick Murchison, looking to the provinces and particularly to the North, saw the emergence of a valuable provincial network of institutions peopled by knowledgeable curators, and containing collections ordered according to the latest stratigraphic principles. One no longer needed to rely upon raw data in the field in order to discern local geology. A scientific traveller could simply compare the museums of Whitby and Scarborough with similar institutions in Bath and Bristol. Together they formed an index to the geology of England. (Knell 2000: 75)

Geology was one of the first modern disciplines to fully realise the museum as a research, reference and networked technology. And because geologists were simultaneously establishing the intellectual framework for their science, and establishing museums as a cornerstone technology of that science, they overcame the problems of interoperability.

Initially, they thought the museum was capable of concretising their actions, beliefs and values; that they really were creating a finite resource. However, they soon came to understand the error of their thinking: 'no-one, who has not experienced it, can form an adequate conception of the labour of reducing into system and method the chaos of a newly-established museum, into which contributions are unceasingly flowing, and where there is as yet no adequate provision made for placing them away' (Jelly 1833: 118; Knell 2000: 93). The continued need to exploit the full range of social practices, which were the lifeblood of the museum, meant that collecting and donation would continue, and new intellectual fashions would be sought. It wasn't that the museum founders were bad planners, unsophisticated or lacked vision, but they had created a cultural institution which inevitably reshaped society and altered social practices, and which could not itself avoid being reshaped by those altered practices as well as by more general external change. The new technologically enhanced museums being developed today have the same relationship to society and the future.

The Gore–Brown vision of the future demonstrates the difficulties of prediction against a background of constant social change:

> Imagine you had a device that combined a telephone, a TV, a camcorder, and a personal computer. No matter where you went or what time it was, your child could see you and talk to you, you could watch a replay of your team's last game, you could browse the latest additions to the library, or you could find the best prices in town on groceries, furniture, clothes – whatever you needed. (USIIFT 1993)

Remarkably, in just ten years, this vision seems to have come to fruition. Nearly all of these things are now possible using technologies. But should we be surprised at this? Just over a decade ago, technology companies were lobbying for access to the Superhighway, and they almost certainly had in mind the kinds of devices discussed in *Agenda for Action*. However, where this vision seems less secure is in its forecast use of these technologies. The camera phone and the phone-mp3 player are not pervasive gadgets but niche products. While it can be argued that it is only a matter of time until these technologies come together, at present the preference remains for particular tools to do particular jobs well. This may also be the case in the future. So, in many respects, the Gore–Brown vision may be as wrong as it is right, though of course all open-ended predictions of the future have time on their side. It should also be noted that this vision had, more than anything, a political purpose: to shake up the social, economic and regulatory frameworks so as to make possible a technological future. In this regard it was highly successful and has led to remarkable technological change. Yet while technologies present us with a range of *possibilities*, which are configured in the visionary's dream of a new world, the market and the consumer determine an *actuality* much closer to the everyday. This is not to suggest that everyday practices cannot be fundamentally altered by technological change, but rather to say that societies operate through embedded cultural practices which are not so easily displaced. So while technologists accurately forecast that media would come together as multi-media, we still watch films, read books, play games, and engage with the Web like we would a vast reference book: the transformation is subtle, sometimes altering the medium without making huge changes to practices. This subtlety of difference across time and space is familiar to historians and cultural geographers; it is what we should expect of the future.

The recent history of the technologies marketplace reveals how this disparity between dream and reality has caused many a visionary to come unstuck: the bursting of the dotcom balloon in 2000 was accompanied by the collapse of the mobile phone and PC markets. 'There was this belief that everything to do with telecoms, media, software was going to be the next Microsoft. And everybody felt they had to join in.'[7] In the marketplace, the iterative nature of technological development can add a further impediment to the technological dream. When confronted by so many competing products and services, wider society seems increasingly disinclined to adopt new technologies simply for the sake of fashion. If a tool seems to do the job well, then it is not updated until technologies have advanced sufficiently to make the leap essential or highly worthwhile. In 2004, low-tech texting remains the most used mobile phone technology and ringtone sales the most profitable phone-related market, while new sales of phones and contracts remain depressed. Did anyone, in 1993, think the technological revolution would lead to such mundanity? Of course, they only needed to look at television to understand how the high ideals of public broadcasting became altered in the increasingly liberated world of popular culture, entrepreneurship and market choice. At the public interface with developing technologies, it is the youth market which has the greatest concentration of disposable income and the greatest need to follow fashion, and thus the mobile phone develops on the back of products and services entirely coloured by the perceived needs of that audience. The technological leap to camera phones with their high resolution colour screens, for example, has been achieved by convincing the young that they extend the possibilities for 'eyeing up' or 'ogling'. The answer to questions about the future, then, lies just as much in the marketplace as it does in technological possibilities: the market is a powerful modifier of ideas; it is the reality check for technological dreams. So if the D-Me world is likely to arrive, will it do so on the back of impressive cultural resources or by locating a niche in the world of fashionable youth?

Despite market experiences, technological innovation continues to inspire optimism: *Technological Landscapes*, for example, was written at a time of great uncertainty but yet remains buoyant and confident. It was in this rather depressed technological environment that the Sixth Framework IST programme also made its bid for political support. It had three essential qualities to make it worthy of patronage. The first was plausibility: technological innovation is iterative and reasonably predictable, and because of this it involves fewer risks. The second was social and economic relevance: westernised society has long headed in the direction of greater technological innovation and thus has associated with it huge potential markets. The EC's own research also suggested that technologies were being replaced on a two to five year cycle, causing major problems for business (European Commission 2002a: 15). Thirdly, the plan is built around a vision which suggests a better future.

However, many of the promises of this new technological future have already been realised in one form or another – we are in an iteration – and the contrast between it and now does not seem as great as it was in 1993 when Gore was speaking to an audience still using MS-DOS. The modern desktop PC, for example, has capabilities beyond the needs of most applications. Technologies are part way through this revolution and they no longer offer the promise of the entirely new so much as the enhanced. It is when technological development gets to this stage that the market seems to put developers under pressure.

It is in business and manufacture – which can be both producers and users – where the sting of technological change is most sorely felt in profit margins. Were most museums involved in a competitive 'cultural economy' akin to the world of manufacture (as *Technological Landscapes*, with its rather too vague notion of 'cultural heritage institutions', implies), the situation would be different but this is not currently the case. As users of technologies, most museums are rather closer to the domestic user. Some may develop systems on a larger scale but the majority will rely upon mainstream technologies with a few bespoke enhancements (such as collection databases). They must make decisions based upon their powers to upgrade and migrate content, but constrained budgets restrict those choices. Fortunately the domestic market seems ready to take up opportunities which are also of great use to museums, such as Wi-Fi. This keeps technologies inexpensive and user-friendly.

What technologists have come to understand is that technologies are not taken up if content is inadequate (hence the rise of texting and the failure of WAP).[8] Future online services require a critical mass of quality content, and the proven popularity of museums on the Web suggests a natural way forward. Certainly there is a relationship of mutual benefit here between those who wish to develop new technological solutions and the content-holding institutions who wish to develop new audiences. And as cultural materials in museums, libraries and archives are traditionally available 'free', they also present a relatively unproblematic resource into which to tap. This relationship has given the

DigiCULT initiative a certain prestige and political weight, but it has also had the benefit of bringing computer scientists into contact with the complex realities of modern museum values of integrity, authenticity, authority and so on, and a whole host of relativities from the humanities. These are notions critical to the development of 'intelligent heritage' and an inclusive 'knowledge-based society'.

The problem for this group, however, is that it must frequently deal with all-embracing concepts, such as the 'cultural heritage institution', which have no real-world basis. The European view tends to focus at this macro level, one of national governments and national museums, and although it calls for support for smaller organisations, the fact is that it is a vision built out of the experiences of a heterogeneous assemblage of larger institutions. In contrast, it is Europe's long-established cultural diversity which gives it great cultural advantage but which is also its greatest impediment to integrated thinking. The repeated assertion, for example, that 'In the Information Society, in the long run, only the digital will survive in the memory of a nation as it is more readily available and accessible than analogue cultural heritage resources' (European Commission 2002a: 38, 45), is a product of this macro perspective. Clearly, cultural heritage is, as far as museums and tourist agencies are concerned, valued primarily for its materiality. Similarly, in a related publication discussing digital objects and authenticity, there seems to be suggestion that cultural materials are entirely composed of easily extractable information (European Commission 2002b). The group discussing this problem, it turns out, was composed entirely of archivists and librarians, and consequently the fundamentally more complex issues of capturing material culture were not discussed (though clearly this is a component of library and archive holdings too).

Digital collecting – unshackling the museum

It is an information scientist's perspective, perhaps, which seems to encourage a belief that the thing only becomes real when it is captured in a digital form and converted into information. However, the next generation of museum professionals might decide that all collecting is a selective process of capturing information, and perhaps the step from collecting real objects to collecting digital representations of them is not too great. While we understand the museum as based around the collection of objects, the burden of collections leads to unwieldy and inflexible organisations unable to live within their means and frequently struggling to achieve their goals. The histories of collecting reveals how successive collection-holding institutions (learned societies, for example) have outgrown the need to collect, locating instead refined intellectual and educational goals which dispense with the need for a repository. The collection is then passed on to other organisations until it achieves the ultimate goal of a place in a publicly funded museum.

Collecting, as a core museum practice, is complex and largely beyond scientific rationalism. It is an act of authorship and connoisseurship. It is a physical interpretation of a set of circumstances or body of potential data. The object is thus placed within a collection according to an individual's beliefs. The power of authorship has been challenged in the museum over the last two decades but collecting is impossible without it. The question then arises, how are things altered if we collect digitally without retaining the real thing? The President of the Bundesarchiv, Germany, believes future archival collecting will be of two types: critically important material will be preserved; other important material will simply be captured in digital form (European Commission 2002b: 9; Knell 2004). In the museum, the photograph or drawing already acts as a surrogate for the real thing; a digital representation will be no different. It is here, where no object is preserved, that the power of authorship becomes critical, so as to ensure that the digital object is authoritative and legitimate, regardless of the inevitable bias and individualism that is found in all authored work. Disciplinary rules and frameworks will become even more important to the collecting exercise in this digital future as the possibilities for re-examination and a second opinion are strictly limited.

One often remarked-upon concern here is the increased potential for forgery in the digital collection. However, it is doubtful that a move to the digital will necessarily pose increased risks for museums in this regard. Forgers have already successfully managed to produce paper documents, which are indistinguishable from the historic examples they are purported to be, and inserted them into museum archives.[9] Similarly, fakers of Chinese ceramics read the scientific papers of the ceramics experts in order to make sure their fakes pass currently favoured authenticity tests (Tseng 2001). In some respects digital collections can be offered greater protection. In museums, a theft or contamination invariably results from the perpetrator gaining physical access to the collections and associated archives, often in the guise of a legitimate visitor. In the digital collection, no user need have access to the master image or record; access is always through the copy which can be destroyed after use (in other words, digital objects become accessible only through a form of publication). A further reduction of risk arises from keeping things (digital objects) which, unlike paintings and sculpture, have no value in the art and antiquities marketplace. In the digital realm of trusted repositories with effective security, perhaps the greater risk is the accidental misrepresentation of the object through errors of interpretation, capture or record making. Recently, technologists have suggested that a record of the processing history be kept, just as museums keep object history files to help them decide questions of authenticity (Research Libraries Group and Online Computer Library Center 2002).

Much of the discussion taking place in Europe has been dominated by librarians and archivists who are confronting the issues of 'born digital' material. This is apparent in the preferred language of Europe where there is frequent reference to 'digital preservation'. This phrase is only useful in the realm of easily transferable information. Museums' material concerns make 'digital preservation' an oxymoron.[10] Similar misunderstandings arise from referring to the museum's digital collection as a 'digital library'. The digital museum collection will be as impenetrable as the physical collection, as it is the result of the same complex disciplinary practices; the museum collection is not like a library, its collections are not so easily read. These important distinctions suggest that the digital futures for the museum and library are also destined to be distinctive.

While computer scientists understand that rapid technological change will require the migration of content onto successive new media, there are other issues that will undermine the permanent value of the digital museum resource. I shall mention just two. The first of these arises from the mutability of the meanings and understandings of collected things. To an audience who has experienced the stomach-churning cine-matography of the 2001 television series *Band of Brothers* or read Antony Beevor's, harrowing 1998, *Stalingrad*, the 1962 film *The Longest Day* will seem a lie and an inauthentic representation of the Second World War. *The Longest Day* crystallised the values and sensibilities of 1960s society; *Band of Brothers* responded to earlier war movie genres with a new desire for authenticity. In these examples, there are subtle differences in the medium and the way it was used. The medium of film changes, responding to a context (cinematography, technology, artistic innovation, fashion, aesthetics and so on), which both alters the author and the medium. And while these examples are constructed narrative tales, the digitised images of cultural objects and sites – although less obviously so – have the same qualities: they are shaped by the medium and by the hand of the author. These, in the same way, date stamp an inter-pretation, in a way that a kept object does not. While both image and object can be reinterpreted, the first is to always be read through the filter of the medium.

While medium of capture places constraints on the outcome, the possibilities for use can also shape the act of capture. This will be my second example. In the museum, the real object is capable of being an archival resource, a site of meaning making, a component in an educational programme, primary data in a research project and so on. But museums tend to select different objects for different jobs; a tattered item of costume might present a researcher with critical clues to an aspect of textile history but will never form an exhibit. The question, then, is how should the object be digitised to preserve its essential characteristics? When we digitise a 1960s miniskirt do we invest in high resolution capture of lining, buttons and zip or just capture an overview? The answer to these questions lies in intended use: if for research then the answer is 'yes', if for display then 'no'. The answer affects both the mode of capture and the quality of the dataset. The contrast between these two uses also extends to the degrees of liberality of interpretation and resolution that become captured in the image-record. This tends to give permanence to acts which only exist temporarily in the museum. The more liberal interpretation of educators and exhibitors exists only for the period of engagement with an audience, while the objects themselves exist for the most part in the world of the specialist where more pedantic forces of integrity and authenticity predominate and, ideally, associ-ate an arcane dataset with the object. Thus the digital object – for the purposes of efficiency – may be a further compromise.

Digitisation, then, offers new possibilities to collect but also new forms of constraint. But it may enable museums to reduce the quantities of objects they collect physically, without sacrificing much in the way of making a record, and thus mitigate some of the high costs of keeping which make collecting expensive. The costs of collecting (acquisition) itself will probably remain unaltered. And while the possi-bilities of storing vast quantities of data cheaply might cause computer scientists to fantasise about the new possibilities of digitally capturing whole archaeological sites and making them available online, such dreams – however real they become – are for the moment exercises in technology. The curator of the digital collection will need to learn new levels of restraint to counter the ease with which a digital camera can be used. Museum costume collections frequently contain the cast off clothes of curators and without a professional framework it would be all too easy for the next generation of costume curator to succumb to the world of the snapshot. So, although these new digital collections, internalised within machines, are remote, the tasks associated with them, as the EC recognises, remain essentially curatorial: objectification, classification, selection, ordering, keeping, exploitation and disposal. While technologists might feel they have the reins of technology, it will be specialists in culture, and more indirectly their political masters and their publics, who will decide which technologies to endorse.

New access, new income

Education, or rather 'the educational market', is seen as driving digitisation programmes (European Commission 2002a: 19). ISTAG clearly saw Ambient Intelligence as contributing significantly to future education and learning, although it was uncertain whether this would deinstitutionalise the sector or strengthen institutional players, such as universities and museums (Ducatel et al. 2001:15). Given the high costs of providing online learning, and the high level of institutional accountability and support required, together with the need for assurances of authority, integrity and authenticity, these institutional players have a strong future provided costs of delivery can be contained. Competition, however, will grow as ease of access increases, a development already seen in the distance education sector but which might also affect the museum provision of online resources to schools. The ISTAG vision suggests that learning will become more diverse, pervasive and accessible, and it places a high value on the increased possibilities of social learning, although technologies already have a proven track record in this area.[11]

Culture will have an increasingly important role as learning becomes more accessible and flexible. The European vision for the culture sector, frequently talks about the 'true value' of culture:

> Thus, European cultural heritage institutions not only hold the key to a treasure chest of unique resources, they also have the potential to turn the key to unlock the true value of our rich cultural heritage. (European Commission 2002a: 12)

Technological Landscapes is not just referring to the power of technologies here. The report repeatedly emphasises the importance of museums' intellectual capital which recognises not just the collections but more particularly the peculiar qualities of the workforce, and indeed those qualities that have been most under attack in the last decade. However, whether technology can unlock *the true* value is not beyond question. Television companies, such as the BBC, which hold archives of past programmes, have new opportunities to realise the commercial worth of their holdings (European Commission 2002a: 11). Closer to the world of museums, libraries may be able to reveal the true value of their collections by converting them to easily searchable e-texts. In contrast, the museum's digitised object is merely a compromise.

The power of the real thing is sacrificed, and replaced by access to an image, even if that image can be manipulated. Is this simply a form of interactive publication or can the digital exhibit really offer something akin to a museum experience? Certainly access is extended as online content is not constrained by the linearity of the publication, delicate objects become visible, the storehouse is opened up and collections become accessible to remote communities. Haptic technologies might even allow those communities to sense that they can hold and touch these virtual objects. Yet, no matter how one animates the digital object or captures it in high resolution, the object received through a monitor seems remote. Its materiality, its being, its existence as proof, as evidence – its true value – remains illusive. The emotive experience of seeing the real requires the real and no surrogate will do. A virtual visitor may understand the thing better and be better prepared to interpret it when they see it but they receive those peculiar attributes of real things only through real world engagement. Haptic technologies seem to offer the potential to dissolve this barrier and give a sense of a tangible reality, but, as yet, that sense of tangibility is simply an illusion no different from 3-D and '4-D' cinema.

If technologies do have the power to open up the true value of the museum object, then, from a contemporary museum perspective, they do so in a complementary fashion. In the comfort of our own homes, interacting with an online resource, a cup of coffee by our side, the chance of a successful learning outcome is heightened. In contrast, during a museum visit, we are not inclined to read labels and soon get tired of walking, standing and staring, and also tired, perhaps, of the curator's singular approach to interpretation. Increasingly, the real things before our eyes lose their appeal as we fight with our body's instincts for more active engagement and more comfortable surroundings. But yet, stood before that Gauguin, Braque or Picasso we see the brushstroke and the illusion of the glossy image of books and webs dissolves into a coarser and more craftsman-like object; the painting moves from art historical icon to something very clearly of human manufacture. This is what we can, in the right circumstances, learn in museums and it seeps in through our every pore provided we are equipped to interpret the object. Unfortunately, to achieve this level of appreciation one needs to go into the gallery with a little information – one cannot appreciate art or anything else museums collect and keep, simply by looking at it, or indeed by touching it. A little prior knowledge enhances the museum visit immeasurably. However, suppose the visitor takes her own D-me into the gallery as her own interpretative assistant. Perhaps now some of the pain is removed: she is given the information she wants and she is told what she should see. The leap to personalised interpretation is not that great – wireless technologies are already making available context-aware information to visitors – and this offers the greatest potential for turning museums into inclusive spaces.[12] The same personalisation of technology also means that networked online information resources can be interpreted according to local context: an English steam locomotive, for example, might be interpreted differently for the viewer in India, Poland or Bolivia. There are, of course, many contentious objects and interpretations in museums – *Enola Gay* being a famous example – which might respond well to this kind of personalised interpretation. However, there are also dangers in permitting the public to hear only what they want to hear, and museums will still want to control the thrust of the interpretation and present their audiences with challenges.

Technologies do open up the possibilities for sophisticated interpretation which can come close to challenging the object in terms of being the ultimate repository of knowledge. A prime example of this is Kevin Kiernan's *Electronic Beowulf*, a project begun in 1993 when its intentions were beyond the capabilities of contemporary technologies. A joint project of the British Library and the University of Kentucky, it was published as a CD-ROM at the end of that decade. High-resolution images of the eleventh-century manuscript were combined with a range of other resources which revealed hidden detail in the object. Although only a composite of images of the real thing, for most uses it is unquestionably more useful than the real thing. The CD-ROM contributes to the preservation of the real thing by leaving it undisturbed and in doing so it largely replaces it as the material culture at the heart of modern English studies.

The digital object, although having weaknesses when compared to the real, can also be manufactured to have superior strengths in terms of usability. In the same fashion, the digital exhibit might then compete successfully with the real experience. David Bearman, of Art Museums Image Consortium (AMICO), USA, sees interactivity as a competitive factor in these virtual environments: 'Those resources that you cannot manipulate will be perceived as second rate ... Moreover, the museums they come from will be perceived as second rate' (European Commission 2002a: 12). We know from the Web that the latest technologies can enhance the overall feel of a site – the semiotics of fashion and novelty may increase the effectiveness of communication – but we also know that quality of information, effective design, comprehensiveness, authority and so on make for reasons to visit. Interactivity was a museum buzzword in the 1970s and 1980s, but it too has been questioned, particularly with the rise of the modern edutainment centre where there is often no logical point to the interaction and no relationship between action and outcome, and where – because there are no real objects – intellectual depth is illusive. However, Bearman is right in flagging up inter-activity as a desirable addition to what is possible in the museum but it is not a concept that has any value in isolation. In the ultimate interactive digital environment – that of 3-D gaming – gamers judge the success of a game not simply in terms of interactivity but in strong narrative, plausibility, creativity, and intellectual and imaginative *depth*. These are also values of museums and of the arts in general. The key to communicative success lies not in the ability of an organisation to construct an educational experience or the technician to make things interactive, but in the intellectual creativity of the organisation. The *Beowulf* project was an act of scholarship but most critically one of considerable creativity and vision. To its great credit the EC's vision repeatedly values these qualities in museums – even if overplaying market possibilities: 'Cultural institu-tions should build on their strengths, authenticity, knowledge-based interpretation and contextualisation, and use new technologies to develop their own niche markets for licensed resources' (European Commission 2002a: 18).

The museum, then, is unlikely to be replaced by a digital entity, just as the electronic book has not eradicated the paper version, and the desktop PC never did create the paperless office. Technologies tend to sit side by side, each ideal for its own task; a view which perpetuates a belief that the future will continue to be one of specific tools for a specific jobs. *Technological Landscapes* frequently refers to cultural institutions becoming hybrids of the real and the digital. Indeed, this marriage might offer the possibility of reshaping a failing and unaffordable museum into a leaner centre for knowledge, expertise and learning. Let me use a traditional small town museum somewhere in the English midlands to explain what I mean. This museum is run by a small team, and occupies an old building with more space than it can maintain. The visitor experience consists of poorly interpreted objects of a kind seen in many local museums in Britain. They do little to stir the imagination. The staff are imaginative but there is clearly too little revenue funding here to really make a go of it, and in the glossy, connected, interactive, immersive, click-of-a-mouse world increasingly available to the majority of its visitors, its future looks bleak. But, on my last visit, there in the corner of one of the galleries, I noticed an old photograph of some ancient urns still in the ground. The picture was from the early twentieth century and showed a street not far away which was then being built. Next to the photograph was one of the pots. Here was an interpreted object, an object which speaks of the historical event of its discovery, and of the deep past it exposed. Suddenly this pot becomes real, concrete and powerful. Clearly, the objects here do still retain their powers but they lay behind a veil of neglected interpretation. Perhaps a better future for this museum is to slim down the enterprise, to put the most important material into compact storage, reduce the size of the buildings and physical holdings, and make a major commitment to online interpretation – narratives and reference materials – and digital collecting. A temporary exhibition space or two could be created and used to cycle themed and well-interpreted displays, support school visits and act as a venue for community activities. If these complementary resources are sold to schools, and better commercial use is made of the photographic archive – perhaps making attempts to exploit the genealogical market by marrying the content of collections with data in the local archive and local studies library – then perhaps a more sustainable and effective museum is created. The audience is extended, technologies and institutions are working in a complementary fashion, and the real, by this means, also gains a more secure future. In the process of responding to new opportunities to improve interpretation and access, the museum is fundamentally redefined and reborn.

The shape of things to come

Before the downturn in the dotcom market, there was much talk of the profits that could be made from online connectivity. There were global markets to be captured and the development of the Superhighway reflected an economic vision. As Bangemann put it, 'Citizens and users will benefit from a broader range of competing services.' The continuing decline in traditional museum revenue streams in many parts of the world has made museums cost aware and opportunity seeking. External pressure to change has pushed them into consultancy and turned their names into brands on everything from greetings cards to household paints. That *Technological Landscapes* detects this economic shift in thinking in the culture sector (European Commission 2002a: 133), and refers to the 'cultural economy', is partly because the European Community is first and foremost an economic partnership, and its research programmes are centred on achieving a healthy environment for market competitiveness. Though they aspire to independent financial solvency, museums rarely operate in a market where direct payment for services secures their funding. The economic value of museums is indirect: a pervasive influence on tourism, education, leisure and a liveable environment, which provides direct economic benefits for a range of businesses but not necessarily for the museums themselves. It is here where the economic benefits of museums are most felt that they remain least measurable or attributable. Contributions of this type, which most justify their economic cost, tend to depend on museums being situated in a specific place. In contrast, digital heritage is often about making resources ubiquitous: the virtual Louvre is available to everyone but it only reaps economic benefits if tourists are drawn to visit Paris. Smaller museums making their high quality exhibits available online could conceivably undermine the potential for visits by providing content which might satisfy the needs of potential visitors or reveal that this museum isn't for them. Without online access even the visitor who enters and leaves in revulsion is a click on the counter, a visitor figure to weigh against the cost of the museum.

It is unclear if museums will be able to generate an income from technologically enhancing their collections and interpretations, but Scottish Cultural Resources Network's (SCRAN) agglomeration of exclusive and enhanced resources may suggest a way ahead. With some £15 million in government pump-priming, SCRAN has rapidly developed a critical mass of digital resources which can be combined in a range of interpretive and educational contexts. Access for schools and individuals is via subscription. Museums benefit from having their digitisation activities externally funded, and preserve other rights. It is an excellent example of creative thinking which for the moment appears to have succeeded (Royan 2000; European Commission 2002a: 54, 123).[13] Yet, as *Technological Landscapes* detects, such enterprises, unless they find a unique niche, are at risk from the activities of 'spoilers' such as New York Public Library, the Library of Congress, and Massachusetts Institute of Technology who, as they receive their income from patronage and other sources, freely put material online. However, SCRAN, like other CultureNets around the world which have secured government funding (e.g. Scandinavia, Mexico, Latvia and Hungary), is now too fundamentally important to Scottish nationhood to be permitted to fail. Free access is, of course, a fundamental philosophical ingredient of the Web. It has also been a long-established belief of the museum and library fraternity.

Like CultureNet developments, the European Commission (EC) necessarily operates at the level of governments, yet culture tends to be locally grown and locally supported. It is built around a sense of identity whether dealing with the science of palaeontology, saving the local canal or reflecting the Scottish nation. Such local enterprises, and the institutions they spawn, put themselves first, and their involvement in collaborative exercises usually results from selfish or mutual concerns (rather than from altruism). For some twenty years museums have operated in this opportunistic way and they will continue to do so. Today, numerous opportunities lie in technologies, and museums will examine them as a means for improving services, achieving efficiencies and generating income. They recognise that involvement will have short-term benefits, but that in a year or two they will need to find some other source of income. By this means, and by exploiting their communities of practice (Wenger 2000; Wenger et al. 2002),[14] (and not inconsiderable government investment) museums have survived.

From a continental perspective, the EC sees a need for paternalistic actions by governments to ensure efficiency, sustainability and inclusion. While such strategic thinking should be met positively, the experiences of museums reveal relatively few sustained examples of strategic planning.[15] Individualism and localism, which create value in culture, are not so open to government control, but while these give the sector a certain strength they also undermine strategic desires for efficiency and sustainability (see European Commission 2002a:13, 43 for structural actions). It may be that strategy might develop only in supporting measures: CultureNet portals represent strategic attempts to bring together a range of resources in highly imaginative ways which also wave the national flag. Consequently, they have proven attractive to governments in terms of both funding and involvement. However, the cultural assets they configure arise out of more chaotic local circumstances.

Seventy years ago, HG Wells published *The Shape of Things to Come*, a novel in which the fictional Dr Philip Raven left to the author notes on 'a history of the future'. It forecast a second world war that would lead to the destruction of the world. Like other artistic visions, it was painted from the palette of his present, configuring a world that also owed much to his past. The actuality of the future echoed Wells' predictions but only in terms of a present successively reconfigured and revisited; for all his social awareness and experience of future predicting he did not describe a future that came to be. *Technological Landscapes* predicts the future using the same tools, it is a rich reflection of the present and inevitably aspects of the present will be inherited by the future, just as they were for Gore and Wells. In Wells' vision, the future landscape is one of remarkable underground cities imaginable in 1933; Ridley Scott's 1980s *Blade Runner* similarly sweeps aside the historic landscape but here constructs a future reflecting the pessimism of that decade. *Technological Landscapes* promises a futuristic landscape of pervasive technologies and arises from the irrepressible optimism of modern science. The revolution, however, is largely one for information and computer scientists who wish to turn the anarchic mass of digital information, currently available to the public, into an intelligent resource of 'semantically rich, adaptive information contexts' (European Commission 2002a: 105; 2003). If they succeed, then a revolution for museums may follow. Their attempts also mirror those of the world that gave birth to the modern museum. Nearly two centuries ago museums emerged from nothing to populate every major conurbation in provincial England. They did so in the timescale of present technological cycles – three to five years. However, it was not long before the circumstances which led to their emergence evaporated and museums then had to find other roles and purposes (Knell 2000: 285). Even today, museums are being born as *new* technologies for identity, communication, learning and social interaction (see, for example, Huang 1999: 249).

The role for museums in the information revolution which lies before them remains unclear. They will be fundamentally affected but their relationship to information is rather different from that of the library and archive; museums are places of authorship and constant reinvention. Museums will face up to this challenge in their usual opportunistic fashion: through institutional and personal adaptability; the pragmatic exploitation of opportunities which arise from change; and the use of long-established collaborative methods of working. *Technological Landscapes* is undoubtedly a rich and complex vision and one that must be welcomed. But it also conceals considerable diversity of provision: it is not a consensus view but a collection of inevitably personal interpretations. By concertinaing this diversity into the term 'cultural heritage institution', the roadmap loses some of its definition. It is as though the rivers, roads and railways on this map have all been coloured the same. For the most part the museum response to this technological revolution will not be strategic or, indeed, necessarily sustainable. It will be one of creativity, diversity, individualism and opportunism. This, at least, is what history tells us about the way museums managed change in the past and there is little reason to think that this won't also be true in the future.

Notes

1 I have reviewed the history of museum desires for the future in a number of publications, and also neglect and decline in 'Collection loss, cultural change and the second law of thermodynamics', presented at the Society for the History of Natural History Conference, *Lost, Stolen or Strayed: The Fate of Missing Natural History Collections*, Leiden, May 2001.

2 The subject for this paper arose from attending a DigiCULT event early in 2003. Here I found a community, distinct from that to be found in the world of museums and museum studies, planning the future of museums, libraries and archives. As someone interested in communities of practice and change in museums, this was clearly an interesting topic for a paper. Aspects of this paper were delivered at the international colloquium to launch *M Museos de México y del Mundo* at the National Museum of Anthropology in Mexico City and at the Museum Directors' Forum at the National Museum of History, Taipei in 2003. I am very grateful to Miguel Fernández Félix, Marco Barrera Bassols and Kuang-nan Huang for inviting me to speak at these events.

3 Seamus Ross, Humanities Advanced Technology and Information Institute, University of Glasgow, correctly expressed the view that this technological development requires the leadership of computer scientists rather than museum professionals (S. Ross on 'Digital preservation research opportunities' speaking at the European Commission IST Digital Culture workshop *Mapping the Future*, Luxembourg, 28 January 2003). But, as I suggest here, this technological leadership does not necessarily extend to the application of these technologies in museums and related organisations.

4 The DigiCULT websites contain a wealth of material: http://www.cordis.lu/ist/ka3/digicult/, http://www.cordis.lu/ist/directorate_e/digicult/index.htm and http://www.digicult.info/pages/ publications.php.

5 The second phase is in Tunisia in 2005. For WSIS, http://www.itu.int/wsis/ For European involvement: Communication from the European Commission to the Council, *Towards a Global Partnership in the Information Society: EU Perspective in the Context of the United Nations WSIS*, Brussels, 19.5.2003 COM(2003) 271 final.

6 For ISTAG reports see http://www.cordis.lu/ist/istag-reports.htm, and for the work of the group more generally see http://www.cordis.lu/ist/istag.htm.

7 Tony Dye, Investment Manager, Phillips and Drew, quoted by Mike Verdin, 'Dot. Com doomsters see more share falls', BBC News, 12 March 2002, http://news.bbc.co.uk/1/hi/ business/1854227.stm.

8   WAP, or wireless application protocol.
9   John Drewe famously contaminated the archives of the Tate Gallery and Victoria & Albert Museum in the 1990s in order to perpetrate a series of art frauds.
10 Paul Fiander makes this point in relation to the migration of the content of vinyl records onto CDs, and the consequent loss of the authentic (in European Commission 2002b: 12).
11 See, for example, the pioneering work of the Jason Project, http://www.jason project.org/. eSchoolnet provides European collaborative learning and was just one example in operation before this ISTAG report was published, http://news.eun.org/eun.org2/eun/en/ index_eschoolnet.html.
12 Tate Modern, London, piloted the use of portable wireless connected interactives in August 2002 but many museums are currently establishing wireless networks for the use of their visitors.
13 See also Technology Advisory Service for Images (TASI), 'SCRAN case study' at http://www.tasi.ac.uk/resources/scran.html.
14 European Commission (2002a: 80) suggests that cultural institutions 'adapt to the network logic' but clearly this has been something at the core of museum practice for more than two centuries.
15 A century of British reports, for example, failed to stimulate action: (Miers 1928; Markham 1938; Rosse 1963; Department of Education and Science 1973; Standing Commission on Museums and Galleries 1979; Resource 2001). In contrast, museums in Spain are currently moving towards an integrated service. At the same time, museums in France enter a more fragmented phase.

References

Department of Education and Science (1973) *Provincial Museums and Galleries*. London: HMSO.

Ducatel, K., Bogdanowicz, M., Scapolo, F., Leijten, J. and Burgelman, J.-C. (2001) *ISTAG: Scenarios for Ambient Intelligence in 2010*, ISTAG report, Brussels: European Commission, ftp://ftp.cordis.lu/pub/ist/docs/istagscenarios2010.pdf.

European Commission (2002a) *Technological Landscapes for Tomorrow's Cultural Economy: Unlocking the Value of Cultural Heritage*, DigiCULT Report, Luxembourg: Official Publications of European Communities, http://www.digicult.info/pages/report.php.

European Commission (2002b) *Integrity and Authenticity of Digital Cultural Heritage Objects*, DigiCULT thematic issue 1, http://www.digicult.info/downloads/thematic_issue_1_final.pdf.

European Commission (2003) *Towards a Semantic Web for Heritage Resources*, DigiCULT Thematic Issue 3, http://www.digicult.info/pages/Themiss.php.

European Council (1994) *Europe and the Global Information Society* (Bangemann Report), Brussels: European Council, http://www.medicif.org/Dig_library/ECdocs/reports/ Bangemann.htm.

European Council (2001) *European Content in Global Networks: Coordination Mechanisms for Digitisation Programmes* (Lund Principles), ftp://ftp.cordis.lu/pub/ist/docs/digicult/ lund_principles-en.pdf.

Huang, K.-N. (1999) *New Visions for Museums*, Taipei: National Museum of History.

J[elly], H. (1833) 'Biographical sketch: J.S. Miller', *Bath and Bristol Magazine or Western Miscellany*, 2: 111–22.

Kiernan, K.S. (1993) 'Digital preservation, restoration, and dissemination of medieval manuscripts', in A. Okerson (ed.) *Scholarly Publishing on the Electronic Networks, Proceedings of the Third Symposium*, http://www.uky.edu/ArtsSciences/English/Beowulf/eBeowulf/main.htm.

Knell, S.J. (1996) 'The roller-coaster of museum geology', in S.M. Pearce (ed.) *Exploring Science in Museums*, New Research in Museum Studies, London: Athlone, 29–56.

Knell, S.J. (2000) *The Culture of English Geology 1815–1851: A Science Revealed Through Its Collecting*, Aldershot: Ashgate.

Knell, S.J. (2001) 'Collecting, conservation and conservatism: late twentieth century changes in the culture of British geology', in D.R. Oldroyd, (ed.) *The Earth Inside and Out: Some Major Contributions to Geology in the Twentieth Century*, London: Geological Society, 329–51.

Knell, S.J. (2004) 'Altered values: searching for a new collecting', *Museums and the Future of Collecting*, Second Edition, Aldershot: Ashgate, 1–46.

Malhotra, Y., Al-Shehri, A. and Jones, J.J. (1995) 'National Information Infrastructure: myths, metaphors and realities', http://www.brint.com/papers/nii/.

Markham, S.F. (1938) *The Museums and Art Galleries of the British Isles*, Edinburgh: CUKT/Constable.

Miers, H.A. (1928) *A Report on the Public Museums of the British Isles*. Edinburgh: Constable.

Research Libraries Group and Online Computer Library Center (2002) *Trusted Digital Repositories: Attributes and Responsibilities*, Mountain View California: RLG, http://www.rlg.org/longterm/repositories.pdf.

Resource (2001) *Renaissance in the Regions: A New Vision for England's Museums*, London: Resource.

Rosse, Earle of (1963) *Survey of Provincial Museums and Galleries*, London: Standing Commission on Museums and Galleries, HMSO.

Royan, B. (2000) 'Scotland in Europe: SCRAN as a Maquette for the European Cultural Heritage Network', *Cultivate Interactive*, 1, http://www.cultivate-int.org/issue1/scran/.

Standing Commission on Museums and Galleries (1979) *Framework for a System of Museums*, London: HMSO.

Tseng, S. (2001) *The Art Market, Collectors and Art Museums in Taiwan since 1949*, unpublished Ph.D. thesis, Leicester: University of Leicester.

US Information Infrastructure Task Force (USIIFT) (1993) *National Information Infrastructure: Agenda for Action*, Washington, DC: National Commission on Libraries and Information Science. http://www.ibiblio.org/nii/toc.html.

Wenger E., McDermott, R.A. and Snyder, W. (2002) *Communities of Practice: A Guide to Managing Knowledge*, Boston: Harvard Business School Press.

Wenger, E. (2000) *Communities of Practice: Learning, Meaning and Identity*, Cambridge: Cambridge University Press.

Whitby Literary and Philosophical Society (1826) *Annual Report*, 3.

Chapter 43

Digital Heritage and the Rise of Theory in Museum Computing

Ross Parry

Introduction

The museologist Tomislav Šola warns us of something called the *technology trap*. This is what we fall into, he explains, when in the museum we pursue technology for its own sake. It is what catches us when we allow technology to become self-serving and we let ourselves be guided by it. Our defence against this, he suggests, is not just the 'know-how' of professional experience, but also (crucially) our critical, analytical apparatus. 'And that', he concludes, 'is theory' (Šola 1997: 225).

The following is about this relationship between technology, theory and the museum – more specifically how in the last decade we have seen writers and commentators, in an effort to avoid self-serving applications of technology in the museum, reaching for the critical apparatus to which Šola refers. The aim here is to acknowledge and chart the emergence of a subject now calling itself *digital heritage* (or sometimes *digital cultural heritage*), to consider where it has come from and in what form it might now progress. The rise of theory within the subject of museum studies is here contrasted with the more practical preoccupations of its sub-discipline, museum computing. The emergence of more sociological and theorised readings of museum computing are then highlighted (the *cultural turn* as it is termed here), alongside the co-ordinated expansion of research activity in this area. It is hoped that through this enquiry, we can begin to identify a number of approaches for the subject. In this regard, some challenges are suggested for digital heritage studies, including an engagement with the concept and management of change and also *technological determinism*, an acknowledgement of the agency of media, recognition of the relationship between old and new media, as well as the value of historical methodologies. The sub-text here is

Source: *Museum Management and Curatorship*, vol. 20, no. 4, 2005, pp. 333–348.

about legitimising this area as a scholarly discipline, and is about advocating to those who work within it the application of a critical rigour, as well as the benefits of using other disciplinary tools.

What is theory, and why should we use it?

When (like Šola) we talk about applying theory to our research, or to theorising our approaches, we mean applying a set of assumptions, terms and methods that together provide the rationalising framework within which informed discussion can function. The thing we call *theory* provides the ideas (the groundwork) upon which a critical approach can be predicated and built. These ideas may be epistemological or ontological in nature – in other words, about how we know, and about what we are. Or they may extend, perhaps, to how we conceive society, or the way meaning is made, or the value of representations. For museum studies, these may be assumptions related to the nature of museum learning, or approaches to museum historiography, or our understanding of the nature of museum space or, perhaps, the social role of the institution itself. Whatever the specific subject may be, it is by drawing upon the assumptions developed by theoreticians (by standing on the shoulders of giants) that we can aim to present a stronger foundation and a clearer starting point for our work.

Theory also equips us with a vocabulary – justified terms of reference – which can help us to articulate our subject with greater clarity and differentiation. Again, within museum studies, this control of language might affect whether we refer to, for instance, the *transmission* or *construction* of knowledge at work in museum learning (Durbin 1996), or whether we follow *effective* or *teleological* histories (Hooper-Greenhill 1992: 9–12), or whether the sector works with *impaired* visitors or *disabling* environments, or both (Delin 2003). In each case, it is theory and the terminology control that comes with it that informs and refines the language that each approach uses.

However, along with a set of assumptions and a vocabulary, theory can also signal priorities and stress associations within our research. To align ourselves to any given theory can frequently determine the direction and objectives of our work. A theory may determine (or at least strongly intimate) where a research project might begin, and even where it might aspire to end. For a scholar of museum studies, this might mean whether precedence should be given to tracing discourses back through an archive, observing and critiquing activities in a gallery, or questioning and interviewing visitors and professionals.

In short, theory should, ideally, provide a piece of analysis with an informed set of assumptions, a consistency and clarity of language, as well as a coherent method and rationale of working. To work in a theoretically informed way is to benefit from this depth, this precision and this logic. It is to work within a critical framework. Yet, and crucially, as much as theory is a lens we hold up to our subject, bringing it into focus (perhaps with more detail and exactitude), it is also, always, a compromise. For as with any lens, with this acuity must come the acceptance that what we see has been to some extent framed and filtered. To work with theory is to agree to abide by a set of rules, and to see the world in a certain way. Theory can give us acumen, but only within set parameters, and only in concordance with the assumptions that we are resolved to accept when we initially subscribe to that theory. This is our Faustian bargain with theory. We might usefully say, therefore, that theory is rigour, but always *conditional* rigour.

The rise of theory in museum studies

Over the last twenty years, the discipline of museum studies has benefited increasingly from applying this sort of theoretical rigour to its work. Museum studies has, in effect, become theorised.

For instance, by drawing upon (amongst others) Jean Baudrillard's comments on the nature of the *hyperreal*, and Marshall McLuhan's ideas on the *sensory bias* of culture, the work of writers such as Lumley (1988) became generously laced with theory. Likewise, Vergo's axiom that existing museology had thought 'too much about museum *methods*, and too little about the purposes of museums', was symptomatic (self-admittedly) of this same shift within the subject (Vergo 1989: 3). Similarly, it was the 'reflexive museology' and 'critical self-awareness' advocated by some contributors that Scaltsa (2001: 42) noted in an appraisal of a major international symposium entitled, significantly, *Museology Towards the 21st Century: Theory and Practice* that took place in Thessaloniki in 1997. To Scaltsa, and to contributors such as Grigoris Paschalidis, museology was now confronting and exploring the ideologies that permeated the design and content of exhibitions, the shape of collections, and policy-making within the museum. In this way the discipline had, Scaltsa argued, 'forged its theory'. However, highlighting the 'pertinence and rich theoretical potential of the museum as an analytical locus for anthropology, sociology and cultural studies', and showing how 'social and cultural theorising can illuminate many contemporary museum issues' (Macdonald 1996: 3), it was perhaps Macdonald and Fyfe's volume of essays published the same year as the Thessaloniki symposium that served as something of a touchstone for these approaches. Within it we see, typically, a practitioner such as Porter (1996) working reflectively with theory imported from literary criticism and cultural studies – her work as much a critique of the value of theoretical approaches within museum studies as it is a study of the representation of women in history museums.

However, within museum studies, the adoption of these new theoretical tools has been far from uniform. Sometimes conspicuous and sometimes implied, sometimes pervasive within a work but sometimes contained, theory continues to be deployed within museum studies in a variety of ways and with varying degrees of influence – not to mention cultural contexts. Here we remember the assertion of Bhatnagar (1999: 128) that museologists and museum professionals of the Indian sub-continent, for example, might not wish to 'follow blindly the concepts of New Museology', but instead might work to mould new models and concepts to suit the region's development.

In some cases, theory has come to shape and inspire a whole work, as when Hooper-Greenhill (1992: 9–12) uses Michel Foucault in her excavation of the genealogy of museums' construction of knowledge. Other times, several theories have dovetailed together to influence a thesis, as when Pearce (1995: 23–27) absorbs Saussurian semiotics and the writings of Baudrillard into her structural/linguistic analysis of collecting, or the way Viv Golding (2005) evokes both Hans George Gadamer and Black women theorists in her application of feminist-hermeneutics to the museum as 'frontier'. Elsewhere, the role of theory has been to provide key definitions or general concepts, as when Duncan (1995: 11) applies anthropologist Victor Turner's concept of 'liminality' to her discussions of the ritualised spaces of the art museum. At other times, theory has also come to be used simply as a specific precision tool for a particular aspect of a study. Consider, for instance, Fyfe (2003) and his reflections on the extent to which Pierre Bourdieu (specifically his notions of cultural capital and symbolic violence) might unlock our understanding of the relationship between art reproductions and museums, or the way Andrea Witcomb (2003: 38–41) introduces Michel de Certeau's notion of the *everyday* in her discussions of the public space of the museum.

Through this variety of approaches, the theorising of museum studies has continued as a productive and expanding project, unpacking and unpicking the museum concept, holding it up to inspection using a variety of critical approaches informed from a variety of disciplines. Museum studies today can be a deeply theorised discipline.

The dearth of theory in museum computing

The same, however, could not be said for *museum computing* – the body of work that takes information and communication technology (ICT) as its main focus. Though information science has had a guiding role to play within this literature (with its focus on the technological aspects of operation and standards), museum computing has only occasionally been exposed to the same rigours of theory enjoyed by the rest of museum studies.

Engagement by museum practitioners with informational technology theory and mass communication theory reaches back as far as the 1970s, and Roger Miles' work on rationalising approaches to exhibition design (Hooper-Greenhill 1995: 4–5). Subsequently, during the 1980s, George MacDonald integrated media theory into his discussions on the role and design of new museums (MacDonald 1992; MacDonald and Alsford 1989). Trained as an anthropologist and archaeologist, MacDonald turned with ease to the theoretical tools of cultural examination, most readily to media studies, and more specifically Marshall McLuhan. Within his study of the then new Canadian Museum of Civilisation, MacDonald's thoughts on entertainment and education (in short, that there is no difference), as well as his historicising of the theatrical and performance discourses of the museum, are all informed by McLuhan. It is McLuhan that MacDonald uses (actually via Šola) to decode the poetic and ritualised nature of museum communication. And, again, it is McLuhan who guides MacDonald's hand when describing the museum as information resource within the context of the 'Information Society'. What we see at play (excitingly) in MacDonald's oeuvre is a simultaneous theorising of museum computing and technologising of museology.

Occasionally, museum computing has become implicated in other theory-driven discussions – especially those concerned with surveying the state of museums in the new millennium. For instance, Hooper-Greenhill's notion of the *postmuseum* (the post-industrial adaptation of the modernist museum) is defined by her in part by the way it dissolves many of the existing notions of the museum as four-walled site. In building this thesis (with its advocacy for a cultural change within museums), she draws into her discussions and definitions of interpretive communities Ananda Mitra's work on diasporic websites, and the way that the Internet can constitute and construct a community of alienated and isolated individuals (Hooper-Greenhill 2000: 121 and 162). Likewise, within Hilde Hein's philosophical exploration into museum histories and museum futures, a similar evocation of new technology is made. As part of her discussion on the shift away from object centredness to a new emphasis on the promotion of experience, Hein uses a reference to virtual reality technology to focus her discussions on what is meant by 'real things'. Seen as a transfiguration of reality, rather than an imitation or replacement of it, and with visitors responding enthusiastically to 'real' interactive spectacles imagined in 'virtual space', she trails the emergence of 'virtually real experiences' within the museum (Hein 2000: vii–ix, 12, 66, 76–77, 151). Yet, for Hein, as with Hooper-Greenhill, these references to the influence of technology and new media are only marginal within a wider and more ambitious thesis. The theorising of museum computing is not the main aim for either author.

This is not so for an author such as Šola (1997), in whose work new technology is integrated intricately and explicitly. Šola argues that, to be active agents and contributors to culture and society, museums should confront the concept and practicalities of change. He suggests that museums might do this by first understanding their operation within a system of *cybernetics* – rationalised and controlled change, based on balancing *threat* with *counteractivity*. Furthermore, theory (as yet undefined but, he argues, something like *heritology* or *mnemosophy*) is also essential in catalysing this process – something to help develop more critical and questioning practitioners. For Šola, the role of ICT within this project of transformation appears to be twofold. First, ICT (and the 'age of the microprocessor') is seen as one of the defining forces changing society, and one of the threats to be counteracted by the museum. This may result, he argues, in the emergence of what he calls 'information-space museums', and might facilitate the creation of the 'total museum', a 'museum without walls' that permeates more deeply into everyday behaviour, with 'curators outside museums, museum action and museum objects in situ and in use'. Second, as the field of cybernetics deals with the control and communication processes in both animals and machines (and involves information processing systems, automation and information theory), ICT forms part of the stimulation and the fundamental logic for the science that Šola thinks will rationalise the model for change within the museum. He argues that the practice and theory of ICT offer the 'final chance to form the general theory of heritage care and communication' (Šola 1997: 173, 218, 268, 273). Whether digital media will actually permeate as deeply as this into theory, as it has into practice, remains tantalising conjecture. Though we may not agree with the full extent of Šola's scientific project (with its ambitious aspirations for a general theory within the subject), his theorising has, nevertheless, the desired catalytic effect of provoking debate and thought.

Yet, until recently, the work of writers such as Šola and MacDonald has largely been the exception. Instead, much of the literature and published research on museum computing has been project-orientated, written largely by museum professionals with a view to best practice and procurement, and it has generally been indisposed to placing new technology within a conspicuous and coherent theoretical context. It is not too controversial to say that, as a body of work, museum computing has not consistently been predicated on clear theoretical models.

One of the first (and in many ways most enduring) sustained works on museum computing was by Williams in 1987. Writing from the perspective of a registrar, Williams gives primacy to documentation within his study. A clear and helpful guide for museum practitioners, providing detail and specificity on software and hardware procurement, the intention was to offer practical advice for the first-time computer user on how to develop a computerised record system. A comparable tone and aim shaped *The MDA Guide to Computers in Museums* written by Gill (1996) almost a decade later. Again, the book targeted users with some or no knowledge of ICT, and (as with Williams) was intended as an introduction to computing, to procurement and software for documentation. Much like Sue Gordon's *Making the Internet Work for Museums* that appeared the same year (Gordon 1996), Gill gave primacy to best practice, substantiated through relevant contemporary case studies. As manuals, practical guides and comments on current practice, these studies were very successful and valuable – essential atlases to navigate the newcomer through the new technological landscape. What they were *not* (and what, to be fair, they had no intention of being) were critical readings, placing new media into a cultural context or a theoretical rationale.

The rise of theory in museum computing

However, towards the end of the 1990s, new studies of museums and new technology were beginning to make important links to other critical approaches. It was *The Wired Museum*, edited by Jones-Garmil (1997), that was the first widely published, edited volume to bring together a series of substantial essays specifically on the subject of museums and new media. Whereas many of its contributions (such as Johnston and Herman) inherited the discourse of Gill, Gordon and Williams, the book is notable in the way some of its authors began to place museum computing into other critical contexts. Most notably, by gravitating towards issues of authority, authenticity and commodification, Besser (1997: 116) drew upon Walter Benjamin's seminal essay on the work of art in the age of mechanical reproduction to consider 'the potential effects of widespread photographic digitisation on the museum, on scholarly research, and on the general public'. The volume was one of the first attempts to provide, as it says itself, 'ways of thinking about the use of technology in museums' (Anderson 1997: 14). In a sense, *The Wired Museum* was the book that helped the profession crystallise many of its thoughts on museums and new media, and identify its needs and its agenda.

Significantly, just a year later, a collection of essays edited by Thomas and Mintz (1998) provided a series of perspectives on the subject of exhibition making and interpretation, and how new media technologies might impact upon these practices. Significantly, some of the volume's authors began to adopt, or at least allude to, the language and the techniques of sociological study. Here we find, perhaps for the first time, a study of museum computing becoming self-reflective: 'This book is a reflection', Thomas explains, 'on the nature of museology in the age of information'. Looking back on her own oeuvre of research, Thomas argues how much more sophisticated the discussion has become in just the few years preceding the publication of the book. Certainly, the questions posed by Thomas (1998) and Mintz (1998: 3, 20, 34) in their own papers in the volume (for instance, the cultural value of the 'virtual object'), even if they were not perhaps answered, were nevertheless testimony to this new level of sophistication. But it is perhaps the arguments set out by Dierking and Falk (1998) in their essay 'Audience and Accessibility' that represents the fullest extent of these new theoretically aware approaches. Building upon solid empirical research (in many cases their own) and mindful of educational theory and theoretical assumptions regarding museums as 'free-choice learning environments', Falk and Dierking make a persuasive case for media, specifically digital multimedia, as a provider of the essential choice and variety that characterise successful exhibitions. Their study provided one of the first real glimpses of what theoretically grounded and critical studies in museum computing could look like.

Now, at the start of this century, a new group of writers has emerged who have begun more systematically to place museum computing into critical contexts informed by cultural theory. Together their work – looking at the value of the digital object, on the management of digital information, on virtual reality and on e-learning – signals a major shift and refocusing within the subject. Working from, for instance, the premise that George Hein's interpretation of constructivist learning is influential on contemporary museum education, Teather and Wilhelm (1999) have cultivated a debate into the ways the well-developed theorising of on-site museum learning might also be applied to web-based learning. Likewise, Hazan (2001), informed by the thinking of Walter Benjamin, Alfred Gell and others, begins to provide helpful perspectives on the status of the 'auratic' museum object online. Benjamin, in particular, she argues, has 'compelling implications' for the electronic duplication of the digital image. Benjamin (and the sense that the ethereal 'aura' traditionally associated with the art object can be challenged and rewired by the technologies of reproduction, generating new codes of access, perception and presentation) is also deployed in Andrea Witcomb's discussions of the 'virtual museum', within her wider reimaginings of the modern museum. However, it is Witcomb's citation of Chesher (2002), a scholar writing at the intersection of new media production and theory, who uses sociology to read new technology, which signifies an important connection within her analysis. To help shape and substantiate her argument on museum virtuality, Witcomb looks towards the literature of new media studies, as much as to that of writers at the core of conventional museum computing literature. At that moment, as Witcomb reaches across the disciplinary divides for Chesher, museum computing is, potentially, re-contextualised within a very different discourse and arena of study and, consequently, is open to very different and theorised readings.

In the area of information management, a similar trans-disciplinary vision and willingness to question essential concepts has been shown by Cameron (2003) in her discussion of how documentation systems and practices might adapt to 'meet the needs of contemporary discourses and audiences'. Cameron advocates the adoption of documentation systems that can be open to multiple interpretations, and that acknowledge how museum objects can hold multiple, sometimes contradictory and cross-disciplinary meanings. This shift from databases being documentation tools to 'knowledge environments' is, in part, based on empirical research (focus groups and interviews with stakeholders), but it also comes, importantly, from her own reflections on the role of documentation within the postmodern condition – where we see both the established indexes of truth and the privileging of material culture within documentation and within the museum as a whole becoming negotiable.

Furthermore, for the first time, a generation of new researchers specifically researching (and theorising) the area of museums and new media is making its way through the increasing number of postgraduate programmes in and around the field of museum studies. Drawing upon, variously, Manuel Castells and his theories of the *informational society* (Arvanitis 2002), Falk and Dierking and their models of gallery-based learning (Galani and Chalmers 2002), as well as Foucault and Benjamin within the analysis of the space of representation and structure of knowledge as presented through multimedia (Gere 1996: 10), this emergent body of work is helping to bring the amount of literature and critical discussion in the area to a critical mass.

The rise of theory as a 'cultural turn' in museum computing

It is significant that by reaching for new approaches (from cultural studies, communication studies, media studies, and from what has become known as *digital theory*), museum computing is following a direction that many other subjects have taken before. In a sense, museum computing is experiencing a moment when cultural theory is having an effect on its methods and perspectives, just as the discipline of history did in different ways during the last quarter of the twentieth century. From the mid-1960s, a transformation began in historical studies, as scholars began to introduce to their work methods from anthropology and social theory (Evans 1997: 38). Then, performing a similar reflection on method, a new generation of historians of culture, during the end of the 1980s, advocated the use of literary techniques to develop their approach to evidence and the past (Hunt, 1989: 14–15). Both moments, in their own way, represented what we have come to call a *cultural turn* within the subject. David Chaney helps us to define a cultural turn as the movement within a subject towards the theories and approaches of cultural studies and sociology, a condition in which 'culture, and a number of related concepts, have become simultaneously both the dominant topic and most productive intellectual resource in ways that lead us to rewrite our understanding of life in the modern world' (Chaney 1994: 1–2). Therefore, with their studies increasingly hinging and focusing on cultural (rather than strictly technical) themes, and with the use of forms of culture (models and theories of cultural construction) informing the assumptions and methodologies of these studies, we might usefully say that museum computing is experiencing the beginnings of its own cultural turn.

The expansion and co-ordination of research activity in museum computing

It is significant that this turn to theory has come about at just the time (in a European context at least) that inter-governmental sponsorship of research activity in the area of ICT and cultural heritage has reached unprecedented levels. To take the example of the UK since 1997, and the election of the new Labour government, the UK has witnessed a procession of high profile, state-funded initiatives to advocate and shape development of ICT in the sector, as digital cultural heritage has become an important agent within both the government's learning agenda and its policy on social inclusion. The need to develop this potential for using new media technologies to enhance museums' educational provision has been endorsed by leading practitioners and museum educationalists (Anderson 1999: 2). Targets have been set for as many virtual visits as real visits to be made to museums, for one in three homes to access digital museums, and for the majority of school children to use museum resources as an integral part of the curriculum (Keene 1999). These visions have been supported by both government standards in digital content creation, as well as practical recommendations (including the cost, training and rights implications) on what is planned to be a sustainable and strategic development in museums' ICT (Resource 2001; Smith, L. 2000; Stiff 2002: 8). The focus now remains on deepening access, broadening participation, utilising learning resources, developing the skills of the museum workforce and (most importantly) cultivating sustainability in all of these.

The ultimate reference point for Europe's approach to the development of ICT is the *eEurope Action Plan* (launched at the Seville European Council in June 2002 and endorsed by the Council of Ministers in the eEurope Resolution of January 2003) and the UNESCO World Summit on the Information Society, Geneva 2003, Tunis 2005. For the European Union, the development of digital cultural heritage is expressed in terms of the socio-economic policy of modernising public services, boosting productivity and increasing participation within the global society. This involves meeting the challenge of the *digital divide* (Parry 2001), and cultivating the individual empowerment that comes from the free flow of, and equitable access to, information (Abid 2002). Underpinning these aims is the drive to increase and rationalise the co-ordination of digital heritage projects at both a national and a European level.

For museum computing, a key change in this strategic, co-ordinated and policy-motivated development has been the fact that, since 1998, cultural heritage has found a clear, defined and permanent home within the European Commission's research and technological development, specifically with respect to providing access to cultural content through the networking of museums, as well as developing strategies for the long-term development and maintenance of digital repositories and the preservation of digital objects (Smith, B. 2000). Europe's systematic approach to digital cultural heritage is characterised not only by its drive to introduce leading edge technologies into the sector, but also by its push to foster strategy and partnership. This is evidenced by the way it has identified education as a key target market, and by the importance it has allotted to the cooperation and the co-ordination of methodological approaches (European Commission Directorate-General Information Society 2002: 13).

In terms of our concern here with the move to theory, this last point is very important. This heightened research activity has given museum computing not only an enhanced identity (now fashioned as *digital heritage* and *digital cultural heritage*), but also a more conspicuous, co-operative and formalised peer group, in addition to a more identifiable and credible research area. For the future growth of the subject, this visibility and legitimacy will prove vital.

Towards a critical framework for digital heritage

As it becomes more theorised, formalised and conspicuous, we might reasonably ask upon what ideas and assumptions this new subject of digital heritage might usefully be predicated. What key concepts might it need to confront? How might these assumptions shape its language and its discourse? Are there clear terms of reference for it to work within? Are there methods of work and objectives that digital heritage might find beneficial? What form, in short, might studies within this new theoretically informed discipline (the discipline of *digital heritage studies*) take?

In many ways, the critical framework for digital heritage is already beginning to take shape. A number of ideas (to do with *change, agency, discourse* and *history*) are already proving important. Certainly, existing museology and existing new media theory, as well as the early studies in digital heritage, are together setting standards and challenges for the subject.

Engaging with the concept of change

In recent years, the profession, and certainly museum computing, has taken a very pragmatic view of *change*, producing very practical measures to manage it (Information Management Associates and The Networked Services Policy Task Group 2003). Moreover, change is understood frequently in quantified terms – through uptake and permeation of specific types of technologies, or numbers of connections, or levels of usage. These sorts of approaches are, of course, very valuable and useful. However, as we have seen here in the work of Hilde Hein and Šola, digital heritage can complement these perspectives (with their deterministic overtones of technology's power changing society) with other readings of technology and change. These are readings that acknowledge the complex interchanges that take place within a culture shaped by technologies that are themselves cultural constructs – what we now capture with the term 'cultural technologies' (Flew 2002: 39–41). Digital heritage will benefit from continuing to confront these debates, and being clear about the assumptions it is making over this relationship between technology and society. It must also be clear as to what extent the impact of technology is constant and to what extent it varies, and to what extent it sees the potential of technology being determined within the capacity of the technology itself, and to what extent it is society that ultimately controls and constructs the value and role of this technology. Last, there must be clarity on its very notion of newness – including the uncertainty and flux that can accompany the emergence of an influential new technology.

Acknowledging the agency of media

Within Witcomb's deliberations on the meaning of digital reproductions, and MacDonald's evocation of McLuhan, we have seen the ways digital heritage is already working to understand the *agency* of new media. This can usefully begin with an acknowledgement of the extent to which media technology is historically specific, culturally constructed and, therefore, continually contested. As a cultural product, media (such as new digital media) is imbued with specific ideas and meanings, and to use this media is to be implicated with these values. Furthermore, any act of communication with this media will itself be shaped in part by the same qualities. Choosing to place text on a computer screen, rather than on a printed label, is itself meaningful. The medium of the computer, with its own cultural associations, not to mention physical orientations, becomes implicated in the content – the message (McLuhan 2001: 7).

Similarly, in Cameron's study of documentation processes (old and new) and Hazan's reflections on reproduction technologies (old and new), we also see digital heritage research mindful of the differences and inheritances of technology. Following new media studies (Lister et al. 2003: 53–55), digital heritage studies such as these are grappling with the extent to which any given new media is reliant upon (derivative of) previous existing media, and/or to what extent it is remedial, an improvement of, and identifiably distinct from these older technologies.

Finding a more nuanced discourse

The critical self-awareness we have seen at play in both Scaltsa's and Thomas' work signals another aspect to digital heritage's new critical framework – the turn to more nuanced ways of thinking and communicating. To date, commentators on museum computing have all too easily adopted the posture of either advocate or sceptic. Advocate discourse (at times the discourse of government strategy) has been of 'digital salvation', seeing ICT as a powerful mechanism, and stressing the potential of the technology for the museum (Fahy 1995: 82; Šola 1997: 270; Wallace 1995: 108). Sceptic (and moderate) discourse, conversely, has seen this, in its more extreme manifestations at least, as a 'naïve and utopian narrative' (Witcomb 2003: 113). Where advocate discourse frequently adopts revolutionary language, sceptic discourse uses the language of besieging–ICT the Trojan horse wheeled into the fortress (Šola 1997: 147–148). With respect to the latter, anxiety tends to surround the end of the physical visit; a loss of authenticity and authority; new media contributing to a dumbing-down in museums; the gimmickry of digital technologies; as well as anxieties over the sustainability of new media initiatives. We might hope that one consequence of refining the terms of reference for digital heritage studies might be a blurring and dissolving of some of this binary and oppositional language.

Valuing a historical view

The method of looking back to understand the present is not new to museum studies (Bennett 1995; Crooke 2000; Knell 2000; Pearce 1995). Similarly, to scholars of media studies and new media studies, historical approaches are now customary. Within communication studies, for instance, Thomas (2002: 82) tries to understand piracy and innovation 'by addressing the historical trajectory that new media have taken, particularly the development of computer software'. Similarly, in order to

understand the cultural status and assumptions that surround the medium of television (and to posit a thesis that it is 'one of the most extreme examples of the instability endemic in media forms'), William Uricchio (2002: 221) chooses to 'look further
back' into its developmental history. In contrast, for discussions of museums and new
media, such an approach is still quite novel. We may note Williams' 'brief history
of museum computerisation' (1987: 1–7), or Bearman and Trant's (1999: 20–24)
narration on the early years of museum website development, or Bowen's (1997:
9–25) account of the origins of the Internet and one key online museum resource,
or Robinson's (1998: 39–42) attempts to place museum ICT into a larger historical context, or even Witcomb's (2003: 104) acknowledgment that recognising the
'longer history' of modern museum media can enrich the base for engaging with
its use. However, these examples of historicised approaches to digital heritage still
remain, on the whole, the exception.

That said, a writer such as Kim Veltman (1996, 2003), working at the heart
of Europe's digital heritage landscape, has not only provided sophisticated historicised readings of modern visual technologies, but also has transplanted this critical
approach and its use of concepts from communication studies and media studies, to
rationalise the future 'roadmap' for research within the European Research Area,
in the field of digital culture. Veltman's approach, like that of other new writers in
this area (Parry and Sawyer 2005), reflects on the past in order to understand the
present. Resisting the approach of much of the literature in this area that has tended
to privilege the present and future tenses (reporting on current practice and speculat-
ing forwards), it is already proving beneficial for digital heritage studies to recognise
the value of historical methodologies, and to understand new media by looking backwards. Digital heritage will benefit from continuing to work from the assumption
that, to understand the language, actions and institutions of current museum practice
in this area, we first need to understand (through historical analysis) what cultural
circumstances and discourses produced these elements and that, perhaps, continue
to be implicated with their use.

Conclusion

Our concern here has been the future of museum computing (recast as *digital heritage*), what it is becoming, what it needs to become to have coherency in itself and to
make a valid contribution to the study and practice of museums, as well as to help us
to avoid Šola's *technology trap*. Developing its important traditional focus on procurement, projects and practice, museum computing is today, as we have seen, experiencing the beginnings of a disciplinary realignment and openness to new modes of thought
and critical tools from areas such as cultural studies, sociology and media studies.
Crucially, this has all taken place at just the same time that heightened investment
and advocacy have increased the amount (and formalised the conduct) of research
activity in this area. It is within this frisson (intellectual, professional, governmental, fiscal), and abetted by this new formality and rigour, that museum computing is
being transformed. Within this transformation, the beginnings of a more robust critical framework for this sub-discipline are starting to emerge. It is a framework that

seems to want to confront the very nature of change, to acknowledge and explore the specific meanings that particular media carry, to place today's use of technology into the context of yesterday, and to articulate all of this with care and subtlety.

As the theorising of museum studies continues amidst the informational society, the value and role of our reflections on computing within the museum become more resonant. The shift described here from museum computing to digital heritage is not just a case of academic posturing – the implications are profound. For digital heritage is beginning to both represent and to facilitate our move to some very different understandings of the museum and its relationship with its publics.

Acknowledgements

The author is grateful to the organisers and delegates of 'Museums and Technology: An International Conference on the Application of New Technology in Museums', at the Graduate Institution of Museology, Tainan National College of the Arts, Taiwan (November 2004), and 'Technology for Cultural Heritage; Management, Education, Communication', the Second International Conference of Museology, University of the Aegean, Greece (June 2004), at which many of the initial ideas for this research were aired and discussed.

References

Abid, A. (2002) UNESCO and the World Summit on the Information Society. Presented to 68th IFLA Council and General Conference, 18–24 August 2002. Retrieved June 17, 2005, from http://www.ifla.org/IV/ifla68/ papers/150–85be.pdf.

Anderson, D. (1999) *A Common Wealth: Museums in the Learning Age*. London: Department of Culture, Media and Sport.

Anderson, M. (1997) In K. Jones-Garmil (ed.), *The Wired Museum: Emerging Technology and Changing Paradigms* (pp. 11–32). Washington DC: American Association of Museums.

Arvanitis, K. (2002) Digital, virtual, cyber or network museum? A search for definitions as an act of interpretation. Paper presented to *Museum, Communication and New Technologies*, 1st International Museology Conference, Department of Cultural Technology & Communication, University of the Aegean, Mytilene, Greece (May 31–June 2, 2002).

Bearman, D. and Trant, J. (1999) Interactivity comes of age: museums and the world wide web. *Museum International, 204*(4): 20–24.

Bennett, T. (1995) *The Birth of the Museum: History, Theory, Politics*. London: Routledge.

Besser, H. (1997) The changing role of photographic collections with the advent of digitization. In K. Jones-Garmil (ed.), *The Wired Museum: Emerging Technology and Changing Paradigms* (pp. 115–127). Washington, DC: American Association of Museums.

Bhatnagar, A. (1999) *Museum, Museology and New Museology*. New Delhi: Sundeep Prakashan.

Bowen, J. (1997) The Virtual Library museums page (VLmp): whence and whither? In D. Bearman, and J. Trant (eds), *Museums and the Web 1997: Selected Papers* (pp. 9–25). Pittsburgh: Archives and Museum Informatics.

Cameron, F. (2003) The next generation: 'knowledge environments' and digital collections', *Museums and the Web 2003*. Retrieved June 17, 2005, from http://www.archimuse.com/mw2003/papers/cameron/cameron.html.

Chaney, D. (1994) *The Cultural Turn: Scene-setting Essays on Contemporary Cultural History*. London: Routledge.

Chesher, C. (2002) What is new media research? In H. Brown, G. Lovink, H. Merrick, N. Rossiter, D. Teh, and M. Willson (eds), *Politics of a Digital Present: An Inventory of Australian Net Culture*. Melbourne: Fibreculture.

Crooke, E. (2000) *Politics, Archaeology and the Creation of a National Museum in Ireland: An Expression of National Life*. Dublin: Irish Academic Press.

Delin, A. (2003) *Disability in Context: The Disability Portfolio, Guide 1*. London: Resource, The Council for Museums, Archives and Libraries.

Dierking, L. D., and Falk, J. H. (1998) Audience and accessibility. In S. Thomas, and A. Mintz (eds), *The Virtual and the Real: Media in the Museum* (pp. 57–70). Washington: American Association of Museums.

Duncan, C. (1995) *Civilising Rituals: Inside Public Art Museums*. London: Routledge.

Durbin, G. (1996) *Developing Museum Exhibitions for Lifelong Learning*. Norwich: TSO.

European Commission Directorate-General Information Society (2002). *The DigiCULT Report Technological Landscapes for Tomorrow's Cultural Economy – Unlocking the Value of Cultural Heritage*. Luxembourg: Office for Official Publications of the European Communities.

Evans, R. J. (1997) *In Defence of History*. London: Granta Books.

Fahy, A. (1995) New technologies for museum communication. In E. Hooper-Greenhill (ed.), *Museum, Media, Message* (pp. 82–96). London: Routledge.

Flew, T. (2002) *New Media: An Introduction*. Oxford: Oxford University Press.

Fyfe, G. (2003) *Museums, Cultural Capital and Art Reproduction: An Historical Sociological Perspective* (1) (p. 2003). University of Leicester: Department of Museum Studies, University of Leicester, October (unpublished paper presented to October (2003)).

Galani, A., and Chalmers, M. (2002) Can you see me?: exploring co-visiting between physical and virtual visitors. In D. Bearman, and J. Trant (eds), *Museums and the Web 2002: Selected Papers* (pp. 31–40). Archives & Museum Informatics.

Gere, C. (1996) *The Computer as Irrational Cabinet*. Middlesex University: unpublished PhD thesis.

Gill, T. (1996) *The MDA Guide to Computers in Museums*. Cambridge: The Museum Documentation Association.

Golding, V. (2005) The museum clearing: a metaphor for new museum practice. In D. Atkinson, and P. Dash (eds), *Social and Critical Practice in Art Education* (pp. 51–66). Stoke on Trent: Trentham Books.

Gordon, S. (1996) *Making the Internet Work for Museums*. Cambridge: The Museum Documentation Association.

Hazan, S. (2001) The virtual aura: is there space for enchantment in a technological world? In *Museums and the Web 2001*. Retrieved June 17, 2005, from http://www.archimuse.com/mw2001/paper/hazan/hazan.html.

Hein, H. S. (2000) *The Museum in Transition: A Philosophical Perspective*. Washington and London: Smithsonian Institute Press.

Hooper-Greenhill, E. (1992) *Museums and the Shaping of Knowledge*. London: Routledge.

Hooper-Greenhill, E. (1995) Museums and communication: an introductory essay. In E. Hooper-Greenhill (ed.), *Museum, Media, Message* (pp. 1–12). London: Routledge.

Hooper-Greenhill, E. (2000) *Museums and the Interpretation of Visual Culture*. London: Routledge.

Hunt, L. (1989) Introduction: history, culture and text. In L. Hunt (ed.), *The New Cultural History* (pp. 1–22). Berkeley: University of California Press.

Information Management Associates and The Networked Services Policy Task Group (2003). *The People's Network Change Management Toolkit*. London: Resource.

Jones-Garmil, K. (1997) *The Wired Museum: Emerging Technology and Changing Paradigms*. Washington, DC: American Association of Museums.

Keene, S. (1999) *A Netful of Jewels: New Museums in the Learning Age*. London: National Museum Directors Conference.

Knell, S. (2000) *The Culture of English Geology, 1815–1851: A Science Revealed Through its Collecting*. Aldershot: Ashgate.

Lister, M., Dovey, J., Giddings, S., Grant, I., and Kelly, K. (2003) *New Media: A Critical Introduction*. London: Routledge.

Lumley, R. (1988) *The Museum Time Machine Putting Cultures on Display*. London: Routledge / Comedia.

MacDonald, G. (1992) Change and challenge: museums in the information society. In L. Karp, C. Mullen Kreamer, and S. D. Lavine (eds), *Museums and Communities: The Politics of Public Culture* (pp. 158–181). Washington: Smithsonian Press.

MacDonald, G., and Alsford, S. (1989) *A Museum for the Global Village*. Hull: Canadian Museum of Civilisation.

Macdonald, S. (1996) Introduction. In S. Macdonald, and G. Fyfe (eds), *Theorising Museums: Representing Identity and Diversity in a Changing World* (pp. 1–18). Oxford and Malden: Blackwell and The Sociological Review.

McLuhan, M. (2001) *Understanding Media: The Extensions of Man*. London: Routledge.

Mintz, A. (1998) Media and museums: a museum perspective. In S. Thomas, and A. Mintz (eds), *The Virtual and the Real: Media in the Museum* (pp. 1–18). Washington: American Association of Museums.

Parry, R. (2001) Including technology. In J. Dodd, and R. Sandell (eds), *Including Museums: Perspectives on Museums, Galleries and Social Inclusion RCMG* (pp. 110–114). Leicester: RCMG.

Parry, R., and Sawyer, A. (2005) Space and the machine: adaptive museums, pervasive technology and the new gallery environment. In S. MacLeod (ed.), *Reshaping Museum Space: Architecture, Design, Exhibitions* (pp. 39–52). London: Routledge.

Pearce, S. M. (1995) *On Collecting: An Investigation into Collecting in the European Tradition*. London: Routledge.

Porter, G. (1996) Seeing through solidity: a feminist perspective on museums. In S. Macdonald, and G. Fyfe (eds), *Theorising Museums: Representing Identity and Diversity in a Changing World* (pp. 105–126). Oxford: Blackwell and The Sociological Review.

Resource (2001) *Information and Communication Technology and the Development of Museums, Libraries and Archives: A Strategic Plan for Action*. London: Resource, the Council for Museums, Archives and Libraries.

Robinson, M. H. (1998) Multimedia in living exhibits: now and then. In S. Thomas, and A. Mintz (eds), *The Virtual and the Real: Media in the Museum* (pp. 37–55). Washington: American Association of Museums.

Scaltsa, M. (2001) Museology towards the 21st century: theory and practice. International Symposium proceedings, Thessaloniki, November 21–24, 1997. Thessaloniki: Endefktirio.

Smith, B. (2000) Digital heritage and cultural content in the new Information Society Technologies Programme. *Cultivate Interactive*, 1 (3 July). Retrieved June 17, 2005, from http://www.cultivate-in.org./issue1/ist/.

Smith, L. (2000) Building the digital museum: a national resource for the learning age. The National Museums Directors' Conference, Resource and MDA. Retrieved June 17, 2005, from http://www.mda.org.uk/digitalmuseums.pdf.

Šola, T. (1997) *Essays on Museums and Their Theory: Towards the Cybernetic Museum*. Helsinki: Finish Museums Association.

Stiff, M. (2002) *Managing New Technology Projects in Museums and Galleries*. Cambridge: MDA.

Teather, L. and Wilhelm, K. (1999). Web musing: evaluating museums on the web from learning theory to methodology, *Museums and the Web 1999*. Retrieved June 17, 2005, from http://www.archimuse.com/mw99/papers/teather/teather.html.

Thomas, D. (2002) Innovation, piracy and the ethos of new media. In D. Harries (ed.), *The New Media Book* (pp. 82–91). London: British Film Institute.

Thomas, S. (1998) Mediated realities: a media perspective. In S. Thomas, and A. Mintz (eds), *The Virtual and the Real: Media in the Museum* (pp. 1–17). Washington: American Association of Museums.

Thomas, S., and Mintz, A. (1998) *The Virtual and the Real: Media in the Museum*. Washington: American Association of Museums.

Uricchio, W. (2002) Old media as new media: television. In D. Harries (ed.), *The New Media Book* (pp. 219–230). London: British Film Institute.

Veltman, K. (1996) The rebirth of perspective and the fragmentation of illusion. In T. Druckery (ed.), *Electronic Culture: Technology and Visual Representation*, 209–227 [Aperture].

Veltman, K. (2003) Roadmaps for research and research topics in digital culture. Presentation at the concentration meeting "Mapping the future", European Commission, Preservation and Enhancement of Cultural Heritage DG INFSO/E, Luxembourg, 28 January 2003. Retrieved June 17, 2005, from ftp://ftp.cordis.lu/pub/ist/docs/digicult/veltman28012003.ppt.

Vergo, P. (1989) *New Museology*. London: Reaktion Books.

Wallace, M. (1995) Changing media, changing messages. In E. Hooper-Greenhill (ed.), *Museum, Media, Message* (pp. 107–123). London: Routledge.

Williams, D. (1987) *Guide to Museum Computing*. Nashville, TN: American Association for State and Local History.

Witcomb, A. (2003) *Re-imagining the Museum: Beyond the Mausoleum*. London: Routledge.

Index